THESE
CANADIANS

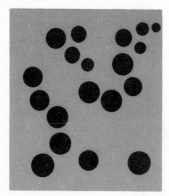

THESE
CANADIANS

A sourcebook of marketing and socio·economic facts

Nariman K. Dhalla

Marketing and Research Director
J. Walter Thompson Co., Ltd., Toronto

McGRAW·HILL COMPANY OF CANADA LIMITED
Toronto New York London Sydney

Contents

PART TWO	**The Canadian Mosaic**

PART THREE	**Regional Analysis**

Continued

94665

Library of Congress Catalog Card Number 66-14580

1 2 3 4 5 6 7 8 9   B66   9 8 7 6

Printed and bound in Canada

Dedicated to my wife, Claude

PREFACE

There are many excellent books on Canada, but only a few deal specifically with Canadians from a socio-economic and marketing viewpoint. Most of the available information is scattered in census reports, government publications, magazine articles, market research studies, and textbooks on marketing and the social sciences. The present work attempts to bring together all the major facts about Canada's population and economy into one easy-to-read volume. Many of the topics in the news today are treated at some length — poverty, unemployment, immigration, education, French Canada, to mention just a few.

The book begins with a short introductory chapter on the geography of Canada that may serve as a backdrop for the subsequent discussions of marketing and socio-economic factors. The text proper that follows is broken into three sections. Part I deals with the emerging trends in Canadian society, particularly those related to population, income, education, family life, retailing, and the labor force. Part II analyzes in detail six aspects of the Canadian mosaic: sex, age, income, social status, ethnic origin, and urban-rural residence. In Part III, the mosaic concept is carried a step further to apply to the sixty-four fairly homogeneous economic regions into which the country can be divided. Each of the three parts is preceded by *a short introduction, suggesting marketing applications of the textual and statistical material.*

The book contains a large dose of tables, but it should not be regarded merely as a statistical abstract. At no time are the numbers allowed to become an end in themselves. They are only the means by which one seeks to interpret what is happening in Canadian society. Wherever possible the current figures are projected to 1970 to show the trends more clearly.

The author is grateful to the management of J. Walter Thompson Company Limited for being able to take some time off to work on the book. However, the views expressed are his own and do not reflect the attitude or policy of the company.

Nariman K. Dhalla

Chapter 1

BACKDROP: THE NATURAL ENVIRONMENT

Location and Size

Canada occupies the upper half of the North American continent, with the exception of Alaska and Greenland. To be geographically precise, the country extends in longitude from Cape Spear, Newfoundland, at 52°37'W. to Mount St. Elias, Yukon Territory, at 141°W., a distance of 3,200 miles. In latitude, it stretches from Middle Island in Lake Erie, at 41°41'N. (the same level as Rome) to the North Pole, a length of about 2,900 miles.

On old-fashioned maps, Canada is shown in the northwest corner of a rectangular world. At a time when Europe was the hub of all activities, this representation had some justification. Today, however, it becomes increasingly necessary to take a new look at the globe, with the center over the Arctic Ocean around which the great world powers are now grouped. Such a map would immediately reveal the strategic position of Canada. She lies on the opposite shores of the Arctic Ocean to Soviet Russia, while in the south she borders the United States separated for more than a thousand miles by just the forty-ninth parallel. In the east, the island of Newfoundland commands the shortest crossing of the North Atlantic Ocean and links Canada geographically with her two mother countries, Britain and France. Similarly in the west, the broad arc of land between Vancouver and Whitehorse provides the quickest route across the Northern Pacific Ocean to the Far East. Canada thus lies at the crossroads of contact with the principal powers and some of the most populous areas of the world — between the U.S.A. and the U.S.S.R. on the one hand, and between China-Japan and Europe on the other.

In size, Canada is the largest country in the world after the Soviet Union, covering some 3,560,238 square miles of land, or some 7% of the land surface of the globe. One province alone, Québec, is larger than France, Germany and Spain combined. A journey from Halifax to Vancouver is of approximately the same length as one from New York to Liverpool and takes the best part of a week by express train. St. John's, Newfoundland, is closer to Paris than to Vancouver.

Population and Marketing

When one values Canada's bridge hand, it is found that she holds a few weak cards. The immense area of the country, coupled with the small size of the population — roughly only one-tenth of the United States — tends to shoot up the distribution costs. A company that can cover the United States with, say, 500 salesmen, cannot get by in Canada with one-tenth as many; it will need probably 100 to 150 personnel to achieve the same degree of penetration. The problem becomes even more acute for the manufacturers of durable goods who have to maintain, in addition to a large sales force, a far-flung chain of service depots.

However, it would not be fair to paint the whole picture only in somber colors. There are many bright spots as well. Nearly 40% of the population is concentrated within the 100-mile radius of the three metropolitan centers of Montréal, Toronto and Vancouver. This simplifies the task of reaching the cream of the market economically. The remaining 60% are, no doubt, thinly spread over the huge continental land mass; but even here it is possible to obtain a satisfactory penetration of the sales message. Canada has many types of national media — consumer magazines, weekend supplements, and network television — that provide an adequate coverage not only of major marketing centers but also of the intervening, less populous areas.

Physiographic and Climatic Regions

Foreigners often mistakenly imagine Canada as a land of long, austere winters where the old ice no sooner shows signs of disappearing than the new one of the next season begins to form. True, large parts of Canada are frozen over six months in the year. But there are also warm regions where it is possible to grow vines and tobacco — crops which one does not usually associate with cold climes.

A Canadian can, without leaving his country, see the physical landscape and experience the climatic conditions prevailing in England, Central Europe, Siberia, and Japan. All he has to do is to take a round trip from Halifax to Dawson, going by the northern route and coming back by the southern. To get a better picture of Canada, it is necessary to examine separately the different physiographic and climatic regions of the country.

APPALACHIAN REGION

On the extreme east, the Appalachian mountain ranges cover the Maritimes, the island of Newfoundland, as well as the Gaspé Peninsula and the Eastern Townships of Québec. This region is rich in mineral deposits and is covered by extensive forests, providing a base for important mining and lumbering industries. The river terraces and valleys are ideal for mixed farming and for the cultivation of potatoes and fruits, especially apples. Large hydro-electric power resources are limited, however, because the drainage basins of the rivers are not generally extensive.

The climate is a mixture of the continental and the marine types. Since the area is under the influence of the Westerlies and cyclonic storms moving east from the great North American land mass, a good deal of the weather is fairly similar to that prevailing in the inland regions. The presence of the ocean nearby, however, helps to exercise an ameliorating influence. Saint John on the New Brunswick coast averages eight degrees more than inland Ottawa in January and seven degrees less in July.

THE LOWER GREAT LAKES–ST. LAWRENCE LOWLANDS

This geographic area extending from Québec City to Lake Huron, a distance of 600 miles, is the smallest in Canada — only 38,000 square miles. It is not endowed with rich mineral deposits, and its timber stands have long been depleted. But, in compensation, it has rich agricultural soils, plentiful water-power sites, excellent means of communication, and an ideal location next to the industrial heartland of the United States. As a result, economic development has progressed further here than in any other part of Canada. The region supports over half of the country's population, and is responsible for the bulk of the nation's manufacturing output. Here are situated the two biggest cities, Montréal and Toronto, plus a host of large industrial centers like Hamilton, Windsor, London, Kitchener, and Trois Rivières.

Climatically, since the Lower Great Lakes region constitutes the southernmost portion of Canada, the winters are milder than those prevailing elsewhere in Canada, except on the Pacific coast. The summers are warm and often quite sultry. It may be humid and oppressive for days at a time. Temperatures of more than 100°F. are not unknown. Autumn sets in gradually. Although the temperature begins to fall in September, it is usually well into October before there are heavy frosts.

In the lower Ottawa Valley and the St. Lawrence lowlands, winters are more severe. This is due to the northerly latitude and the remoteness from the moderating influence of the Great Lakes. In January, on the average, Montréal is nine degrees colder than Toronto. The winters are also long, and the frost lasts till the end of April. Spring is so short and sudden that often the winter seems to give way immediately to summer. Heat waves do occur, but they are not as numerous nor as prolonged as those in the Lower Great Lakes region.

The snowfall increases as one moves eastward. The average rises from 55 inches in Toronto to 80 in Ottawa, 100 in Montréal, and 124 in Québec. In southwestern Ontario, winter thaws are frequent, but in the St. Lawrence lowlands the countryside has a fairly persistent snow cover of one to three feet till March.

CANADIAN SHIELD

Probably so called because of its shieldlike shape on the map, this is the largest physiographic region, covering 1,850,000 square miles, or almost half of

Canada. This vast, lake-stippled expanse of rock, bush and bog criss-crosses through the country, encompassing Labrador, the vast northern areas of Québec, Ontario, Manitoba and Saskatchewan, the northeast corner of Alberta, the district of Keewatin, and the area to the east of the Great Slave and Great Bear Lakes in the Mackenzie Territory. The region constitutes the oldest part of the earth's crust and as such is one of the world's greatest storehouses of minerals, containing as yet unknown reserves of iron, nickel, copper, lead, zinc, and other metals. It also has vast forest and water-power resources, but no good soils for agriculture except in the small areas of the clay belts south of James Bay.

The climatic conditions are too severe for large-scale settlements. The relief of the land is such as to offer no major barrier to the southward sweep of the arctic air masses. Consequently, below-zero readings may be expected every month from October to May at latitudes as low as that of London, England. Snow covers the ground for more than six months of the year. The warm season is short, the length of the frost-free period in many parts being less than 90 days. As a result, population in this vast region is very sparse, being mostly located in the major centers of mining and forest industries.

THE INTERIOR PLAINS

Lying west of the Canadian Shield are the Interior Plains. They stretch from the U.S. frontier in a northwest direction to the Arctic Ocean, covering in their span southern Manitoba and Saskatchewan, most of Alberta, and part of the Northwest Territories. On the southern reaches of these plains are the rich prairie farmlands that have made Canada one of the greatest grain producers in the world. In addition to the extremely fertile soil, nature's gifts for the region also include rich deposits of fuel minerals — coal, oil and natural gas. In recent years, these deposits have helped considerably to diversify the economy of the area and to reduce excessive dependence on agriculture.

The climate on the prairies is of the middle-latitude, steppe type. The great western Cordilleran chain effectively prevents the moderating influence of the Pacific Ocean from reaching this region. Thus, Lethbridge on the east side of the mountains is 20 degrees cooler on an average January day than Vancouver on the west, although both cities lie on the same latitude. As one goes east, the winters become progressively more severe. This is clearly brought out by the decreasing January mean temperatures of the following cities arranged from west to east: Calgary 16°F., Swift Current 10°F., Regina 2°F., and Winnipeg 1°F.

The weather is not always favorable to the farmer. Severe blizzards in spring, destructive hail storms in midsummer, freezing temperatures in August, lack of precipitation during the crop-growing season — any one of these can wreck the hopes of a good harvest.

CORDILLERAN REGION

The Cordilleran mountain ranges cover almost all of British Columbia and the Yukon. They include the Rockies, the numerous interior plateaus and troughs, as well as the coastal chain bordering the Pacific. The most important natural resources of the region are the dense coniferous forests on the mountain slopes and the vast hydro-electric power potential from numerous rivers. Unlike the Appalachians, which have been reduced by erosion, the Cordilleras are, geologically speaking, of recent up-folding and consequently still retain great height. Transportation through them is difficult, and many areas are still relatively inaccessible.

The Pacific coast, the off-shore islands, and a small portion of the open lower Fraser Valley enjoy a marine climate, very much like the one prevailing in the United Kingdom and France. Extremes of weather, so common in other parts of Canada, are here unknown. At very few places do mean monthly temperatures ever drop below 32°F., or exceed 65°F. Victoria, for example, is as warm in winter as Richmond, Virginia, while its summers are as cool as the winters of St. Petersburg, Florida.

Since the mountains run at right angles to the wind, the oceanic influence does not penetrate far inland. In the interior mountainous terrain, the climate is a transition between the marine type in the west and the continental type in the east. Temperatures are higher in summer and lower in winter than those on the Pacific coast, but the difference between midsummer and midwinter is not so great as in the Prairies.

THE THREE NORTHERN REGIONS

The Innuitian region, the Hudson Bay Lowlands, and the Arctic Lowlands and Plateaus constitute the so-called "Frozen North," the least developed part of Canada. The Innuitian region was not even mapped until about 20 years ago. The winters are too long and severe, but some settlements may be expected in the distant future to exploit the vast untapped mineral wealth of this area.

Economic Effects of Climate

Since nearly seven-eighths of the country experiences below-zero temperatures in January, no Canadian town of any appreciable size is found along the northern latitudes. About half the population is located within 125 miles of the U.S. border, 90% within 225 miles of it. However, because of recent technological developments it is becoming slowly possible to establish fairly comfortable living conditions in the North. The construction of the Distant Early Warning line has demonstrated that, even within the furthest reaches of the Arctic, operations involving a great deal of outdoor work can be carried on successfully. As science advances and mankind learns to overcome the rigors of winter, climate will become less and less of a barrier to the development of northern resources.

DISTANCES BETWEEN PRINCIPAL POINTS IN CANADA

Place	St. John's	Charlotte-town	Halifax	Moncton	Saint John	Fredericton	Québec	Montréal	Sherbrooke	Three Rivers	Ottawa	Kingston	Toronto	Hamilton
St. John's	0	894	933	994	1,083	1,099	1,467	1,559	1,451	1,545	1,663	1,725	1,886	1,925
Charlottetown	894	0	239	126	215	230	600	684	583	677	795	857	1,018	1,057
Halifax	933	239	0	189	278	292	662	747	646	740	858	920	1,081	1,120
Moncton	994	126	189	0	89	104	473	558	457	551	669	731	892	931
Saint John	1,083	215	278	89	0	67	426	476	375	503	587	649	810	849
Fredericton	1,099	230	292	104	67	0	403	454	353	481	565	627	788	827
Québec	1,467	600	662	473	426	403	0	169	127	78	280	342	503	542
Montréal	1,559	684	747	558	476	454	169	0	101	95	111	173	334	373
Sherbrooke	1,451	583	646	457	375	353	127	101	0	196	212	274	435	474
Three Rivers	1,545	677	740	551	503	481	78	95	196	0	206	268	429	468
Ottawa	1,663	795	858	669	587	565	280	111	212	206	0	112	247	286
Kingston	1,725	857	920	731	649	627	342	173	274	268	112	0	161	200
Toronto	1,886	1,018	1,081	892	810	788	503	334	435	429	247	161	0	39
Hamilton	1,925	1,057	1,120	931	849	827	542	373	474	468	286	200	39	0
London	2,001	1,133	1,196	1,007	925	903	618	449	550	544	362	276	115	80
Windsor	2,111	1,243	1,306	1,117	1,035	1,013	728	559	660	654	472	386	225	190
Fort William	2,521	1,653	1,716	1,527	1,445	1,423	1,079	969	1,070	1,064	858	908	811	850
Winnipeg	2,817	1,950	2,012	1,823	1,776	1,753	1,350	1,353	1,454	1,448	1,242	1,292	1,207	1,246
Brandon	2,951	2,084	2,146	1,957	1,910	1,887	1,484	1,486	1,587	1,581	1,375	1,426	1,340	1,379
Churchill	3,796	2,929	2,991	2,802	2,755	2,732	2,329	2,331	2,432	2,426	2,220	2,270	2,185	2,224
Regina	3,172	2,305	2,367	2,178	2,131	2,108	1,705	1,707	1,808	1,802	1,596	1,647	1,562	1,601
Saskatoon	3,288	2,421	2,483	2,294	2,247	2,224	1,821	1,823	1,924	1,918	1,712	1,763	1,677	1,716
Calgary	3,639	2,772	2,834	2,645	2,598	2,575	2,172	2,174	2,275	2,269	2,063	2,113	2,028	2,067
Edmonton	3,618	2,751	2,813	2,624	2,577	2,554	2,151	2,153	2,254	2,248	2,042	2,093	2,008	2,047
Vancouver	4,280	3,413	3,475	3,286	3,239	3,216	2,813	2,815	2,916	2,910	2,704	2,754	2,670	2,709
Victoria	4,365	3,498	3,560	3,371	3,324	3,301	2,898	2,900	3,001	2,995	2,789	2,839	2,755	2,794
Prince Rupert	4,574	3,707	3,769	3,580	3,533	3,510	3,107	3,109	3,210	3,205	2,998	3,049	2,964	3,003

DISTANCES BETWEEN PRINCIPAL POINTS IN CANADA (continued)

Place	London	Windsor	Fort William	Winnipeg	Brandon	Churchill	Regina	Saskatoon	Calgary	Edmonton	Vancouver	Victoria	Prince Rupert
St. John's	2,001	2,111	2,521	2,817	2,951	3,796	3,172	3,288	3,639	3,618	4,280	4,365	4,574
Charlottetown	1,133	1,243	1,653	1,950	2,084	2,929	2,305	2,421	2,772	2,751	3,413	3,498	3,707
Halifax	1,196	1,306	1,716	2,012	2,146	2,991	2,367	2,483	2,834	2,813	3,475	3,560	3,769
Moncton	1,007	1,117	1,527	1,823	1,957	2,802	2,178	2,294	2,645	2,624	3,286	3,371	3,580
Saint John	925	1,035	1,445	1,776	1,910	2,755	2,131	2,247	2,598	2,577	3,239	3,324	3,533
Fredericton	903	1,013	1,423	1,753	1,887	2,732	2,108	2,224	2,575	2,554	3,216	3,301	3,510
Québec	618	728	1,079	1,350	1,484	2,329	1,705	1,821	2,172	2,151	2,813	2,898	3,107
Montréal	449	559	969	1,353	1,486	2,331	1,707	1,823	2,174	2,153	2,815	2,900	3,109
Sherbrooke	550	660	1,070	1,454	1,587	2,432	1,808	1,924	2,275	2,254	2,916	3,001	3,210
Three Rivers	544	654	1,064	1,448	1,581	2,426	1,802	1,918	2,269	2,248	2,910	2,995	3,205
Ottawa	362	472	858	1,242	1,375	2,220	1,596	1,712	2,063	2,042	2,704	2,789	2,998
Kingston	276	386	908	1,292	1,426	2,270	1,647	1,763	2,113	2,093	2,754	2,839	3,049
Toronto	115	225	811	1,207	1,340	2,185	1,562	1,677	2,028	2,008	2,670	2,755	2,964
Hamilton	80	190	850	1,246	1,379	2,224	1,601	1,716	2,067	2,047	2,709	2,794	3,003
London	0	110	926	1,322	1,455	2,300	1,677	1,792	2,143	2,123	2,785	2,870	3,079
Windsor	110	0	1,036	1,432	1,565	2,410	1,787	1,902	2,253	2,233	2,895	2,980	3,189
Fort William	926	1,036	0	419	552	1,397	774	889	1,240	1,220	1,882	1,967	2,176
Winnipeg	1,322	1,432	419	0	133	978	355	470	821	801	1,463	1,548	1,757
Brandon	1,455	1,565	552	133	0	937	221	384	688	715	1,330	1,415	1,671
Churchill	2,300	2,410	1,397	978	937	0	845	813	1,217	1,144	1,859	1,944	2,100
Regina	1,677	1,787	774	355	221	845	0	163	467	493	1,108	1,193	1,449
Saskatoon	1,792	1,902	889	470	384	813	163	0	404	330	1,046	1,131	1,287
Calgary	2,143	2,253	1,240	821	688	1,217	467	404	0	194	642	727	1,150
Edmonton	2,123	2,233	1,220	801	715	1,144	493	330	194	0	761	846	956
Vancouver	2,785	2,895	1,882	1,463	1,330	1,859	1,108	1,046	642	761	0	85	1,158
Victoria	2,870	2,980	1,967	1,548	1,415	1,944	1,193	1,131	727	846	85	0	1,243
Prince Rupert	3,079	3,189	2,176	1,757	1,671	2,100	1,449	1,287	1,150	956	1,158	1,243	0

Note: Generally, the distances given are the shortest by railway.

(Source: Prepared under the direction of Surveyor General, Department of Mines and Technical Surveys, Ottawa.)

LONG-TERM AVERAGE MONTHLY TEMPERATURE IN FAHRENHEIT FOR SELECTED PLACES

	Jan.	Feb.	Mar.	Apr.	May	June	July	Aug.	Sept.	Oct.	Nov.	Dec.	Year
Atlantic Provinces													
St. John's	24.0	21.6	27.5	34.8	43.0	52.4	60.0	60.7	54.4	46.4	37.6	29.5	41.0
Charlottetown	18.8	17.6	26.9	37.0	48.6	58.4	66.6	65.9	58.4	48.4	37.7	25.2	42.5
Halifax	24.4	23.4	31.2	39.5	49.5	58.1	65.0	65.1	59.2	50.0	40.2	29.0	44.6
Sydney	22.7	19.8	27.6	36.5	46.6	56.2	65.0	64.8	58.0	48.6	39.0	28.7	42.8
Moncton	16.1	16.3	26.5	37.3	49.6	58.4	65.8	64.2	56.3	46.1	34.8	21.7	41.1
Saint John	19.8	20.2	29.5	38.9	48.9	56.6	61.8	62.2	56.6	47.8	37.2	24.6	42.0
Québec													
Knob Lake	−11.9	−6.7	7.0	21.3	34.0	48.7	55.1	51.4	42.2	30.8	15.8	−0.4	23.9
Sept Iles	3.2	6.9	17.8	30.9	41.5	51.8	59.2	57.8	49.1	38.6	26.5	12.0	33.0
Québec	12.0	13.4	24.8	37.9	52.0	62.4	67.6	65.3	56.8	45.4	32.0	17.5	40.6
Montréal	15.4	16.4	28.0	41.6	55.6	65.6	70.4	68.2	59.6	48.0	35.2	20.7	43.7
Ontario													
Ottawa	12.0	12.7	25.2	40.5	54.2	64.1	68.6	66.4	58.4	46.1	33.0	17.4	41.6
Toronto	24.5	24.0	32.2	43.8	55.1	65.5	70.8	69.0	61.6	50.2	39.2	28.4	47.0
London	22.5	22.2	31.5	43.2	54.5	64.9	69.6	68.0	60.9	49.2	37.0	26.2	45.8
North Bay	10.5	12.4	23.8	38.0	51.6	62.0	66.8	64.8	56.2	44.9	31.5	16.3	39.9
Kapuskasing	−1.3	2.4	14.4	30.8	45.7	57.3	62.8	60.4	51.4	39.9	22.7	7.5	32.8
Fort William-Port Arthur	7.6	10.2	21.2	35.4	47.4	57.2	63.4	61.9	53.4	42.6	27.0	13.7	36.8
Prairie Provinces													
Winnipeg	0.6	4.3	18.6	38.0	52.4	62.0	68.4	65.8	55.4	42.9	23.2	8.0	36.6
Churchill	−17.3	−16.7	−4.4	10.6	28.4	42.4	54.7	53.0	43.1	29.6	9.6	−9.1	18.7
Regina	2.3	5.5	19.2	38.6	52.0	59.8	66.6	63.7	53.2	40.9	22.0	8.8	36.1
Saskatoon	0.8	4.6	18.7	38.4	51.8	59.8	66.4	63.2	52.5	40.6	21.1	7.4	35.4
Calgary	15.8	17.3	26.2	39.4	50.1	56.2	62.4	59.8	51.6	42.1	27.9	18.8	39.0
Edmonton	7.7	11.2	23.4	39.6	51.7	57.9	62.9	59.6	50.6	40.8	24.2	11.6	36.8
Grande Prairie	5.6	6.4	20.4	37.3	50.3	56.4	60.7	58.5	49.8	39.3	21.8	9.3	34.7

LONG-TERM AVERAGE MONTHLY TEMPERATURE IN FAHRENHEIT FOR SELECTED PLACES (continued)

	Jan.	Feb.	Mar.	Apr.	May	June	July	Aug.	Sept.	Oct.	Nov.	Dec.	Year
British Columbia													
Penticton	26.7	31.0	39.8	48.6	56.6	63.4	68.7	66.4	58.4	48.2	37.6	31.0	48.0
Vancouver	37.6	40.0	44.0	49.8	55.6	60.8	64.4	64.1	58.5	51.7	44.0	39.5	50.8
Victoria	39.2	41.5	45.0	49.2	53.8	57.4	60.0	60.2	57.4	51.7	45.1	41.4	50.2
Prince Rupert	35.7	36.5	39.4	43.4	48.8	53.4	56.2	57.4	53.8	47.8	41.6	36.8	45.9
Prince George	14.6	19.4	30.4	40.6	50.0	56.4	59.6	58.2	50.4	41.3	28.4	18.2	38.9
Northwest Territories													
Whitehorse	5.2	6.8	21.3	31.8	45.5	54.6	56.2	53.6	46.0	34.4	14.6	3.2	31.1
Yellowknife	−14.7	−14.2	1.4	17.3	38.9	53.3	60.9	56.7	44.9	31.0	7.2	−12.9	22.5

(Source: Dominion Bureau of Statistics, *Canada Year Book, 1960*.)

LONG-TERM AVERAGE MONTHLY PRECIPITATION* IN INCHES FOR SELECTED PLACES

	Jan.	Feb.	Mar.	Apr.	May	June	July	Aug.	Sept.	Oct.	Nov.	Dec.	Year
Atlantic Provinces													
St. John's	5.31	5.13	4.64	3.77	3.85	3.13	3.14	3.97	3.73	4.76	5.71	5.95	53.09
Charlottetown	4.09	3.36	3.30	2.83	3.14	2.97	2.85	3.48	4.12	4.17	4.16	4.66	43.13
Halifax	5.16	3.96	4.33	4.48	4.36	4.32	3.62	4.06	4.61	5.12	5.03	5.21	54.26
Sydney	4.86	4.41	4.15	3.77	3.67	3.18	2.98	3.92	4.30	5.22	4.98	5.17	50.61
Moncton	2.96	3.58	3.15	3.16	3.41	3.66	2.94	3.24	3.80	3.24	4.33	3.50	40.97
Saint John	4.55	3.42	3.93	3.62	3.42	3.64	3.28	3.89	4.19	4.47	4.61	4.37	47.39
Québec													
Knob Lake	1.59	1.58	1.90	1.36	1.26	3.11	3.52	3.48	3.07	2.94	2.52	1.22	27.55
Sept Iles	4.13	3.74	3.09	2.19	3.15	2.95	4.47	3.34	3.73	3.07	3.99	4.09	41.94
Québec	3.63	2.80	2.95	3.29	3.55	4.50	4.40	4.41	4.21	3.72	4.00	3.30	44.76
Montréal	3.54	2.72	3.26	3.37	3.30	3.76	3.97	3.48	3.72	3.40	3.92	3.36	41.80

* Precipitation figures are for the precipitation of rain and snow combined. For winter months, one inch of precipitation is equivalent to ten inches of snow.

	Jan.	Feb.	Mar.	Apr.	May	June	July	Aug.	Sept.	Oct.	Nov.	Dec.	Year
Ontario													
Ottawa	2.67	2.20	2.81	2.62	2.84	3.43	3.53	2.97	3.12	2.70	2.97	3.03	34.89
Toronto	2.72	2.31	2.58	2.55	2.65	2.70	3.23	2.39	2.67	2.29	2.55	2.29	30.93
London	3.45	2.81	2.91	2.97	3.05	3.40	3.71	2.78	3.51	2.84	3.51	3.30	38.24
North Bay	2.02	1.68	2.02	2.32	2.87	3.39	3.85	2.66	3.84	2.91	2.79	2.10	32.45
Kapuskasing	1.99	1.37	1.64	1.65	2.29	2.79	3.32	3.17	3.23	2.11	2.36	2.07	27.99
Fort William-Port Arthur	2.28	1.42	1.96	2.15	2.65	4.12	2.89	3.68	3.34	2.58	2.50	2.05	31.62
Prairie Provinces													
Winnipeg	0.93	0.81	1.13	1.20	2.07	2.64	2.72	2.49	2.32	1.44	1.11	0.86	19.72
Churchill	0.32	0.42	0.58	0.75	1.04	1.27	2.37	2.58	2.24	1.48	1.20	0.76	15.01
Regina	0.65	0.59	0.78	0.81	1.60	3.24	2.13	1.74	1.22	0.85	0.86	0.62	15.09
Saskatoon	0.58	0.64	0.56	0.83	1.45	2.73	2.54	1.63	1.30	0.89	0.69	0.56	14.40
Calgary	0.55	0.66	1.12	1.26	1.94	3.48	2.41	1.96	1.79	0.89	0.79	0.62	17.47
Edmonton	0.90	0.77	0.85	1.10	1.82	2.97	3.11	2.27	1.16	0.84	0.91	0.93	17.63
Grande Prairie	1.35	1.37	0.74	0.82	1.52	2.00	2.48	1.68	1.28	0.98	1.22	1.36	16.80
British Columbia													
Penticton	0.98	0.81	0.75	0.83	1.00	1.36	0.78	0.83	0.89	0.98	1.05	1.24	11.50
Vancouver	7.92	6.04	5.25	3.63	2.71	2.13	1.36	1.63	3.15	6.59	6.89	9.53	56.83
Victoria	4.05	3.13	2.15	1.17	0.98	0.91	0.49	0.65	1.28	2.90	3.63	4.85	26.19
Prince Rupert	9.44	7.45	7.93	6.82	5.13	3.95	4.67	5.46	8.04	12.32	12.27	10.52	94.00
Prince George	1.85	1.48	1.25	0.96	1.53	2.20	2.14	2.25	2.20	2.12	2.13	2.05	22.16
Northwest Territories													
Whitehorse	0.64	0.47	0.60	0.41	0.57	1.00	1.63	1.53	1.34	0.71	1.00	0.77	10.67
Yellowknife	0.54	0.46	0.39	0.36	0.59	0.73	1.15	1.02	0.92	0.99	0.69	0.61	8.45

(Source: Dominion Bureau of Statistics, *Canada Year Book, 1960.*)

LONG-TERM MONTHLY AVERAGES ON THE NUMBER OF HOURS OF BRIGHT SUNSHINE FOR SELECTED CITIES*

	Jan.	Feb.	Mar.	Apr.	May	June	July	Aug.	Sept.	Oct.	Nov.	Dec.	Year
St. John's	66	80	97	101	166	173	232	181	151	108	58	51	1,464
Charlottetown	89	111	140	156	212	221	244	236	177	134	78	59	1,857
Halifax	95	113	148	152	200	212	239	219	169	152	89	88	1,876
Sydney	69	97	122	139	182	208	258	218	173	144	73	62	1,745
Moncton	105	123	144	162	207	205	228	219	159	145	92	88	1,877
Saint John	113	127	156	162	204	202	211	210	168	147	100	102	1,902
Québec	82	104	142	161	191	200	221	206	155	119	67	66	1,714
Montréal	79	102	145	167	203	222	244	223	170	126	69	61	1,811
Ottawa	92	116	151	185	228	250	274	249	177	137	78	73	2,010
Toronto	77	106	149	184	223	263	286	256	201	151	84	67	2,047
London	61	90	129	167	234	242	278	253	175	153	76	64	1,922
Kapuskasing	75	103	133	170	202	216	234	196	132	90	45	50	1,646
Fort William-Port Arthur	96	126	156	183	205	206	251	226	134	94	50	70	1,797
Winnipeg	100	130	167	204	245	250	294	263	178	133	84	78	2,126
Churchill	73	117	171	182	155	200	273	236	92	64	36	47	1,646
Regina	104	119	158	216	258	236	329	288	203	171	94	88	2,264
Saskatoon	97	123	191	218	267	268	338	305	213	169	94	84	2,367
Calgary	106	126	153	191	242	236	315	268	189	164	114	96	2,200
Edmonton	81	117	168	219	253	251	302	268	188	154	97	75	2,173
Grande Prairie	78	109	157	215	266	263	299	255	180	137	80	66	2,105
Penticton	52	90	150	198	238	247	312	279	204	140	59	40	2,009
Vancouver	48	80	126	168	226	223	280	254	178	110	53	38	1,784
Victoria	66	94	148	197	252	263	322	287	205	130	72	57	2,093
Prince Rupert	40	59	81	103	138	125	125	125	97	54	40	31	1,018
Prince George	57	88	133	175	242	240	254	244	161	100	53	38	1,785

(Source: Dominion Bureau of Statistics, *Canada Year Book, 1960.*)

* The list is shorter than in the previous two tables because the figures for certain cities are not available.

PART ONE

THE EMERGING TRENDS

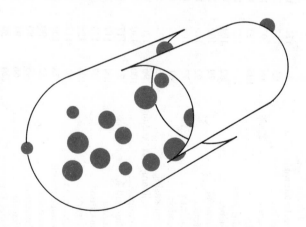

INTRODUCTION

The Roman Emperor Constantius issued a decree forbidding "anyone to consult a soothsayer, a mathematician, or a fortuneteller. May curiosity to foretell the future be silenced for ever." Despite this death penalty, forecasters continued to thrive in ancient Rome. They are still with us at present, with one major difference: they practice their profession, not in the back alleys and dark corners, but in the hallowed halls of universities and the executive suites of big corporations. Economic forecasting today is as unrelated to soothsaying as chemistry is to alchemy, astronomy to astrology, or chess to checkers.

Of course, no prediction can be a hundred per cent accurate, but one can come fairly close to the mark. This is because the future does not suddenly appear full-grown, like Minerva springing from the head of Jupiter. It emerges slowly from the amalgamation of varied forces that are already at work. Hence, the shape of the economy in the next few years need not be perceived dimly through the crystal ball. It can be sketched in broad outlines by analyzing and projecting from the present.

Developing such forecasts is a "must" in business life. Change is the keynote of the present era. Despite much talk about human nature being always the same, consumers are constantly modifying their tastes, preferences, and the standards by which they judge products and services. Rich rewards await the company that knows how to anticipate these changes and act on them at the right time and in the right way.

In Part One of this book an attempt is made to analyze the emerging trends in the following areas:

- Population
- Income and consumption
- Education
- Family life
- Retailing
- Labor force

Knowing clearly what Canadians are doing and where they are going provides a solid base for developing any long-term plan for the future. Unless management is aware of marketing and socio-economic trends, it will operate in a fog, using as guidelines what is nothing more than an agglomeration of folklore, outmoded maxims, and generalizations from particularistic experiences.

These are the years of challenge for marketing. Survival depends more and more on developing product lines, distribution techniques and advertising strategies that go hand in hand with the emerging trends. A firm that ignores this basic fact, sentences itself to a humdrum life of a passive follower. It will be always trailing in the rear, until one day it falls so far behind that it has to drop out of the race. The annals of business are full of records of once strong and prosperous companies that died — if not with a bang, at least with a whimper — because the top executives did not have their radar sets tuned in to the market place and so could not see the signals of change early enough.

Chapter 2

TRENDS IN POPULATION

The Postwar Increase

All long-term economic and marketing analyses start with population. More people mean more consumers, higher demand, bigger markets. Rapidly growing population eliminates the danger of serious depressions and serves as a backstop against overexpansion of factory capacities. In this respect, Canada's performance during the postwar era has been quite encouraging. In 1946, the country had 12,292,000 inhabitants; in 1965, there were 19,571,000 — a jump of 7.3 million in 19 years. This is, indeed, a healthy rise when it is remembered that from 1901 till the end of World War II the population increased by only 6.7 million.

The postwar gain is attributable both to high natural increase (excess of births over deaths) and heavy net immigration (excess of immigration over emigration). The improvement in health conditions has resulted in a steady decline of the death rate (i.e., deaths per 1,000 people) from 9.4 in 1946 to 7.5 in 1965. On the other hand, because of the demographic changes in the proportion of women in the reproductive age group, the crude birth rate has fluctuated from 28.5 in 1954 to 21.4 in 1965. However, even at the low level it is far above that prevailing in many industrialized nations. In fact, between 1946 and 1965 no less than 8,300,000 children were born in Canada. This means that more than two out of five persons living in the country were not even around at the end of World War II. On top of natural increase is the high rate of net immigration. Between 1946 and 1965 Canada received 2,504,020 newcomers from other countries. About 1,097,000 emigrated, mostly to the United States, resulting in an average net benefit from immigration of 70,350 persons a year.

Projections for Future Growth

Will this growth continue? Forecasting the future of population is a parlous business at best, and no one knows that better than the demographers who have tried it in the past. Fortunately, in recent years, the techniques have been considerably improved, and if the assumptions are realistic, the degree of error can be reduced to a few percentage points.

The Economic Council of Canada, in its *First Annual Review,* has prepared estimates of Canada's population for 1970. The projections are based on the following assumptions:

- There will be no major war with ballistic missiles carrying nuclear warheads. Obviously, it is pointless to consider what Canada's population growth would be in a world laid waste by radioactive dust.

- Minor cyclical swings will not be eliminated, but the country will be spared the havoc of a deep or protracted depression like that of the Thirties, with prolonged periods of mass unemployment.

- The target year 1970 will be reasonably "normal" — that is, it will be neither at the top of a cycle nor at the bottom, but somewhere along the trend line.

- Net immigration between 1965 and 1970 will average 50,000 a year (immigration 125,000 and emigration 75,000). The age and sex distribution of the immigrants will follow closely the current pattern.

- The mortality rates for different age groups will go on declining as in the past because of better medical facilities and improved sanitary conditions.

- The use of contraceptive devices will not be more extensive than at present, and the fertility ratios of females 15 to 49 years old will be about the same as in 1963 and 1964. The age at which women marry has been falling, and this trend will continue.

No one, of course, can tell whether all these assumptions will be validated as the years go by. If they are, then Canada's population will rise from 19,571,000 in 1965 to 21,729,200 in 1970. This implies an annual growth of 2.2%, a very high rate that can be matched by only a few nations in the world. In fact, if this rate were to continue for long, Canadian population would double itself within the lifetime of most of today's teen-agers. Even during the short span of 1965 to 1970, there will be 2,158,000 more people in the country, which is almost equivalent to adding a city about the size of Metropolitan Montréal.

Although large-scale development of natural resources may lead to the establishment of new communities in the hinterland, the majority of Canadians will reside in urban areas, especially in the large metropolitan centers. Suburban growth will continue, filling up the empty spaces between adjoining cities and leading to the emergence of a new type of highly urbanized society called "megalopolis."

	1965 (000)	1970 (000)	% increase
Atlantic Provinces	1,990	2,132	7.1
Québec	5,657	6,269	10.8
Ontario	6,731	7,566	12.4
Prairie Provinces	3,364	3,690	9.7
British Columbia	1,789	2,025	13.2
Yukon and Northwest Territories	40	47	17.5
Canada	19,571	21,729	11.0

Every province will register a sharp rise in population, but the rate of gain will vary considerably. Ontario will be the fastest growing province, followed by British Columbia and Québec. In the Prairies and the Atlantic Provinces, growth will be slower than the Canadian average. The preceding estimates have been prepared by extrapolating past trends.

In addition to projections on population, it is useful to know how many new families and households will be formed. Such information is of obvious significance for anticipating new residential construction and for determining the demand for all the things that go to equip a home — ranges, refrigerators, radios, TV sets, furniture, and the like. Here are the estimates for the first and second half of the Sixties prepared in Staff Study No. 4 of the Economic Council of Canada. (Illing, Wolfgang, M.: *Housing Demand to 1970.*)

	Average annual increase	
	1961–1966	1966–1971
Family households	77,700	113,400
Non-family households	34,500	31,500
Total households	112,200	144,900
Total families	72,000	108,200
Total marriages	137,880	178,740

Note: A family, as defined by the DBS, consists of a husband and wife, or a husband and wife and any children who have never married, or a person with any children who have never married, living together in the same dwelling. A household consists of one person or a group of persons occupying one dwelling. It usually contains a single family, but it may consist of a group of unrelated persons, of two or more families sharing a dwelling, or of one person living alone.

The sharp jump in new family formation in the later half of the Sixties will be the result of the "baby boom" of the Forties and thus will be largely independent of immigration. Even if not a single family migrated to Canada between 1966 and 1971, the annual net family formation would none the less amount to 95,000, a figure still 30% higher than the 1961-1966 rate.

Family households are expected to rise faster than families because, with growing prosperity, a large number of low-incomed families now sharing accommodation together will be able to establish separate households of their own. Among the non-family households, the sharpest increase will be in the ones headed by women living alone, chiefly widows. Females continue to have lower death rates than males at all ages, and in older groups the differentials seem to be widening.

Implications of Growth

What are the implications of this population growth to the future economy of the country? First and foremost, the consumer markets will expand. Secondary manufacturing industries are now operating under a handicap because of limited demand. With 2.2 million more people by 1970, a higher degree of specialization will become possible in many cases. Overhead costs, including research, design and tooling expenses, will come down. More and more manufacturers will be able to afford huge machinery, economic only with large runs.

The new population score card will also help to strike it rich for the farmer. Domestic demand will replace external demand as the main stimulus to agriculture. This will lead to significant shifts in production, so that, even on the Prairies, farming will become more diversified, and hence less risky.

Rapidly increasing population will also contribute to general economic prosperity through the high level of investment that it will necessitate, particularly in such forms of social capital as houses and schools. Furthermore, a great impetus will be given to technological changes and innovations. With the volume of demand rising, it will be easier for businessmen to scrap old plants and build new ones. "The gale of creative destruction," to use Professor Schumpeter's colorful expression, will blow more freely, bringing with it increased productivity, and hence added per capita real income.

Age Groups

The growth of population will, of course, not be uniform. This can be clearly seen by comparing the 1970 age structure, as estimated by the Economic Council of Canada, with the one prevailing in 1965. (See table at the end of this section.) Certain age groups are likely to expand rapidly, others moderately, while others still may even show a decline. These differential rates of growth will mean varying degrees of market expansion for diverse commodities.

The second baby boom, forecast for the late Sixties, will bring extra business to the producers of infant foods and toys as well as to the operators of diaper services. On the other hand, the recent drop in birth rate will be reflected in the below-average rise for the 5–14 age group. This will ease the pressure on elementary schools, but it will not be good news to the manufacturers of candies and children's clothing.

The 15–19 group will stay in the limelight, as in the past few years, but it will take on an even more gold-plated sheen than before. So far, the majority of this group has consisted of youngsters in their early teens who have helped the economy only as consumers. In the coming years, there will be a larger proportion of the older teens in this group, transforming it into a more pervasive consuming-earning-spending type. To the business community, this will mean greatly expanded markets for sports clothes, dance records, and various other youth-oriented items.

The most spectacular increase will be in the 20–24 age group — three times more than the average for the entire population. The colleges are soon going to feel the pinch, necessitating more provincial and, ultimately, federal aid to institutions of higher learning. The pressure will mount on business, too, to help support the large numbers of poor-but-deserving high school graduates who want to have their sheepskins.

The years 20 to 24 are also the period of family formation. Many wedding bells will start ringing, bringing joy to the hearts of jewelers, caterers, and proprietors of honeymoon resorts whose business is directly related to the marriage curve. Since very few of the newly-weds will be able to afford the down-payment for a home of their own, apartments will constitute a larger share of new residential dwellings. Manufacturers of appliances, therefore, will have to beam their selling strategy more to builders than to consumers. Also, on account of the limited floor space in apartments, compactness will be the feature prized most by the buyers of household goods.

The young adults will affect marketing in other fields as well. No strangers to change, they will be receptive to product innovation and, in a youth-oriented society, will probably set the trends for older age groups to follow. Furthermore, being reared in a period of prosperity, they will come to accept many one-time luxuries as necessities. Nor will their limited purchasing power put a damper on their unquenchable appetites. Lavish use will be made of credit. For those who lament the present size of consumer debt, there will be cause for more despair as tomorrow's young households perform the last rites over the puritanic ideals of thrift and frugality. If credit is not readily available, they will rent rather than purchase the big-ticket items needed for setting up a household. In this way, they will avoid using sizable chunks of cash and at the same time will have greater leeway for getting new models.

While the 20–24 group will hold the spotlight, the 25–29-year-olds will also post a provocative growth rate. Their swelling numbers will boost sales for a wide range of household goods. It is at this period that the move from an apartment to a house usually takes place, triggering a buying spree that embraces gadgets, furnishings and major appliances. However, since the average family income will be still below par, the private home-builders, to attract this market, will have to produce more low-cost dwellings and devise easier ways of financing. The answer may perhaps lie in prefabricated houses, or at least in the extensive use of fabricated components.

The upward trend presented so far will almost make a U-turn with the 30–44 age group. These are the persons born in the late Twenties and Thirties when the birth rate had fallen to an all-time low. Between 1965 and 1970 their numbers will actually decline by 36,100, and the drop will be keenly felt by marketers catering to this group. Here is one more reason why businessmen may find it more profitable to direct their sales pitches to the younger households.

Things brighten up a bit in the 45–64 group. Its growth will be slightly above average. The news is encouraging especially when one remembers that it is in this category that families reach the height of their earning power. The rise in well-heeled households can mean bigger markets for luxury goods, expensive houses, high-priced automobiles and other similar items.

The increase in the over-65 group will just about match the par for the whole population. The marketing implications are not so much in the numbers as in the better financial position of tomorrow's senior citizens, due to significant advances in medicare and improvements in private and public pension plans. Some executives see a glittering array of special markets opening up to cater to the elderly — "retirement villages," vacation resorts, "golden age" clubs, geriatric aids, and a long list of leisure goods and services from do-it-yourself kits to home-study courses.

POPULATION BY SEX AND AGE GROUPS, 1965 AND 1970

Age groups	Males		Females		Persons		% change
	1965	1970	1965	1970	1965	1970	
0– 4	1,156,000	1,310,700	1,103,900	1,250,300	2,259,900	2,561,000	+13.3
5– 9	1,132,100	1,192,900	1,081,800	1,141,500	2,213,900	2,334,400	+ 5.4
10–14	1,044,000	1,143,400	996,000	1,094,900	2,040,000	2,238,300	+ 9.7
15–19	908,000	1,048,900	871,100	1,001,900	1,779,100	2,050,800	+15.3
20–24	694,900	929,500	682,400	891,300	1,377,300	1,820,800	+32.2
25–29	590,700	730,400	594,200	713,700	1,184,900	1,444,100	+21.9
30–34	624,500	603,700	601,500	608,800	1,226,000	1,212,500	− 1.1
35–39	644,200	624,400	633,500	604,000	1,277,700	1,228,400	− 3.9
40–44	613,300	636,100	625,100	629,000	1,238,400	1,265,100	+ 2.2
45–49	537,200	599,800	537,400	617,900	1,074,600	1,217,700	+13.3
50–54	486,700	520,900	477,300	529,000	964,000	1,049,900	+ 8.9
55–59	406,000	460,100	394,900	463,700	800,900	923,800	+15.3
60–64	320,100	369,100	319,600	376,300	639,700	745,400	+16.5
65–69	249,800	277,400	265,300	295,100	515,100	572,500	+11.1
Over 69	455,400	472,000	524,100	592,500	979,500	1,064,500	+ 8.7
Total	9,862,900	10,919,300	9,708,100	10,809,900	19,571,000	21,729,200	+11.0

(Sources: DBS: 1) *Estimated Population by Sex and Age Group for Canada and Provinces, 1965*, catalogue No. 91-202; 2) Staff Study No. 1 prepared for the Economic Council of Canada by Frank T. Denton, Yoshiko Kasahara and Sylvia Ostry: *Population and Labour Force Projections to 1970*.)

BIBLIOGRAPHY

Caves, Richard E., and Richard H. Holton: *The Canadian Economy: Prospect and Retrospect*. Harvard University Press, Cambridge, Massachusetts, 1959.

Economic Council of Canada: *Economic Goals for Canada to 1970*. First Annual Review. Queen's Printer, Ottawa, December, 1964.

Royal Commission on Canada's Economic Prospects (Gordon Commission): *Final Report*, Queen's Printer, Ottawa, November, 1957.

Taylor, Thayer C.: "Coming Up, the Third Postwar Boom Decade," *Sales Management*, November 10, 1965.

Wilson, George W.; Scott Gordon; Stanislaw Judek: *Canada: An Appraisal of Its Needs and Resources*. The Twentieth Century Fund study, University of Toronto Press, Toronto, 1965.

Chapter 3

TRENDS IN INCOME AND CONSUMPTION

Changes in Income, Purchasing Patterns and Marketing

Throughout the course of human history, poverty has been the rule, riches the exception. Even in the wealthy countries of the past, only the ruling classes lived in abundance and luxury; the great majority of people struggled for mere subsistence. High incomes meant palaces for living kings and pyramids for dead ones, but hovels and hunger for the mass of mankind. Today in Canada, as in the other parts of the Western World, the situation has completely changed. The common man is now able to enjoy a standard of living that in the days gone by was reserved only for the upper economic layer. The term "affluence" has acquired a new meaning of more for the many rather than much for the few. Here is a society in which the basic material wants have been satisfied in some measure for almost everybody, and met in real abundance for many.

There has been a steady rise in the level of income earned by Canadians. In 1964, the per capita disposable income was $1,640. Just after the war (average income of 1946-1950), the corresponding figure was only $838. Although part of the increase was offset by a decline in the value of the dollar, roughly 32% of the gain represented a rise in real purchasing power. Perhaps one of the most realistic yardsticks for indicating this improvement is a comparison for the two periods of the quantity of food purchasable *with one hour of work*. For every single pound bought in the 1946-50 period, an industrial laborer could get in 1964 1.2 pounds of flour, 1.4 pounds of round steak, 1.5 pounds of cheese, 1.7 pounds of peaches, 1.8 pounds of bacon, and 2.3 pounds of butter. Here is a clear example of how increased productivity can augment the standard of living for everyone.

Furthermore, the average work week has steadily declined, and Canadian laborers have gained a number of the so-called "fringe benefits," such as longer vacations and increased employer contributions to medical and pension plans. In 1939, a typical blue-collar laborer was a man on an assembly line whose job was intensely monotonous. Today, a large proportion of such persons are highly skilled. Many exercise a great deal of judgment and are entrusted with the care and operation of some very sophisticated kinds of equipment. The white-collar personnel, especially those in the clerical and sales professions, have not fared as well, but due to the booming economy, even they have gradually moved up the income ladder. If most Canadians still cannot afford $150 suits, summer cottages, *and* winter trips to Florida, they can have some of these things some of the time. What is more significant, the majority of individuals, especially among the younger age groups, are optimistic about the future and are confident that still higher levels of opulence can be attained.

For 1964, the income distribution pattern has been estimated as follows:

	Households	% of the total
Under $2,000	807,200	16.8
$2,000–2,999	508,700	10.6
$3,000–3,999	602,200	12.5
$4,000–4,999	748,400	15.6
$5,000–5,999	674,300	14.0
$6,000–9,999	1,097,000	22.8
$10,000 and over	367,200	7.7
Total	4,805,000	100.0

The shape of the income structure resembles a diamond rather than the conventional pyramid, with the majority of the households concentrated in the lower and middle income brackets ($3,000–$9,999). Progressive taxation at the top and welfare payments at the bottom have reduced the numbers at the extremes of the income scale. Only a small minority — the aged, the uneducated, the unskilled — are not able to meet the minimum standards for nutrition, housing and clothing. However, even here, when compared to the situation a generation ago, the sharp edge of poverty has been blunted. At the same time, the rich have learned to be discreet, almost reticent, in exhibiting their wealth. In a sense, conspicuous consumers have given way to conspicuous producers, for, by and large, it is the corporations that have taken the place of individuals in displaying wealth. They build palatial structures, called offices or factories, provide private airplanes for the top personnel, and have fancy lodges for their convening executives. In fact, much of the dining and wining today is done by free-spending "organization men" with their liberal expense accounts.

Hedonism

During the last two decades, the consumer market has been affected by several social and economic forces which have changed Canadians' attitudes towards life. The puritanical traits of frugality and hard work are slowly being discarded. In the metropolitan areas at least, hedonism has become the guiding philosophy and is gaining more and more adherents. The younger generation especially has been inculcated with a love for possessions and a zest for finding momentary pleasures. They have broken out of the old-fashioned inhibitions of their parents and learned to "live it up." The progressive disintegration of respect for authority, the gradual acceptance of Freudian psychology (or its popularized version), the postwar lowering of religious barriers, the peril of nuclear annihilation — all these factors have contributed greatly to the live-for-the-moment attitude, the new mood of self-indulgence, the permissive spirit of care-free spending. Faith and principle are far from dead, but self-denial is increasingly seen as foolishness rather than a virtue. The current view is very much akin to what was expressed by John Cleland in his long-suppressed novel, *Fanny Hill,* where one of the principal characters mentions that pleasure of one sort or another is the universal port of destination and every wind that blows thither a good one, provided it blows nobody any harm.*

A Changed Attitude Towards Money

Another by-product of hedonism is a transformation in the attitude towards money. In the years gone by, money was respected for its own sake as a working tool, something to invest and beget more money, which in turn would produce more power, higher social status, a larger estate. A prudent man of means would no more have thought of selling off his 6% bonds to take an extended vacation than a carpenter would have disposed of his tools to buy a Model T. Capital was held inviolate, and to dip into it was sacrilegious.

In the society of today, money is meant for spending. Savings, in the usual sense of the word, are no longer as important. Pension plans and social security lessen the urgency of providing for old age. Medical and hospitalization plans and other forms of insurance guard against emergencies. Supplementary unemployment benefits are a further step in the same direction.

The broad lower- and middle-income class not only saves little for the proverbial rainy day, but it does not at all regard it shameful to go into debt. Today's consumer insists on having whatever he or she wants at once — whether it be a house, an automobile, a power mower, or an Easter bonnet — and paying for it out of income yet to be earned. The current philosophy is: "Why deny yourself? Give vent to your whims and desires."

In this attitude, the public has been abetted to a considerable extent by business. Consumption is fast becoming a hallowed word alongside with Democracy and Motherhood. The economy is dependent on mass production, which can

---

* Another outcome of this trend has been the steady disintegration of once-cherished ideals on sex-discipline and virginity. Canada is undergoing a revolution of mores and an erosion of morals that is turning it into a "sex-affirming culture." Today, sex seems to be emerging from everywhere — from the stage and screen, books and magazines, as well as the words and rhythms of "pop" music. True, Canada is a long way from the rugged debaucheries of Restoration England or the perfumed corruption of the Louis XV era in France, but during the last few years the trend towards sexual permissiveness has been indeed rapid. John O'Hara, whose writing until recently was criticized as "sex-obsessed," appears positively Platonic alongside the authors of today's paperback fiction, who describe unashamedly in detail actions that used to be mentioned primarily in scientific works and even there only in Latin.

only be maintained if the products which roll from the assembly lines are immediately consumed and not accumulated into inventories. Credit is a very useful tool in this respect. It turns people into better prospects. The selling task is eased; customers tend to buy more when they do not have to put up the money immediately.* Indeed, since the family income reaches its peak when the head is between 35–55, and since most households face their heaviest needs much earlier, appropriate use of installment payments can be quite helpful in bridging the gap.

The Market for "Seconds"

Credit is just one weapon in the marketing arsenal. Another method that has been tried with great success is the creation of the need for "seconds." Like a hospitable hostess, the industry is urging consumers to "do have another"; and families are now buying more of each product than would have been deemed rational or prudent in earlier years. This is brought out clearly in the survey of household facilities and equipment conducted every year by the Dominion Bureau of Statistics.

	1960	1965
Percentage of total households in Canada having:		
Two or more radios	32.7	41.3
Two or more television sets	3.4	10.9
Two or more telephones	7.2	13.2
Two or more automobiles	7.4	12.5

Perhaps the ultimate development of this two-or-more-of-a-kind concept — which began so humbly in the Twenties with the political promise of two chickens in every pot — is the promotion of the idea of two homes per family: a town house and a country cottage. This idea is slowly catching on, opening up tremendous markets for builders, building-material suppliers, appliance manufacturers, and the like.

Obsolescence

Marketers have also met with remarkable success in developing the throwaway spirit among consumers. People are now no longer attached to old things. They do not hold on to their possessions as if they were heirlooms. Psychological obsolescence has become a part of life. Originally an item was considered outmoded only when something new was introduced that performed the function better. Now a product, even though sound in terms of quality and performance, still gets "worn out" in consumers' minds simply because styling or some other innovation has made it less desirable. Women's fashion designers and automobile manufacturers popularized this phenomenon of planned obsolescence,

* Also, many retailers are discovering to their delight that they can often make more money on the interest charges in financing the purchase than on the sale of the item itself.

and other industries have not been slow to take a cue from them. Even the male apparel field has succumbed to this trend. Men no longer want a suit; they want a certain look of elegance, sophistication and success, and this "look" changes every few years.

Convenience

Among the other factors that affect marketing is the trend towards convenience. Canadians today are less price-conscious, more convenience-conscious. They want things that are ready to use, ready to wear, ready to plug in, ready to serve. The opportunities for pleasure and enjoyment are so great that the general tendency is to get the necessary tasks over with, in the fastest and the easiest way. Here are seven forms of convenience which the consumers now expect almost as a matter of course:

- *Readiness convenience.* The housewife wants her spinach chopped and cleaned, her chicken cut up and ready to fry, her beef steaks cubed, her sausage precooked, her potatoes sliced into French fries, her TV dinners ready to be served in a matter of minutes. She demands a variety of prepared mixes which will produce everything from cakes and cookies to puddings and pie crusts merely by adding water. Food processors burn the midnight oil figuring out ways to make "instant foods" still more instantaneous.

- *Form convenience.* Many toilet preparations are now available in liquid, paste, powder, lotion, or spray form. In the tobacco field, smokers have a choice of plain or filtered cigarettes, king size or regular, made with straight tobacco or mentholated.

- *Place convenience.* With the exodus to the suburbs, a large part of the consumer's retail dollar is spent in the shopping centers designed to offer one-stop shopping for just about every home and family need. Convenience of place is also evidenced by the shift in patronage from hotels to motels, and from restaurants to diners and drive-ins.

- *Time convenience.* Since many married women are working, retail stores have been forced to remain open in the evenings and at other odd hours. Time convenience has also led to the growth of self-service outlets and vending machines. In the future, this trend may provide a stimulus for other retailing developments, such as direct-to-consumer selling, catalog and telephone selling, and perhaps a combination of television and telephone selling. In the United States one bank is experimenting with a computerized dialing system that enables customers to pay bills by phone.

- *Packaging convenience.* Depending on the nature of the item, its package must be easy to find on the shelf, easy to carry in the pocket or handbag, easy to store, easy to open, easy to use, easy to dispose of, or serve as re-usable purpose. The plastic squeeze bottles, the cellophane wraps, the aerosol cans, represent some recent ingenious break-throughs in packaging convenience.

TOTAL CANADIAN EXPENDITURES ON CONSUMER GOODS
AND SERVICES, 1964 constant dollars
(Figures in millions of dollars, except the last column)

Consumer goods and services	Average 1949– 1953	Average 1954– 1958	Average 1959– 1963	1964	% rise 1964 over 1949–53
Food	*4,141*	*5,220*	*6,217*	*6,693*	*61.6*
Tobacco and alcoholic beverages	*1,115*	*1,422*	*1,749*	*1,904*	*70.8*
Tobacco products	484	592	768	812	67.8
Alcoholic beverages	631	830	981	1,092	73.1
Clothing and personal furnishings	*1,914*	*2,236*	*2,603*	*2,807*	*46.7*
Men's and boys' clothing	448	503	578	638	42.4
Women's and children's clothing	806	955	1,101	1,190	47.6
Footwear	241	271	330	339	40.7
Laundry and dry cleaning	124	172	206	233	87.9
Other	295	335	388	407	38.0
Shelter	*2,298*	*2,965*	*3,890*	*4,564*	*98.6*
Gross rents paid by tenants	671	824	1,050	1,261	87.9
Expenses of owner-occupants	740	1,020	1,533	1,922	159.7
Net imputed residential rent and capital consumption allowances	623	878	1,043	1,103	77.0
Other	264	243	264	278	5.3
Household operation	*1,872*	*2,534*	*3,104*	*3,548*	*89.5*
Fuel	330	406	453	457	38.5
Electricity	140	243	351	407	190.7
Gas	39	58	124	163	317.9
Telephone	133	226	338	417	213.5
Furniture	228	304	326	357	56.6
Home furnishings	208	248	292	356	71.2
Appliances, radios and TV sets	343	489	509	562	63.8
Other	451	560	711	829	83.8
Transportation	*1,626*	*2,309*	*2,967*	*3,656*	*124.8*
Street-car, railway, other fares	345	363	424	485	40.6
New and used automobiles, trailers	745	1,101	1,356	1,835	146.3
Automotive operating expenses	536	845	1,187	1,336	149.3
Personal and medical care	*1,283*	*1,626*	*2,200*	*2,563*	*99.8*
Medical and dental care	264	343	453	512	93.9
Hospital care, medical insurance, etc.	417	616	968	1,227	194.2
Other	602	667	779	824	36.9
Miscellaneous	*2,508*	*2,873*	*3,028*	*3,696*	*47.4*
Grand totals	*16,757*	*21,185*	*25,758*	*29,431*	*75.6*

(Source: DBS, *National Accounts, Income and Expenditure* reports. Catalogue No. 13-201. Figures converted into 1964 dollars by using the price indices mentioned in the report for each of the categories.)

• *Selection convenience.* The consumer wants a wide range of forms, sizes, patterns, models, colors, flavors, styles, and prices in just about everything he or she buys. Automobiles provide a good example. They come in a regular galaxy of colors, with different types of optional equipment to suit anybody's needs or whims. There is an ample choice in size as well — large, standard, intermediate, compact, and small.

• *Automatic operations convenience.* Typical examples are appliances for washing and drying clothes, thermostatic devices for regulating room temperature, gadgets that automatically start the radio in the morning, and gas ranges that can turn the heat on and off at predetermined times. Nor are such facilities confined to the home. Cars are equipped with automatic gear shifts, power steering, and power brakes. The 1966 Thunderbird model makes motoring even more relaxing by offering a unique "highway pilot" which enables the driver to maintain a chosen cruising speed on expressways.

Thus, a tidal wave of craving for convenience is sweeping the country. Consumers are constantly on the lookout for products, ideas and services that make their all-too-many tasks easier and less time-consuming. It is therefore safe to say that any type of business, whether it be in the field of production or distribution, can expand its markets considerably by applying fresh and imaginative inventiveness in one or more of the above areas of convenience.

ANNUAL EXPENDITURES ON CONSUMER GOODS AND SERVICES PER HOUSEHOLD

(Figures in 1964 constant dollars)

Consumer goods and services	Average 1949-53 household expenditures $	%	Average 1954-58 household expenditures $	%	Average 1959-63 household expenditures $	%	1964 household expenditures $	%
Food	1,212	24.7	1,328	24.6	1,374	24.1	1,393	22.7
Tobacco and alcoholic beverages	326	6.7	362	6.7	386	6.8	396	6.5
Tobacco products	141	2.9	151	2.8	169	3.0	169	2.8
Alcoholic beverages	185	3.8	211	3.9	217	3.8	227	3.7
Clothing and personal furnishings	560	11.4	569	10.6	575	10.1	584	9.5
Men's and boys' clothing	131	2.7	128	2.4	128	2.2	133	2.2
Women's and children's clothing	236	4.8	243	4.5	243	4.3	248	4.0
Footwear	71	1.4	69	1.3	73	1.3	70	1.1
Laundry and dry cleaning	36	0.7	44	0.8	45	0.8	48	0.8
Other	86	1.8	85	1.6	86	1.5	85	1.4

ANNUAL EXPENDITURES ON CONSUMER GOODS

AND SERVICES PER HOUSEHOLD (continued)

Consumer goods and services	Average 1949–53 household expenditures $	%	Average 1954–58 household expenditures $	%	Average 1959–63 household expenditures $	%	1964 household expenditures $	%
Shelter	672	13.7	754	14.0	860	15.1	950	15.5
Gross rents paid by tenants	196	4.0	210	3.9	232	4.1	262	4.3
Expenses of owner-occupants	217	4.4	259	4.8	339	5.9	400	6.5
Net imputed residential rent and capital consumption allowances	182	3.7	223	4.1	231	4.1	230	3.8
Other	77	1.6	62	1.2	58	1.0	58	0.9
Household operation	548	11.2	644	11.9	686	12.1	738	12.1
Fuel	97	2.0	103	1.9	100	1.7	95	1.6
Electricity	41	0.8	62	1.1	78	1.4	85	1.4
Gas	11	0.2	15	0.3	27	0.5	34	0.6
Telephone	39	0.8	58	1.1	75	1.3	87	1.4
Furniture	67	1.4	77	1.4	72	1.3	74	1.2
Home furnishings	61	1.3	63	1.2	65	1.1	74	1.2
Appliances, radios and TV sets	100	2.0	124	2.3	112	2.0	117	1.9
Other	132	2.7	142	2.6	157	2.8	172	2.8
Transportation	476	9.7	587	10.9	656	11.5	761	12.4
Street-car, railway, other fares	101	2.1	92	1.7	94	1.6	101	1.7
New and used automobiles, trailers	218	4.4	280	5.2	300	5.3	382	6.2
Automotive operating expenses	157	3.2	215	4.0	262	4.6	278	4.5
Personal and medical care	375	7.6	413	7.7	486	8.5	534	8.7
Medical and dental care	77	1.5	87	1.6	100	1.7	107	1.7
Hospital care, medical insurance, etc.	122	2.5	157	2.9	214	3.8	255	4.2
Other	176	3.6	169	3.2	172	3.0	172	2.8
Miscellaneous	734	15.0	731	13.6	669	11.8	769	12.6
Motion picture theatres	39	0.8	27	0.5	16	0.3	13	0.2
Newspapers and magazines	62	1.3	62	1.2	58	1.0	61	1.0
Net expenditure abroad	4	0.1	59	1.1	40	0.7	18	0.3
Other	629	12.8	583	10.8	555	9.8	677	11.1
Grand totals	4,903	100.0	5,388	100.0	5,692	100.0	6,125	100.0

Note: The average number of households was estimated at: 3,418,000 for 1949–53; 3,932,000 for 1954–58; 4,525,000 for 1959–63; and 4,805,000 in 1964.

(Source: DBS, *National Accounts, Income and Expenditure* reports. Catalogue No. 13-201.)

Outlook for 1970

What will the picture be like in 1970? Much will depend on the amount of money available for spending on different goods and services. This in turn will hinge on the size of the Gross National Product in 1970. Forecasting is always difficult, and probably the most realistic approach that can be adopted here is the one taken by the Economic Council of Canada. Rather than trying to predict events which cannot be foreseen, the Council has set a certain number of targets for 1970, based on the realization of five basic goals: full employment, sustained economic growth, reasonable price stability, a viable balance of payments position, and balanced regional development.

Assuming that these goals are attained, the Gross National Product, in 1964 constant dollars, will reach $63,937 million in 1970, compared to $47,003 million in 1964. This is the total volume of production that Canada can achieve by the end of the decade if there is a reasonably full and efficient use of her economic resources. To quote the Council's words: "It is a calculation of the possible — in a sense, a target to be aimed at — not a projection of the probable. Moreover, it does not represent the highest possible level of attainment under the best of all possible circumstances, but rather an indication of productive capabilities under reasonable expectations of performance."*

As they say along the Atlantic Coast, "The rising tide lifts all the boats." If the Gross National Product reaches its target of $63.9 billion, personal disposable income should be in the neighborhood of $42 billion by 1970 (in 1964 constant dollars). The distribution pattern by income groups would be approximately as follows:

	Households	% of the total
Under $2,000	436,000	8.0
$2,000–2,999	216,000	3.9
$3,000–3,999	334,000	6.1
$4,000–4,999	454,000	8.3
$5,000–5,999	1,023,000	18.6
$6,000–9,999	2,200,000	40.1
$10,000 and over	824,000	15.0
Total	5,487,000	100.0

The consumer market's center of gravity will shift from the lower to the middle income brackets, with a sizeable number of families reaching the five-figure mark. This will not only represent a bigger aggregate demand for all sorts of

* Economic Council of Canada: *Economic Goals for Canada for 1970*. First Annual Review. Queen's Printer, Ottawa, December, 1964. Page 31.

products and services, but will also result in a significant change in the composition of demand on account of the reshuffle in purchasing power.

The increased income will allow many individuals to choose the kind of life they wish to lead. When families pass beyond the $10,000 line, a large portion of their income is discretionary, and the range of options is so wide that it is no

TOTAL AND PER CAPITA PERSONAL DISPOSABLE INCOME IN 1964 CONSTANT DOLLARS

Province	Average 1949– 1953	Average 1954– 1958	Average 1959– 1963	1964	Esti- mate 1970
A. Total income (million dollars)					
Newfoundland	239	325	418	492	672
Prince Edward Island	73	82	104	125	168
Nova Scotia	605	726	870	967	1,260
New Brunswick	448	520	623	718	882
Québec	4,383	5,553	6,956	8,124	10,794
Ontario	6,933	8,879	10,901	12,423	16,716
Manitoba	998	1,145	1,390	1,565	2,016
Saskatchewan	1,172	1,102	1,351	1,456	1,806
Alberta	1,341	1,652	2,087	2,355	3,192
British Columbia	1,779	2,376	2,853	3,263	4,410
Yukon and N.W. Territories	25	38	45	49	84
Canada	17,996	22,398	27,598	31,537	42,000
B. Per capita income (dollars)					
Newfoundland	658	785	909	1,002	1,233
Prince Edward Island	745	820	1,000	1,168	1,541
Nova Scotia	938	1,049	1,180	1,272	1,546
New Brunswick	863	937	1,042	1,164	1,330
Québec	1,077	1,197	1,324	1,461	1,722
Ontario	1,496	1,629	1,752	1,886	2,209
Manitoba	1,276	1,347	1,509	1,634	1,940
Saskatchewan	1,395	1,251	1,465	1,544	1,826
Alberta	1,421	1,465	1,570	1,645	1,921
British Columbia	1,517	1,684	1,750	1,877	2,178
Yukon and N.W. Territories	1,000	1,267	1,216	1,195	1,787
Canada	1,277	1,387	1,515	1,640	1,933

(Source: DBS, *National Accounts, Income and Expenditure* [Different years]. The estimates for 1970 have been prepared by the author. The figures in current dollars were converted to 1964 constant dollars by using the implicit price index for personal expenditures on consumer goods and services published in the above DBS reports. Excluded from Canada's total is the income of Canadians who are temporarily abroad; e.g., pay and allowances of Canadian Armed Forces overseas.)

longer a question of this purchase or that purchase, but of selecting a complete style of living. A skilled craftsman with an annual income of over $10,000 may choose to live like a junior executive in his own $20,000 suburban home, or he may continue to stay in a "working-class" neighborhood and use the savings for his children's college education. Wealth thus permits a large measure of choice, and anyone who tries to forecast exactly what will happen in the coming years is sure to stub his toe. The new category of affluent masses may alternatively confer their favors from boats to overseas travel, from psychoanalysis to a host of other interests that endlessly come and go. But while it is impossible to be specific about a particular market, one can chart the broad directions of the changes that will take place as a result of higher income, better education, faster communications, and increased urbanization.

Mass Culture Market

A mass market will be created for what is loosely called "culture." In a society whose dynamics are switching from scarcity to abundance, from self-denial to self-fulfillment, from conformity to individuality, the public will demand the sort of standards that the "class" market now expects. With greater leisure, both from employment and from household chores, more attention will be paid to cultural development and creative hobbies. It is quite probable that tomorrow's typical conversation pieces and even status symbols will be art work, literary composition, and ingenious items developed in the studio or home workshop. The opera and classical music concerts will no longer be just for the white-tie-and-tails set. The mental horizons of the masses will broaden as communications and technological innovations shrink the world's boundaries and increase the cross-fertilization of culture and ideas. Consequently, the selling base of mass merchandising will shift from function to styling. With the growth of public taste, the designer — an almost unknown breed a decade or so ago — will assume a position of responsibility and will enjoy far more freedom. Manufacturers will experiment with new styles unthinkable today.

The rising tide of individual self-expression will result in a greater fragmentation of the market. Indeed, despite all the pressure to conformity emanating from mass-media advertising and suburban living, the consumer will look for diversity, not uniformity, in the goods he purchases. Feeling like a small cog in a world that is growing exceedingly complex, he will rely on consumption as the one area where he can reaffirm his individuality.

The trend toward individualized products will open up new vistas for small businessmen. As a rule, the larger manufacturers can only aim at the mass market to support their heavy investment in machinery and organizational overhead. The small firms, hence, would be free to cater to those customers who are not satisfied with mass-produced items and are on the lookout for something distinctively different.

New Products

By 1970, almost every manufacturer will be forced to enter the new product race. Either he makes new products the major concern of his business, or he will suffer the attrition of time and aggressive competition. It will no longer be possible to live in a sealed continuum and try to play it safe by systematically rejecting radical new ideas in favor of the respectable virtues of the here and now. Planning for growth without a new product program will be, indeed, like planting acorns in a flower pot.

Most successful firms in the future will have the following characteristics:

• They will spend large sums of money to seek out and develop new products and new markets at the right time and in the right way.

• They will be anxious to convert their lab-hatched technological eggs into practical consumer omelets. New ideas will not have to wend their laborious way tortuously upward through successive committee layers before coming up for final approval at the top.

• They will be customer-oriented and not product-oriented; they will bring out new products which the customers want to buy, not what the production and engineering departments are equipped to sell.

• Their top-management slots will be staffed with enthusiastic leaders who, by word and deed, will create an atmosphere of effervescent high adventure and fearless risk-taking.

• Their marketing will be centripetal, not centrifugal. There will be a man at the top entrusted with the task of co-ordinating the work of the various departments, so that the total communications program is able to achieve one overwhelming, self-reinforcing cumulative effect.

Growth of Leasing

Another development, now in its infancy, but likely to grow in importance, is the trend towards leasing rather than buying. In the past, people placed value on ownership because there were not enough goods to go around. But, in an affluent society where all can live like kings, the trappings of royalty lose much of their luster. Consumers increasingly come to realize that they are not interested in the things per se, but rather in their use in a convenient and worry-free manner through leasing.

The boon to the rental industry is obvious. Auto rental companies blazed the trail, and other retail outlets are slowly following their lead. Already one large department store in the United States advertises the availability of hundreds of items for rent, among them dishwashers, linens, china, power tools, and wheelchairs. Big manufacturers, too, are toying with the idea of renting appliances to apartment-house builders. Not only will refrigerators, air conditioners, washers and dryers be rented, but they will also be serviced and replaced by newer models after a specific period.

Some sociologists envision the time when the family, instead of buying, will rent the house and all its major furnishings and appliances. The only possessions owned will be those which give the home a stamp of individuality — paintings, personal accessories, "objets d'art," and so forth. Home builders have begun talking excitedly about the House of Tomorrow, which will come in removable sections, with annual model changes available for the discontented.

If this burgeoning trend really gathers momentum, it will have far-reaching repercussions on the economy. In fact, it may go a long way to curing one of capitalism's worst headaches — the instability of employment. Obviously, the adverse effects of the business cycle can be mitigated if production is steady and continuous, and this can to a large extent be achieved if individuals spend their money at a fairly even rate. What can be more promising than involving families in long-term commitments paid for at regular intervals? For example, under a contract selling plan, an automobile manufacturer could stipulate that he will provide a customer with a new car every three years. The amount paid each month would be fixed, and the all-important delivery date would be left to the discretion of the manufacturer. This would permit the factory managers to plan production on a long-range basis without the violent ups and downs in output that cause sharp fluctuations in employment. Even the consumers may benefit because the reduction in the costs of production may be passed on to them.

BIBLIOGRAPHY

Ansoff, Igor H.: "The Firm of the Future," *Harvard Business Review*. September-October, 1965.

Business Week: "For Americans Today — Money is to Spend." June 16, 1956.

Business Week: "The New Customer — Skilled, Choosy, Culture-Hungry." May 4, 1957.

Business Week: "Selling the Consumer on Need for Seconds." September 5, 1959.

Editors of *Fortune: The Changing American Market.* Hanover House, Garden City, N.Y., 1953.

Editors of *Fortune: Markets of the Sixties.* Harper & Brothers, New York, 1960.

Firestone, O. J.: *Problems of Economic Growth.* University of Ottawa Press, Ottawa, 1965.

Katona, George: *The Mass Consumption Society.* McGraw-Hill Book Company, Inc., New York, 1964.

Levitt, Theodore: *Innovation in Marketing.* McGraw-Hill Book Company, Inc., New York, 1962.

Mauser, Ferdinand F.: *Modern Marketing Management.* McGraw-Hill Book Company, Inc., New York, 1961.

Mauser, Ferdinand F., and Robert C. Garretson: "The Future Challenges Marketing," *Harvard Business Review.* November-December, 1963.

Mortimer, Charles G.: *The Creative Factor in Marketing.* Fifteenth Annual Parlin Memorial Lecture, May 13, 1959, Philadelphia Chapter of the American Marketing Association.

Packard, Vance: *The Waste Makers.* David McKay Company, Inc., 1960.

Rose, Albert: "Canada: The Design of Social Change," Chapter I in *Marketing: Canada,* edited by Isaiah A. Litvak and Bruce E. Mallen. McGraw-Hill Company of Canada Limited, Toronto, 1964.

Chapter 4

TRENDS IN EDUCATION

The Culture Boom

The attitude towards education, particularly higher learning, has taken almost a 180-degree turn. Apathy, indifference, and even hostility, have been replaced by eager enthusiasm. A generation or so ago, the Canadian ideal was not a man of letters but a man of action — the self-taught pragmatist, the graduate of life, the entrepreneur who achieved progress through intuition and persistence. Except in French Canada, the intellectual was dismissed as a cultural adornment, living in an ivory tower, far removed from the realities of life.

How different is the situation today! Anti-eggheadry is at an all-time low. The intellectuals' place is everywhere. They have, for example, burst out of the academic halls into government circles. So many have gone to work for the federal civil service that in some respects, as Professor John Porter remarks, the conference rooms of Ottawa have become more university-like than the universities. Almost one-fifth of the bureaucratic elite were once university teachers, many having a distinguished scholastic career before becoming public servants.*

The intellectuals' new influence is not confined just to government. They have invaded other fields as well. Professors do consulting work for business firms, often earning more than their academic salaries. Philosophers and novelists are not exactly swamped with management job offers, but their TV appearances are more frequent, their lecture fees more munificent, and, what with paperbacks, they can not only get their manuscripts published, but published for gold.

Many Canadians too are on a culture spree, especially in the big cities. This is manifested in several ways — in the alacrity with which they rush to act in a community theater, to daub at canvas, to manipulate clay, to purchase paintings by new and relatively unknown artists, or merely to spend some leisure hours at concerts, ballets, theaters, museums, or chamber-music recitals. To proclaim an interest in the arts no longer makes one a snob. In many circles, in fact, it is a passport to status.

The evidence of the culture boom is noticeable everywhere. Libraries are doing a thriving business. The number of volumes in public libraries has jumped from 6,925,000 in 1949 to 16,609,000 in 1963. Nor are these just gathering dust. Total circulation reached a record high of 70,418,478 in 1963, which means the borrowing of roughly 4 books per person compared to only 2 in 1949.

* John Porter, *The Vertical Mosaic*, University of Toronto Press, Toronto, 1965, pp. 434 and 435.

The "paperback explosion" has made the literary classics as well as the critical works on literature, music, aesthetics, and art readily available to the man in the street. The Muses, so to speak, have been democratized. They have been brought down from their Olympic abode to the supermarket shelf.

Canadians are delighting their ears as well as nourishing their minds. Young couples buy classical records along with their frozen vegetables at the nearby grocery stores. They discuss the merits of compositions which not too long ago were derisively termed "long hair stuff." They listen avidly to FM radio stations, some of them devoted almost entirely to serious music and to talks on art, literature, and related subjects.

Movies, too, show an upsurge in artistry. While Hollywood generally has been in the doldrums, the European studios have been faring quite well. The trend is toward out-of-the-way films shown in somewhat exclusive cinemas. Some of these productions have attracted so much public attention that they have been screened afterwards in downtown and neighborhood theaters.

True, this exciting culture boom is still confined to a small segment in the major metropolitan areas. But its influence is fast spreading. Fueling this acceleration is the steady rise in the education level of the population. In 1931, an average adult had spent 7.1 years at school; by 1961 the figure had shot up to over 8.5 years. The same upward movement is seen even more dramatically in the following table from the latest census:

Age of head	% of total households in each age group where the head has completed at least high school
Under 25	29.4%
25–34	29.1
35–44	26.4
45–54	22.2
55–64	17.2
65 and over	14.4
Average	22.9

(Source: DBS, *Census of Canada, 1961*. Bulletin 93-512.)

The younger the head of the household, the better is his education. Over a quarter have at least high school diplomas. A sizeable proportion of these have even been to university.

Of course, the educative process does not stop abruptly once a person is out of school or college. More and more, it is looked upon as a continuing operation that goes on during the individual's entire work life. Adult education, as a result, is gaining in popularity. Hundreds of thousands of Canadians participate in study programs in order to broaden themselves intellectually, occupationally, or culturally. With the growth of leisure, many attend "how-to-do-it" classes to utilize their spare time more creatively. They learn to paint, to make jewelry, to do fancy woodwork, to write short stories, or to be bilingual. A special DBS survey back in June 1960 found that about 4% of non-school population had taken part in some form of educational activity during the previous nine months. Of those reporting, nearly 60% were men and about two-thirds were married. Their median age was 31 years and, what is more significant, the majority had completed grade 12 or better. It would appear that persons with fairly sound schooling are more inclined to continue learning in adult years. Education breeds more education.

In this sudden thirst for knowledge, self-improvement, and fuller life, the mass media are playing an important role. Consumer magazines and specialty journals help to up-grade the taste and stimulate an interest in culture among its readers. The Canadian Broadcasting Corporation, through its educational programs, makes such subjects as arts and adventures of the mind exciting to millions without talking down or unduly simplifying. Also, many libraries claim that television encourages more reading. Any story which appears on TV creates a demand for the book. Particularly, dramatizations of the classics inspire people to read or reread the play.

In addition, more and more persons* are thronging to public lectures, discussion groups, special film showings, art exhibits, culture tours, drama and music festivals, and the like. Also, with the ease of overseas travel and the new developments in communications (e.g., Telestar linking Europe and North America), a large number of Canadians are coming to know what people in foreign lands are thinking and doing.

The effect of all this informal learning is difficult to evaluate. None the less, it cannot be denied that, despite their low level of formal education, many young urbanites in the middle class are well informed about the world around them, discuss current events, and are familiar to some extent with the developments in art and music. Also, they look on "foreign" products and services with less suspicion and accept innovations more readily. They like to taste and cook exotic dishes, and their homes reflect the color and artistry they have learned to appreciate in their travels. In short, tastes and desires are more cosmopolitan, more sophisticated, than a decade or two ago.

To many critics this sudden widening of interest in culture is merely superficial — an urge to move up the social ladder. There is probably a modicum of truth: some are attracted to art more by a need to impress others than by any passionate longing for the aesthetic experience. Crude status striving undoubtedly exists and lends a sulphurous odor to an otherwise healthy movement. But even the people pursuing culture for the wrong reasons are inadvertently devel-

* Conservatively estimated by the DBS at nearly four million in 1963.

oping taste and selectivity. They are educating and refining themselves, and expanding their mental horizons.

Need for Higher Education

One beneficial outcome at least has been that the parents are becoming more and more aware of the need for keeping their children longer at school. This is clearly reflected in the following figures on enrolment for the age group 15 to 24.

| | % of the total males and females in that age group attending school | | | |
| | 15–19 | | 20–24 | |
	Males	Females	Males	Females
1931	32.2	35.1	3.6	2.0
1941	33.8	37.0	4.5	2.8
1951	40.8	40.1	6.4	3.3
1961	61.2	55.7	11.3	4.6

(Source: DBS, *Census of Canada, 1961.* Bulletin 99-520.)

Between 1931 and 1961 the percentage of males continuing their education has almost doubled in the age group 15 to 19, and more than tripled in the age group 20 to 24. The increases for females, though less spectacular, have been equally significant.

The thirst for higher learning seems to be endless. More and more young Canadians are concluding that a college education — the traditional stepping-stone to the executive job — is worth going after. Full-time enrolment at universities jumped from 63,040 in 1952-53 academic year to 178,200 in 1964-65. By 1969-70, it may be close to 312,400, according to a forecast prepared by the Canadian Universities Foundation. If past experience is a guide, this estimate, if anything, may prove to be too conservative.

The universities are bracing themselves for this campus explosion. Their capital expenditures have been steadily mounting from $115 million in 1962 to $138 million in 1963, $165 million in 1964, and an estimated $270 million in 1965. Along with a major expansion of facilities at established institutions, brand new universities are being set up, and existing colleges are being grouped to form other new universities.

The possibility of making more intensive use of the available staff is also being examined. Experiments are conducted with closed-circuit television which would permit one teacher's lectures to be heard in a number of rooms at the same time. Another proposal is for a year-round operation. Such a system, adopted in a number of U.S. universities, has been partially introduced in Canada as well. The new Simon Fraser University intends to have three 16-week terms a year, with the third term optional for those who wish to complete a four-year program in two and two-thirds years.

The need for higher learning has never been greater. The changed complexion of society, with technological and scientific advances, is eliminating a vast number of unskilled and semiskilled jobs. Yesterday a high-school diploma was enough to get one into a blue-collar job with career possibilities. Today, and even more so tomorrow, the college degree is the master key for meeting the stiffer manpower requirements of both industry and business. With the frontiers of knowledge being pushed farther and farther into the unknown, travelers in this more complex universe must carry greater intellectual baggage. Even those pinning their hopes to business careers find that such new areas as econometrics, cybernetics, critical path methods, and business simulation techniques require some kind of postgraduate preparation.

In the past, immigration has played a major role in replenishing the "brain shortage" in the country. This can be seen from the table below, prepared by the Economic Council of Canada.

AVERAGE ANNUAL MIGRATION OF PROFESSIONAL AND
TECHNICAL WORKERS, 1950 TO 1963

Inflow from United States to Canada	+1,230
Outflow from Canada to United States	−4,681
Net loss	−3,451
Inflows from rest of world	+6,560
Net gain from migrations	+3,109

It is far from certain that the net "brain gain" can be maintained in the years ahead. The demand for highly skilled and professional workers in the United States is estimated to be growing faster than domestic sources of supply. In these circumstances, the U.S. market will be tight and therefore relatively attractive to Canadians. At the same time, prosperity in Europe will make it increasingly difficult for Canada to continue to rely on overseas countries as much as before. The only solution lies in training a larger proportion of our young people in the levels of skills required by a modern industrial society. Fortunately, both the authorities and the students are aware of this need for good education. It has been estimated that by 1970 roughly three or four out of every 10 people will come into the period of family formation with a high school diploma. Another 12% to 15% will enter the market with a university degree.

Implications for 1970

This great proliferation of education is bound to have far-reaching effects in many areas. The average citizen will be more sophisticated, one able to deal better with abstractions and to understand more subtle levels of communication. Also, the old moral and traditional standards will loosen their hold. Life will become more liberal, relying less on cult, dogma, and the established order. Women will feel dissatisfied with their role as housewives, with jobs confined mainly to rearing children, washing clothes and dishes, and performing the regular household chores. More and more well-educated wives will seek employment, not just to increase family income, but also to avoid boredom. Women will realize that they have certain skills and abilities, and they will insist on a chance to exercise them.

The nation will also move into a new age of elegance. Gone will be the traditional family congregation around the kitchen table, with father in his undershirt belching his pre-dinner beer and reading the sports page. Gone also will be the widespread income level that can support only a one-week vacation, via the battered family automobile, to a nearby picnic and camping site.

Undoubtedly, pockets of gray life will continue to exist, but, as a whole, the consumers of the future will have much brighter expectations. Here are the trends of things to come: gourmet foods, vintage wines, and soft music in a candlelit dining room; month-long vacations, often to distant parts of the world; two homes and two automobiles; a growing appreciation of good form and design in durable goods; and the broadening of interest in avant-garde literature, music, and art. Indeed, the household of the next decade will reflect an awareness of taste and gracious living, as well as the resources to pay the tab.

With educational and cultural levels up, consumers will be more receptive to the new, the different, the experimental and the unusual. Of course, traditional forms and ideas and habits are not going to be thrown away overnight. People cling to the familiar even while exploring the unknown. But there will definitely be a trend away from mass conformity toward individuality and self-expression. In other words, a high level of education will demand from merchandisers more competition by innovation, less competition by imitation.

The growing level of education will also have great effect on communications. Already, the researchers say that the average citizen is exposed to 1,600 advertising messages a day. The effort to be heard and noted above the background noise of advertising is one of the major problems the communicators face today. In future, the noise will grow louder, and the competition will become keener. The Canadian eye and ear will be bombarded in all directions by every kind of concentrated stimulus known to man. The advertiser will not succeed unless he is different and exciting, provocative and intriguing, challenging and arresting. The future consumer just won't waste his time any more with the banal, the dull, and the ordinary.

The new sophistication will also have another effect. The average man will have to be appealed to more directly and intelligently than ever before. The advertiser must say what he wants to say quickly and straightforwardly, and treat his readers or viewers as intelligent beings. This means that generality will be out, the fact in; pomposity will be out, honesty in; the "sledgehammer" approach will be out, the soft sell in. The copywriter will no longer have to descend to the abracadabra of meaningless claims to make the product stand out. The selling will be indirect, subtle, soothing, and unobtrusive. The advertising will appeal to the senses with significant images, stimulating colors, inspiring music, dramatic movement, and meaningful symbols.

BIBLIOGRAPHY

Bank of Nova Scotia: "Closing the Gap in Higher Education," Monthly Review, March, 1964.

Dominion Bureau of Statistics: *Canada Year Book, 1965,* Queen's Printer, Ottawa, 1965.

Dominion Bureau of Statistics: *A Graphic Presentation of Canadian Education,* (81-515 occasional) Queen's Printer, 1961.

Economic Council of Canada: *Economic Goals for Canada to 1970,* First Annual Review, Queen's Printer, Ottawa, December, 1964.

Economic Council of Canada: *Towards Sustained and Balanced Economic Growth,* Second Annual Review, Queen's Printer, Ottawa, December, 1965.

Leighton, David, S. R.: "Education and the Canadian Consumer," in Isaiah A. Litvak and Bruce E. Mallen, *Marketing: Canada,* Chapter 2, McGraw-Hill Company of Canada Limited, Toronto, 1964.

Miller, Herman P.: *Rich Man, Poor Man,* Thomas Y. Crowell Company, New York, 1964.

Toffler, Alvin: *The Culture Consumers,* St. Martin's Press, New York, 1964.

Chapter 5

TRENDS IN FAMILY LIFE

Two trends in family life are discussed in this chapter: togetherness and the decline in the prestige of the housewife.

Togetherness

For countless generations, family life depended on having a mother at the hearth and a father bringing home the bacon. Men and women had clear-cut roles spelled out for them, and both knew the patterns they were supposed to adhere to.

Today, especially in the upper and middle classes, the situation has changed considerably. The husband is still expected to go to work and earn the living. But he is also called upon to perform many small tasks around the house — do the laundry, wash and dry the dishes, dress and feed the babies, sit up with the sick or sleepless child, and in general help his wife in her numerous household chores.

In turn, the modern wife is expected to carry the major burden of managing the house. But her role is not confined to cooking, cleaning, sewing, and raising children. She golfs, swims, sails, gardens, drives the family car, paints the spare bedroom, fulfills the community obligations. Furthermore, she takes interest in her husband's work, discusses his office problems, and tries to make the necessary social contacts to further his career.

Whereas it was once a question of: "Who wears the pants in this family?", it is now a matter of pants all around, and the children are apt to cling as much to the father's apron strings as to the mother's. The husband, formerly known as "the head of the household," is now only a partner in the family firm. Families are operating as "democratic units" rather than as patriarchies.

The key feature in today's middle-class life is "togetherness." The trend is towards joint living — in working, playing, praying as a group rather than individually. Families have barbecues in the backyard together, take drives together on weekends, do the dishes together, spend summers at a lake-side cottage together, go to church together. There is oneness of family participation in almost every area.

The reasons behind this collective living are not far to seek. The insecurity created by threats of war, the danger of nuclear annihilation, the disenchantment with government due to corruption and petty squabbling, the smallness of the individual in relation to the giant corporations — all these factors have made men and women alike, fall back on the home which alone seems permanent and worthwhile in the vast, changing, impersonal world. Furthermore, longer vacations and weekends, greater leisure through time-saving devices, and more discretionary income for household purchases, have all worked towards the spending of more time in and around the home. Television too helped to draw the whole family back to the living room.*

As a result, for an increasing number of expenditures, the trend is toward group rather than individual decisions. No matter how appealing a candle-lit dinner table may look in an illustration in *Chatelaine,* the housewife will not go out and buy so much as one candle if she knows that her husband hates dim light while eating and does not like "fuss" at dinner time. The woman may be the main purchaser, but often what she buys is largely determined by the individual preferences of each member of her family. Sometimes she dare not acquire a dress or a coat for herself without thinking how that will affect the whole household. Will it mean one less family outing? Should the money be saved for a second television set instead?

Many businesses, realizing the greater sense of family unity, have jumped on the "togetherness" bandwagon. *McCall's* calls itself "the Magazine of Togetherness." Automobile companies have utilized this emotional appeal in much of their advertising by picturing the whole family enjoying a new car. Many of the advertisements for outboard motors have also stressed family fun by showing photographs of children and parents participating in boating.

The interchangeable roles of men and women mean that sex differences in attitudes and tastes are less pronounced than in the past. Male and female interests in buying are becoming more alike in many fields. The beauty market, for example, is not confined to women only. Men, too, now care how they look. In the past, the words "dude" and "dandy" were common epithets to shame any member of the masculine sex who used fancy toiletries. Today, the Canadian male is appropriating the bathroom medicine chest and filling it with men's deodorants, men's shampoos, and men's colognes. The makers of men's toiletries are enjoying a market unequalled since the days of wigs and knee breeches. The notion is fast disappearing that a man has to smell of witch hazel and old cigars to be masculine. The accent is on good grooming, and the smell of a well-groomed male is not stale. Indeed, the application of pre- and after-shave lotions as a habitual, everyday act has resulted in greater consumption of fragrance by men than by women.

---

* However, the increased family unity here is passive rather than active. While TV may be credited with augmenting the family's fund of common experience and shared interests, it can also be blamed for destroying the pleasant art of conversation and face-to-face interaction.

Not everybody is happy with the trend towards togetherness. Many social scientists blame women for the marked decline in masculine self-esteem and for the resulting psychological tensions. Specifically, the wife is accused of reversing the established order of male sexual dominance and female passivity. She is said to have subdued the old pioneer spirit of self-reliance and to have set the patterns of conformity which are damaging to free enterprise. Margaret Mead, the U.S. anthropologist, warns that the emphasis on family is being so overdone that it inhibits the development of men of adventure and daring. Already, she says, feminization of the male is evidenced by his increased preoccupation with security, high salaries, residence in a good suburb, prestige memberships in community organizations, and his affirmation of home life as an end rather than a part of human life.

Despite these complaints, it is doubtful whether it would be possible to set the clock back and return to the patriarchal structure. Times have changed and with them society's notions about concepts of masculinity. Fast dying, if not already dead, is the old image of the pioneer man. Today, the premium is on earning a living with brains rather than with brawn. In industry, for example, to an increasing extent, technicians are replacing the heavy labor group — a trend which is being accentuated with automation.

Consequently, it is not fair to brand the North American woman as a potent sorceress transforming the male into a protean creature that can be molded according to her moods. Various social and economic factors have led to "togetherness," and to accuse the female of stealing male authority is somewhat like blaming the scientists for the catastrophies resulting from their discoveries.

Decline in the Prestige of the Housewife

In recent years, the female world has been shaken by a new wave of militant feminism. Some call it the second revolution of the century. It differs significantly from the first revolt of six decades ago when the suffragettes chained themselves to lampposts in order to win the right to vote and to own property. In the current fight, the goals are more abstract, the combatants less aggressive, and the battlelines more fluid. The drive now is not for legal but psychological freedom — the right of every woman, even with young children, to free herself from the tyranny of domesticity and to seek a fuller life in an executive suite, factory, studio, or laboratory. This yearning is growing so rapidly in intensity that it may, in the end, not only change society, as the early feminism did, but also produce a New Woman, as the earlier feminism promised but failed to achieve.*

The modern feminists find it a strange paradox that although all professions

* Most of the remarks in this section apply to the upper and upper-middle classes of English-speaking Canada.

are finally opened to females, the word "career woman" does not have good connotation; that while universities are ready to receive anyone with basic qualifications, higher education has become so suspect that more and more girls discontinue their studies after high school to marry and have babies; that despite the many roles the women can play in a modern complex society, they have got themselves anchored to the home like stand-by watchmen.

The root of all this trouble lies in "the feminine mystique," the phrase made famous by Betty Friedan. It puts motherhood on the pedestal and glorifies the role of the housewife. In hundreds of books and magazine articles, women are taught that real fulfillment comes in sexual passivity, male domination and nurturing mother love. All their energies should be devoted to their husbands and children. If they want to excel in something, it should be within the confines of the home; e.g., cooking more exotic dishes, making the living room more attractive, dressing and acting in a more feminine way, providing the tender care that will keep the husband from dying young and the son from becoming a delinquent.

However, lately many cracks have started appearing in this idyllic picture. The term "housewife" is slowly losing its prestige, particularly in the upper and middle classes. This is because more and more work that was originally performed at home is now rarely done; e.g., canning, baking bread, weaving cloth, nursing the sick, taking care of the aged. Even cooking no longer requires as much time as it used to, for foods come pre-washed and pre-prepared. A great deal of energy is now spent at little, unrewarding tasks — making beds, ironing the clothes, emptying the wastebaskets, vacuum-cleaning the floors. Many women find the routine exhausting and unstimulating, resulting in extreme boredom and in some cases even mental illness.

In one motivation study, a projective technique was used, and women were asked to complete the following sentence: "The job of a housewife . . . ." There was no reason at all why the completions should be loaded in any direction. Yet a large number of women expressed the view that being a housewife was arduous, irritating and unending. Here were some typical replies:
— is a million things.
— stinks.
— is never done.
— is a drudgery.
— is twelve to fifteen hours a day.

Depth interviewing has revealed the same attitudes. The following two replies of housewives are quite characteristic:

• "Who am I? I begin to feel I have no personality. I'm a server of food and putter-on of pants and a bedmaker, somebody who can be called on when you want something. At times it seems as though the world is going past my door while I just sit and watch."

• "In the past 60 years we have come full circle and the housewife is once again trapped in a squirrel cage. If the cage is now a plate-glass-and-broadloom ranch house or a luxurious modern apartment, the situation is no less painful than when her grandmother sat over an embroidery hoop in her gilt-and-plush parlor and muttered angrily about women's rights."

This sense of frustration is highest among the talented, well-educated women. Like shut-ins, they feel isolated and stifled in their homes, especially if they have spent many years of study in the sciences, arts, or professional courses. The transition from Freud to Frigidaire, from Sophocles to Spock, is not smooth and easy, as Betty Friedan remarks.

Some women vainly try to escape the boredom by putting more frantic efforts into the housework. They move from the city apartment into a spacious dwelling in the suburbs. The new house takes longer to clean, and the shopping, gardening, and socializing with neighbors are so time-consuming that the emptiness seems dispelled. But eventually, with the home furnished, the children at school, and the family's place in the community formalized, the vacuous feeling returns. The woman tries to escape from it by plunging more deeply into her household work: cooking fancy dishes, redecorating, waxing the floor more often than necessary. But all these distractions bring no lasting relief. Some suburban housewives have been so badly caught in the trap that they have started taking tranquillizers as casually as cough drops.

The solution, according to many female leaders, lies in discarding the feminine mystique. They emphasize that the true basis of a happy home lies in woman's personality, not in her broom, stove or dishpan. To expect a woman to get a rewarding sense of total fulfillment from her multiple, monotonous household chores is as irrational as for an assembly-line worker to feel pride in the building of an automobile just because he has tightened a bolt. The only way for a woman to discover herself is by taking an interesting job where she can utilize her talents. A woman cannot find her identity through others — her husband, her children.

MARRIED WOMEN IN THE LABOR FORCE

Statistics show that this advice has not fallen on deaf ears. Canadian housewives have emerged from their homes in ever increasing numbers to enter man's world of work. In 1941, only one married woman in 20 was in the labor force. By 1951, the proportion had doubled to one in ten; by 1961, it had doubled again to one in five; by 1970, according to the Economic Council of Canada, it will be one in three.

Secretarial and clerical work, of course, remains women's gateway into business. But more and more females are climbing into higher jobs. Increasing numbers hold professional and semiprofessional posts in retailing, banking, insurance, investment, and real estate. Manufacturing is still a difficult field to break into. But even here, wherever skilled personnel is scarce, industry is beginning to overlook its traditional objections.

No doubt, many married women work for strictly financial reasons — a hankering for a better home, a second car, a European vacation, and, in many cases, to help their children through college. Others are forced to earn a living — widows, divorcees and wives with husbands handicapped, ill or alcoholic. But more and more are leaving the home out of a sense of frustration. The children are in school; today's appliances make housework a part-time task; PTA meetings fail to fill the void. The women desire a change in living habits and pace. They want to get back in the stream of life, especially if they had worked before marriage.

That money is not a primary consideration can be seen from the fact that in several cases it is financially more rewarding to stay at home than to go to work. Personal expenses rise very rapidly when women seek outside employment. First, there is the need for a more extensive wardrobe. This is costly to maintain with extra dry-cleaning bills, shoe repairs, and nylon stocking replacements. Then there are transportation fares, contributions to office collections, club or union dues, restaurant bills for luncheons, and sometimes impulse buying during the noon recess. Additional costs are incurred for domestic help and day nurseries. Moreover, income taxes may go up, if the wife's earnings put the family in a higher bracket.

MARKETING IMPLICATIONS

The marketing implications of the influx of women into the labor force are far-reaching. The trend affects the sales of all types of goods and services. More working wives mean a greater market for ready-made clothes, laundry services, labor-saving appliances, and other items designed to make housekeeping easier. Besides, the extra family income creates a demand for better equipped homes, newer furniture, bigger cars, and more expensive vacations.

The food industry, too, stands to benefit. With ample money in her purse, the working woman is likely to give little thought to the few additional pennies she leaves at the supermarket in return for the myriad built-in services she takes home in her shopping bag. Hence, one may expect a growing popularity of such items as pre-cooked frozen dishes, cook-in pouches of gourmet foods, and other ready-made items.

The clothing industry is affected as well. Though the working woman represents 31% of the total female population over 14, she accounts for about 45% of all women's apparel purchases. Her job requires three wardrobes — one for home activities, one for social affairs, and the third for her job. She consumes more stockings, girdles, shoes, handbags, coats, and hats than her housewife counterpart.

Working wives are very enthusiastic about adopting new fashions, trying new hair styles, and using new cosmetic preparations. Of course, all members of the fair sex give attention to these matters, but the interest of the working wife is intensified by the fact that she has to be elegant every morning when leaving home for work.

New types of services are also becoming popular. Even now, metropolitan areas have home-meal delivery service, providing complete hot meals to people's homes on a regular route basis. The customer has a fairly wide menu choice for each dinner seven days of the week. The entire ready-to-eat, three-course dinner is delivered to the home at the hour specified, with satisfaction guaranteed. This can be an ideal solution to a working wife's problem.

There is more need for other services, too, like day-care facilities for both pre-school and school-age children. Ontario has over 350 licensed day nurseries and their number is increasing by 10 to 15 a year. While many are municipally supported, intended for low-income families where the mother generally is the sole support, there are also several private centers which charge $50 to $60 a month per child. Some women trade unionists are now pressing for more subsidized nurseries and day-care centers for children. They also want income-tax exemptions for working mothers who have to employ persons to supervise their children.

The real estate firms are also indirectly affected by the decline of the feminine mystique. Families in which the wife intends to pursue a definite professional goal are likely to move back to the city from the suburbs. The downtown areas offer more and better jobs; more evening courses geared to women who want to improve their academic qualifications; as well as more nursery schools, day-care centers, after-school play programs, and part-time facilities for maid services.

Equally significant are the changes taking place in retailing. A new kind of shopper is coming into prominence, one with more money, more needs, but less time. The trend toward night opening of stores is already well established, but, in numerous other areas too, retailers are trying to increase shopping convenience for the working woman. Services, such as pay-check cashing, adequate lunch-hour selling staff, telephone ordering, and delivery of packages, are growing in importance as store owners vie with one another to win the patronage of the working wives.

Finally, there are the subtle changes difficult to pinpoint. When a married woman has an interesting job which utilizes her talents and intelligence, she wants to be judged as a person in her own right, and not only as a homemaker. As a result, she is likely to develop new living habits, new spending patterns, new psychological needs, and new status symbols. She no longer finds social significance in keeping her home impeccably clean, or creative fulfillment in baking a cake without the help of a cake-mix. In the past, thanks to the artful manipulation of communications experts, bored housewives were able to get a sense of identity, purpose, and creativity by loading their homes with different types of durable and nondurable goods. The situation is different now. A career woman, who frankly dislikes household chores, has little interest in a new wax that will give an extra-brilliant luster to her floor, or a new soap powder that will make her clothes whiter than white. In fact, material possessions no longer provide the magic antidote for subduing discontent and boredom. The overwhelming desire is for immaterial items, those intellectual and spiritual values and activities that give meaning and purpose to life.

Of course, it would be unrealistic to assume that the new wave of feminism is sweeping the land, surmounting all the obstacles that stand in the way. Not every woman has a yearning to "fulfill" herself by using her brains in creative work. Much depends upon her education and her talents. At present, a large percentage of wives, especially among the lower socio-economic classes, still falls into the category of what sociologists call "the true housewife type." For such a woman, from the psychological point of view, housekeeping is the dominating interest. She gets pride and satisfaction from maintaining a comfortable and well-run home for her family. Consciously or subconsciously she feels that she is indispensable and that no one else can take over her job. She has little, if any, desire for a position outside the home, and if she does seek employment, it is through the force of circumstances or necessity.

However, it is apparent that this group is diminishing and probably will continue to do so as new activities, interests, and education opportunities open more avenues to women. The feminine mystique no longer has the undisputed sway it had in the Fifties, and businessmen will have to take that into careful consideration when formulating their marketing plans for the years to come.

BIBLIOGRAPHY

Business Week: "Back from the home to business," October 7, 1961.
Friedan, Betty: *The Feminine Mystique,* W. M. Norton and Company, Inc., New York, 1963.
Fulford, Robert: "The second Revolt of 'Modern' Women," *Maclean's,* July 25, 1964.
Life: "The American Woman: Her Achievements and Troubles," Special two-in-one issue, December 24, 1956.
Time: "Help Wanted: Maybe Mary Poppins, Inc.," Time Essay, July 9, 1965.
Wolff, Janet: *What Makes Women Buy,* McGraw-Hill Company, Inc., New York, 1958.

Chapter 6

TRENDS IN RETAILING

Introduction

The whole field of retailing is in a state of ferment. New ways of selling are being tested. New types of stores are being opened. New methods of distribution are being developed to move the vast variety of products that flow from the factories and farms.

The pace of change has quickened considerably in the last few years. Competition and the profit-squeeze are forcing retailers to become more efficient and to attract more consumer traffic. In order not to be left out of the race, retailers all across the country are revamping every aspect of their merchandising policy — the way their stores are laid out, the type of goods they carry, the services they offer, the prices they charge.

Shopping Centers

The locations of today's new stores are not the same as those of a decade or two ago. People are moving from the downtown areas to the suburbs, and retailers have followed suit to be close to their customers. Hence, shopping centers have become a familiar sight on the fringes of big cities. Their success depends on such factors as one-stop shopping, ample parking space, freedom from downtown congestion, the opportunity to purchase at leisure, and a reasonable variety of merchandise which is competitively priced and of good quality.

There were 346 shopping centers in Canada in 1963, with sales totaling $1,340,188,739, compared to only 67 in 1956 with sales of $237,501,828. If retailers not common to shopping centers are excluded (e.g., general stores, motor vehicle dealers, lumber and building material dealers, and farm supply stores), the business transacted in such centers amounted in 1963 to 9.6% of all retail trade. The ratio ranged from 4.1% in the Atlantic Provinces to 12.4% in Ontario.

In the beginning, shopping centers were no more than strip developments with an ill-assorted collection of new stores and branches of downtown chains. The rate of failure was high, due mainly to the lack of prior planning and research of sales potential and customers' preferences. In most of the new centers currently being opened, great care is taken in choosing locations, studying competition, providing adequate parking space, selecting tenants, and preparing promotions. Much attention is given to the designing of the layout of the area and the appearance of the stores, in an attempt to offer to today's more sophisticated customer, variety without confusion, color without garishness, and gaiety without vulgarity.

RETAIL SALES IN SHOPPING CENTERS BY PROVINCES, 1963
(thousand dollars)

Type of store	Québec	Ontario	Alberta	British Columbia	Other provinces	Canada
Grocery and combination stores.	137,193	292,647	43,771	55,308	40,631	569,550
Other food and beverage stores.	2,899	40,615	12,269	10,853	8,664	75,300
Department stores	*	*	*	*	*	248,408
Variety stores	22,364	35,370	5,531	4,337	8,823	76,425
Garage and service stations	*	*	2,018	1,885	*	9,041
Men's clothing stores	6,398	14,803	1,065	941	1,420	24,627
Family clothing stores	7,492	3,392	*	*	869	14,709
Women's clothing stores	14,194	28,614	2,622	3,937	3,358	52,725
Shoe stores	9,273	16,102	1,628	1,774	1,793	30,570
Hardware stores	10,893	10,115	1,094	1,895	1,225	25,222
Furniture, appliance and radio stores	1,195	12,138	1,589	967	2,053	17,942
Restaurants	5,176	12,723	1,896	2,557	2,089	24,441
Drug stores	10,086	29,075	4,796	6,630	4,229	54,816
Jewelry stores	1,920	4,607	489	1,108	1,109	9,233
Miscellaneous	29,932	63,122	4,874	3,346	5,906	107,180
Total of all trades	279,885	678,315	129,308	150,238	102,443	1,340,189

* Figures withheld by DBS to avoid disclosing individual operations but included in total. (Source: DBS, *Shopping Centres in Canada, 1961–63*. Catalogue No. 63-214.)

The mushrooming of shopping centers has seriously injured downtown trade. In many cities, reassessed property values in central districts have dropped sharply because of the cancerous growth of blighted areas and the exodus of several well-known firms to outlying zones. At the same time, downtown traffic has been rising, clogging main business streets and hampering the free movement of shoppers.

Fortunately, many progressive cities are aware of this situation and are wasting no time in adjusting their structures and facilities to meet the changed demands of the automotive age. Owners of downtown stores are joining with other interests — banks, insurance companies, transit operators, real estate firms, and civic officials — in formulating blueprints for rejuvenating the core areas. There are ambitious projects for clearing the slums, improving public transportation, augmenting parking facilities, and building expressways to the heart of the city. Plans also call for the construction of shopping malls, free of automobile traffic, and festooned with greenery, statuary, fountains, and, in some cases, even moving sidewalks. Proponents of these projects visualize future city centers that would have more to offer to the human spirit than the spectacle of huge, mono-

RETAIL SALES IN SHOPPING CENTERS BY TYPE AND SIZE, 1963
(thousand dollars)

Type of store	Type			Size			
	Inde-pendent	Chain	Total	5–15 stores	16–30 stores	Over 30 stores	Total
Grocery and com-bination stores......	49,073	520,477	569,550	284,354	196,815	88,381	569,550
Other food and beverage stores......	14,085	61,215	75,300	30,402	21,941	22,957	75,300
Department stores....	248,408	—	248,408	*	*	*	248,408
Variety stores...........	2,325	74,100	76,425	19,774	35,289	21,362	76,425
Garage and service stations..................	7,831	1,210	9,041	*	*	*	9,041
Men's clothing stores.....................	14,479	10,148	24,627	5,530	10,640	8,457	24,627
Family clothing stores.....................	5,742	8,967	14,709	3,320	7,113	4,276	14,709
Women's clothing stores.....................	18,567	34,158	52,725	10,898	21,549	20,278	52,725
Shoe stores..............	6,389	24,181	30,570	7,250	13,345	9,975	30,570
Hardware stores.......	13,509	11,713	25,222	8,788	10,688	5,746	25,222
Furniture, appliance and radio stores....	12,240	5,702	17,942	4,231	6,665	7,046	17,942
Restaurants..............	24,441	—	24,441	8,944	9,538	5,959	24,441
Drug stores..............	38,352	16,464	54,816	29,986	17,073	7,757	54,816
Jewelry stores...........	5,323	3,910	9,233	1,556	3,567	4,110	9,233
Miscellaneous...........	77,713	29,467	107,180	26,005	50,818	30,357	107,180
Total of all trades......	538,477	801,712	1,340,189	457,689	458,794	423,706	1,340,189

* Figures withheld by DBS to avoid disclosing individual operations but included in totals.
(Source: DBS, *Shopping Centres in Canada, 1961–63*. Catalogue no. 63-214.)

tonously regimented blocks of physical capital. New and more interesting groupings of buildings are being planned, to make their appearance gradually. Special areas are allocated to parks and plazas, theaters, concert halls, and other recreational facilities. All these improvements would give new life to the downtown area, and consequently be a shot in the arm to retailing.

Scrambled Merchandising

Competition for the customer's dollar has become so intense that many retail establishments are broadening their lines — in fact, poaching on each other's traditional preserves — in order to provide one-stop shopping facilities to the public. Supermarkets are crowding out their groceries with aisles of hardware goods and health and beauty preparations. Department stores are experimenting with selling small European cars. Drug stores are carrying all sorts of general merchandise, from tobacco to photographic equipment, electric shavers, clocks, and chinaware. Some of the old five-and-ten-cent stores are busy transforming themselves into junior department stores, where customers can buy big-ticket merchandise, such as lawn furniture, radios and phonographs.

In fact, the whole movement toward scrambled merchandising has gone so far that the traditional dividing lines in retailing are getting completely blurred. Luxury goods are carried in mass outlets, and knick-knacks in luxury stores. Every retailer, it seems, is experimenting to find out which kinds of wares mix and which don't. One of the latest examples of a tentative crossing of boundaries is a two-way affair which has a nice sense of justice about it; some service stations are testing the handling of food items through vending machines, while food stores are seriously thinking of adding gas stations and auto accessory stores near their parking lots to draw additional revenue from the traffic already coming there.

Two factors have hastened the trend toward scrambled merchandising. One is the leasing of stores to qualified specialists (e.g., Loblaw Groceterias in the United States rent space in some of their stores to the catalog-order offices of Montgomery Ward). The other development is "rack jobbing" in supermarkets. Here the rack jobber, for a specified cut of the profits, guarantees the sales of non-food items. He prices the merchandise, sets it up on the shelves, keeps the display clean and filled, and takes care of the mark-ups and mark-downs when necessary. If the items do not sell, back they go to his warehouse. The only responsibility of the supermarket manager is to allocate space and ring up the sales at the checkout counter.

Where will all this scrambled merchandising end? According to some, all outlets will continue to broaden their merchandise lines, and will eventually meet on a common ground to blend into an amorphous, everything-for-everybody store. However, this seems rather doubtful. Trying to be everybody's store for everything can turn out to be an unprofitable business, as many operators have learned from bitter experience. With a certain fixed area of floor space, a fixed amount of merchandise investment, and a fixed limit of specialized know-how, it is not easy to extend the fringe lines without placing a dangerous strain on the supporting center base.

Food stores, which started the trend toward diversification, are now coming to the inescapable conclusion that as long as the average family in Canada spends a quarter of its budget on food, therein lies their true mine of diamonds. Few supermarkets — excepting the armory type units of recent years — have anything like the space they need for the numerous new food products coming into the market. Nor is there sufficient place for the refrigeration equipment required for all frozen foods and packaged meats. Hence, more attention to complete stocks of food is likely to pay off better than diverting efforts to general merchandise. Also, fat margins do not make up for a slow turnover. Although the non-foods have better gross-profit ratios, the mark-downs are also higher, so that, even with lower mark-ups, the food lines may show a better net profit. In fact, already in some quarters, "bantams," or scaled-down versions of the supermarket, are proving popular. These are located usually in crowded areas where desirable sites for large stores are scarce. Several operators feel that a scientifically designed small outlet, carrying only the fastest selling brands in all product categories, may have a strong appeal for many types of shoppers.

Similarly, it is doubtful that variety stores will continue to spread their wings into new lines. While some of the new, ultramodern, multi-floor outlets of Woolworth or Kresge may continue to capture the news headlines, for the average stores the foremost problem will be to digest their present, wide assortments. Rather than lock competitive horns with other types of retail outlets, many variety stores will likely find it more profitable to emphasize their proven sellers, such as toys, piece goods, stationery, notions, housewares, hosiery, toiletries, glassware, and women's and children's apparel.

The danger of living up to the reputation of "carrying everything" is being recognized even by the department store owners. With the enormous proliferation of shapes, styles, colors, and patterns coming out of the factories, the traditional policy of great breadth of stock has gone beyond the point of diminishing returns. The stores now have wider selections than the majority of their customers normally need or want. As a result, their inventory investment per dollar of sales has gradually increased, while their turnover rates have steadily declined — a major cause of the profit erosion.

All this is not meant to imply that retailing in the future will move into watertight compartments. Stores will continue to raid each other's better lines. But the cold stare of the profit and loss statement will force many operators to reinforce the depths of their basic lines rather than spread, wide and thin, over too horizontal a merchandise base. Most probably, the coming drive will be to stratify into the naturally profitable areas, peculiar to each retail outlet.

Private Brands

While the problem of improving the "profit mix" will act as a brake on the trend towards scrambled merchandising, it will accelerate development in another area: the field of private brands. Also called distributor-controlled brands, these are the items sold by one retailer exclusively, as opposed to the national brands available to all or most of the retailers.

Generally three conditions are required to assure the success of a private brand: it must be in a product category where the sales volume is large and not volatile; it must offer the consumer better value by being of the same quality as the national brand at a lower price; and it must bring a higher profit than the national brand.

Department stores and mail-order houses have flirted with private brands for years. At present, Simpson-Sears Limited has about 40 of its own labels in its catalogs, and they produce nearly 90% of the total sales. T. Eaton Company's private-label trade, too, is growing at a substantial rate, several times faster than the sales of general-consumer goods. To make the customer more aware of its products, the company has slashed the number of its own brands from 30 to 16 and has redesigned its trademarks so that the name Eaton is prominent in each.*

In the food stores, private brands are strongest in beverages, bakery products, canned fruits and vegetables, ice cream, salad dressing, peanut butter, cheese, jams and jellies. IGA (Independent Grocers' Alliance Limited) has probably moved more heavily into private labels than any other supermarket organization. Steinberg's Limited, too, is heavily committed. It stocks 400 to 500 lines produced to its own specifications and sold as a rule under its own name. Also, work has begun in Montréal on an $8-million Steinberg's bakery. When completed in the fall of 1966, it will be the largest and most fully automated plant in Canada and will supply about 90% of the bakery products sold in the company's supermarkets.

Most experts seem to agree that private brand retailing will rise sharply in the next decade.

• Automation will encourage mass-production methods, and private-label contracts will become almost mandatory for some manufacturers to utilize excess capacity and to schedule the work in the factory on a more even basis. This will make it easier for retailers to obtain standard products under a private label at a favorable price.

• At present, many housewives are still suspicious of private brands and dismiss them as inferior to national brands. But these inhibitions will slowly disappear. Retail giants are steadily improving their corporate image, and hence, even on the "prestige" front, private brands will be well received by the consumers.

• Manufacturers' efforts to increase sales through contests, premiums and cents-off deals have quickened the erosion of brand loyalty. As national-brand preference becomes weaker, the task of promoting private brands will become correspondingly easier.

• Shopping in a self-service store is getting to be more impulsive, more of a split-second affair. By manipulation of facings, shelf heights or location, the retailer will be able to back up his own brand with a selling force that at times can be more powerful than the advertising support given to the national brands.

• Almost all big chains will be marketing nationally, and so will be able to use for their brands national media, like magazines and network television, that are not now economical. In fact, most private brands will not be "private" any more. They will be as well-known to the public as the national brands.

For these reasons, the private label will be on the ascent, and by 1970, its

* Gibson, Paul: "Private-label selling getting big new push," *Financial Post,* August 14, 1965.

volume in many product categories may equal or even exceed that of the national brands. At one time, the retailer worried that he might become a satellite of the manufacturer. Tomorrow, the shoe may be on the other foot.

Self-service

The profit squeeze, which has given impetus to private-brand development, is also accelerating the trend towards self-service. Many retailers have found that they could reduce their operating expenses only by getting rid of high-priced sales help. Most of today's new stores are self-serviced. Some of the old stores, too, are converting to this system. By eliminating the conventional clerk aisles and by adopting more efficient refixturing, they have been able to double their display space and to make it yield more sales per square foot.

Self-service is not just a means of reducing selling expenses; it actually increases in some ways convenience to the customer. Survey after survey has shown that when one has to wait for clerks, the service is hurried, and the pressure of other customers tends to make one reduce the shopping list. By contrast, a self-service store actually provides a different but more desirable kind of service — a service built around low selling prices, attractive layout and displays, and open assortments of related items for inspection and comparison.

Three factors have contributed greatly to the success of self-service: advertising, packaging, and display. National advertising is preselling goods to a greater extent every year, and thus diminishing the need for personal selling on the retail floor. Attractive and informative packaging lets the product sell itself, without having to depend on the recommendations of the salesclerk. The layouts and interior display arrangements of modern stores are so geared to impulse buying and the fast flow of traffic that the sales person only becomes an obstacle between the customer and the merchandise. A public that must be *persuaded* to buy requires intelligent and courteous floor selling; but with a public *presold* on brands, self-service is often the most effective selling technique.

Self-service got its baptism in the supermarkets, and it enabled the food merchandisers to move into the big league. Many of them at present do as much business in a month as they did in a year in the personal-selling era — a fact that has completely transformed the character of the industry, which once consisted only of mom-'n-pop stores. As is bound to happen, success breeds imitators, and the example of the supermarket is now copied in some form or another by variety, drug, hardware, stationery, and women's clothing stores. Most of these retail establishments have found that self-service results in a higher volume yield per customer, per employee, per fixture, per square foot of floor space.

Discount Retailing

The most recent application of the self-service technique is by the discount stores. They are trying to adapt to soft goods the same methods which supermarkets applied so successfully to groceries a decade or two ago. Their business policy is quite simple: replace paid salesmen with pushcarts, use low prices to lure customers, and make up for reduced profit margins through high volume and quick turnover. A discount house that has retained its original character-istic is noted for its frugality — a contempt for carpeted floors and frills, a mini-mum of investment in physical facilities, and the paring of services to the bare essentials. This permits the store to operate on gross margins of 20% to 25%, compared with 35% to 40% for conventional general-merchandise outlets. The department store's motto is: "Think on the best, thin on the rest." The dis-counter, on the other hand, operates on the principle, "Thick on the best, to hell with the rest."

The rise of the discount or self-service department stores in Canada has been quite spectacular. From virtual non-existence in 1960, sales shot up to $106.9 million in 1962, and two years later to $207.6 million, with a good prospect of continuing growth. The discounters' share of total department store sales has increased from practically nothing in 1960 to 11.5% in 1964. The following are the major merchandise categories, consisting primarily of convenience goods, in which the discounters have made significant inroads into the business of tradi-tional department stores.

Merchandise category	Discounters' share of total department store sales, 1964
Photographic equipment and supplies	44.5%
Toiletries, cosmetics, drugs	28.4
Stationery, books, magazines	24.6
Toys, gifts, pets and miscellaneous goods	18.7
Men's and boys' shoes	16.3
Boys' clothing and furnishings	16.2
Men's clothing	15.7
Millinery	14.4
Linens and domestics	13.5
Girls' and infants' wear	13.0
Food and kindred products, candy	13.0
Women's, misses' and children's shoes	12.6
Jewelry	12.4
Hardware and housewares	12.3

(Source: DBS, *Department Store Sales and Stocks*. Catalogue No. 63-002.)

The big national advertisers have unconsciously abetted the discount houses in building their business. The public has been led to rely on the manufacturer's honesty and fabricating skill, rather than on the retailer's knowledge and judg-ment. Consequently, consumers do not hesitate to buy in an outlet which offers the best price, especially if the product is guaranteed by the manufacturer and can be easily taken to his service depot for repairs.

DISCOUNT DEPARTMENT STORE SALES BY DEPARTMENTS

Department	1962	1963	1964	% change 1962–1964
Women's and misses' dresses............ $	3,463,456	$ 3,364,895	$ 4,649,781	34.3
Women's and misses' coats and suits..	2,437,367	3,449,908	5,125,450	110.3
Women's and misses' sportswear.......	2,902,515	4,692,487	5,534,414	90.7
Furs.........	47,619	49,919	42,286	−11.2
Girls' and infants' wear......................	5,157,262	8,758,623	11,683,000	126.5
Lingerie and corsets.........................	2,033,795	4,467,364	5,977,176	193.9
Aprons, housedresses and uniforms..	442,463	384,810	495,401	12.0
Millinery.................................	1,023,585	1,099,368	1,430,557	39.8
Hosiery and apparel accessories.........	2,041,589	4,414,656	6,060,527	196.9
Women's, misses' and children's shoes................................	3,210,798	5,853,016	7,671,871	138.9
Men's clothing................................	6,337,997	7,711,727	9,699,518	53.0
Men's furnishings...........................	5,927,945	7,168,136	9,613,626	62.2
Boys' clothing and furnishings...........	2,850,017	5,347,850	7,023,387	146.4
Men's and boys' shoes.......................	2,508,584	3,353,746	4,581,990	82.7
Food and kindred products...............	8,882,866	11,294,253	12,029,100	35.4
Toiletries, cosmetics and drugs...........	7,230,824	11,193,514	15,528,145	114.7
Photographic equipment and supplies..	2,660,496	3,788,568	5,316,402	99.8
Piece goods....................................	635,435	1,469,121	1,997,604	214.4
Linens and domestics........................	3,618,871	5,959,892	7,209,346	99.2
Smallwares....................................	653,115	1,919,689	2,458,429	276.4
China and glassware.........................	667,929	1,513,192	1,767,051	164.6
Home furnishings.............................	2,202,733	3,990,122	4,725,539	114.5
Furniture......................................	4,229,989	4,893,947	6,155,047	45.5
Major appliances.............................	1,391,220	3,294,473	4,507,563	224.0
Radio and music..............................	2,281,374	2,801,728	3,920,840	71.9
Hardware and housewares..................	9,900,714	13,448,125	17,345,646	75.2
Jewelry...	1,939,600	3,116,544	4,071,029	109.9
Sporting goods and luggage...............	6,920,226	4,934,965	6,054,755	−12.5
Stationery, books and magazines........	2,000,237	7,349,733	8,933,304	346.6
All other departments........................	11,308,237	19,099,211	26,006,959	130.0
Total of all departments....................	$106,908,858	$160,183,582	$207,615,743	94.2

(Source: DBS, *Department Store Sales and Stocks, February 1964 and June 1965*. Catalogue no 63-002. The following firms are considered by the DBS as operating discount stores: Allied Towers Merchants Ltd.; Clarke-Gamble of Canada Ltd.; Frederick's Department Stores; Freimart Stores; G E M Stores; Hamilton Harvey & Son; K. Mart; Miracle Mart; Mon-Mart Discount Department Stores; Riteway Ltd.; Save-Mart; Sayvette Limited; Sentry Department Stores; Topps Discount Department Stores; Woolco Department Stores.)

The outmoded operating methods of the old-line stores have also helped the discounters. In particular, the department stores have created an unnecessary price umbrella for many goods by offering the same package of services with each item and marking everything up by the same percentage, regardless of the costs incurred or the elasticity of consumer demand. One survey has shown that a $10 purchase by a housewife in a traditional department store includes 92 cents for sales service, although she makes her own selection; 22 cents for the credit department, even if she pays cash; and 11 cents for delivery, despite the fact that she carries away the parcel herself. The discount stores have found here a wonderful opportunity which they have exploited to the full. They selected merchandise with a high mark-up which does not require special services, and slashed the prices to the bone, depending on volume to generate the profits. Credit, delivery, and installment services, if available, are provided on the "user-pay" principle. The policy of no exchanges and no refunds is generally enforced, except when the product is faulty. And, needless to say, the merchandise is not gift-wrapped.

Although one might sometimes see chauffeur-driven Lincolns in the parking lots, the mainstays of the discount stores are the Ford, Chevrolet, and Pontiac owners, persons earning $6,000 or less a year. In spite of their growing income, the household heads in this group are under more economic pressure than ever before. There is the mortgage on the home, the doctor's bills, the education of the children, and the installment payments on the car. They need to stretch their dollar as much as possible, and discount stores are right down their alley. The discounters realize this, and some of them even run their entire food departments as "loss leaders," hoping that this would generate traffic in other parts of the store where their real profits lie.

Price, however, is not the only cause of the popularity of discount stores. There are other reasons as well, such as convenient location, good parking, self-service, evening openings which permit family shopping, and informal atmosphere where one can paw and maul the merchandise to the heart's content without being browbeaten by a clerk.

The traditional type of department stores, which have borne the brunt of the attack, have started to fight back vigorously. Some are following the well-known technique of, "if you can't beat them, join them," and are themselves jumping on the discount bandwagon, by adopting discount methods, by converting their warehouses to bargain centers, or by setting up their own "twig" stores in the suburbs on a self-service, discount basis. Once again the old battle cry reverberates across the land: "We'll not be knowingly undersold."

A large number of other established stores are going the opposite way by emphasizing their strong points and striking at the enemy's weak spots. To give a few examples:

• The discounter does not give personal selling service; so they do. And they make sure the service is all that it is supposed to be. They hire better clerks, friendly and courteous, who know how to serve customers properly.

• The discount house is a Coney Island type of place. Its vast, elbowing crowds can be irritating and a bit hard on the nerves. As an offset, many conventional merchants are emphasizing an inviting, relaxing atmosphere.

• The discounter generally sells for cash, though some steer customers to finance companies to work out budget-payment plans on large purchases. Many traditional department stores are, therefore, liberalizing their own credit plans.

As the old-line retailers fight back, the original discounters are finding new ways of adjusting themselves. Some are venturing into fashion merchandise in order to broaden their appeal. Others are trying to cultivate the patronage of the growing middle and upper-income groups by adding customer services, upgrading physical facilities, and copying the decor of the conventional department store. Needless to say, with all these improvements, their operating costs are mounting, making it more difficult for them to sell at bargain rates.

With the discount store moving in the direction of orthodoxy and the orthodox competitors trying to imitate the discounters, the maverick and the traditional retailing organizations are tending to meet on some middle ground. The result is that when anyone discounts, nearly everybody else follows suit. Soon the term "discount" will have no more special significance for discount houses than "self-service" has for grocery stores.

Automatic Vending

Another retailing trend that has been prominent of late is automatic vending. Push-button selling is a logical extension of the principle of self-service. In the vending machine, one has a salesman who never sleeps, who does not require social security, fringe benefits, or paid vacations to add to the cost of retailing. In many respects, robot vending is to distribution what automation is to production.

The list of products which these silent salesmen can offer is growing larger year after year. For a long time, vending-machine sales were confined to cigarettes, confectionery, and beverages. These are still the bread-and-butter lines. But today the vending machines are so far advanced that they can dispense almost anything, from peanuts and panties to insurance policies, onion soup, a spray of French perfume, or a 30-second sniff of oxygen to ease hangovers.

Recently, the most spectacular gain has been in the field of employee food service. Already a few large companies have discontinued their costly cafeterias and installed instead a bank of vending machines providing a wide variety of hot and cold foods. Soon this method is likely to be adopted by most of the big industrial plants. Management is also finding in these machines a satisfactory solution to the perennial problem of coffee-breaks.

Vending machine operators have also been eyeing for some time the semi-captive market of apartment dwellers. Currently, apartment buildings have only the coin-operated automatic washing and drying machines. But soon installations will probably be made to vend a host of food and non-food items, including milk, bread, fruit juice, soft drinks, baked goods, cigarettes, household products, and health and beauty aids.

Recently, one company has placed in the basements of large apartment buildings, freezer units containing all kinds of frozen foods. Tenants are invited to join a "food club." Each receives colored tokens of various values, which, when inserted in the slide unit attached to the freezer, activate the mechanism that releases the food package selected. The tokens are the equivalent of "credit cards" and are numbered to identify the customer. At the end of the month, the tenant is billed for the total value of the tokens deposited during the month.

NUMBER OF VENDING MACHINES BY TYPE AND LOCATION
AS OF DECEMBER 31, 1963

Type of machine	Indus-trial plants	Busi-ness offices	Amuse-ment centres	Hotels, motels, etc.	Gaso-line service stations	Other loca-tions	Total of all loca-tions
Cigarette and cigar machines	2,772	730	1,633	8,003	2,193	999	16,330
Frozen refreshment machines	133	5	15	3	1	67	224
Bottled or canned drink machines	1,220	308	151	171	303	590	2,743
Cartoned milk or juice machines	370	16	8	—	1	168	563
Cup-vending machines:							
Milk	366	13	9	27	55	132	602
Other cold drinks:							
Post-mix	1,717	199	414	53	30	437	2,850
Pre-mix	436	99	125	27	30	159	876
Hot drinks	3,272	775	284	69	488	768	5,656
Combination hot and cold	179	9	1	—	4	57	250
Confectionery machines:							
Bulk (unwrapped)	1,252	487	3,025	5,253	11,526	12,623	34,166
Packaged confectionery	1,970	292	1,095	151	349	778	4,635
Pastries	1,104	106	19	11	5	345	1,590
Canned hot food machines	747	50	6	4	1	145	953
Fresh food machines:							
Heated	98	—	2	6	—	7	113
Refrigerated	456	52	20	3	4	57	592
No temperature control	48	3	1	—	—	—	52
Other machines	21	27	43	211	45	186	533
Total of all machines	16,161	3,171	6,851	13,992	15,035	17,518	72,728

(Source: DBS, *Vending Machine Operators, 1963*. Catalogue no. 63-213.)

So far the greatest roadblock to automatic selling has been the inability of machines to accept paper money. But now change-makers for dollar bills are available. The next step will be to incorporate the changers within the selling units themselves. Already, there is a machine in experimental use that accepts any amount of money up to $9.99 in coins and dollar bills, records the amount of purchases, and gives out the proper change at the end. This opens the way for selling high-priced items. It also encourages sales of multiple units (e.g., a complete carton rather than just a pack of cigarettes).

SALES BY VENDING MACHINE OPERATORS, 1963
(thousand dollars)

Products	Atlantic Provs.	Québec	Ontario	Prairie Provs.	British Columbia	Canada
Tobacco products	1,967	13,168	13,108	4,683	6,222	39,148
Frozen refreshments	*	72	79	*	12	258
Milk and milk products	22	349	1,283	102	13	1,769
Cold drinks						
Vended in bottles, cans or cartons	379	883	524	186	104	2,076
Vended in disposable cups	381	1,856	3,216	476	287	6,216
Hot drinks (coffee, tea, hot chocolate, and cup-vended soup)	177	2,589	5,888	811	327	9,792
Bulk (unwrapped) confectionery	134	642	505	154	36	1,471
Packaged confectionery	171	838	1,322	250	182	2,763
Pastries	65	869	641	29	8	1,612
Sandwiches (hot and cold)	43	439	1,088	25	15	1,610
Canned hot foods and canned soup	19	202	457	47	10	735
Other hot foods	*	*	*	—	*	105
Other cold foods	—	*	*	—	—	5
Other non-food items	—	4	9	*	*	20
Total of all products	3,468	21,959	28,146	6,779	7,228	67,580

* Figures withheld in order to avoid disclosure.
(Source: DBS, *Vending Machine Operators, 1963*. Catalogue no. 63-213.)

Technological breakthroughs in this field are constantly occurring. It is not inconceivable that in the years to come engineers may develop a machine that can accept a credit card, check its validity, and record purchases made. A few years ago, this idea would probably have been classified along with the imaginary exploits of Buck Rogers. Today the knowledge necessary for this type of operation is at hand. All one has to do is apply it.

How far will automated selling go? One expert believes that telephone buying may be the pattern of future retailing. The housewife would select from samples shown on closed circuit TV, and the merchandise would be delivered within the hour by a jet copter from automated warehouses.

Whether retailing will ever reach this stage, it is difficult now to forecast. However, one development seems reasonably certain in the near future — the establishment of a fully automated store, based on IBM records. Prototypes of it already exist in an experimental form in both Canada and the United States. Here is how it works:

A sample of each item to be sold is mounted on a display board with a number tacked above it. At the top of the fixture are racks of IBM cards with corresponding numbers for every item shown. When the customer makes his selection, he takes the card and moves on to the next purchase. Two or more units of the same item require two or more cards. When the shopping is completed, all the cards collected are carried to the cashier, where they are fed into a billing machine which prints the invoice in triplicate. One copy is handed to the customer, the other goes to the store's inventory files, while the third is whisked through a pneumatic air chute to the stock room where the order is quickly filled and rushed to the pickup window.

Some retailing researchers believe that this system will be adopted fairly widely in the future because of its certain inherent advantages:

• The method of display permits the shopper to find quickly the item he wants; there is no hidden merchandise.

• The customer has no carts to push about; nor does he have to carry an armful of goods in the store.

• Shopping becomes faster, and peak-hour traffic can be easily handled.

• Rapid turnover, reduced payroll costs, and elimination of pilferage permit a lowering of prices on the goods carried.

• Constant electronic inventory control reduces the costly out-of-stock headache.

• Store personnel do not have to look after the stock or do a lot of cleaning.

BIBLIOGRAPHY

Business Week: "The Not So Silent Salesmen," November 21, 1964.

Federal Reserve Bank of Philadelphia: "What's Behind the Discount Rumpus in Retailing?" *Business Review,* November, 1961.

Hamill, Katharine: "The Squeeze on Shopping Centers," *Fortune,* September, 1963.

Hughes, Lawrence M.: "The 'Secret' Hand in Private Brands," *Sales Management,* September 16, 1960.

Morse, Leon: "The Battle of Brands," *Sales Management,* May, 1964.

Moyer, M. S.: "Renaissance in Canadian Retailing," *The Marketer,* Fall/Winter 1965 issue.

Newman, Peter C.: "The Revolution That's Changing Your Shopping Habits," *Maclean's Magazine,* September 1, 1956.

Silberman, Charles E.: 1) "The Revolutionists of Retailing"; 2) "The Discounters Choose Their Weapons"; 3) "The Department Stores are Waking Up." *Fortune,* April 1962, May 1962, June 1962. (Series on "The Distribution Upheaval.")

Thomas, Wayne: "National Brands — 'Chain' Gang Victims," *Marketing,* September 14, 1962.

Weiss, E. B.: *Merchandising for Tomorrow,* McGraw-Hill Book Company, Inc., New York, 1961.

Chapter 7

TRENDS IN THE LABOR FORCE

Trends in Employment and Unemployment

DEFINITIONS

Of all the official statistical reports released periodically, few have so much economic and political significance as the announcements concerning the labor force, employment, and unemployment. The information, based on a monthly survey among 30,000 households across Canada, serves as a barometer of the country's economic health and indicates how well the nation is utilizing its most precious resource — manpower.

Before analyzing the figures, one must be clear on what they represent, since popular conception and official terminology do not always jibe. The labor force covers that portion of the civilian population, 14 years of age and over, which at the time of the survey was employed or seeking employment. Normally excluded are students, housewives, and old people, unless such persons are working part-time or looking for a job.

Counted as employed are all those who during the week of the survey:

a) did any work for pay or profit;

b) helped in running a farm or business operated by a related member of the household; or

c) had a job, but were not at work, because of bad weather, illness, industrial dispute, vacation, or some other reason.

Unemployed include persons who were without work and seeking part-time or full-time jobs as well as those on temporary layoff up to 30 days.

THE LABOR FORCE

The labor force has shown a healthy increase in the last 15 years, from 5,163,-000 in 1950 to 7,141,000 in 1965. This growth is impressive in itself, but it becomes even more so when one considers that agriculture has been declining as a source of employment. Not only has all the gain been in nonagricultural industries, but in addition this sector has been called upon to absorb another 424,000 people for whom farming would no longer provide jobs.

At various times in the past, immigration has made a substantial contribution to the nation's reservoir of productive manpower. This was particularly so in the 1950's when the domestic supply of young people was severely limited by the low prewar birth rates. It is estimated that net immigration accounted for two-thirds of the total labor force increase between 1950 and 1955 and for about half of the gain for the decade as a whole. In the early Sixties the situation was reversed, with the immigrants in a distinct minority.

AVERAGE ANNUAL INCREASE IN LABOR FORCE

	1950–1955	1955–1960	1960–1965*
Net immigration	60,000	55,000	15,000
Domestic population	30,000	105,000	131,000
Total growth per year	90,000	160,000	146,000

* Figures for 1960–1965 were estimated.

There have been sharp changes in participation rates by age groups. In 1950, 56% of the male teen-agers were in the labor force; in 1965 the proportion was only 39%. Thus, while the total male population of 14 to 19 years of age soared from 630,000 to 1,086,000, the work force in this age group varied very little, from 352,000 to 420,000. The reason, of course, is the prolongation of schooling. Instead of coming into the labor market at, say, 15 or 16, the young men are now entering it at 17 or 18 or even later. Many reasons can be cited for this: a radical switch in public attitudes towards education; the expansion of training facilities throughout the country; the shift in population from farms to cities (a much larger proportion of youngsters finish high school in urban than in rural areas); and the rise in family income, enabling parents to finance their children's university education.

Not only are the males joining the labor force later, but they are moving out of it earlier. In the past, the participation rates among the elderly were high due to the large number of agricultural workers. It is well known that old farmers are like old soldiers; they sometimes die, but they seldom retire. With the shift away from agriculture, the proportion of over-65-year-old males in the labor force has fallen considerably. There has also been a slight decline in the age group of 55 to 64. A growing number of companies now permit or even encourage their employees to retire before 65. This helps to get rid of a worker in a "red circle" job; that is, one about to be eliminated by attrition. Often, in the age of automation, a fattened-up pension may cost a firm less than keeping a man on the payroll until he retires.

If different factors have contributed to check the size of the male labor force, no such restraints have been in operation in the female sector. The number of working women shot up by 87% between 1950 and 1965, from 1,112,000 to 2,076,000. The fair sex now accounts for over 29% of the labor force, compared to only 22% fifteen years ago. The most dramatic increase has been in the age groups of 35 to 64 — a jump from 372,000 to 988,000 — reflecting the rising proportion of married women who want to earn money after the early child-bearing years. Social attitudes have changed and ostracism against females going to work has nearly disappeared. Employment opportunities, too, have been plentiful. There have been many new openings in the wholesale and retail trade, as well as in finance, teaching, and government — fields noted for having a large proportion of women on the payrolls. It is not surprising, therefore, that in the early Sixties (1960-1965) one and a half times more females than males entered the labor force.

LABOR FORCE (thousands)

	Males	Females	Total
1965	5,065	2,076	7,141
1960	4,754	1,657	6,411
Increase 1961 to 1965	311	419	730

The growth in the labor force has not been uniform across the country. The sharpest gains have been in British Columbia and Ontario, while the Atlantic Provinces have shown the least increase.

LABOR FORCE (thousands)

	1950	1965	% increase
Atlantic Provinces	524	611	16.6
Québec	1,433	2,022	41.1
Ontario	1,826	2,614	43.2
Prairie Provinces	951	1,228	29.1
British Columbia	429	666	55.2
Canada	5,163	7,141	38.3

These wide differences are due to inter-regional population movements and the concentration of postwar immigrants in certain areas. Ontario and British Columbia have benefited from the influx, while the Atlantic Provinces have suffered, because many young adults have left home to seek better opportunities in greener pastures elsewhere.

EMPLOYMENT

Between 1950 and 1965, the number of employed edged up from 4,976,000 to 6,862,000. As may be expected, some significant changes occurred in the structure of employment. Some industries expanded at a rapid rate, while in others the opportunities for work shrank considerably.

The most outstanding drop has been in agriculture. Less than one person out of 11 is now engaged in farming compared to one out of five in 1950. The introduction of new equipment and better techniques of cultivation have substantially reduced manpower requirements. This, together with the relative attractiveness of opportunities in urban areas, has encouraged young people to leave the farms in large numbers.

	Employed (000)		% distribution		% change
	1950	1965	1950	1965	1950–65
Goods-producing industries					
Agriculture	1,018	594	20.5	8.7	− 41.7
Forestry	82	77	1.6	1.1	− 6.1
Fishing, trapping	39	23	0.8	0.3	− 41.0
Mines, quarries, oil wells	75	134	1.5	1.9	+ 78.7
Manufacturing	1,272	1,637	25.6	23.9	+ 28.7
Construction	307	463	6.2	6.7	+ 50.8
Service-producing industries					
Transport, storage, communication	421	540	8.5	7.9	+ 28.3
Electric power, gas, water utilities	46	77	0.9	1.1	+ 67.4
Wholesale and retail trade	671	1,145	13.5	16.7	+ 70.6
Finance, insurance, real estate	142	280	2.8	4.1	+ 97.2
Services: community, business, personal, government	903	1,892	18.1	27.6	+109.5
Total	4,976	6,862	100.0	100.0	+ 37.9

(Source: DBS, *The Labor Force.* The 1950 figures have been adjusted to conform to the Standard Industrial Classification.)

The percentage of employed in other goods-producing industries has also tended to decline. The steadily increasing use of larger, faster, and more powerful machinery and equipment has cut down the demand for labor in forestry, fishing, and trapping. In manufacturing, too, the number of workers per unit of production has declined, as older facilities have been replaced by more advanced mechanical equipment capable of integrating different production processes. On the whole, out of the total of 1,886,000 new jobs created between 1950 and 1965, the goods-producing industries provided only 135,000. The remaining 1,751,000 came from the service-producing industries. Certain sectors, like finance, and community, business, and government services, registered percentage gains about three times more than the national average.

UNEMPLOYMENT

Unemployment is a result of an imbalance or disjuncture between the supply of labor and its demand. In some respects, it is inevitable in a society where there is no central economic planning and state control, and hence no integration of production and employment policies of individual firms and industries. Even in countries experiencing intense labor shortage, a small fraction of the working population at any given time will be out of work as long as employers retain their privilege to fire and the employees their freedom to quit. Frictional unemployment of this type is a part of the constant process by which labor resources are allocated and reallocated in response to market stimuli and the changing requirements of a dynamic economy.

There is no accepted standard as to how high this level of unavoidable unemployment should be in a healthy economy. The Economic Council of Canada has suggested a rate of 3%. This is slightly above the level of 1946 and 1953 when unemployment was on the average only 2.8% of the labor force.

Unfortunately, since 1954, Canada's record has been quite discouraging. The ratio has hovered consistently above the 3% mark. What is even more disconcerting is that at each successive recession, unemployment has been higher; and at each recovery, the drop has been less steep than during the preceding business cycle. A good many of those out of work are in areas where there are no longer job opportunities in the types of work for which they are qualified.

The problem is serious. Unemployment in 1965 cost the nation $2.1 billion in the loss of goods and services. Its magnitude can be seen from the fact that if it had been distributed over the total work force at one time, rather than borne by the minority wholly or partly employed during the year, it would have resulted in the shutting down of the entire country — with no production, no services, no pay — for no less than 15 days.* Because it is spread out in bits and pieces and in unequal loads, its impact is less observable and less troubling to the nation's sense of husbandry than a concentrated shutdown. None the less, it is still a chronic malady sapping the vitality of the country. Both the individual and society suffer: the individual through cuts in income, depletion or elimination of savings, hardship for the family, erosion of unused skills, and sickness of spirit which may be lastingly harmful; and society through unrealized output, reduced demand, and the social costs of poverty.

Before steps can be taken to ameliorate the malady, it is necessary to identify the symptoms and find out which parts of the country are most affected. Fortunately, in recent years, the Dominion Bureau of Statistics has gathered (though not always published) a substantial amount of information on who and where the unemployed are. An examination of these statistics lends a great deal of depth to an otherwise hazy picture and focuses attention on some prominent points. One can see clearly that the incidence of unemployment is strikingly uneven. The national average tends to conceal sharp variations from region to region and from group to group. The information given below is only for 1965, but the situation was very much the same in the preceding years. Unemployment rates for the various groups have moved up and down more or less in unison.

---

* Estimated Gross National Product per year $51,500,000,000
Gross National Product per day (÷ 365) $141,096,000
Gross National Product per employed worker (6,862,000 employed) $7,505
Gross National Product lost (7,505 x 280,000 unemployed) $2,101,400,000
Number of days of Gross National Product lost
(2,101,400,000 ÷ 141,096,000) 15

Unemployment rate by sex:

Males	4.4%
Females	2.7
Average	3.9%

Female unemployment is below the average because of the greater concentration of women in the service-producing industries where job opportunities have been expanding both rapidly and smoothly. To some extent, the lower rate may also be attributable to the tendency on the part of married women out of work to report themselves at the time of the survey as housewives rather than as unemployed.

Unemployment rate by age-groups:

14 – 19	8.8%
20 – 24	4.7%
25 – 34	3.1%
35 – 44	2.9%
45 – 54	3.0%
55 – 64	3.7%
65 & over	4.5%
Average	3.9%

The incidence of unemployment is heaviest among the youngest group. This is partly due to the application of seniority principles by employers when laying off part of the staff. Also, teen-agers switch their jobs quite frequently, with the result that at any given time a large proportion may be out of work simply because they have left their old jobs and not yet obtained new ones. The lack of experience and skill is another contributing factor. Alarming numbers of our youth today do not have the educational preparation necessary for the new job opportunities that are opening up. Often the training received is out of step with the requirements of the technological era.

Unemployment rate by marital status:

Single	6.5%
Married	2.9%
Widowed, separated or divorced	3.8%
Average	3.9%

Many single persons are unemployed probably because a sizeable number are between 14 and 24 years of age, looking for their first job. Frictional unemployment is also apt to be high. Since they have little or no family responsibilities, single persons tend to give up their jobs quite easily when they find the working conditions unsatisfactory.

Unemployment rate by industries:

Primary industries 4.3%
Manufacturing 3.4%
Construction 10.7%
Transportation and other utilities 3.9%
Trade 2.6%
Service 2.4%
Average 3.9%

By far the worst record is held by the construction industry. The seasonal nature of the work, the disruptions due to bad weather, the overcrowding of the industry with unskilled immigrants, the loose attachment of employees to particular employers, all contribute to the high incidence of unemployment.

Unemployment rate by occupations:

White-collar occupations 1.4%
Blue-collar occupations
   Craftsmen, production process, related
     workers 4.6%
   Unskilled laborers 13.4%
Other occupations
   Primary industries 4.1%
   Transport and communication 5.1%
   Service and recreation 3.5%
Average 3.9%

The country is moving from a blue-collar to a white-collar economy, one which offers fewer and fewer opportunities to untrained persons. This trend plus the technological changes, particularly automation, are making it more and more difficult for unskilled laborers to obtain jobs. In fact, unemployment is almost inversely correlated to the level of education.

Unemployment rate by provinces:

Atlantic Provinces 7.4%
Québec 5.4%
Ontario 2.5%
Prairie Provinces 2.6%
British Columbia 4.1%
Average 3.9%

The Atlantic Provinces have the highest rate of unemployment. They are handicapped by a combination of adverse factors, such as heavy dependence on seasonal occupations, lack of economic opportunities, dispersal of population in small rural communities, and absence of an important manufacturing complex around which tertiary industries can grow.

Unemployment rate by months:

January	5.9%
February	5.8%
March	5.6%
April	5.3%
May	3.7%
June	3.5%
July	3.3%
August	2.8%
September	2.5%
October	2.4%
November	3.1%
December	3.5%
Average	3.9%

Seasonal unemployment is a perennial problem in Canada, and a major one. Over twice as many people are out of jobs during the first quarter of the year as in the third. The Department of Labour has calculated that, even under reasonably full employment conditions, about 4% of the labor force is likely to be seasonally unemployed at mid-winter. This is the penalty that Canadians have to pay for living in the northern clime.

FUTURE OUTLOOK

According to the Economic Council of Canada, the labor force will grow from 7,141,000 in 1965 to 8,127,000 in 1970. This estimate has been prepared after taking into consideration the age and sex composition of the population as well as the social conditions and attitudes that would influence participation rates within each group. The results are shown graphically in Chart 3.

In the age group of 25 to 54, the proportion of males in the labor force will remain the same as before. A longer period of schooling will cut down the participation rates of teen-agers and adolescents, while adequate provisions for private and public pensions will encourage earlier retirement of males over 55. Housewives will continue to seek outside employment in large numbers, most of the increase being concentrated among those aged 35 to 64. Probably, by the end of the decade one-third of the married women will be working, compared to slightly over a quarter in 1965.

On the basis of these assumptions, the Economic Council of Canada forecasts that the labor force in the next few years will grow as shown at the top of p. 71.

Thus, between 1965 and 1970, on the average 197,000 new members will be added to the working force every year. This is substantially higher than average increase of 124,800 per year in the Fifties and of 146,000 between 1960 and 1965. In fact, the annual growth rate of 2.7% expected for the later Sixties is one of the biggest that Canada has ever experienced in her entire history and way beyond that anticipated for any other industrial nation in the world.

LABOR FORCE (in thousands)

	Males	Females	Persons	Annual Growth
1965	5,065	2,076	7,141	—
1966	5,152	2,138	7,290	149
1967	5,257	2,235	7,492	202
1968	5,367	2,331	7,698	206
1969	5,482	2,430	7,912	214
1970	5,599	2,528	8,127	215
Average	—	—	—	197

Most of the gain will originate from the domestic population. In sharp contrast to the previous decade, immigration will play a far less significant role in the expansion of the labor force, as shown below:

ANNUAL GROWTH OF LABOR FORCE (000)

	Average 1955–60	Average 1965–70
Net immigration	55	30
Domestic population	105	167
Total labor force growth	160	197

As a result, there will be a reduced reliance on the supplies of skilled and professional personnel from abroad, and a greater dependence on the development of such manpower at home. The implication of these changes on the Canadian economy can be far-reaching.

The table on page 72 shows the participation rates in the labor force by sex and age groups for 1965 and 1970. It is clear from the last column that over 40% of the total increase in the labor force (395,000 out of 986,000) will come from persons under 25, despite their lower participation rates. So far, the effect of the early postwar baby boom has been modified and delayed by the tendency of the young people to continue their education further. But this has acted only as a temporary brake. Very shortly the full impact will be felt, the bulk of the pressure stemming from those between 20 and 24. Between 1965 and 1970, 299,000 persons in that age group will enter the labor force, compared to only 52,000 from 1950 to 1960. In other words, the average increase *each year* will exceed the growth which took place over the *whole decade* of the Fifties.

Changes in the age structure of the population will also bring about sharp variations in other sectors of the labor force. Because of the low birth rates during the Great Depression and the anticipated drop in immigration, there will be no increase in the number of male workers 35 to 44 years old. On the other hand,

LABOR FORCE BY AGE GROUPS, 1965 AND 1970

	1965 Population 14 and over (000)	1965 Labor force (000)	1965 Partici- pation rate %	1970 (estimated) Population 14 and over (000)	1970 (estimated) Labor force (000)	1970 (estimated) Partici- pation rate %	Increase in labor force 1965–1970 Per cent	Increase in labor force 1965–1970 No. (000)
14–19								
Persons..........	2,139	738	34.5	2,450	834	34.0	+13.0	96
Males..............	1,086	420	38.7	1,246	462	37.1	+10.0	42
Females..........	1,053	318	30.2	1,204	372	30.9	+17.0	54
20–24								
Persons..........	1,339	935	69.8	1,776	1,234	69.5	+32.0	299
Males..............	660	578	87.6	891	779	87.4	+34.8	201
Females..........	679	357	52.6	885	455	51.4	+27.5	98
25–34								
Persons..........	2,341	1,496	63.9	2,578	1,671	64.8	+11.7	175
Males..............	1,157	1,128	97.5	1,271	1,240	97.6	+ 9.9	112
Females..........	1,184	368	31.1	1,307	431	33.0	+17.1	63
35–44								
Persons..........	2,461	1,611	65.5	2,433	1,637	67.3	+ 1.6	26
Males..............	1,214	1,186	97.7	1,213	1,186	97.8	—	—
Females..........	1,247	425	34.1	1,220	451	37.0	+ 6.1	26
45–54								
Persons..........	2,007	1,331	66.3	2,234	1,548	69.3	+16.3	217
Males..............	1,001	959	95.8	1,098	1,054	96.0	+ 9.9	95
Females..........	1,006	372	37.0	1,136	494	43.5	+32.8	122
55–64								
Persons..........	1,422	808	56.8	1,648	965	58.6	+19.4	157
Males..............	715	617	86.3	817	699	85.6	+13.3	82
Females..........	707	191	27.0	831	266	32.0	+39.3	75
65 and over								
Persons..........	1,419	222	15.6	1,553	238	15.3	+ 7.2	16
Males..............	672	177	26.3	714	179	25.1	+ 1.1	2
Females..........	747	45	6.0	839	59	7.0	+31.1	14
Total								
Persons..........	13,128	7,141	54.4	14,672	8,127	55.4	+13.8	986
Males..............	6,505	5,065	77.9	7,250	5,599	77.2	+10.5	534
Females..........	6,623	2,076	31.3	7,422	2,528	34.1	+21.8	452

(Source: DBS, *The Labour Force* (special tables) and *Population and Labour Force Projections to 1970* by F. Denton, Y. Kasahara, and S. Ostry. Staff Study No. 1 prepared for the Economic Council of Canada.)

EMPLOYMENT BY INDUSTRIES AND OCCUPATIONS, 1965 AND 1970

	Employed (000)		% distribution		Change 1965–1970	
					Per cent	Actual (000)
	1965	1970	1965	1970		
A. Industries						
Agriculture	594	543	8.7	6.9	− 8.6	−51
Other primary industries	234	197	3.4	2.5	−15.8	−37
Manufacturing	1,637	1,884	23.8	23.9	+15.1	247
Construction	463	520	6.7	6.6	+12.3	57
Transportation, communication, utilities	617	717	9.0	9.1	+16.2	100
Wholesale and retail trade	1,145	1,357	16.7	17.2	+18.5	212
Finance, insurance, real estate	280	347	4.1	4.4	+23.9	67
Community, business, personal service	1,489	1,878	21.7	23.8	+26.1	389
Public administration, defence	403	440	5.9	5.6	+ 9.2	37
Total	6,862	7,883	100.0	100.0	+14.9	1,021
B. Occupations						
White-collar occupations						
Managerial	637	718	9.3	9.1	+12.7	81
Professional and technical	782	930	11.4	11.8	+18.9	148
Clerical	920	1,072	13.4	13.6	+16.5	152
Sales	482	591	7.0	7.5	+22.6	109
Blue-collar occupations						
Craftsmen production process, related workers	1,730	2,010	25.2	25.5	+16.2	280
Unskilled laborers	335	378	4.9	4.8	+12.8	43
Other occupations						
Service and recreation	793	1,009	11.6	12.8	+27.2	216
Operators and kindred workers in transport and communication fields	432	473	6.3	6.0	+ 9.5	41
Manual laborers in primary industries	751	702	10.9	8.9	− 6.5	−49
Total	6,862	7,883	100.0	100.0	+14.9	1,021

(Source: DBS, *Labour Force* for 1965. Estimates for 1970 were prepared by the author.)

above-average gains are expected for the age category of 54 to 64. In short, manpower requirements in the later Sixties will have to be met in a large measure by younger and older workers. This will necessitate many adjustments in training facilities, personnel policies, and wage contracts.

As regards employment, the Economic Council of Canada has set as one of its targets the reduction of those out of work to 3% of the labor force — the minimum to take care of frictional, seasonal, and structural maladjustments. On this basis, the total employment in 1970 will reach 7,883,000, compared to 6,862,000 in 1965. This means a net addition of 1,021,000 new jobs. Such an increase is equivalent to an average growth of 3% per year, quite a high figure when it is remembered that it is almost double the corresponding rate of 1.6% between 1956 and 1963.

In the table on p. 73, an attempt has been made to break down the total employment figure of 7,883,000 in 1970 by industries and by occupations. These estimates are only approximations, but they serve to indicate that employment opportunities will vary sharply from industry to industry and from occupation to occupation, due to the changes in demand and the advances in technology.

An actual decline in jobs is expected for primary industries. In agriculture, subsistence income from small farms will cause many rural youths to migrate to urban areas for work. Even on large farms, further mechanization will result in less need for hired help. The reduction of employment opportunities in other primary industries will not be as drastic, but it will still be substantial. These industries, such as forestry, fishing and mining, are heavily dependent on exports, and, according to the Economic Council of Canada, their output is not expected to grow as fast as the Gross National Product. Besides, the trend towards heavy capital investment will sharply curtail the requirements for unskilled labor.

Employment in white-collar jobs will increase rapidly because of the expansion of such industries as business service, banking, insurance, trade, and public administration. On the other hand, mechanization and automation will cut down the rate of growth in the blue-collar jobs. There will be a steady shift from direct-production labor to indirect labor and from non-office to office employment. Engineers, scientists, administrators, and computer programers will replace men on the production line, whether that production line be a factory, an airline-reservations system, a telephone network, a power generating plant, or a life insurance office.

One area which will not be affected by automation and where the job opportunities will be plentiful is the service and recreation field. More policemen and firemen will be needed for the mushrooming urban and suburban communities; more nurses and health attendants will be in demand at hospitals and medical institutions about to be built; more personal service workers, like waiters, bartenders, hairdressers, and dry cleaners, will be required to satisfy the diverse needs of a society that is getting more affluent and pleasure-oriented.

It must always be remembered that all these future estimates of employment by industry and occupation are based on one very important assumption: that by 1970 the economy will be operating at its full potential, with unemployment reduced to 3% of the labor force. This is the goal which the Economic Council has set. It is not unrealistic, but it will not be achieved automatically. Certain steps will have to be taken by both the private and the public sectors of the economy. Some of these measures are discussed in the following section.

Measures for Alleviating Unemployment

Canada faces a formidable task in the years ahead. The country will have to create 1,021,000 new jobs between 1965 and 1970 to provide employment not only for the anticipated gain in the labor force but also for a substantial portion of those currently on the jobless list.

Meeting this objective is difficult but not unrealizable. Success will depend on sustained and co-ordinated efforts by all sectors of the economy. Sporadic incursions into the problem and random flourishes are not going to bring results. What is needed is the formulation and implementation of an active and positive labor market policy by the federal government, so that the manpower resources of the country can be most productively utilized. War will have to be waged on many fronts, but the grand strategy may be epitomized as follows:

1) Permit the economy to operate at its full potential through a healthy increase in productivity.
2) Cut down seasonal swings in unemployment.
3) Reduce cyclical fluctuations in the economy.
4) Provide more jobs for the younger workers.
5) Mitigate the structural maladjustments in the demand and supply of labor.
6) Revitalize the depressed areas which have been cut off from the main currents of economic progress.

ECONOMIC GROWTH AND PRODUCTIVITY

In the past, the country's prosperity has to a great extent depended on productivity—that is, the level of output in relation to the labor input. In the future, too, the performance of the economy will be conditional mainly upon this factor. According to the Economic Council of Canada, productivity during the remainder of the Sixties should increase by at least 2.3% a year if the country is to achieve the goal of full employment. This means that the output per worker will have to amount to $7,999 in 1970, compared to $6,985 in 1964.

At first sight it may seem strange that a rise in productivity is required to generate more employment. If each worker produces more, obviously less manpower is needed to perform certain fixed tasks. But this is true only during the short period of adjustment. In the long run, more jobs are created than lost. In very simple terms, here is how the process works.

When a company installs a new, highly efficient machine, some workers are no longer wanted, but those that remain become more productive. This reduces cost per unit of output. Lower costs mean one or a combination of three things: higher wages for the remaining workers, which augment their purchasing power; lower prices, which enable consumers at any given level of income to buy more goods and services; greater profits, which mean more spending by the company and its stockholders. The group with the strongest bargaining strength will get the lion's share of the benefit, but the basic effect is much the same — an increase in the total demand for, as well as the capacity to produce, goods and services.

This extra spending or demand, as it courses through the various trade channels, creates new jobs and often more of them than were eliminated by the machine. On the whole, as society becomes more affluent, a larger percentage of income is spent on types of goods and services which are not particularly adaptable to automation — education, health, entertainment, personal services, and individualized products. Then, of course, additional jobs open up in companies that make and service the new equipment. In short, productivity increase may lead to some displacement of labor, but at the same time it results in lower levels of unemployment because of the stimulating interaction between technical progress and industrial and consumer demand.

The table on p. 77 highlights this point succinctly. There is clearly an inverse correlation between productivity and unemployment. The rise in one is accompanied by a drop in the other. For example, between 1950 and 1953, when productivity increased at an annual average of 4.3%, full employment conditions prevailed. Between 1958 and 1961, the gain in productivity was barely 1% a year, and unemployment shot up to 6.8%. Since 1962, the performance of productivity has been more encouraging, but it is still below the level reached in the early Fifties. The relative number of jobless has also fallen, but the country is still far from its full employment level.

Some labor unions try to stall the trend toward increased productivity (e.g., by slowing down the introduction of new machinery) in order to prevent likely unemployment. Of course, mechanization produces many dislocations and hardships in individual cases, but it can be said in broad, general terms that it will not be in the interest of Canada to check technological progress. Most European and Japanese producers, who had to rebuild their factories completely from the ruins of World War II, have now installed the most up-to-date equipment. In the United States, too, millions of dollars are spent every year on research and development. If the Canadian firms are to succeed in export markets, as well as to meet competition from imported products at home, they have to keep abreast of the most advanced technology and pursue a policy of constant innovation and development. Only in this way can they attain a satisfactory rate of growth and hold their own against the industrial giants of the world.

UNEMPLOYMENT INCREASES AS THE GROWTH IN PRODUCTIVITY DECLINES

	Total employment including armed forces (000)	Gross national product in 1964 dollars (million)	Gross national product per worker	Annual increase in output per worker (%)	Unemployment rate (%)
1950	5,028	26,073	$5,186	5.4	3.6
1951	5,175	27,671	5,347	3.1	2.4
1952	5,267	29,908	5,678	6.2	2.9
1953	5,340	31,048	5,814	2.4	3.0
1954	5,357	30,133	5,625	−3.3	4.6
1955	5,481	32,732	5,972	6.2	4.4
1956	5,702	35,541	6,233	4.4	3.4
1957	5,848	35,993	6,155	−1.3	4.6
1958	5,826	36,416	6,251	1.6	7.0
1959	5,990	37,673	6,289	0.6	6.0
1960	6,084	38,578	6,341	0.8	7.0
1961	6,176	39,571	6,407	1.0	7.1
1962	6,351	42,200	6,645	3.7	5.9
1963	6,498	44,156	6,795	2.3	5.5
1964	6,729	47,003	6,985	2.8	4.7
1970 (target)	7,993	63,937	7,999	2.3	3.0
Av. 1950–53				4.3	3.0
Av. 1954–57				1.5	4.3
Av. 1958–61				1.0	6.8
Av. 1962–64				2.9	5.4

(Source: Based on the suggestions made by B. J. Drabble in *Potential Output 1946 to 1970*. Staff Study No. 2 prepared for the Economic Council of Canada.)

The present situation can be viewed as a race — a race between the job-eliminating forces of automation and the job-creating forces of research, new products, growing foreign trade, and increased demand from business and consumers. Rather than hobbling the job-eliminating forces and thereby foregoing the potential benefits of technology, it is better to spur on the job-creating forces and sharpen our economic reflexes.

While the bulk of the increase in productivity comes from technological progress, one should not overlook the other factors that help to augment the output per worker. These include higher standards of health and education, improved managerial competence, more harmonious industrial relations, greater specialization, and wider adoption of large-scale production techniques. Some attention should be given to all these forces, if Canada is to forge ahead in the future.

However, productivity alone is not going to solve automatically all manpower problems. Unemployment is not like ice that melts away when business expands.

It resembles rather a rock that requires a great deal of patience and effort to remove. What makes the situation even more complicated is that unemployment manifests itself in not one but several forms — seasonal unemployment, cyclical unemployment, teen-age unemployment, structural unemployment, and regional unemployment. This calls for a war on many fronts. No doubt, there is a considerable amount of overlapping, and measures designed to alleviate one kind of unemployment will affect the others as well. However, in order to have a clearer picture, one has to deal separately with each major facet of unemployment. The broad, general approach has its value, but it is not effective enough in the campaign to cut down the number of jobless in the nation.

SEASONAL UNEMPLOYMENT

This type of unemployment is the curse of the northern climate. Invariably, through good times and bad, the number of persons out of work starts to increase in the fall, slowly at first, and later more and more rapidly as the temperature drops. By about February or March, a maximum is reached. Then, as winter gives way to spring, the pendulum swings back with equal predictability, and unemployment starts to decline again. So it goes from one year to the next with almost clock-like regularity.

A rough estimate indicates that seasonal factors are responsible for about one-half of all winter unemployment, or approximately one-third of total joblessness as a year-round average. Some areas, because of the severity of the climate, are more adversely affected, but no province is completely spared, and from one end of the country to the other the annual toll is heavy in terms of enforced idleness and wasted manpower.

There is no standard method of measuring seasonal unemployment. The simplest way is to take the differences in unemployment rates between the first and the third quarters. A large part of these variations may be reasonably attributed to seasonal influences.

The table on p. 79 shows the trend in seasonal unemployment from 1954 to 1965.

Despite the fluctuations from year to year, the three-year averages reveal a steady upward trend from 1954 to 1962. Since then, the adverse effect of the seasonal factor has been somewhat mitigated.

Taking the 1954–1965 period as a unit, the first-quarter rate comes out to be more than double that of the third. This provides a reasonably good indication of the magnitude of the seasonal problem. If employment could somehow be maintained at its third-quarter level throughout the whole year, winter layoffs would be cut roughly in half. This may appear to be wishful thinking, at least for the foreseeable future; but it does serve to indicate that, if effective measures to reduce seasonal unemployment can be found and implemented, the rewards will be great in terms of the utilization of wasted manpower and the recovery of lost output.

	Unemployment rate (%)			
	First quarter	Third quarter	Differ-ence	Three-year average
1954	6.2	3.3	2.9	
1955	7.5	2.6	4.9	3.9
1956	5.8	1.9	3.9	
1957	6.1	3.2	2.9	
1958	10.1	4.8	5.3	4.6
1959	9.3	3.8	5.5	
1960	9.4	5.1	4.3	
1961	11.0	4.9	6.1	5.0
1962	8.7	4.1	4.6	
1963	8.4	3.9	4.5	
1964	6.9	3.4	3.5	3.7
1965	5.8	2.8	3.0	
Average: 1954–1965	7.9	3.6	4.3	

Where is the incidence of seasonal unemployment felt most? This can be best analyzed by industries, occupations, provinces, and age groups. The following figures are for 1965, computed from the DBS monthly report, *The Labour Force.*

SEASONAL UNEMPLOYMENT BY INDUSTRIES

	Unemployment rate (%)		
	First quarter	Third quarter	Differ-ence
Agriculture, forestry, fishing, mining	7.3	1.9	5.4
Manufacturing	5.0	2.6	2.4
Construction	19.1	5.5	13.6
Transportation, communication, utilities	6.8	2.3	4.5
Wholesale and retail trade	3.8	1.9	1.9
Community, business, personal and government service, finance, insurance, real estate	3.1	1.9	1.2
All industries	5.8	2.8	3.0

The construction industry is the worst hit by changes in climate. Its seasonal fluctuation is four times greater than the over-all average. The service-producing industries have the least seasonal swings. Employment in manufacturing, too, does not fluctuate, and this helps to impart an element of stability to the economy. Of course, the reference here is to manufacturing taken as a whole. Certain sectors, such as fish canning and fruit and vegetable processing, are highly seasonal, and when some of these plants are concentrated in a certain area, the work force may be subjected to a substantial amount of winter unemployment.

SEASONAL UNEMPLOYMENT BY OCCUPATIONS

| | Unemployment rate (%) | | |
	First quarter	Third quarter	Differ-ence
White-collar occupations	1.8	1.2	0.6
Blue-collar occupations			
Craftsmen, production process and related workers	7.3	2.8	4.5
Unskilled laborers	21.1	8.1	13.0
Other occupations			
Manual laborers, primary industries	7.1	1.9	5.2
Operators and kindred workers in transport and communications	9.0	2.8	6.2
Service and recreation	4.4	3.1	1.3
All occupations	5.8	2.8	3.0

As may be expected, white-collar employees are affected the least and un-skilled laborers the most by seasonal fluctuations. Thus the greatest impact of winter unemployment is felt by persons who are least able financially to with-stand it. Since the wages of the unskilled are generally low, they cannot earn enough, even with overtime, during warm weather to be able to sit back and take it easy in the winter.

SEASONAL UNEMPLOYMENT BY PROVINCES

| | Unemployment rate (%) | | |
	First quarter	Third quarter	Differ-ence
Atlantic Provinces	12.1	4.2	7.9
Québec	7.8	4.0	3.8
Ontario	3.6	2.1	1.5
Prairie Provinces	4.1	1.6	2.5
British Columbia	5.7	3.3	2.4
Canada	5.8	2.8	3.0

The differences among provinces are due partly to climate and partly to in-dustrial composition. In the Atlantic region, the weather, combined with a heavy dependence on the seasonally volatile primary industries (logging and fishing), tends to produce a sharp reduction of activity during the cold months. Manufacturing is not as yet sufficiently developed to act as a stabilizing factor. The few plants that exist are connected mainly with wood products and fish processing, the least stable members of the manufacturing group. On the other hand, in Ontario, where secondary manufacturing and service industries pre-dominate, the influence of the seasonal factors is watered down considerably.

In fact, the winter unemployment rate in Ontario is lower than the summer unemployment rate in the Atlantic Provinces.

SEASONAL UNEMPLOYMENT BY AGE-GROUP AND SEX

	Unemployment rate (%)		
	First quarter	Third quarter	Difference
Males			
14–19	14.2	7.7	6.5
20–24	9.0	4.0	5.0
25–34	6.0	2.2	3.8
35–44	5.2	2.0	3.2
45–54	5.7	2.0	3.7
55–64	7.0	2.7	4.3
65 and over	5.8	3.5	2.3
Average	6.8	3.0	3.8
Females			
14–19	6.9	6.7	0.2
20–24	3.4	2.4	1.0
25–34	2.3	1.6	0.7
35–44	2.7	1.5	1.2
45–54	2.3	1.1	1.2
55–64	2.4	0.9	1.5
65 and over	2.9	1.6	1.3
Average	3.2	2.5	0.7

Seasonal unemployment is primarily a male problem, and hence relatively the more serious from a social point of view. The occupations which provide steady year-round jobs — the service, the trade, and the finance group of industries — are staffed mainly by women. By age groups, the younger male workers, of 14 to 24 years of age, are the most affected.

REMEDIES

To a considerable extent, seasonal unemployment is unavoidable. Canadians have to accept it as a part of the price of living in the northern latitude, in the same way as they have to spend more for clothing, home heating, and snow-plowing. The difficulties of working outdoors in winter are considerable, and barring some unexpected technological breakthroughs, employment in primary industries and transportation is bound to vary with the temperature. The only remedies that can be suggested in this case are:

• Shortening the inactive season in winter (e.g., through new ice-breaking devices, cutting down the period the St. Lawrence Seaway is closed).

- Establishing a better balance between the peak periods of some industries and the slack season of others (e.g., developing a winter tourist industry or other forms of enterprise to provide counter-seasonal employment).
- Creating new jobs by stimulating the growth of nonseasonal industries in areas where seasonality is a problem.
- Providing education and training facilities so that the unskilled and semi-skilled workers dependent on seasonal industries can find other temporary jobs during the slack season.

In the construction industry, where the work is not always outdoors, more remedial measures are possible, and it is here that Ottawa has concentrated most of its efforts. The government pays 50% of the on-site payroll costs through the Municipal Winter Works Incentive Program. Also, a bonus of $500 is given for each house built between November 15 and April 15 under the Winter Home Building Incentive Program. At the same time, during cold weather, an extensive publicity campaign is waged, urging builders and home owners to "Do It Now."

These are useful measures, but more steps are yet required to be taken. For example, Norway and Sweden, with climates similar to Canada's, have been able to cut down the seasonal drop of employment in construction to less than 10%. This has been achieved by classifying all the jobs into those that are possible in winter and others that can be carried out only during the less severe weather. Building permits are issued in such a way that the work which can be done in any month of the year is allowed to be undertaken only in winter. This procedure might be unpopular in Canada, as smacking too much of governmental interference; but if some alternative means of education or persuasion could be found to continue construction projects all through the cold months, Canada would be able to wipe out a substantial portion of seasonal unemployment. It would be possible to take thousands of persons off the jobless lists every winter and turn them into all-year-round earners.

CYCLICAL UNEMPLOYMENT

This type of unemployment is the result of the ups and downs of the whole economy rather than of a specific industry. It oscillates between the peaks and troughs of the business cycle, reaching its maximum at the period of recession and its minimum during general business expansion.

Several factors are responsible for cyclical fluctuations, such as variations in the production of capital goods, waves of pessimism and optimism among consumers, changes in foreign-market conditions, and expansions and contractions of monetary supply and credit facilities. Booms and busts are inevitable in a capitalistic society where there is no rigid state control and the generating force of the economy comes from the unco-ordinated plans (and concomitantly the mistakes) of myriads of individuals operating their own small enterprises.

Business cycles have continued to occur in the postwar era. No common procedure exists for dating the exact peaks and troughs, but it may roughly be said that the first major recession lasted from April 1953 till June 1954, a period of about 14 months. Then, there were two other slow-downs from May 1957 to April 1958 and from February 1960 to March 1961. These declines in business tempo were accompanied by substantial reductions in employment, the greatest effect being felt in durable-goods manufacturing and construction.

Since the Great Depression of the 1930's, numerous "built-in stabilizers" have been incorporated into the economy to prevent any recurrence of that catastrophe. Old-age pensions, unemployment compensation, and agricultural price supports, buttress incomes. Federal insurance of bank deposits and home-mortgage loans protects financial assets. Private pension schemes, medical-care plans, and insurance savings, help to keep the wolf away from the door of workers and their families. The progressive tax system reduces personal taxes proportionately more than the drop in income.

Along with these built-in stabilizers, the government has other weapons in its arsenal to prevent a moderate recession from catapulting into a major depression. Some of the tools available are reduction of personal and business taxes, easing of credit, encouragement of new housing, and development of public-works programs. However, in the past the authorities have not always been prompt in using these devices, and unemployment of a cyclical nature has persisted longer than it would have otherwise.

Nor is the private sector of the economy free from blame. Many of the postwar recessions have been triggered by fluctuations in business inventories. Involuntary accumulations of unsold goods have been followed by drastic cutdowns in production. This has had a snowball effect, curtailing output in various sectors of the economy and resulting in a loss of confidence all around.

Obviously, there would be less disruption if inventories were kept relatively low as a normal practice. This means a need for strict inventory control. It also implies a stable price level, without which companies are encouraged to build up stocks in order to avoid paying more for the raw materials later on. A government that seeks to promote economic growth in order to reduce unemployment may very largely defeat its own objective if, in doing so, it resorts to inflationary policies. Clearly, a delicate balance between maximum growth and minimum price inflation must be maintained at all times.

UNEMPLOYMENT OF YOUNG WORKERS

In 1965, persons in the age group of 14 to 24 constituted only 23% of the labor force but accounted for no less than 39% of total unemployment. In other words, roughly two out of every five job-hunters were teen-agers and young adults.

To a certain extent, high unemployment rates among young people are inevitable. They are especially vulnerable to layoffs because of their lack of seniority, their relative inexperience, and their unwillingness or inability to adjust to the routine and discipline of a job. They also frequently quit work on their own account, as part of the process of finding a satisfactory career field. Furthermore, many teen-agers under 18 are still at school, and their chief interest is some casual summer job, which is not always easy to get.

However, these factors do not tell the whole story. The heavy incidence of unemployment in recent years is in a large measure due to the scarcity of those bottom-rung occupations through which young people with little education or no training traditionally entered the labor market. Even where the technical requirements of the jobs have not changed, employers have tended to raise the educational qualifications for new recruits. A high-school diploma has become a prerequisite in many cases, simply as a screening device to cut down the number of people who have to be interviewed. Also, to a certain extent, the nationwide publicity campaign to persuade youngsters to stay in school is rendering it difficult for those who have quit to find work. A few firms are beginning to feel that drop-outs are unemployable, and they insist on hiring only high-school graduates, even for dead-end tasks.

The situation is serious and calls for a speedy remedy. Sociologists point out that the psychological scars of prolonged unemployment can be particularly deep, with effects that may blight the entire lifetime. To a youngster, especially if he has an impoverished background, unemployment seems only to confirm his well-grounded suspicion that he "can't make it" — that decent jobs are not available to persons of his color, or his nationality, or his social class. The prospects for a "good life" through the right channels become dim, and the seeds are sown for juvenile delinquency.

Since the teen-age unemployment problem is rooted in the dwindling opportunities for the uneducated and untrained, formal education and training have become young people's only valid passport for entry into the world of business. Already in many quarters an opinion is voiced that an additional two years of school attendance be made compulsory.

Even if that were not possible, young people should be encouraged to get all the education they can absorb. Large numbers of boys and girls who have above-average mental ability do not enter college; other capable youngsters drop out of school because they are not interested in the conventional types of academic courses. If each youngster could be persuaded and assisted to reach his full potential, the resulting benefits to the individual, the economy, and the entire society would be rich indeed.

In addition, some governmental assistance is required for the expansion of vocational training services to jobless out-of-school young people, so that they will be better qualified to meet the new, stringent requirements of the labor market.

Private industry should also be induced to provide more apprenticeship and on-the-job training to unskilled young people.

TECHNOLOGICAL AND STRUCTURAL UNEMPLOYMENT

Perhaps the most serious type of unemployment is of a structural nature, arising from the inability of the labor supply to adjust to the changes in the demand for manpower. Economic progress necessarily implies the expansion of some activities and the withering of others, the emergence of new products and the decline of existing ones, the development of new knowledge and better techniques and the obsolescence of traditional skills and established methods. In a sense this is the continuation of the process initiated by the Industrial Revolution. The substitution of manpower by computers today is not much different in principle from the replacement of weavers with Jacquard's loom or Hargreave's jennie.

In recent years much has been written in a pessimistic, almost panicky vein about the dire effects of automation and "cybernation," a newly coined term to refer to the marriage of computers with automatic machinery. According to some, the country is in for a period of unemployment in comparison with which the depression of the 1930's will seem a joke. Automation, they prophesy, will create an economy in which a potentially unlimited output will be achieved by complicated machines requiring little assistance from human beings. The nation will be caught in the horn of plenty. The unskilled and the poorly educated will be condemned to a vast human slag heap. There will not even be enough jobs of the conventional kind to go around.

However, this highly pessimistic forecast takes a grossly exaggerated view of the economic impact of automation, and completely loses sight of the realities of every-day life. As *Fortune** points out in one of its articles, the discussions on the future of science and technology have turned into a "competition in ominousness." A vast gap exists between scientific possibility and economic feasibility. Even today machines can replace men in many jobs, but in a majority of cases it is still less costly and more profitable to employ human beings. This partly explains why the civilian application of military and space research has been so far disappointingly small.

Theoretically, automation or cybernation means a system in which a computer controls all aspects of the processes, from injection of the raw materials to the emergence of the final products. It determines the proper mix and flow of materials, senses deviations from the desired operating conditions, and corrects these deviations as they occur or even before they occur. So far, no fully automated process of this type exists in any industry in Canada or the United States. Nor is any in prospect in the near future. As one management consultant

* Charles E. Silberman, "The Real News About Automation," *Fortune,* January, 1965.

has wisely observed: "There's no substitute for the brewmaster's nose." Automation is not and cannot be a system of machines operating without men; it can only be a symbiosis of the two. The computers can merely perform the tasks programmed for them by trained minds.

One result of automation is worth mentioning. It relieves people from the routine, the repetitive, the dull, and the unchallenging tasks. In this respect it reverses the principle upon which much of the improved standard of living has been based since the Industrial Revolution — the principle which called for the division and subdivision of tasks, so that the individual might produce at a high rate by monotonous repetition of one small set of motions as his part in the production line. Automation turns the repetitive task over to automatically controlled machinery. Rather than narrowing the job span, it tends to widen the ordinary workaday horizon.

Despite these advantages, the fact remains that automation displaces many workers and "twists" the labor market by creating shortages of brainpower and surpluses of musclepower. Since it is not advisable to hold back the clock of progress, the remedy lies in increasing the mobility of labor in all its forms: occupational, industrial, and geographical. Lack of such mobility not only prolongs unemployment in localities with declining industries, but it also deprives the expanding industries elsewhere of needed manpower.

A high level of mobility can be obtained only through an all-out effort on diverse fronts. There is little point in retraining a worker for a job that exists outside of his locality unless he is provided with the financial resources to move with his family. Likewise, it is useless for a worker to migrate if he is uninformed about the labor-market conditions in the new area, or is technically unequipped to take advantage of existing job opportunities once he gets there. Effective mobility cannot be achieved in this piecemeal fashion. Nor can any local community be expected to assume the entire financial burden of training and retraining its displaced workers, when such workers may have to move elsewhere for re-employment. The dimensions of the problem are such that they can be tackled adequately only by the federal government. The newly-created Department of Manpower is a step in the right direction.

REGIONAL UNEMPLOYMENT

The incidence of unemployment is not uniform throughout the country. Certain regions suffer more than others. The Department of Labour has picked out 65 National Employment Service Office areas and 16 counties or census divisions where the situation is so serious that they have been designated to receive special federal assistance. These areas are shown in the following table.

Many of these communities have been "depressed" throughout most of the postwar period, in good years as well as bad. The high number of jobless is due to a variety of reasons, such as the over-dependence on seasonal industries, the

AREAS THAT QUALIFY FOR SPECIAL ASSISTANCE FROM THE FEDERAL GOVERNMENT BECAUSE OF HIGH AND CHRONIC UNEMPLOYMENT AND LOW FAMILY INCOMES

Newfoundland
Corner Brook
Grand Falls
St. John's

Prince Edward Island
Charlottetown
Summerside

Nova Scotia
Amherst
Bridgewater
Inverness
Kentville
Liverpool
New Glasgow
Springhill
Sydney
Sydney Mines
Truro
Yarmouth

New Brunswick
Bathurst
Campbellton
Edmundston
Minto
Moncton
Newcastle
St. Stephen
Sussex
Woodstock
County: Queen's

Québec
Alma
Causapscal
Chandler
Chicoutimi
Dolbeau
Gaspé
Jonquière
La Malbaie
La Tuque
Louiseville
Maniwaki
Matane
Mégantic
Mont Laurier
Montmagny
New Richmond
Port Alfred
Roberval
Rimouski
Rivière du Loup
Shawinigan
Ville St. Georges
County: Beauce
County: Labelle
County: Pontiac

Ontario
Bracebridge
Collingwood
Elliot Lake
Midland
Owen Sound
Parry Sound

Ontario (continued)
Sturgeon Falls
County: Haliburton
County: Manitoulin Island
County: Parry Sound

Manitoba
Brandon
Dauphin
The Pas
Census Division 10
Census Division 12
Census Division 18
Census Division 19

Saskatchewan
Lloydminster
North Battleford
Prince Albert
Yorkton
Census Division 5
Census Division 10
Census Division 13

Alberta
Blairmore
Census Division 12
Census Division 13

British Columbia
Kelowna
Penticton
Vernon

Note: The above areas contain 16% of the national labor force.

depletion of natural resources, the transfer of local plants to other areas, or the fall in demand for a commodity in which the area had specialized.

On both humanitarian and economic grounds, the redevelopment of distressed localities is a must, to wipe out the inequities that exist within the nation. The task, however, is not easy because of the so-called "negative multiplier effect." It is almost like a vicious circle. As an area becomes depressed and economic activities diminish, the loss of tax revenue and the community's low credit rating often make it impossible to expand or even to maintain adequate public services and facilities. This, in turn, discourages the entry of new industries and speeds up the decline of the existing ones.

Since the local economies are unable to correct the situation, help must come from outside. The federal government has a responsibility in this field. No goal of full employment can be attained as long as the depressed areas are allowed to persist. An over-all full employment policy, by necessity, must include special provisions to deal with those localities which lag behind the national progress.

In the long run, excessive local unemployment can be cured in two broad ways: by moving workers to the jobs or jobs to the workers. The first approach does not in any sense imply a forced exodus of population. Such a drastic remedy is unthinkable except in a few isolated cases where the area is considered absolutely hopeless for further development. However, encouragement of voluntary migration from depressed to prosperous communities is always worthwhile, since it helps to bring about a better balance between the demand and supply of manpower.

To facilitate the geographical mobility of labor, the federal government is prepared to give outright grants to all persons who have been without work for any four or more of the preceding six months. Others who have been unemployed for a shorter period, but have no prospect of getting a job within their locality, can obtain loans at 6% interest repayable in two years. Such loans are also available for employed workers who face imminent permanent layoffs and do not expect to find other openings within a commuting distance. These loans or grants — which, incidentally, are given without any means test — cover actual transportation costs for the worker, his family, and household effects, plus a resettlement allowance of up to $1,000. The latter is calculated on the basis of $200 for the worker, $200 for his wife, and $100 for each child up to six children.

However, Ottawa realizes that, despite all its grants and loans, no mass migrations from depressed communities are likely to occur. Consequently, efforts are also made to stimulate new jobs in the "designated areas" of labor surplus. Since 1963, the companies locating in such areas get a three-year corporation-tax holiday, plus accelerated depreciation that permits them to write off their machinery and equipment in two years and their buildings in five years. So far, the outcome has been fairly encouraging. In 1964, it resulted in the creation of about 18,000 new jobs.

This program of tax incentives is expected to end by March 1967. Its place has already been taken by a new and even more sweeping plan. Under it, a firm desiring to locate in a designated area can obtain grants of up to 33⅓% on the first $250,000 of private investment, 25% on the next $750,000, and 20% on investment above $1,000,000. The maximum given for any one project is $5,000,000 on an investment of $24,600,000 or more.

These grants are available for new manufacturing and processing plants, as well as for the expansion of existing plants that contribute appreciably to the improvement of income and employment in the area. To dangle the carrot even closer, such grants are not treated as income for tax purposes, nor do they have to be deducted from the capital investment against which capital cost allowances are claimed.

In addition to the federal government, the provincial governments, too, are trying to attract new industries in retarded areas through special types of grants, loans, tax concessions, licensing policies, and preferential treatments in the awarding of public contracts. One method gaining in popularity is the creation of industrial estates. The provincial governments, through their developing agencies, improve and subdivide tracts of land, and frequently erect factory buildings for sale or lease to industrial firms at relatively low cost. Utilities, such as streets, rail leads, and sewers, are usually installed, and a variety of other services are provided. Such industrial estates are particularly attractive to small and medium-sized companies with limited capital. Renting a factory permits a capital cost to be converted into an operational expenditure and releases funds for the purchase of machinery and equipment. Also, the risks are reduced, since the firm leasing the premises can easily pull out of an unsuccessful venture.

Obviously, providing incentives to industries is only one part of the solution. The available manpower in the depressed localities must also be able to perform the necessary skilled work demanded by modern manufacturing. Otherwise, trained workers from other areas will move in, and local unemployment will not be alleviated.

Unfortunately, progress in this field has been rather discouraging. No doubt, the federal government, in co-operation with the provinces, has greatly expanded its vocational education and training programs. But despite that, very few of the hard-core unemployed have availed themselves of these opportunities. In one survey conducted by the Economic Council of Canada, it was found that 88% of the jobless had not taken any of the training courses and less than 5% had completed the full curriculum.

Experience has shown that the training programs alone are not enough. The public has to know about them. This calls for continuing publicity on a large scale, using all the available communications media. Also, many jobless do not understand the value of education, nor do they have the financial means to maintain themselves and their families through the retraining period. It would be highly desirable if the National Employment Service, through its local offices, were to contact such people, advise them on the kinds of facilities available, and make appropriate financial arrangements with the local educational authorities responsible for administering the programs.

All this emphasis on the obligations of governments is in no way intended to underrate the role which private business can play in the conquest of poverty and distress. Of course, the businessman's primary concern is to earn profits, but his responsibility does not end there. In an age of automation, it is his moral duty to retrain workers for other occupations in his firm when he sees the changes coming. Beyond that, he should share even more than he does today in alleviating the trials and tribulations caused in his local community by technological advances.

Like any other person, a businessman is a citizen, and it is through a reawakened civic sense that many a distressed area of today may achieve a brighter outlook tomorrow. This means more gifts to educational, philanthropic, and religious organizations of all kinds. The churches in particular are in need of more funds. Anyone who has visited the darker alleys of rundown communities knows that some of the human problems are too deep to be wholly cured by unemployment-insurance checks. The government clerk is no substitute for the social worker, and the social worker is no replacement for the priest or minister who knows his parish.

BIBLIOGRAPHY

Denton, Frank T., Yoshiko Kasahara, and Sylvia Ostry: *Population and Labour Force Projections to 1970.* Staff Study No. 1 prepared for the Economic Council of Canada, Queen's Printer, Ottawa, 1965.

Denton, Frank T. and Sylvia Ostry: *An Analysis of Post-War Unemployment.* Staff Study No. 3 prepared for the Economic Council of Canada, Queen's Printer, Ottawa, 1965.

Department of Labour: *Labour Gazette.* Monthly bulletins.

Dominion Bureau of Statistics: *The Labour Force.* Catalogue No. 71-001. Monthly bulletins and special tables not published but available on request.

Dominion Bureau of Statistics: *Unemployment in Canada.* Tables and Charts. Catalogue No. 71-503 Occasional (1962).

Drabble, B. J.: *Potential Output 1946 to 1970.* Staff Study No. 2 prepared for the Economic Council of Canada, Queen's Printer, Ottawa, 1965.

Economic Council of Canada: *Economic Goals for Canada to 1970.* First Annual Review, Queen's Printer, Ottawa, 1964.

International Labour Office: *Unemployment and Structural Change,* Geneva, Switzerland, 1962.

National Industrial Conference Board: "The Employment Challenge in the 1960's" by Roy A. Matthews. (Printed in the August and September 1963 issues of *Business Management Record.*)

Silberman, Charles E.: Series on "Technology and the Labor Market" in *Fortune Magazine.* 1. "The Reals News about Automation" (January 1965). 2. "The Comeback of the Blue-Collar Worker" (February 1965). 3. "What Hit the Teenagers" (April 1965). 4. "The Drift to Early Retirement" (May 1965).

The Senate of Canada: *Proceedings of the Special Committee of the Senate on Manpower and Employment,* Nos. 1-24, Queen's Printer, Ottawa, 1960-1961.

The Senate of Canada: *Final Report of the Special Committee of the Senate on Manpower and Employment,* June 1961, Queen's Printer, Ottawa, 1961.

The United States Department of Labor: *Manpower Report of the President and a Report on Manpower Requirements, Resources, Utilization, and Training,* U.S. Government Printing Office, Washington 25, D.C., 1963 and 1964.

The Story of Manpower in Charts

1. GROWTH OF THE LABOR FORCE, 1950–1970

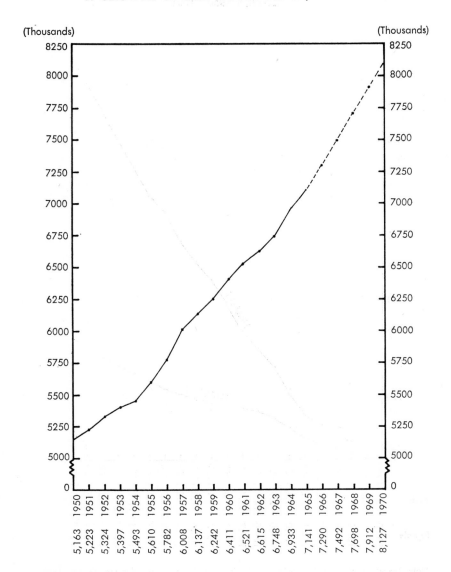

(Thousands)

1950	1951	1952	1953	1954	1955	1956	1957	1958	1959	1960	1961	1962	1963	1964	1965	1966	1967	1968	1969	1970
5,163	5,223	5,324	5,397	5,493	5,610	5,782	6,008	6,137	6,242	6,411	6,521	6,615	6,748	6,933	7,141	7,290	7,492	7,698	7,912	8,127

Note: In the Fifties, the labor force increased annually by 124,800 persons. From 1960-1965, it grew more rapidly at 146,000 per year. During the remaining Sixties, because of the postwar baby boom, the rise would be even steeper at 197,000 persons per year.

(Source: DBS and Economic Council of Canada).

2. RELATIVE GROWTH OF MALES AND FEMALES IN THE LABOR FORCE, 1950–1970

(INDEX 1950 = 100)

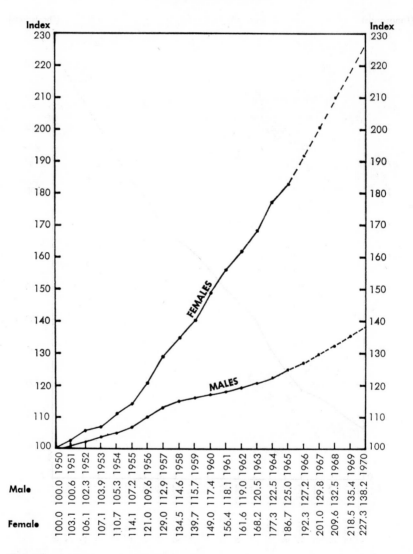

	1950	1951	1952	1953	1954	1955	1956	1957	1958	1959	1960	1961	1962	1963	1964	1965	1966	1967	1968	1969	1970
Male	100.0	100.6	102.3	103.9	105.3	107.2	109.6	112.9	114.6	115.7	117.4	118.1	119.0	120.5	122.5	125.0	127.2	129.8	132.5	135.4	138.2
Female	100.0	103.1	106.1	107.1	110.7	114.1	121.0	129.0	134.5	139.7	149.0	156.4	161.6	168.2	177.3	186.7	192.3	201.0	209.6	218.5	227.3

Note: The number of women in the labor force has been growing much faster than men. Between 1950 and 1965, the female participation increased by 86.7%, the male only by 25.0%. By 1970, females are expected to comprise 31% of the labor force compared to 29% in 1965 and 22% in 1950.

(Source: DBS and Economic Council of Canada).

3. CIVILIAN PARTICIPATION RATES

PERCENTAGE OF THE POPULATION IN THE LABOR FORCE BY SEX AND AGE GROUPS

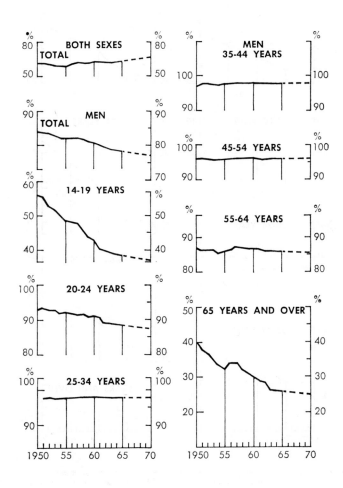

3. CIVILIAN PARTICIPATION RATES (continued)

PERCENTAGE OF THE POPULATION IN THE LABOR FORCE BY SEX AND AGE GROUPS

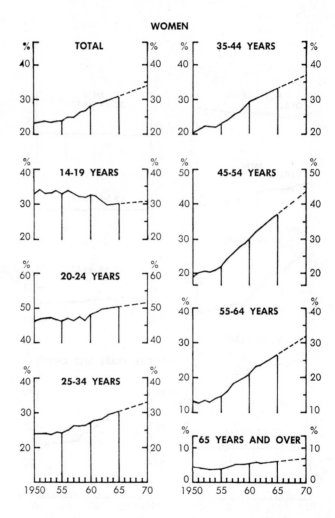

WOMEN

Note: Among males there has been a sharp decline in the participation rates at the two ends of the age spectrum — 14 to 24 on account of increased schooling and 55 and over because of better pension plans. In the other age groups, the rates have remained fairly constant at over 95% level. The participation of females in the labor force has risen for all age groups except 14-19. The most dramatic growth has been among those between 35 and 64, reflecting a growing proportion of married women who want to earn money after the early child-bearing ages.

Source: Canadian participation rates based on data from DBS Labour Force Survey and estimates or projections by Economic Council of Canada.

4. GROWTH OF THE LABOR FORCE BY AGE GROUPS, 1950–1964 AND 1964–1970

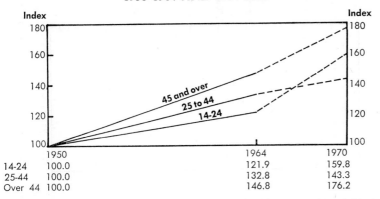

	1950	1964	1970
14-24	100.0	121.9	159.8
25-44	100.0	132.8	143.3
Over 44	100.0	146.8	176.2

Note: Between 1950 and 1964, persons between 14 to 24 in the labor force increased very slightly due to the low birth rates at the time of the Great Depression. During the remainder of the Sixties this will be the fastest growing group. Substantial gains are also expected for the age category of 45 to 64. Thus from now till 1970, manpower requirements will have to be met in a large measure by the younger and older workers.

(Source: DBS and Economic Council of Canada).

5. UNEMPLOYMENT AS A PERCENTAGE OF THE LABOR FORCE, 1950–1970

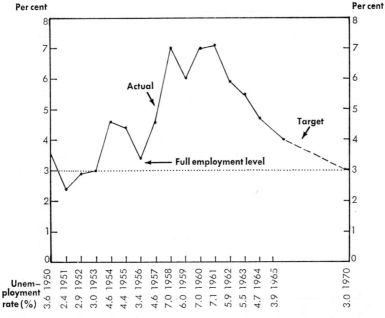

	1950	1951	1952	1953	1954	1955	1956	1957	1958	1959	1960	1961	1962	1963	1964	1965	1970
Unemployment rate (%)	3.6	2.4	2.9	3.0	4.6	4.4	3.4	4.6	7.0	6.0	7.0	7.1	5.9	5.5	4.7	3.9	3.0

Note: The average of unemployment in 1950-1953 was 3%. It rose by more than 40% to an average of 4.3% in 1954-1957, and then again by over 50% to an average of 6.8% in 1958-1961. Since 1962, the trend has been encouraging downwards, but Canada has still far to go to reach the full employment level of 3%.

(Source: DBS and Economic Council of Canada).

6. TRENDS IN EMPLOYMENT BY MAJOR INDUSTRIES, 1950–1970

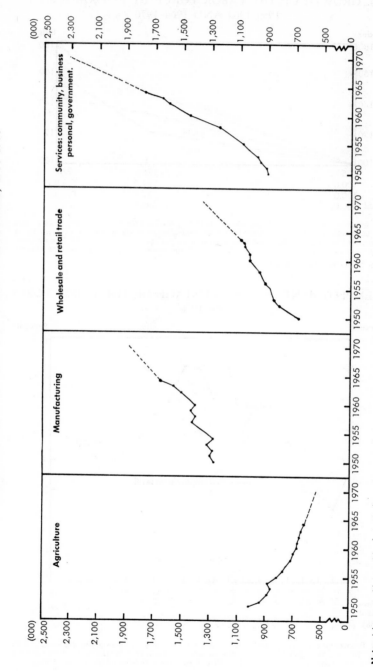

Note: Job opportunities are rising fastest in the service-group of industries. There is also a healthy upward trend in manufacturing and trade, while agriculture is experiencing a steady decline.

Source: DBS: Projections from 1966 to 1970 prepared by the author.

7. BREAKDOWN OF EMPLOYMENT AND UNEMPLOYMENT, 1965

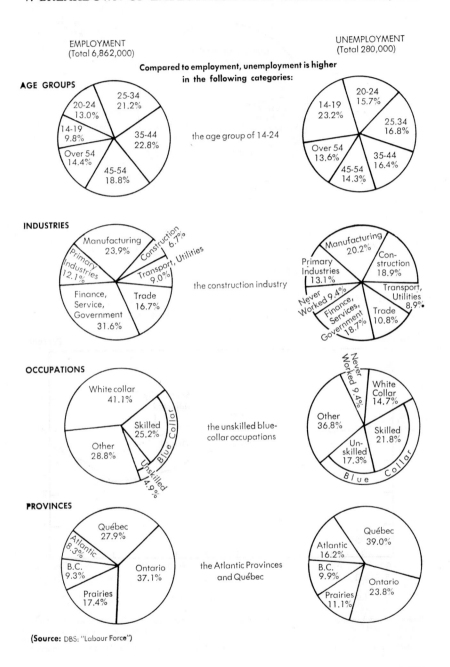

EMPLOYMENT
(Total 6,862,000)

UNEMPLOYMENT
(Total 280,000)

Compared to employment, unemployment is higher
in the following categories:

AGE GROUPS

25-34 21.2%
20-24 13.0%
14-19 9.8%
Over 54 14.4%
35-44 22.8%
45-54 18.8%

the age group of 14-24

20-24 15.7%
14-19 23.2%
25.34 16.8%
Over 54 13.6%
35-44 16.4%
45-54 14.3%

INDUSTRIES

Manufacturing 23.9%
Construction 6.7%
Primary Industries 12.1%
Transport, Utilities 9.0%
Finance, Service, Government 31.6%
Trade 16.7%

the construction industry

Manufacturing 20.2%
Construction 18.9%
Primary Industries 13.1%
Transport, Utilities 8.9%
Never Worked 9.4%
Finance, Services, Government 18.7%
Trade 10.8%

OCCUPATIONS

White collar 41.1%
Skilled 25.2%
Other 28.8%
Blue Collar
Unskilled 4.9%

the unskilled blue-collar occupations

Never Worked 9.4%
White Collar 14.7%
Other 36.8%
Skilled 21.8%
Unskilled 17.3%
Blue Collar

PROVINCES

Québec 27.9%
Atlantic 8.3%
B.C. 9.3%
Ontario 37.1%
Prairies 17.4%

the Atlantic Provinces and Québec

Québec 39.0%
Atlantic 16.2%
B.C. 9.9%
Ontario 23.8%
Prairies 11.1%

(**Source:** DBS: "Labour Force")

8. HOW LONG THE UNEMPLOYED WERE WITHOUT JOBS, 1965

*Includes persons on temporary lay off for a maximum of 30 days.

Note: The most disconcerting feature is the high percentage for hard-core unemployment. Of those out of work, nearly a third were idle for over four months.

(Source: DBS "Labour Force")

9. SEASONAL UNEMPLOYMENT

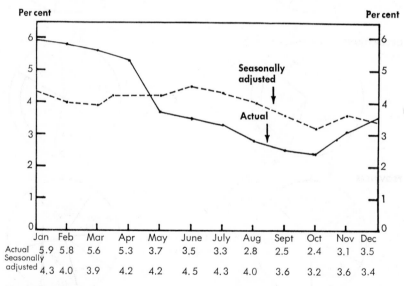

	Jan	Feb	Mar	Apr	May	June	July	Aug	Sept	Oct	Nov	Dec
Actual	5.9	5.8	5.6	5.3	3.7	3.5	3.3	2.8	2.5	2.4	3.1	3.5
Seasonally adjusted	4.3	4.0	3.9	4.2	4.2	4.5	4.3	4.0	3.6	3.2	3.6	3.4

Note: Seasonal unemployment is a perennial problem in Canada, and a major one. Invariably, through good times and bad, the number of persons out of work starts to increase in the fall, slowly at first, and later more and more rapidly as the temperature drops. By about February a maximum is reached. Then, as the winter gives way to spring, the pendulum swings back with equal predictability and unemployment starts to decline again.

(Source: DBS: "Labour Force")

10. UNEMPLOYMENT BY PROVINCES

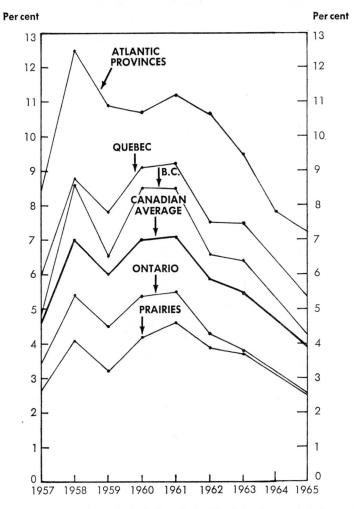

Note: Unemployment has been consistently the highest in the Atlantic Provinces and the lowest in the Prairies.

(Source: DBS: "Labour Force")

	Atlantic	Quebec	Ontario	Prairies	British Columbia	Canada
1957	8.4	6.0	3.4	2.6	5.0	4.6
1958	12.5	8.8	5.4	4.1	8.6	7.0
1959	10.9	7.8	4.5	3.2	6.5	6.0
1960	10.7	9.1	5.4	4.2	8.5	7.0
1961	11.2	9.2	5.5	4.6	8.5	7.1
1962	10.7	7.5	4.3	3.9	6.6	5.9
1963	9.5	7.5	3.8	3.7	6.4	5.5
1964	7.8	6.4	3.2	3.1	5.3	4.7
1965	7.3	5.4	2.5	2.5	4.2	3.9

PART TWO

THE CANADIAN MOSAIC

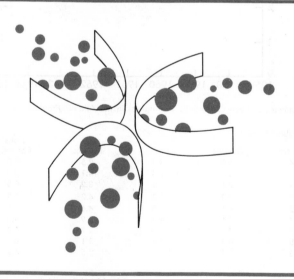

INTRODUCTION

Back in the 18th century Alexander Pope, a high priest of the Age of Reason, in one of his more Delphic moments laid down the cardinal principle for 20th century marketers, economists and sociologists: "The proper study of mankind is a man." One may slightly rephrase that dictum and say that the proper study of Canada is Canadians — Canadians in all their diversity and multifariousness, constituting a mosaic of different worlds which in part blend with one another, but in part and for a time remain segregated or even come into direct conflict.

Social scientists have long realized that Canadians form innumerable tight little islands, each with its own sub-culture, taste and behavior pattern. Now businessmen, too, are gradually shifting away from the popular but nebulous notion of national market or average consumer. They are beginning to realize that divergence rather than convergence is the rule and that more than lip service needs to be paid to the concept of "typological marketing."

Experience has repeatedly shown that, instead of an all-purpose product which serves no purpose well, it is far better to have an item that stands out from the faceless crowd and is geared to the particular likes or desires of a specialized group. "This rifle" approach (as opposed to "a shotgun" approach) not only results in high consumer satisfaction and loyalty, but it also prevents the various brands of the same company from cannibalizing each other.

Consequently, one of the first steps in successful marketing is the detailed examination of the number of ways in which the Canadian market can be broken down. Part II of this book deals with six aspects of the Canadian mosaic:

- Sex,
- Age groups,
- Socio-economic classes,
- Income groups,

- Ethnic groups,
- Urban-rural residents.

Each classification represents certain social roles around which cluster patterns of hopes, dreams, aspirations, and expectations that to a significant degree influence the conduct of the consumer.

Once the manufacturer has discovered the most meaningful segment or segments to work with, the foundation is laid for the beginning of a sound marketing strategy. He can use the classification scheme to appraise competitive strengths and vulnerabilities, to plan his product line, to determine his advertising and selling approaches, and to set precise marketing objectives against which performance can later be measured.

One of the major causes of the "profit squeeze" — in some industries as big a factor as rising labor and material costs — is that the average individual brand cannot command as large a share of the market as it once did. There are too many choices, too many look-alike products in the store. The main hope for the future lies in capturing bigger pieces of fewer markets, instead of scrambling about for a smaller share of every market in sight.

Chapter 8

MOSAIC BY SEX

Male-Female Differences

Among the various segments into which a market can be broken, the classification by sex is one of the most important. From the beginning of life, man and woman differ in almost every particular from the smallest cell to the deepest id. Women are passive, subjective, intuitive, identificationists, and try to escape reality through indulgence in fantasy. Men are aggressive, objective, realists, and go by rationalization. Women subconsciously like to cling, and men consciously love to command. Of course, as in most things, it is not a matter of black and white. There are women who have masculine traits and men who have feminine instincts. But, on the whole, the male pattern of thought is quite unlike the feminine make-up.

Characteristics generally regarded as "manly" are leadership, aggressiveness, emancipation from trivialities, and lack of fear, timidity or embarrassment. Psychological tests designed to measure dominance have consistently revealed that, compared to females, males tend to be more violent, to become angry more often, to have a greater desire for power. Even though women feel rivalry with one another, they seldom engage in direct and open competition or behave aggressively.

The environmental factors, too, explain the lack in females of a strong desire for domination. According to present social standards, the "ideal" girl is one who is intelligent enough to do well in school, but not so brilliant as to get all A's; capable of handling a job properly, but not so involved in her occupation as to need it for happiness; able to stand on her own two feet and earn a living, but not so competitive as to lose her feminity and jeopardize her chances of getting married.

On the other hand, the boy is taught to glorify achievement. The heroes placed before him are the successful: those who have accumulated the greatest wealth, made the most startling inventions, established the largest number of speed records, sustained the longest in endurance contests. The biblical teachings of meekness and humility are almost forgotten in the exaltation of the drive for assertiveness and aggressiveness.

These differences between sexes affect many fields of marketing. A good example is the automobile. For a man, a car is obviously a lot more than a means of transportation. It is an extension of his ego; its power is his power. It makes him feel more substantial, more achieving, more masculine. Even a downtrodden male, when speeding on the highway, gets a sensation of being a rolling potentate. His car responds to every whim — something nobody else does. It enables him to rush forward and leave other people behind, to assert himself successfully. That is why men have the itch to buy a car at least one notch beyond what they can afford; that is why cars keep getting longer in length and higher in horsepower.

By contrast, most women have a down-to-earth attitude towards the automobile. In fact, research studies have shown that the female role in purchasing is often negative. Furnishing the home, saving money, providing better education for the children are given precedence over having a new car. Even when both husband and wife decide to make a purchase together, the features which appeal to them are somewhat different. Females are relatively more interested in such items as styling, color, trim, automatic transmission, ease of parking, trunk space, and safety features for children. Males are more concerned with engineering, performance, road holding, depreciation, and service costs.

In view of so many dissimilarities, men and women require diverse types of advertising; they will not be influenced to buy unless approached in the right manner. Fortunately, thanks to anthropologists, psychologists, and sociologists, both sexes have been thoroughly x-rayed. The seven veils of woman have been swept aside by the intrepid social scientists. Nor has the male escaped from their prying eyes. They have observed him clinically, analyzed him emotionally, pegged him statistically, till he has lost most of his protective armor.

The Male Market

A large proportion of the purchases in this country are made by women, and businessmen therefore tend not to pay sufficient attention to the male market, except for products directly oriented to men, such as cigars, shaving preparations, sports equipment, and the like. This is unfortunate, since men play a significant role in many areas generally overlooked. As the major bread-earners, they initiate the purchasing decisions and are responsible for the brand choice of many big-ticket items, even though the actual buying may be done by women. Also, with more and more wives working, the husbands quite frequently find themselves pushing shopping carts up and down the supermarket aisles. A shorter work-week and convenient store hours have helped to accelerate this trend. Hence, the male influence cannot be completely ignored even for such items as food and toiletries, once exclusively within the female domain.

Thus, it behooves the marketers to direct more efforts at the male customers by revamping their conservative product concepts and out-dated distribution and merchandising practices. There are still plenty of areas with unexploited potential, where rich rewards await those willing to research men's needs and market the products with a truly masculine approach.

What are the selling appeals that activate males and put them in a buying mood? It is impossible to be specific. There are all types of men — patricians and plebians, playboys and puritans, extroverts and introverts, avant-garde artists and antiquated backwoodsmen. In the face of all this, absolute statements are foolhardy. The following observations are broad generalizations.

Men are extremely responsive to flattering depictions of themselves. This is pointed out by the Schwerin Research Corporation in one of its bulletins (Vol. X, No. 9). In the category of men's toiletries, advertising that stresses only the ingredients of the product is found to be far less motivating than that with a well-developed amatory sequence. Even when the romantic rewards are highly exaggerated, the impact is not lost. A typical successful commercial has the well-groomed hero surrounded by a bevy of beautiful damsels, or nuzzled by a lovely model, or otherwise romantically occupied in scenes that always lead to the same, obvious conclusion: that one can be a Don Juan by using the product.

Schwerin also hints that in male-oriented commercials the man's virility, like Caesar's wife, should be above suspicion. There is a cool, if not a negative, reaction to any implication of weakness or sentimentality. Men are not apt to be influenced by human-interest pictures and hearth-and-home scenes. Their interest is roused by illustrations dealing with cars, tools, cameras, sports, the outdoors, and the like. Another time-tested successful approach is the endorsement of the product by a sports celebrity.

With increasing sophistication, men appreciate fresh, creative, and sometimes offbeat approaches with touches of wit or comedy. However, even in jocularity, the man should never be depicted as losing the battle of the sexes. Humorous representations featuring males as bumblers or being trounced by women cause resentment, resignation, and apathy which may eventually affect the purchase of the product. Some experts do not even recommend the "togetherness" theme since in the eyes of many males it represents the decline of the masculine prestige.

Along the same lines, it is wise to avoid situations which show men as apprentices or plain novices. Most males are proud of their know-how. They believe they have special knowledge or insight into something, whether it be engineering, carpentry, medicine, politics, or economics. When purchasing big-ticket items, they want to know all the facts. In an experiment tried by a boating company, two advertisements were run: one of a prestige nature with a big illustration, the other of a nuts-and-bolts type with tightly packed technical copy relieved only by tiny, explanatory drawings. The former produced only 70 to 90 inquiries a month, while the latter drew over 400.

SOCIAL CHARACTER

So far the emphasis has been on individual characteristics. Equally important is the social environment which plays a major role in molding the character of the male, and thereby indirectly affecting his buying behavior.

One of the most monumental works in this field, which marketers have put to good use, is David Riesman's *The Lonely Crowd*.* According to him, the male heads of households can be divided into three "ideal types" of character: tradition-directed, inner-directed, and other-directed. These groups sometimes are overlapping, but the classification can be of great help in understanding how a man behaves.

THE TRADITION-DIRECTED MALE

Tradition-directed males are found in societies characterized by general slowness of change, dependence on family and kin organization, low social mobility, and a tight web of values. Good examples are rural communities of French Canadians, Hutterites, Doukhobors, Indians, and Eskimos. Here the boys are taught to follow the footsteps of their fathers. The culture provides the ritual and the routine to occupy and orient everyone. All important relationships of life are controlled by careful and rigid etiquette. Little energy is expended toward discovering new solutions to the age-old problems.

The tradition-directed male hardly regards himself as a distinct personality. Still less does it occur to him that he might shape his own destiny in terms of personal, lifelong goals. He is not sufficiently separated psychologically from himself, his family or group to think in these terms. His contemporaries expect him not to be a certain type of person but to behave in a certain way.

THE INNER-DIRECTED MALE

The second classification of Riesman, the inner-directed male, is the product of the early twentieth century capitalism, with its emphasis on free enterprise, unrestricted competition and ostensible consumption. The source of direction is "inner" in the sense that the goals towards which the individual is steered have been implanted in him from childhood by elders. The main difference from the tradition-directed male is that the principles rather than the details of life, are internalized. The strong tendency here is to glorify achievement and to make a fetish of success. Any given male may be passive or sterile, but the basic masculine philosophy is of strength and progress — to initiate, to procreate, to plant seed in the earth, to press for technological achievements, to subjugate the forces of nature, to design and build the world in one's own image. The motto, set from childhood, is: *ad astra per aspera*. The stars may be far away, but the inner-directed male still aims for them because his is a lifelong commitment to

* David Riesman with Nathan Glazer and Reuel Denney: *The Lonely Crowd*. The following paragraphs summarize the highlights from this book, sometimes in the author's own words. In some respects, the remarks apply to both sexes, but they are quite appropriate in this section since the male generally is the head of the household and his social behavior sets the pattern for the whole family to follow.

a certain goal, be it money, power, fame, or some lasting achievement in the arts or the professions.*

In the inner-directed society, the emphasis is on technological and intellectual processes rather than on human co-operation. Relations among industries and between industry and the outside world are supposed to be managed by the "invisible hand" — Adam Smith's favorite phrase for co-ordination through the free market. All attention is concentrated on the product itself, not the use made of it by the consumer. The problem of marketing recedes into the psychological background before the obduracy of the technical tasks themselves.

THE OTHER-DIRECTED MALE

The third type in Riesman's classification is the other-directed male. Here getting along with people is the magic key to accomplishment. The pressure is toward social competence, with the concurrent playing down of technical competence. While the inner-directed man is job-oriented, the other-directed is people-oriented. His sources of direction are his contemporaries, either those known to him directly or their stand-ins, the mass media. He is always paying close attention to the signals from others. Unlike the inner-directed male, he seeks not fame but the respect and, above all, the affection of a jury of peers. No doubt, everybody wants and needs to be liked by some of the people some of the time, but it is only the other-directed types who make this their main source of direction and their chief area of sensitivity.

* In fact, this image of man is nothing new. It has existed for centuries in the Western World. The tragic poet of ancient Greece, Sophocles, expressed this idea very well in the following verse:

Many are the wonders of the world but none so wonderful as man,
Man makes his way through the perilous sea,
Steering his bark over the waters,
While the waves break over his head.
He ploughs the earth and makes it yield food;
He snares the birds of the air, tames tribes of savage beasts,
And traps the creatures of the deep;
He shelters himself from frost and rain,
And devises remedies for sickness.
He is resourceful and has good counsel;
Language he has learned;
He has made cities and is sworn to keep law and justice.
Only death he cannot avoid.

This is significantly different from philosophy in other parts of the globe, especially the Far East, where the man is considered insignificant, and the only hope lies in Nirvana in which the soul — unnamed, unnumbered, unidentified — achieves a blessed reunion with the cosmic spirit. The sacredness of individual personality, the cardinal philosophy of North America, is conspicuous by its absence in the East. Here there is no need to glorify individualism, since each soul is supposed to mingle with another like smoke. The inhabitants take their environment as something given, and try to adapt themselves as best they can.

The other-directed person resembles the tradition-directed in one respect: both live in a group milieu and lack the inner-directed person's capacity to go it alone. The nature of this group milieu, however, differs radically in the two cases. The tradition-directed person takes his signal from others, but they come in a cultural monotone. The distinction between the familiar and the strange is clearly marked. The former is permissible; the latter is taboo. In the case of the other-directed person, this line of demarcation has broken down. He is able to receive signals from far and near; the sources are many, the changes rapid.

In an other-directed culture, the home is no longer the sole agent in implanting the social values; the peer group is as important. The parents make the child feel guilty not so much for the violation of inner standards as for the failure to be popular with other children. In education, co-operation and "getting along" are stressed rather than intellectual pursuits and academic excellence. In economic, political, and religious matters, unbridled competition is replaced by collaboration, individual autonomy by the ideal of unity and ecumenicity.

Of course, as pointed out before, these three types of Riesman are to some extent overlapping. It would be difficult to find a male wholly dependent on tradition-direction, inner-direction, or other-direction. No individual can exist without a reliance on tradition, much as he may appear to be influenced by the day-to-day swings of fashion. Similarly, all males are inner-directed since they are bound to have acquired and internalized some permanent orientations from their elders. And, conversely, all persons are other-directed in the sense that they take their cue from their peers at some time or other. The question is to what degree an individual or a social group places reliance on one or another of the three available mechanisms.

DIFFERENCES IN PURCHASING PATTERNS

For marketing purposes, the important distinction is between the inner-directed and the other-directed. The tradition-directed, for the most part, reside in distant, thinly-settled rural communities untouched by industrialization. In view of the expenses involved and the time required, it is usually not deemed worthwhile to make specific efforts to reach this market.

The purchasing patterns of the other-directed and the inner-directed vary considerably. The former has reduced the art of consumption almost to a science. He avoids splurging too much in order not to arouse the neighbors' envy, and at the same time he hesitates to spend too little for the fear of being pegged too low by others. His behavior is to a considerable extent prescribed by group norms and folkways. He must live in a certain size house in a certain section of the city, drive a car within a certain range of models, have certain types of appliances in his home, belong to a certain club, go to a certain church, even have a certain number of children. The range of choice within this prescribed "package" is often surprisingly narrow.

The behavior of inner-directed males is more difficult to predict. Some carry into consumption the same ideals of acquisition that are manifested in the field of production. Others seek in consumption some sort of escape from the work they are engrossed in.

The "acquisitive" male is declining in numbers, but one can still find his type among the nouveau-riche and certain other groups in society. Such a person buys, not for the sake of consumption, but for status and prestige as a pathway to success. His big, chrome-plated car may provide him with a means of transportation, but it also conveys an eloquent message which he expects to be understood by the Joneses up and down the street. The mink coat he gets for his wife may happen to keep her warm in winter, but it also sets him apart and shows in unmistakable terms that he has "arrived." In extreme cases, he may lavish money and energy on a house to a point where it may resemble a department store; or go in for yachts, diamonds, libraries, or treasures of Europe (including a titled son-in-law).

Such a person, though anxious to "keep up with the Joneses" or rather with the "best people" in his milieu, is not other-directed in the strict sense. All he tries to do is to fit into a role demanded by his station, or hoped-for station in life. By contrast, the other-directed consumer seeks experiences rather than things and yearns to be guided by others rather than to dazzle them with display. His desire to outshine is clearly muted.

The second type of inner-directed male is almost diametrically opposite to the acquisitive consumer. He does not care too much for public opinion. All he looks for in consumption is some sort of relief from the stress and strain of work. This escape may be either down or up the cultural scale. Some find pleasure in visiting beer parlors, watching Westerns on television, or reading dime novels dealing with sex, sadism and murder.

More often, thanks to the diffusion of culture, the movement is up. The individual tries to gratify his aesthetic hunger on a steady diet of exquisite, soul-satisfying hobbies like painting, gardening, boating, golfing, traveling, and studying for its own sake without any material rewards. His real goal in life is self-development, the full realization of self-potential. Like an artist, he desires to recreate and re-experience the world around him in his own image. He does not want it handed to him on a platter. Such a type of inner-directed male buys "genuine" articles even though the neighbors might never be able to tell the difference. He goes to the theater, not to be seen or to be able to talk about a play, but to obtain mental stimulation. He is much less concerned with the possession of furniture which will impress the visitors than with pieces which please him personally.

PRESENT AND FUTURE TRENDS

No definite research has been done to determine what percentage of males in Canada are inner-directed and other-directed. Inner-directed types seem to be dominant in rural areas and small towns, other-directed in metropolitan cities. Much also depends on the occupation of the individual. The inner-directed types are the lawyers, the doctors, the bankers, the small entrepreneurs, the technically oriented engineers, the work-minded craftsmen, and others who do not care to move with the crowd. Big business and big government also have niches for inner-directed rate-busters — for instance, men who can say no without going through an elaborate song and dance ritual.

Other-directed individuals are the bureaucrats, organization men, the marketing and sales executives, and all those with jobs where success depends on getting along with others. The trend towards other-direction has been accentuated in recent years by the economy of abundance, where the main problem is not producing but selling the product. The path to success in many areas lies in merchandising a pleasing personality, in catering to the wants and needs of the consumers, in supressing pugnacity and self-assertiveness and co-operating with the group.

In the future, however, with the growth of education, income and leisure, the trend is likely to be toward culture-oriented, inner-directed individuals. Right now, their voice may not be very loud yet, but it is bound to gather strength as the years pass by. This will have far-reaching implications for marketers. In the new-value system, status seeking will wane in importance, and appeals to prestige and social advancement will no longer be so effective. Advertisers will have to pay greater attention to the aesthetic pleasure, the glow of happiness, the inner satisfaction which their products provide. To the nutritious steak will have to be added the sizzle of refinement, artistry, and spiritual enrichment.

BIBLIOGRAPHY

Boomer, Peggy: "Male Market: Big, Rich but Tough". *Printers' Ink,* July 20, 1962.

Demos, Raphael: "The American Image of Success". *Harvard Business Review,* March-April 1961.

Dichter, Ernest: "Discovering the 'Inner Jones'". *Harvard Business Review,* May-June 1965.

Martineau, Pierre: *Motivation in Advertising.* McGraw-Hill Book Company, Inc., New York, 1957.

Riesman, David, Nathan Glazer, and Reuel Denney: *The Lonely Crowd.* Doubleday Anchor Book (A16). Doubleday & Company, Inc., Garden City, New York, 1950.

Schwerin Research Corporation *The Neglected Sex.* Bulletin Vol. X, No. 9. September 1962.

The Female Market

Women have a dominating influence over consumer expenditures, which keep in motion the wheels of the economy. They are the purchasing agents for the country's biggest institution — the home. In their hands rests the bulk of the discretionary spending dollar. True, that dollar may have been his to begin with, but for all practical purposes it is hers to dispose of. In many households the wives have taken over the management of all the finances and reign supreme as queens of the family exchequer. Hence their influence is felt on a wide variety of goods and services. In some department stores, women shoppers are credited with as much as 85% of men's-wear purchases. In the office equipment field it is often necessary for a salesman to devote as much time to convince the secretary as the boss. Real estate agents say that when it comes to selling a house, "it's the woman three to one; she can often make or break the sale." Females have also entered other areas that used to be male's exclusive domain, like what brand of beer or wine to buy or what kind of life insurance to get. It is not surprising, therefore, that in business writings and marketing discussions the word "consumer" has taken on a feminine gender.

The woman's role is not just confined to being the disbursing agent for the family. Feminine wealth has accumulated through inheritance, earnings, gifts, and plain thrift. One outcome is the increasing number of female investors. Despite the lack of precise statistical information, many stockbrokers believe that Canadian women are responsible, directly and indirectly, for a good portion of the fifty per cent increase in share ownership over the past ten years. Shareholders' lists of some of Canada's blue-chip corporations are beginning to show a predominance of feminine names. For example, one analysis showed that 35.3% of Bell Telephone's Canadian-held shares were owned by women, 26.4% by men, and the remainder by institutions. Similarly, more than half of the shareholders of Abitibi Power and Paper were women. Fat, dividend-paying stocks are now apparently competing with diamonds as a girl's best friend.

To sell profitably to the female of the species, it is necessary to have a sympathetic understanding of the reasons behind her actions and attitudes — to know her needs and desires, her interests and enthusiasms, her habits and preferences. For countless generations, poets and writers have tended to shroud the woman in a veil of mystery. She has been called as enigmatic as the Sphinx, as full of riddles as the Oracle of Delphi, as unfathomable as the Mona Lisa smile. Fortunately, with the development of psychology and other social sciences, the secrets of the female mind have been more and more exposed. These findings are extremely valuable to businessmen, since they help to strike the right chord and provide the key to bigger and better sales.*

---

* One of the most exhaustive analyses of this topic is found in Janet Wolff's *What Makes Women Buy*. An attempt is made here to cull the highlights from that book.

PHYSICAL CHARACTERISTICS

Most women, of course, are acutely aware of their personal appearance. They are interested in beauty preparations, clothes and other products and services that promise to make them beautiful, youthful and sexually attractive. However, when sex is used as a selling theme, it must always be employed with caution. Ideas, photographs, and words that are overly sexy are not apt to evoke much response. A typical woman is not so keenly interested in winning the admiring glances from men as in having reassurances of her femininity and good taste. Probably, the most effective method is to create an atmosphere of romance, an aura of happiness in companionship, the feeling of loving and being loved. Also, motherhood means more to a woman than wifehood. Both physically and mentally, she is intimately and inextricably bound to her creation. As a result, advertising campaigns revolving around pictures and stories of mothers and children seldom fail to gain immediate attention.

Women's senses are more developed than men's, and they use them more extensively. For example, when shopping for clothes, they "feel" the material, trying to judge its quality from the finish. Smart retailers know that if they prepack the merchandise, they must leave a sample open and loose so that it can be freely handled.

In color perception, too, women are far superior to men. Color blindness is found in eight times as many males as females, and even among individuals of normal vision, women excel in tests of color discrimination. To men, blue is simply blue. To women, blue can be navy blue, aquamarine, azure, turquoise, royal blue, sky blue, blue violet, midnight blue, and so on. Furthermore, psychological tests have consistently shown that a woman is more responsive and sensitive to color than men. Often her choice is influenced by the color of the product or the package. Manufacturers have tried to capitalize on this, and many household items, like paper towels, sheets, toilet soaps, light bulbs, which once used to be in white only, now come in a riot of colors.

Due to their highly developed senses, women fare exceptionally well at detailed work. In fact, they become so preoccupied with small items that they sometimes fail to tell the forest from the trees. This tendency can be an advantage or drawback in selling. Small, perfect details can completely capture a woman's attention and imagination. She is appreciative of fine stitching on the collar of a dress, or is captivated by a delicate design on the flower vase in an advertisement for a desk or coffee table. Even though these things are not vital, she is aware of the atmosphere, associates it with the product, and is put in a proper buying mood because of it. At the same time, imperfect details in a message cause her to reject the entire sales story and the product as well. Words that are out of character or unconvincing, elements of a picture that are incoherent or unbelievable, catch her attention right away. In one TV commercial, a model, supposed to be taking care of her baby, forgot to wear a wedding ring.

The picture was flashed on the screen for only a matter of seconds, yet hundreds of women noticed this slip and sent unfavorable letters to the television station. It follows, therefore, that when selling to women every element of a design, package, advertisement, promotion, or direct sale must be carefully checked. One word, one gesture, or one detail striking a discordant note can break the spell and ruin an otherwise convincing impression.

PSYCHOLOGICAL CHARACTERISTICS

Perhaps the most prominent feminine characteristic is the tendency to personalize. A man by nature follows an objective line of reasoning. A woman by contrast, is inclined to look at each person, each product, each idea, each remark personally and emotionally. Her thinking is largely subjective. She translates everything into concrete personal terms. A theoretical discussion, for example, on the regulation of international trade may soon disintegrate into an argument about the family budget.

On account of this tendency to think in concrete terms, women find it almost impossible to separate a speaker from his advice, a writer from his ideas. If they do not like the person, they usually do not like also what he says. The lesson is clear. The first requisite of the salesman is to ensure that he does not antagonize the female shopper. Then, he must try to sell the product by personalizing it. How can it be made a part of her life? What can it do for her family? How is it more suited to her than anyone else? At the same time, to keep her in a buying frame of mind, he must not criticize or belittle anything or anybody, for chances are she will figure out some way to apply it to herself.

Another point to note is that, compared to a man, a woman has a lower level of self-confidence and self-sufficiency, and concomitantly a greater desire for self-esteem and social approval. She yearns for recognition and acceptance from others — mainly from her close relatives, friends and neighbors. She is anxious to be considered as a good wife, mother, and homemaker, and looks for affection and appreciation from those around her.

However, the circumstances are not always favorable. Her husband, more often than not, thinks that a moron can accomplish the work to which she is mostly committed — making beds, cleaning dishes, loading and unloading the washing machine. Also, her opportunities for recognition are few. A man gets promoted, obtains more salary, wins at golf, shows off his skill at hunting or fishing. His wife, on the other hand, labors day in and day out over the same monotonous treadmill within the four narrow walls. Furthermore, she is expected to carry out her housework as a duty, and matter of course. She scrubs and mops all day long, and not one soul in the world ever notices it. Her washing goes on all alone in the basement or utility room, with clammy floors and dripping pipes. Nobody thanks her for it; no one even is aware of the effort.

Faced with this vacuum, women devise all sorts of ways to gain approval and self-esteem. Some seek satisfaction by taking a job outside the home. Others participate in committee work, help at the hospital, get involved in church affairs. The majority, however, try to glorify their occupation as a homemaker. They endeavor to demonstrate their creativity to the non-perceptive opposite sex through cooking, sewing*, home decorating, and child rearing.

Many Canadian publications are aware of this inner need and frequently run articles quoting figures intended to boost the morale of the female readers. Here is an example published in *Chatelaine*.

"How much are you worth? Even leaving aside the incalculables — for instance, your blue eyes and smiling face, your role as family comforter and psychologist — it's an impressive amount. Suppose yours is a city family in a middle-income bracket ($5,000 to $8,000), three children, living in a moderate-priced home. Now, you take a month off. Here's what your husband would have to pay out in cold hard cash — and, if anything, our figures veer to the conservative."**

The figure arrived at is $257.65 per month, broken down as follows:

Housekeeper	$140.00
Cleaning woman	30.00
Laundress	9.00
Home economist and shopper	5.00
Chauffeur	5.00
Baby sitter	20.00
Handyman	3.00
Seamstress	5.00
Cleaner	2.00
Hostess	17.00
Gardener and groundkeeper	5.00
Tax deduction	16.65
TOTAL	$257.65

Statements of this nature enhance the ego of the housewife and prove to her that she is doing something worthwhile. Intelligent advertising can help her farther along these lines. It can, through believable indirection, exalt her role and make her realize that her household performance has a wider significance, a more important role in the social structure. This assuages her emptiness and takes the edge out from the thanklessness of her job. She does not consider herself a drudge, an unpaid servant, alone and meaningless.

* According to surveys reported by Simplicity Pattern Company, most women do not sew to pinch pennies. The first and main reason is the urge to create. A second is to get a particular kind of dress that they want. Economy is third in importance.

** Cynthia Steers, "How much are you worth to your husband?" *Chatelaine*, April 1959.

Unfortunately, too little advertising shows awareness of this fact. It confines itself to shouting about the virtues of the brand, ignoring the real needs of the woman. No doubt, product claims are essential. However, they should be supported by other motives which would give the housewife pleasure in keeping the home, provide her with a sense of achievement in getting things done, and, wherever possible, make her feel that by using the product she is doing something which the others do appreciate and esteem in spite of their seeming indifference. One detergent advertisement scored high in readership because it showed the husband putting his arm affectionately around his wife and admiring his clean shirts. Obviously, this was not a literal situation; probably few husbands do this. But the illustration had a considerable impact and indirectly contributed to the higher sales of the product.

OTHER SELLING APPEALS

While selling to woman, one must also remember that because of her relatively routine daily existence she has a tendency to indulge frequently in reveries. She proceeds to build a more exciting life, imagining all sorts of romantic and wonderful things that may happen to her. Businessmen can take advantage of this fact. No matter what the product or service, a woman can be led to weave a story with skillful suggestions. Many advertisements have made unromantic items of woman's real world a big part of her imaginary world. However, in selling via the fantasy route, one should be careful not to go too far. Unlike men, whose daydreams are far fetched, as making a million dollars, going on a safari to darkest Africa, or blasting off in a rocket to outer space, the feminine imagination is rather confined to people close-by, like family, friends or neighbors.

Another distinctive female trait is sociability. Women love to mix with other persons, discuss local events, swap gossip. Readership surveys of print advertising have consistently shown that men exhibit high interest in pictures relating to objects, women to illustrations of people, particularly members of their own sex. On advertising labor-saving devices, an appeal suggesting to women the possibility of extra "time" for socializing with others is generally more effective than one promising to save elbow grease.

While women like to be social, they also desire to stress their individuality. This is clearly seen when it comes to shopping for apparel. To quote the sociologist, Gregory Stone, clothing is the woman's equivalent of heraldry, a colorful means of telling the world about herself as a person. It is a symbolic statement of her social position, of her mood, and especially of her individual identity. Men in their clothing are more interested in aligning themselves with some category — their professional group, their fellow office or factory workers — so that the male costuming becomes something like a uniform. But the woman goes in exactly the opposite direction in order to emphasize her personal identity; she tries *not* to wear the same dress as anyone else.*

To satisfy this female desire for individuality, it is often necessary to offer most products within a wide range of choices — a whole spectrum of colors, a wealth of styles, a dozen possible models and combinations. However, because of her low self-confidence, a woman experiences a terrible tension when the time comes for selection. The manufacturer can help to render the decision-making easy for her by explaining clearly the distinguishing features of each type of product.

Such facts must be presented honestly and straightforwardly. A woman resents violently any attempt to bamboozle her. Nothing infuriates her so much as the feeling that she has been fooled. If a salesman has been misleading, if an advertisement does not deliver what it promises, she will not only abstain from repurchasing the product but will start a campaign to persuade others not to buy it as well.

The modern housewife is no push-over. She no longer falls for comparisons that compare nothing, for claims that assume she is either an incompetent or an ignoramus. Nor does she like being shouted at or talked down to. While a woman might desire a strong and influential authority in her life and may even display certain masochistic tendencies, there is enough evidence to show that she will not tolerate being bullied by strangers. She wants to be asked to buy rather than be bluntly commanded to buy. She prefers a quiet approach, a soft sell, low-pitched voices, natural, "real" commercials that explain things as one would to a friend. An ounce of charm is worth more than a pound of pressure.

Women are also sympathetic towards the problems and sufferings of other people. They are moved by sickness, injustice, misery and poverty. They, therefore, dislike TV commercials or other illustrations that glorify violence, cruelty, or aggressiveness. They are touched by appeals that stress compassion, selflessness, and reverence for life.

Furthermore, women take the problem of buying very seriously. This makes a cartoon or light approach to them comparatively risky, unless the technique is well executed in order not to offend. In expensive products especially, humor is almost invariably a mistake. Women are not apt to be casual in the purchase of a refrigerator, a car, or a house.

To help its advertisers, *The Ladies Home Journal* made a detailed analysis, comparing 318 ads which received the highest with another 318 that had the

* This urge for self-expression reaches its limit while shopping for hats. Everybody knows that ladies' hats defy all rules of logic and laws of common sense. So a woman, when shopping, can be entirely on her own; she cares naught for the world and its judgments. One respondent told a motivation researcher that when she is particularly depressed and purposeless, she finds no tonic better than looking for hats.

lowest Starch "noted" ratings. The following are some of the highlights culled from that study.*

• Have a strong focal point or center of interest which captures attention quickly and induces the person to read on.

• If four-color ads are being preferred, use strong colors with dramatic contrasts for emphasis.

• Choose photographs instead of artwork. Realistic illustrations are more effective in reaching a female reader.

• Prepare the layouts in a simple and orderly fashion, providing the reader with quick, easy comprehension.

• Concentrate only on few elements in the ad, preferably a forceful presentation of a single selling point, devoid of extras.

• Avoid having the textual material cover more than a quarter of the size of the ad.

• Make headlines moderate in tone, less inclined to boast, exhort or scream. Don't use exclamation points when wooing a lady through ad copy; she generally objects to being "shouted at in print."

• Relate the product to the reader's needs; e.g., health, security or comfort of the family.

• Stay away from creating ads that are generally unrealistic, lack self-identification, employ humor or whimsy, are out of proportion or perspective, or place the merchandise in an unnatural environment.

BIBLIOGRAPHY

Conway, Jeannette: "Women Reap Share of Dividends," *The Globe and Mail,* October 31, 1963.

Friedan, Betty: *The Feminine Mystique,* W. M. Norton and Company Inc., New York, 1963.

Hepner, Harry. W.: *Advertising — Creative Communication with Consumers.* McGraw-Hill, Inc., 1964.

Martineau, Pierre: *Motivation in Advertising.* McGraw-Hill Inc., New York, 1957.

Steers, Cynthia: "How much are you worth to your husband?" *Chatelaine,* April 1959.

Wolff, Janet L.: *What Makes Women Buy?"* McGraw Hill Inc., New York, 1958.

* *Printers' Ink,* February 17, 1961.

Chapter 9

MOSAIC BY AGE GROUPS

Characteristics of Households By Age Groups

One important way of analyzing Canadian markets is through a breakdown of the households by the age of the head. A businessman often discovers from a consumer survey that his product appeals to a specific age group. In order to pinpoint his selling effort, he must know what the households in that particular age class are like, where they live, how much money they earn, what their educational levels are, how their spending dollar is distributed. Data relating to these and similar questions lie scattered through the different reports of the Dominion Bureau of Statistics. They have been grouped together for quick perusal in the tables at the end of this section. Much of the information refers to 1961. However, since the ratios shown vary slightly from year to year, the data may be considered current for all practical purposes. The highlights of the distinctive characteristics of the various age groups are summarized below.

HOUSEHOLD HEAD: UNDER 25 *

The transition from organized school life, home protection, and adolescent romances has occurred. The young persons are busily engaged in making adjustments to the adult world — getting their feet wet on the first job, settling in new living quarters, establishing fresh and more lasting contacts. Over 80% of the household heads are married, and those who are not generally room with friends or relatives. Just 10% of the households are very small, consisting of one person.

As would be anticipated, these young families are on the move. Each year, nearly three out of five change their residence, some going from one place to another in the same neighborhood, others traveling to the opposite end of the country. The exodus from rural areas is clearly reflected in the fact that only 5.1% of the households are on farms, half the national average of 10.3%. Because of this extreme mobility, the home-ownership ratio is very low. The majority are apartment dwellers. About 2% live in mobile trailers.

Educational attainment is above par but not so impressive as that of the next group because of many "dropouts." Seven out of ten youngsters failed to complete high school. Students going to universities are not likely to be well represented here, since they usually reside with their parents and form a separate household later on in life.

---

* For more information on this age group, refer also to "The College Market" and "The Young Newlywed Market" sections in this chapter.

The deficiency in schooling is reflected in the occupation figures. Many individuals are at the bottom rung of the ladder. Though 9.2% are in professional and technical category (higher than national level of 8.6%), there is an above-average concentration in low-paying clerical, service, and unskilled jobs. As a result, the earning power is quite modest. The non-farm family income is 24% below the Canadian average, even though in over a quarter of the homes the wife is working. Roughly 70% of the families earn under $5,000 annually, barely 8% more than $7,000. About 27% live in dwellings where they have no exclusive use of bath or shower.

A fairly large slice of the budget is eaten up by the purchase of furniture and appliances required for setting up of the new home. This necessitates restraint on some other expenditures, like food, clothing, smoking, and alcoholic beverages. However, the zest for living is not lost, and the group ranks tops in outlays for recreation.

HOUSEHOLD HEAD: 25–34

At this stage, the earnings are up sharply, but they are still below the Canadian average. As a rule, the family has just one breadwinner, the wife being incapacitated from working on account of children in the pre-school age. This group is the best educated. One out of ten had some exposure to college, and more than half that number traveled the full course. Consequently, the proportion of family heads engaged in professional and technical pursuits exceeds that of any other age classification.

The mobility ratio is still above par, though the pace has slowed down considerably compared to the previous age group. Only a quarter changed their residence during the span of the year. Over a third of the families have three or more children, and a relatively large number live in the suburbs. Nearly half own their homes, the median value being close to $11,800.

As for consumer expenditures, a substantial part of the budget is earmarked for the purchase of durables, but the ratio is not as high as for the younger families. Food bills climb up because of the children, but expenditures on clothing are rather modest.

On account of the differences in the age structure of the population across the country, there is an above-average proportion of these households in Québec and below-average proportions in Manitoba and Saskatchewan. 15.8% of the households are headed by New Canadians, significantly more than the national par of 9.5%.

HOUSEHOLD HEAD: 35–44

In terms of size, this group is the most important, accounting for nearly a fourth of the nation's households. It also wields considerable influence from the point of view of purchasing power. The families are well-heeled, one out of four earning more than $7,000 annually, and better than one out of two over $5,000.

As regards children, this is the peak period with a larger number at home than for any other age group. 52% of the families comprise of five or more persons, compared to an over-all average of 32%. However, the households with youngsters under six have declined sharply, releasing many mothers for outside work. Some 24% of the wives are in the labor force.

The family now appears to have settled down, barely 14% changing residence in the course of the year. Because of the children, a relatively large proportion reside in the suburbs. Over two-thirds own their homes, the median value being around $12,400, by far the highest among all age classifications.

The educational level is only slightly less than the record high for the preceding age group. As a result these households are well represented in the managerial and professional occupations: 22.6% versus Canadian par of 21.0%.

On account of many children at home, the income left over for discretionary spending is somewhat curtailed. The expenditures on food and clothing are considerably above the average level. Security payments, mainly insurance, also take up a bigger chunk of the budget than for any other age group.

HOUSEHOLD HEAD: 45–54

In general, the adults in this life cycle are at the height of their careers. The early years of struggle are only memories. They are able to look back upon their efforts with pride and satisfaction. Some have established themselves so well that the mortgages have been paid off and their financial responsibilities to children adequately met.

Many parents glow inwardly as their offspring go off to college or careers, pleased with the job they have done and basking in the reflected glory of their children's achievements. Often, the men turn their attention to public service, or undertake long-postponed activities. The women seek employment outside the home. Sometimes the reason is to pay big bills (e.g., university education for their youngsters), but in many cases it is to fill the void and feel "useful." Significantly, families in this category have a very high percentage of working wives, second only to the newly married couples under 25.

Nearly one out of six household heads are in managerial positions, the largest ratio for all age groups. However, they are below average in professional and technical categories, on account of a relatively low educational level. This is to be expected, since the great depression of the Thirties prevented many individuals from continuing their studies after high school.

Most families own their homes (73.2%), but it is not as important any more to live in the suburbs for the sake of the children. The median value of the non-farm home is $11,631, 5.5% above the Canadian average.

This group, undoubtedly, constitutes the most affluent market. The income level reaches its peak here. Nearly one family in eight earns over $10,000 a year. As a result the average consumer expenditures are highest for many items, such as clothing, personal care, education, smoking and alcoholic beverages, and above all, automobiles. Bigger, more luxurious cars appear in the driveway, and trade-ins become more frequent.

HOUSEHOLD HEAD: 55–64

This segment is often referred to as the "unfettered" or "empty nest" market. For years, the children had been the focus of activities and family expenditures. Now the offspring have grown up and started a new life cycle of their own. Consequently, nearly half the household consists of one or two persons.

Normally, this period offers the first real opportunity for leisure since marriage and the rearing of children. Husband and wife find new relaxations together, and renew, in a mellow tone, the romance of mutual companionship. They also reach out into the community for new satisfactions and experiences.

Yet many men find this period particularly painful. They begin to experience a psychological desertion. With the departure of children and the loss of certain friends through death, their sources for obtaining love, support, and esteem become more and more restricted. Besides, they start to realize that their position at work is not likely to improve. If they have not already attained the pinnacles to which they aspired at 21, the probabilities of reaching them grow less with increasing years.

The income patterns are affected by the fact that many individuals over 60 are retired or semi-retired. There is a substantial clustering at the low end of the income scale; close to a fourth of the families earn less than $3,000 a year. The low income is also a reflection of the poor level of education. More than six out of ten persons did not proceed further than elementary school. This generation grew up in an era where formal training received very little emphasis. At the same time, maturity and experience, in many instances, are yielding good rewards. The largest percentage of those earning over $15,000 are found here, helping thereby to push the average income figure to the second highest level among all age groups.

Three out of four families own their homes, but the median value of the non-farm dwelling is 4% below average, being only $10,500. 31.9% of the household heads are prewar immigrants, more than double the over-all average of 15.5%. Since agriculture is one of their primary occupations, there is an above-par concentration of this age group on farms: 14.5% compared to 10.3% for the country as a whole.

Urban family expenditures reveal certain peculiarities. A larger than average share of the budget goes into:

• Medical care (health cannot anymore be taken for granted).
• Transportation other than by automobile (vacations no longer pivot on car trips to the summer cottage with children).
• Gifts and contributions (grandparents love to splurge on the small fry in the family; also if the parents of the 54–65's are alive, they are likely to need care and financial support).

With money, time, and new vistas opening up, the empty nesters are promising customers. When they shop, they can pick what pleases them, not just what is economical. Also social security and company pension plans have made them somewhat less concerned about their financial future. Here is a market for luxury items, for comfort, convenience and preparations for retirement.

HOUSEHOLD HEAD: 65 AND OVER*

This is for the most part the retired generation. Three-fourths of the household heads are not in the labor force, and among those who still work, farming is the major occupation. This does not necessarily mean an increased hankering for this profession with age. Persons engaged in industry are forced to retire, while those in agriculture can continue to work performing reduced chores.

Annual income is very meager. Over half the families get below $3,000 a year; only 13% have more than $7,000. The situation of non-family households is even more depressing; 50% have to manage with an annual income of less than $1,000, and another 26% receive only between $1,000 to $2,000. It is not, therefore, surprising that 16% live in dwellings without running water, and 30% without bath or shower.

The composition of the household has also changed radically. There are fewer husband-and-wife families, more instances where a widow or widower is living alone or with a relative. On account of the longer life expectancy of females, nearly a third of the households are headed by women. Mobility is very low; 60% have not moved from their present dwellings for more than 10 years.

Home ownership is high, but the median value of the home is 22% below the Canadian average. Relatively few reside in the suburbs; the ratio is only about one in six. 34% of the households are in rural areas, compared to the national average of 28%. Also, due to the mild climate on the Pacific coast, there is an above-par concentration of the senior citizens in British Columbia.

The comments made in connection with the educational attainments of the previous age class apply even more strongly here. Fewer than a third of all household heads have gone beyond elementary school; 5% have had no schooling whatsoever.

The expenditure patterns of the aged differ considerably from those of other consumers. Because of their lower income, a relatively larger share of the budget goes into basic necessities — food, housing, and household operation. These items account for 50% of the total expenditures, far higher than the Canadian average of 44%. Medical bills take up another substantial portion of their meager income. But despite their financial difficulties, the old folks still love to spoil their grandchildren with all sorts of gifts.

* For more information on this age group, refer also to "The Old Age Market" section in this chapter.

SELECTED HOUSEHOLD CHARACTERISTICS BY AGE GROUPS

	All households	Age of the head of household					
		Under 25	25–34	35–44	45–54	55–64	65 and over
SEX							
Male head	87.0%	88.7%	95.3%	93.4%	88.9%	82.0%	69.1%
Female head	13.0	11.3	4.7	6.6	11.1	18.0	30.9
Total	100.0%	100.0%	100.0%	100.0%	100.0%	100.0%	100.0%
Number	4,554,736	179,725	938,389	1,072,159	936,625	681,014	746,824

(Source: DBS, *Census of Canada, 1961.* Bulletin 93-512.)

	All households	Under 25	25–34	35–44	45–54	55–64	65 and over
RESIDENCE BY PROVINCE							
Newfoundland	1.9%	1.6%	1.9%	2.0%	2.1%	1.9%	1.8%
Prince Edward Island	0.5	0.4	0.4	0.4	0.5	0.6	0.8
Nova Scotia	3.8	4.0	3.3	3.6	4.0	3.9	4.7
New Brunswick	2.9	3.0	2.5	2.8	3.0	3.0	3.4
Québec	26.2	25.8	28.8	27.7	26.9	25.7	20.1
Ontario	36.0	34.2	35.8	36.4	35.7	36.6	36.1
Manitoba	5.3	5.1	4.7	5.0	5.3	5.5	6.3
Saskatchewan	5.4	5.6	4.6	4.9	5.2	5.6	7.0
Alberta	7.7	10.2	8.4	7.5	7.1	7.3	7.4
British Columbia	10.1	9.8	9.3	9.5	10.0	9.8	12.3
Yukon and Northwest Territories	0.2	0.3	0.3	0.2	0.2	0.1	0.1
Canada	100.0%	100.0%	100.0%	100.0%	100.0%	100.0%	100.0%
Number	4,554,736	179,725	938,389	1,072,159	936,625	681,014	746,824

(Source: DBS, *Census of Canada, 1961.* Bulletin 93-512.)

SELECTED HOUSEHOLD CHARACTERISTICS BY AGE GROUPS (continued)

	All households	Age of the head of household					
		Under 25	25–34	35–44	45–54	55–64	65 and over
RESIDENCE: URBAN-RURAL (FAMILIES)							
Metropolitan areas:							
City proper	25.7%	27.1%	25.8%	24.7%	25.6%	26.8%	26.0%
Suburbs	21.6	19.4	24.6	24.4	21.2	18.1	15.6
Other urban	24.7	28.6	25.3	24.3	24.3	23.7	24.6
Rural: non-farm	17.7	19.8	17.7	16.8	16.4	16.9	21.8
Rural: farm	10.3	5.1	6.6	9.8	12.5	14.5	12.0
Total	100.0%	100.0%	100.0%	100.0%	100.0%	100.0%	100.0%
Number	4,147,444	187,077	958,084	1,053,323	867,479	565,209	516,272

(Source: DBS, *Census of Canada, 1961.* Bulletin 93-515.)

	All households	Age of the head of household					
		Under 25	25–34	35–44	45–54	55–64	65 and over
MARITAL STATUS							
Never married	6.3%	17.5%	5.7%	4.2%	5.5%	7.4%	7.5%
Married	83.0	82.1	93.3	92.6	86.9	76.5	57.1
Widowed	10.1	0.2	0.6	2.4	6.7	15.4	35.1
Divorced	0.6	0.2	0.4	0.8	0.9	0.7	0.3
Total	100.0%	100.0%	100.0%	100.0%	100.0%	100.0%	100.0%
Number	4,554,736	179,725	938,389	1,072,159	936,625	681,014	746,824

	All households	Age of the head of household					
		Under 25	25–34	35–44	45–54	55–64	65 and over
TYPE OF HOUSEHOLD							
Family households							
One family	83.0%	80.3%	90.5%	91.2%	86.3%	76.8%	64.2%
Two or more families	3.7	1.8	3.0	3.0	4.0	5.0	4.3
Non-family households	13.3	17.9	6.5	5.8	9.7	18.2	31.5
Total	100.0%	100.0%	100.0%	100.0%	100.0%	100.0%	100.0%
Number	4,554,736	179,725	938,389	1,072,159	936,625	681,014	746,824

(Source: DBS, *Census of Canada, 1961.* Bulletin 93-512.)

SIZE OF HOUSEHOLD

Very small (1)	9.3%	9.6%	4.3%	4.2%	6.8%	12.6%	23.1%
Small (2)	22.2	33.4	14.0	8.7	16.5	34.6	45.3
Medium (3 to 4)	36.2	48.1	44.8	34.7	38.5	34.0	23.3
Large (5–8)	28.7	8.6	34.9	46.0	32.3	16.4	7.5
Very large (over 8)	3.6	0.3	2.0	6.4	5.9	2.4	0.8
Total	100.0%	100.0%	100.0%	100.0%	100.0%	100.0%	100.0%
Number	4,554,736	179,725	938,389	1,072,159	936,625	681,014	746,824
Average size of household	3.9	2.9	4.1	4.9	4.3	3.2	2.4
Average number of children	1.9	1.0	2.0	2.8	2.3	1.0	0.2

(Source: DBS, *Census of Canada, 1961*. Bulletins 93-512 and 93-516.)

NATIVE AND FOREIGN BORN

Immigrated:							
Before 1946	15.5%	0.5%	1.8%	5.3%	13.7%	31.9%	38.0%
1946–1955	6.5	3.5	9.3	10.3	6.8	3.3	0.9
1956–1961	3.0	5.7	6.5	3.6	1.8	0.9	0.4
Born in Canada	75.0	90.3	82.4	80.8	77.7	63.9	60.7
Total	100.0%	100.0%	100.0%	100.0%	100.0%	100.0%	100.0%
Number	4,554,736	179,725	938,389	1,072,159	936,625	681,014	746,824

(Source: DBS, *Census of Canada, 1961*. Bulletin 93-512.)

MOBILITY

Residing in present dwelling:							
Less than a year	15.3%	56.9%	27.4%	14.3%	9.7%	7.5%	5.8%
1 to 5 years	36.7	37.4	56.3	43.3	31.2	24.6	20.1
6 to 10 years	16.6	1.9	11.4	22.0	20.1	17.0	14.4
More than 10 years	31.4	3.8	4.9	20.4	39.0	50.9	59.7
Total	100.0%	100.0%	100.0%	100.0%	100.0%	100.0%	100.0%
Number	4,554,493	179,714	938,335	1,072,098	936,571	680,983	746,792

(Source: DBS, *Census of Canada, 1961*. Bulletin 93-530.)

SELECTED HOUSEHOLD CHARACTERISTICS BY AGE GROUPS (continued)

	All households		Age of the head of household					
		Under 25	25–34	35–44	45–54	55–64	65 and over
RESIDENCE BY TYPE OF DWELLING							
Single detached	65.4%	37.8%	57.2%	69.0%	69.8%	67.9%	69.5%
Single attached	8.9	9.6	9.7	9.0	8.4	8.6	8.4
Apartment or flat	25.3	51.1	32.1	21.7	21.5	23.3	22.0
Mobile	0.4	1.5	1.0	0.3	0.3	0.2	0.1
Total	100.0%	100.0%	100.0%	100.0%	100.0%	100.0%	100.0%
Number	4,554,493	179,714	938,335	1,072,098	936,571	680,983	746,792

(Source: DBS, *Census of Canada, 1961.* Bulletin 93-530.)

HOUSING STATUS							
Own home	66.0%	23.9%	49.8%	67.5%	73.2%	75.1%	77.0%
Pay rent	34.0	76.1	50.2	32.5	26.8	24.9	23.0
Total	100.0%	100.0%	100.0%	100.0%	100.0%	100.0%	100.0%
Number	4,554,493	179,714	938,335	1,072,098	936,571	680,983	746,792
Median value of non-farm home ($)	11,021	7,986	11,797	12,397	11,631	10,531	8,610
Average monthly rent, non-farm ($)	65	62	65	65	65	65	64

(Source: DBS, *Census of Canada, 1961.* Bulletin 93-530.)

INDICATIONS OF POVERTY							
% of households living in dwellings that are:							
Without running water	10.9%	10.7%	8.7%	8.7%	10.4%	12.9%	15.6%
Without bath or shower	22.9	26.9	20.5	19.4	21.5	25.3	29.5
In need of major repair	5.6	6.3	5.3	5.3	5.5	5.6	6.6
Number	4,554,493	179,714	938,335	1,072,098	936,571	680,983	746,792

(Source: DBS, *Census of Canada, 1961.* Bulletin 93-530.)

TOTAL INCOME

A. Family households (non-farm)

	Total						
Under $2,000	11.7%	11.2%	7.0%	6.8%	7.9%	13.3%	35.7%
$2,000–$2,999	10.2	16.0	9.8	8.0	8.2	10.8	16.4
$3,000–$3,999	15.0	23.4	17.7	14.5	12.8	14.5	13.1
$4,000–$4,999	16.7	20.3	21.4	18.2	14.7	14.0	9.8
$5,000–$5,999	14.0	12.9	17.1	16.6	13.6	11.5	6.9
$6,000–$6,999	9.9	8.3	10.5	11.6	11.1	8.7	4.8
$7,000–$9,999	14.3	6.9	12.5	16.0	19.0	15.1	7.2
$10,000–$14,999	5.5	0.7	2.9	5.6	8.7	7.9	3.8
$15,000 and over	2.7	0.3	1.1	2.7	4.0	4.2	2.3
Total	100.0%	100.0%	100.0%	100.0%	100.0%	100.0%	100.0%
Number	3,504,692	136,373	810,728	912,018	746,392	470,027	429,154
Average income per household ($)	5,559	4,216	5,131	5,895	6,430	5,966	4,124

B. Non-family households (non-farm)

	Total						
Without income	4.8%	2.6%	2.8%	3.9%	6.1%	9.4%	2.8%
Under $1,000	28.6	10.4	6.3	9.4	14.1	23.3	47.9
$1,000–$1,999	20.3	18.5	11.1	13.2	16.3	20.0	25.8
$2,000–$2,999	14.9	32.5	19.3	17.2	17.9	15.2	10.3
$3,000–$3,999	13.5	24.2	27.4	22.9	18.8	13.1	5.2
$4,000–$4,999	7.5	7.3	15.0	14.4	11.7	7.6	2.8
$5,000–$9,999	8.7	4.1	16.4	16.4	13.0	9.5	3.8
$10,000 and over	1.7	0.4	1.7	2.6	2.1	1.9	1.4
Total	100.0%	100.0%	100.0%	100.0%	100.0%	100.0%	100.0%
Number	551,287	26,745	49,617	52,581	80,393	113,790	228,161
Average income per household ($)	2,473	2,532	3,534	3,520	3,082	2,489	1,773

(Source: DBS, *Census of Canada, 1961*. Bulletin 98-506.)

SELECTED HOUSEHOLD CHARACTERISTICS BY AGE GROUPS (continued)

	All households	Age of the head of household					
		Under 25	25–34	35–44	45–54	55–64	65 and over
EDUCATION							
No schooling	1.5%	0.3%	0.4%	0.6%	1.0%	2.3%	4.5%
Elementary: 1–4 years	8.6	1.6	3.1	5.7	8.9	13.4	16.6
Above 4 years	38.8	26.2	32.7	35.5	40.2	45.7	46.1
Secondary: 1–3 years	28.2	42.5	34.6	31.8	27.7	21.4	18.4
4–5 years	14.5	21.4	18.5	16.1	14.0	10.6	9.7
University: Some	3.6	5.1	4.5	4.1	3.5	2.9	2.3
Degree	4.8	2.9	6.2	6.2	4.7	3.7	2.4
Total	100.0%	100.0%	100.0%	100.0%	100.0%	100.0%	100.0%
Number	4,554,736	179,725	938,389	1,072,159	936,625	681,014	746,824
OCCUPATION							
White collar							
Managerial	12.4%	3.9%	9.1%	13.5%	15.5%	13.4%	13.5%
Professional and technical	8.6	9.2	10.4	9.1	7.4	6.8	6.8
Clerical	7.5	13.4	7.5	6.8	7.2	7.8	6.8
Sales	5.6	6.8	6.6	5.7	5.0	4.3	5.1
Blue collar							
Craftsmen, production process, etc.	29.0	30.0	31.4	30.4	29.0	26.5	16.2
Unskilled laborers	4.6	6.6	4.6	4.3	4.5	5.0	3.4
Other occupations							
Service and recreation	8.8	10.5	8.6	7.9	7.8	10.1	14.4
Transport and communications	7.4	9.6	9.7	8.1	6.4	5.1	2.4
Farmers and farm workers	11.3	5.0	6.5	9.4	12.6	16.8	28.7
Other primary industries	3.1	3.7	3.6	3.2	3.0	2.7	1.6
Not stated	1.7	1.3	2.0	1.6	1.6	1.5	1.1
Total	100.0%	100.0%	100.0%	100.0%	100.0%	100.0%	100.0%
Number in labor force	3,641,750	170,498	898,082	1,012,327	848,774	524,412	187,657

(Source: DBS. *Census of Canada, 1961.* Bulletin 93-512.)

WIFE WORKING

	Total						
Wife in labor force	20.8%	25.9%	20.3%	23.9%	24.7%	14.6%	3.2%
Wife not in labor force	79.2	74.1	79.7	76.1	75.3	85.4	96.8
Total	100.0%	100.0%	100.0%	100.0%	100.0%	100.0%	100.0%
Number of husband-wife families	3,800,026	393,216	1,013,430	1,007,948	709,447	410,159	265.826

(Source: DBS, *Census of Canada, 1961.* Bulletin 93-520.)

ANNUAL URBAN FAMILY EXPENDITURES

A. *Average per family*

Food	$1,323	$1,022	$1,276	$1,461	$1,492	$1,270	$1,032
Housing, fuel, light, water	911	830	962	928	941	844	836
Household operation	214	183	221	228	226	209	171
Furnishings and equipment	277	334	304	296	296	252	167
Clothing	508	413	435	572	650	515	316
Automobile	518	550	558	537	583	524	269
Other transportation	112	112	96	90	131	163	103
Medical care	237	174	213	251	244	261	238
Personal care	118	88	111	127	139	118	89
Recreation	160	188	171	180	169	143	103
Reading	35	24	33	37	36	41	33
Education	39	18	20	45	78	35	10
Smoking and alcoholic drinks	230	137	223	248	274	241	153
Other	69	45	75	65	61	82	68
All current consumption	4,751	4,118	4,698	5,065	5,320	4,698	3,588
Gifts and contributions	170	90	136	179	180	228	162
Personal taxes	378	274	378	404	446	392	233
Security	271	210	248	323	323	272	140
Total expenditures	$5,570	$4,692	$5,460	$5,971	$6,269	$5,590	$4,123

	All households	Age of the head of household					
		Under 25	25–34	35–44	45–54	55–64	65 and over
B. Percentage distribution							
Food	23.8%	21.8%	23.4%	24.5%	23.8%	22.7%	25.0%
Housing, fuel, light, water	16.4	17.7	17.6	15.5	15.0	15.1	20.3
Household operation	3.8	3.9	4.0	3.8	3.6	3.7	4.1
Furnishings and equipment	5.0	7.1	5.6	4.9	4.7	4.5	4.1
Clothing	9.1	8.8	8.0	9.6	10.4	9.2	7.7
Automobile	9.3	11.7	10.2	9.0	9.3	9.4	6.5
Other transportation	2.0	2.4	1.8	1.5	2.1	2.9	2.5
Medical care	4.3	3.7	3.9	4.2	3.9	4.7	5.8
Personal care	2.1	1.9	2.0	2.1	2.2	2.1	2.2
Recreation	2.9	4.0	3.1	3.0	2.7	2.6	2.5
Reading	0.6	0.5	0.6	0.6	0.6	0.7	0.8
Education	0.7	0.4	0.4	0.8	1.2	0.6	0.2
Smoking and alcoholic drinks	4.1	2.9	4.1	4.2	4.4	4.3	3.7
Other	1.2	1.0	1.4	1.1	1.0	1.5	1.6
All current consumption	85.3	87.8	86.1	84.8	84.9	84.0	87.0
Gifts and contributions	3.0	1.9	2.5	3.0	2.9	4.1	3.9
Personal taxes	6.8	5.8	6.9	6.8	7.1	7.0	5.7
Security	4.9	4.5	4.5	5.4	5.1	4.9	3.4
Total expenditures	100.0%	100.0%	100.0%	100.0%	100.0%	100.0%	100.0%

(Source: DBS, *Urban Family Expenditures, 1959.* Bulletin 62-521.)

The Youth Market

Today, wherever one turns, the accent is on youth. In other cultures, young people can hardly wait to enter the adult world. They hate to be called children, dislike most of all to be adolescents. In North America, youngsters are in no hurry to leave such an agreeable, status-endowed existence for the dubious pleasures of adulthood. Instinct (and the evidence before their eyes) tells them that they will never have it so good again. So why give up something pleasant?

Most adults, as they advance in years, yearn like Faust to relive their youth just once more for a brief period. But, while in the past, the middle-aged man kept his secret wishes buried deeply in private fantasies, today he lets them out and goes part of the way along Faust's troubled trail. He tries to show that he is mentally young by wearing a trench coat, driving a sports car, dancing the frug and the watussi, and in other ways imitating the teen-age style of living.

Many facets of female behavior bear the same stamp. A woman of 40 or 50 adopts a young-girl's hair style and takes Metrecal instead of food to shrink to the size of the thin young models. Department store sales personnel report that women are out to fit the clothes instead of vice versa.

With youth being thus set up on the pedestal, youngsters everywhere are realizing their importance and claim for a preferential treatment in the market place. Businessmen have not been slow to take the hint. Many design their products solely for this segment, and appeal to the youngsters directly rather than through their parents.

In terms of size, persons under 25 account for 49% of the country's population. In this respect, practically half of the Canadian market can be classified as the youth market. For detailed analysis it is convenient to break it up into the five major segments, some of which are overlapping.

The infant market (age roughly 0-5);
The juvenile market (age roughly 6-12);
The teen-age market (age roughly 13-19);
The college market (age roughly 18-24);
The young newly-wed market (age roughly 18-24).

Each group has its own needs and motivations, and requires different sales approaches through different media. There is very little similarity between a 5-year-old kindergartener and a 24-year-old collegian. However, one common streak runs through the entire market — the desire for newness. The young are the accelerators of change. They expect it, accept it, and effect it. Many products that now have wide acceptance first gained their foothold among young people, particularly those in high school and college. Youth's influence on adult clothing is generally recognized. Perhaps not so well known is the fact that many other items — canned soft drinks, frozen TV dinners, and filter cigarettes, to mention a few — established beachheads in the youth market before branching out to the general public.

THE INFANT MARKET (0-5)

Parents are not the only ones to get ecstatic over babies. Marketing men love them too. Estimates vary as to the volume of business depending directly on babies, but it runs into millions of dollars. An average baby, during its first year, generates a demand for goods and services anywhere from $700 to $1,000. This includes food, clothing, toys, drugs, cribs, carriages, playpens, high chairs, diaper services, babysitter fees, and other odds and ends — not to overlook the rolls and rolls of photographic film purchased by proud parents.

To give an example, T. G. McCormack, president, Dominion Stores Limited, once stated that a new-born baby during the first 12 months of his existence consumes on the average $200 worth of food. "He devours, among other things, 675 jars of prepared baby foods, 30 cans of tomato or pineapple juice, ten boxes of zwieback, 15 pounds of potatoes, ten dozen eggs, four pounds of bacon, six packages of cereal, 337 cans of evaporated milk, and 22 pounds of sugar or corn syrup. And that's only the first year. After that he gets teeth and really starts eating!"

The following table shows the value of factory shipments in 1961 of some industries producing directly for the infant market.

VALUE OF FACTORY SHIPMENTS OF SELECTED INDUSTRIES PRODUCING DIRECTLY FOR THE INFANT MARKET, 1961

Products	Value
Food, infant and junior	$24,641,364
Toys	20,378,889
Infants' wear	17,303,948
Babies' footwear	5,485,735
Carriages, strollers, etc., baby	3,080,695
Carriages, doll	948,808
Babies' equipment and supplies, miscellaneous	964,780

(Source: DBS, *Products Shipped By Canadian Manufacturers, 1961*. catalogue no. 31-211.)

Thus, infants provide business to hundreds of firms, and jobs to thousands of Canadians. The market, furthermore, is fast-growing and secure — fast-growing because of the continuing population explosion, and secure because mom and dad will do without many items themselves rather than deprive their little ones of the things they need or want.

Of course, the buying decisions here are made entirely by the adults, and the selling appeals have to be directed solely at them. The market is characterized by strong brand consciousness, and acceptance of new items seems to be in proportion to the parent's confidence in the maker's name.

THE JUVENILE MARKET (6-12)

One of the main characteristics of modern life is the emphasis placed on children. Friends, recreation, home and neighborhood, all revolve around the young ones' needs. Part of this doting is due to the growing popularity of psychological theories which stress that many of the mental ills and maladjustments of later life are caused by the frustrations suffered during childhood. It is important for a youngster to feel successful, popular and happy if he is to grow up into a well-balanced adult.

One by-product of this admonition from psychologists is that children have lots of freedom and are given the things they desire most of the time. Rather than dispute with her highly emotional offspring, a mother will forgo the brand she prefers and buy the one he wants with a premium offer of a space helmet for 10 boxtops. Marketing men have not been slow to exploit this opportunity. More and more it is realized that the best route to sales is through children. Advertising in many cases is beamed to them directly and not through parents.

The most potent medium for etching messages on young brains is, undoubtedly, television. Children not only repeat the merit of an advertised product, but they do it with a gusto rarely displayed by even the enthusiastic announcers. And, what is more, they go on mentioning it all day long at no extra cost. Unlike the set, they cannot be turned off at will.

Television, therefore, has opened up undreamed-of vistas for influencing young children. However, an advertiser must select his program with care. A show may be just right for a nine-year-old, but too complicated for one three years younger and too infantile for another three years older. Similarly, the commercial must be in tune with the audience reached. There is a significant variation in the method of approach to the six- and seven-year-olds as opposed to those of 11 and 12 years of age.

The other broadcast medium, radio, is mainly used in the juvenile market for well-known brands that need only reminder advertising to keep the name humming around in the listener's mind. For describing a new product, like a toy, the radio is not very suitable because the verbal method of communication fails to rouse the interest of the child.

The print media are often ruled out since a vast majority of six- and seven-year-olds, while being avid TV fans, are too young to read or have only a limited vocabulary. For the older boys and girls, the most important vehicle is the "comics," appearing in weekend supplements. They have a wide readership, each copy being perused intensively and then passed along to others.

The following are some of the considerations for good advertisements, suggested by Eugene Gilbert and other experts on the juvenile market.

• Have a setting that is quite familiar. The more projectable the situation, the greater is the degree of impact. This means avoiding emphasis on the adults.

Youngsters prefer to see other children, hear children's voices, get involved in children's activities.

- Show the product in a realistic setting. Contrived and artificial demonstrations of the product are usually rejected by juvenile viewers. While youngsters will often admit to a preference for animated commercials over live action types, they tend to pay more attention to the latter, especially if it really shows them how to do something.
- Avoid references, similes, or analogies that are not likely to be part of a youngster's personal or general information.
- Provide strong physical action. All children seem to have a real predilection for commercials that depict dynamic situations in which characters are actually involved in highly active roles.
- Make the copy simple enough to read aloud. A young child often moves his lips when reading, pronouncing all the syllables of the words to himself. However, research has shown that, unlike their parents, children show no disinclination to avoid a "busy" print ad; in fact, they may savor each luscious adjective.
- Concentrate on one main theme. A young person's mind is clear-cut and direct. He should be given all the information as concisely as possible. Various appeals should be integrated so that the message appears as one unit, one demand for action.
- Cater to the parents. Using a child's credulity to club a parent into buying something is highly annoying and only serves to create a bad image for the product. Slight changes in the text can avoid irritating the parents without losing the interest of the children.

Advertising is just one means of persuading children to buy. Another method equally effective is sales promotion, especially premiums. From unusual hats and balloons to large gifts through coupons like bicycles or transistor radios, the "something extra" which premiums offer means more to the 6- to 12-year-olds than to any other age group. The parents, as a rule, are not opposed to such promotions because they obviate some of the need for constant toy purchases.

A good premium should tie in with the current sports figures, fads, and idols of the younger set. When the Davy Crockett fad was at its height, one dealer offered free play tents with every appliance purchase, thus giving the children the opportunity to "camp out just like Davy."

The premium must also have some value. If the child opens the box and can hardly find the toy, although on the outside it is lavishly illustrated, a good deal of disappointment results. Nothing frustrates the young consumer more than to feel he has been taken in. For self-liquidating premiums, 25 cents need not be the limit. Bona-fide offers going for a dollar and over have been well received.

Prompt delivery is equally important. When such words as "Don't delay,"

"Rush," "Act now" decorate a box top, and the children in full faith perform as requested, the manufacturer should see that the article is sent within a reasonable amount of time. One should always avoid giving the youngster a sense of disillusionment. As each day passes, the wild enthusiasm slowly dissipates, and by the time the premium arrives the child may have lost all interest in it.

BIBLIOGRAPHY

Gilbert, Eugene: *Advertising and Marketing to Young People.* Printers' Ink Books, Pleasantville, New York, 1957.
Helitzer, Melvin: "Media buying to reach children," *Media/Scope,* November 1963.
Jack and Jill Magazine: "Hypothesizing the Children's Market." Research conducted for that magazine by E. L. Reilly Co. Inc.
Sales Management: "The Changing Face of the Children's Market," December 18, 1964.
Packard, Vance: *The Hidden Persuaders.* David McKay Company, Inc., New York, 1957.

THE TEEN-AGE MARKET (13–19)

The teen-age market is complex and often confusing, but there is pay dirt in it for businessmen who attempt to cultivate it. This is, truly speaking, the frontier market — young, wild, sprouting everywhere, and just barely being exploited. If ever there was a market to test the mettle of the adventurous, here is one. It is important for three significant reasons: for its own purchasing power now; for the role it plays in influencing the family spending; and for its rich potential as an adult market of tomorrow.

The younger generation today measures its wealth, not by pennies in the piggybanks, but by fairly substantial figures in the savings account passbooks. At present, more than 735,000 youngsters, or over one-third of the population in the age group of 14 – 19, are in the labor force. Even assuming their average annual earnings to be as low as $1,000 (exact figures are not available), this means that they have nearly three-fourths of a billion dollars for spending. In addition, they are permitted frequent access to their mother's charge account and their dad's billfold. Their parents, because of the age cycle, are usually in the above-average income groups. A man with teen-age children is generally at his peak earning power; also, more working mothers have children in their teens than in any other age group.

Though not so affluent, the teen-agers who go to school are not badly off financially either. Part-time work, summer jobs, and odd tasks in the neighborhood, plus the usual allowances from their parents, keep their pockets jingling with ready cash. A Canadian High News Survey conducted in 1962 revealed that the average high school student makes through income and allowances $555 a year, $662 for the boys and $448 for the girls. Since about a million students are in high school now, their total income would be around $550 million.

On the basis of these calculations, the purchasing power of all teen-agers, in or out of the labor force, would reach a staggering figure of over a billion dollars.

And a substantial portion of this pot of gold, it is important to add, is discretionary spending money. In most cases, no strings are attached to the teen-ager's income. The boys and girls have few adult expenses, such as rent, grocery bills, insurance premiums, and taxes. Their earnings are almost 100 per cent expendible.

The following table shows how high school boys and girls spend and save their money in Canada and the United States. The figures are expressed as percentage of income.

PERCENTAGE OF INCOME SPENT AND SAVED BY HIGH SCHOOL
STUDENTS IN CANADA AND THE U.S.A.

	Boys		Girls	
	Canada	U.S.A.	Canada	U.S.A.
Food	21%	32%	17%	26%
Entertainment, music, records	16	22	14	11
Clothing	4	7	21	19
Books and school supplies	6	11	6	14
Sports	12	11	4	6
Car and gas	4	4	—	—
Grooming	3	2	8	7
Other	6	4	8	8
Saving	28	7	22	9

(Source: *Marketing*, March 15, 1963.)

Many industries, therefore, stand to gain if they make a special pitch to woo the teen-agers. Youth is not a difficult field to cultivate. Young people are not money-hoarders; they are money-spenders. The adult market is a depression-conscious market. Even those who did not suffer financially are nevertheless aware of what they term "extravagant" purchases. Teen-agers, on the other hand, have never known a non-prosperous world. What their parents consider a luxury, they regard as a necessity to keep pace with today's living.

Some surprising sales are being rung up because of teen-agers' free-spending. A good example is contact lenses which cost about five or six times as much as frame glasses. Despite this, one optical house reports that more than half these lenses are bought by persons between the ages of 15 and 19.

TEEN-AGERS' INFLUENCE ON FAMILY PURCHASES

In addition to their own purchases, the teen-agers have tremendous influence on the family's buying habits. For example, their opinions on cars, furniture, appliances, TV sets, recreation equipment and the like carry a great weight when the time comes to purchase these items. Because parents have to rule negatively on cigarettes, liquor, late hours, and other disciplinary matters, they do not mind giving in to their children in such matters as the choice of a product or the switch of a brand. Consequently, an advertiser who touches a responsive chord in the youngsters can generally count on the parents to finally buy the product.

The teen-age influence on family purchases is well described by Eugene Gilbert, a U.S. expert who has done extensive research in this field. In his book, *Advertising and Marketing to Young People,** Mr. Gilbert points out that the youth market exerts a pressure which ranks with that of the most powerfully organized lobby. Logically, the teen-ager is the most ideal carrier of new ideas into the home. When he is sold on a product and feels that his family may reject it, he resorts to such a subtle and controlled selling campaign that the family finds itself thinking of that particular product as their next purchase. Capturing the mercurial tastes of youngsters is, thus, an excellent method of killing two birds with one stone — the young person on his own purchases and his influence on his parents.

GROWTH POTENTIAL OF THE TEEN-AGE MARKET

Nor should one overlook the teen-age market for its growth potential. Today's big-spending teen-ager is tomorrow's bigger-spending adult. Marketers can build loyalty that will mean increased future sales when these boys and girls grow into men and women. The field is wide open. Young people are impressionable. They are open-minded and desire to learn. They have no established patterns, no backlog of items, no inventory of treasured, irreplaceable objects. They have not spent a lifetime learning to love the products of the competitor. In short, they are not set *in* their ways; they want to be set *on* their ways — right towards the goods of the manufacturer who knows how to approach them in a proper way.

This is borne out to some extent by a unique experiment conducted in the United States by Eugene Gilbert. In 1954, he recorded the preferences of two sample age groups, 8–14 and 15–19, for three products: fountain pens, cameras, and typewriters. Nine years later he contacted again the same group of students to see how the buying pattern in 1963 corresponded with the declared preferences of 1954. The results were as follows:

PERCENTAGE WHO BOUGHT LAST TIME THE SAME BRAND
THEY PREFERRED 9 YEARS AGO

	8–14 in 1954	15–19 in 1954
Fountain pen	32.3%	53.7%
Camera	40.3	67.5
Typewriter	28.6	41.4
Average brand preference longevity	33.7	52.3

* Eugene Gilbert, *Advertising and Marketing to Young People,* Printers' Ink Books, Pleasantville, New York, 1957, p. 41-43.

This would seem to indicate that while the younger children's likes and dislikes are subject to change, among the older teen-agers the brand loyalties are established to a much higher degree. It is important, therefore, to influence teen-age purchases now so as to build an attachment toward the brand that hopefully will be carried over into adulthood.

CHARACTERISTICS OF THE TEEN-AGE MARKET

Given the wealth and importance of the teen-age market, what is the businessman to do about it? How can he come to understand it, and, better still, sell to it?

The adolescent market has certain characteristics which have given ulcers to many executives. Marketing to youth is quite unlike marketing to adults. Capturing the quicksilver tastes of millions of youngsters requires deep insight into their habits, their ideas and their thoughts.

Before probing below the surface into the psychological and sociological factors that affect teen-age behavior, it is necessary first to sweep away a few cobwebs. In certain quarters, the teen-age generation is a source of personal indignation and a good deal of dismay and disquietude. The picture usually conjured is one of boys in leather jackets and girls in tight slacks, very "beat" and disillusioned and caring only for beach parties, pop art and the most dreadful music. A large number are supposed to be sexually promiscuous at altogether precocious ages, their whole outlook conditioned by film actors and actresses, whose sordid, adolescent romances seem to them the height of adventurous glory and excitement.

These impressions are generally based on personal inexperience and a few sensational stories in the press, which always has a tendency to play up the volatile and the violent. It is not fair to generalize from a few isolated cases of misbehavior on the part of some juvenile delinquents. For every young radical whose picture makes the front page of the paper, there are a hundred young conformists whose lives flow along the well-greased tracks of normality. The majority of the teen-agers are decent youngsters who handle their tasks with honesty, diligence, and aplomb.

The main reason for so much misunderstanding is that adults fail to take into consideration the psychological make-up of the adolescents. Teen-agers face many problems peculiar to their age. The teen years are major change years — the years of puberty, adolescence and early maturity, with the physical and psychological awakening and upheaval that these mean. There are new needs, new interests, new experiences, and since everything is in a highly formative stage, the behavior often tends to be unstable and even contradictory. Laughter comes as easily and quickly as anger. Elation and depression closely follow each other. Egocentrism and sociability, ascendancy and submissiveness, heightened ambitions and loss of interest — all these manifest themselves at one time or another, and sometimes with equal fervor in rapid succession. There is often no relationship between the importance of the situation and the violence of the reaction. Behavior is more transitory and less stable than at later stages of life. Yesterday's enthusiasms become matters of boredom today. The heart's desire one day may be to become a missionary; ere long this is completely forgotten, and the goal of life is to achieve renown as a dancer. Such contrasting moods make it very difficult to predict an individual's behavior during adolescence. They also explain the rapid emergence of fads and fancies, a constant source of frustration to parents and businessmen alike.

Teen-agers have many problems, and the need for security is one of the greatest. The world of teen-agers enlarges from the limited scope of a child's horizon to the broad realm of the adult universe. Suddenly teen-agers are faced with a variety of new situations with little idea of how to behave. Their self-confidence is always being threatened because of their lack of experience and knowledge.

They do not want to rely on parents for guidance. In fact, they want to be fully independent. They tend to turn to friends for direction, solace or discussion of things that matter to them. In this way, they gain the feeling of security, identity, understanding, and mutual acceptance they need so badly.

Conformity to the group is of utmost importance. No matter how radically the teen-ager may disagree with his parents and the adult world, he is conservative where his friends of the same age are concerned. If the group frowns upon noble ideals, he will tend to frown upon such ideals; if the group keeps late hours, he will be bent upon keeping late hours; and if the group swears and uses slang, he will do it too. There is at this stage a keen desire to follow the herd and to avoid being marked as "different." To be "liked" and to be "alike" is the creed of the typical teen-ager. This attitude of conformity stands out above almost everything else at this period of life.

MARKETING TO TEEN-AGERS

Based on these characteristics, here are a few practical examples of the steps that can be taken to score a success in this market.

• *Talk to, not down to, teen-agers.* The teen-ager should always be regarded as a thinking, intelligent youngster who, in the process of growing up, tries consciously or unconsciously to emulate the adult. If a commercial approaches him from a "kid" angle, he is apt to feel that the message is intended for his younger sibling rather than for himself. Also, it is not wise to resort to teen-age jive talk in the copy. Youngsters resent adult intrusion into their world. Besides, this jargon is strictly local and is likely to change so swiftly that what is contemporary when the ad is written may be gauche by the time it appears in print.

• *Capitalize on the teen-agers' desire to attract the opposite sex.* Ideas which offer ways to attract the opposite sex are usually well-received. They may be connected with improving physical appearance or personality; teens are extremely concerned with both. To girls, especially, romance and eventual marriage are emotionally all-consuming; they dream of the day they will walk down the aisle all dressed in white. Appeals in this direction can be potent.

- *Be sincere and honest.* Young people can easily detect inaccuracies and discrepancies in advertising and are quick to expose a hoax. The copy must always be sincere, believable and convincing. Once the word gets around that a product does not live up to its claim, the market is lost.

- *Avoid sophistication.* An overly sophisticated ad may inhibit the teen-ager's ability to identify, for his range of experience is strictly limited. What seems fashionable to the average copy writer, often appears bizarre to the naïve youngster. The most effective approach is to depict young people in group activity, provided the situation is a familiar one. An illustration portraying a boy and girl enjoying "pop" at a soda fountain would be far more acceptable than one showing them dining in an obviously expensive restaurant with the dash and glamor of sophisticated living.

- *Win over the leaders at school.* An authoritative, wise-mother approach is not likely to succeed with teen-agers. They do not want to be treated as little children any more. It is far better to attempt to cultivate the patronage of the leaders in school. What they approve counts for more than what dad or mom say at home.

- *Associate the product with a national hero.* Though it is usually best to avoid picturing adults in teen-age ads, youngsters are hero worshippers, and testimonials can be extremely effective if the over-all popularity of the "personality" is well established. However, timing is extremely important due to the transience of this age group's adoration for an individual. A fad can raise an idol to the heights, but it can also dump him the next moment into a waste heap.

- *Be conscious of different teen-age groups.* The teens cover a wide span of years, and interests within the group vary with age. Thus, the subteens resent being lumped with the "children." Similarly, the older teen-ager does not like to be associated with the subteen. Each group wants its own spot to buy in. Department stores have found that it pays to set up separate counters catering to these different groups.

- *Have your package look modern.* Young people abhor anything that smacks of being old-fashioned. If the package does not appeal, all the preliminary advertising efforts to get the youngster to the point of purchase will be wasted. Teens are fond of vibrant and buoyant colors and are attracted by new shades and tones.

- *Make frequent use of premiums.* Most market studies show that teen-agers respond more readily to premiums and trading stamps than older people. A premium with its notion of "something extra" means a good deal to young people because their wants are many and their means are relatively slim. However, premiums offered must be attractive, of good quality, and representing a demonstrable value. Teen-agers today have pretty high standards and a fairly keen sense of market values.

- *Run teen-age contests whenever possible.* Contests, if properly conducted, can prove extremely useful in augmenting sales. The prizes offered should be realistic, providing immediate rewards rather than future benefits. Since many youngsters do not go on to college, a college scholarship as a prize in a high school contest is certain to arouse less interest than a free trip to a favorite vacation spot. Also, it must be remembered that young people love presents. Even a small item is exciting to them. Consequently they are more likely to enter contests where many small prizes are given away, because they feel there is a greater chance to win. Ten bicycles would be definitely a more attractive offer than one television console.

- *Use appropriate advertising media.* The mighty power of television, which holds its grip on the child market, loses out to some extent with maturing age. Adolescents still watch television, especially plays, drama, westerns, and variety shows. However, other media begin to exert greater influence. Radio listening, for the most part to popular music, becomes a favorite form of entertainment, and the new compact transistors are carried practically everywhere. Reading, too, assumes greater importance as the level of education increases. U.S. evidence seems to suggest that young people read publications devoted to their particular interests more thoroughly than they do general magazines. The following are some of the publications introduced fairly recently to cover the teen-age market:

> *Miss Chatelaine,* a consumer magazine for the teen-age girl.
> *Canadian Boy,* a consumer magazine for the younger teen-age boy.
> *After Four,* a weekly tabloid for teen-agers, distributed with the Toronto Telegram.
> *Teen Talk,* a weekly tabloid, distributed in all of the Thompson Newspapers.
> *Teen Scene,* a tabloid carried every other week in the *London Free Press.*

A few proponents strongly recommend direct mail (e.g., "Mailbag" with *Canadian High News*). Young people, it is pointed out, get very little mail; so they are excited and receptive when some arrives bearing their name.

SPECIFIC TEEN-AGE MARKETS

So far, the discussion has been in general terms. The extent to which an individual manufacturer can cash in on this effulgent, effervescent youth market depends, of course, on his type of business. Here are a few concrete examples of how certain industries have been beneficially affected.

FOOD

Young people are the best customers for between-meal items, like hot dogs, hamburgers, milk shakes, cokes, candy bars, popcorn, and chewing gum. The market for other foods also stands to benefit indirectly. Because of rapid growth, youngsters consume prodigious amounts of food. A teen-age boy requires 3,000 calories a day, and a girl 2,500 — considerably more than the 2,400 needed by their father and the 2,000 by their mother. Many manufacturers are aware of this fact, and try to capture a healthy slice of the teen-age market by stressing the nutritional value of their food products to parents, or by instructing the youth directly through advertising and educational literature.

CLOTHING

During the adolescent period, appearance assumes great importance. Unlike the adult who selects his clothing by its becomingness and quality, the teen-ager chooses it in terms of what others of his kind are wearing. Adult approval is usually of little significance to him. He is mainly interested in the appropriateness of his appearance as judged by the standards of his peer group. Boys, for example, favor an informal style of dressing. They prefer a sports jacket to a suit, a windbreaker to a topcoat, blue jeans to well-cut slacks, and a sports shirt to a regular shirt. However, as every clothing manufacturer knows from experience, there is nothing hard-and-fast about the teen-agers' tastes. They veer from fad to fad, and it takes a brave man indeed to say what style will be a "hit" tomorrow.

TOILETRIES

Teen-age girls are heavy users of cosmetics, such as face make-up, talcum powders, colognes, deodorants, and bubble baths. They are also interested in products that would remove skin blemishes, reduce overweight, and beautify their hair, complexion, and nails. In general, they like to conform to the current standards of feminine beauty and to what they consider to be the latest mode for their age-group, as exemplified by the movies and cover girls. Boys, too, care for good grooming. They experiment with various styles of hair cuts and extensively apply hair oils and pomades.

RECREATION

The recreation market gets a large share of the teen-age dollar, extending all the way from bowling alleys and spectator sports to portable phonographs and pocket-size adventure books. In fact, certain sectors are dependent almost exclusively on youngsters. Teen-agers have saved the movie industry, accounting for perhaps half or more of the cinema attendance. They are the mainstays of the record and radio business. One spokesman for the record industry estimates that 70% of the single records and about half of the albums of popular music are bought by teen-agers.

AUTOMOBILES

Boys and girls in most parts of the country receive driver's licenses by the age of 16. Although they probably will not own a car for several years, they are quite influential when it comes to persuading the family to get a new car. Many a parent can attest to the buying pressures stimulated by a few well-aimed kicks at the tires of the family car and several sarcastic remarks about that "old crate." Even though the youngster may be driving an old, rebuilt jalopy, he feels that the family car should be the latest model, one that indicates a successful father.

"SECOND" MARKETS

Teen-agers breed a demand for extra facilities at home. They create a profitable "second" market for automobiles, radios, TV sets, bathroom installations, and telephones (i.e., new lines and not just extensions). They thus help to build up the economy and shove back the barriers of saturation, which otherwise would hinder the expansion of many industries.

BIBLIOGRAPHY

Business Week: "Catching the Customers at the Most Critical Age," October 25, 1957.

Cateora, Philip, R.: *An Analysis of the Teen-Age Market,* Bureau of Business Research, The University of Texas, Austin, 1963.

Clare, John: "The Scramble for the Teen-age Dollar," *Maclean's,* September 14, 1957.

Gilbert, Eugene: *Advertising and Marketing to Young People,* Printers' Ink Books, Pleasantville, New York, 1957.

Media/Scope: "Youth: The Frontier Market," June, 1964.

Printers' Ink: "Do ad men understand teen-agers?" July 29, 1960.

Small Marketers Aids (No. 80): "Building Sales to Younger Customers," Small Business Administration, Washington D.C., June, 1962.

Smith, Paul E.: "Merchandising for the teen-age market," *Journal of Retailing,* Summer, 1961.

THE COLLEGE MARKET

The nation's spacious campuses and ivied walls are locales for one of today's most explosive gilt-edged growth markets, one whose impact will continue to be felt for many years to come. Numerically, the college group may be the smallest segment of the youth market, but potentially, it is replete with opportunities. These student-consumers, in their late teens and dewy twenties, are a special breed of taste-makers, be it for cars, cosmetics, clothes, coiffures, or in-fads. Currently, they have widespread influence on the purchasing habits of friends and relatives, and, looking further, as opinion leaders and style setters of tomorrow, their consumption patterns will probably set the mold for the others to follow.

Most experts agree that the campus serves as a major launching site for several important product innovations. As experimental consumers, the collegians in the United States were first to stamp their approval on filter cigarettes, beer in cans, electric shavers, and several other new ideas that have since been well accepted by the general public. Thus, by wooing the students when their tastes and attitudes are still malleable, a company can not only build up strong product affinities, but may also have on its side an influential group that can be a trailblazer for the whole country.

As a market, the collegians straddle many age groups. Since a large percentage of students are under 20, a sizeable segment of the market may be called "teen-agers." Their academic life is a blend of fun and books with emphasis on the former. However, college teens differ significantly from those in high school and will go to extremes to avoid identification with the younger group. Similarly, the "over 20" group might be lumped technically with the "young adult" classification. But from a marketing point of view, the collegians are a breed unto themselves.

Within the college market, there are many overlapping segments:

• Graduates who, as a rule, try to stay aloof from campus life, usually concentrating on studies to the exclusion of nearly everything else.

• Married students, some with children, carrying on their family and scholastic responsibilities at the same time.

• Commuting students who are still subject to family influence and are somewhat removed from campus opinions and mores.

• The "hard core," those who live on campus, are subject to group conformity, and are truly collegiate.

However, almost all these students have a common distinction — better education. This makes them broad in outlook, open to new experience, independent and disciplined in their thinking, and possessed of convictions based on understanding of the world and their own role in it.

The campus market, of late, has been growing by leaps and bounds. Within a decade, full-time enrolment in Canadian universities and colleges jumped by two and a half times as shown below:

FULL-TIME ENROLMENT IN CANADIAN UNIVERSITIES AND COLLEGES

Academic year	Under-graduate (000)	Graduate (000)	Total (000)	Total enrolment as % of population 18–24
1955–56	69.3	3.4	72.7	4.7
1956–57	75.0	3.5	78.5	5.0
1957–58	82.6	4.1	86.7	5.4
1958–59	90.4	4.6	95.0	5.8
1959–60	96.7	5.2	101.9	6.1
1960–61	107.4	6.5	113.9	6.7
1961–62	121.6	7.3	128.9	7.5
1962–63	133.0	8.4	141.4	8.0
1963–64	147.3	11.1	158.4	8.6
1964–65	164.4	13.8	178.2	9.2

(Source: Association of Universities and Colleges of Canada, *Financing Higher Education in Canada*, the Bladen Commission.)

What is behind the sheepskin explosion? Population make-up is one catalyst. The huge postwar baby crop that brought bonanza sales to moppet and teen-age markets is now hitting the campuses. During the last few years, the 18 to 24 age groups, the chief reservoir of college registrants, has expanded more rapidly than the total population. However, these demographic changes have provided only a partial explanation. Had the same proportion of young people attended universities in 1964-65 as in 1955-56, enrolment would have increased as a result of baby boom only to 90,200. The fact that it reached 178,200 indicates that a greater proportion of 18- to 24-year-olds are continuing their studies after high school.

This rapidly growing desire to enter university is not just one form of escapism — a longing to seek the sylvan calm of the campus quadrangle in place of the hustle and bustle of the commercial rat race. There are other more compelling reasons: the craving to move up the social ladder, the fears of unemployment in an age of automation, and the recognition of the high financial reward that can be expected from investment in education. Also, the strong and constant admonition from governmental circles, "don't be a drop-out," has not fallen on deaf ears. More and more students are becoming keenly aware that in today's competitive world any additional training will mean so much more in dollars and cents on the job later on. They realize that even a B.A. is no longer enough to meet the new rigid requirements of business and industry. Now, to stand out and, above all, to have a shot at the managerial seat, one needs an M.A. or even a Ph.D. All these factors have combined to double the chances of a Canadian going to university. In 1950, about one in twelve primary-school pupils entered university. In 1964, the proportion had risen to about one in six; and by the end of the decade, according to the Bladen Commission, it may be as high as one in four.*

PROFILE OF COLLEGE STUDENTS

One of the most exhaustive studies on the profiles of the college students is the one undertaken by the Dominion Bureau of Statistics a few years ago. The results have been published in a three-part report entitled *University Student Expenditure and Income in Canada* (Catalog Nos. 81-519 to 81-521). Part I deals with non-Canadian students, Part II with Canadian undergraduates, and Part III with Canadian graduates. The statistics below have been obtained from the last two parts. The averages for the whole country have been computed from

---

* Canada has one of the highest rates of university attendance in the world. This is clearly borne out by the Bladen Commission: "The chance that a child born in 1945 will enter university is one in three if he is a citizen of the United States, one in six if he is a Canadian, one in nine if he is an Australian, one in twelve if he is French, and one in twenty if he is English. These differences are certainly not a reflection of relative intelligence; they represent variations in social philosophy and in per capita income. Until recently Britain has carefully selected a small intellectual *elite* and given them, largely at public expense, a very specialized education of high quality. It did not even pretend that university was available to all who could benefit from it. In consequence, British universities have had a very low "wastage" rate. In contrast, Canada, Australia, and above all, the United States give much greater attention to the student of average ability. These countries are more tolerant toward the late developer, the persistent worker, the product of the less sophisticated country school. It is assumed that the less able should be eliminated only after they have been given a chance."

the separate data of different faculties. The figures show only the percentages. To get the actual numbers, these percentages have to be applied to the total of 121,547 for undergraduate and 7,347 for graduate students. This is for the academic year 1961-62, the period during which the survey was taken. In 1964-65, enrolment was 164,441 for undergraduates and 13,797 for graduates.

Here are some of the highlights from the survey:

GENERAL CHARACTERISTICS OF CANADIAN UNIVERSITY STUDENTS, 1961-62

	Under-graduate students (%)	Graduate students (%)
Residence and marital status		
Single living in:		
Parent's home	44.8	25.1
Rented house or apartment	9.6	19.7
Private home, boarding house	17.1	11.8
College residence	20.1	6.6
Married, living with spouse	7.6	34.3
All other	0.8	2.5
Total	100.0	100.0
Wife's activities		
Working full-time	43.5	40.5
At university full-time	7.3	4.8
Working and attending university	0.5	2.8
Keeping house	39.3	45.1
Other	9.4	6.8
Total	100.0	100.0

(Source: DBS, *University Student Expenditure and Income in Canada*, catalogue nos. 81-519 to 81-521.)

The above tables show that:

• Over a third of the graduates and about one-twelfth of the undergraduates are married. In over 40% of the cases the wives work full-time to provide monetary assistance to the husbands for completion of their studies.

• Among the single students, nearly half of the undergraduates and about 25% of the graduates live in their parents' home.

When it comes to socio-economic grouping, the campus reflects its middle and upper class make-up. While it is a basic credo that education should be available to all who want or deserve it, today's college students as a rule are from better-

SOCIO-ECONOMIC CHARACTERISTICS OF PARENTS OF
CANADIAN UNIVERSITY STUDENTS, 1961–62

	Under-graduate (%)	Graduate (%)	Canadian average (%)
Parent's income level			
Below $3,000	14.0	23.3	36.5
$3,000–$4,999	24.6	25.4	41.7
$5,000–$5,999	14.1	11.0	9.4
$6,000–$7,999	16.0	13.7	7.1
$8,000–$9,999	10.5	8.6	2.3
$10,000–$14,999	11.4	9.6	1.8
$15,000 and over	9.4	8.4	1.2
Total	100.0	100.0	100.0
Median income	$5,901	$5,103	$3,646
Father's education			
University degree	18.9	22.9	4.9
Some university	7.9	6.7	4.3
High school graduation	18.3	17.6	15.3
Some high school	22.7	18.0	31.1
Elementary school	32.2	34.8	44.4
Total	100.0	100.0	100.0
Father's occupation			
White collar			
Owners and managers	24.1	26.4	9.9
Professional	18.6	18.7	7.6
Commercial and financial	7.3	6.5	5.6
Clerical	5.2	6.9	6.9
Blue collar			
Manufacturing and mechanical	11.1	10.9	22.0
Construction	4.7	3.7	6.3
Laborers	2.0	1.7	9.6
Other			
Transportation and communication	5.6	4.5	8.0
Service and recreation	5.3	4.8	8.5
Farmers	9.9	10.2	8.2
Other primary	3.2	1.7	3.8
All other and not stated	3.0	4.0	3.6
Total	100.0	100.0	100.0

(Source: DBS, *University Student Expenditure and Income in Canada*, catalogue nos. 81-519 to 81-521.)

income homes. Canadian income tax statistics show that 36.5% of all taxpayers earn less than $3,000 a year. Families in this income bracket send a disproportionately small number of children to university. In the categories from $5,000 up, the percentage of young people going to college is above the Canadian average, and as income increases, the chances of entering university are improved. For example, 3% of taxpayers earned $10,000 or more, but 21% of undergraduates and 18% of the graduates were from this group.

A high degree of correlation also exists between college enrolment and father's educational attainment. This is to be expected. Well-educated parents are in a better position than others to realize the value of university training for their children. Less than 5% of the males in the labor force have completed college, while 19% of the undergraduates and 23% of the graduates have fathers with university degrees.

Regarding parents' occupations, college students are from the upper echelons of the white collar community, their fathers being managers, owners, or in learned professions. (The DBS survey also reveals the extent to which children follow the father's occupation. Education students reported 5% of the fathers in education; law students, 9% of the fathers in the legal profession; medical students, 11% of the fathers as physicians and surgeons; pharmacy students, 7% of the fathers as pharmacists; dentistry students, 4% of fathers as dentists; and engineering students, 4.5% of fathers as engineers.)

Though there is a distinct class orientation, it would not be fair to conclude that the campus constitutes an exclusive club. Nearly a quarter of the graduates come from families earning below $3,000 a year. A third of the students had fathers with no more than elementary-school training. The Alger Hiss story has not as yet lost its glamor, and the North American ideal of bettering oneself through hard work and good grades is still in operation.

ATTITUDE TOWARDS LIFE

The DBS survey is strictly quantitative. It does not delve into qualitative aspects, the way students think and behave, their beliefs, hopes and aspirations. Information on these points is very skimpy. Besides, more than any other adult group, this market defies tabulation. It has a distinctive characteristic all its own: the chameleon-like quality of youth. Slot them into one tidy pigeon-hole now, and they will probably squirm into another next year. Trying to pin a tag on some 200,000 collegians is an exercise very similar to that of the blind men in the fable attempting to describe an elephant. At best, one can analyze general statements made by experts who have studied life on the campus. These are, of course, subjective evaluations rather than quantified research findings. However, they can be valuable to a businessman who wants to understand and communicate successfully to college students.

Perhaps the most conspicuous feature which many sociologists have noted is the preoccupation of youth with the material aspects of their existence. The collegians seem to be primarily concerned with maintaining the *status quo* — a very comfortable one which makes them the sought-after darlings of business and industry. They know pretty specifically the kind of rich, full life they want for themselves and their families. To an astonishingly large extent, they look forward to well-paying prestige jobs and luxurious suburban homes equipped with all the paraphernalia of modern living — a stereophonic set, an outdoor barbecue, a recreation den, and a garage for two cars. Very few speak of a career in public service, or of a desire to pursue knowledge for its own sake, no matter what the cost. Money is the prime lure, and as most students pay their way through college, cold cash takes on added importance. The following remark by a McGill undergraduate is typical: "I can't wait to get my hands on a decent paycheck. My tastes run high — maybe too high — and I've had enough of grubby living."

Many students are convinced that the wrongs of the world will gradually right themselves with little or no direct intervention on their part. By and large, they do not expect to achieve fame, make an enduring contribution to society, pioneer new frontiers, or otherwise create ripples in the placid order of things. The key note is conservatism. Most observers have noted with surprise that the young people are stability-minded and security-oriented. They clamor for more protection and look to the government for solving many of their problems.

However, one cannot blame today's youth for their intense "privatism," their urge to get married quickly, their preoccupation with their own small world. The environment in which they live is not very favorable. When looking outside from their campus windows, they find little joy in what they see. The H-bomb and the intercontinental ballistic missile cast an ugly shadow across the land. Brinkmanship has been made into an adroit art. The danger is ever present that somewhere out in the vast reaches of the Pentagon or the Kremlin, some maniac may seize power and push the ultimate button that may wipe out all mankind.

Even for less serious things, the outlook is not bright. As one collegian remarks: "Society orbits around the mediocrity of men. If we are apathetic, it's in relation to society which is apathetic." Many believe that their fathers, by becoming "organization men," have sold their birthright for a mass of pottage. During the recent disturbances at Berkeley, California, picketers carried signs reading: "I am a human being; do not fold, bend or mutilate" — a protest against excessive dehumanization, the tendency to reduce everyone into a number on an IBM card. But most students realize that it is too late now to turn back the tide. Hence, the prevalent sense of frustration, a pervasive lack of enthusiasm, a craving for security, a reluctance to talk about the future except in material terms, an apparently studied effort to avoid controversy. Here is a generation that is troubled, worried, confused and alienated, and has tried to adjust itself by retiring to a shell of indifference and getting preoccupied with material things. Many consider this not only a logical but even a virtuous step. To quote one graduate: "The big world is too vast and complicated. Individual crusades aren't the answer. So you parcel out life into bits that you can handle. If everyone controls his own small piece of living, maybe the larger problems will solve themselves."

Lately, there are indications that the materialistic philosophy is slowly losing its hold even among the non-conformists. Students are beginning to champion certain causes, such as political equality (e.g., the Separatist movement in Québec) or social reform (e.g., the abolition of racial discrimination, the fight against poverty and hunger, the crusade for world peace). Their demonstrations, picket lines, parades, marches, and sit-downs bespeak an excitement and idealism that have been absent from the campus life for over a decade.

True, these agitators are still in a minority, but they cannot be dismissed as flippant adolescents looking for "kicks." They are intelligent and dedicated, hoping and planning to change the world. They can't be bought off, they can't even be intimidated by threats of imprisonment. They have developed a new and powerful democratic technique, non-violent direct action. This method is not only effective in redressing many wrongs; it also ennobles the spirit of the participator. It is, indeed, comforting to note that not every collegian has been completely swallowed up in the quicksand of materialism, self-indulgence, cynicism, and selfishness. A new flame may have been kindled that augurs well for future progress.

FUTURE UNIVERSITY ENROLMENT

All the experts agree that the college market will expand greatly in the future. Since Canada is striving to come gradually closer to the U.S. participation rates, university enrolment is bound to grow at an accelerating rate during the next decade. Here are the *minimum* estimates published in the Bladen Commission Report, based on the projections prepared by Dr. E. F. Sheffield.

PROJECTED UNIVERSITY ENROLMENT FOR NEXT DECADE

Academic year	Male (000)	Female (000)	Total (000)
1966–67	164.8	64.3	229.1
1967–68	180.9	73.3	254.2
1968–69	199.7	83.9	283.6
1969–70	217.6	94.8	312.4
1970–71	234.1	106.3	340.4
1971–72	253.1	118.3	371.4
1972–73	265.5	130.5	396.0
1973–74	275.5	142.1	417.6
1974–75	286.7	152.8	439.5
1975–76	296.0	165.0	461.0

The breakdown of total enrolment by regions has been estimated as follows:

COMPARISON OF ACTUAL AND PROJECTED
UNIVERSITY ENROLMENT BY REGIONS

	Actual	Projected	
	1964–65 (000)	1970–71 (000)	1975–76 (000)
Atlantic Provinces	17.7	30.0	40.0
Québec	59.4	113.0	138.0
Ontario	50.8	105.0	155.0
Prairies	31.7	62.2	88.0
British Columbia	18.6	30.2	40.0
Canada	178.2	340.4	461.0

Another important enrolment breakdown is by undergraduates and graduates. The need to augment the number of students in graduate schools is very urgent, particularly because of the very large number of well-trained personnel required to staff universities and colleges and to fill research positions in government and business. Also, Canada is getting increasingly conscious of the difficulty, not to say propriety, of relying on other countries to provide advanced training.

After analyzing the recent trend in the ratio between undergraduate and graduate enrolment, the Bladen Commission has arrived at the following estimates:

COMPARISON OF UNDERGRADUATE AND GRADUATE
UNIVERSITY ENROLMENT

	Actual	Projected	
	1964–65 (000)	1970–71 (000)	1975–76 (000)
Undergraduate	164.4	309.9	406.0
Graduate	13.8	30.5	55.0
Total	178.2	340.4	461.0

The Bladen Commission has not considered it worth while at this juncture to estimate separately the enrolment in new types of proposed post-secondary institutions, such as junior colleges, community colleges and the institutes recommended by the Parent Commission in Québec. In so far as these students are of university level and are following courses of a university type, they have been included in the projections.

In view of this student explosion, the universities will be hard strained for funds. Both their operating and capital expenditures will expand by leaps and bounds, as can be seen from the following projections made by the Bladen Commission.

PROJECTED EXPENDITURES OF UNIVERSITY STUDENTS

Academic year	Operating expenditures (million)	Capital expenditures (million)	Total expenditures (million)
1964–65	$ 337	$200	$ 537
1965–66	407	247	654
1966–67	492	263	755
1967–68	579	289	868
1968–69	685	325	1,010
1969–70	799	342	1,141
1970–71	924	390	1,314
1971–72	1,068	338	1,406
1972–73	1,207	315	1,522
1973–74	1,350	334	1,684
1974–75	1,506	338	1,844
1975–76	1,675	357	2,032

BIBLIOGRAPHY

Association of Universities and Colleges of Canada: *Financing Higher Education in Canada* (The Bladen Commission Report), University of Toronto Press, Toronto, 1965.

Borovoy, Alan A.: "With Concern for Young Idealists," *Saturday Night,* September, 1965.

Business Week: "War Babies with Diplomas," June 15, 1963.

Dominion Bureau of Statistics: *University Student Expenditure and Income in Canada, 1961-62.* Part II — Canadian Undergraduate Students. Part III — Canadian Graduate Students (catalog numbers 81-520 and 81-521 Occasional), Queen's Printer, Ottawa, August 1963 and March 1964.

Friedan, Betty: *The Feminine Mystique,* W. M. Norton and Company, Inc., New York, 1963.

Gilbert, Eugene: *Advertising and Marketing to Young People,* Printers' Ink Books, Pleasantville, New York, 1957.

Kent, Shirley: "How to Reach the College Market," *Printers' Ink,* May 17, 1963.

McReynolds, David: "The Majority Generation," *Saturday Night,* September, 1965.

Sales Management: "The Mercurial Consumer," December 6, 1963.

Taylor, Thayer C.: "Now It's Campus Explosion," *Sales Management,* May 21, 1965.

THE YOUNG NEWLYWED MARKET

The bumper baby boom crop of the early Forties is getting ripe for the harvest. The first wave of those born during the war has already made it to the altar. The real surge will come in the near future when the effects of the high birth rates in the immediate postwar years begin to be felt. But any businessman with his eye on the market to come, can forearm himself by seeing how today's young newlyweds live and spend.

In several respects, these young adults bear a unique stamp. First, they are marrying at an earlier age. Over a third of the brides are now under 20. The DBS statistics show that from 1947 to 1963 the median age for marriages declined substantially — from 22.4 to 21.2 for brides and from 25.3 to 23.8 for bridegrooms. A generation ago over 10% of all weddings occurred after the woman was past 30; now merely 5% wait that long. Young girls, often in their teens, yearn for what they believe is the easy, secure life of a married woman. They long for the element of success and prestige that marriage connotes under current social values. Their greatest fear is to become "old maids."

Financially, too, things are not the same as when the mother was a bride. The young adults are relatively well off. Their only acquaintance with depressions, want, breadlines, and soup kitchens is stories told by parents or read in books. They have always known prosperity and wear their affluence as part of their daily apparel.

Furthermore, they are extremely mobile. Physically, they do not mind packing up their belongings and changing their residence at a short notice to take advantage of opportunities that open up at the other end of the country. Economically, they are on the move as well. They are optimistic about making more money and do not hesitate to go into debt to enjoy right away the material benefits of life. Psychologically, they are moving, too, as they evolve from frivolous teen-agers to serious home makers.

WEDDING BELLS

All this spells bonanza for businessmen. In fact, the rich vein of this orebody flows from the very start — right from the time of the wedding. The two little words "I do" are perhaps the most expensive in the English language. When a lad and lass prepare to marry, cash outlays shoot up at a dazzling rate. The bride and the groom spend, their parents spend, and their well-wishers spend. No wonder the bridal market is one of the most sought-after in the country. Once the engagement has been announced, brides-to-be are usually inundated by direct-mail advertising. One girl typically received enough solicitations from photographers, dress shops, travel agents, florists, limousine rental services, and furniture stores to fill a weekend suitcase.

Exactly how much expenditure an average marriage generates is hard to pin down because of the regional, economic and ethnic differences. By most estimates, weddings generally range in cost from $400 in rural areas to $3,400 in wealthy suburbs of metropolitan cities. The national average is about $1,500. That's just to get the bride and groom out of the church to their honeymoon, and does not include costs of setting up a household.

Many objections have been voiced by clergymen and sociologists against large expensive weddings. But these have fallen mostly on deaf ears. An elaborate ceremony for her daughter is often the dream of a mother who was a World War II bride and had only an army-base chapel as a memory. Her daughter's grand wedding almost becomes her wedding again. As a result, more and more money is being poured into the coffers of the bridal marketers.

Most large department stores have consultants or counselors to assist the bride in planning for the big occasion. The services provided include trousseau, travel bureau, catering, and gift registry (where the bride lists her gift preferences from the merchandise carried by the store, so that her friends and relatives know what to choose without any duplication).

June is popularly regarded as the best month for bridal marketers. The custom goes back to Roman mythology and the goddess Juno, the protectress of marriages. However, there are enough weddings in other months to keep the businessmen happy, as shown in the following data for 1965.

January	5.5%
February	4.4
March	4.9
April	4.9
May	7.2
June	9.2
July	11.9
August	12.4
September	12.7
October	11.4
November	8.8
December	6.7
Total	100.0%
Total marriages	145,567

SETTING UP A HOME

While engagement announcements and wedding bells bring cheer into the hearts of jewelers, dressmakers and owners of holiday resorts, the crucial thing is what happens when the honeymoon is over and the lovers settle down to transform an empty cubicle into a gadget-bedecked home. Here the market reveals certain characteristics, indicating a transition from the adolescent to the fully adult stature.

Despite the advantages of an equity in a house, lack of capital and uncertainty about the future dictate a strong preference for apartments to start with. Nevertheless, the newlyweds tend to stretch their purses when looking for a place to live. According to finance companies, they do not hesitate to spend up to 40% of their income for a luxurious apartment, with wall-to-wall carpeting.

Major appliances generally rate pretty far down the list. Apartments usually provide the basics, anyway. The heavy pressures for washing machines and dishwashers come a few years later, when the children arrive. If they do have to buy a refrigerator, the newlyweds are likely to shop for a reconditioned one. The situation, however, is completely different for small household appliances — blenders, irons, vacuum cleaners, radios, television sets, and the like. They are purchased as soon as possible, in most cases on credit. Though quality is not overlooked, price looms fairly high in the buying decision. Remarks one salesman in a department store: "We can talk of style and other plus factors till we're blue in the face. The vital question is 'How much?' " This is not surprising, because the income of the family at this stage is relatively meager.

As regards home furnishing, there are two schools of thought. Some newlyweds play for keeps and buy the best. They feel that if they wait, they will get stuck with junk. In the case of others, mobility outweighs pride of possession. They purchase modestly because sooner or later they expect to discard the lot. When they get their house, they hope to trade up.

In view of the heavy expenditures on durable goods, food and clothing take a smaller than average slice of the budget. The newlyweds do not skimp on food, but they consume more inexpensive items. Also, since the courting is over, eating out shifts from glamor spots to ordinary restaurants. Beer replaces costlier potations. If they splurge on a party, they try to make up by paring on the weekly food bill.

Clothing may be no problem at the start, thanks to the trousseau. But a young man on the way up the ladder must look right. His wife wants to reflect credit on her husband. They, therefore, tend to buy the best at the cheapest price available. This means watching for sales, or purchasing less often.

Once settled in the new abode, saving a bit of the weekly paycheck ranks almost as high as spending. Practically every young couple has a dream object up its sleeve: a house, a big new car, a beautiful piece of furniture, or a trip to Europe before the baby arrives. Here the working wife gives a big assist; they bank her paycheck, try to live on his.

MARKETING APPROACHES

The basic characteristic of a modern young wife is her lack of experience in managing the household. Contrary to the earlier generations, adolescent girls today are almost detached from the family hearth, and do not depend on their parents for education into the ways of life. As a result, a bride does not automatically enter the role of housewife with a full store of know-how. She has not been in the kitchen long enough to acquire the routine skills which her mother in her own youth considered essential to womanhood. Her confusion is further compounded by the new types of goods and services that constantly appear on the market. Supermarket shelves are filled with all kinds of soaps and detergents. How can she find out which one is the best? If she wants to buy a small appliance, she is offered a wide variety of brands and models. Which one should she select?

Advertising can and does give her a lot of information. It introduces her to new products, points out differences, and acquaints her with the characteristics of a particular brand. However, many advertisements fail to include all the relevant facts. For example, a new type of coffee table may be beautifully shown and glowingly described, without mention being made of its being stain-proof. Possibly it is, but if the manufacturer does not let this be known, perhaps no one else will, and sales may be lost. Readership surveys show that women find the time to read extensive advertising copy if it is helpful — copy that stresses specifics, not unbelievable superlatives; copy that gives them a "how-to" approach, not far-fetched adjectives.

When making their purchases, the young couples display a liking for the new, a desire to try anything that offers betterment. They are constantly looking for a change and are anxious to develop their own style of life, without being bound by the consumption patterns followed in their parents' homes. However, side by side with the yearning for difference is a drive toward conformity. The young consumers are ever ready to move on to greener pastures; yet eccentricity and unusual behavior are frowned upon and discouraged. This means that the newness of the product should be kept within the bounds of convention. Too wide a departure from the accepted pattern will not be generally acceptable.

Also, while the newlywed couples are very receptive to new concepts, they also sometimes reveal a tendency to get nostalgic over the past. This can be clearly seen in eating habits. A young housewife is susceptible to the idea of new foods, new dietary practices, new ways of cooking. Yet, she has an occasional suppressed hankering for some of the meals she was fond of in childhood. Food tastes developed in youth are extremely difficult to change. This suggests that a promotion developed round the theme "like mother used to make," if properly presented, would probably catch on. In other words, a manufacturer can be successful by going into opposite directions at the same time — the new and experimental, the old and traditional.

BIBLIOGRAPHY

Business Week: "Many hands slice the wedding cake," June 2, 1962.

Business Week: "Newlyweds — a market unto themselves," November 2, 1963.

Gilbert, Eugene: *Advertising and Marketing to Young People,* Printers' Ink Books, Pleasantville, New York, 1957.

Levitt, Theodore: *Innovation in Marketing,* McGraw-Hill Book Company, Inc., New York, 1962.

Wolff, Janet: "New Directions in Marketing: Answering Woman's Hunger for Information," *Sales Management,* November 10, 1959.

The Old Age Market (over 65)

The aged and aging are much in the news today. Not too long ago it used to be sarcastically and intemperately remarked that the only persons interested in the over-65's were the morticians. Today, society is taking a more tolerant and humane attitude. Free medical care and hospitalization are provided to those in need, and old age pensions are given as a matter of right at the age of 70, and will soon be available at 65. Experts are writing learned treatises on gerontology. In Ontario, the provincial government has gone so far as to appoint a Select Committee on the Aging, with fairly broad terms of reference: to inquire into the problems inherent in the field of geriatrics; to examine all government and non-government programs and policies affecting the senior citizens; and to determine what facilities are needed to aid old persons to fulfill a satisfying role in society.

The influence of the aged is being felt not only in the halls of the legislative assemblies but in the marts of trade as well. The reason is simple: the old age market has more than doubled in the course of a generation. In 1931, persons over 65 numbered 576,000; in 1965 the figure was up to 1,494,600 and is gradually growing. The chemistry of aging has been slowed and the life span expanded, thanks to improved public health services, higher nutritional standards, more sanitary working conditions, and reduction of debilitating physical labor.

Thus, the over-65's represent a sizable and an influential market. Yet both manufacturers and retailers have been slow to recognize its potentialities and to promote directly to it. Their hesitancy is to a great extent due to the lack of purchasing power among the senior citizens. After 65, the diamond-shaped income pattern of the working population, with the broadest segment in the middle income, changes to a triangle with the largest number in the low-income groups clustered at the base.

No doubt, the bulk of elderly people are hard pinched for cash, but it would be a mistake to write them off as sales potentials. As many businessmen are slowly beginning to realize, income is not a very reliable yardstick to judge the market. A rising executive, with $10,000 a year, five children, and a double mortgage on his home has little discretionary spending power. By contrast, a retired person has very few obligations. The children no longer have to be educated, clothed and supported; work-related expenses are curtailed; the home is generally free from mortgage; most of the furniture and appliances have already been acquired. The income may be low, but it is steady and stable, originating from one or many sources, such as employee retirement programs, dividends, life insurance policies, veterans' allowances, and government old-age pensions. In addition, grandparents are frequent recipients of gifts from their offspring and other relatives. A relatively high level of assets also helps somewhat to alleviate the economic situation. In a survey conducted a few years ago by the DBS, it was found that while the average liquid-asset holdings of families in all age-groups were only $1,688, those of families over 65 were as high as $4,509, most of them consisting of readily convertible securities.

PATTERN OF EXPENDITURE

Of course, older folks buy most of the things that younger people do, but they have special needs and desires which provide profitable opportunities to certain types of businessmen. Here are a few examples:

MEDICAL AND PERSONAL CARE

As may be expected, the elderly constitute a steady market for health items, like vitamin pills, drugs, ointments, ophthalmic goods, hearing aids, and geriatric foods. They spend less on general toiletries and cosmetics, but they are good prospects for specialized products such as medicinal or mild soaps, ache-ameliorating preparations, and a variety of aids to foot comfort. Older women like to hide the ravages of time, and some manufacturers have done well by promoting therapeutic creams designed to ward off aging of the skin.

RECREATION

Senior citizens have plenty of time on their hands, and due to improving health standards, they have still enough energy to indulge in varied kinds of physical and mental activities. Hence, the field is wide open for a whole gamut of products and services catering to the leisure market — garden implements, games, books, periodicals, home-decorating materials, do-it-yourself kits, and the like. Hobbies become the center of retired persons' lives. Some turn to the visual arts, others to music, while others still take up crafts — weaving, pottery, dress designing, wood-working, furniture making, and diverse other activities. Traveling is also a popular pastime. Many travel agencies report doing brisk business with the over-65's. The preference is for conducted tours with people in the same age group. Cruises — long, leisurely and relaxing — have a particularly strong appeal.

CLOTHING

Because of his varied recreational activities, an elderly male looks for durable, casual, and comfortable trousers, shirts, jackets, and sweaters. He is not as conventional as generally expected. He likes his flashy socks and is addicted to gaudy shirts and sportswear. He had to dress conservatively when working; upon retirement, he cuts loose. The elderly woman, too, puts comfort ahead of fashion. She goes for "soft, full" lines, flattering lace, and long sleeves. She demands certain propriety of style; she does not want her grandchildren snickering at her. Some research into old people's requirements is in order. Many of them are baffled and frustrated by so-called standard sizes, lengths and girths. They also have frequent foot problems, but few manufacturers of footwear have seriously taken this into consideration.

HOUSING

Many old couples have mortgage-free houses, but since the cost of up-keep is high, often they prefer to sell them and move to small homes or apartments. Builders providing such accommodation can find rich diggings in this field. Of course, for low income groups, public housing or church or union projects generally seem to be the only answer. But there are enough well-to-do senior citizens to provide lucrative business to private builders. However, the dwellings must be tailored to meet the special needs and desires of this market. The most important requisites are safety and convenience features: non-skid flooring in bathrooms and kitchens; grab-rails in the bathtub and shower to facilitate getting in and out; elimination of thresholds to lessen the danger of tripping; wall-to-wall carpeting in living rooms and bedrooms for safety and added warmth; bright but diffused general lighting to soothe the aging eyes; low kitchen counters for sit-down meal preparation; built-in cabinets and shelves that are easy to reach without undue stooping or stretching. Other welcome features are maid and nurse services shared with other occupants. Restaurant-type facilities can be an enticement as well.

The debate is still going on as to whether it is wise to isolate the elderly from other groups. Many senior citizens do not like to be segregated, and sociologists, too, are warning about the dangers of developing ghettos of the aged. But experience has shown that elaborate projects providing some sort of meal service, health care and the like, can only operate efficiently and economically if the old people are grouped together. However, such developments must be close to established communities and recreation centers, with public transportation readily available. Locations too far off the beaten track are seldom looked upon with favor.

PSYCHOLOGICAL FACTORS

The over-65 age group thus offers numerous marketing opportunities. How can a businessman enter this market and carve out a profitable segment for himself? Success to a great extent will depend on learning more about the interests, the problems, and the psychology of the oldsters.

A wide gulf exists between the outlook of the new generation and the old. Young people are adventurous and confident of what the future will bring in the form of expanding opportunities and purchasing power. Old people tend to be more conservative, more fearful of the oncoming years and less hospitable to new ideas, new commodities, new services, new ways of doing things. They are not anxious to engage in action for action's sake, to tolerate change and possible ensuing inconvenience just for the fun of experiencing new sensations. Failing sinews and creaking joints contribute to physical inertia which all too often obstructs the mental processes as well. Health, with its accompanying sense of abundant physical well-being, ceases to be an unrecognized blessing taken for granted, and becomes instead a goal earnestly and persistently sought, although never quite achieved.

Then there is the feeling of loneliness, a painful consciousness of being no longer wanted. In a society that tends to judge a man by what he does, the retired person suffers a special stress. Nobody ever suddenly becomes Negro or Jew, but people do suddenly stop working. They become a minority almost overnight, and it hits them hard. Retirement for an individual does not mean just a loss of income; it leads to a whole series of changes — in his position in the society, in community activities, and in professional organizations. Particularly disturbing is the loss of the "identification tag"; someone accustomed to thinking of himself as a foreman or a sales manager is often seriously disoriented when he finds that he is no longer anything at all.

What makes the loneliness still worse is that few elderly couples any longer reside with their children. The extended family unit of the past, with three generations living under one roof, has been increasingly replaced by the nuclear family of husband, wife and unmarried children. In contemporary culture, the newly-married firmly believe that they have an inherent right to lead their own lives, unencumbered by any ties to the older generation. The parents are quietly shunted off, the few visits being confined to feast days and anniversaries.

As a result, old folks often find themselves cut off from the mainstream of life and begin to sense that they have no longer any meaningful and satisfying role to play. Often they move into a back-street boardinghouse or walk-up flat, clinging to the places they have known, while the winters grow colder and the friends fewer. They feel increasingly isolated and rejected, seeing their doctor more and more often, penny-pinching their fixed income against the upward-creeping cost of living, and trying to keep something by against the high cost of dying. The alleged "golden years" turn out to be a badly tarnished imitation, a period of frustration and loneliness rather than of happiness and fulfilment.

Of course, it would not be correct to paint this gloomy picture for all old people. Several surveys have shown that many of the elderly have led fairly productive lives, looked after the grandchildren so that their daughter or daughter-in-law can accept a full-time job, and in general taken the initiative to be helpful all around and to seek a new "modus vivendi." However, for many aging people in Canada today, the psychological problems are quite serious, even though they may be financially well off.

SALES APPROACHES

In view of all these factors, experts have consistently warned the businessmen to tread the ground gently when selling to this market. There are many traps for those who try to be patronizing, or use the jocular, the sentimental, or the fake-respectful approach. The older a person grows, the more he wants to be treated like anybody else. He hates being put on the shelf, and any merchandiser who takes him off it is apt to find a ready welcome. In fact retailers point out that the quickest way to make sure that the sale would flop would be to label: "This dress is for ladies 65 and over." Old people are sensitive about their age and resent being categorized. Manufacturers report the same experience. One advertising campaign for geriatric salt-free foods was a failure because of the blatant hard-sell, with emphasis on age and infirmity. As a result, companies now take a more tangential approach. They emphasize quality, comfort, convenience, and other desirable features and downgrade the stereotype illustration of the silver-haired couple growing old gracefully.

Here are some factors which can help to strike the right chord when selling to senior citizens.

• Appeals to good health. (The threat of steady physical and mental deterioration hangs like the sword of Damocles over their heads.)

• Methods of retaining physical attractiveness and camouflaging tell-tale signs of age. (The urge to look beautiful never dies in the female heart.)

• Promises of economic security, ways of making small incomes go further, plans for remaining financially independent. (Dependence on children for monetary aid is often a bitter pill to swallow.)

• Sales stories which suggest leisure-time interests and offer to fill the void with worthwhile activities. (There is no unhappier person than one who having led an active and productive life suddenly finds himself on the outside of affairs, a lonesome drone in the human hive.)

FUTURE PROSPECTS

In future years, the senior market will warrant an even closer attention. Health-education campaigns, safety programs, regular medical examinations, control of obesity, and early treatment of degenerative conditions will lower still further the mortality rates among the elderly. According to an estimate prepared by the Economic Council of Canada, persons 65 years of age and over will increase from 1,494,600 in 1965 to 1,637,000 in 1970, a rise of 9.5%. Thus, by the end of the decade the old age market will consist of more customers than the current combined population of the three Maritime Provinces.

Sheer numerical size will not be the only positive factor. Most probably, the market will have higher discretionary income because of the cumulative effects of several forces all operating at the same time.

Thanks to the prosperity of the last two decades, many persons will be retiring in the next few years with a healthy nest egg. They will have succeeded in building up a sufficiently large bank balance or investment portfolio to help them pass the remaining years of their lives in reasonable comfort.

The greatest increase in wealth, however, will come from the private pension plans. The trend is toward more extensive coverage and larger benefits. In 1964, 1,337,000 persons were covered by 2,119 trusteed pension plans, whose assets were worth $5,820 million and were growing at the rate of $640 million a year.* By 1970, the majority of Canadian employees will be sheltered under a broad

* DBS: Daily Bulletin, December 16, 1965.

financial umbrella. Thus, when they step over the threshold into the new world of retirement, they will not be so short of spendable funds as they are now.

Also, the trend is toward greater public assistance to the aged, as can be seen in the recent liberalization of the government pension plan. In future, as this group gains numerical strength to make its voice heard in the legislative chambers, it will become vociferous in its demands for more aid from the treasury.

The number one issue is medicare. The elderly fear contracting a long and expensive illness that would throw them at the mercy of their families or force them into the charity wards. They do not dare to spend their money freely, feeling compelled to scrape and save every penny against the day they may fall ill. It is this fear that has made medicare, in one form or another, an urgent social need and a political issue. Legislation to that effect has already been passed in the United States, and most probably it will be introduced in Canada also in the not too distant future. Thus, with the threat of crippling doctor and hospital bills out of the way, many oldsters will be able to enjoy their remaining years fruitfully, if modestly, on their retirement incomes.

EMPLOYMENT

Regarding employment of persons over 65, the outlook is uncertain. The trend during the last few years has been towards early retirement. For over a decade, the over-all jobless rate in the country has been well above the full-employment level of 3%. Consequently, the unions have found it difficult to encourage the retention of older workers when good openings are not readily available for young men about to start raising families. Also, many elderly laborers themselves are not deeply attached to their jobs and, provided they are assured of an adequate pension, look forward to the day when they can retire. Indeed, the fact that their working wives are also eligible for full pension and other benefits has prompted many males to leave the labor force even before 65. In view of all these factors, the Economic Council of Canada has estimated that in 1970 the participation rate of males over 64 in the labor force will be 25.1%, compared to 26.3% in 1965.

However, one should not overlook the other side of the story. For many men and women, work is not only a source of income, but also a means of personality enhancement without which they fear loss of prestige, social participation, and above all, sense of worth. If allowed to, they would willingly defer their retirement. Mandatory retirement policies in industry are unfair because they let chronological age determine whether an individual is to be "forced to the sidelines." Also, from an economic point of view, there is a danger that unless many old people are permitted to contribute to their own support through work, the maintenance of the aged can become such a crushing burden on the society and state as to force down the general standard of living.

One may, no doubt, cite many administrative advantages of a uniform retirement age. But counterbalancing them is the important factor that the outlay on pensions is delayed for each year the employee defers his retirement. The employer also gains from being able to retain the services of good workers. Numerous studies have shown that old persons have many points in their favor; for example:

- They have a definite desire to work.
- They have the stability that comes with maturity.
- They do not waste time on their assignments.
- They have a sense of responsibility and are loyal to their job and their employer.
- They generally have steadier work habits.
- They usually require less supervision.
- They are less distracted by outside influences, and consequently capable of greater concentration.

The way the industrial society is presently constituted, it is not easy to secure increased participation of the aged in the labor force. Nevertheless, all efforts to maintain the continued employment (or to secure re-employment) of those who are able and willing to work should be encouraged and effectively supported. The country today is faced with the paradox of increasing life expectancy and decreasing work expectancy. Of course, there is an ultimate peak in every man's capabilities. But, unfortunately, in the contemporary society the tendency is to put that peak too early in life and to assume that the descent from it is more rapid than it actually is.

BIBLIOGRAPHY

Business Week: "14-Million Americans Over 65: a Neglected Market," February 4, 1956.
Business Week: "How the Old Age Market Looks," February 13, 1960.
Department of Labor, Economics and Research Branch: *The Aging Worker in the Canadian Economy,* Queen's Printer, Ottawa, 1959.
Dun's Review and Modern Industry: "Old Folks: An Overlooked Market," April, 1964.
Ellis, W. H.: "Facts You Can Use to Reach the Senior Citizen Market," *Canadian Business,* July, 1961.
Gridlow, E.: "The Senior Market," *Sales Management,* October, 1961.
Laskin, Richard (editor): *Social Problems: A Canadian Profile,* Section 36, H. G. Page's "Our Older Population," McGraw-Hill Company of Canada Limited, Toronto, 1964.
Reed, Vergil D. and Ruth R. Reed: "What Our Aging Population Means to Marketing," *Advertising Agency,* March and April, 1952.
Spurgeon, David: "Age in a Youth-Oriented Society," *Globe and Mail Magazine,* January 4, 1964.
Unemployment Insurance Commission: *How Old is Old?,* Queen's Printer, Ottawa, 1959.
United States Senate: Committee on Labor and Public Welfare: *The Aged and Aging in the United States: A National Problem,* United States Government Printing Office, Washington, 1960.
Wolff, Janet: *What Makes Women Buy,* McGraw-Hill Book Company, Inc., New York, 1958.

Chapter 10

MOSAIC BY SOCIO-ECONOMIC CLASSES

Class Structure in Canada

Since Karl Marx first used the term, the word "class" has acquired unpleasant connotations. It brings to mind undesirable innuendoes of bloody revolutions, proletarian struggles, and historical destinies. North American philosophy has strongly supported the notion that this continent is a unique place where any person, despite his humble origin, can rise to the top. According to this theory, there is no hereditary aristocracy, no legal discrimination in education, no obvious barriers to the selection of an occupation. Perhaps one may find a thin lower layer of underprivileged poor — no doubt on the way up, and a narrow upper crust of overprivileged rich — probably on the way down. The vast majority, however, are believed to belong to one huge group, so broad that it can hardly be called a class at all.

Lately, a number of eminent social scientists have been taking a closer look at this question and are convinced that Canada definitely has a class structure. Admittedly, it is not like the Indian caste system which brands the individual's place in the community from his very birth. Ours is an "open" society with a high degree of fluidity. But the fact that the various strata are not clearly defined does not mean that class distinctions do not exist. Like Molière's M. Jourdain who had been using prose all his life without knowing it, Canadians live within a class structure even though they may not be consciously aware of it.

Class affects many aspects of life. It creates a social mold so inclusive that an individual is seldom free from it. The disciplinary pressures of approval and disapproval, of belonging and ostracism, make most members of the same class similar in motives, attitudes, and purchasing behavior. So great is this pressure towards conformity that it can influence the type of neighborhood a person lives in, the nature of his employment, the selection of his friends, the value he puts on university education for his children, and even such details as whether he plays bridge or bingo, drinks espresso or instant coffee.

Social Research Inc. reports a not atypical history of a man who in his lifetime passed through an interesting series of changes in food habits. He came from a very poor Italian immigrant family, and as a lad he was raised on minestrone, pizza, spaghetti, and red wine. After completing high school, he began working in logging camps where, anxious to be accepted, he soon learned to have beef, beer, and beans. Later, he joined a big corporation and went up quickly on the management ladder. In his new executive role, he found himself cultivating the favorite foods and drinks of other executives: steak, lobster, and whiskey. Ultimately, he gained acceptance in the city's upper class. Whereupon he began winning admiration from individuals in his elite social set by going back to his Italian knowledge of cooking, and serving them (with the aid of a butler) authentic Italian treats, such as minestrone, pizza, spaghetti, and red wine!

Many businessmen believe that the steady rise in discretionary spending power is making everybody equal. But class has several faces, and income is just one of them. True, with the general diffusion of wealth and the widespread use of credit, such one-time upper-class symbols as limousines and mink coats are available to a variety of people. But a rich man is not simply a poor man with more money; nor is a poor man, given the same income, likely to behave like a rich man. Though clerical and production workers may earn the same amount, the two have different ideals, different personality drives, different standards of conduct, different reactions to advertising and sales appeals.

Even in their fantasies, they are governed by class membership. In one survey, a sample of housewives were asked what they would like to be turned into if a magician were to change them into something other than a human being. The most common type of response from the working-class woman was along these lines:

- A French poodle — it's well fed, brushed, and people pet it.
- The bed my children lie on so that I could still be close to them.
- A house so I could watch people's lives.

By contrast, typical replies from middle-class women were:

- A bird, for it can fly wherever it wants and see the world.
- A cloud because it is so light and frothy and free.
- A cow so that I could just lie around and eat grass.
- A flower that blooms for years.

Middle-class women often think only of themselves in fantasies. Working-class women indicate a desire to continue to be with people, to nurture them, and to be nurtured by them. They do not want "to get away from it all."

Each individual is so absorbed in the ideology and culture of his background, that it seldom dawns on him that somebody else may have a different system of standards. Hence it is only normal for a businessman to assume that he can make judgments about the best appeals and methods to reach working-class families in the light of his own outlook on the world. But even a superficial probing on the surface will reveal that all classes are not alike. There are sharp differences in attitudes and motive forces, in sophistication and moral viewpoints. The symbols that upper-class executives use in promoting their products are sometimes completely meaningless to those who will form the market for their goods.

Consequently, when formulating marketing strategies, the class system has to be carefully considered. Before a businessman can predict behavior or try to influence it through counselling, education, promotion, or advertising, he must have a clear understanding of what the class order is, how it works, and what it does to the lives and personalities of those who are in it.

MAJOR SOCIO-ECONOMIC CLASSES

As a rule, most writers on the subject divide the social classes into six categories. For marketing purposes, they can be grouped as follows:

Affluent market: upper-upper; lower-upper; upper-middle.

Mass market: lower-middle; upper-lower.

Depressed market: lower-lower.

This grouping is essentially a matter of convenience. No social scientist claims that everyone falls neatly and squarely into one of these six classes. It is more accurate to view the population as being arranged along a vertical axis with any number of arbitrary cutting points. But while there is a continuum, people do tend to cluster together, creating a series of bulges and contractions. The major bulges are what sociologists call the class groupings.

Another way to picture the situation is to imagine a host of people strung along a mountainside. At several points, the trail becomes so narrow that only a few people can pass at a time. Between these difficult passages are broad, gentle inclines, where large numbers of people can spread out. Some always like to go on climbing higher. A few find the air at the top too rarefied and are forced to retreat to lower bases. A large proportion, however, show no inclination to move up or down, and pitch their tents at different levels convenient to them.

Below is a brief description of the six social classes. The generalizations are based on investigations conducted by numerous social scientists in universities and market research firms. Taken together, all these studies — requiring several hundred thousand manhours of work — represent a lode of fascinating and valuable information about how people really behave. Of course, not each and every person in the grouping would have all the characteristics here set forth. Still, the picture presented is reasonably typical for each class as a whole. The cast may change, the scenery may vary from town to town, but generally the plot and the outcome are as standard and predetermined as in an old-time melodrama.

UPPER-UPPER

This is the "social register" class, the Canadian equivalent of aristocracy. Its members display a minute interest in genealogies and take great pride in their distinguished ancestry. They try to be very exclusive and, as far as possible, keep their marriages within the clan. In rural communities, they are likely to be gentlemen farmers, with great estates, model farms, and a type of living patterned after the nobility of England.

In actual numbers, this class is insignificant, probably less than one-half of one per cent. Many towns and villages would hardly have a single aristocratic family. But, though small, these people have considerable influence and do a lot for the community. They have, through inheritance, heavy investments in land, industry, universities, and the like. They subsidize local theaters and orchestras, serve on the boards of charitable organizations, and contribute to various social enterprises.

The basic values of this class are to uphold the family reputation, to reflect the excellence of one's breeding, and to display a sense of community responsibility. The members try to create an impression that wealth has little bearing on their social pre-eminence. Rather, it is the gracious, leisurely way of life they have achieved as a result of their innate good taste and high breeding. Their reference group is the British upper class. Their clothing shows strong British influence, and British sports, such as sailing, polo, and riding, are their favorites.

As a rule, the upper-upper class families are oriented to the past, and tend to be highly ritualized in their behavior. They often live in big, old houses, sanctified by historic traditions. Dining arrangements, and even gatherings of the immediate family in the living room, are stylized. The child is trained to a code of behavior appropriate to his position as a member of the distinguished lineage.

Their consumption patterns do not reflect a desire for status symbols. Their position is so secure that their is no need to live ostentatiously. They tend to avoid mass-produced, mass-marketed goods, and spend their money on such items as paintings, sculptures, stamp collections, old maps, rare books, and the like. Also, they are not heavy purchasers of durable goods. Many of their belongings are inherited. It is rare indeed to find an upper-upper couple who cannot set up their first home completely from ancestral furniture and wedding presents.

LOWER-UPPER

This class includes people of great power and influence — the executive elite, the owners of large businesses, and the well-to-do lawyers, doctors, architects, and other high-prestige professionals. (Millionaire undertakers are not as a rule accepted.) Compared to upper-uppers, the members of this class usually have larger incomes, higher education, better housing, and more expensive automobiles and other durables. But their wealth is new, much to new, and this, coupled with their lack of family background, tends to exclude them from the social summit. They may pass the "means test," but they are not able to meet the "lineage test" of the established families.

The culture of the lower-uppers is heavily permeated by the North American dream of material abundance, to be achieved and maintained by unremitting struggle and constant sacrifice. Happiness appears to be a blend of material well-being, success in occupation, and high social position. A man is judged largely by the number and quality of things he owns. Status is validated in the acquisition and exhibition of material and non-material objects — house, cars, clothes, jewelry, gadgets, furniture, works of art, membership in exclusive clubs, enrollment of children in private schools.

There is a tendency among lower-uppers to emulate the upper-uppers. But since their rise has been far too recent, they have not had time to age to the proper mellowness for the aristocratic style of living. Consequently, they often lack the true grace, the right taste, and the correct social rituals. They do things too perfectly, too elaborately, and too much for effect. Hence, they are sometimes labelled the "nouveaux riches" or "parvenus."

UPPER-MIDDLE

The major difference between upper-middle and the lower-upper class is in the degree of "success" at career and the extent to which this has been translated into gracious living. Compared to the class above them, the upper-middles have less glamorous occupations, lower incomes, poorer education, and fewer opportunities to participate in prestige-giving activities. They comprise moderately successful professional men and women, owners of medium-sized businesses, and "organization men" at the managerial level. They are "solid" folk but not "society." In many small communities, where the two upper classes do not exist, this group may be at the top of the social hierarchy.

The upper-middles are very conscious of status symbols. These are the people who make their coffee in espresso machines, cook barbecue dinners in their backyards, specialize in buffet-style entertaining, play bridge and scrabble, and belong to golf clubs, yacht clubs, and college clubs. They appreciate good plays and music, and frequently attend the theater and concerts. They talk well and are quite at home on the platform. They realize the value of education and try to send their children to college.

The upper-middle-class wife, even of a junior executive, usually buys most of her clothes at specialty shops or in the exclusive department stores. She feels constrained to choose her wardrobe according to rather carefully prescribed standards of appropriateness. In furnishing her home, she thoughtfully considers whether a given piece or combination of pieces will serve as adequate testament to her aesthetic sensitivities. She pays careful attention to the best shelter magazines, the interior decorators in town, and the homes of other women around her, particularly the boss's wife.

In order to have enough money for the prestige extras, the upper-middles have developed many skills at economizing. The wife will make some of her children's clothes, upholster furniture, or refurbish antiques bought at auctions. The husband will paint or paper the walls, do carpentry work, and drive to the office in a model of car that shows several years' wear.

Both husband and wife are hyperactive civic boosters. He plays a major role in service clubs, and she initiates many local charity drives. Being avid social climbers, they hope that their good deeds will somehow be recognized far beyond the usual pat on the back, and that they will be invited to upper-class cliques and exclusive clubs. The fact that this rarely happens, seldom stops them from continuing to try.

MASS MARKET

The next two classes, lower-middle and upper-lower, constitute the mass market, or what sociologist William Lloyd Warner calls "the level of the Common Man." The "collar color" criterion is often used as a dividing line between the two. The upper-lower is the blue-collar class, where the breadwinner of the family earns his livelihood at some manual task and is paid by the hour or by piecework. The lower-middle is the white-collar class where employees work with their "heads" or through relationship with other people, like, for example, the salesman. They receive salaries and commissions which are regarded as socially superior to wages.

However, the recent upheaval of our economic system has resulted in a considerable blurring of the prestige line between white- and blue-collar workers. In hundreds of companies, there has been a sharp downgrading in the amount of skill and dignity associated with the average clerical job. The introduction of office machinery has been creating working conditions very similar to those in the plant. Many white-collar office workers — billing clerks, key-punch operators — are actually machine attendants, manual workers in any honest nomenclature. Even the layout of a large office is getting to look like a factory — with its straight-line flow of work, and each person doing a fragment of the complete operation. The tasks of some clerical people are so routinized, repetitive, and simple that employees are often chosen for their special capacity to endure boredom.

While the status of white-collar jobs has gone down, that of blue-collar occupations has steadily risen. Many blue-collar workers are now skilled, exercise a great deal of judgment, and are entrusted with the operation of some very sophisticated equipment. One modern oil refinery, for example, requires a high school education for production workers, and hires only foremen with engineering degrees. Some of these ex-proletarians live in new suburban communities where they are exposed to and espouse middle-class values. The wives, too, urge them to move up. Several hold secretarial jobs in offices where they come into contact with the middle-class style of life which they want to imitate. As a result, the color of the collar has lost some, though not all, of its significance as a class label.

LOWER-MIDDLE

This class, to use a military parallel, consists of the non-commissioned officers of our society. Included within its folds are the lower ranks of the white-collar world — non-managerial office staff, small business owners, salesmen, and the like — plus the higher ranks of the blue-collar world — senior foremen and other aristocrats of labor, anxious to be accepted in white-collar circles. In rural communities, lower-middles are those farmers who sell between $5,000 to $15,000 worth of products annually.

As a rule, the families in this class have sufficient income for the conveniences, if not the luxuries, of life. They live on the side streets of good neighborhoods, where they have rows of clean little bungalows, with neat lawns and gardens lovingly tended. If they cannot afford a rug, they have at least a linoleum covering on the living room floor. By careful allocation of funds, they manage to get, in time, most of the items associated with the North American standard of living — automobiles, electrical appliances, and annual two weeks' vacations.

The two key words in understanding their character are "striving" and "respectability." They are continually trying to succeed in their businesses or jobs, to save for a better future, to give their children the educational and other opportunities they themselves missed in childhood. They are active members of many associations and show great eagerness to get elected to an office or to serve on a committee. They hope by this involvement to curry favor with those above them and somehow accumulate a reserve of social goodness that might some day be cashed in for a more material status advance.

While striving to get ahead, they want at the same time to present to the world a solid front of respectability. They place great store in demonstrating that they are moral, cultured, and socially above the "working classes." Modesty, propriety, cleanliness, integrity, and strict adherence to moral codes are the values highly prized. Without this class, many church activities, such as study groups, missionary societies, and welfare organizations, would not be kept alive.

UPPER-LOWER

This is the ordinary "working class" of popular parlance. Most of the members are skilled and semi-skilled operatives who constitute the backbone of the industrial unions. Others are truck drivers, miners, small farmers, barbers, launderers, service station attendants, and the like. Usually their jobs do not require too much formal education. Their work is often boring, especially when it is of a repetitive nature, and they live for the pleasures their paychecks can buy.

Their earnings, however, are not steady. Much depends on the swings of the business cycle. Layoffs, strikes, or reductions in the hours of work may unexpectedly cut off the income and even bring the wolf close to the door.

This financial insecurity affects their buying behavior. Working-class families display a strong desire to save money for a rainy day. They steel themselves against the temptations of immediate fun and frivolity. For example, they show no particular interest in spending large amounts of money on recreation or vacations. Although such expenditures might relieve the monotony of their daily routine, they would still rather save in order to make sure that monotony is not supplanted by misery.

Their methods of saving are somewhat different from the classes above. They are not particularly attracted towards security through greater insurance. It seems to them too intangible a way of providing for the future. They prefer more tangible investments, like ownership of real estate, farm, or business. Also, many housewives find it relatively meaningless to abstractly earmark cash in the bank account for saving. Instead, they may put it in an envelope or a tin can. To them, an empty can more dramatically commands "thou shalt not spend" than does a red bank balance.

But despite their good resolutions to save, the temptations are frequently much too strong to resist. They resort to time payments, against their better judgment, whenever their desire for some durable becomes overwhelmingly great. Also, the women do not have enough will power to withstand impulse buying of "cute little objects" which they see in the stores. Often, it is their indiscretions at the one-dollar level, rather than the failure of resolutions in the $100-range, that render it difficult for them to make the two ends meet.

LOWER-LOWER

If the upper-uppers are the contemporary versions of the aristocracy, then the lower-lowers are the equivalents of the "untouchables," rejected by the caste system. Sordid poverty still exists side by side with affluence. But, unlike the hungry Thirties, when graduate engineers rubbed shoulders with factory workers in soup lines, today's poor are confined to special problem groups — the unskilled, the uneducated, the unfortunate (e.g., widows with small children), the discriminated (e.g., native Indians), the old, and the handicapped.

Right now, the poor eat the bitter bread of existence. They may work hard, but their life is like a treadmill. They are the last hired, the first fired. Lacking saleable skills or educational qualifications, they are forced to take the most menial and the dirtiest of jobs, at ridiculously low wages.

The simple problems of day-to-day existence are so engrossing that the poor have little time or energy for the amenities of life. If they have a roof over their heads, they are unconcerned at not having a rug under their feet. As long as they have food to eat, they do not ask for a tablecloth. They are too weak to demand life on their own terms and too helpless to pull themselves up by their bootstraps.

This economic deprivation shapes their social life at various levels. It forces them to live in dilapidated houses and to sublet their already cramped quarters. It stimulates borrowing between neighbors and buying from the corner grocery store where credit is often provided. It induces parents to take children out of school and send them to work in unskilled jobs.

In rural areas, too, the lot of the lower-lowers is not enviable. They not only have inadequate incomes; they suffer from the isolation that comes of having descended from generation after generation of poor ancestors — a heritage of debilitating want that leaves them without the energy or the vision to see beyond their own tumbledown fences. The education that might have raised their sights has been denied to them. The schools to which their children go are often as primitive as the farm homes from which they come.

The lower-lowers, both in city slums and rural outposts, know that they are looked down upon by the rest of society. They react to this ostracism in different ways. Some become apathetic and fatalistic, following the philosophy of living for the moment and of getting their kicks whenever they can. Others feel bitter, and they give vent to their frustrations in verbal or physical violence, such as tavern fights, or in escape patterns, like heavy drinking and sexual promiscuity. Many also lose their sense of social responsibility, centering their whole world around the gang at the pub. They show no interest in welfare organizations aimed at improving their lot. As for middle-class morality standards, they have nothing but general contempt, very much like that expressed by Eliza Doolittle's reprobate father in "My Fair Lady."

EXTENT OF MOBILITY WITHIN THE CLASSES

As Canada grows older and more complex, the six class breakdowns described above tend to get more rigid. There is a significant hardening of the arteries of the social system. Several factors are at work reducing the fluidity and openness for which the country was once noted.

In the old days, the factory was so organized that a laborer at the bottom could, by gradual steps, become a skilled worker, a foreman, and then a manager. Today, with automation, the employees fall into two levels: the semi-skilled workers on the one hand, and the trained and educated engineers and researchers on the other. The gap between the two is quite wide and not easy to jump.

The same change is taking place in the office as well. Once upon a time, a clerk could work his way up to bookkeeper, then to accountant, and finally perhaps to controller. But now, with complex accounting machines, the clerk just pushes the button and feeds the tape. He does not learn much about bookkeeping. The person who gets to be accountant and then controller is a graduate of a business school who comes into the company by what is called a lateral entry.

The big labor unions, too, are sometimes responsible for freezing men and women to their jobs, in return for security, recognition, and dignity. Initiative beyond the call of duty becomes pointless when promotions to better-paying jobs are available on the basis of impersonal seniority rules.

The result is that the old route up through the shop is closing. The worker is unionized, the manager professionalized, and, as these lines get firmer, the boy from the shanty town has less chance than before of crossing over the tracks. The Horatio Alger drama of the climb from rags to riches is becoming more an article of faith than a social reality.

Education, too, seems to work in such a way as to hinder social mobility. Though everyone has a common right to education, it is not an equal right. The educational conveyor belt drops lower class children at the beginning of the route while it carries those from the higher classes a longer distance, with nearly all the upper class children going to the end of the line. As one sociologist points out, a decision to go to college is influenced far more by the father's occupation than by the son's I.Q. One reason is unquestionably the cost of attending university. Higher education, the key to better jobs, must be bought with money. And money is the very commodity which the lower classes lack.

Even if finances were no problem, the environment in which the youngster from the lower classes is brought up does not encourage him to aspire to go to university. The most tempting goal in his life is to "get by" and "live it up." He wants to have income of his own quickly so that he can buy a car, have fun with the girls, and become independent of his parents. Higher education, in his eyes, has not much meaning since he can start out making what seems like excellent pay — almost as much as his semi-skilled father is earning after several decades. What he does not realize, till it is too late, is that he will be getting the same pay twenty years hence, except for possible across-the-board raises in the "scale."

THE TRICKLE-DOWN THEORY

While society is becoming more stratified at the occupational and educational levels, there is one avenue still open: with increased earning power, families can upgrade themselves (at least in their own minds) by adopting the consumption patterns of those above them. New cars, appliances, and furniture are seen as confirmations of "getting ahead."

Advertising and promotion experts have not been slow to exploit this upgrading urge. For solid business reasons, they are the most ardent champions of an open-class society, and they have succeeded well in their efforts. Through an education of taste and by a definite steering of preferences and wants into new directions, they have managed to convert one-time expensive and sophisticated products of the luxury market into necessities of the mass markets.

However, this device of dangling products as status symbols to lower classes must be used with considerable care. It must not be forgotten that a vast majority of the people are content to live and die within the boundaries and tastes of their own class. They have no desire whatsoever to take on new habits, new modes of living, new addresses, new affiliations, and new friends — and, what is still worse, discard the old ones. They realize very well that the resolute striver is a lonely soul making his way on a slippery slope.

Even when there is an upgrading urge, it is usually confined to the next rung in the ladder. People seldom emulate those who are several steps above them. In fact, it is sheer snobbery to think that a laborer is eager to ape the tastes and foibles of the elite. The "trickle-down" theory may be true for certain kinds of products; but for many convenience and shopping goods the flow of communications and ideas is horizontal, not vertical. The normal pattern is to seek information and guidance from others in the same class rather than from those above.

In television commercials, bejewelled women, dressed in the latest Paris fashions and talking with a broad "a," will scarcely be regarded by the lower socioeconomic status women as voices of authority. In the same vein, testimonials by celebrated authors or stage stars have little meaning to those who have no acquaintance with the legitimate theater or new developments in literature.

Similarly, the kind of super-sophisticated and clever advertising which appears in the "New Yorker" and "Montrealer" is almost meaningless to the lower status people. They cannot comprehend the subtle humor; they are baffled by the bizarre art. In no sense does this imply that they lack intelligence or wit; it is merely that their communication skills have been pressed into a different mold.

To an alert businessman, the significance of these differences is fairly obvious. He cannot successfully sell his goods to a specific class unless he takes into account the motivations of that class. People are open to suggestions and amenable to guidance, but only when these are conveyed in their language and with the symbols they know. For example, the affluent market will be attracted by live television performances presented within the symbolic format of the classical theater. To reach the mass market, it may be necessary to show the same ideas, the same human dilemmas, and at times the same plots within the outward form of a soap opera.

Hence, in the interests of sound marketing, it is necessary to study further the salient behavior patterns of the members of various socio-economic groups. Each class has its own value system, its own type of sophistication, its own way of reacting to advertising messages. An executive who is aware of these facts has a good deal of valuable information on which to formulate his marketing strategies. For instance, even for the same product, he may use one appeal in the affluent market and another one in the mass market. In other words, different brand images may be created among members of different social classes. (This is not difficult since people at different levels tend to be exposed to different media.)

Characteristics of the Affluent Market

The top three classes constitute the affluent market. For the most part, one can ignore the upper-upper group. Despite its wealth, it is numerically insignificant. The two other classes, lower-upper and upper-middle, have a somewhat similar style of life and can be examined together. It is difficult to document all the behavior patterns of the members of this group. The information available is far too scanty. However, by putting together such fragmentary statistics as do exist, by analyzing the published and unpublished reports of market researchers, and by relying upon the impressions of a few well-placed observers, one can depict in broad outline some of the salient characteristics of this affluent market.

• *Worship of youth.* Formerly teen-agers copied the styles of adults; now, more and more, it is the other way around. The young are held up on a pedestal. The Fountain of Youth is the favorite spa. Even though they are way past their twenties, males in the upper strata go bareheaded, get boyish hair cuts, and exhibit a penchant for trench coats, sports cars, and convertibles. The same is even more true of females. A mother of 40 or 50 dyes her hair, avoids starches to retain her slimness, and dresses to look like her teen-age daughter.

• *Interchangeability in sex roles.* The husband is not strictly the "head" of the household; he is just another member. "Togetherness" is the cardinal philosophy. The male does not mind participating in female chores such as shopping, cooking, and housecleaning. The wife is not uneasy about undertaking masculine tasks like repairing, painting, yard work, and shovelling of snow. As a result of this interchangeability in sex roles, the men no longer consider it effeminate to wear bright-colored sports shirts, to have fancy drinks, or to use scented hair tonics and perfumed shaving lotions. The women, for their part, no more act like delicate females. They drink whiskey during the cocktail hour, wear pants while doing the housework, and take part in such manly sports as golfing and curling.

• *Disregard of tradition.* In this rocket and space age, the passionate desire is to have the very latest items — just off the drawing boards. "What's new?" is more than a by-word; it is an attitude towards life. The past, no matter how glamorous, is no longer eulogized. Trademarks, packages, and advertising formats that are meant to glorify tradition may become instead cues for something old-fashioned, out-of-date, stodgy, and dull. Psychological obsolescence may well prove to be fatal for a product.

• *Decline of the Protestant ethic.* With the breakdown of tradition, the Protestant ethic, so long the dominant force in the country, is fast losing its grip. Hedonism is taking the place of Puritanism; pleasure is considered a right instead of a privilege; self-denial is seen as foolishness rather than a virtue. Freudianism is gaining in popularity, and repression, not licence, is looked upon as the greater evil. Ernest Hemingway's one-sentence manifesto has, in many cases, become the accepted code: "What is moral is what you feel good after, and what is immoral is what you feel bad after." A generation ago, a man who boasted that he had not taken a vacation in ten years could confidently expect to be admired all around. Today people in the upper levels no longer make a fetish out of work or subscribe to the old dictum that idleness is sin and the incubator of mischief.

To the businessman, the directions are clear: stress not so much the basic ingredients of the product as the pleasure obtained from the use of it. "Sell the sizzle, not the steak" is an effective way of communicating to the affluent market. Also, with the current trend to a natural, if sometimes amoral, attitude toward sex, a sophisticated use of sexual symbolism can prove a potent sales promoter. (Such an approach would be dangerous in the mass market, where sex is still taboo.)

• *Improvement in taste.* Broader educational opportunities (both formal and informal), better communication facilities, and greater overseas travel have led to a tremendous "growing up" in taste. The time was when the "nouveau riche" did not know the difference between a Picasso and a piccolo, nor cared for it either. Today there is a strong emphasis on a cultured style of living. Take, for example, the eating habits: they have become quite sophisticated. The upper levels, as a rule, prefer wine to beer; hard-crust rolls to plain white bread; cucumbers in sour cream to ordinary sweet pickles; and exotic, off-beat gourmet foods to the standard bill of fare. They serve coffee in demi-tasses, debate the merits of Pink Squirrels, Singapore Slings, Daquiris, and Gimlets, and consider it sacrilegious to ask for ginger ale with their whiskey. This sophistication is not just confined to eating and drinking. The individuals in the affluent market look for smartness in packages, chic in clothes, elegance in automobiles, and distinctiveness in furniture. Successful products are those that are outstanding not only functionally but aesthetically as well. In advertising, this sophistication calls for a soft sell rather than a hard-hitting approach. Humor is especially appreciated, provided it has a light touch and is not allowed to grow stale through too much repetition.

  • *Striving for status.* The upper-levels have an unquenchable thirst for status. Their homes are tangible symbols of success and showcases of culture. Inside them they display antiques, paintings, old family portraits, leather-bound books, and hand-made products (e.g., Eskimo carvings). However, keeping up with the Joneses — those arbiters of taste — is not as simple as it used to be. As more and more people have been able to adopt a higher standard of living, it is becoming increasingly difficult to say what items are the badges of success. No longer are automobiles and fur coats the cherished symbols of the well-bred and the well-heeled. Gone, too, are the days when an electronic marvel, such as a hi-fi set, would cause neighbors to look on with admiring eyes. To achieve status now, one has to be distinctive; he must get away from the masses. In an age when thousands can travel abroad, it makes a world of difference whether one takes a three-week economy trip to London-Paris-Rome or a six-week trip taking in Athens, Istanbul, and Cairo. Thus businessmen catering to the affluent market will have to put more and more emphasis on the uncommon and the unusual. The mass producers may have to provide more variety, as indeed the auto industry is already doing. A small company may have to concentrate on one-of-a-kind merchandise — an item that is "different," has a certain distinctiveness or a special feature which can be talked about.

  • *Appreciation of leisure.* Leisure activity plays a major role in the style of living of the higher status groups. Photography, assembling of a stereo system, working with home power tools, and a host of various do-it-yourself activities provide an outlet for creativity and an opportunity to relax from the stress and strain of daily work. Other current vogues are power boating, skiing, curling, golfing, trapshooting, and duck hunting. A survey conducted in the United States by *Sports Illustrated* shows that 80% of the sporting goods sold are bought by families with incomes over $7,500 and residing in metropolitan areas. The same may be true in Canada as well. All these trends have great significance for businessmen, even those not directly connected with the leisure market. They result in people's taking life less seriously, being more casual, and therefore more easily swayed by advertising themes that are light-hearted, gay, and have a "fun" motif.

• *Interest in high fashion.* Most of the leaders of "haute couture" come from the affluent society, though not necessarily from its highest strata. The upper-uppers maintain a certain independence of the current dictates of fashion; to them there is grace and charm in continuity, and they see vulgarity in constant change. The lower-uppers and the upper-middles, on the other hand, are the strong exponents of high fashion. They love to be pace-setters, and some of them patronize the "original" designers in the big fashion centers of the world. Yet, since people in this group are aware of the class above, and are perhaps trying to gain entrance into it, they seek to combine opulence with quiet elegance. They like to give the impression of being well-bred and do not dare to go to extremes. Advertising directed to them should, therefore, stress the pose of assured distinction, effortless superiority, and inbred elegance. The suitable expressions for prestige are "sophistication" and "chic." The word "glamor" is "cheap."

The above are some main features of the urban style of life of the higher status families. They are intangible and difficult to document statistically, but they exert tremendous influence on buying behavior and hence on marketing. Obviously, a product aimed at the affluent market has a good chance of riding the crest of sales popularity if it flows with the tide and captures to some extent the expression of the current social values.

Characteristics of the Mass Market

The lower-middles and the upper-lowers constitute the mass market. However, unlike the quality market, these two classes do not form a homogeneous group. Many businessmen erroneously conclude that since the working class is prosperous and rather well-educated compared to earlier years, it exists no longer and its members can be lumped together with the white-collar group. However, various studies by leading social scientists have consistently shown that the upper-lowers continue to differ from the lower-middles in their style of life, regardless of income. True, a carpenter or a bricklayer may now earn two or three times more than he did in 1940, but that does not mean he has acquired a burning desire to pattern his life after that of the middle class. His tastes and preferences in consumer products are very much what they were 25 years ago. Long-established mental habits are not readily altered. Hence, for marketing purposes, the differences between the lower and middle classes must be clearly recognized and documented.*

* In the subsequent paragraphs, the abbreviations "middle" and "lower" are used for "lower-middle" and "upper-lower" respectively. Sometimes these classes are also called by their popular nomenclature, "white-collar class" and "blue-collar class" or "working class."

PSYCHOLOGICAL DIFFERENCES

A vast psychological gulf exists between the two groups, both among men and women. The middle-class male is self-confident, has a strong sense of choice-making, plans for the future, and is culturally motivated to suffer, to renounce, to postpone gratifications in order to improve his or his children's position. Also, being well-educated, he stresses rationality, is abstract in his thinking, and takes an interest in local and national happenings.

The lower-class male is more oriented to the present than to the future. Because of his limited education, he has little interest in relatively abstract concepts, most of his attention being confined to the trivial and day-to-day interests of life. His mental horizons are fairly narrow, and he remains more or less incapsulated in the small world of family and next-of-kin. Also, he does not put high value on university education. When plans for the future come up, he tries to get his son into a craft union where family ties are quite important.

Women, too, are different in the two classes. To a middle-class housewife, life is not a chancy affair. She does not wait for what it brings to her door; rather she marks out her own path. Because of a great number of avocational and outside interests, her life tends to be varied, exciting, and rich in inner fulfillment. She has a sense of going somewhere, of developing.

The lower-class housewife, though not lacking in physical energy, is psychologically a passive person. She accepts things as given. She has little interest, energy, or skill to probe into things for herself. Mental activity is arduous for her. Her energy goes into maintaining life and improving it within the framework which is taken for granted, rather than altering that framework. She does not venture to experiment on her own initiative.

As a result, her daily life is busy, crowded, humdrum, and dull. Her chief concerns are elemental in character: feeding the family, keeping the home and clothes clean, and mothering the children. Everybody has these occupations to some extent, but they tend to be more important for the lower-class woman. She has little time for or interest in any other activity, except perhaps watching television. Rarely does she join a woman's club or some other social organization. In fact, she is discriminated against by her peers if she has ambitions along those lines.

EARNING CAPACITIES

Middle-class males are optimistic about their financial future. They expect their incomes to go up comfortably as they get better opportunities to utilize their talents. Nor do they fear that adverse swings in the business cycle will throw them out of work or in any way jeopardize their standard of living.

By contrast, working-class males are constantly worried about a depression. They feel that their fortunes are too much at the mercy of the over-all economic situation, which they cannot control or even mitigate. Also, they are realistic enough to expect no substantial improvement in their future financial position.

The type of work they do now will remain roughly the same ten years hence, and their pay envelopes will be fatter only if the union succeeds in getting a wage raise for their job category.

LEISURE

The middle class lead a rich and varied life, depending on the time of the year. Winter is the "social" season, the time for parties and dances, football and hockey games, school affairs and civic activities. Summer is for more personal pleasures, like gardening, or a drive to the lake-cottage for swimming and boating.

In the lower class, the seasons create very little difference in the lives of the families. Most of their leisure hours throughout the year are spent at home, watching television, fixing things up, and, for men especially, cleaning and repairing the car. Dropping in on friends and relatives is also common. The family does not travel for travel's sake, as is often the case with the middle class. An extended trip may be made for a definite purpose, such as visiting a relative, but these trips are not viewed as pleasurable in themselves, but only as a means of renewing family ties.

HUSBAND-WIFE RELATIONSHIP

In the middle class, the housewife has rebelled against the old structure of the patriarchal family, which set up the husband as lord and master. She is not prepared to sacrifice her own interests in order to pamper his whims. She considers herself as a partner and confidante and not a meek drudge. Often, her interests extend to the husband's job as well. She takes interest in his work, listens to his problems, and tries her best to represent him well socially to his colleagues, clients, and the boss.

The situation is not the same in a working-class family. The male is emotionally dominant, physically aggressive, and mentally self-seeking. He is accustomed to having his own way, and does not like to be tied to the apron strings of any woman, including his wife.

As a result, a pattern of separateness, rather than sharing, characterizes the household responsibilities. The work inside and outside the house is sharply demarcated. The husband may take over some of the indoor chores if the wife has a good excuse for not working, as when she is ill or has a new baby. But this is recognized as an exception to the normal, accepted way of doing things. The couple's day is spent in isolated activities, with a minimum of time devoted to shared interests. Often the woman stays at home while the man has some "fun." Even vacations are not always family affairs.

The wife does not get involved in her husband's work. She does not think he could benefit from any advice she may give. Rather, she believes that she can be of greater assistance by leaving him alone and "tending to her own knitting" — which is to keep the house clean, the children neat, and the clothes of everybody in good shape.

CHILD REARING

Middle-class parents take interest in their children's grades, insist on high-school graduation, and emphasize the advantages of postponing marriage in order to obtain a university education. They are also concerned with the purely social character of the experiences their children are exposed to. Recreational activities are closely supervised, respect for law and order is inculcated, taboos are placed on sexual activities, and considerable attention is paid to the teaching of correct manners. While physical aggressiveness is punished, aggressive competition for social and economic gains is strongly encouraged. The parents want their children to grow up into well-adjusted and self-confident adults, who are successful in their careers and comfortable in a wide variety of social situations.

Lower-class parents, on the other hand, do not place much value on education and are somewhat unconcerned about their children finishing high school. Child-rearing patterns are different too. Recreation is not closely supervised, and the boys are encouraged to be aggressive and fight for their rights. Fear rather than respect for the law is taught, and relatively few taboos are placed on sexual interests. In social relations, the emphasis is on honesty and frankness rather than on tact and etiquette. Also, lower-class children are often very much "spoiled." While middle-class mothers may spend money on extra items considered helpful in personality development — e.g., books, music lessons, hobbies, sports equipment — working-class women tend to shower their children with toys intended for pleasure only. The former more deliberately strive to invest in their children; the latter are more inclined to indulge them.

HOUSING

The middle-class individual prefers a home with distinctive architecture or at least with some element of luxury in appearance. In addition, he likes to be located near a wealthy or fashionable neighborhood, and does not mind loading himself with extra commuting burdens to live in such a place.

The blue-collar worker does not care too much for the locality. He is satisfied with one which has a friendly atmosphere, where he can feel socially comfortable and not be outclassed. He also wants a place close to his job. Commuting in traffic jams is to him a sheer waste of time. Regarding the external appearance of the home, he is somewhat indifferent, as long as the building is in good condition. He prefers to save on the purchase price of the house so that he can furnish it more liberally.

The young white-collar family usually regards its first home as a temporary lodging on the way to a better one. The blue-collar worker sees it as his anchor to the world and his security for old age. For this reason, he is much more interested in getting something durable, and once he has it, he loads it down with hardware. His kitchen is filled with more appliances and his living room with more furniture than one finds in a middle-class home.

FURNISHINGS

In home furniture and furnishings, the middle-class housewife is primarily moved by aesthetic considerations, the lower-class woman by labor-saving features. For example, in the case of a wall-to-wall carpet, the former would justify the purchase on the grounds of the luxurious appearance of her living quarters. The latter would stress more the fact that the job of cleaning the floor would be simplified. Of course, working-class women are not opposed to the idea of beautifying their homes. They simply feel that they are not in the economic brackets where such concerns can be at the forefront. They would rather have more articles than better-styled articles, and they want to get more done with less energy.

The middle-class housewife usually has a definite style in mind for furnishing her home, and she strives to adopt it with the help of various magazines on home improvement and interior decoration. The lower-class woman simply follows the lead of newspaper advertising and furniture displays in stores. What she likes is something sturdy that will take a beating from children and at the same time be attractive enough to provide a pleasant introduction to her home when friends and relatives drop in. She is not too concerned with the clash of colors and moods. She stays away from the ultra-modern in style; her tastes do not run along avant-garde lines. At the same time, she abhors the antique. She has had too much forced experience with hand-me-downs to grasp the subtlety of honoring dated objects.

Sharp variations also exist in tastes for colors and designs. A middle-class woman, as a rule, favors muted and neutral colors and austere and plain designs, and she wants everything to match properly. The working-class wife, on the other hand, thinks in terms of "decoration" rather than "decor." She uses bright colors and bold patterns, with frills on everything. Muted tones and severe lines are too cold for her taste. What might seem garish to a white-collar woman is "warm" or "cheerful" to her. In one study it was found that the middle classes for the most part prefer solid-color rugs, whereas patterned rugs become more popular as one goes down the scale.

FOOD

In food habits, too, there are differences between the two classes. Unlike the middle-class woman, a working-class housewife is more concerned with pleasing her family than with following the dictates of dietary experts. She does not want to count the calories so rigorously nor calculate the vitamins so determinedly that her meals become a treatment instead of a treat. A strong believer in the philosophy that the way to a man's heart is through his stomach, she tries to stimulate her husband's affection by preparing rich sauces and high-caloried desserts which are his favorites.

However, she is not entranced with the notion of creative cookery. Not being variety minded, she is not as anxious to follow the hints of culinary artists as some middle-class women appear to be. Also, she likes to save time and has no objection to using cake mixes, frozen foods, and other "instants." She is inclined to scoff at any deficiencies in the taste appeal of these foods — at least to a greater degree than middle-class women.

CLOTHING

In fashions, the middle-class woman has a distaste for high style, for what is daring or unusual. Respectability is the standard. Parisian creations are considered too extreme to wear to PTA meetings or for afternoon shopping. Clothes have to be "smart," meaning thereby what everyone else in one's social circle is wearing. The important thing is to be in fashion, not ahead of it.

The lower-class woman is not so conservative. While the middle-class woman carefully dresses to conform with rigid social expectations about what is right and proper on any given occasion, the working-class woman dresses more to please her secret fantasies of what makes her look her best. She sees herself as a Cinderella who is a slave to her home but is always hopeful of being transformed into a beautiful princess. Thus, unlike the middle-class woman who is afraid to follow a new mode until she is sure of its widespread acceptance, the working-class woman would espouse it quickly as the "new hope." But, since her budget is limited, she has to put up with inferior fabrics, poor workmanship, and sometimes tasteless imitations. That is why she is scorned by those above her as being a slave to cheap glamor.

SHOPPING

The working-class woman's preference for a personalized world influences her shopping patterns. While middle-class women frequent downtown shopping districts, the lower-class woman generally confines herself to those neighborhood stores where experience has taught her she will neither be "taken in" nor snubbed by the storekeeper and salesmen. She prefers to make her big-ticket purchases through "connections," such as relatives or long-time friends who run businesses themselves or have contacts with people who do.

ADVERTISING AND MERCHANDISING APPEALS

Each class has its own set of social mores, customs, and inhibitions, which a businessman must keep in mind when preparing his advertising and merchandising appeals. Professor G. H. Smith, in *Motivation Research*, gives a striking example of an advertisement that ran head on into the rather prim morality standards of the lower middle class. A company producing perfume wanted to introduce a new fragrance called Naomi for the mass market. The advertising agency, with the idea of creating an enticing exotic atmosphere, thought of illustrating Naomi with one of Gauguin's famous paintings of South Sea Island belles. The girls in the painting were unquestionably seductive by upper-class standards, but some of the more cautious ad men worried about the wisdom of using the painting, since the girls depicted were natives with bare bosoms.

A decision was made to pre-test the ad by conducting a depth interview among a representative sample of lower-middle-class housewives who would comprise the main market for the fragrance. The study clearly indicated that these women saw nothing glamorous in the Gauguin Tahitian beauties. They called them dirty, heavy, sweaty creatures, maybe Africans. The housewives were then shown another picture of a young American blonde holding flowers. That produced many emotionally warm, admiring responses. Needless to say, Gauguin's masterpiece was scuttled. The illustration selected was of a blonde, pale-skinned girl against a South Sea backdrop.

In the case of the lower classes, it is imperative that businessmen do not use the orthodox sales appeals normally directed to white-collar consumers. Advertising must be closely related to the basic goals which activate consumption patterns of the blue-collar housewife. Here are a few specific guidelines:

The working-class housewife, because of her limited education, has very little interest in abstract concepts. She tends to personalize everything. For example, she sees not the institution of law, but the policeman on the beat; not education itself, but the teacher in the local school; not medicine as such, but the doctor who treats her. In other words, her world is defined in terms of the people she knows and the events which are close to home. Thus, advertising which is "people-oriented" is, in most cases, much more meaningful to her than that which is impersonal, technical, or too objective.

An equally important desire of the working-class woman is to create an attractive environment. This is not surprising, for prettying up herself and her home is the only way she has of alleviating some of the harsher aspects of her life. By buying a knick-knack for the house, or a ribbon for the hair, she is able to get out of her rut and brighten her daily existence. Advertising will be more appealing when it caters to these propensities, by conveying some of this prettied-up atmosphere, than when it is purely factual and practical in its presentation.

The working-class woman violently resents being identified with the shiftless, irresponsible lower-lower class. She likes to be treated as Mrs. Average Housewife, a member of the mass market to which a majority of the people belong. However, she does not know how to go about achieving that goal. Being uncertain and self-conscious, she requires, even craves, explicit guidance. Hence, in many cases, advertising may have to play a strong educational role. It has not only to communicate to her that an object is a normal part of common man's possessions, but also teach her how it will fit into her life. For example, a woman who grew up in a home that never had a coffee table needs to learn how to use one. Educating her is as important as showing how the coffee table will pretty up her environment.

Another basic drive of the working-class housewife is the search for social and economic security. More than a white-collar woman, she needs to be assured that her buying decisions are sound, her product choice is wise, and her trust in merchandise purchased is justified. In the absence of personal recommendations from close friends or relatives, she does not mind paying premium prices to buy well-known brands. This is an important factor upon which a national advertiser can capitalize. He can provide her with economic security by emphasizing that, in a market full of uncertain values, his own brand is reliable, and the company is prepared to back up all advertising claims. Also, he can confer upon her social security, by pointing out that the product is part of "the good life" (not sophisticated life) and is being used by thousands of average women like her across the country.

If the product being marketed is a labor-saver, that fact should not be ignored. The working-class housewife has an arduous job. She has a big family and no outside help, with the result that her life is an unending round of household chores. Hence, she is always on the look-out for products which can simplify her task and lessen the wear and tear on her. For example, in furniture, she will be less attracted by the appeal that stresses the aesthetic lines of a piece and more by the one that concentrates on its durable, easy-to-clean qualities.

However, it is important to emphasize that, though the lower-class woman wishes to be relieved from her irksome household tasks, she does not want the free time to idly enjoy herself. She has an almost compulsive need to be busy. This seems to satisfy her psychologically about her worthiness and her love for her family. Thus, while advertising should strive to make her feel less pressed and burdened, it should also communicate to her a sense of being important and essential to her family. The saving of labor must be compensated for by something worthwhile, such as the possibility of giving more time to children and husband.

Method for Measuring Socio-Economic Classes

Granting the importance of class for marketing purposes, how can one analyze it in detail? The task is admittedly difficult. Some market-research firms try to get around it by asking the interviewer to assess the status of the respondents. This is undoubtedly risky. Class is a concept that evokes strong personal feelings, and an interviewer's subjective estimate of a respondent's class position is probably just as reflective of the interviewer's own status as of the respondent's. The following remarks made by a field worker in a market research firm are fairly typical:

"I rank my people alphabetically from A to E. E's live in slums and they smell. D's are cozy, have fringes on their lamps, fancy cookie jars in their kitchens, and embedded wagon wheels full of flowers on their front lawns. C's are shrill and less open. They are very concerned with what the neighbors think; they either don't want to commit themselves on what they buy or they are loudly over-critical. B's are a mixed group; they can be mildly flamboyant or intellectual and reserved. If I come upon what I think is an A house, I don't bother to knock; I'd only get the maid."

Obviously, what is needed is some sort of an index to reflect the respondent's social-class position. Such a yardstick, in order to be objective, must satisfy certain requirements:

• It must be standardized; i.e., it can be applied in precisely the same way all across the country.

• It must be reliable; i.e., it must give the same results no matter how many different people use it.

• It must be scalar; i.e., it must permit graduation in ascending or descending order.

• It must be convenient; i.e., it can be easily handled in the field, requiring only a minimum amount of additional interviewer training.

One can compile such an index by taking into consideration income, education and occupation. All three factors are important for assessing socio-economic status. The total income obtained from different sources reveals the purchasing power of the household. Obviously, it is pointless to market a product among a group that has not the wherewithal to buy it. Education is a good indicator of the taste and the mental horizon of an individual. It separates one social level from another by laying stress, not just on any knowledge, but on knowledge that is systematized and generalized. For example, a butcher can be a storehouse of information about meat cuts; yet he does not have the kind of systematic knowledge of animal anatomy expected from a biologist.

Occupation is an even better indicator of social status. The work a man does, the dignity of the job, the authority and knowledge required, and the financial remuneration received, determine in a great measure his consumption patterns. To know that an individual is a professor, a sales clerk or a bricklayer immediately brings to mind an apperceptive mass of ideas about the kind of person he is. Each has a distinct pattern of life — economically as well as intellectually and socially.

It has been sometimes suggested that the total score for social class should include also source of income, dwelling area and house type. These extra factors, however, do not lend themselves well to market-research work.

Source of income is the favorite of many social scientists. One, for example, suggests the following rating:

• Inherited wealth;
• Earned wealth (an individual who has amassed sufficient money and does not have to work);
• Profits from business and fees from the practice of profession;
• Salaries and commissions;
• Wages;
• Private relief (e.g., from relatives, friends, churches, etc.);
• Public relief and non-respectable income (e.g., from gambling or prostitution).

This classification has a rather limited application. In some respects it is superfluous, since occupation reveals the source of income. Ordinarily, professionals receive fees, office employees salaries, factory workers wages, and people running their own business profits. Also, in many cases a person may be reluctant to tell to the interviewer his source of income. This is true, particularly, at the extremes of the scale where the majority of income is from inherited wealth or from public relief. Furthermore, many individuals, especially in the higher levels, have two equally important sources of income; e.g., salary as well as interest on securities. In such cases, the ranking becomes somewhat difficult.

Dwelling area and house type, the two other factors suggested, are likewise not very satisfactory. They lack the key requirements of a good index: standardization and reliability. Houses and neighborhoods differ from one part of the country to another. Also, when ranking is left to the discretion of the interviewers, there is too much bias and variability introduced to warrant proper comparisons. Consequently, it is best to use only the three key yardsticks: income, education and occupation.

In market-research work the following method may be applied to establish objectively and inexpensively the social level of everyone in the sample. Each head of the household is assigned a score by virtue of his or her occupation, educational attainment, and total household income. The household, rather than the individual, is selected as a unit of measurement because in the majority of cases the status of all the members within a household is the same as that of the head.

INCOME

The following score may be used for total income; i.e., the income of all members from all sources and not just the earnings of the major breadwinner:

Score 1	$15,000 and over
2	$10,000–$14,999
3	$ 6,000–$ 9,999
4	$ 3,000–$ 5,999
5	Below $3,000

EDUCATION

The education score may be computed from the highest grade attended (or completed) by the head of the household.

Score 1	University degree.
2	From one to four years of university.
3	Three or more years of secondary school but no university.
4	From five years of elementary school to two years of secondary school.
5	Four years or less of elementary school, including those with no schooling.

OCCUPATION

Occupation is more difficult to scale. To determine the score, an attempt has been made, in the accompanying table, to group some 275 occupations into five classes on the basis of income and education. (See table entitled "Occupations of Males Ranked According to the Combined Scores of Income and Education.")

Score 1, Class A   (Income $9,000 and more; education 12 or more years of schooling.)

     2, Class B   (Income $7,000–$9,000; education 10–12 years of schooling.)

     3, Class C   (Income $5,000–$7,000; education 9–10 years of schooling.)

     4, Class D   (Income $3,000–$5,000; education 6–9 years of schooling.)

     5, Class E   (Income $3,000 or less; education 6 or less years of schooling.)

The final step in obtaining the social status of a household is to add together the scores on income, education, and occupation, and then to apply the following conversion table:

Total Score	Social Class
3– 4	Two upper
5– 7	Upper-middle
8–10	Lower-middle
11–13	Upper-lower
14–15	Lower-lower

Here is a typical example of this three-factor social ranking. A head of the household, with two years of secondary school, is a photoengraver in a printing plant, making $6,000 a year. His wife, at a clerical job in an insurance firm, earns $45 a week or $2,340 annually. The total family income is thus $8,340. On this basis, the household gets a score of 3 for income, 4 for education, and 3 for occupation, adding up to 10 or lower-middle class. (When the head of the household is not in the labor force, his score on education is generally assigned as his score on occupation.)

This is the ideal way of ascertaining the socio-economic status of the household. Unfortunately, the 1961 census does not provide all the statistics needed to apply this technique in its entirety. The three-way cross-tabulation by occupation, income and education is not available in the form required. An attempt is made to circumvent the problem by relying solely on occupation. This is by far the most realistic yardstick. Since in the following table on male occupations (pages 188 to 195) the ranking has been obtained by multiplying average income by average education, it indirectly takes into consideration these two other factors.

These statistics are based on males in the labor force. The calculations exclude females in the labor force (some of whom may maintain their own households) as well as household heads not in the labor force (e.g., college students and retired persons). Hence the figures may be presumed to underestimate to some extent the proportion in the lower classes. However, the bias introduced is not believed to be great, since in the male occupations are included many persons in the low-status jobs who are not likely to be heads of households.

OCCUPATIONS OF MALES RANKED ACCORDING TO THE COMBINED SCORES OF INCOME AND EDUCATION, CANADA, 1961

Occupations	Number working	Average income ($)	Average years of schooling	Average age
Class A (mainly two upper classes)				
Physicians and surgeons	19,835	15,822	17	42
Dentists	5,234	13,409	17	46
Law professionals	12,594	12,495	17	44
Optometrists	1,160	10,064	16	44
Professors and college principals	8,779	9,247	17	40
Owners or managers: primary metal industries	1,978	11,848	13	46
Architects	2,874	9,389	16	39
Owners or managers: paper and allied industries	3,241	11,280	13	47
Veterinarians	1,498	9,092	16	40
Owners or managers: chemical and chemical products industries	3,859	11,000	13	45
Chemical engineers	2,982	8,375	17	35
Mining engineers	2,347	8,846	16	38
Osteopaths and chiropractors	1,019	8,760	16	42
Owners or managers: services to business management	5,431	10,712	13	44
Geologists	2,716	8,077	17	35
Owners or managers: electrical products industries	3,126	10,531	13	44
Physicists	673	7,956	17	35
Physical scientists, n.e.s.*	1,380	8,385	16	36
Owners or managers: textile manufacturing	2,096	10,924	12	46
Owners or managers: mines, quarries and oil wells	3,717	10,878	12	45
Professional engineers, n.e.s.	4,928	8,045	16	39
Owners or managers: petroleum and coal products industries	879	9,876	13	44
Civil engineers	11,888	7,981	16	37
Electrical engineers	8,723	7,798	16	37
Owners or managers: education and related services	766	8,258	15	46
Pharmacists	6,443	7,702	16	43
Owners or managers: machinery industries	2,606	10,048	12	44

* Note: *n.e.s.* stands for "not elsewhere specified".

Occupations	Number working	Average income ($)	Average years of schooling	Average age
Owners or managers: transportation equipment industries	2,942	10,004	12	45
Owners or managers: printing and publishing	5,168	9,980	12	46
Owners or managers: finance, insurance, real estate	32,180	9,802	12	45
Mechanical engineers	8,122	7,823	15	38
Economists	2,026	7,760	15	37
Owners or managers: knitting mills	679	10,303	11	47
Advertising managers	2,176	8,621	13	39
Biological scientists	1,397	6,977	16	37
Air pilots, navigators, flight engineers	2,739	9,285	12	35
Owners or managers: leather manufacturing	1,217	10,063	11	47
Industrial engineers	3,960	7,798	14	39
Owners or managers: miscellaneous manufacturing	3,972	9,087	12	45
Farmers with annual value of products sold over $25,000	9,507	—	—	—
Total of Class A	198,857	—	—	—
Percentage of all occupations	4.2%	—	—	—

Class B (mainly upper-middle)

Occupations	Number working	Average income ($)	Average years of schooling	Average age
Owners or managers: rubber manufacturing	575	8,998	12	45
Chemists	5,702	6,682	16	37
Accountants and auditors	29,121	7,324	14	40
Owners or managers: metal fabricating	6,155	9,303	11	45
Sales managers	22,636	8,230	12	41
Owners or managers: non-metallic mineral products	2,708	8,933	11	44
Commissioned officers, military	17,523	6,944	14	35
Actuaries and statisticians	2,479	6,893	14	38
Security salesmen and brokers	5,151	7,215	13	41
Owners or managers: clothing	4,010	9,348	10	47
Owners or managers: food and beverage	11,966	8,477	11	46
Owners or managers: wholesale trade	42,701	8,462	11	45
School teachers	49,219	6,115	15	36
Owners or managers: health and welfare services	2,756	7,503	12	46
Owners or managers: transport, communications, utilities	24,102	7,999	11	44
Agricultural professionals, n.e.s.	2,681	5,845	15	40
Authors, editors, journalists	9,717	6,558	13	39
Health professionals, n.e.s.	451	6,263	13	45
Computer programmers	666	5,753	14	32
Owners or managers: public administration	27,470	6,571	12	46
Office managers	12,646	6,548	12	41

OCCUPATIONS OF MALES RANKED ACCORDING TO THE COMBINED SCORES OF INCOME AND EDUCATION, CANADA, 1961 (continued)

Occupations	Number working	Average income ($)	Average years of schooling	Average age
Librarians	630	5,235	15	41
Professional occupations, n.e.s.	23,165	6,014	13	39
Owners or managers: furniture and fixtures	2,409	7,797	10	44
Owners or managers: construction industry	35,812	7,642	10	43
Inspectors and foremen, communications	2,344	6,679	11	43
Owners or managers: miscellaneous services	7,489	6,675	11	45
Funeral directors and embalmers	2,633	6,639	11	42
Radio and television announcers	1,552	5,563	13	29
Credit managers	4,277	6,005	12	39
Insurance salesmen and agents	26,373	5,997	12	39
Farmers with annual value of products sold between $15,000 and $24,999	13,300	—	—	—
Total of Class B	400,419	—	—	—
Percentage of all occupations	8.5%	—	—	—

Class C (mainly lower-middle)

Occupations	Number working	Average income ($)	Average years of schooling	Average age
Owners or managers: wood manufacturing	5,981	6,932	10	46
Advertising salesmen and agents	2,811	5,771	12	37
Brokers, agents and appraisers, n.e.s.	5,315	5,736	12	40
Purchasing agents and buyers	13,078	6,137	11	41
Owners or managers: forestry and logging	3,389	7,441	9	45
Owners or managers: all other industries	4,292	6,586	10	45
Artists, commercial	4,294	5,465	12	36
Commercial travellers	73,548	5,845	11	39
Other artists, art teachers	1,454	5,323	12	41
Foremen: transportation equipment industries	4,305	6,034	10	44
Owners or managers: retail trade	126,371	5,972	10	44
Photoengravers	1,132	5,964	10	37
Real estate salesmen and agents	9,801	5,383	11	46
Social welfare workers	5,071	4,543	13	39
Teachers and instructors, n.e.s.	5,196	5,307	11	40
Foremen: primary metal industries	4,409	6,469	9	44
Owners or managers: motion picture or recreation services	6,308	5,822	10	45
Musicians and music teachers	4,469	4,826	12	38
Physical, occupational therapists	633	4,820	12	44
Locomotive engineers	7,575	6,337	9	47
Stenographers	4,704	4,730	12	40
Draughtsmen	19,757	4,727	12	33
Science and engineering technicians, n.e.s.	35,889	4,717	12	33
Radio and television equipment operators	3,342	5,019	11	33
Photographers	3,335	5,000	11	37
Foremen: mine, quarry, petroleum well	5,626	6,096	9	43
Auctioneers	346	5,486	10	44

Occupations	Number working	Average income ($)	Average years of schooling	Average age
Foremen: paper and allied industries	3,785	6,025	9	46
Ticket, station and express agents, transport	7,258	4,910	11	40
Lithographic and photo-offset occupations	2,926	5,264	10	33
Religion professionals	23,982	3,463	15	43
Conductors, railroad	5,725	5,767	9	47
Medical and dental technicians	4,643	4,300	12	36
Athletes, entertainers, and related workers	4,228	4,679	11	34
Foremen: electric power, gas and water utilities	3,176	5,687	9	43
Surveyors	8,384	4,255	12	30
Foremen: other manufacturing industries	20,234	5,515	9	43
Foremen: trade	8,078	4,957	10	39
Owners or managers: personal services	35,254	5,235	9	46
Nurses, graduate	2,354	3,926	12	39
Inspectors—construction	3,887	4,644	10	44
Locomotive firemen	3,744	5,142	9	37
Compositors and typesetters	15,320	4,600	10	36
Brakemen, railroad	7,713	5,077	9	39
Inspectors, examiners, gaugers, n.e.s.—metal	12,201	4,548	10	41
Bookkeepers and cashiers	59,050	3,775	12	35
Telephone operators	1,714	4,525	10	40
Farmers with annual volume of products sold between $5,000 and $14,999	111,827	—	—	—
Total of Class C	707,914	—	—	—
Percentage of all occupations	15.1%	—	—	—

Class D (mainly upper-lower)

Occupations	Number working	Average income ($)	Average years of schooling	Average age
Foremen: all other industries	15,138	4,994	9	43
Electricians and related electrical and electronics workers	101,600	4,488	10	36
Interior decorators, window dressers	2,382	4,078	11	35
Postmasters	2,961	4,482	10	49
Operators, electric street railway	1,342	4,964	9	41
Office appliance operators	6,007	4,020	11	30
Telegraph operators	3,923	4,422	10	36
Inspectors and foremen, transport	17,813	4,882	9	43
Printing workers, n.e.s.	1,912	4,880	9	35
Foremen: food and beverage industries	6,663	4,850	9	43
Foremen: textile and clothing industries	4,086	4,784	9	43
Well-drillers and related workers	5,745	4,773	9	33
Foremen: wood and furniture industries	3,966	4,764	9	43
Pressmen, printing	8,354	4,733	9	36
Inspectors, graders and samplers, n.e.s.	3,066	4,254	10	41
Lens grinders and polishers; opticians	1,537	4,138	10	35
Clerical occupations, n.e.s.	158,114	3,709	11	36

Occupations	Number working	Average income ($)	Average years of schooling	Average age
Class D (continued)				
Patternmakers, except paper	1,927	4,507	9	41
Canvassers and other door-to-door salesmen	8,649	4,050	10	40
Beverage processors	2,875	4,447	9	39
Bookbinders	1,363	4,393	9	37
Switchmen and signalmen	3,473	4,386	9	39
General foremen—construction	18,313	4,923	8	43
Typists and clerk-typists	2,319	3,483	11	29
Paper makers, still operators, chemical and related workers	36,783	4,662	8	38
Civilian protective service occupations	77,853	4,125	9	43
Baggagemen and expressmen, transport	1,819	4,048	9	43
Farm managers and foremen	3,242	4,025	9	43
Stock clerks and storekeepers	33,064	3,598	10	38
Armed forces, non-commissioned	95,353	3,530	10	29
Photographic processing occupations	1,734	3,530	10	33
Jewelers, watchmakers, engravers	5,248	3,906	9	41
Furnacemen, moulders, blacksmiths, and related metal workers	31,671	4,384	8	42
Other occupations in bookbinding	549	3,875	9	35
Operators, water transport	17,787	4,304	8	38
Postmen and mail carriers	12,792	3,804	9	41
Inspectors, graders, scalers—log and lumber	6,279	3,794	9	39
Other sales occupations	149	3,406	10	35
Bus drivers	18,106	4,224	8	41
Machinists, plumbers, sheet metal workers, related workers	216,784	4,224	8	38
Stationary engine and excavating and lifting equipment operators and related workers	120,577	4,219	8	40
Occupation not stated, whole group	123,042	3,643	9	38
Millmen	4,708	4,076	8	38
Sales clerks	96,397	3,212	10	34
Mechanics and repairmen, except electrical and electronic	179,984	4,000	8	38
Logging foremen	2,997	4,543	7	45
Stewards	4,035	3,506	9	44
Tire builders, vulcanizers and other rubber workers	8,618	3,931	8	38
Shipping and receiving clerks	52,476	3,482	9	37
Miners, n.e.s.	26,330	4,476	7	36
Laborers: primary metal industries	10,292	3,902	8	37
Insulation appliers	2,367	3,893	8	34
Timbermen	2,005	4,333	7	42
Furriers	2,711	3,778	8	41
Clay, glass and stone workers, n.e.s.	6,685	3,771	8	36

Occupations	Number working	Average income ($)	Average years of schooling	Average age
Butchers and meat cutters	21,776	3,768	8	38
Tobacco preparers and products makers	1,397	3,731	8	39
Paper products makers	5,812	3,728	8	34
Meat canners, curers, packers	2,862	3,707	8	37
Painters, except construction and maintenance	7,422	3,660	8	37
Truck drivers	160,242	3,632	8	35
Nurses-in-training	326	2,641	11	24
Driver-salesmen	51,612	3,217	9	32
Quarriers and related workers, n.e.s.	4,930	4,018	7	40
Other food processing occupations	5,443	3,507	8	38
Barbers, hairdressers, manicurists	18,840	3,489	8	43
Transport occupations, n.e.s.	1,797	3,488	8	46
Cutters, markers—textiles; garment and glove leather	4,962	3,482	8	38
Upholsterers	5,392	3,466	8	37
Plasterers and lathers	10,051	3,442	8	35
Nursing assistants and aides	13,177	3,032	9	39
Prospectors	855	3,016	9	45
Tailors	5,937	3,380	8	44
Bakers	11,228	3,367	8	37
Production process and related workers, n.e.s.	11,736	3,353	8	36
Furnacemen and kilnmen, ceramics and glass	1,167	3,821	7	41
Milk processors	5,899	3,266	8	35
Cabinet and furniture makers—wood	8,009	3,238	8	39
Bleachers and dyers—textile	1,833	3,238	8	38
Laborers, mine	14,920	3,685	7	36
Service workers, n.e.s.	3,427	2,857	9	40
Painters (construction and maintenance), paper-hangers and glaziers	43,164	3,183	8	40
Millers of grain and flour	2,233	3,590	7	39
Porters, baggage and pullman	5,090	2,791	9	37
Fruit and vegetable canners and packers	1,498	3,128	8	37
Taxi drivers and chauffeurs	21,706	3,104	8	41
Tanners and tannery operatives	2,317	3,536	7	40
Woodworking occupations, n.e.s.	11,252	3,081	8	38
Bricklayers, stonemasons, tile-setters	20,762	3,516	7	36
Laborers, paper and allied industries	11,321	3,454	7	37
Bartenders	9,163	3,007	8	40
Longshoremen and stevedores	12,265	3,425	7	40
Laborers, railway and transport	10,287	3,419	7	41
Loom fixers and loom preparers	1,459	3,410	7	39
Carpenters	122,126	3,400	7	42
Laborers, communication and storage	2,776	2,912	8	36
Launderers and dry cleaners	9,047	2,889	8	38
Knitters	1,977	2,870	8	33

Occupations	Number working	Average income ($)	Average years of schooling	Average age
Class D (continued)				
Stone cutters and dressers	1,695	3,280	7	39
Warehousemen and freight handlers, n.e.s.	30,348	2,862	8	34
Cement and concrete finishers	6,267	3,268	7	38
Bottlers, wrappers, labelers	20,046	2,841	8	33
Cooks	25,207	2,840	8	40
Finishers and calenderers	1,701	3,223	7	36
Woodworking machine operators, n.e.s.	9,407	3,210	7	38
Construction workers, n.e.s.	13,500	3,186	7	36
Laborers, transportation equipment industries	6,802	3,177	7	41
Weavers	3,225	3,127	7	35
Hawkers and pedlars	1,353	3,059	7	43
Forest rangers and cruisers	7,580	2,672	8	38
Apparel and related products makers, n.e.s.	4,663	3,050	7	39
Sawyers	13,186	3,043	7	38
Elevator tenders, building	3,857	3,035	7	49
Dressmakers—not in factory	683	3,035	7	44
Other textile occupations	5,021	3,019	7	36
Service station attendants	19,525	2,340	9	28
Farmers with annual value of products sold between $2,500 and $4,999	114,650	—	—	—
Total of Class D	2,544,176	—	—	—
Percentage of all occupations	54.1%	—	—	—
Class E (mainly lower-lower)				
Spinners and twisters	1,907	2,988	7	34
Sewers and sewing machine operators	5,290	2,981	7	40
Carders, combers and other fibre preparers	1,354	2,933	7	39
Janitors and cleaners, building	69,383	2,913	7	49
Laborers, electric power, gas and water utilities	7,454	2,908	7	37
Sectionmen and trackmen	23,195	3,344	6	43
Other agricultural occupations	4,785	2,486	8	37
Leather cutters, lasters, sewers, and other leather workers	14,085	2,803	7	40
Laborers, other manufacturing	26,201	2,753	7	35
Gardeners, except farm, and groundskeepers	24,411	2,363	8	43
Laborers, public administration and defence	33,098	2,683	7	41
Waiters	16,810	2,311	8	35
Winders, reelers	753	2,624	7	30
Laborers, food and beverage manufacturing	15,046	2,587	7	34
Lodging and boarding housekeepers	1,069	2,457	7	59
Laborers, textile and clothing manufacturing	4,852	2,371	7	34
Laborers, wood manufacturing	20,172	2,367	7	35

OCCUPATIONS OF MALES RANKED ACCORDING TO THE COMBINED SCORES OF INCOME AND EDUCATION, CANADA, 1961 (continued)

Occupations	Number working	Average income ($)	Average years of schooling	Average age
Messengers	6,427	2,001	8	32
Laborers, trade	33,660	1,939	8	29
Laborers, transportation, except railway	16,895	2,203	7	39
Laborers, construction	70,006	2,175	7	34
Laborers, all other industries	25,197	2,129	7	36
Lumbermen, including laborers in logging	68,249	2,376	6	34
Teamsters	1,268	2,326	6	40
Fishermen, trappers, and hunters (whole group)	35,648	2,129	6	39
Farm laborers	156,250	1,585	8	30
Kitchen helpers and related service workers, n.e.s.	16,370	1,735	7	36
Attendants, recreation and amusement	4,160	1,326	9	30
Guides	2,851	1,865	6	38
Fish canners, curers, packers	6,124	1,825	6	36
Newsvendors	5,733	701	9	20
Babysitters	323	562	9	23
Farmers with annual value of products sold less than $2,500	135,126	—	—	—
Total of Class E	854,152	—	—	—
Percentage of all occupations	18.1%	—	—	—
Total of all occupations	*4,705,518*	*4,500*	*9*	*39**

*Note:

The compilation of this table involved the following steps:

- Since the DBS does not provide in detail the occupations by the heads of the households, the occupations of males were used as a substitute.

- The 1961 Census (Bulletin 94-509, Table 17) breaks down each occupation by education. The average years of schooling were computed from this report by applying the following weights:

	Weight
Elementary less than 5	2.5
Elementary 5 and over	6.5
Secondary 1 or 2	9.5
Secondary 3	11.0
Secondary 4–5	12.5
Some university	15.0
University degree	17.0

- The average income for each occupation was obtained from another 1961 Census report (Bulletin 98-502, Table B-4). The "income" figure here refers to the total income and not just employment earnings. Both employees and self-employed are included.

- The average income was multiplied by average years of schooling to derive a combined score, and then all the occupations were arranged in a descending order on the basis of that score. On the top of the list were physicians and surgeons with a score of 268,974 (average income $15,822 multiplied by 17, the number of years of schooling).

• The occupations were then classified into five groups. Those that scored 108,000 or more (at least 12 years of schooling and $9,000 of income) were put in the A class. Those that obtained a score below 108,000 but higher than 70,000 (at least 10 years of schooling and $7,000 of income) fell into the B class. The C class included those who scored below 70,000 but higher than 45,000 (at least 9 years of schooling and $5,000 of income). The score for the D class ranged from a high of 44,999 to a low of 21,000 (at least 7 years of schooling and $3,000 of income). Any occupation that scored below 21,000 was placed in the final E class.

• The farmers, and stockraisers were treated separately. Since they range all the way from very rich to very poor, it would have been unrealistic to lump all of them in one category. The annual value of products sold was used as a guide, and the following formula adopted:

    A class: Over $25,000
    B class: $15,000–$24,999
    C class: $5,000–$14,999
    D class: $2,500–$4,999
    E class: Below $2,500

• Because the income forms part of the score, some occupations, like religious professionals, suffer to a great extent. Ideally, no doubt, it would be desirable to take the factor of prestige into consideration, but from the practical point of view this is not possible, since no adequate basis exists for deriving prestige ratings.

In market research work, this table can prove a valuable working tool when a decision has to be made as to what score the head of the household should receive for his occupation. Incidentally, it must be remembered that when occupation is used as a yardstick for assessing social status it is not enough to confine oneself to broad designations as managers, professionals, craftsmen, and the like. More detailed information is required. The interviewers must be instructed to find out where the respondents work and what type of job they are engaged in.

SOCIAL CLASS ESTIMATES BY PROVINCES, 1961

Province	A Mainly two upper classes	B Mainly upper-middle	C Mainly lower-middle	D Mainly upper-lower	E Mainly lower-lower	Total
NUMBER						
Canada	198,857	400,419	707,914	2,544,176	854,152	4,705,518
Newfoundland	1,535	5,258	8,922	47,750	25,237	88,702
Prince Edward Island	520	1,512	3,093	11,200	9,743	26,068
Nova Scotia	4,888	13,049	19,751	103,395	37,476	178,559
New Brunswick	3,530	9,314	14,958	70,151	34,596	132,549
Québec	54,635	97,523	178,882	722,421	235,964	1,289,425
Ontario	84,318	160,471	268,315	943,293	244,170	1,700,567
Manitoba	8,096	21,242	39,771	125,453	51,636	246,198
Saskatchewan	6,369	18,258	52,699	106,161	64,992	248,479
Alberta	16,744	32,963	62,354	173,011	76,889	361,961
British Columbia	17,887	40,217	57,929	235,283	70,470	421,786
Yukon and N.W. Territories	335	612	1,240	6,058	2,979	11,224

SOCIAL CLASS ESTIMATES BY PROVINCES, 1961 (continued)

Province	A Mainly two upper classes	B Mainly upper-middle	C Mainly lower-middle	D Mainly upper-lower	E Mainly lower-lower	Total
PERCENTAGE DISTRIBUTION						
Canada	4.2	8.5	15.0	54.1	18.2	100.0
Newfoundland	1.7	5.9	10.1	53.8	28.5	100.0
Prince Edward Island	2.0	5.8	11.9	42.9	37.4	100 0
Nova Scotia	2.7	7.3	11.1	57.9	21.0	100.0
New Brunswick	2.7	7.0	11.3	52.9	26.1	100.0
Québec	4.2	7.6	13.9	56.0	18.3	100.0
Ontario	5.0	9.4	15.8	55.5	14.3	100.0
Manitoba	3.3	8.6	16.1	51.0	21.0	100.0
Saskatchewan	2.6	7.3	21.2	42.7	26.2	100.0
Alberta	4.6	9.1	17.2	47.8	21.3	100.0
British Columbia	4.3	9.5	13.7	55.8	16.7	100.0
Yukon and N.W. Territories	3.0	5.5	11.0	54.0	26.5	100.0

Note: The computations are based on the preceding table of "Occupations of Males Ranked According to the Combined Scores of Income and Education," which ranked occupations in the descending order by classes. The same breaks were used for provinces.

(Source: DBS, *Census of Canada, 1961*, Bulletins 94-509 to 94-512.)

ESTIMATES OF IMMIGRANTS AND NATIVE-BORN IN DIFFERENT SOCIAL CLASSES, 1961

	A Mainly two upper classes	B Mainly upper-middle	C Mainly lower-middle	D Mainly upper-lower	E Mainly lower-lower	Total
NUMBER						
Canada	198,857	400,419	707,914	2,544,176	854,152	4,705,518
Born in Canada	150,281	317,885	555,859	1,999,786	661,883	3,685,694
Foreign-born						
Immigrated before 1946	20,225	43,001	82,524	221,807	83,116	450,673
Immigrated after 1946	28,351	39,533	69,531	322,583	109,153	569,151
PERCENTAGE DISTRIBUTION						
Canada	4.2	8.5	15.0	54.1	18.2	100.0
Born in Canada	4.1	8.6	15.1	54.3	17.9	100.0
Foreign born						
Immigrated before 1946	4.5	9.5	18.3	49.2	18.5	100.0
Immigrated after 1946	5.0	6.9	12.2	56.7	19.2	100.0

Note: The computations are based on the preceding table of "Occupations of Males Ranked According to the Combined Scores of Income and Education," which ranked occupations in the descending order by classes. The same breaks were used for immigrant and native-born males in the labor force.

(Source: DBS, *Census of Canada, 1961*. Bulletin 94-515.)

SOCIAL CLASS ESTIMATES BY METROPOLITAN CENTERS, 1961

Metropolitan Centers	A Mainly two upper classes	B Mainly upper-middle	C Mainly lower-middle	D Mainly upper-lower	E Mainly lower-lower	Total
NUMBER						
Calgary	6,073	8,897	12,436	41,546	7,699	76,651
Edmonton	5,627	10,527	13,611	51,082	9,968	90,815
Halifax	2,291	5,910	5,590	33,700	3,980	51,471
Hamilton	5,134	8,894	16,110	68,035	10,469	108,642
Kitchener	1,981	3,896	5,983	26,608	5,313	43,781
London	2,819	5,114	7,984	27,695	5,120	48,732
Montréal	34,642	57,285	88,047	328,422	57,571	565,967
Ottawa	6,756	17,338	16,736	61,192	10,512	112,534
Québec	4,531	8,519	13,917	50,238	9,048	86,253
Regina	1,841	3,887	5,068	16,830	3,134	30,760
Saint John	898	2,226	3,073	14,679	2,146	23,022
St. John's	771	2,200	2,896	12,507	1,841	20,215
Sudbury	1,029	1,601	3,265	21,716	2,455	30,066
Toronto	36,618	62,122	88,410	287,784	54,084	529,018
Vancouver	11,363	23,267	28,988	115,585	25,059	204,262
Victoria	1,660	4,196	4,779	23,744	4,328	38,707
Windsor	2,397	4,498	7,082	30,651	4,538	49,166
Winnipeg	6,154	14,311	20,060	75,170	13,426	129,121
Total metropolitan centers	132,585	244,688	344,035	1,287,184	230,691	2,239,183
PERCENTAGE DISTRIBUTION						
Calgary	7.9	11.6	16.2	54.2	10.1	100.0
Edmonton	6.2	11.6	15.0	56.2	11.0	100.0
Halifax	4.4	11.5	10.9	65.5	7.7	100.0
Hamilton	4.7	8.2	14.8	62.6	9.7	100.0
Kitchener	4.5	8.9	13.7	60.8	12.1	100.0
London	5.8	10.5	16.4	56.8	10.5	100.0
Montréal	6.1	10.1	15.6	58.0	10.2	100.0
Ottawa	6.0	15.4	14.9	54.4	9.3	100.0
Québec	5.3	9.9	16.1	58.2	10.5	100.0
Regina	6.0	12.6	16.5	54.7	10.2	100.0
Saint John	3.9	9.7	13.3	63.8	9.3	100.0
St. John's	3.8	10.9	14.3	61.9	9.1	100.0
Sudbury	3.4	5.3	10.9	72.2	8.2	100.0
Toronto	6.9	11.8	16.7	54.4	10.2	100.0
Vancouver	5.5	11.4	14.2	56.6	12.3	100.0
Victoria	4.3	10.8	12.4	61.3	11.2	100.0
Windsor	4.9	9.2	14.4	62.3	9.2	100.0
Winnipeg	4.8	11.1	15.5	58.2	10.4	100.0
Total metropolitan centers	5.9	10.9	15.4	57.5	10.3	100.0

(Source: DBS, *Census of Canada, 1961.* Bulletin 94-504.)

SOCIAL CLASS ESTIMATES BY ETHNIC GROUPS, 1961

Ethnic groups	A Mainly two upper classes	B Mainly upper-middle	C Mainly lower-middle	D Mainly upper-lower	E Mainly lower-lower	Total
NUMBER						
Canada	198,857	400,419	707,914	2,544,176	854,152	4,705,518
British	116,038	228,489	343,999	1,082,502	300,389	2,071,417
French	35,634	78,476	169,090	759,098	260,982	1,303,280
German	9,151	20,633	43,688	163,265	60,266	297,003
Hungarian	1,703	2,316	5,607	22,407	10,503	42,536
Italian	1,767	5,680	10,387	82,710	36,527	137,071
Jewish	6,171	11,077	15,088	15,055	2,429	49,820
Dutch	3,600	8,353	16,466	59,921	26,732	115,072
Polish	3,615	6,078	14,059	53,476	18,872	96,100
Russian	1,971	3,274	5,960	14,719	6,647	32,571
Scandinavian	3,918	8,685	16,962	56,894	23,969	110,428
Ukrainian	3,422	7,998	21,249	72,691	30,627	135,987
Other European	6,632	10,781	26,088	99,810	41,627	184,938
Asiatic	2,011	2,245	9,356	16,548	7,360	37,520
Native Indian	85	255	882	8,525	17,230	26,977
Others	3,139	6,079	9,033	36,555	9,992	64,798
PERCENTAGE DISTRIBUTION						
Canada	4.2	8.5	15.0	54.1	18.2	100.0
British	5.6	11.0	16.6	52.3	14.5	100.0
French	2.7	6.0	13.0	58.3	20.0	100.0
German	3.1	6.9	14.7	55.0	20.3	100.0
Hungarian	4.0	5.4	13.2	52.7	24.7	100.0
Italian	1.3	4.1	7.6	60.3	26.7	100.0
Jewish	12.4	22.2	30.3	30.2	4.9	100.0
Dutch	3.1	7.3	14.3	52.1	23.2	100.0
Polish	3.8	6.3	14.6	55.7	19.6	100.0
Russian	6.0	10.1	18.3	45.2	20.4	100.0
Scandinavian	3.5	7.9	15.4	51.5	21.7	100.0
Ukrainian	2.5	5.9	15.6	53.5	22.5	100.0
Other European	3.6	5.8	14.1	54.0	22.5	100.0
Asiatic	5.4	6.0	24.9	44.1	19.6	100.0
Native Indian	0.3	0.9	3.3	31.6	63.9	100.0
Others	4.9	9.4	13.9	56.4	15.4	100.0

Note: The computations are based on the preceding table of "Occupations of Males Ranked According to the Combined Scores of Income and Education," which ranked occupations in the descending order by classes. The same breaks were used for males in the labor force by ethnic groups.

Source: DBS, *Census of Canada, 1961.* Bulletin 94-515.)

BIBLIOGRAPHY

Barber, Bernard: *Social Stratification,* Harcourt, Brace and Company, New York, 1957.

Bendix, Reinhard and Seymour Martin Lipset (editors): *Class Status and Power,* The Free Press, Glencoe, Illinois, 1953. Particularly the following chapters: 1) "Selected Characteristics of Classes in a Modern Middle Western Community" by August B. Hollingshead; 2) "The Warner Approach to Social Stratification" by Ruth Rosner Koruhauser; 3) "Portrait of the Underdog" by Genevieve Knupfer; 4) "Class Differences in Family Stability" by August B. Hollingshead; 5) "Fashion in Women's Clothes and the American Social System" by Bernard Barber and Lyle S. Lobel.

Blishen, Bernard R.: "The Construction and Use of an Occupational Class Scale," *Canadian Journal of Economics and Political Science,* November, 1958.

Chicago Tribune: The New Consumer, The Research Division of the Chicago Tribune, 1957.

Clark, S. D. (editor): *Urbanism and the Changing Canadian Society.* Particularly the chapter, "The Social System of a Slum: the Lower Ward, Toronto" by W. E. Mann. University of Toronto Press, 1961.

Coleman, Richard P.: "The Significance of Social Stratification in Selling," published in *Marketing: A Maturing Discipline.* Proceedings of the December 1960 Conference of the American Marketing Association, edited by Martin L. Bell.

Editors of *Fortune: Markets of the Sixties,* Harper and Brothers, New York, 1960. (Particularly Chapters VI and VII.)

Kemm, Thomas: "Defining Markets: Who belongs to which social class and what are his wants?" *Printers' Ink,* Vol. 264 (August 29, 1958).

Martineau, Pierre: "Social Classes and Spending Behavior," *The Journal of Marketing,* Volume 23, No. 2, October, 1958, published by the American Marketing Association.

Packard, Vance: *The Hidden Persuaders* and *The Status Seekers,* David McKay Company, Inc., New York, 1957 and 1959.

Pirie, Margaret C.: "Marketing and Social Classes: An Anthropologist's View," published in *The Management Review,* September, 1960.

Rainwater, Lee; Richard P. Coleman; and Gerald Handel: *Workingman's Wife,* MacFadden-Bartell Corp., New York, 1962.

Reissman, Leonard: *Class in American Society,* The Free Press of Glencoe, Illinois, 1959.

Smith, Lynn and C. A. McMahan: *The Sociology of Urban Life,* Dryden Press, New York, 1951.

True Story Women's Group: *The Invisible Wall, The Familiar Stranger* and *The Golden Triangle,* MacFadden Publications Inc., New York, 1960.

Warner, William Lloyd; Marchia Meeker; and Kenneth Eells: *Social Class in America,* Harper Torchbooks, Harper and Row Publishers, Inc., New York, 1960.

Chapter 11

MOSAIC BY INCOME GROUPS

Problem of Poverty

The famous Biblical pronouncement, "Ye have the poor with you always," holds true even for an affluent country like Canada. Despite a steady rise in income, want and privation still exist, keeping millions from sharing in the advantages and opportunities that the rest of the nation enjoys. To them, the affluent society is no longer a reality or a hope; it is, in fact, a mockery.

During the Depression nearly everybody was deprived, and there was a national fellowship of the poor. Today the situation is different. The poor are those who have been left stranded on the by-road, while the country as a whole has been moving ahead rapidly on the highway to prosperity. It is a small comfort to tell them that the average income of the Canadian is the second highest in the world, just as it is no consolation for a drowning man to know that the average depth of the lake is only four and a half feet.

However, "poverty" is one of those emotionally charged words that can trap a person if he is not careful. There is no objective definition of poverty, any more than there is an objective definition of art or beauty. The standards of poverty are established by society. They vary from place to place and from time to time within the same place.

Obviously, compared with the nineteenth-century poor, so bitingly described in literature — Zola's Gervaise was quite prepared to dispute with a dog for a bone — the Canadian poor are well off. They would be considered rich by most Red Chinese, whose per capita annual income averages far less than $100. In southern Italy and Sicily, thousands of *nullatenenti* (have-nots) are forced to live in caves or open trenches. Poverty is too soft a word to describe the maimed beggars that are common sights in some parts of Asia and Africa.

Nevertheless, Canada has its frustrated poor. People who are fairly well off tend to think of indigence in absolute, merely materialistic terms of Dickensian squalor. But poverty has to be measured in relation to the rising standards of living, the expectations of the individual, and the nation's capacity to produce wealth. Poverty is the condition — and the awareness — of being economically left behind while everyone else is marching forward. The "poor" are those who cannot *now* maintain a decent standard of living — a standard that includes not some food, but sufficient nutriment; not mere shelter, but decent housing; not just bare necessities but also nonessentials required for normal existence. Even if this poverty is not like any earlier poverty nor that prevalent in the rest of the world, it is still worth declaring a war on.

The general North American standard for measuring privation in non-farm areas is an annual income of less than $3,000 for families and of less than $1,500 for individuals not in families. To a certain extent, these are of course crude measures. Refined analysis would require the income cut-off to vary by family size, location, and other indications of needs and costs. Unfortunately, such breakdowns are not available from the official statistics.

For practical purposes, however, the dividing line selected for non-farm areas is not unrealistic. Budget studies frequently confirm the fact that persons below the level of $3,000 are hard-pressed and unable to cope with adverse contingencies, such as illness or unemployment. For example, a DBS survey shows that a city family with an average income of $2,577 has to spend $846 on food and $604 on housing, fuel, light, and water. This leaves $1,127, or less than $22 per week, to cover all other expenses including transportation, home furnishings and supplies, health care, and school books.

To complete the picture on poverty, one has to take into consideration the farm population as well. Since the cost of running a household is much lower on a farm than in urban areas, the cut-off figure usually taken is the annual gross income of $2,500, which nets in the neighborhood of $1,000. This is the level adopted by the Agricultural Rehabilitation and Development Administration (ARDA), set up by the federal government in 1961 to combat rural poverty.

WHO ARE THE POOR?

Analysis of the figures from the 1961 census indicate that today's have-nots are confined to special problem groups. Many are unskilled laborers. It is ironic that the technological revolution, which has been the key to prosperity for the majority, has also shut the door in the face of a sizeable minority. The hardest hit are those with less than 5 years of schooling, the so-called "functionally illiterate" who are incapable of reading and writing to the extent required for all but the most menial tasks. Such workers find it extremely difficult to win a niche for themselves in this fast-paced mechanized world. All they can look forward to is a succession of low-paid and frequently demeaning jobs. They do not share in the gains of good times, and invariably suffer the hardships of bad times.

The elderly are also caught in the web of poverty. Over half of the over-65-group families and nearly three-fourths of the individuals not in families have incomes below the minimum level. Medical science has helped to prolong their lives, but they are deprived of opportunities to fill the added years with material satisfactions. Many persons, now retired, were at the peak of their earning power during the Depression, and probably did not get a chance to build up a normal nest egg.

Equally harsh is the lot of the family that does not have a male breadwinner. Over 50% of the broken families headed by women are poor, compared to only 21% for normal families. The mother, who suddenly is forced to support her young children, probably lacks the skill and the time for a normal job. She may also encounter salary discrimination on account of her sex.

Disability is another major contributory cause of poverty. About 1.3 million Canadians have a permanent physical handicap of some degree. Although the majority are in the working age, only one in four has earnings from employment. The others have to depend on welfare, where their cases are often dealt with in a dilatory manner. In a report to the Federal-Provincial Conference on Poverty and Opportunity, the Canadian Welfare Council pointed out that hundreds of handicapped persons have actually been known to have died before government bureaucrats got around to making a decision on their applications.

Unfair racial discrimination also leads to distress and suffering. The hardest hit ethnic group is, ironically, the one that owned Canada before the white man arrived. The native Indians are the most destitute of the poverty-stricken in the country. The Indian Affairs Branch of the federal government reports that among the registered Indians, some 50% of the families have an annual income of $1,000 or less, while 75% of all the families earn below $2,000 a year. The average age of death for Indian males is 33.3 years and for females 34.7 years — far below the national mean of 60.5 years for men and 64.1 years for women. What is still more shocking, one of the main causes of death is from wholly preventable maladies like pneumonia. Thus, tucked away in city slums or in their desolate reservations, the Indians suffer from all the adverse effects of poverty — unsuitable and primitive housing, serious ill health, and dead ambitions that lead to apathy, immobility and hopelessness.

Many farmers, too, are on the low rung of the income ladder. The wave of affluence has swept by, leaving them and their families in eddies of poverty. The following table, based on the 1961 census, points out the large percentage of commercial and non-commercial farms that have difficulty in making their two ends meet.

	Farms with gross income below $2,500	% of total farms in the province
Newfoundland	1,471	84.0
Prince Edward Island	4,449	60.6
Nova Scotia	9,502	75.9
New Brunswick	8,713	73.9
Québec	56,850	59.3
Ontario	51,666	42.5
Manitoba	19,020	43.9
Saskatchewan	30,378	32.3
Alberta	28,009	38.2
British Columbia	11,784	59.1
Yukon and N.W. Territories	24	92.4
Canada	221,866	46.1

The under-$2,500 farmers are generally small operators working on holdings too tiny to warrant the use of machinery. They cannot expand because they are rarely able to secure farm credit of the kind or the amount required. The term "golden harvest" in this case is but an empty cliché. No doubt, farmers traditionally have a hard row to hoe, but that does not make their poverty easier to bear.

The lot of hired farm laborers is even worse. These migrant workers are not covered by the Minimum Wage Act or the Unemployment Insurance Act. Their average annual earnings are less than $1,200 a year, almost at a level of destitution. It has become a custom for corporation farms and large farmers to contract out work and thereby absolve themselves of the responsibility for housing and feeding migrant workers. Since these contractors are not licensed, there are no enforceable government regulations or standards by which the farm laborers can be protected.

Thus, poverty in Canada is far greater than most people imagine or are willing to accept. On the basis of the 1961 census, the count comes to 847,940 families (or 2,915,672 persons) and 687,857 persons not in families in non-farm areas; plus 221,866 farm households, (or 1,020,584 persons). The grand total is 4,624,113 or 25.4% of the nation's population. It is doubtful that this percentage may have gone down considerably since 1961. Past experience has shown that the general rise in the level of personal income, benefits mostly the middle and upper income groups.

Since poverty breeds poverty, it tends to be self-perpetuating. On account of discrimination, lack of education, and the conviction that the cards are stacked against them, the children of the poor are too often condemned to repeat their parents' fate. Squalid housing, with its accompanying frustrations, does not provide the suitable environment for bringing up a new generation that will play a constructive role in modern society. Clearly, poverty is a significant enough malady to make its alleviation a prime social and a national goal.

ALLEVIATING POVERTY

Praising the Lord and passing the alms, man has tried to fight social injustice for more than a thousand years. Hinduism and Buddhism encouraged almsgiving but reconciled themselves to poverty by suggesting that it was a requisite for man's prime goal: the enrichment of spirit instead of body. The early Christians adopted a similar attitude, as exemplified in the famous phrase, "Blessed are the poor." It is only recently, with the advent of technology and increased productivity, that the goal of abolishing want and distress has come within the reach of realization. The experience of Scandinavia indicates that one can not only balm the wounds of the poor but also reshape their skills, attitudes and even their personalities.

In the recent Federal-Provincial Conference on Poverty and Opportunity, a brief submitted by the Government of Manitoba pointed out that only about

25% of the poor in Canada are hard-core or unavoidable cases. Included in this category are elderly people, mothers with young children and no male bread-winner, as well as persons suffering from serious social, physical or mental disabilities. Here, increased welfare payments and enlightened social policies are probably the best remedies. They can at least alleviate the misery, if not remove it.

For the other 75% of the cases, the problem is essentially economic as distinct from social. Given a sound strategy and the proper mobilization of resources, a successful attack can be mounted in a comparatively short time. Some of the measures needed include removal of slums; elimination of all forms of discrimination in social and economic life; increase in the minimum wage and extension of its coverage; financial help to the dependent children of the unemployed; federal assistance to vitalize the economies of depressed areas; and a comprehensive educational program, ranging from job-training camps for high-school drop-outs to vocational courses for slum adults. For the small farmers, the best solution probably lies in the consolidation of uneconomic farms and their conversion, where necessary, to more suitable uses, such as woodlots or pastures. This implies the need for special farm credit, improved guidance in farm management, and re-establishment allowances, as well as vocational and technical training for those who may be obliged to leave the farms.

As regards long-range plans, utmost efforts would have to be made to see that the children of the poor get a much better education than their parents received. The cost of such a program would be high, but it is one of the best investments our nation can undertake. In addition to providing the tools to meet the challenge of the technological revolution, education broadens mental perspectives, turns lethargy into ambition, and generates the desire to attain a higher standard of living. In fact, some experts believe that children from slum homes should be voluntarily transferred to free boarding schools, so that they can have the opportunity to be educated away from the unfavorable environment and perverse influences of a squalid, indifferent home life.

Along the same lines, suggestions have been made that more should be spent per pupil in poor communities than in the rich suburbs — the reverse of the current situation. This would tend to lift the horizons of poor children and enable them to compete on a more equal footing. At present, because of the decentralized character of public education, economic inequality is compounded by geographic inequality. Many poor children are concentrated in school districts with a low tax base, and most of the poor school districts, in turn, are in provinces that cannot afford to give these communities enough assistance to overcome the handicap. Federal aid to education is a major weapon in Ottawa's war on poverty, but most of the programs envisage grants to *all* schools. It would be better, though politically difficult, to concentrate the bulk of the federal funds in those counties and census divisions where the median family income is under $3,000 a year.

Whatever the answers, it is clear that stamping out want and deprivation is not an easy matter. Poverty is too complex to lend itself to general cures. It is a pocket blight, and each pocket needs its own peculiar medication. The enemy has to be fought in every corner and crevice, and in every form that it manifests itself, either apparent or disguised.

The measures taken so far have not been adequate. In fact, quite often, the so-called welfare legislation does not primarily benefit the poor. The farm price-support program is intended to boost the low incomes of agriculturists; but the poorest of the farm families — those that grow crops for their own subsistence — get almost no aid. Other welfare institutions also tend to ignore those who need help the most. The National Employment Service offices have little contact with the very poor. Urban renewal more often than not results in uprooting the slum dwellers to provide housing for the middle-income families. Huge sums are spent in building hospitals which are of little help to people who cannot afford health insurance. The bulk of the federal-provincial vocational training programs require a minimum of high school education, and therefore bypass the unskilled who most need to learn a new trade but do not have the academic qualifications to enroll for the classes.

Even when the poor are directly involved, they are rarely consulted on what services should be offered to them, or how they are to be run. In fact, the officers in charge seldom take kindly the suggestions from the recipients of the handouts. All too often, by conveying to the poor the message that they are helpless and inferior, the social workers manage to create or reinforce the very sense of dependency they are supposed to eliminate.

What is needed is something equivalent to the U.S. Community Action Program, which mobilizes the poor themselves, organizing people of rundown neighborhoods to manage their own child-care centers and basic education courses, and to conduct self-help drives to improve housing and sanitation. The purpose of such programs is not to deliver more or better social services, but to get the poor involved and to persuade them that they can control their own environment. Only then is the tragic effect of paternalism removed. "I warn you against doing good to people" a British social worker said two hundred years ago. "One does good, if at all, *with* people, not *to* them." The warning still holds.

No doubt, it is difficult to encourage initiative on the part of those who have been brought up in destitute, broken homes where the father does not go to work every morning. Even the technical training sometimes fails to accomplish its purpose of making the unemployed more employable, when the unemployed in question have built a way of life around getting the most out of various kinds of relief. However, the research done by the Canadian Welfare Council indicates that such cases are the exception rather than the rule. The country's poor are not lazy and irresponsible. The majority work hard for their low incomes, and they do not like to live on handouts. The have-nots cannot pull themselves up by their own boot straps simply because their environment has done little to prepare them to cope with the realities of today. So, when an opportunity for improvement does present itself, they are not equipped to grasp it.

What would it cost to alleviate poverty? Exhaustive studies in the United States have shown that by spending 2% of the Gross National Product, it would be possible to bring all poor families up to a minimum income level of $3,000 a year. No corresponding estimates are available for Canada, but the proportion in relation to the Gross National Product would be slightly higher since a larger percentage of the population is below the poverty line.

There are good social and economic reasons why Canadians can and should allocate this amount to relieve distress. True, ethical considerations demand that society should provide equal opportunities to the poor and the rich alike. But, what is more significant, the measures designed to lift up the poor, if sensibly devised and efficiently administered, can bring great economic benefits as well. Obviously, very little can be sold to persons who are unemployed or get below-subsistence wages. If their earnings rise to a desirable level, they acquire the urge to improve their standard of living. In the process of spending their increased income, they buy more products from the farmer and the businessman and so, in turn, provide more jobs for other Canadians. In short, winning the war on poverty not only helps the poor, it also promotes continued economic growth, raises the employment and income levels for *all,* and strengthens the fabric of the nation as a whole.

A DBS survey on urban consumer expenditures indicates that when a family moves up the income bracket, from below $3,000 to $3,000–$3,999, it spends:

- 20% more on housing, fuel, light, water
- 32% more on food
- 36% more on household operation
- 42% more on medical care
- 45% more on reading
- 61% more on smoking and alcoholic drinks
- 64% more on personal care
- 68% more on furnishings and equipment
- 83% on recreation
- 84% more on clothing
- 100% more on education
- 137% more on security
- 198% more on automobiles.

When one remembers that over a fifth of the non-farm families earn below $3,000 a year, the new markets that can open up through elimination of poverty almost stagger the imagination. As one economist remarks: "Our greatest untapped market lies not in the Far North, but right at our very doorstep among the needy poor."

THE PROFILE OF CANADA'S POOR (NON-FARM), 1961

	Families			Persons not in families		
	Total of all families	Families below $3,000	Per cent of all families	Total of all persons	Persons below $1,500	Per cent of all persons
Sex						
Male head	3,409,942	716,280	21.0	622,821	239,090	38.4
Female head	247,026	131,660	53.3	784,455	448,767	57.2
Total	3,656,968	847,940	23.2	1,407,276	687,857	48.9

(Source: DBS, *Census of Canada, 1961*. Bulletin 98-504.)

Residence by province						
Newfoundland	86,458	44,273	51.2	24,683	18,213	73.8
Prince Edward Island	14,386	6,447	44.8	6,574	4,414	67.1
Nova Scotia	146,825	54,929	37.4	59,731	37,247	62.4
New Brunswick	110,715	43,118	38.9	39,714	24,761	62.3
Québec	993,738	241,552	24.3	359,705	178,627	49.7
Ontario	1,376,148	245,396	17.8	534,805	240,077	44.9
Manitoba	175,311	41,631	23.7	71,693	35,348	49.3
Saskatchewan	142,203	44,923	31.6	61,735	32,794	53.1
Alberta	239,607	49,560	20.7	95,341	41,885	43.9
British Columbia	368,773	75,674	20.5	152,083	74,052	48.7
Yukon	2,804	437	15.6	1,212	439	36.2
Canada	3,656,968	847,940	23.2	1,407,276	687,857	48.9

(Source: DBS, *Census of Canada, 1961*. Bulletin 98-503.)

Residence: Urban-Rural						
Metropolitan areas						
City proper	1,046,717	198,205	18.9	580,163	234,826	40.5
Suburbs	873,190	110,397	12.6	227,072	104,823	46.2
Other urban	1,033,548	240,517	23.3	374,523	193,839	51.8
Rural non-farm	703,513	298,821	42.5	225,518	154,369	68.5
Total	3,656,968	847,940	23.2	1,407,276	687,857	48.9

(Source: DBS, *Census of Canada, 1961*. Bulletin 98-503.)

Age of family head						
Under 25	168,311	54,321	32.3	224,276	91,323	40.7
25–34	869,222	162,615	18.7	189,650	43,489	22.9
35–44	935,893	148,135	15.8	141,703	39,070	27.6
45–54	756,787	126,511	16.7	171,197	61,292	35.8
55–64	477,732	118,323	24.8	219,671	110,245	50.2
65 and over	449,023	238,035	53.0	460,779	342,438	74.3
Total	3,656,968	847,940	23.2	1,407,276	687,857	48.9

(Source: DBS, *Census of Canada, 1961*. Bulletin 98-504.)

THE PROFILE OF CANADA'S POOR (NON-FARM), 1961 (continued)

	Families			Persons not in families		
	Total of all families	Families below $3,000	Per cent of all families	Total of all persons	Persons below $1,500	Per cent of all persons
Education of family head						
No schooling	46,308	31,681	68.4	33,769	28,548	84.5
Elementary	1,646,666	554,724	33.7	669,193	415,055	62.0
Secondary	1,636,268	241,219	14.7	603,197	221,113	36.7
Some university	137,573	12,183	8.9	56,252	14,801	26.3
University degree	190,153	8,133	4.3	44,865	8,340	18.6
Total	3,656,968	847,940	23.2	1,407,276	687,857	48.9

(Source: DBS, *Census of Canada, 1961*. Bulletin 98-504.)

	Total of all families	Families below $3,000	Per cent of all families	Total of all persons	Persons below $1,500	Per cent of all persons
Occupation of family head						
White collar						
Managerial	427,349	36,026	8.4	37,851	5,991	15.8
Professional and technical	266,687	10,306	3.9	102,591	12,417	12.1
Clerical	229,460	24,391	10.6	145,065	15,889	11.0
Sales	193,436	22,943	11.9	44,174	10,646	24.1
Blue collar						
Craftsmen, production process, and related workers	1,024,824	140,338	13.7	167,696	29,840	17.8
Unskilled laborers	156,360	54,559	34.9	42,878	14,269	33.3
Other occupations						
Service and recreation	277,875	60,048	21.6	145,295	74,071	51.0
Transport and communications	265,863	46,010	17.3	37,573	6,393	17.0
Primary industries	161,518	69,672	43.1	26,988	12,259	45.4
Not stated	41,658	8,556	20.5	28,788	4,765	16.6
Sub-total heads in labor force	3,045,030	472,849	15.5	778,899	186,540	23.9
Heads not in labor force	611,938	375,091	61.3	628,377	501,317	79.8
Total	3,656,968	847,940	23.2	1,407,276	687,857	48.9

(Source: DBS, *Census of Canada, 1961*. Bulletin 98-504.)

Interpretation: Out of the total of 3,656,968 non-farm families in Canada, 847,940 or 23.2% have an annual income from all sources of less than $3,000. Similarly, 1,407,276 persons are not in families; that is, living alone, living with unrelated individuals as lodgers or employees, or living with relatives but not in a husband-wife or parent-child relationship. Of these 1,407,276 persons, 687,857 or 48.9% have an annual income of below $1,500. These two percentages, 23.2% and 48.9%, constitute the yardsticks against which other percentages should be measured to assess the extent of poverty. For example, 53.3% of all families with female heads are poor, which is 2.3 times higher than the average of 23.2%. Similarly, in Newfoundland, 73.8% of persons not in families fall under the poverty definition. This percentage is almost 24 points higher than the Canadian average of 48.9%.

ANNUAL CONSUMPTION EXPENDITURES OF POOR URBAN FAMILIES
COMPARED WITH THE AVERAGE FOR ALL FAMILIES, 1959

Items of expenditure	Average expenditures ($)		Percentage distribution	
	All families	Families under $3,000	All families	Families under $3,000
Food	1,323	846	23.8%	32.8%
Housing, fuel, light water	911	604	16.4	23.4
Household operation	214	118	3.8	4.6
Furnishings and equipment	277	123	5.0	4.8
Clothing	508	183	9.1	7.1
Automobile	518	82	9.3	3.2
Other transportation	112	61	2.0	2.4
Medical care	237	142	4.3	5.5
Personal care	118	55	2.1	2.1
Recreation	160	59	2.9	2.3
Reading	35	20	0.6	0.8
Education	39	5	0.7	0.2
Smoking and alcoholic drinks	230	105	4.1	4.1
Other	69	31	1.2	1.2
All current consumption	4,751	2,434	85.3	94.5
Gifts and contributions	170	66	3.0	2.5
Personal taxes	378	15	6.8	0.6
Security	271	62	4.9	2.4
Total expenditures	5,570	2,577	100.0%	100.0%

(Source: DBS, *Urban Family Expenditures, 1959*. Catalog no. 62-521.)

Characteristics of Non-farm Families Above the Poverty Line

The families above the $3,000 poverty mark can be roughly classified into three broad categories:

- Lower income: $3,000–$5,999
- Middle income: $6,000–$9,999
- Upper income: $10,000 and over

The tables at the end of this section highlight the profiles of non-farm families in each of these three income groups. The figures have been compiled from the latest available 1961 census reports and from the DBS survey, *Urban Family Expenditure, 1959*. Although a few years old, it is unlikely that the tables are out-of-date. The actual number of families in each class would, of course, differ with the passage of time, but, since the socio-economic traits of the population change very slowly, the percentages shown are apt to remain very much the same.*

The following is a brief résumé of these tables. The aim is to bring out the striking characteristics of the family heads in each income group by age, occupation, education, residence, place of birth, and the like — in short, to convert the statistics into recognizable people.

LOWER INCOME: $3,000–$5,999

This by far is the largest segment of the market. The educational level is fairly low, and consequently two-thirds of the families are headed by the so-called "working-class" types: craftsmen, foremen, skilled and unskilled operators in factories, and workers in service, transportation and primary industries. In 54.8% of the cases the husband is the sole breadwinner, compared to only 30.6% in the middle income bracket. This is because the wife is often compelled to stay at home to look after the young children. 34.3% of the family heads are under 35, nine percentage points higher than that for the next group. In this respect, the lower income class may, to a certain extent, be regarded as the younger version of the middle-income class, poised to rise eventually as experience and seniority, plus the extra worker in the family, augment its earnings.

About 44% of the annual budget has to be devoted to the two basic necessities, food and shelter, compared to only 37% for the middle-income group. As a result, a relatively smaller proportion is left over for nonessentials. Nevertheless, these households do not as a rule suffer from severe hardships. 96% have refrigerators, 90% television sets, 74% automobiles, and 60% homes of their own. Over a third of these single-detached homes are valued above $12,500.

MIDDLE INCOME: $6,000-$9,999

The families here begin to have what the economists call "discretionary spending power." Unfortunately, this expression is one of those loose terms for which it is possible to get six different definitions from half a dozen experts. Broadly speaking, it represents the stage at which a family can use most of its money to purchase things it would like to have rather than what it must have. Admittedly, much depends on the size and composition of the household. Also, one man's need may be another man's discretion. Hence, the dividing line between discretionary and nondiscretionary income is somewhat arbitrary. However, it can be roughly set at the $6,000 level. At that point quantity slowly changes into quality. The average-sized family is no longer solely preoccupied

* The 1961 census also provides statistics on persons not in families, but no special tabulations have been prepared for them, since they do not constitute an important segment of the consumer market. Their average income is very low because of the high concentration at the two extremes of the age scale — the very young and the very old.

with obtaining the basic necessities, for it has now the extra money to exercise a number of options. It can buy better food and drinks, acquire a new car instead of a used one, or take a small flyer in the stock market.

The family heads in the middle-income class are not young any more. 55.7% are between 35 and 54 years of age, considerably above the norm of 46.3%. About seven out of ten have homes of their own, and nearly a third reside in the suburbs of metropolitan areas.

A large number in this class would tumble sharply down the income ladder if all married men had to support their families on what they alone earned. The total purchasing power is boosted in many cases by wives, and sometimes even by grown-up children, bringing home the paycheck. Only 30.9% of the families in this income bracket have one person working, far below the average of 48.8%; 50.4% have two income recipients and 18.7% even three or more.

The educational record, on the whole, is better than the norm. Close to 70% have continued at school beyond the elementary level; however, the fraction that pushed on to college is not significant. As a result, though there is a general upgrading in occupational pursuits, with above-par representations in managerial, professional and sales positions, over half the family heads have non-white-collar jobs. In other words, the group consists, to a startling extent, of persons hitherto identified as proletarians. The old stereotype of the middle-income class comprising mainly of the "petty bourgeoisie" no longer holds true.

The percentage distribution of expenditures in the consumer's budget broadly parallels the average for all families. The only noteworthy differences are above-par spending on automobiles and below-par on food and housing. The group has sufficient purchasing power to enjoy most of the comforts and conveniences of life. 74.9% have at least one automobile and another 11.3% two or more. 58.8% own single-detached homes, of which 66.7% are of postwar construction and 64.1% valued over $12,500.

UPPER INCOME: $10,000 AND OVER

This sector constitutes the cream of the market. It owns most of the wealth, does most of the saving, and is primarily responsible for investments, which are the key to prosperity and full employment. It is frequently imagined that large numbers in this bracket make their living by clipping coupons, but nothing could be farther from the truth. Only 5% have their main income other than from employment — interests, dividends, rents, royalties, and the like. The remaining 95% are dependent primarily on earnings from their jobs or businesses. In fact, many would never have qualified for inclusion in the affluent class were it not for the pooling of the salaries of several members. 31.3% of the upper-crust families have three or more income recipients, three times above the norm of 10.8%. Father works, mother works, and in many cases the children, too, contribute something to the family exchequer. Many women married to successful men are well trained themselves and are not satisfied to do menial jobs around the house or to bask in the glory of their husbands' accomplishments. They seek intellectual stimulation, which an interesting job often provides. The earnings from the children are, however, temporary. This means that the number in this income group is continuously fluctuating. When working youngsters leave to form households of their own, the family often falls into a lower bracket; while in other homes, children enter the labor force and improve the family's income status.

Nearly two-thirds of the family heads are managers, proprietors, or professionals. This group is the reservoir of some of the best talent in the country — doctors, lawyers, engineers, professors, business tycoons, and top executives directing the fortunes of large corporations. Their skills are much in demand, and therefore they have a high earning potential. As may be expected, the education record is quite impressive. Over a quarter of the family heads hold a university degree, while another 8% have at least some college training. Experience also plays a major role; 61.8% of the heads have passed the age of 45. Very few young households (under 35) are found in this group.

The gold-plated families, geographically speaking, tend to bunch up in large clusters, making it relatively easy to track them down. Over two-thirds are located in the 17 DBS metropolitan centers, and within these centers over half live in the suburbs. The new income elite seek more fashionable neighborhoods, most of which are outside the cities' cores. When the figures are analysed by provinces, Ontario has more than its normal share of upper income groups, while the Atlantic Provinces are considerably underrepresented.

Families in the more rarefied income atmosphere are always heady prospects for marketing executives. These prized targets siphon off about three times more of the income pie than their numbers suggest. Besides, since only a small proportion of their income is devoted to basic necessities, a substantial amount is left over to be spent on the vast array of goods and services that make up "the good life." 29.3% have two or more cars, and 16.6% two or more television sets. Above two-thirds own single-detached homes of which 35.4% are valued over $22,500.

It must, of course, be remembered that in the upper portion there is a juxtaposition of the old-rich and the new-rich. The former, with several generations of money and social position behind them, consider it somewhat boorish and crude to display wealth, even to talk about it. They spend money, but the results are not publicly seen. The newly rich families constitute the brassy lower portion of the upper class. They look upon the piling up of possessions as badges of honor and compete with each other in exhibitionist spending. As consumers, they are therefore the darlings of the marketers.

Income and Education

One feature that emerges clearly from these statistics is the close relationship between income and education. As a rule, the more educated the person is, the greater are his earnings. This can be seen in the following table which indicates the average income of the non-farm population in Canada by age, sex, and schooling.

AVERAGE INCOME OF THE NON-FARM POPULATION IN CANADA BY AGE, SEX AND SCHOOLING, 1961

Age groups	Average for all groups	No schooling	Ele-mentary	Second-ary (1–3 yrs.)	Second-ary (4–5 yrs.)	Some uni-versity	Uni-versity degree
Males							
15–24	$1,972	$1,426	$1,854	$1,966	$2,150	$1,711	$ 3,055
25–34	4,273	1,768	3,415	4,271	4,886	5,179	6,994
35–44	5,081	2,036	3,834	4,857	6,019	6,888	10,355
45–54	4,977	2,176	3,742	4,912	6,397	7,229	11,430
55–64	4,393	2,141	3,396	4,637	6,136	7,012	11,425
65–69	3,163	1,609	2,412	3,669	4,651	5,543	9,605
Over 69	2,071	1,123	1,644	2,473	3,532	4,153	6,188
Average	$3,999	$1,715	$3,134	$3,943	$4,825	$4,995	$9,048
Index	100	43	78	99	121	125	226
Females							
15–24	$1,455	$1,072	$1,115	$1,351	$1,741	$1,681	$ 2,362
25–34	1,914	953	1,516	1,768	2,216	2,584	3,149
35–44	1,864	972	1,510	1,718	2,179	2,731	3,468
45–54	1,919	1,015	1,445	1,780	2,397	3,149	4,037
55–64	1,746	966	1,273	1,771	2,416	3,241	4,294
65–69	1,328	845	992	1,497	2,106	2,324	3,365
Over 69	1,154	811	954	1,247	1,796	2,891	2,592
Average	$1,651	$ 888	$1,247	$1,589	$2,080	$2,535	$ 3,384
Index	100	54	76	96	126	154	205

(Source: DBS, *Census of Canada, 1961*. Bulletin 98-501.)

In every case, within the same age and sex grouping, the income increases as one moves up the education scale. The only exception is in the younger age group (15-24) where persons having some university training earn less than those with high school diplomas. But this is because a large number attend classes during the year and can only work part-time. It is in no way a reflection on their earning capacity.

Another important fact is that the maximum earning power is reached later in life for those with better academic qualifications. For males who have just completed elementary school, highest earnings ($3,834) are in the 35-44 age bracket. For those with a university degree, income increases significantly at each age level, reaching a peak in the age group of 45 to 64. The implications of this analysis are fairly clear. While there may be some short-term financial gain in curtailing one's schooling to get a paying job, over the full span of a normal working life the advantage is with a person who has acquired a university education. This is brought out distinctly in the table below.

EDUCATION AND LIFETIME EARNINGS (FROM AGE 15 TO 65)
FOR MALES

Level of schooling	Income	Above or below average
Average for all groups	$206,960	—
No schooling	95,470	−111,490
Elementary	162,410	− 44,550
Secondary: 1–3 years	206,430	− 530
4 or 5 years	255,880	+ 48,920
Some university	280,190	+ 73,230
University degree	432,590	+225,630

(Computed from previous table.)

The difference between the expected lifetime earnings of the male with average elementary school and high school education is quite striking — $93,470. But the greatest gains appear at the university-degree level. A college graduate can hope to earn about $432,590 during his normal working lifetime as compared with $255,880 for an average high school graduate. Even when these earnings are matched against the high cost of college training — a cost often borne by the parents — the rate of return is still obviously substantial.

To sum up, education and affluence go hand in hand. There are many exceptions, to be sure. Differences in talent, imagination, drive, home environment, family connections, or just plain good luck, cause some people to do well and others poorly, despite the same level of formal schooling. But, on the whole, education has a distinct bearing on the individual's level of income. "Let ignorance talk as it will, learning has its value." So expressed the French essayist La Fontaine 300 years ago. These words hold true even more today in this age of technological revolution.

BIBLIOGRAPHY

Faltermayer, Edmund W.: "Who Are the American Poor?" *Fortune,* March, 1964.
Federal Reserve Bank of Philadelphia: "The New Poverty." A pamphlet forming part of the *Series for Economic Education,* September, 1964.
Firestone, O. J.: *Problems of Economic Growth,* University of Ottawa Press, Ottawa, 1965.
Fortune: "The Mixed-Up War on Poverty," August, 1965.
Indian Affairs Branch: *Statement for Federal-Provincial Conference on Poverty,* December, 1965.
Ontario Federation of Labour: *Poverty in Ontario, 1964.* A report prepared by the Research Department for the 8th annual convention held at North Bay in October, 1964.
Time: "The Poor Amidst Prosperity." Time Essay, October 1, 1965.

SOCIO-ECONOMIC CHARACTERISTICS OF NON-FARM FAMILIES
WITH INCOME OVER $3,000, 1961

	Average income ($)	Average for all families	Total family income		
			$3,000 –5,999	$6,000 –9,999	$10,000 and over
Sex					
Male head	5,590	93.2%	95.2%	96.8%	97.0%
Female head	3,500	6.8	4.8	3.2	3.0
Total	5,449	100.0%	100.0%	100.0%	100.0%
Number of families	—	3,656,968	1,663,022	858,921	287,085

(Source: DBS, *Census of Canada, 1961.* Bulletin 98-504.)

	Average income ($)	Average for all families	Total family income		
			$3,000 –5,999	$6,000 –9,999	$10,000 and over
Income recipients: Number					
One income recipient	4,586	48.8%	56.2%	30.9%	28.3%
2 income recipients	5,803	40.1	37.1	50.4	40.4
3 or more income recipients	8,218	10.8	6.7	18.7	31.3
No income	—	0.3	—	—	—
Total	5,449	100.0%	100.0%	100.0%	100.0%
Number of families	—	3,656,968	1,663,022	858,921	287,085

(Source: DBS, *Census of Canada, 1961.* Bulletin 98-503.)

	Average income ($)	Average for all families	Total family income		
			$3,000 –5,999	$6,000 –9,999	$10,000 and over
Income recipients: Relationship					
Husband only	4,779	45.4%	54.8%	30.6%	28.0%
Husband and wife	5,824	30.1	27.6	38.4	29.8
Husband, wife and children	8,398	6.3	4.0	11.0	18.1
Husband and children	6,984	10.7	8.6	16.7	21.0
All other	3,484	7.2	5.0	3.3	3.1
No income	—	0.3	—	—	—
Total	5,449	100.0%	100.0%	100.0%	100.0%
Number of families	—	3,656,968	1,663,022	858,921	287,085

(Source: DBS, *Census of Canada, 1961.* Bulletin 98-503.)

	Average income ($)	Average for all families	Total family income		
			$3,000 –5,999	$6,000 –9,999	$10,000 and over
Age of family head					
Under 25	3,970	4.6%	5.4%	2.7%	0.5%
25–34	5,020	23.8	28.9	22.5	11.5
35–44	5,810	25.6	27.6	29.5	26.2
45–54	6,373	20.7	18.7	26.2	32.9
55–64	5,895	13.1	11.5	13.0	19.7
65–69	4,533	4.6	3.4	2.8	4.4
70 and over	3,750	7.6	4.5	3.3	4.8
Total	5,449	100.0%	100.0%	100.0%	100.0%
Number of families	—	3,656,968	1,663,022	858,921	287,085

(Source: DBS, *Census of Canada, 1961.* Bulletin 98-504.)

SOCIO-ECONOMIC CHARACTERISTICS OF NON-FARM FAMILIES WITH INCOME OVER $3,000 (continued)

	Average income ($)	Average for all families	Total family income $3,000–5,999	Total family income $6,000–9,999	Total family income $10,000 and over
Family size					
2 persons	4,615	29.3%	24.9%	24.1%	20.5%
3 persons	5,388	20.9	21.8	21.5	18.7
4 persons	5,919	21.0	22.5	23.9	24.4
5 persons	6,103	13.4	14.5	14.9	17.3
6 or more persons	5,913	15.4	16.3	15.6	19.1
Total	5,449	100.0%	100.0%	100.0%	100.0%
Number of families	—	3,656,968	1,663,022	858,921	287,085

(Source: DBS, *Census of Canada, 1961.* Bulletin 98-503.)

	Average income ($)	Average for all families	Total family income $3,000–5,999	Total family income $6,000–9,999	Total family income $10,000 and over
Education of family head					
No schooling	2,778	1.3%	0.7%	0.3%	0.3%
Elementary	4,381	45.0	46.2	30.0	22.6
Secondary	5,790	44.7	48.2	54.6	43.2
Some university	7,499	3.8	3.0	6.2	8.0
University	10,925	5.2	1.9	8.9	25.9
Total	5,449	100.0%	100.0%	100.0%	100.0%
Number of families	—	3,656,968	1,663,022	858,921	287,085

(Source: DBS, *Census of Canada, 1961.* Bulletin 98-504.)

	Average income ($)	Average for all families	Total family income $3,000–5,999	Total family income $6,000–9,999	Total family income $10,000 and over
Occupation of family head					
White collar					
Managerial	8,629	14.0%	8.9%	18.8%	40.2%
Professional and technical	8,728	8.8	5.2	14.2	24.3
Clerical	5,262	7.5	9.1	7.4	3.0
Sales	6,173	6.4	5.8	8.0	7.1
Blue collar					
Craftsmen, production process, etc.	5,197	33.7	39.7	31.2	13.7
Unskilled laborers	3,915	5.1	5.5	2.1	1.0
Other occupations					
Service and recreation	4,819	9.1	10.2	6.9	3.6
Transport and communications	5,117	8.7	9.8	7.6	4.3
Primary industries	3,447	5.3	4.3	2.7	1.8
Not stated	4,842	1.4	1.5	1.1	1.0
Total	5,850	100.0%	100.0%	100.0%	100.0%
No. of families in labor force	—	3,045,030	1,505,543	802,196	264,442

(Source: DBS, *Census of Canada, 1961.* Bulletin 98-504.)

SOCIO-ECONOMIC CHARACTERISTICS OF NON-FARM FAMILIES
WITH INCOME OVER $3,000 (continued)

	Average income ($)	Average for all families	Total family income		
			$3,000 –5,999	$6,000 –9,999	$10,000 and over
Residence: By province					
Newfoundland	3,673	2.4%	1.8%	1.1%	1.0%
Prince Edward Island	3,919	0.4	0.3	0.2	0.2
Nova Scotia	4,260	4.0	3.9	2.5	2.0
New Brunswick	4,155	3.0	2.9	1.7	1.4
Québec	5,387	27.2	28.0	23.5	29.3
Ontario	5,868	37.6	37.9	44.2	42.3
Manitoba	5,260	4.8	5.0	4.6	4.1
Saskatchewan	4,803	3.9	3.6	3.3	2.9
Alberta	5,602	6.5	6.6	7.1	6.8
British Columbia	5,618	10.1	9.9	11.7	9.9
Yukon	6,473	0.1	0.1	0.1	0.1
Canada	5,449	100.0%	100.0%	100.0%	100.0%
Number of families	—	3,656,968	1,663,022	858,921	287,085

(Source: DBS, *Census of Canada, 1961.* Bulletin 98-503.)

	Average income ($)	Average for all families	Total family income		
			$3,000 –5,999	$6,000 –9,999	$10,000 and over
Residence: Urban-rural					
Metropolitan centers					
City proper	5,768	28.6%	29.3%	31.0%	32.8%
Suburbs	6,534	23.9	23.2	31.9	35.9
Other urban	5,201	28.3	30.0	26.6	22.9
Rural non-farm	3,990	19.2	17.5	10.5	8.4
Total	5,449	100.0%	100.0%	100.0%	100.0%
Number of families	—	3,656,968	1,663,022	858,921	287,085

(Source: DBS, *Census of Canada, 1961.* Bulletin 98-503.)

	Average income ($)	Average for all families	Total family income		
			$3,000 –5,999	$6,000 –9,999	$10,000 and over
Native and foreign born					
Immigrated					
Before 1946	5,457	13.4%	11.4%	13.0%	16.0%
1946–1955	5,594	7.5	8.6	8.4	6.3
1956–1961	4,963	3.7	4.0	3.5	2.2
Born in Canada	5,460	75.4	76.0	75.1	75.5
Total	5,449	100.0%	100.0%	100.0%	100.0%
Number of families	—	3,656,968	1,663,022	858,921	287,085

(Source: DBS, *Census of Canada, 1961.* Bulletin 98-504.)

HOUSING CHARACTERISTICS OF NON-FARM FAMILY HOUSEHOLDS WITH INCOME OVER $3,000, 1961

	Average income ($)	Average for all families	Total family income		
			$3,000 –5,999	$6,000 –9,999	$10,000 and over
Tenure					
Owned					
Single detached	5,904	54.5%	49.9%	58.8%	67.4%
Other	5,834	10.2	10.0	10.6	12.2
Rented	4,948	35.3	40.1	30.6	20.4
Total	5,560	100.0%	100.0%	100.0%	100.0%
Number of family households....	—	3,504,692	1,604,113	847,081	287,616
Monthly cash rent					
No cash rent	4,360	5.8%	5.5%	4.4%	3.8%
Under $ 20	3,377	2.6	2.1	1.0	0.8
$ 20–$ 39	3,785	15.6	14.7	7.2	6.2
$ 40–$ 59	4,388	26.5	29.5	18.8	13.4
$ 60–$ 79	4,962	24.4	27.6	24.9	17.0
$ 80–$ 99	5,660	12.4	12.3	18.7	13.4
$100–$119	6,369	7.3	5.7	14.8	13.3
$120–$129	7,271	2.3	1.4	4.9	7.9
$130–$149	8,300	1.6	0.7	3.4	9.0
$150 and over	11,731	1.5	0.5	1.9	15.2
Total	4,948	100.0%	100.0%	100.0%	100.0%
Number of family households that are tenants	—	1,236,493	642,888	258,939	58,720
Value of dwelling					
Under $ 3,000	2,665	8.4%	5.5%	1.3%	1.0%
$ 3,000–$ 7,499	3,916	19.7	22.0	8.8	4.4
$ 7,500–$12,499	5,116	28.6	36.3	25.8	12.7
$12,500–$17,499	6,467	25.8	26.7	39.0	23.6
$17,500–$22,499	7,992	10.7	7.1	17.9	22.9
$22,500 and over	13,542	6.8	2.4	7.2	35.4
Total	5,904	100.0%	100.0%	100.0%	100.0%
No. of family households owning single-detached homes	—	1,910,367	799,869	497,880	193,981
Period of construction					
Before 1920	4,873	19.3%	19.3%	12.7%	12.3%
1920–1945	5,780	24.1	24.0	20.6	24.3
1946–1959	6,318	52.0	52.0	61.1	59.0
1960–1961	6,202	4.6	4.7	5.6	4.4
Total	5,904	100.0%	100.0%	100.0%	100.0%
No. of family households owning single-detached homes	—	1,910,367	799,869	497,880	193,981

HOUSING CHARACTERISTICS OF NON-FARM FAMILY HOUSEHOLDS WITH INCOME OVER $3,000, 1961 (continued)

	Average income ($)	Average for all families	Total family income		
			$3,000 –5,999	$6,000 –9,999	$10,000 and over
Condition of dwelling					
In good condition......................	6,335	80.3%	79.4%	88.9%	93.5%
In need of minor repair.............	4,311	15.8	17.0	9.7	5.8
In need of major repair.............	3,489	3.9	3.6	1.4	0.7
Total............................	5,904	100.0%	100.0%	100.0%	100.0%
No. of family households owning single-detached homes......	—	1,910,367	799,869	497,880	193,981

(Source: DBS, *Census of Canada, 1961*. Bulletin 98-505.)

STANDARD OF LIVING OF NON-FARM FAMILY HOUSEHOLDS WITH INCOME OVER $3,000, 1961

	Average income ($)	Average for all families	Total family income		
			$3,000 –5,999	$6,000 –9,999	$10,000 and over
Refrigeration facilities					
None...................................	2,876	5.8%	3.6%	1.4%	1.2%
Ice box..............................	3,470	0.8	0.6	0.3	0.2
Mechanical........................	5,743	93.4	95.8	98.3	98.6
Total............................	5,560	100.0%	100.0%	100.0%	100.0%
Number of family households....	—	3,504,692	1,604,113	847,081	287,616
Television set					
None...................................	3,993	12.9%	10.4%	7.6%	6.1%
One.....................................	5,562	82.2	86.2	85.8	77.3
Two or more.......................	9,607	4.9	3.4	6.6	16.6
Total............................	5,560	100.0%	100.0%	100.0%	100.0%
Number of family households....	—	3,504,692	1,604,113	847,081	287,616
Passenger automobile					
None...................................	3,850	27.3%	25.8%	13.8%	8.8%
One.....................................	5,762	65.1	69.8	74.9	61.9
Two or more.......................	9,980	7.6	4.4	11.3	29.3
Total............................	5,560	100.0%	100.0%	100.0%	100.0%
Number of family households....	—	3,504,692	1,604,113	847,081	287,616

(Source: DBS, *Census of Canada, 1961*. Bulletin 98-505.)

ANNUAL URBAN FAMILY EXPENDITURES BY INCOME GROUPS, 1959

Items of expenditure	All income groups	$3,000 –5,999	$6,000 –9,999	$10,000 and over
A. *Average per family* ($)				
Food	1,323	1,232	1,541	2,081
Housing, fuel, light, water	911	840	1,070	1,421
Household operation	214	180	260	507
Furnishings and equipment	277	242	347	587
Clothing	508	405	704	1,145
Automobile	518	410	754	1,235
Other transportation	112	84	151	303
Medical care	237	216	281	404
Personal care	118	104	147	232
Recreation	160	125	220	391
Reading	35	31	44	65
Education	39	21	59	169
Smoking and alcoholic drinks	230	204	293	425
Other	69	57	91	139
All current consumption	4,751	4,151	5,962	9,104
Gifts and contributions	170	117	229	575
Personal taxes	378	214	582	1,613
Security	271	217	356	784
Total expenditures	5,570	4,699	7,129	12,076
B. *Percentage distribution*				
Food	23.8%	26.2%	21.6%	17.2%
Housing, fuel, light, water	16.4	17.9	15.0	11.8
Household operation	3.8	3.8	3.6	4.2
Furnishings and equipment	5.0	5.2	4.9	4.9
Clothing	9.1	8.6	9.9	9.5
Automobile	9.3	8.7	10.6	10.2
Other transportation	2.0	1.8	2.1	2.5
Medical care	4.3	4.6	3.9	3.4
Personal care	2.1	2.2	2.1	1.9
Recreation	2.9	2.7	3.1	3.2
Reading	0.6	0.7	0.6	0.5
Education	0.7	0.4	0.8	1.4
Smoking and alcoholic drinks	4.1	4.3	4.1	3.5
Other	1.2	1.2	1.3	1.2
All current consumption	85.3	88.3	83.6	75.4
Gifts and contributions	3.0	2.5	3.2	4.8
Personal taxes	6.8	4.6	8.2	13.3
Security	4.9	4.6	5.0	6.5
Total expenditures	100.0%	100.0%	100.0%	100.0%

(Source: DBS, *Urban Family Expenditures, 1959.* Catalogue no. 62-521.)

Chapter 12

MOSAIC BY ETHNIC GROUPS

The General Picture

When Sir Wilfrid Laurier remarked over half a century ago that Canada was the most anomalous nation that ever existed, he was referring to the people as well as the land. The search for a Canadian character and a Canadian soul has been going on since Confederation. It has been the subject of countless plays, radio talks, magazine articles, and weighty books, yet it almost defies proper definition. A representative Canadian "type" is as difficult to find as a typical Canadian scene.

In the first place, there is French Canada. To every suggestion of assimilation to a common denominator, the French Canadians as a group have remained doggedly opposed. United culturally by language and religion, and represented politically by Québec, they have succeeded, as has no other ethnic group in North America, in maintaining their distinctiveness through every vicissitude of fortune.

Although there is less bigotry and more tolerance than in the days when Lord Durham found "two nations warring in the bosom of a single state," the English and French cultures are still far from blended. They co-exist side by side, almost in isolation, neither exerting a perceptible influence on the other. Canada as a political entity is largely a result of adjustment between two parties whose association has often been referred to as a *mariage de raison* or a *modus vivendi,* without cordiality.

As regards other minor ethnic groups, they too have been able to preserve to some extent their own identity. If the "melting pot" is a model for the United States, in Canada perhaps the "salad bowl" is a more appropriate term. No attempt is made to preach the supremacy of the Canadian way of life, no force exerted to beat all men into a single pattern of conformity. In the United States a Briton, to be fully accepted, is forced to become a good American. In Canada he can comfortably remain a good Briton. The presence of a powerful neighbor to the south partly accounts for this tolerant attitude. Since complete assimilation of all ethnic groups would mean an increasing adoption of the U.S. values of life and standards of behavior, the preservation of the Canadian nation, paradoxically, depends to a certain extent on discouraging too strong a nationalism. If no subtle pressure is brought to bear on the Slavic housewife to give up her "babushka," or on a Nova Scotian Scot to stop speaking his Gaelic, the indirect purpose is to check the onrush of American influence in Canadian life. Lord

Tweedsmuir's aphorism that "to be a good Ukrainian in Canada is to be a better Canadian" is still backed, if not by everybody, at least by the majority of what one might call opinion leaders.

No marketing analysis is complete unless one takes into consideration the heterogeneous character of Canadian consumers. The distinction among ethnic groups does not lie just in the language spoken. It is a difference in cultural patterns and outlook toward life. Hence a marketing strategy which is successful with one group may fail with another because it inadvertently touches upon some sensitive spot. As the president of one large corporation has aptly remarked: "We are swiftly moving from an era when business was our culture into an era when culture will be our business."

At the same time, one should not go to the other extreme and over-emphasize the importance of minor ethnic groups. Though national differences are permitted to exist, Canada is not a patch-work quilt, with various communities segregated in cultural ghettos. Because of the influence of schools, work groups, social clubs, and mass media, many nationals lose the customs and traditions of their homeland and adopt something closer to English-Canadian culture — and to a minor extent the French-Canadian pattern in Québec.

The process is more akin to "integration" than "assimilation." Assimilation usually means the complete absorption of the newcomer by the dominant culture. In the course of this operation, the cultural and social differences are worn off and a more or less homogeneous society emerges. The integration system followed in this country is far less drastic. No attempt is made to cast all the species in a rigid mold stamped "made in Canada." The emphasis is on the gradual absorption, without any overt pressure, of the culture of the adopted land.

MOTHER TONGUE

It is difficult to measure statistically the extent of integration among minor ethnic groups in Canada. The closest one can get is through data on the mother tongue, that is, the language first learned in childhood and still understood. If the mother tongue is other than English or French, then the person may be presumed to have retained certain traits of the country of his origin. This is not an unrealistic assumption, for, of all the channels through which customs and traditions are communicated, language is the most effective. It is the key which opens the rest of the cultural treasure-house. When certain members of an ethnic community break away from their mother tongue and speak only English, they are cut off from the most important source through which symbolic values are imparted. They tend to lose feelings of group consciousness, rapport, and solidarity, and become predominantly Anglo-Saxon in their outlook.

The table below shows the different mother tongues of the population in Canada as reported by the 1961 Census. Only 13% of the inhabitants converse at home in some language other than English or French. The most important foreign tongues, in descending order of importance, are German, Ukrainian, Italian, Dutch, Indian and Eskimo dialects, and Polish.

MOTHER TONGUES OF THE POPULATION IN CANADA, 1961

Mother tongue	Persons speaking	% of total	Mother tongue	Persons speaking	% of total
English	10,660,534	58.45	Finnish	44,785	0.24
French	5,123,151	28.09	Russian	42,903	0.24
German	563,713	3.09	Slovak	42,546	0.23
Ukrainian	361,496	1.98	Greek	40,455	0.22
Italian	339,626	1.86	Serbo-Croatian	28,866	0.16
Dutch	170,177	0.93	Japanese	17,856	0.10
Indian and Eskimo	166,531	0.91	Lithuanian	14,997	0.08
Polish	161,720	0.89	Flemish	14,304	0.08
Scandinavian	116,714	0.64	Lettish	14,062	0.08
Norwegian	(40,054)	(0.22)	Estonian	13,830	0.08
Danish	(35,035)	(0.19)	Syrian and Arabic	12,999	0.07
Swedish	(32,632)	(0.18)	Roumanian	10,165	0.06
Icelandic	(8,993)	(0.05)	Gaelic	7,533	0.04
Magyar	85,939	0.47	Welsh	3,040	0.02
Yiddish	82,448	0.45	Other	48,758	0.27
Chinese	49,099	0.27			
			Total	18,238,247	100.00

(Source: DBS, *Census of Canada, 1961*. Bulletin 92-549.)

ETHNIC GROUPS

Except for the data in the table above and on page 227, very little information is available from the 1961 census about mother tongue. The basis used by the DBS for analyzing the characteristics of different nationals is not mother tongue but ethnic group; that is, the cultural entity to which a person or his ancestor on the male side belonged when first coming to this continent. This is not an ideal criterion, for it overlooks the psychological aspect — the feeling of belonging to a particular group. Perhaps, through the generations, the ethnic consciousness is lost, and the individual now, no matter what his paternal ancestry, feels "Canadian." Or perhaps the great-grandfather was Irish, but the descendants have been brought up to feel French Canadian. Except for these limitations, the census figures on ethnic groups are extremely valuable for throwing some badly-needed light on various pieces of the Canadian mosaic. The information, culled from numerous DBS publications, is summarized for the whole of Canada in the tables on pages 228 and 229. Here are some of the highlights worth noting:

OFFICIAL LANGUAGE

The official language figures are interesting for two reasons: they show which ethnic groups are highly bilingual and which groups have a large proportion of members not understanding either of the two official languages.

POPULATION IN CANADA BY ETHNIC GROUPS, 1961

Ethnic origin	Population	% of total	Ethnic origin	Population	% of total
British			Other Europeans (cont'd)		
English	4,195,175	23.00	Estonian	18,550	0.10
Irish	1,753,351	9.61	Finnish	59,436	0.33
Scottish	1,902,302	10.43	Greek	56,475	0.31
Welsh	143,942	0.79	Hungarian	126,220	0.69
Other	1,899	0.01	Latvian	18,194	0.10
French	5,540,346	30.38	Lithuanian	27,629	0.15
German	1,049,599	5.76	Roumanian	43,805	0.24
Italian	450,351	2.47	Slovak	24,720	0.13
Jewish	173,344	0.95	Yugoslavic	68,587	0.37
Dutch	429,679	2.36	Other	51,446	0.28
Polish	323,517	1.77	Asiatic		
Russian	119,168	0.65	Chinese	58,197	0.32
Scandinavian			East Indian	6,774	0.04
Danish	85,473	0.47	Japanese	29,157	0.16
Icelandic	30,623	0.17	Syrian-Lebanese	19,374	0.11
Norwegian	148,681	0.81	Other	8,251	0.04
Swedish	121,757	0.67	Other		
Ukrainian	473,337	2.60	Eskimo	11,835	0.07
Other European			Native Indian	208,286	1.14
Austrian	106,535	0.59	Negro	32,127	0.18
Belgian	61,382	0.34	Other & not stated	210,382	1.15
Czech	48,341	0.26			
			Total	18,238,247	100.00

(Source: DBS, *Census of Canada, 1961.* Bulletin 92-545.)

Since the Canadian nation theoretically is supposed to be a partnership between English and French, complete bilingualism is an ideal which the country should strive for. But after nearly one hundred years of Confederation, very little progress has been made towards that goal. In fact, during the last generation, the proportion of Canadians fluent in both languages has not grown but actually slightly declined (12.7% in 1931 to 12.3% in 1961). Bilingualism has become a one-way street with nearly a third of *les Canadiens* speaking English, but hardly 4% of *les Anglais* understanding French.

These percentages are, of course, no surprise. They conform to ordinary experience. The hard fact is that Canadians of all ethnic groups, except for a minority of intellectuals and pursuers of culture and erudition, learn the second language only when it is required in business, politics, or social relations. This necessity, for self-evident reasons, arises far more often for English than for French. Hence, among the various minor ethnic groups, very few are well-versed in both official languages.

FOREIGN-BORN AND MOTHER TONGUE

The French group is almost entirely native-born, while the other groups, excepting of course Indians and Eskimos, are replenished by new arrivals from abroad. The Italians have the largest proportion of foreign-born, most of whom have come to Canada during the postwar era.

The process of Canadianization goes on among all minor ethnic communities, but the pace varies from one group to another. Among the Germans, the Dutch, and the Polish, over half the number have forgotten the language of their ancestors and speak only English. The nationals that have succeeded fairly well in preserving their mother tongues are the Ukrainians, the Italians, and the Indians and Eskimos. It is also interesting to note that only 1% of the British have lost their mother tongue and speak French, while conversely 10% of the French have become completely anglicized.

ENDOGAMOUS MARRIAGES AND FERTILITY RATIO

Intermarriage, or endogamy, is used by some sociologists as another index of acculturation. The more the members of an ethnic group select mates from outside, the greater is the possibility of their losing their original cultural patterns. By this criterion, the French and the Italians are the most ethnic-conscious, for they have the largest percentage marrying within the group. On the other hand, only about half the marriages among the Germans, the Polish, and the Dutch are endogamous.

The rate at which different ethnic groups are growing can be seen from the analysis of the fertility ratio. This is computed as follows:

$$\frac{\text{Number of children under 5 x 1000}}{\text{Number of women 15 to 44}}$$

The above formula is much more scientific than the crude birth rate, since any difference in the age and sex of the population are automatically eliminated. The figures indicate that the Indians and the Eskimos have the highest fertility ratio (981). The French Canadians at present are not as prolific as generally imagined. Their ratio is below that for the Italians and the Dutch; in fact, it is only 5% above the Canadian average.

MALE WORKERS IN DIFFERENT INDUSTRIES AND OCCUPATIONS

Compared to the national average, the Germans, the Ukrainians, and the Dutch have a significantly higher proportion of male workers in agriculture; the French in forestry; the Italians in construction; the Polish in manufacturing; and the Native Indians in fishing and trapping.

When the figures are examined by occupations, the British score above average marks in managerial and professional positions, while all other Europeans are over-represented in blue-collar jobs.

	Total population	English	French	German	Ukrainian	Italian	Dutch	Indian, Eskimo	Polish
Metro cities									
Calgary	1.53%	2.15%	0.07%	2.86%	1.23%	1.01%	3.07%	0.06%	1.41%
Edmonton	1.85	2.28	0.22	4.20	7.75	1.05	4.61	0.55	3.25
Halifax	1.01	1.63	0.12	0.12	0.06	0.12	0.31	0.02	0.13
Hamilton	2.17	2.96	0.12	1.91	2.07	5.41	4.81	0.12	5.27
Kitchener	0.85	1.15	0.03	3.64	0.39	0.24	0.92	0.01	1.55
London	0.99	1.51	0.03	0.70	0.32	0.62	2.25	0.02	1.17
Montréal	11.57	4.64	26.67	4.70	3.31	25.13	2.51	0.99	10.62
Ottawa	2.36	2.24	3.16	1.08	0.53	1.98	1.46	0.04	1.32
Québec	1.96	0.12	6.66	0.07	—	0.19	0.05	0.01	0.06
Regina	0.61	0.81	0.04	2.18	0.98	0.12	0.40	0.07	0.65
Saint John	0.52	0.83	0.12	0.07	0.02	0.02	0.11	—	0.04
St. John's	0.50	0.84	—	0.03	0.01	0.01	0.04	—	0.02
Saskatoon	0.52	0.69	0.04	1.28	1.87	0.08	0.71	0.06	0.47
Sudbury	0.61	0.52	0.66	0.41	0.98	1.81	0.19	0.07	1.12
Toronto	10.00	13.12	0.51	10.83	9.66	34.28	8.94	0.23	19.84
Vancouver	4.33	6.08	0.26	5.63	2.93	3.50	6.02	0.32	2.99
Victoria	0.85	1.31	0.03	0.43	0.20	0.19	0.84	0.19	0.32
Windsor	1.06	1.31	0.39	0.96	1.13	2.66	0.41	0.01	2.07
Winnipeg	2.61	3.03	0.54	6.29	10.95	1.16	3.49	0.35	7.68
Total metro cities	45.90	47.22	39.67	47.39	44.39	79.58	41.14	3.12	59.98
Other urban	23.73	23.30	28.67	15.47	15.74	16.65	17.11	3.74	18.39
Total urban	69.63	70.52	68.34	62.86	60.13	96.23	58.25	6.86	78.37
Rural—non-farm	19.00	19.47	19.06	14.42	13.87	2.98	18.39	86.21	9.58
Rural—farm	11.37	10.01	12.60	22.72	26.00	0.79	23.36	6.93	12.05
Canada, percentage	100.00%	100.00%	100.00%	100.00%	100.00%	100.00%	100.00%	100.00%	100.00%
Canada (in 000's) Population 1961	18,238	10,661	5,123	564	361	340	170	167	162

Source: DBS, *Census of Canada, 1961.* Bulletin 92-549.

SOCIO-ECONOMIC CHARACTERISTICS OF MAJOR ETHNIC GROUPS, 1961

	All ethnic groups	British	French	German	Ukrainian	Italian	Dutch	Polish	Indian and Eskimo
Official language spoken									
English only	67.4%	95.5%	8.6%	95.7%	94.6%	65.2%	95.3%	91.3%	76.7%
French only	19.1	0.4	61.2	0.4	0.3	6.8	0.2	0.7	2.3
Both English and French	12.2	4.0	30.1	2.6	2.6	10.6	2.9	5.5	1.8
Neither English nor French	1.3	0.1	0.1	1.3	2.5	17.4	1.6	2.5	19.2
Total	100.0%	100.0%	100.0%	100.0%	100.0%	100.0%	100.0%	100.0%	100.0%
Number of persons (000)	18,238.2	7,996.7	5,540.3	1,049.6	473.3	450.4	429.7	323.5	220.1

(Source: DBS, *Census of Canada, 1961*. Bulletin 92-561.)

	All ethnic groups	British	French	German	Ukrainian	Italian	Dutch	Polish	Indian and Eskimo
Mother tongue and immigration									
Number of persons in the ethnic group (000)	18,238.2	7,996.7	5,540.3	1,049.6	473.3	450.4	429.7	323.5	220.1
% retaining the mother tongue	n.a.*	98.7%	89.6%	53.7%	76.4%	75.4%	39.6%	50.0%	71.4%
% who are immigrants	15.6	16.5	1.5	30.4	25.9	57.2	31.1	33.6	—
% who are postwar immigrants	8.3	6.3	0.8	21.4	7.8	50.8	28.7	19.3	—

* Not applicable

(Source: DBS, *Census of Canada, 1961*. Bulletins 92-545, 92-549, 92-561, 92-562.)

	All ethnic groups	British	French	German	Ukrainian	Italian	Dutch	Polish	Indian and Eskimo
Endogamous marriages	76.7%	81.2%	88.3%	52.0%	61.8%	76.6%	54.9%	49.0%	60.9%*

* Indian, Eskimo and Negro.

(Source: *Census of Canada, 1961*. Bulletin 93-520.)

	All ethnic groups	British	French	German	Ukrainian	Italian	Dutch	Polish	Indian and Eskimo
Fertility ratio	606	575	639	610	542	656	745	558	981

(Source: DBS, *Census of Canada, 1961*. Bulletin 92-553.)

	All ethnic groups	British	French	German	Ukrainian	Italian	Dutch	Polish	Native Indian
Industries									
Agriculture	11.9%	10.5%	10.7%	20.8%	22.6%	2.2%	22.0%	13.6%	19.0%
Forestry	2.3	1.5	4.2	1.1	0.9	0.7	1.0	1.4	12.7
Fishing and trapping	0.8	0.9	0.5	0.3	0.1	0.1	0.6	0.1	15.8
Mines, quarries, oil wells	2.5	2.4	2.6	2.3	2.9	2.5	1.6	3.6	1.6
Manufacturing	23.4	22.7	23.9	22.9	21.3	31.0	22.1	29.7	13.5
Construction	8.9	6.7	10.3	11.0	7.9	25.6	10.6	8.9	8.1
Transport, communications, other utilities	11.1	12.6	10.7	8.6	12.5	7.9	8.2	9.8	7.6
Wholesale and retail trade	14.7	15.3	14.2	14.4	12.1	11.6	14.3	12.9	4.2
Finance, insurance, and real estate	2.6	3.5	2.1	1.9	1.4	1.3	2.0	1.6	0.1
Community, business and personal services	10.9	10.6	10.4	8.9	10.5	10.8	9.5	10.5	8.1
Public administration and defence	8.4	10.8	7.6	5.8	5.7	3.7	6.2	5.2	6.1
Miscellaneous	2.5	2.5	2.8	2.0	2.1	2.6	1.9	2.7	3.2
Total males in labor force (%)	100.0%	100.0%	100.0%	100.0%	100.0%	100.0%	100.0%	100.0%	100.0%
Occupations									
Managerial	10.2%	12.1%	7.6%	8.3%	7.1%	6.6%	7.9%	9.2%	1.2%
Professional and technical	7.6	9.3	5.9	6.1	5.8	2.8	6.9	6.7	1.1
Clerical	6.9	8.2	6.7	5.0	5.6	3.7	5.2	5.2	1.0
Sales	5.6	6.6	5.2	4.4	3.5	3.2	4.5	3.8	0.9
Service and recreation	8.5	9.2	7.7	6.4	7.3	8.5	6.7	7.3	7.8
Workers in transport and communications	7.5	8.0	8.9	6.2	6.4	4.7	6.7	4.8	3.8
Workers in primary industries	16.1	13.8	16.1	23.3	25.6	4.9	24.4	17.6	49.3
Workers, mostly skilled, in second. industries	28.8	25.6	31.4	32.5	29.6	43.7	29.6	35.1	17.7
Workers, mostly unskilled, in second. industries	6.2	4.6	7.5	5.6	6.9	19.3	6.1	7.5	14.3
Miscellaneous (not stated)	2.6	2.6	3.0	2.2	2.2	2.6	2.0	2.8	2.9
Total males in labor force (%)	100.0%	100.0%	100.0%	100.0%	100.0%	100.0%	100.0%	100.0%	100.0%
Number of males in labor force (000)	4,705.5	2,071.4	1,303.3	297.0	136.0	137.1	115.1	96.1	27.0

(Source: DBS, *Census of Canada, 1961.* Bulletins 94-527 and 94-515.)

Specific Ethnic Groups

On the basis of the mother tongue, the six important ethnic groups in Canada, besides British and French, are Germans, Ukrainians, Italians, Dutch, Poles, and Native Indians and Eskimos.

GERMANS

People of German origin form the largest ethnic group, after the British and the French. Their first arrival dates back to 1750 when the sailing ship *Anne* left Rotterdam for Nova Scotia with 312 Germans aboard. At that time, Halifax, the first major British settlement in Canada, was itself only one year old. In 1753, about 1,500 Germans from the Halifax area moved down the Nova Scotia coast and established a colony of their own which they called Lunenburg. Their descendants are still there and have made a name for themselves as expert shipbuilders, sailors, and fishermen.

Since that early migration, successive waves of Germans have come to Canada. Prominent among these were the Mennonites who, between 1800 and 1837, left the eastern seaboard of the United States and settled in and around the county of Waterloo in Ontario. (They have sometimes been called the "Pennsylvania Dutch," a misnomer resulting probably from the similarity of sound between the word "Dutch" and the German "Deutsch.") Later these settlers were joined by immigrants from Germany. They were not Mennonites, but they were eager to work in a German-speaking environment. Together, they developed the extensive agricultural resources of the region and gradually started establishing important industries. Their principal town was called Berlin until 1916, when it was renamed Kitchener.

The German immigrants who arrived in the latter half of the 19th Century played a major role in the development of the vast western prairies. Most of them were farmers coming from German communities in Russia, Russian Poland, Hungary, Roumania, and various parts of the Austro-Hungarian Empire. This influx of peasant immigration was halted when the First World War broke out, but it commenced again after the termination of hostilities and remained strong until the Depression brought all immigration to a standstill.

After the Second World War, over 10,000 German-speaking refugees from eastern Europe were allowed to enter Canada as displaced persons. In early 1950 a change in Canadian regulations permitted German nationals, who until then had been classified as enemy aliens, to be eligible again for immigration. Between 1956 and 1965 nearly 125,000 persons from the Bonn Republic entered Canada. Most of them were technicians or businessmen, and they settled down in the major cities of Ontario, which provided the best opportunities for their specialized skills.

Persons of German origin have been active in all phases of Canadian life. Taken as a group, their largest contribution has been in the field of agriculture in Western Canada. The Mennonites, who came from southern Russia in the 1870's, were among the first immigrants to demonstrate that large-scale settlement in the open prairies was feasible. In this, they put to good use the experience they had gained on the Russian steppes.

The concentration on farming has continued to this day. The 1961 Census shows that 22% of the German-speaking people are on farms (twice the national average of all ethnic groups), and that in the Prairie Provinces 35.2% of German males in the labor force are engaged in agriculture.

The Germans have also made their mark in manufacturing. Many early artisans brought with them special skills from their home country, and the small factories they started have now grown into prosperous enterprises. Products such as Heintzman pianos, Knechtel and Krug furniture, Schneider meats, and Breithaupt leather are but a few of the great variety of goods manufactured in Canadian plants founded by people of German origin.

PUBLICATIONS IN GERMAN

Name of publication	Place of publication	Frequency of issue	Circulation (including free)
1. Der Courier (The Courier)	Toronto	Weekly	16,907 (ABC)
2. Mennonitische Rundschau (Mennonite Review)	Winnipeg	Weekly	Not available
3. Montrealer Nachrichten (Montreal News)	Montréal	Weekly	12,200 (sworn)
4. Montrealer Zeitung	Winnipeg	Weekly	2,250 (sworn)
5. Der Nordwesten	Winnipeg	Weekly	16,500 (sworn)
6. Die Post	Steinbach	Weekly	4,629 (ABC)
7. Torontoer Zeitung (Toronto News)	Toronto	Weekly	8,250 (sworn)
8. Die Zeit (The Times)	Toronto	Weekly	6,905 (sworn)

Note: Circulation data for all foreign language publications in this section are 1964 estimates. For the most recent figures, consult the latest issue of *Canadian Advertising*.

UKRAINIANS

The 75th anniversary of the arrival of the first two Ukrainian immigrants falls in 1966. In the years since 1891 when Vasyl Elyniak and Ivan Pylypiw set foot on Canadian soil, the population of Ukrainian origin has risen to nearly half a million.

The majority of the early immigrants were illiterate peasants who settled in Western Canada. Their self-sufficiency, frugal mode of living, resourcefulness, and tenacity enabled them to endure great privations and hardships on the lonely unbroken prairie. Despite several handicaps — lack of knowledge of English, insufficient capital, differences in farming methods between Europe and Canada

PUBLICATIONS IN UKRAINIAN

Name of publication	Place of publication	Frequency of issue	Circulation (including free)
1. Batkivshchyna (Our Country)	Toronto	Bi-weekly	4,005 (claim)
2. The Canadian Farmer	Winnipeg	Weekly	15,666 (sworn)
3. Homin Ukrainy (Ukrainian Echo)	Toronto	Weekly	8,722 (claim)
4. My I Svit (We and the World)	Toronto	Monthly	5,000 (claim)
5. Nasha Meta (Our Aim)	Toronto	Weekly	8,157 (claim)
6. Novi Dni (New Days)	Toronto	Monthly	2,100 (sworn)
7. Novy Shliakh (New Pathway)	Winnipeg	Weekly	12,353 (sworn)
8. Postup (Progress)	Winnipeg	Weekly	7,156 (claim)
9. Svitlo (The Light)	Toronto	Monthly	5,370 (claim)
10. Ukrainske Zhyttia (Ukrainian Life)	Toronto	Weekly	Not available
11. Ukrainsky Holos (Ukrainian Voice)	Winnipeg	Weekly	15,992 (claim)
12. Ukrainsky Visti (Ukrainian News)	Edmonton	Weekly	9,372 (sworn)
13. Vilne Slovo (Free Word)	Toronto	Weekly	8,500 (sworn)
14. Yevanhelski Ranok (Evangelical Morning)	Toronto	Monthly	1,150 (claim)
15. Zinochy Svit (Woman's World)	Winnipeg	Monthly	2,850 (sworn)

— most of the early pioneers were able in a relatively short space of time to clear the land and establish prosperous farms.

Ukrainian immigration continued to be strong in the 1920's, but the composition of the new arrivals changed. Only a few were peasants. A large proportion were laborers, discharged soldiers, political refugees, or university professors. They preferred to settle in Ontario rather than on the Prairies.

After the Second World War another large batch of Ukrainian immigrants entered Canada. The majority were displaced persons — those who had been sent into Germany as forced laborers or who had fled there at the end of the war to escape Communist domination. They represented every cross-section of life, from unskilled workers to scientists, musicians, and artists. The Iron Curtain has now cut off practically all immigration. Between 1956 to 1964, the Ukrainian community in Canada was replenished by only 2,800 newcomers.

Ukrainians are found in every walk of life, but a large proportion, 22.6%, are still engaged in agriculture. It is in this field that they have made their most important contribution. Ukrainian farmers have participated in international competitions and frequently won world championships for Canada. Also, a relatively large proportion of agricultural scientists in the country are of Ukrainian descent.

Ukrainians have always been interested in maintaining their culture and identity. Their associations are found all across the country, and numerous books have been written on their history, folklore, and poetry. The language is a focal point of interest, and there is a strong movement in predominantly Ukrainian communities to teach it to the children at school. As a result, nearly

76% of persons of Ukrainian origin have retained their mother tongue, the highest percentage among the European ethnic groups.

This strong love for the mother tongue is evidenced by the extraordinary number of newspapers and periodicals produced by the Ukrainians. Since 1903, when *The Canadian Farmer* made its first appearance, about 135 papers have been published at one time or another. Many were short-lived, others lasted a few years, but a handful of hardy ones have been able to withstand financial difficulties and become well established and successful publications.

ITALIANS

The 1961 Census shows 340,000 people in Canada whose mother tongue is Italian. More than 80% of them have come to this country since 1946. They are essentially urban dwellers, four out of five living in the metropolitan centers. The Italian population in rural areas is practically negligible, less than 4% of the total.

The city that has attracted most Italians is Toronto. In fact, one section of the downtown area has practically earned the nickname of "Little Italy." Here English is rarely spoken and few Anglo-Saxon faces are seen. For a newly-arrived immigrant, it is almost like finding his home transplanted in a foreign soil. He can stroll past the shops that sell Italian clothes and shoes, visit a restaurant that keeps its pizza ovens hot until three or four in the morning, listen to the soccer arguments in front of the Roma Sport Club, catch the strains of operatic arias drifting from a record shop, or go to a movie where Sophia Loren speaks her native tongue without sub-titles.

Each ethnic group has his stereotype. A typical Italian, in the public imagination, is a dark, clannish, spaghetti-eating worker, who is lazy, frequently gets into trouble with the police, and in general has a gay time in a cold climate. But this popular image is far off the mark.

The Italians are as different in appearance, outlook, and cuisine as the different provinces that make up Italy itself. Though they stick together in families, they are perhaps the most unorganized of all ethnic groups. Those who arrived 30 years ago dislike the newcomers; the northerners despise the southerners; the southerners are split between Sicilians and Celabrese. Even those born in the same districts are divided according to the town or village they came from. As a result, their various organizations prefer to remain independent rather than form a federation which would speak for all nationals.

By temperament, the Italians are easy-going, but in Canada they have to wage an uphill battle in order to survive. Sociological surveys have frequently shown that they are among the most hard-pressed of all ethnic groups. Many of the sponsored immigrants arrive in this country with a single suitcase, unable to speak English or French properly, and lacking technical skill or training in a trade. During the first few years, they sacrifice their leisure, their privacy, their

PUBLICATIONS IN ITALIAN

Name of publication	Place of publication	Frequency of issue	Circulation (including free)
1. Il Cittadino Canadese (Canadian Citizen)...	Montréal	Weekly	24,478 (sworn)
2. Corriere Canadese (Canadian Courier)..	Toronto	Weekly	10,066 (ABC)
3. Corriere Del Niagara (Niagara Courier)	Hamilton	Weekly	8,250 (sworn)
4. Corriere Del Quebec (Quebec Courier)..	Montréal	Weekly	10,215 (sworn)
5. Corriere Illustrato (Illustrated Courier).	Toronto	Weekly	9,641 (ABC)
6. Corriere Italiano (Italian Courier)..........	Montréal	Weekly	36,500 (sworn)
7. L'Eco D'Italia (The Echo of Italy)........	Vancouver	Weekly	6,457 (sworn)
8. Selezione (Selections).............................	Toronto	Monthly	10,892 (sworn)
9. La Tribuna Italiana (Italian Tribune)....	Montréal	Weekly	15,000 (sworn)

comfort — everything, indeed, but their dignity — to make the two ends meet. The hours of work are long, the wages low, and the tenure of employment highly uncertain.

Why is it that the Italians are willing to put up with so many hardships? Though the situation is bad in Canada, it is still better than what it was in their homeland. Besides, the intention of many immigrants is to get rich quickly so that they can return to their villages later on as persons of affluence and esteem. But once here, they find it takes longer than expected to accumulate as much money as they would like. In the meantime, they improve their position and get used to North American life. Their children grow up as Canadians and have little interest in the old native land. As a result, many eventually decide to stay permanently in this country.

People of Italian origin have made many important contributions to Canadian life, not only in the fields of music and the other arts, but also in the building trades, architecture, fashion design, and food manufacturing.

Over a quarter of the Italian males are engaged in construction. Through their hard work in building subways, highways, industrial plants, and office buildings, they are helping to transform Canada into a modern industrial nation. Hundreds of new Italian construction companies have mushroomed since 1946, and though some of them have turned out to be fly-by-night operations, many have fared remarkably well.

Several Italians have brought with them from their home country special knowledge of mosaic and stucco work as well as marble cutting. Most of the functional and decorative work of this type on Canadian public buildings has been done by Italian artisans.

The restaurant business has also attracted large numbers. In major metropolitan centers, Canadians have been introduced to typically Italian dishes and have come to appreciate the Italian style of cooking.

In the manufacture of food products, a number of Italians have gained prominence. The names of Catelli and Gattuso have become familiar to most Canadian housewives.

Italians also work as tailors and dressmakers or in the manufacture of clothing and textiles. With their strong flair for design, they excel in various branches of the apparel industry. Today many of the large clothing and dressmaking firms in Montréal and Toronto employ Italians as shop foremen, cutters, and designers.

DUTCH

According to the 1961 Census, 170,000 people have Dutch as their mother tongue. Immigration from the Netherlands goes back nearly 200 years. The first settlers were the United Empire Loyalists who fled from the United States during and after the American Revolution. They were not much different from their fellow Loyalists of English or Scottish origin. They quickly adapted themselves to pioneer conditions in the Maritimes or Upper Canada and melted imperceptibly into the Canadian scene.

Direct immigration to Canada from the Netherlands did not start till the opening of the West. In 1894 the first group of Dutch immigrants, about 80, entered Canada. From then on their numbers steadily grew. Many of the early colonists were successful farmers in their own country, and they became adjusted to the new life on the Prairies without too much difficulty. Place names such as Edam, Amsterdam, Zealandia, and Neerlandia are reminders of these pioneer communities.

In the period between the two world wars, the Prairies continued to attract Dutch immigrants. However, a number settled in Ontario as well, particularly in the southwestern section, where they pioneered sugar-beet and tobacco farming. It was also at this time that a start was made in market gardening in Holland Marsh, about 50 miles north of Toronto.

Since the end of the Second World War, the Dutch have arrived in larger numbers than ever before. The 1961 Census shows 133,500 postwar immigrants of Dutch origin, a figure surpassed only by the British, the Italians, and the Germans. Their prior knowledge of English, their technical skills, their willingness to accept hard work, plus their lack of strong ethnic consciousness, have enabled them to assimilate quickly with the native population.

As may be expected, the most important contribution of the Dutch has been to augment agricultural production, particularly in the field of dairy farming, sugar-beet growing, market gardening, and horticulture. Their experience at home in developing rich farming districts from bog areas has proved a valuable asset when similar problems were tackled in Canada. The Dutch have been largely responsible for converting Holland Marsh and Thedford Marsh in Ontario into vegetable-producing land, and Pitt Polder in the Fraser Valley into a dairy district.

Some of the more recent immigrants have gone into manufacturing. Several food-processing plants have been established. Dutch bakeries, too, are becoming a feature of many cities and towns. One example is Voortman's Bakery at Aldershot, Ontario, which sells its products as far afield as British Columbia. Its specialty is pumpernickel bread.

Dutch communities seem to feel very little need of grouping themselves as separate entities. Before the Second World War there were no Dutch language publications. However, the large postwar wave of immigrants has created sufficient potential readers to make the founding of a few weeklies and monthlies possible. Some of those which first came out in the early 1950's have already disappeared, but others have been established to take their place.

PUBLICATIONS IN DUTCH

Name of publication	Place of publication	Frequency of issue	Circulation (including free)
1. Calvinist-Contact	Hamilton	Weekly	6,554 (ABC)
2. Compass-Onder Ons	London	Monthly	1,800 (sworn)
3. Dutch Free Press	Chatham	Weekly	2,000 (claim)
4. Hollandia-News	Chatham	Weekly	5,264 (claim)
5. De Nederlandse Courant	Willowdale	Weekly	3,925 (sworn)
6. De Nederlandse Post	Montréal	Monthly	9,224 (claim)
7. Pioneer	Hamilton	Monthly	2,600 (sworn)

POLES

The history of Poland in the 18th and 19th centuries was replete with wars, partitions, and struggles for independence. Each unsuccessful uprising resulted in a mass exodus of refugees, some of whom settled in Canada. After 1890 the economic rather than the political factor induced many to leave Poland. Most of the immigrants were peasant farmers who flooded into the newly-opened West. The First World War interrupted the flow, but it started again on a limited scale after 1918.

At the commencement of the hostilities in 1939, several hundred skilled Polish technicians and engineers were admitted to Canada on a temporary basis to assist the Allies in war work. When the peace was signed most of them chose to remain in this country permanently. They were soon joined by other immigrants, mostly Polish veterans, political émigrés, and refugees from displaced-persons camps. Between 1946 and 1950, about 36,500 Poles entered Canada from various countries where they had been temporary postwar residents.

Although the first major immigration was mainly to the agricultural West, the Polish-speaking people are now predominantly urban, with only 12% living on farms. The Prairies at present account for less than a third of the Polish population. Over 50% reside in Ontario, particularly in the industrialized Toronto-Hamilton area.

From the beginning of their settlement, the Poles have formed a multitude of societies — fraternal, cultural, religious, and political. In 1944, an over-all association, the Canadian Polish Congress, was formed to represent the whole Polish community, except the extreme left wing. Today most Polish organizations, about 130, are affiliated with this Congress.

As a group, the Poles have left their mark both in agriculture and industry. Their energy, ingenuity, and determination helped to open up the vast farming areas of the West. Those who were drawn to the manufacturing centers of the East have, by their engineering and technical skill, contributed to the country's industrial growth.

The part which Polish engineers and pilots have played in the Canadian aircraft industry is well known. B. W. Sznycer constructed the first certified Canadian helicopter. W. J. Jakimiuk was responsible for the design of the two internationally famous planes — the Chipmunk and the Beaver. J. Zurakowski, an outstanding test pilot, was first to break the sound barrier with an aircraft fully developed in Canada, the CF-100.

The Polish language spoken by the average Canadian of Polish origin has undergone considerable change. It contains an abundance of English words, adapted to Polish grammar and pronunciation. Many Poles do not look upon this trend with favor, and if they are not well-versed in the literary tongue, prefer rather to use English in conversation with other Polish Canadians.

PUBLICATIONS IN POLISH

Name of publication	Place of publication	Frequency of issue	Circulation (including free)
1. Czas (Polish Times)	Winnipeg	Weekly	7,322 (sworn)
2. Glos Polski—Gazeta Polska (Polish Voice-Gazette)	Toronto	Weekly	5,770 (ABC)
3. Zwiazkowiec (Alliancer)	Toronto	Semiweekly	6,865 (ABC)

NATIVE INDIANS

In much of Canada today, Indian place names are all that remain to remind one that the land was once occupied by the red man. However, the Indians are not a dying race, as is popularly believed. In fact, they are the fastest growing ethnic group in Canada, with a fertility ratio of 981 compared to the Canadian average of 606. From an ebbing 100,000 early in the century, their population has now risen to more than 200,000, back to the size it was at the outset of the 17th century, when colonization of Canada began.

Some two-thirds of the Indians live in 2,200 reserves or Crown lands set aside for their exclusive use. About 16% have moved to urban areas and live in white communities. The rest are in the Yukon and the Northwest Territories where there are no reserves.

The Indians are not all cut from the same piece of cloth. They are divided into 562 bands, ranging in size from a dozen to 7,000 members. Many of these bands have separate languages, cultures, and ways of life. At a place called Caughnawaga, near Montréal, lives a tribe, a branch of the once ferocious Iroquois, whose members, it has been discovered, are immune to vertigo. Today they are found perched on skyscraper girders all over North America, and they probably have the highest per capita income of any Canadian Indian today. These westernized Caughnawaga Indians have little in common with the proud and magnificent Blackfoot and Stony Indians of the Prairies, contented to live disdainfully on their reserves, appearing once a year in all their finery at the Calgary Stampede. These Plains Indians, too, bear slight resemblance to the depressed and indigent Dogrib and Slave tribes of the Northwest Territories. Still more different are the Indians of the Pacific Coast, with their round faces, their highly-developed totem-pole art, and their long record of successful fishing operations.

From the marketing point of view, the unfortunate fact of life is that the original inhabitants of Canada are now the poorest and most abject of all ethnic groups. Penned in their segregated slums, called reserves, or adrift in cities and towns, the majority of Indians live in silent desperation, a reproach to a nation's neglect. More than half of all Indian families occupy shacks of three rooms or less, without electricity. While close to 90% of white homes have sewerage, indoor toilets and baths, a tiny minority of Indians — about one in nine — have such ordinary facilities for health and civilized living.

In recent years, life in the reserves has become hopelessly cramped and highly uneconomic. Everywhere industrialization is slowly advancing, bulldozing the traditional hunting and trapping grounds of the Indians, polluting the inlets and streams where they once fished, and automating many unskilled jobs in the factories where they once earned their meager livelihood.

Nevertheless, an Indian is reluctant to quit his reserve, for it means leaving behind his lifelong friends and familiar surroundings for a new and strange environment. By both education and experience, he is unprepared for urban, industrial life. He lacks ambition, self-reliance, and competitiveness — qualities badly needed for success in big-city society. His traditional attitude towards life is living from day to day. The white man's philosophy of saving now to buy desirable goods tomorrow seems to him confusing and somehow unacceptable.

Despite this, the Indian Affairs Branch estimates that about 32,000 Indians have so far abandoned their reserves. Some have integrated into the mainstream of national life and have proved their ability to take an equal place alongside other Canadians in various types of careers. The vast majority, however, squat on the fringes of white settlements, condemned to a no-man's land, out of touch both with the modern world and the old ways of the reserve. They are displaced persons and they suffer from all the frustrations of the homeless.

To improve the future lot of the Indians, the federal government is pinning its hope on massive education of Indian children, preferably in non-Indian schools, and about $30 million are spent annually on this project. But it is an uphill fight. To an Indian slum child, who sees no connection between his own experience and the things he learns at school, education in the company of white students is often a confusion rather than an inspiration. Language is another problem. The medium of instruction is English or French, but the Indian children are usually brought up to speak their own tongues which are structurally different from the European languages. Most think in their native dialects and use them commonly at home. To make matters worse, sickness and, in the north, the steady necessity for wood-gathering to sustain life throughout the long sub-Arctic winter keep school attendance low.

To sum up, the history of Canada's efforts to give its Indian population a decent standard of living — either as integrated members of the white man's society or at arm's length on reserves — is strewn with the sun-bleached bones of failure. It is unfortunate that both sides regard each other with mutual incomprehension, bewilderment and suspicion. The Indian is dismayed by the methods of his would-be healers which often have consisted of deciding what is good for him and then spooning in the appropriate medicine. The white man, for his part, is perplexed to find that so many good ministrations could cure so few ailments, and, failing to see what went wrong, concludes that the Indian is shiftless, uncooperative, and congenitally lazy.

It seems obvious that the solution lies in breaking away from the old concepts of paternalism. Fortunately, the Indian Affairs Branch has realized this and initiated large-scale community development programs. Their objective is to bring the majority of the reserves to a social and economic level comparable with the neighboring white communities. There is no rushing after panaceas, no domineering insistence on what is right for the Indian. The emphasis is on self-help through persuasion and unobstructive advice. One of the results expected is the acceptance by Indian communities of new responsibilities and obligations in the management of their affairs and a greatly reduced dependence on Ottawa hand-outs.

ESKIMOS

The Eskimos are one of the smallest ethnic groups, numbering in 1961 11,835 or 0.1% of the population. But they are in many respects unique and have been the subject of intensive studies by anthropologists. Few other races, with so limited resources, have accomplished so much. For thousands of years they have been able to maintain themselves, with only primitive implements, in a land where until recently the white man, in spite of his technical equipment, could scarcely survive a season. These natives of the North are an outstanding example of the adaptation of human beings to their environment — having developed snow houses, kayaks, traction by dogs, and warm light clothing of skin and fur.

Both the Indians and the Eskimos belong to the Mongolian stock, but there are vast physical and cultural differences between the two. The Indians of the North feel at home in the forest, and they seldom venture above the treeline. The Eskimos, on the other hand, do not like to be fenced in, preferring the barrens to the balsam. Originally, they must have been sea people, for, with the exception of a few hundred who live inland west of Hudson Bay, they have never wandered far from the salt water. Practically everything they need for subsistence has come from the sea.

As an ethnic group, the Eskimos have developed a civilization and pattern of living which has consistently won the admiration of the world outside. They have no history of warfare whatever. Dishonesty is almost foreign to their nature. The children are never punished, not so much as by a harsh word. Their hospitality is well-known. A stranger entering an igloo can expect nothing but the best. Whether it is a piece of seal tenderloin or the lump of pork from a can of pork and beans, the guest can be certain of the choicest morsel in the dinner pot. If he stays the night, he will get the center spot on the sleeping platform: it is the warmest.

Many Eskimos still subsist by hunting and fishing, and live and travel in small family groups. This is necessary, because normally there is not enough game in one district to support a large tribe. But the economic conditions are changing rapidly with the advent of a different civilization from the south. Each year an increasing number of Eskimos give up their nomadic life. Defence construction, governmental administration, and mining and stevedoring operations have created many well-paying jobs. Several Eskimos now work as truck drivers, miners, bulldozer operators, and machine tenders. They have turned out to be natural mechanics. Once shown how, they can easily operate a complicated piece of machinery, or even tear it down and put it back together again.

Recently, a new source of revenue has opened up, the shipment of frozen Arctic char (one of North America's finest eating and game fish) to gourmet restaurants across Canada. With the help from the federal government which provided the freezing equipment, the Eskimos have set up several fishing co-operatives to catch and market char. Their venture so far has been immensely successful.

Lately, too, a lucrative market has developed for their art work. The Eskimo is gifted with great imagination and very sensitive powers of observation. Without any lessons, without any tools except those used in his daily work, he has created masterpieces from native stone and ivory that have been acclaimed the world over. This art of carving is not new. Some figures near Igloolik, off the northeast coast of Melville Peninsula, are estimated to be at least 2,000 years old. Originally, these sculptures had religious significance and were supposed to bring luck in hunting. Today, carving is done mainly for its own sake — and to bring in money.

As a result of all these developments, many Eskimos today are reasonably well off, some earning as much as $5,000 a year. A number of families, who once lived in a twilight world of little food and government charity, now reside in frame houses, own cooking stoves, and are eager to upgrade their living standards, a few even going so far as to order from Eaton's and Simpsons-Sears' mail order catalogs. As a Minister of Northern Affairs and National Resources once remarked: "The day is fast coming when sales of refrigerators to Eskimos may no longer be a joke but a fact."

The Hudson's Bay Company, through its 183 trading posts across the Arctic, has for generations enjoyed a near monopoly in the northern market. Now this is slowly disappearing. In the last few years, Ottawa has helped Eskimos in establishing over a dozen co-operatives, some of which also run their own retail outlets and stock most of the goods one might find in a rural general store.

Eskimos buying habits vary according to the location of the settlement and amount of work available. In most villages, Eskimos still buy only the essentials. Studies at Port Harrison show that the natives there spend 50 cents of every dollar on food. The remainder is divided between yard goods, clothing, rifles and ammunition, and cooking utensils. At Frobisher Bay, however, where incomes are greater because year-round work is available, Eskimos spend 25% of their dollar on food, 17% on clothing, 11% on household goods, including furniture and appliances, and 29% on non-edible luxury items, such as watches, cameras, record players, and tape machines.*

* *Financial Post:* "Money in their parkas, Eskimos eager to buy," January 27, 1962.

BIBLIOGRAPHY ON ETHNIC GROUPS

Audrey, Gill: "Money in Their Parkas, Eskimos Eager to Buy," *Financial Post,* January 27, 1962.

Canadian Advertising, Section on Foreign Language Papers. Maclean-Hunter Publishing Company Limited.

Department of Citizenship and Immigration: *Notes on the Canadian Family Tree,* Queen's Printer, Ottawa, 1960.

Encyclopedia Canadiana, The Grolier Society of Canada, Limited, Ottawa, 1958.

Indian Affairs Branch, Department of Citizenship and Immigration: *The Indian Today,* Queen's Printer, Ottawa, 1962.

Locke, Jeannine: "The Canadian Indians." Four-part series in *Canadian Weekly,* September 19, September 26, October 3, and October 10, 1964.

Phillips, R. A., and G. F. Parsons: *This is Arctic,* Department of Northern Affairs and National Resources, 1958.

Shields, Roy: "Toronto's Little Italy," *The Star Weekly,* Toronto, September 12, 1964.

DISTRIBUTION OF GERMAN POPULATION IN CANADA BY ETHNIC ORIGIN, MOTHER TONGUE, TOTAL IMMIGRANTS, AND POSTWAR IMMIGRANTS, 1961

	Number of persons				Per cent of Canada			
	Ethnic origin	Mother tongue	Total immigrants	Postwar immigrants	Ethnic origin	Mother tongue	Total immigrants	Postwar immigrants
By provinces								
Atlantic provinces	55,320	3,427	2,389	1,905	5.27	0.61	0.75	0.85
Québec	39,457	31,589	27,950	24,127	3.75	5.60	8.75	10.72
Ontario	400,717	183,789	129,645	111,017	38.18	32.60	40.60	49.34
Manitoba	91,846	83,994	30,205	18,491	8.75	14.90	9.46	8.22
Saskatchewan	158,209	89,650	29,143	6,821	15.08	15.90	9.13	3.03
Alberta	183,314	97,666	51,416	30,112	17.47	17.33	16.10	13.38
British Columbia	118,926	72,473	47,735	31,785	11.33	12.86	14.95	14.13
Yukon and N.W. Territories	1,810	1,125	834	744	0.17	0.20	0.26	0.33
Canada	1,049,599	563,713	319,317	225,002	100.00	100.00	100.00	100.00
By urban-rural areas								
DBS metropolitan cities								
Calgary	31,760	16,128	10,784	8,490	3.03	2.86	3.38	3.77
Edmonton	41,422	23,652	15,370	12,122	3.95	4.20	4.81	5.39
Halifax	9,427	655	513	433	0.90	0.12	0.16	0.19
Hamilton	21,594	10,774	9,065	8,025	2.06	1.91	2.84	3.57
Kitchener	54,450	20,539	12,126	9,504	5.19	3.64	3.80	4.23
London	10,427	3,962	3,356	2,974	0.99	0.70	1.05	1.32
Montréal	27,873	26,491	23,817	20,528	2.66	4.70	7.46	9.12
Ottawa	12,300	6,084	4,669	4,221	1.17	1.08	1.46	1.88
Québec	996	411	364	340	0.09	0.07	0.11	0.15

DISTRIBUTION OF GERMAN POPULATION IN CANADA BY ETHNIC ORIGIN, MOTHER TONGUE, TOTAL IMMIGRANTS, AND POSTWAR IMMIGRANTS, 1961 (continued)

	Number of Persons				Per cent of Canada			
	Ethnic origin	Mother tongue	Total immigrants	Postwar immigrants	Ethnic origin	Mother tongue	Total immigrants	Postwar immigrants
Regina	22,370	12,273	5,202	2,656	2.13	2.18	1.63	1.18
Saint John	1,378	363	286	248	0.13	0.07	0.09	0.11
St. John's	564	195	151	136	0.05	0.03	0.05	0.06
Saskatoon	14,023	7,188	2,564	1,262	1.34	1.28	0.80	0.56
Sudbury	4,215	2,299	1,645	1,515	0.40	0.41	0.51	0.67
Toronto	80,300	61,020	53,483	48,953	7.65	10.83	16.75	21.76
Vancouver	51,056	31,752	23,096	17,276	4.86	5.63	7.23	7.68
Victoria	5,341	2,422	1,838	1,403	0.51	0.43	0.58	0.62
Windsor	9,944	5,433	4,280	2,929	0.95	0.96	1.34	1.30
Winnipeg	50,206	35,483	20,713	15,356	4.78	6.29	6.49	6.83
Sub-total	449,646	267,124	193,322	158,371	42.84	47.39	60.54	70.39
Other urban	199,044	87,220	49,000	31,125	18.96	15.47	15.35	13.83
Total urban	648,690	354,344	242,322	189,496	61.80	62.86	75.89	84.22
Rural non-farm	197,619	81,314	38,389	21,382	18.83	14.42	12.02	9.50
Rural farm	203,290	128,055	38,606	14,124	19.37	22.72	12.09	6.28
Canada	1,049,599	563,713	319,317	225,002	100.00	100.00	100.00	100.00

(Source: DBS, *Census of Canada, 1961*. Bulletins 92-545; 92-549; 92-562; 92-563. The figures on immigration refer to persons with German as mother tongue.)

DISTRIBUTION OF UKRAINIAN POPULATION IN CANADA BY ETHNIC ORIGIN, MOTHER TONGUE, TOTAL IMMIGRANTS AND POSTWAR IMMIGRANTS, 1961

	Number of persons				Per cent of Canada			
	Ethnic origin	Mother tongue	Total immigrants	Postwar immigrants	Ethnic origin	Mother tongue	Total immigrants	Postwar immigrants
By provinces								
Atlantic provinces	2,349	1,605	584	97	0.50	0.44	0.47	0.26
Québec	16,588	13,424	7,968	4,512	3.50	3.71	6.50	12.15
Ontario	127,911	89,766	45,729	22,708	27.02	24.83	37.30	61.15
Manitoba	105,372	85,173	23,844	4,002	22.26	23.56	19.45	10.78
Saskatchewan	78,851	67,087	15,622	1,079	16.66	18.56	12.74	2.90
Alberta	105,923	83,923	22,186	3,573	22.38	23.22	18.10	9.62
British Columbia	35,640	20,101	6,592	1,139	7.53	5.56	5.38	3.07
Yukon and N.W. Territories	703	417	73	25	0.15	0.12	0.06	0.07
Canada	473,337	361,496	122,598	37,135	100.00	100.00	100.00	100.00
By urban-rural areas								
DBS metropolitan cities								
Calgary	8,033	4,446	1,465	477	1.70	1.23	1.20	1.28
Edmonton	38,164	28,021	7,324	1,934	8.06	7.75	5.97	5.21
Halifax	432	204	78	28	0.09	0.06	0.06	0.08
Hamilton	10,931	7,476	3,871	2,202	2.31	2.07	3.16	5.93
Kitchener	2,163	1,408	754	381	0.46	0.39	0.62	1.03
London	1,834	1,167	736	574	0.39	0.32	0.60	1.55
Montréal	14,519	11,963	7,138	4,119	3.07	3.31	5.82	11.09
Ottawa	2,985	1,900	850	403	0.63	0.53	0.69	1.08
Québec	56	20	5	1	0.01	—	—	—

DISTRIBUTION OF UKRAINIAN POPULATION IN CANADA BY ETHNIC ORIGIN, MOTHER TONGUE, TOTAL IMMIGRANTS AND POSTWAR IMMIGRANTS, 1961 (continued)

	Number of persons				Per cent of Canada			
	Ethnic origin	Mother tongue	Total immigrants	Postwar immigrants	Ethnic origin	Mother tongue	Total immigrants	Postwar immigrants
Regina	5,741	3,543	819	159	1.21	0.98	0.67	0.43
Saint John	100	82	27	4	0.02	0.02	0.02	0.01
St. John's	44	22	6	—	0.01	0.01	0.01	—
Saskatoon	9,072	6,776	1,622	291	1.92	1.87	1.32	0.78
Sudbury	4,942	3,562	1,416	715	1.04	0.98	1.16	1.93
Toronto	46,650	34,917	20,312	12,093	9.86	9.66	16.57	32.56
Vancouver	18,712	10,583	3,574	579	3.95	2.93	2.92	1.56
Victoria	1,509	720	233	56	0.32	0.20	0.19	0.15
Windsor	5,508	4,075	1,917	485	1.16	1.13	1.56	1.31
Winnipeg	53,918	39,591	13,206	3,308	11.39	10.95	10.77	8.91
Sub-total	225,313	160,476	65,353	27,809	47.60	44.39	53.31	74.89
Other urban	83,213	56,884	20,923	5,742	17.58	15.74	17.06	15.46
Total urban	308,526	217,360	86,276	33,551	65.18	60.13	70.37	90.35
Rural—non-farm	65,868	50,132	16,080	1,873	13.92	13.87	13.12	5.04
Rural—farm	98,943	94,004	20,242	1,711	20.90	26.00	16.51	4.61
Canada	473,337	361,496	122,598	37,135	100.00	100.00	100.00	100.00

(Source: DBS, *Census of Canada, 1961.* Bulletins 92-545; 92-549; 92-562; 92-563. The figures on immigration refer to persons with Ukrainian as mother tongue.)

DISTRIBUTION OF ITALIAN POPULATION IN CANADA, BY ETHNIC ORIGIN, MOTHER TONGUE, TOTAL IMMIGRANTS AND POSTWAR IMMIGRANTS, 1961

	Number of persons				Per cent of Canada			
	Ethnic origin	Mother tongue	Total immigrants	Postwar immigrants	Ethnic origin	Mother tongue	Total immigrants	Postwar immigrants
By provinces								
Atlantic provinces	5,278	1,840	1,273	946	1.17	0.54	0.49	0.41
Québec	108,552	89,806	65,133	58,799	24.10	26.44	25.27	25.67
Ontario	273,864	207,937	161,128	144,916	60.81	61.23	62.50	63.28
Manitoba	6,476	4,362	3,276	2,780	1.44	1.28	1.27	1.21
Saskatchewan	2,413	1,369	920	716	0.53	0.40	0.36	0.31
Alberta	15,025	9,881	7,483	6,236	3.34	2.91	2.90	2.72
British Columbia	38,399	24,168	18,362	14,418	8.53	7.12	7.12	6.30
Yukon and N.W. Territories	344	263	228	218	0.08	0.08	0.09	0.10
Canada	450,351	339,626	257,803	229,029	100.00	100.00	100.00	100.00
By urban-rural areas								
DBS metropolitan cities								
Calgary	4,994	3,440	2,739	2,476	1.11	1.01	1.06	1.08
Edmonton	4,712	3,582	2,797	2,597	1.05	1.05	1.08	1.13
Halifax	955	411	339	316	0.21	0.12	0.13	0.14
Hamilton	25,560	18,366	13,784	11,824	5.68	5.41	5.35	5.16
Kitchener	1,709	811	633	552	0.38	0.24	0.25	0.24
London	3,467	2,088	1,708	1,509	0.77	0.62	0.66	0.66
Montréal	101,466	85,347	62,219	56,386	22.53	25.13	24.13	24.62
Ottawa	9,094	6,739	5,197	4,895	2.02	1.98	2.02	2.14
Québec	1,080	657	467	410	0.24	0.19	0.18	0.18

DISTRIBUTION OF ITALIAN POPULATION IN CANADA, BY ETHNIC ORIGIN, MOTHER TONGUE, TOTAL IMMIGRANTS AND POSTWAR IMMIGRANTS, 1961 (continued)

	Number of persons				Per cent of Canada			
	Ethnic origin	Mother tongue	Total immigrants	Postwar immigrants	Ethnic Origin	Mother tongue	Total immigrants	Postwar immigrants
Regina	638	416	333	310	0.14	0.12	0.13	0.14
Saint John	259	82	61	47	0.06	0.02	0.02	0.02
St. John's	75	39	24	23	0.02	0.01	0.01	0.01
Saskatoon	420	254	190	138	0.09	0.08	0.07	0.06
Sudbury	8,080	6,145	3,966	3,125	1.79	1.81	1.54	1.36
Toronto	140,378	116,422	93,961	88,829	31.17	34.28	36.45	38.79
Vancouver	18,300	11,878	9,163	7,615	4.06	3.50	3.55	3.33
Victoria	1,265	637	503	411	0.28	0.19	0.20	0.18
Windsor	11,511	9,040	6,847	5,778	2.56	2.66	2.66	2.52
Winnipeg	5,785	3,936	3,017	2,573	1.28	1.16	1.17	1.12
Sub-total	339,748	270,290	207,948	189,814	75.44	79.58	80.66	82.88
Other urban	86,744	56,540	40,827	32,420	19.26	16.65	15.84	14.15
Total urban	426,492	326,830	248,775	222,234	94.70	96.23	96.50	97.03
Rural—non-farm	18,418	10,111	7,291	5,714	4.09	2.98	2.83	2.50
Rural—farm	5,441	2,685	1,737	1,081	1.21	0.79	0.67	0.47
Canada	450,351	339,626	257,803	229,029	100.00	100.00	100.00	100.00

(Source: DBS, Census of Canada, 1961. Bulletins 92-545; 92-549; 92-562; 92-563. The figures on immigration refer to persons with Italian as mother tongue.)

DISTRIBUTION OF DUTCH POPULATION IN CANADA BY ETHNIC ORIGIN, MOTHER TONGUE, TOTAL IMMIGRANTS, AND POSTWAR IMMIGRANTS, 1961

	Number of persons				Per cent of Canada			
	Ethnic origin	Mother tongue	Total immigrants	Postwar immigrants	Ethnic origin	Mother tongue	Total immigrants	Postwar immigrants
By provinces								
Atlantic provinces	34,883	4,078	3,372	3,253	8.12	2.40	2.52	2.63
Québec	10,442	6,059	5,204	4,863	2.43	3.56	3.89	3.94
Ontario	191,017	90,051	77,896	74,167	44.46	52.92	58.27	60.06
Manitoba	47,780	13,363	5,837	4,751	11.12	7.85	4.37	3.85
Saskatchewan	29,325	8,054	3,047	2,144	6.83	4.73	2.28	1.74
Alberta	55,530	24,640	19,404	17,673	12.92	14.48	14.51	14.31
British Columbia	60,176	23,793	18,815	16,532	14.00	13.98	14.07	13.39
Yukon and N.W. Territories	526	139	113	100	0.12	0.08	0.09	0.08
Canada	429,679	170,177	133,688	123,483	100.00	100.00	100.00	100.00
By urban-rural areas								
DBS metropolitan cities								
Calgary	11,159	5,231	4,428	4,189	2.60	3.07	3.31	3.39
Edmonton	13,829	7,844	6,665	6,360	3.22	4.61	4.99	5.15
Halifax	6,756	519	463	437	1.57	0.31	0.35	0.35
Hamilton	15,005	8,176	7,169	6,957	3.49	4.81	5.36	5.63
Kitchener	3,235	1,564	1,406	1,340	0.75	0.92	1.05	1.09
London	7,045	3,830	3,501	3,385	1.64	2.25	2.62	2.74
Montréal	7,138	4,269	3,773	3,511	1.66	2.51	2.82	2.84
Ottawa	5,585	2,482	2,185	2,121	1.30	1.46	1.64	1.72
Québec	187	89	72	67	0.04	0.05	0.05	0.05

DISTRIBUTION OF DUTCH POPULATION IN CANADA BY ETHNIC ORIGIN, MOTHER TONGUE, TOTAL IMMIGRANTS, AND POSTWAR IMMIGRANTS, 1961 (continued)

	Number of persons				Per cent of Canada			
	Ethnic origin	Mother tongue	Total immigrants	Postwar immigrants	Ethnic origin	Mother tongue	Total immigrants	Postwar immigrants
Regina	2,138	687	577	527	0.50	0.40	0.43	0.43
Saint John	1,553	194	164	155	0.36	0.11	0.12	0.13
St. John's	121	62	44	37	0.03	0.04	0.03	0.03
Saskatoon	4,186	1,206	637	543	0.98	0.71	0.48	0.44
Sudbury	1,064	328	282	265	0.25	0.19	0.21	0.22
Toronto	33,434	15,213	13,557	12,926	7.78	8.94	10.14	10.47
Vancouver	23,946	10,243	8,627	7,660	5.57	6.02	6.45	6.20
Victoria	3,211	1,427	1,285	1,183	0.75	0.84	0.96	0.96
Windsor	2,346	702	609	526	0.55	0.41	0.46	0.43
Winnipeg	14,881	5,936	3,794	3,262	3.46	3.49	2.84	2.64
Sub-total	156,819	70,002	59,238	55,451	36.50	41.14	44.31	44.91
Other urban	82,288	29,125	23,831	21,785	19.15	17.11	17.83	17.64
Total urban	239,107	99,127	83,069	77,236	55.65	58.25	62.14	62.55
Rural—non-farm	95,624	31,299	23,861	22,075	22.25	18.39	17.85	17.88
Rural—farm	94,948	39,751	26,758	24,172	22.10	23.36	20.01	19.57
Canada	429,679	170,177	133,688	123,483	100.00	100.00	100.00	100.00

(Source: DBS, *Census of Canada, 1961*. Bulletins 92-545; 92-549; 92-562; 92-563. The figures on immigration refer to persons with Dutch as mother tongue.)

DISTRIBUTION OF POLISH POPULATION IN CANADA BY ETHNIC ORIGIN, MOTHER TONGUE, TOTAL IMMIGRANTS AND POSTWAR IMMIGRANTS, 1961

	Number of persons				Per cent of Canada			
	Ethnic origin	Mother tongue	Total immigrants	Postwar immigrants	Ethnic origin	Mother tongue	Total immigrants	Postwar immigrants
By provinces								
Atlantic provinces	4,064	1,534	898	431	1.26	0.95	0.83	0.69
Québec	30,790	19,827	15,544	11,100	9.52	12.26	14.32	17.80
Ontario	149,524	83,214	58,765	37,980	46.22	51.46	54.12	60.90
Manitoba	44,371	20,652	10,687	3,896	13.71	12.77	9.84	6.25
Saskatchewan	28,951	10,585	5,604	1,284	8.95	6.54	5.16	2.06
Alberta	40,539	16,755	10,472	4,621	12.53	10.36	9.65	7.41
British Columbia	24,870	8,978	6,507	2,987	7.69	5.55	5.99	4.79
Yukon and N.W. Territories	408	175	96	60	0.12	0.11	0.09	0.10
Canada	323,517	161,720	108,573	62,359	100.00	100.00	100.00	100.00
By urban-rural areas								
DBS metropolitan cities								
Calgary	5,819	2,280	1,573	1,010	1.80	1.41	1.45	1.62
Edmonton	12,900	5,250	3,399	1,824	3.99	3.25	3.13	2.92
Halifax	665	216	173	108	0.20	0.13	0.16	0.17
Hamilton	14,315	8,514	5,973	3,386	4.42	5.27	5.50	5.43
Kitchener	5,233	2,514	1,637	978	1.62	1.55	1.51	1.57
London	3,358	1,896	1,508	1,147	1.04	1.17	1.39	1.84
Montréal	26,347	17,182	13,630	9,638	8.14	10.62	12.55	15.46
Ottawa	4,243	2,132	1,535	1,239	1.31	1.32	1.41	1.99
Québec	224	97	84	60	0.07	0.06	0.08	0.10

DISTRIBUTION OF POLISH POPULATION IN CANADA BY ETHNIC ORIGIN, MOTHER TONGUE, TOTAL IMMIGRANTS, AND POSTWAR IMMIGRANTS, 1961 (continued)

	Number of persons				Per cent of Canada			
	Ethnic origin	Mother tongue	Total immigrants	Postwar immigrants	Ethnic origin	Mother tongue	Total immigrants	Postwar immigrants
Regina	3,034	1,049	572	284	0.94	0.65	0.53	0.45
Saint John	180	57	42	19	0.06	0.04	0.04	0.03
St. John's	93	39	33	27	0.03	0.02	0.03	0.04
Saskatoon	2,624	762	463	147	0.81	0.47	0.43	0.24
Sudbury	2,845	1,816	1,249	934	0.88	1.12	1.15	1.50
Toronto	58,578	32,077	24,945	16,660	18.11	19.84	22.97	26.72
Vancouver	12,861	4,833	3,565	1,618	3.97	2.99	3.28	2.59
Victoria	1,446	521	384	222	0.45	0.32	0.35	0.36
Windsor	5,997	3,345	2,309	851	1.85	2.07	2.13	1.36
Winnipeg	24,904	12,416	7,132	3,280	7.70	7.68	6.57	5.26
Sub-total	185,666	96,996	70,206	43,432	57.39	59.98	64.66	69.65
Other urban	60,257	29,733	19,789	11,762	18.63	18.39	18.23	18.86
Total urban	245,923	126,729	89,995	55,194	76.02	78.37	82.89	88.51
Rural—non-farm	35,695	15,498	8,846	4,044	11.03	9.58	8.15	6.49
Rural—farm	41,899	19,493	9,732	3,121	12.95	12.05	8.96	5.00
Canada	323,517	161,720	108,573	62,359	100.00	100.00	100.00	100.00

(Source: DBS, *Census of Canada, 1961*. Bulletins 92-545; 92-549; 92-562; 92-563. The figures on immigration refer to persons with Polish as mother tongue.)

Postwar Immigrants

Canada has always attracted immigrants from abroad. They come for a variety of reasons. Some have been torn from their homes by war, or are fleeing from political or religious persecutions. Others are just temporary residents; they like to see the world, crave adventure, or have a wanderlust. Still others are motivated by economic factors. They are looking for more profitable avenues to exploit their talents, and see better opportunities for themselves and their children in a young and dynamic nation.

Since the end of the Second World War, over two million immigrants have landed in Canada. These newcomers have influenced the economy in various ways — by contributing manpower, by establishing new industries, by repopulating the farms, by investing huge sums of money in housing, and above all, by providing as consumers important markets for different goods and services.

Without immigration, Canada's postwar population growth would have been fairly slow. This can be seen from the following computations:

Population in Canada, June 1, 1961 18,238,000
Population in Canada, Jan. 1, 1946 12,527,000
Growth of population between 1946 and 1961 5,711,000
Postwar immigrant population 1,507,000
Immigrants' contribution to population growth 26.4%

The New Canadians have been responsible for 26.4% of the gain in population during the postwar era. In other words, without them the expansion of the domestic market would have been only three-fourths as rapid. Immigration is providing the extra momentum that makes the difference between accelerated growth and the 2% a year pace that is normally regarded as adequate for an industrial economy. The impact on the consumer market has been tremendous, like the sudden addition of a province larger than Alberta. It is not, therefore, surprising that many economists regard immigration as one of the key factors in Canada's postwar business expansion.

The New Canadian market is fairly well documented statistically. Buried in the voluminous reports of the 1961 Census, there is a mine of valuable information which can be put to good use. An attempt is made in the tables included in this section to extract all the relevant statistics and present them in a compact form. To give more meaning to the figures, the position of the postwar immigrants is usually compared with the rest of the population. The latter includes the native-born plus the prewar immigrants, most of whom may be presumed to have merged into the general tempo of Canadian life.

One striking feature which emerges is that the postwar immigrants are predominantly urban dwellers, with 71% residing in the metropolitan centers and only 4.5% on farms. In fact, over a quarter, 26.9%, are in Toronto alone.

One-third of the New Canadians have English as their mother tongue. This is to be expected, since 27% are born in the United Kingdom and 5% in the

United States. Lately a gradual but significant change has been taking place in the ethnic composition of the new arrivals. Compared to the early Fifties, a proportionately larger number are coming from southern than from northwestern Europe. At one period, for four years continuously (1958 to 1961), the immigrants from Italy even outnumbered those from the British Isles. On account of the prosperity which the Bonn Republic is enjoying, the influx from West Germany has dropped considerably. This has been compensated to some extent by a sharp rise in immigration from Spain, Portugal, and Greece, where overpopulation and chronic uncertainty of employment are forcing young people to go abroad to seek greater economic opportunities.

NEW CANADIANS AND THE LABOR FORCE

Under the present law, all persons possessing requisite skill and ability are admissible to Canada provided they have sufficient means to maintain themselves till they find a job, or are coming forward to assured employment, or are sponsored by relatives who are Canadian citizens. As the regulations now stand, the emphasis is on brain, not brawn. Excepting the sponsored immigrants, very few unskilled workers are given permission to enter the country. This is clearly reflected in the census figures on occupation of male workers. Among the postwar immigrants 10.1% are professionals and 39.2% are engaged in fairly skilled jobs in secondary industries. The corresponding figures for native-born and prewar immigrants are only 7.2% and 27.3% respectively. As regards distribution by industries, the postwar immigrants are concentrated in manufacturing, construction, and personal services. They are relatively scarce, compared to the rest of the population, in agriculture, forestry, transport and communications, and public administration.

Despite complaints from the trade unions, in very few cases have the immigrants actually aggravated unemployment. Generally, they have filled the gaps for professional and highly-skilled personnel and so broken bottlenecks in production. It must also not be forgotten that without immigration the labor force in the Fifties would have increased hardly at all. Because of the low birthrates during the Depression, the numbers of native-born reaching working age were relatively few, hardly enough to compensate for those retiring.

In fact, some of the postwar immigrants have been even responsible for creating new jobs. The Department of Citizenship and Immigration reports that over a 13-year period from 1950 to 1963, more than 11,000 New Canadians started small businesses of their own, providing employment for some 45,000 persons. These cases do not include the large-scale enterprises where the entrepreneurs had sufficient resources and did not approach the Department for advice or other assistance.

Although the immigrant farmers are in a minority, they are nevertheless making a vital contribution to the economy. Their purchases of farms have offset to

POSTWAR IMMIGRANTS BY PROVINCES AND
URBAN-RURAL AREAS, 1961

	Postwar immigrants	% of Canada	% of the total population of each area
Province			
Atlantic provinces	32,346	2.1	1.7
Québec	247,762	16.4	4.7
Ontario	833,303	55.3	13.4
Manitoba	62,498	4.2	6.8
Saskatchewan	28,993	1.9	3.1
Alberta	121,559	8.1	9.1
British Columbia	177,544	11.8	10.9
Yukon and N.W. Territories	3,111	0.2	8.3
Canada	1,507,116	100.0	8.3
Urban-Rural areas			
Calgary	38,094	2.5	13.6
Edmonton	44,429	2.9	13.2
Halifax	7,413	0.5	4.0
Hamilton	65,585	4.3	16.6
Kitchener	20,580	1.4	13.3
London	23,146	1.5	12.8
Montréal	214,128	14.2	10.1
Ottawa	33,930	2.2	7.9
Québec	4,509	0.3	1.3
Regina	7,772	0.5	6.9
Saint John	2,296	0.2	2.4
St. John's	1,492	0.1	1.6
Saskatoon	5,703	0.4	6.0
Sudbury	11,467	0.8	10.4
Toronto	404,704	26.9	22.2
Vancouver	99,150	6.6	12.5
Victoria	15,009	1.0	9.7
Windsor	20,881	1.4	10.8
Winnipeg	49,516	3.3	10.4
Sub-total	1,069,804	71.0	12.8
Other urban	233,069	15.5	5.4
Total urban	1,302,873	86.5	10.3
Rural non-farm	135,928	9.0	3.9
Rural farm	68,315	4.5	3.3
Canada	1,507,116	100.0	8.3

(Source: DBS, *Census of Canada, 1961.* Catalogue no. 92-548.)

IMMIGRATION TO CANADA, BY COUNTRY OF LAST PERMANENT RESIDENCE, 1946-1965

	Total	United Kingdom	Germany	Italy	Netherlands	France	United States	West Indies	Asia	Others
1946	71,719	50,482	354	49	2,234	354	11,474	440	274	6,058
1947	64,127	35,486	267	78	2,738	539	9,444	406	600	14,569
1948	125,414	45,595	2,475	3,204	6,997	1,326	7,393	475	819	57,130
1949	95,217	20,737	2,941	7,728	6,828	1,163	7,756	463	1,357	46,244
1950	73,912	12,669	3,815	8,993	7,169	1,399	7,821	447	2,292	29,307
1951	194,391	31,559	29,196	23,426	19,266	8,279	7,755	802	4,420	69,688
1952	164,498	45,255	25,716	20,651	21,068	5,395	9,333	851	6,044	30,185
1953	168,868	46,793	34,193	23,704	20,341	4,045	9,407	1,005	4,581	24,799
1954	154,227	43,381	28,479	23,780	16,182	3,672	10,131	932	3,075	24,595
1955	109,946	29,382	17,630	19,139	6,759	2,869	10,395	878	3,724	19,170
1956	164,857	50,390	26,061	27,939	7,792	3,809	9,777	1,127	3,577	34,385
1957	282,164	108,989	28,430	27,740	11,934	5,869	11,008	1,257	3,373	83,564
1958	124,851	24,777	13,888	27,043	7,420	2,727	10,846	1,292	4,450	32,408
1959	106,928	18,222	10,423	25,655	5,243	2,153	11,338	1,314	5,585	26,995
1960	104,111	19,585	10,774	20,681	5,429	2,944	11,247	1,276	4,218	27,957
1961	71,689	11,870	6,231	14,161	1,787	2,330	11,516	1,263	2,901	19,630
1962	74,586	15,603	5,548	13,641	1,555	2,674	11,643	1,586	2,733	19,603
1963	93,151	24,603	6,744	14,427	1,728	3,569	11,736	2,354	3,912	24,078
1964	112,606	29,279	5,992	19,297	2,029	4,542	12,565	2,420	6,526	29,956
1965	146,758	39,857	8,927	26,398	2,619	5,225	15,143	3,095	11,684	33,810
Total	2,504,020	704,514	268,084	347,734	157,118	64,883	207,728	23,683	76,145	654,131
Per Cent	100.0	28.1	10.7	13.9	6.3	2.6	8.3	1.0	3.0	26.1

(Source: DBS, *Canadian Statistical Review*, Historical Summary, 1963 and December 1965 issue. Catalogue no. 11-003 and 11-502.)

some extent the exodus of the native-born from rural to urban areas. Many of the new owners are experienced in agricultural operations, and their skill and determination have brought abandoned farms back to fruition again.

The newcomers also add a useful degree of mobility to the labor force. As a rule, native Canadians, settled in one place with a job and family, are reluctant to move to a mining camp in northern Manitoba or to a lumbering community in the virgin forests of British Columbia. Many adventurous young immigrants, eager to make a stake for themselves, are willing to work in the bush and in the mines far away in the hinterland. After a few years, no doubt, they move south and settle in the larger cities; but, in the meantime, they have helped in some measure to push back the northern frontier.

POSTWAR IMMIGRANTS AS CONSUMERS

While the postwar immigrants have played a major role as workers or entrepreneurs, it is actually as consumers that they have exerted their greatest impact on the economy. From the very first month of their arrival, they become important consumers of goods and services. As a rule, they come to Canada with very few material possessions. The average value of the household goods per immigrant is $250–$275, with cash assets amounting to $600–$700. Thus, furniture, appliances, and even clothes, which they once owned in Europe, have to be bought over again. Nor is this all. There is a tendency on the part of many newcomers, once they have got a reasonably good job, to indulge in conspicuous consumption. Within a short time after his departure to Canada, it is not uncommon for the parents in the home country to receive a photograph of their boy in front of his newly-acquired used car. Because they are so insecure, the immigrants, especially from southern and eastern Europe, become very materialistic and strive to collect symbols of their success as quickly as possible. This helps them, they feel, to acquire status in the eyes of fellow-nationals and native-born Canadians.

The 1961 Census shows that within the first seventeen months of their arrival the recent immigrants had purchased no less than 3,440 homes worth on the average $14,645. In the durable goods field, they created a market for at least 14,667 refrigerators, 10,035 television sets, 8,625 passenger cars, and 1,164 home freezers (DBS Bulletin 93-532). Add to this their expenditures on food, clothing, drugs, and toiletries, and the magnitude of their tangible contribution to domestic trade and industry becomes really impressive. It is almost like an export market brought home, the dollar value being far greater than Canada's total sales to several small European countries.

SELLING TO NEW IMMIGRANTS

Selling to the new immigrants is not always easy. Those who understand English or French can, without difficulty, be covered by normal advertising in print or broadcast media. But many of the Europeans cannot be reached this way because of the language barrier. The 1961 Census shows that among those who have been in the country for five years or less and whose mother tongue is not English or French, 14.6% of the males and 26.8% of the females do not speak either one of the two official languages. Many more may understand a few words, but would not be in a position to grasp the sales message in a language still new to them. Since these Europeans are not, as a rule, familiar with the local brand names, they tend to buy imported items from their homelands, even though Canadian goods may be lower priced and of better quality.

Businessmen, therefore, are expanding their efforts to reach the new immigrants in their own tongue. The banks do it through the written word — printing banking forms and booklets in foreign languages. The insurance companies depend more on the spoken word — having New Canadians as agents in districts where their countrymen reside. Supermarkets and chain stores rely on pure convenience to do the trick. Language does not matter when self-service is available.

Merchants, too, have been quick to recognize the bonanza. In communities most affected by the flood of immigration, scores of specialty stores have sprung up. Customers are served in their own language and find their familiar European food specialties, patent medicines, and hundreds of other items.

Canadian manufacturers, on the other hand, have been comparatively slow in tapping this rich market. Only when the import statistics for the items similar to what they are producing begin to show spectacular increases do they realize that a special effort is needed.

Any large scale program to cover the immigrant population is best confined to the major cities where there is a high concentration of New Canadians. One way of reaching them is through advertising in a few of Canada's foreign language semi-weeklies, weeklies, monthlies, published in over 25 different languages.

The ethnic press, by providing a bridge between the new world and the old, fills a very important gap in the life of the new arrivals. It facilitates the adjustment to their adopted land. It not only keeps them in contact with the activities of their former countrymen, but it also tries to interpret the Canadian scene in terms they understand. Often the editor acquires an omnipotent father image whose duty it is to act as a teacher, friend, and guide in a foreign world. The readers consult him if they want to rent a room, buy a car, hire a baby sitter, locate their lost relatives, or even seek a mate for matrimony.

In quality, the ethnic papers range from badly mimeographed sheets that appear at irregular intervals to informative and well-edited journals that enjoy a high reputation in their communities. Some have reliable audited circulations, while others give out "publisher's statements" that may be grossly exaggerated. All this makes their selection for advertising purposes rather complicated, necessitating expert skill and guidance. It must also be remembered that many immigrants after a few years get tired of their ethnic papers and switch to English or French language dailies. Hence the foreign press is most effective in reaching new arrivals and those housewives who, despite their long residence, have not been able to learn English.

Another medium popular among New Canadians is the foreign-language radio program. This fact is clearly brought out by a survey in the Toronto-Hamilton area, sponsored by the Canadian Broadcasting Corporation.

USE OF RADIO BY NEW CANADIANS, TORONTO-HAMILTON AREA

Nationality	Listening regularly to foreign language broadcasts	Listening to English broadcasts only	Do not use radio	Total
Dutch	48%	38%	14%	100%
Germans	59	25	16	100
Hungarians	36	64	—	100
Italians	87	13	—	100
Poles	87	13	—	100
Ukrainians	95	5	—	100

(Source: Canadian Broadcasting Corporation: *Broadcasting and the New Canadian: An Interpretation of Two Recent Surveys in the Toronto-Hamilton Area*, Ottawa, April 1961.)

High production costs have so far prevented television from becoming a large-scale medium in foreign language advertising. However, there have been a few Italian, German, and Ukrainian TV shows, using mostly filmed material, with foreign-language spot commercials.

When mass media are not suitable, recourse may be had to direct mail. The mailing lists can be compiled after consulting the consulates, immigrant aid societies, citizenship councils, and ethnic associations.

In sales promotion, the most effective method is selective sampling among a representative cross-section of New Canadians. As a rule, in big cities the cost is not prohibitive because of the concentration of new arrivals in the ethnic colonies.

SPECIAL FEATURES OF THE MARKET

To develop an intelligent program for selling to the immigrants, it is desirable to take into consideration their different cultural patterns and the difficulties they encounter while trying to adjust themselves to the Canadian way of life.

For an ordinary immigrant, especially of a *non-British origin,* the process of integration is a constant uphill fight. He faces all types of problems—homesickness, difficulty of finding a job, humiliation of being thought different, and the slow process of making friends and entering into Canadian social life. Often he feels like a fifth wheel on the wagon — foresaken, frustrated, fenced in, and even useless. A company can easily win his steadfast loyalty to its products if it sponsors a public relations program intended in some way to overcome his initial hurdles and to lessen his psychological tensions and irritations.

It must also be remembered that an immigrant's culture and set of values remain with him for a long time, even when he is transplanted to an alien soil. Man is not a piece of moulding clay which can be quickly and easily fashioned into various forms. He cannot shed his identity as he does his shirt. Consequently, when selling to the New Canadians, it is not enough to translate the message into another language. One has to translate the whole approach.

Here are a few broad areas where the cultures of the two continents differ.

• In the European family, the boundary lines are clearly defined as to the relative position of each member. The father demands respect and obedience from his children, and harsh punishments are inflicted even for minor transgressions. The parents also object to many aspects of Canadian teen-age life, particularly dating and unchaperoned evening excursions to the movies and dances.

• The immigrant household often consists of more than husband, wife, and children. Many relatives live together under the same roof. The family works as a functional unit designed to meet every crisis and provide for every emergency — unemployment, sickness, old age. The welfare of the family group supersedes that of the individual members. Old people are usually respected and exercise some authority over their children and grandchildren as long as they live.

• Education is eulogized among Europeans. The professional man rates high in the social scale. Intellectuals are esteemed more than successful businessmen. Great value is also placed on certain cultural or philosophical pursuits. Material comforts may even be sacrificed in order to enjoy aesthetic pleasures.

• As a consumer the immigrant is more cautious than his Canadian counterpart. He is not an "impulse buyer" but falls more into the "shop-around" category. High pressure selling is usually resented. If he is disappointed with a product, it will be difficult to win him back later on. If satisfied, he will prove an extremely faithful customer and not switch his brand as easily as the novelty-hungry native. Winning his confidence is therefore more important than whetting his appetite for something new and different.

• Unlike a Canadian, the European does not adopt a predominantly pragmatic approach to life. Being conditioned by his own distinctive history and tradition, he tends to act more from consciously defined principles and ideas. For him, all modes of behavior are somewhat set and stable. This difference may be compared to the one between a well-matured, seasoned, exact, accomplished but somewhat disillusioned father and an over-confident youth who has all sorts of plans for doing big things. When the two have to live in the same house, the fur of both is rubbed the wrong way once in a while.

INTEGRATION

How long does it take an immigrant to lose his distinctive characteristics and become integrated in the Canadian way of life? The rate of acculturation depends primarily on the immigrant's attitude concerning his place in the new country.

It is frequently assumed that the people from the British Isles make the best immigrants. However, a recent study of the Department of Citizenship and Immigration by Professor Anthony H. Richmond throws some doubt on the validity of this assumption. A comparison of the postwar immigrants from the United Kingdom and other countries shows that the British are more dissatisfied with their life and work in Canada and less likely to settle permanently.

Many immigrants from Europe, especially the political refugees, are grateful for the non-material benefits of the Canadian way of life, mainly the freedom from fear and persecution, which the British take for granted. Some others from southern Europe had experienced such a degree of poverty in their home country that even an unskilled laborer's wage in Canada seems riches to them. These immigrants expected life to be difficult at first and are not unduly perturbed if this proves to be the case. On the other hand, most British do not anticipate any serious problems of economic adjustment, and, if things do not go well, they are more inclined to react unfavorably.

Also, many of the British are temporary residents. Though they have entered with immigrant visas — a normal requirement for those intending to work in Canada for a year or more — some have no intention of settling permanently This is borne out by the following table based on the 1961 Census.

Ethnic origin	No. of immigrants arriving in Canada 1946–1961 (000)	No. of postwar immigrants residing in Canada, 1961 (000)	% of immigrants still in Canada
British	632	426	67%
Dutch	145	134	92
French	49	37	76
German	251	199	79
Italian	264	234	89
Polish-Russian-Ukrainian	120	119	99
Scandinavian	47	34	72
Others	378	324	86
Total	1,886	1,507	80%

Between January 1946 and May 1961, 1,927,000 immigrants entered Canada. After allowing for normal death rates, there should have been 1,886,000 postwar immigrants in the country at the time of the 1961 Census. However, only 1,507,000 were counted by census enumerators. This means that 20% must have either returned home or re-emigrated, most probably to the United States. Examination of figures by ethnic origin shows that Canada retained only two-thirds of the immigrants of British origin, compared to 92% for Dutch and 99% for the Polish-Russian-Ukrainian group.

FUTURE OUTLOOK

Forecasting the future of immigration is a hazardous task. Much will depend upon the forces operating in the country of emigration ("push" factors) and the conditions prevailing in the country of immigration ("pull" factors).

Here are some possible "push" factors that may help Canada:

• Increasing possibility of migrating on a "trial" basis, as a result of better communications, cheaper passage fares (in relation to average income), and, in general, greater fluidity in the international labor market.

• Continued economic stagnation or slow rate of industrial progress in the nations of southern Europe, like Spain, Portugal, Yugoslavia, Greece, and Italy (particularly Sicily).

• Likelihood of political upheavals in South Africa as well as Rhodesia and other countries where native inhabitants resent the rule by a minority of white settlers.

• Overpopulation and underemployment in many Commonwealth countries, like India, Pakistan, West Indies, and Hong Kong, creating frustration among many young people with Western education.

• Liberalization of emigration rules by the Soviet Union and other Communist governments as relations between the East and the West improve.

One "push" factor working strongly against Canada is the prevalence of full employment in the United Kingdom, West Germany, Netherlands, and Scandinavia. These countries face a bright economic future, with expanding industries creating plentiful jobs. Furthermore, their inhabitants have grown accustomed to a comprehensive system of social security in which Canada is still years behind. As a result, there is more likely to be a dearth than a plethora of would-be immigrants of ethnic origins that have been traditionally favored.

Coming to the "pull" factors, much depends upon the image projected by Canada overseas. Some of the features which have made this nation so attractive to millions of newcomers in the past will probably continue to exert their influence in future. To mention just a few:

• A rapidly growing country with immense resources and job openings in a variety of occupations.

• High wages and satisfactory working conditions, with ample opportunities to move up the social ladder and to acquire within a short time many of the amenities of life — an automobile, modern appliances, a home of one's own.

• Stable political institutions with governmental interference reduced to a minimum.

• Sound monetary policies with inflation kept reasonably in check.

• A reasonable level of corporate taxation, and no restrictions on international transfer of money and securities.

At the same time, several other forces will be working in the opposite direction. Competition from other countries for desirable immigrants is becoming more severe. Australia and New Zealand are intensifying their efforts to attract more British nationals. In many European countries, particularly West Germany, the demand for manpower has become so great that manufacturers are being forced to look abroad for skilled workers, in some cases as far as Turkey.

In Canada, too, opposition is likely to continue in certain quarters against liberalization of immigration rules. Many influential groups in the country object to admitting unrestricted numbers from abroad. Organized labor, for example, has been constantly on guard against what it terms excessive immigration. The strongest criticisms come from the locals where there is a constant fear that an over-supply of workers in a particular field will increase job competition and depress wages. The national congresses of labor, of course, take a much broader view and realize the benefits of immigration to the Canadian economy. But even they may be expected to clamor for the closing of the floodgates every time the business cycle takes a downturn and unemployment becomes serious.

French Canada also exerts a negative influence. Since the assimilation of the newcomers usually works in favor of the Anglo-Saxon race, immigration is cynically regarded as an English-Canadian device to ensure their majority, no matter how zealously the other race may pursue *la revanche des berceaux.*

In view of these currents and cross-currents, it is extremely difficult to forecast the exact size of future immigration. Perhaps the most realistic prediction is the one made by the Economic Council of Canada. It estimates that between 1965 and 1970 the average annual gross immigration would be 125,000, average annual emigration 75,000, resulting in an average annual net immigration of 50,-000. At this rate, the New Canadians would be responsible for 12% of the total population growth between 1965 and 1970.

These expectations may be realized provided certain conditions are fulfilled. Ottawa must make an attempt to maintain a stable immigration policy and resist the temptation to turn the administrative tap off and on with every change in business conditions. The days are gone when Canada was in the fortunate position of a buyer in a seller's market. She can no longer get the people she wants when she wants them. A systematic concerted effort is required.

Also, if it becomes difficult to obtain sufficient numbers from preferred nations, the government must be prepared to open its gates wider and permit a heavier inflow from southern Europe, Asia, and the West Indies. No doubt there will be some problems of orderly integration at the beginning, but in the long run the country will benefit. Almost all economists and business leaders agree that Canada needs more and more qualified people — including those whose social customs, cultural patterns, and skin pigmentation are different from the existing pieces of the mosaic.

	Canada	Atlantic Prov.	Québec	Ontario	Mani-toba	Saskat-chewan	Alberta	British Columbia	Yukon & N.W. Ter.
No. of postwar immigrants, 1961 (000)	1,507.1	32.3	247.8	833.3	62.5	29.0	121.6	177.5	3.1
A. Place of birth									
U.K. and other Commonwealth countries	26.6%	44.7%	15.9%	28.4%	22.3%	28.5%	22.6%	33.9%	27.7%
Germany	11.1	9.3	8.0	10.3	18.1	15.1	16.8	12.2	19.2
Italy	15.2	3.0	23.6	17.4	4.4	2.4	5.2	8.1	7.1
Poland	5.5	1.5	6.0	5.2	11.2	7.3	7.5	2.9	2.5
U.S.S.R.	5.2	1.3	3.7	5.8	10.8	5.5	4.9	3.4	2.0
Other European countries	28.5	21.4	33.2	27.3	25.0	27.4	32.2	28.1	30.4
U.S.A.	4.7	15.6	5.1	3.6	4.2	7.0	7.1	5.2	8.3
Asiatic countries	2.3	2.6	2.4	1.4	1.6	6.1	3.1	5.3	2.5
Other countries	0.9	0.6	2.1	0.6	2.4	0.7	0.6	0.9	0.3
Total postwar immigrants	100.0%	100.0%	100.0%	100.0%	100.0%	100.0%	100.0%	100.0%	100.0%
B. Mother tongue									
English	33.6%	66.4%	21.8%	34.5%	29.0%	39.1%	32.9%	41.1%	39.4%
French	2.8	3.7	12.7	0.8	1.2	0.9	0.8	0.8	2.3
German	14.9	5.9	9.7	13.3	29.6	23.5	24.8	17.9	23.9
Italian	15.2	2.9	23.7	17.4	4.5	2.5	5.1	8.1	7.0
Magyar	3.1	1.4	4.5	2.8	3.5	3.8	3.2	2.7	5.2
Dutch	8.2	10.1	2.0	8.9	7.6	7.4	14.5	9.3	3.2
Polish	4.1	1.3	4.5	4.6	6.2	4.4	3.8	1.7	1.9
Scandinavian	1.9	1.3	0.7	1.2	1.8	2.7	4.2	5.2	4.8
Ukrainian	2.5	0.3	1.8	2.7	6.4	3.7	2.9	0.6	0.8
Others	13.7	6.7	18.6	13.8	10.2	12.0	7.8	12.6	11.5
Total postwar immigrants	100.0%	100.0%	100.0%	100.0%	100.0%	100.0%	100.0%	100.0%	100.0%

(Source: DBS, *Census of Canada, 1961.* Bulletin 92-562.)

HOUSEHOLD CHARACTERISTICS

	Canada	Atlantic Prov.	Québec	Ontario	Manitoba	Saskatchewan	Alberta	British Columbia	Yukon & N.W. Ter
Total number of postwar immigrant households 1961 (000)	433.1	6.9	76.0	233.4	17.2	7.6	37.3	53.9	0.8
Total number of households of prewar immigrants and native-born, 1961 (000)	4,121.6	413.0	1,115.5	1,407.5	222.5	237.8	312.5	405.7	7.1

A. AGE OF HEAD OF HOUSEHOLD

Postwar immigrant households:

	Canada	Atlantic Prov.	Québec	Ontario	Manitoba	Saskatchewan	Alberta	British Columbia	Yukon & N.W. Ter
Under 25 years	3.8%	4.4%	4.0%	3.4%	4.0%	4.5%	5.3%	4.3%	8.3%
25–34 years	34.2	35.1	34.8	33.1	32.2	35.5	37.6	36.2	48.4
35–44 years	34.3	35.2	33.4	35.8	33.7	31.0	31.2	31.9	28.4
45–54 years	18.7	16.0	18.9	19.3	19.0	17.0	16.6	17.6	10.1
55–64 years	6.7	5.6	6.7	6.5	7.9	7.3	6.9	6.7	3.4
65 years and over	2.3	3.7	2.2	1.9	3.2	4.7	2.4	3.3	1.4
Total households	100.0%	100.0%	100.0%	100.0%	100.0%	100.0%	100.0%	100.0%	100.0%

Other households:

	Canada	Atlantic Prov.	Québec	Ontario	Manitoba	Saskatchewan	Alberta	British Columbia	Yukon & N.W. Ter
Under 25 years	3.9%	3.9%	3.9%	3.8%	3.8%	4.1%	5.2%	3.8%	7.6%
25–34 years	19.2	17.8	21.9	18.4	17.1	17.1	20.9	16.7	28.7
35–44 years	22.4	22.4	24.3	21.8	21.3	20.9	22.2	20.9	25.6
45–54 years	20.8	21.5	21.3	20.5	20.9	20.2	19.2	20.8	18.8
55–64 years	15.8	15.3	15.3	16.7	16.2	15.8	15.0	15.5	10.9
65 years and over	17.9	19.1	13.3	18.8	20.7	21.9	17.5	22.3	8.4
Total households	100.0%	100.0%	100.0%	100.0%	100.0%	100.0%	100.0%	100.0%	100.0%

B. Size of Households

	Canada	Atlantic Prov.	Québec	Ontario	Mani-toba	Saskat-chewan	Alberta	British Columbia	Yukon & N.W. Ter.
Postwar immigrant households:									
Very small (1 person)	5.8%	5.4%	7.4%	4.2%	5.3%	9.4%	7.7%	8.8%	15.2%
Small (2 persons)	17.8	18.3	20.3	16.6	17.0	18.7	17.5	20.0	25.6
Medium (3 or 4 persons)	43.5	43.5	44.9	43.1	43.0	41.3	43.4	43.7	39.5
Large (5–8 persons)	29.8	30.6	25.7	31.9	31.4	28.8	29.8	26.0	19.2
Very large (over 8 persons)	3.1	2.2	1.7	4.2	3.3	1.8	1.6	1.5	0.5
Total households	100.0%	100.0%	100.0%	100.0%	100.0%	100.0%	100.0%	100.0%	100.0%
Other households:									
Very small (1 person)	9.7%	7.4%	7.0%	9.9%	10.6%	12.9%	12.6%	14.1%	11.6%
Small (2 persons)	22.7	18.9	19.0	25.1	24.1	23.2	22.3	27.3	16.3
Medium (3 or 4 persons)	35.3	33.0	35.1	36.8	36.1	34.1	35.1	34.1	31.7
Large (5–8 persons)	28.6	33.7	32.6	26.1	26.7	27.4	27.9	23.1	34.1
Very large (over 8 persons)	3.7	7.0	6.3	2.1	2.5	2.4	2.1	1.4	6.3
Total households	100.0%	100.0%	100.0%	100.0%	100.0%	100.0%	100.0%	100.0%	100.0%

(Source: DBS, *Census of Canada, 1961*. Bulletins 93-512 and 93-513.)

PARTICIPATION IN LABOR FORCE

	Canada	Atlantic Prov.	Québec	Ontario	Manitoba	Saskatchewan	Alberta	British Columbia	Yukon & N.W. Ter.
Postwar immigrants, 1961:									
% of males, 15 and over, in labor force	88.9	83.4	88.3	89.6	88.8	87.6	89.9	87.0	95.8
% of females, 15 and over, in labor force	39.2	25.3	41.0	41.2	41.4	32.2	35.1	33.5	41.6
% of families with wives in labor force	34.8	19.7	33.2	37.3	38.5	29.9	31.0	28.6	30.7
% of persons age 15–24 still studying and hence not in labor force:									
1) Between 15 and 18	72.9	78.6	64.8	72.2	75.7	83.2	77.8	80.3	80.7
2) Between 19 and 24	21.5	26.9	19.2	20.8	22.5	32.9	21.8	27.2	39.1
Rest of the population, 1961:									
% of males, 15 and over, in labor force	76.4	70.6	75.9	79.0	77.2	77.7	79.4	72.1	80.5
% of females, 15 and over, in labor force	28.4	23.2	27.1	31.0	30.6	26.2	30.3	27.5	24.4
% of families with wives in labor force	19.1	14.4	11.9	24.0	23.1	20.6	23.9	21.0	17.3
% of persons age 15–24 still studying and hence not in labor force:									
1) Between 15 and 18	70.5	68.8	59.2	76.9	76.0	79.1	81.3	82.3	54.4
2) Between 19 and 24	19.9	15.5	14.2	26.1	21.9	24.3	25.8	27.9	10.2

(Source: DBS, *Census of Canada, 1961.* Bulletins 92-542; 92-562; 93-517; 93-520; and 94-527.)

Occupations	Canada	Atlantic Prov.	Québec	Ontario	Manitoba	Saskatchewan	Alberta	British Columbia	Yukon & N.W. Ter.
Postwar immigrants, 1961									
Managerial	7.8%	11.0%	9.9%	7.2%	6.3%	8.5%	8.2%	7.5%	6.9%
Professional and technical	10.1	18.0	14.0	8.7	8.9	14.6	10.3	9.8	10.7
Clerical	5.5	3.2	6.4	5.7	4.4	3.1	4.4	4.7	3.3
Sales	4.0	4.0	4.4	3.9	3.2	2.7	3.8	4.6	1.4
Service and recreation	10.0	23.8	11.2	9.4	10.2	10.6	9.6	9.6	10.7
Workers in transport and communications	3.6	3.1	3.2	3.6	3.3	2.3	4.0	4.2	7.1
Workers in primary industries	8.1	9.4	3.5	8.1	7.2	14.3	11.8	9.9	29.3
Workers, mostly skilled, in second. industries	39.2	19.5	36.4	41.4	43.2	33.7	36.2	37.4	24.6
Workers, mostly unskilled, in second. industries	9.4	2.9	8.4	9.8	11.2	6.8	10.0	9.7	4.4
Miscellaneous	2.3	5.1	2.6	2.2	2.1	3.4	1.7	2.6	1.6
Total males in labor force (%)	100.0%	100.0%	100.0%	100.0%	100.0%	100.0%	100.0%	100.0%	100.0%
Number of males in labor force (000)	569.2	9.0	93.4	318.0	23.4	10.5	46.7	66.3	1.9
Prewar immigrants and native-born, 1961									
Managerial	10.6%	8.5%	9.5%	12.0%	9.8%	8.5%	10.8%	12.6%	7.1%
Professional and technical	7.2	5.1	7.3	8.3	6.2	5.2	6.9	7.5	6.6
Clerical	7.1	5.6	7.9	8.1	7.3	4.0	5.5	5.9	3.3
Sales	5.8	4.5	5.9	6.4	5.3	4.2	5.8	6.4	1.4
Service and recreation	8.3	11.6	7.2	8.4	9.0	5.0	7.7	9.8	12.3
Workers in transport and communications	8.1	8.7	8.5	8.0	7.6	5.3	7.4	8.8	10.3
Workers in primary industries	17.1	20.1	13.5	11.8	25.0	46.2	29.8	10.5	24.9
Workers, mostly skilled, in second. industries	27.3	25.8	30.6	29.2	21.9	15.8	19.4	29.6	19.5
Workers, mostly unskilled, in second. industries	5.8	7.8	6.6	5.3	5.5	3.7	4.4	5.8	8.3
Miscellaneous	2.7	2.3	3.0	2.5	2.4	2.1	2.3	3.1	6.3
Total males in labor force (%)	100.0%	100.0%	100.0%	100.0%	100.0%	100.0%	100.0%	100.0%	100.0%
Number of males in labor force (000)	4,136.4	416.8	1,196.1	1,382.6	222.8	238.0	315.2	355.5	9.4

(Source: DBS, *Census of Canada, 1961.* Bulletin 94-515.)

DISTRIBUTION OF NON-FARM INCOME

	Canada	Atlantic Prov.	Québec	Ontario	Manitoba	Saskatchewan	Alberta	British Columbia
A. FAMILIES BY SIZE OF TOTAL INCOME								
Postwar immigrant families, 1961:								
Less than $3,000	18.0%	19.8%	20.9%	17.5%	17.5%	19.5%	15.7%	17.1%
$3,000–$5,999	51.0	44.5	47.2	51.3	58.2	48.8	54.1	51.8
$6,000–$9,999	25.0	27.6	23.7	25.8	20.3	24.2	23.2	25.5
$10,000–$14,999	4.3	5.9	5.7	4.0	2.9	4.9	4.5	4.1
$15,000 and over	1.7	2.2	2.5	1.4	1.1	2.6	2.5	1.5
Total non-farm families (%)	100.0%	100.0%	100.0%	100.0%	100.0%	100.0%	100.0%	100.0%
Number of non-farm families (000)	409.3	5.6	68.9	235.1	16.6	6.2	31.8	44.9
Prewar immigrant and native-born families, 1961:								
Less than $3,000	23.9%	41.9%	24.5%	17.9%	24.4%	32.1%	21.5%	21.0%
$3,000–$5,999	44.8	41.6	46.9	44.6	46.0	42.0	44.6	43.5
$6,000–$9,999	23.3	12.9	20.1	27.9	22.6	20.0	25.7	27.5
$10,000–$14,999	5.4	2.4	5.6	6.5	4.6	3.9	5.7	5.5
$15,000 and over	2.6	1.2	2.9	3.1	2.4	2.0	2.5	2.5
Total non-farm families (%)	100.0%	100.0%	100.0%	100.0%	100.0%	100.0%	100.0%	100.0%
Number of non-farm families (000)	3,247.6	352.8	924.8	1,141.0	158.8	136.0	207.8	323.9

B. PERSONS NOT IN FAMILIES BY SIZE OF TOTAL INCOME
(Persons without income excluded)

Postwar immigrants, 1961:

	Canada	Atlantic Prov.	Québec	Ontario	Manitoba	Saskatchewan	Alberta	British Columbia
Less than $1,500	27.4%	33.7%	27.2%	26.5%	30.9%	30.1%	28.5%	28.9%
$1,500–$2,999	32.0	27.2	34.9	31.8	34.2	33.7	32.2	27.6
$3,000–$5,999	36.2	31.7	32.6	37.6	32.0	28.9	35.6	38.8
$6,000–$9,999	3.5	6.4	4.1	3.4	2.5	5.8	3.0	3.8
$10,000 and over	0.9	1.0	1.2	0.7	0.4	1.5	0.7	0.9
Total persons, non-farm (%)	100.0%	100.0%	100.0%	100.0%	100.0%	100.0%	100.0%	100.0%
Total number of persons, non-farm (000)	142.5	1.5	27.1	76.5	5.8	2.8	10.7	17.6

Prewar immigrants and native-born, 1961:

	Canada	Atlantic Prov.	Québec	Ontario	Manitoba	Saskatchewan	Alberta	British Columbia
Less than $1,500	47.1%	59.2%	46.1%	43.6%	47.4%	50.7%	42.7%	48.1%
$1,500–$2,999	24.7	23.4	27.3	23.8	27.1	24.9	25.5	22.0
$3,000–$5,999	24.1	15.2	23.0	27.2	22.5	21.1	27.3	25.6
$6,000–$9,999	3.1	1.6	2.6	4.1	2.3	2.5	3.6	3.4
$10,000 and over	1.0	0.6	1.0	1.3	0.7	0.8	0.9	0.9
Total persons, non-farm (%)	100.0%	100.0%	100.0%	100.0%	100.0%	100.0%	100.0%	100.0%
Total number of persons, non-farm (000)	1,163.5	89.4	299.3	423.0	61.6	54.8	79.9	126.3

Note: Canada includes Yukon. For persons not in families, figures for Atlantic Provinces refer only to Nova Scotia and New Brunswick.

(Source: DBS, *Census of Canada, 1961.* Bulletin 98-504.)

INDICATORS OF HARDSHIP AND SUB-STANDARD LIVING

	Canada	Québec	Ontario	Mani-toba	Saskat-chewan	Alberta	British Columbia
A. Inability to speak English or French							
Of the persons whose mother tongue is not English or French, % who cannot speak either of two official languages, 1961:							
Postwar immigrants in the country for:							
Less than 5.5 years (1956–1961)	20.5%	29.0%	21.3%	14.8%	11.4%	11.3%	11.7%
5.5–10.4 years (1951–1955)	4.9	7.9	4.9	3.5	3.3	2.5	3.2
10.5–15.4 years (1946–1950)	3.3	4.6	2.9	4.0	4.3	3.2	3.3
Average for postwar immigrants	11.0	17.8	11.1	8.0	6.6	5.8	6.8
Average for prewar immigrants	3.8	3.7	2.3	5.9	5.3	3.7	4.9
Average for persons born in Canada	10.7	31.8	13.0	7.1	5.2	4.8	5.4
B. Income below subsistence level							
Of all non-farm families, % with total income of less than $3,000 a year, 1961:							
Postwar immigrant families in the country for:							
Less than 1.5 years (1960–1961)	53.9%	58.3%	54.5%	51.4%	45.1%	48.2%	48.6%
1.5–3.4 years (1958–1959)	29.0	29.9	30.4	22.0	23.8	24.6	27.0
3.5–5.4 years (1956–1957)	17.1	20.3	16.6	15.0	20.6	16.4	15.4
5.5–10.4 years (1951–1955)	14.4	15.5	14.3	14.9	15.5	12.0	15.0
10.5–15.4 years (1946–1950)	14.6	14.9	13.8	16.1	19.4	14.3	16.4
Average for postwar immigrant families	17.9	20.9	17.5	17.5	19.5	15.7	17.1
Average for prewar immigrant families	29.1	22.3	23.5	35.6	48.7	34.0	32.9
Average for non-immigrant families	22.9	24.7	16.7	21.0	26.7	17.3	16.3

C. Crowded living quarters

Of total households, % living in dwellings with more than one person per room, 1961:

	Canada	Québec	Ontario	Mani-toba	Saskat-chewan	Alberta	British Columbia
Postwar immigrant households in the country for:							
Less than 1.5 years (1960–1961)	21.0%	23.5%	20.9%	15.4%	30.8%	23.6%	15.5%
1.5–5.4 years (1956–1959)	19.4	21.8	19.1	20.5	20.8	20.3	16.0
5.5–10.4 years (1951–1955)	17.9	17.7	18.0	18.4	20.9	19.7	15.8
10.5–15.4 years (1946–1950)	13.5	12.2	12.9	15.1	19.6	17.9	12.8
Average for postwar immigrant households	17.3	18.3	17.1	17.8	20.9	19.6	15.2
Average for prewar immigrant households	6.6	7.5	4.9	7.4	9.1	9.3	5.4
Average for non-immigrant households	18.4	23.1	12.4	20.0	22.6	20.7	14.7

D. Dilapidated dwellings

Of total households, % living in dwellings in need of major repair, 1961:

	Canada	Québec	Ontario	Mani-toba	Saskat-chewan	Alberta	British Columbia
Postwar immigrant households in the country for:							
Less than 1.5 years (1960–1961)	4.8%	2.5%	4.6%	7.9%	11.2%	6.1%	7.2%
1.5–5.4 years (1956–1959)	4.5	2.7	3.9	6.7	8.2	6.8	6.7
5.5–10.4 years (1951–1955)	3.3	2.1	3.0	5.1	6.0	4.8	4.5
10.5–15.4 years (1946–1950)	3.4	2.2	3.0	5.3	6.4	5.5	3.9
Average for postwar immigrant households	3.7	2.3	3.3	5.7	6.9	5.6	5.1
Average for prewar immigrant households	5.6	3.0	3.8	7.4	9.2	9.0	5.3
Average for non-immigrant households	5.8	4.4	4.9	8.0	9.0	7.6	5.7

Note: Canada includes Atlantic Provinces and Yukon and Northwest Territories. No percentages are shown for these areas because the number of postwar immigrants residing there is insignificant.

(Source: DBS, *Census of Canada, 1961*. Bulletins 92-549; 92-562; 93-532; and 98-504.)

INDICATORS OF STANDARD OF LIVING

	Canada	Québec	Ontario	Mani-toba	Saskat-chewan	Alberta	British Columbia
A. Family income							
Average annual income of non-farm families, 1961:							
Postwar immigrant families in the country for:							
Less than 1.5 years (1960–1961)	$4,298	$3,499	$3,429	$3,786	$3,847	$4,349	$3,965
1.5–3.4 years (1958–1959)	4,672	4,706	4,529	4,577	5,104	5,256	4,823
3.5–5.4 years (1956–1957)	5,225	5,268	5,220	4,893	5,405	5,386	5,136
5.5–10.4 years (1951–1955)	5,505	5,739	5,445	5,031	5,717	5,645	5,470
10.5–15.4 years (1946–1950)	5,769	6,427	5,743	5,166	5,405	5,576	5,585
Average for postwar immigrant families	5,363	5,492	5,317	5,164	5,440	5,502	5,335
Average for prewar immigrant families	5,457	6,679	5,805	4,939	3,943	4,997	4,998
Average for non-immigrant families	5,460	5,295	6,020	5,372	5,048	5,822	5,916
B. Value of home							
Median value of single detached home owned by non-farm households, 1961:							
Postwar immigrant households in the country for:							
Less than 1.5 years (1960–1961)	$14,645	$20,599	$14,754	$12,151	$11,335	$14,238	$13,181
1.5–5.4 years (1956–1959)	13,150	14,961	13,831	11,844	9,481	13,068	11,443
5.5–10.4 years (1951–1955)	13,574	14,611	14,088	12,261	10,741	13,199	11,861
10.5–15.4 years (1946–1950)	14,000	15,373	14,522	12,341	9,976	13,664	12,745
Average for postwar immigrant households	13,640	14,910	14,187	12,218	10,262	13,303	12,004
Average for prewar immigrant households	11,054	13,608	12,845	9,651	6,248	9,831	10,904
Average for non-immigrant households	10,679	9,630	12,704	10,511	8,030	12,978	12,227

C. Monthly rent

Average monthly cash rent paid by non-farm households, 1961:

Postwar immigrant households in the country for:

	Canada	Québec	Ontario	Mani-toba	Saskat-chewan	Alberta	British Columbia
Less than 1.5 years (1960–1961)	$84	$83	$90	$83	$69	$77	$77
1.5–5.4 years (1956–1959)	78	77	84	68	70	71	68
5.5–10.4 years (1951–1955)	78	77	83	69	63	70	66
10.5–15.4 years (1946–1950)	77	81	80	68	62	62	66
Average for postwar immigrant households	78	78	83	69	66	70	67
Average for prewar immigrant households	69	74	78	61	47	55	62
Average for non-immigrant households	62	56	74	64	55	66	66

D. Home ownership

% of households owning a home, 1961:

Postwar immigrant households in the country for:

	Canada	Québec	Ontario	Mani-toba	Saskat-chewan	Alberta	British Columbia
Less than 1.5 years (1960–1961)	21.6%	10.1%	24.1%	32.0%	19.3%	23.2%	34.1%
1.5–5.4 years (1956–1959)	34.0	12.1	39.2	41.8	39.6	37.3	44.3
5.5–10.4 years (1951–1955)	62.4	34.5	69.0	68.9	67.3	67.2	66.2
10.5–15.4 years (1946–1950)	73.8	47.9	79.2	81.3	74.9	76.4	74.2
Average for postwar immigrant households	55.8	28.2	62.7	64.1	60.1	59.5	60.5
Average for prewar immigrant households	77.8	49.4	80.0	81.1	86.7	83.9	78.3
Average for non-immigrant households	64.9	50.5	70.0	71.8	73.3	67.5	69.5

INDICATORS OF STANDARD OF LIVING (continued)

	Canada	Québec	Ontario	Manitoba	Saskatchewan	Alberta	British Columbia
E. Ownership of refrigerator							
% of households owning a mechanical refrigerator, 1961:							
Postwar immigrant households in the country for:							
Less than 1.5 years (1960–1961)	92.0%	94.1%	94.3%	90.4%	84.7%	87.9%	84.3%
1.5–5.4 years (1956–1959)	95.4	96.9	97.4	94.5	88.4	90.8	90.4
5.5–10.4 years (1951–1955)	96.4	97.4	98.1	94.9	89.4	92.3	92.5
10.5–15.4 years (1946–1950)	96.3	97.5	98.1	94.7	85.6	90.5	93.6
Average for postwar immigrant households	95.9	97.1	97.8	94.6	87.9	91.3	91.9
Average for prewar immigrant households	91.2	96.1	96.8	90.4	78.6	82.9	90.7
Average for non-immigrant households	90.4	91.1	96.6	91.3	83.6	88.8	92.7
F. Ownership of home freezer							
% of households owning a home freezer, 1961:							
Postwar immigrant households in the country for:							
Less than 1.5 years (1960–1961)	7.3%	4.9%	6.4%	8.8%	14.0%	12.2%	11.6%
1.5–5.4 years (1956–1959)	6.4	4.8	5.8	8.4	12.7	10.9	7.0
5.5–10.4 years (1951–1955)	8.6	6.0	7.1	11.5	17.5	15.8	11.3
10.5–15.4 years (1946–1950)	10.7	6.6	8.9	14.1	25.6	20.6	13.2
Average for postwar immigrant households	8.5	5.7	7.2	11.4	18.4	15.5	10.5
Average for prewar immigrant households	15.5	7.1	9.7	20.0	30.6	28.1	13.6
Average for non-immigrant households	15.6	9.8	15.7	28.2	35.8	32.8	18.0

G. Ownership of television set

% of households owning a television set, 1961:

	Canada	Québec	Ontario	Manitoba	Saskatchewan	Alberta	British Columbia
Postwar immigrant households in the country for:							
Less than 1.5 years (1960–1961)	62.9%	62.3%	68.7%	59.0%	52.3%	54.2%	55.0%
1.5–5.4 years (1956–1959)	78.5	78.9	83.6	77.4	67.9	71.9	66.4
5.5–10.4 years (1951–1955)	81.3	85.0	85.7	78.6	70.9	72.7	66.0
10.5–15.4 years (1946–1950)	83.4	87.4	87.2	81.3	71.5	72.2	72.1
Average for postwar immigrant households	80.4	82.1	85.1	78.3	69.5	71.7	67.2
Average for prewar immigrant households	78.7	89.9	89.5	73.4	60.3	65.3	72.6
Average for non-immigrant households	83.5	89.1	89.4	75.8	69.5	74.5	75.4

H. Ownership of passenger car

% of households owning a passenger car, 1961:

	Canada	Québec	Ontario	Manitoba	Saskatchewan	Alberta	British Columbia
Postwar immigrant households in the country for:							
Less than 1.5 years (1960–1961)	54.1%	37.2%	58.3%	59.4%	71.7%	66.6%	61.3%
1.5–5.4 years (1956–1959)	67.2	46.1	72.7	65.2	71.5	75.8	74.1
5.5–10.4 years (1951–1955)	73.0	56.1	76.3	72.0	75.0	80.1	75.8
10.5–15.4 years (1946–1950)	72.4	54.6	76.4	66.8	71.6	74.6	74.7
Average for postwar immigrant households	70.5	51.4	74.9	68.1	72.9	77.1	74.5
Average for prewar immigrant households	60.7	48.9	64.8	56.5	64.1	62.8	57.5
Average for non-immigrant households	69.7	58.5	78.8	74.9	78.6	79.3	78.1

Note: Canada includes Atlantic Provinces, Yukon, and Northwest Territories. No figures are shown for these areas because the number of postwar immigrants residing there is insignificant.

(Source: DBS, *Census of Canada, 1961*. Bulletins 92-562, 93-532, and 98-504.)

BIBLIOGRAPHY ON POSTWAR IMMIGRATION

Blishen, B., F. Jones, K. Naegele, and J. Porter (editors): *Canadian Society,* The Free Press of Glencoe, Inc., New York, 1961.

Camu, P., E. P. Weeks, and Z. W. Sametz: *Economic Geography of Canada,* Macmillan of Canada, Toronto, 1964.

Corbett, David C.: *Canada's Immigration Policy,* University of Toronto Press, Toronto, 1957.

Department of Citizenship and Immigration: *Immigration* (Annual reports).

Dominion Bureau of Statistics: *Census of Canada, 1961,* Bulletins 92-542, 92-549, 92-562, 93-512, 93-513, 93-517, 93-520, 93-532, 94-515, 94-515, 94-527, 98-504.

Laskin, Richard (editor): *Social Problems: A Canadian Profile,* McGraw-Hill Company of Canada Limited, Toronto, 1964.

New Canadian Publications: *Story of a Million,* Toronto, 1959.

Parai, Louis: *Immigration and Emigration of Professional and Skilled Manpower During the Postwar Period.* Special Study No. 1 prepared by the Economic Council of Canada. Queen's Printer, Ottawa, 1965.

Petersen, William: *Planned Migration: The Social Determinants of the Dutch-Canadian Movement,* University of California Press, Berkeley, 1955.

Reynolds, Lloyd G.: *The British Immigrant: His Social and Economic Adjustment in Canada,* Oxford University Press, 1935.

Richmond, Anthony H.: "Are British Ideal Canadian Citizens?" *The Globe and Mail,* Magazine section, October 10 and 17, Toronto, 1964. (Dr. Richmond's research was sponsored by the federal Department of Citizenship and Immigration, the Canada Council, the Koerner Foundation, and the Milbank Memorial Fund.)

Royal Commission on Canada's Economic Prospects: *The Final Report,* Queen's Printer, Ottawa, 1957.

Waengler, Ernest: "The New Canadian Market Deserves Your Attention," *Industrial Canada,* November, 1958.

French Canada

French Canadians are found all across the country, but the real citadel of Gallic culture is Québec. This province is the heartland of French Canada, a fulcrum for the whole French Canadian community — in fact, a nation within a nation. Here, for more than two centuries, the descendants of the first permanent white settlers north of the Rio Grande have fought to preserve their language, their religion, their unique set of values against the onslaught of the English-speaking world. For most French Canadians, Canada is just the state of Québec. They see themselves mirrored in it. Once away from home, they are no longer a compact group with a strong government backing. Eventually they lose their distinctive identity and are assimilated with the English-speaking population. The 1961 Census shows that, of the 1,298,992 Canadians of French descent outside the boundaries of Québec, only 800,699 have French as their mother tongue. Thus, out of Québec, nearly one "French" Canadian in every three learns English at his mother's knee.

Because of the language and psychological barriers, which often make contacts difficult, if not impossible, French and English Canada have grown side by side without understanding each other. To many English, Québec is still a land of *habitants* with large families, taming the land in a harsh climate and shepherded from the evils of the world by the benevolent village curé. The mind conjures up images of wayside shrines, of twin-spired Louis XV churches with their white and gold interiors, of black- and brown-robed priests and nuns walking silently down the narrow cobbled streets, and of rows and rows of striped farms each with a slender ration of river frontage.

SOCIO-CULTURAL CHANGES

But Québec is no longer a precious museum piece. The social upheaval brought about by industrialization has radically altered the picture. The tradition of stubborn conservatism has given way to a critical reappraisal of all time-honored methods and institutions. Today's French Canadians are not content with just defending their way of life; they also see the need of modernizing it. The quaint French Canada of yesterday exists only in a few shrinking pockets and in the tourist advertisements of travel agencies.

The spread of urbanism has been rapid. Nearly 60% of the inhabitants now live in places with over 30,000 population. The urban French Canadian is a new kind of man, compared to his compatriot on the farm. His tradition may be old, and he may love it; but he is not at home with it, as his grandfather or even his father was.

He does not believe that Québec can survive by fighting off all the influences from the outside world. On the contrary, he feels strongly that the cause of French culture in Canada can be effectively advanced only through major social changes. The old watchword "notre maître le passé" is yielding to the newer cry "notre maître, l'avenir."

Even the Québec farmer has lost the security of his old isolation. He has had a television set in his home for over a decade; and, if the electronic medium has not introduced him to a better world, it has at least showed him a new one.

This does not imply the disintegration of society in Québec. Although not completely satisfied with tradition, French Canadians remain loyal to the interests of their community. Their ethnic consciousness is extremely strong, and they want to further the cause of their own culture even, if need be, at the expense of breaking up Confederation.

CHARACTERISTICS OF FRENCH-CANADIAN CULTURE

First and foremost, it is a willed culture rather than one of spontaneous development. It is a product of a single environment, of a firm and closely knit religion, and of a society trying to protect itself from the full onslaught of North Americanism. Survival has been the key concept of French-Canadian history, and it remains the chief psychological preoccupation of a community set in a

linguistically different continent. Hence, French-Canadian culture is characterized by a sense of loneliness and insecurity. This to a great extent explains its
frequent tendency to turn inward upon itself. The French Canadian is generally
on the defensive, with the attitude of a child deserted by his parents.

One result of the severance of any link with the mother country is that Québec
is the French Canadian's only home. He proudly calls himself the true *Canadien*
and regards the English-speaking inhabitants as *les Anglais,* more attached to
the United Kingdom than to the country of their birth. During the last few years
the cultural ties between Québec's government and Gaullist France have considerably improved, but an average French Canadian still has little love to spare
for Marianne beyond the Atlantic. He is firmly convinced that if Louis XV had
not abandoned his forbears to the British and *quelques arpents de neige* (few
acres of snow), the Tri-color would be flying on Parliament Hill. Moreover, his
devout Roman Catholicism makes him feel that he alone has maintained the
pure Christian traditions in French culture, unsullied by the radicalism and
amorality current in present-day thinking in France.

Therefore, it is not surprising that the French Canadian's attachment is to his
own soil and no other. His folksongs are of his life and people. His authors and
painters are concerned with depicting "La Belle Province." His heroes are not
the heroes of France, but the explorers and priests who discovered the interior
of this continent and were betrayed by the corrupt court at Versailles. Behind the
high wall of his language, he has developed a culture that is indigeneous to
the banks of the St. Lawrence and unique in North America. Québec is not
"New France" as the tourist boosters insistently proclaim; it is French-speaking
Canada.

THE CHURCH

The Church is the major pillar in the social edifice. Québec is a stronghold of
Roman Catholicism. The French Empire began almost as an experiment in theo-
cratic ecclesiastical control. Not only were Huguenots excluded from the colony,
but immigration was restricted to those who, in the eyes of the Jesuits, were
good Catholics. The priests accompanied the first explorers, took part in the first
convoy of settlers, and were present at the foundation of first settlements.

When the French Empire collapsed, religion assumed an even greater importance as a mortar which could hold the social structure together. The Catholicism of Québec is particularly Canadian in its character, for it is heavily laced
with the disciplines and puritanism of the frontier. It is also strongly messianic
in its outlook and at times considers itself the only true spiritual beacon in the
materialistic Anglo-Saxon North American society. The oft-quoted remarks of
Monseigneur L. A. Paquet made in 1902 are regarded by some as appropriate
even today.

"We are not only a civilized race, we are the pioneers of civilization; we are
not only a religious people, we are the messengers of the religious idea; we are

not only the submissive sons of the Church, we are its defenders, and its apostles. Our mission is not so much to manipulate capital as to change ideas, not so much to light the fires of the factories as to maintain and make radiate the luminous flame of religion and thought."

Even in the middle of the twentieth century, the Church holds a dominating place in the social life of French Canadians. The parish is often the first public institution to be organized when a new territory is opened up. The other institutions, such as the municipality and the school board, come later and generally find it quite natural to fit themselves into the convenient framework of the parish. That is the main reason why so many rural municipalities have a saint's name. The curé here is a "father" to his people in fact as well as in appellation, and his advice can be very close to a command.

The Church has played a major role in the preservation of the French people. Its emphasis on family and its opposition to birth control has made for a prolific race. In 1763, when Québec became British, there were only 60,000 *Canadiens*. Today there are five million in Canada. Due to this reproductivity, the proportion of French-speaking Canadians in the country is just about what it was at the time of Confederation, despite the heavy influx of English-speaking immigrants.

Outside observers have always been struck by the broad extent of the social role of the clergy in Québec. The Church enters into almost every phase of life, from the administration of relief to the formation of labor unions. The livelihood and careers of hundreds of thousands of people depend upon it. It controls hospitals, schools, and colleges, and undertakes most of the social welfare projects in the community.

The cultural patterns of the race have been considerably affected by this dominant position of the Church. The emphasis on the spiritual rather than the material is a distinguishing mark of the French-Canadian character. The *Canadien* tends to stress order and stability, rather than progress. Indeed, he regards the aggressiveness of North American commercial life with a certain disdain. Partly because of the Church's insistence on authority and discipline, labor in Québec has been traditionally low-paid and uncomplaining, and the province, till a decade ago, was regarded as an employer's paradise.

Furthermore, the humanistic education encouraged by the Church has perpetuated an intellectual tradition which tends to give priority to ideas over techniques, to analysis over synthesis, to moral values over empirical evidence. The system turns educated *Canadiens* into distinguished teachers, lawyers, priests, and men of letters rather than scientists, engineers, technicians, or business administrators. This explains why almost all of private industry in Québec is owned or controlled by the Anglo-Saxons. It is an unhealthy situation which the provincial government is anxious to rectify as soon as possible.

All French Canadians are conscious of the great debt they owe to their clergy for ensuring cultural survival in the post-conquest period. But there is a growing feeling that this debt has been abundantly repaid and that the clergy's intervention in secular affairs, while perhaps once necessary, is now outmoded and harmful. The young French Canadian of today, especially if he has received a college education, is likely to be anticlerical. He remains a good Catholic but feels that the present all-encompassing role of the clergy should be dramatically modified. The Church is still in the position of a father to him, but a father who, he thinks, is behind the times, excessively demanding, and unwilling to allow the son to grow up. As one professor of sociology remarked: "The young men don't want a religion in which God is a kind of policeman; they want a religion in which the individual is vital."

However, the Church too is changing. A few old-fashioned bishops continue to resist Québec's quiet revolution, but many are trying to swim with the new current. In fact, some of the most radical social thinking today has originated from the leading universities controlled by the Church. Many prominent clerics openly advocate that, in the field of education and health, non-denominational institutions encouraged by the government should exist side by side with religious ones. Because of this flexible attitude, the Church still plays a major role. It may have lost somewhat in numbers — in teeming industrial cities it cannot exert its influence to the extent that it does in the small communities — but it has gained in spiritual strength. If perhaps weaker in outward appearances, it is stronger in basic essentials.

THE FAMILY

Another distinguishing feature of society in Québec is the emphasis on kinship. The family has always been a strong and revered unit in French Canada. Because of the urgent need to preserve ethnic consciousness, the maintenance of a healthy home life has been actively supported by religion, law, and other institutions. As a result, industrialization and urbanism have disrupted far less the close family ties in Québec than elsewhere in Canada. A sociological survey by the University of Montréal shows that even when some members migrate to other places they still maintain a high degree of contact with those left behind.

The strong ties of kinship are also indicated by the many "family associations" prevalent in French Canada. Members of the same family origin organize a club, and all sorts of occasions — birthdays, anniversaries, religious holidays — are used as pretexts to see each other. Sometimes these meetings are quite formal and can number several thousand people at the same time. At a recent reunion of one family group at Ste-Anne-de-Beaupré, more than 7,000 people gathered together for one day.

Because of this powerful hold of the family, the French Canadian has a strong sense of tradition. He is proud of his ancestors who first made the St. Lawrence Valley their homeland. Genealogy, a mere pastime for most English people, is taken seriously by Québecers. It is not unusual to find in a lawyer's or a doctor's office, or even in the home of a parish priest, a picture of the family tree hanging on the wall in an ornate frame.

The Church has always favored strong familial solidarity. Divorce is prohibited and a high birth rate encouraged. Also, the roles of the male and female are clearly demarcated. There is less egalitarian relationship. Authority, protection, and economic support are considered the man's domain. The wife's role is more passive; it is to understand her husband's behavior, be ready to listen to his problems, satisfy his emotional needs, and look after the welfare of the children.

One result of this demarcation of roles is that the proportion of wives in the labor force is lower in Québec than elsewhere in Canada. The man who lets his wife go out to work finds himself blaming his own inadequacy: he has failed in his duty to provide his dependants with the necessities they expect of him. A recent sociological study indicates that it is primarily this factor which prevents many married women from working. An extremely large number interviewed admitted they would like to take outside jobs but could not because their husbands forbade them to do so.

However, many social scientists feel that as time goes on the cultural climate will become more conducive to married women's participation in the labor force. The main reason is financial. Faced with more and more urgent wants aroused by mass-media advertising, the husband's salary will no longer be sufficient to maintain the standard of living desired by the family. Thus, in the next few years, the percentage of married French women in the labor force may tend to follow the North American pattern.

NATIONALISM

After Church and family, the third characteristic of the French Canadian is his nationalism. During the last few years this has assumed violent manifestations, such as the throwing of bombs and the looting of arsenals. No doubt, the terrorist activities are restricted to a limited group of young men, but it cannot be denied that these acts are to some extent outward symptoms of a deeper and more aggravating *malaise*. More and more French Canadians are beginning to feel that the time has come to redress the wrongs they have suffered since the Conquest.

Their complaints are manifold. Basically, they revolve around better treatment from the British majority. In the economic sphere they find that, since most large companies in Québec are English-owned, it is very difficult for them to rise above a certain level unless they are thoroughly anglicized. They are even more bitter at the fact that these companies have no respect for the French language and culture. The same firms which operate in Spanish in South America, in Italian in Italy, conduct their Québec operations in English without a trace of scruple.

In the political field the complaint is mainly against Ottawa. Although Canada is officially a bilingual and bicultural country, French Canadians feel that in actual practice the federal government is running the country for the benefit of the

English-speaking majority. Lip service is paid to "the presence in our midst of a different culture which adds greatly to the intellectual riches of Canada"; but precious little is being done to give it meaning. Fine words butter no parsnips.

Criticism is also levelled against the provincial governments for attempting to erase all traces of French culture from their territories. "Canadiens" resent the fact that the French-speaking communities in the other provinces are not granted the same rights as those Québec has given to its own English-speaking minorities. In Ontario, for example, when the French Canadians tried to campaign for separate public schools in their own language, they met only with rebuff. A school trustee of one large city remarked: "We have no good reason to spend vast sums of money to accommodate those who should have learned English 300 years ago." As a result, the French consider themselves strangers in their own land.

Unfortunately, because of the "two solitudes," to use the phrase of Hugh MacLennan, many English Canadians are not aware of French Canadian grievances or simply dismiss them as erratic and temporary outbursts of a few "angry young men." They still cling to Lord Durham's dream that if old minorities don't exactly die, they are bound to fade away. Their fond hope is that, given enough time, the Québecer's individuality will disappear under the seepage of an alien culture; that, eventually he will become another North American, like so many other minority ethnic groups on this continent.

But this view is contrary to history and sociologically erroneous. French Canadians constitute a minority of a special kind. They have a deep consciousness of having been in the country first. Many can look back on at least eight, and some as many as twelve, generations. Being in the position of charter members, they believe that they have a special claim on Canada. In their eyes the British North America Act is not just a legislation of the Imperial government binding the provinces into a federal unit. It is also a covenant between the English majority and the French minority, wherein the latter obtained recognition of their status as partners in the government and life of the whole nation.

Many French Canadians feel that the English have not kept their part of the covenant and that the time has now come for Québec to establish itself as a sovereign state. A survey conducted in August 1963 by Montréal's Groupe de Recherche Sociale indicates that 13% of the French population favor breaking away from Canada. Although a small minority, it is an influential one. A special breakdown of the data shows that the strength of the separatists lies principally among the metropolitan young, better-educated people. One of every four professionals is a separatist; so is one of every four persons making over $6,000 a year. In Montréal, the size of the separatist group jumps to nearly 16%; outside Montréal it is only 11%. Clearly the people who want to cut off ties with the rest of Canada are those who lead opinion rather than follow it.*

* *Maclean's,* November 2, 1963.

Even among non-separatists, the motto "Québec first" has come to be generally accepted. This means not only that Québec must exercise all the prerogatives it has by virtue of the Constitution, but also that it must try to acquire a wider margin of sovereignty in every field. In the conflicts with Ottawa and with other provinces, Québec's own claims must be advanced and defended, even against the greater interests of Canada as a whole. This is the gist of René Lévesque's thesis of "by itself, for itself."

Nationalistic movements are not new to Québec. The spirit of independence can be traced far back into the 19th century. What makes the current wave particularly dangerous is that it is backed by strong winds of social revolution going on in the province. During the last decade the concept of the good life has radically changed. Gone is the old vision of self-sufficient farm families linked together by parish institutions. In the new urban model, good life means a comfortable city home, a luxurious car, an executive job, and a part in decision making at the top corporate level. When Westmount and St. James Street were only status symbols that were not particularly desirable, the fact that they were populated almost exclusively by English Canadians was only an occasional source of irritation. But when Westmount affluence becomes everyone's goal, when more and more people aspire to St. James Street jobs, then the whole situation is charged with explosive potential.

The atrophy of the rural ideal has also meant a new view of the "Etat National." The provincial government is no longer regarded as just a repository of jealously guarded but largely unused powers — a bulwark against Ottawa's encroachment into an area of minimal rule. Rather, it is looked upon now as a medium for collective self-realization, a vital instrument for the community's cultural, economic, and social progress. It can take over the private power companies and appoint a new set of French-Canadian managers and directors. It can establish a steel industry and introduce a provincial pension plan. It can ease out the traditional elite that has kept education from developing to meet fully the needs of the new society.

To quote René Lévesque, Minister of Welfare in the Lesage government: "It is especially necessary for us to use the economic power of the State as we are one of Canada's have-not minorities. The private sector of our economy is too weak to provide us with the rocket launchers that can blast us off the ramp of our debilitating poverty. Our principal capitalist for the moment — and for as far into the future as we can see — must therefore be the State. It must be more than a participant in the economic development and emancipation of Québec; it must be a creative agent. Otherwise, we can do no more than we have been doing so far, i.e., wait meekly for the capital and the initiative of others. The others, of course, will come, but for their own sake, not for ours. It is through our State alone that we can become masters in our own house."*

* *Le Devoir,* July 5, 1963. Interviewed by Jean-Marc Léger.

Obviously the forces released by Québec's social revolution cannot achieve results fast enough to keep up with burgeoning demand. The young and the impatient look for a scapegoat and a quick solution. They feel that ties with English Canada are a barrier to progress; political independence will clear the way. Separatism, they believe, will lead to great things — to independence, liberty, fulfilment of the nation, French dignity in the New World.

WHAT DOES QUEBEC WANT?

As this spirit of separatism grows among French Canadians, one is reminded of Sir John A. Macdonald's classic admonition: "Treat them as a nation, and they will act as a free people generally do. Call them a faction, and they will become factious." If Canada is to survive in a recognizable form — and this is not putting the point too strongly — English Canada may have to satisfy the major demands of Québec.

Economically, the aim is "être maîtres chez nous" (to be masters in our own house). This means Québec would have more say in financial matters than it does now — enough to establish primary control over its economic destiny, while remaining within a common Canadian monetary, fiscal, and tariff system. Also, the competent French Canadians would be given senior positions in Québec's business hierarchy. The era of picking up crumbs from the rich table, of being hewers of wood and drawers of water, is at an end.

Culturally, Québec wants French Canadians everywhere in the country to enjoy the privileges of a separate school system. It also expects more than lip service to be paid to the cause of bilingualism. Obviously, this does not imply that a clerk in a drug store in Vancouver should break into fluent French when a tourist from Rimouski comes in for a bottle of aspirin. But it does mean that a law graduate from British Columbia, who aspires to a career in the Department of Justice at Ottawa, should be able to understand presentations in French from his Québec colleagues. In other words, the top officials in the civil service and in the Crown corporations have to be well-versed in French.

Politically, Québec, as an embodiment of French Canadian culture, does not like to be treated like any other province. It wants changes in the constitution of the country, so that on certain issues it would have an equal voice with the rest of the nation. This need not result in the abandonment of the federal structure. The concept of an "associate state" is dismissed by many serious-thinking French Canadians as highly unrealistic. It is realized that one cannot in the twentieth century reincarnate the Austro-Hungarian Dual Monarchy or the medieval Holy Roman Empire; nor can one create a "Canada of National Fatherlands" à la de Gaulle. Such political monstrosities would be completely unworkable. To many French Canadians, the maintenance of federal ties offers many distinct advantages, as long as Québec enjoys all the autonomy it needs for the development of its own life and institutions.

In the long run, it would be in the national interest to take steps to accommodate French Canadians. The consequences of Québec secession would be severely damaging to the rest of Canada. Nearly one-third of the market and industrial capacity would be automatically subtracted from the country. The St. Lawrence Valley and Hudson Bay would become almost foreign territories. Canada would be divided into two pieces, with the Atlantic region separated by hundreds of miles from the rest of the nation. Under such circumstances, many provinces might well decide to give up and join the United States.

It is too often forgotten that Canada's binationalism, more than anything else, gives this country its distinguishing characteristic. Many English-Canadians fail to realize that without Québec, Canada makes no sense as a nation and may end up as a carbon copy of the United States.

On the other hand, "les Québecois" must also concede that they, too, have much to gain from a unified country. Some price will have to be paid for this, but the cost will not be nearly so great as it would be if Québec were stranded by independence on a hostile continent of 200 million English-speaking people. Reason would dictate a compromise on both sides. But sadly enough, reason does not always rule in politics. The experience of Pakistan has clearly shown that once a movement based on emotions has been started, there is no knowing where it will end.

MARKETING ASPECTS

How does the special character of Québec affect the sale of consumer goods and services in that province? On the surface at least, French Canadians behave like other North Americans. They worship at the continental shrines of coke, juke box, and credit. The men drive big cars and eagerly watch baseball games. The women are influenced by the newest fads from south of the border.

However, deeper probing indicates that cultural differences do influence consumption habits. First of all, there is the strong spirit of nationalism. It finds its way into the market place in the form of consumer support for local institutions. Lately, an attempt has been made in business circles to take advantage of this factor. An organization called *Le Conseil d'Expansion Economique* is actively engaged in trying to persuade Québecers to deal only with firms which are at least 51% French owned and controlled. Their campaign to "Buy French Canadian" has met with some success. It has been reported that within two weeks after the group began urging bank depositors to support the Québec-owned *Banque Canadienne Nationale* and *Banque Provinciale du Canada,* some $55 million worth of individual savings were transferred from "English" institutions to the two banks.* The *Conseil* also claims that in the past five years, premiums from French-Canadian life insurance companies (at least 51% French owned) have increased by 23%, while others have gone up by only 4%.**

* *Maclean's,* June 1, 1963.
** *Financial Post,* December 21, 1963.

Even without nationalism, the Québec market would still remain different because of the Latin temperament of the inhabitants. Color provides a good example. French Canadians prefer bright, even loud, colors. While a blonde English woman would generally select for her dress a tone that does not attract attention (like beige or gray or pale blue), the French brunette wants to be daring and chic with *chatoyant* materials in vivid and sophisticated colors. In packages and point-of-sale displays, the French Canadians are more attracted by bright and saturated colors — the intense reds and oranges — than by shades and halftones. A balanced package is not so important for the French market as for the English. The love of color also affects the purchase of cars. Montréal has more two-toned automobiles than any other city in Canada.*

One should not get the impression that French Canadians are impulsive in their purchases. Québec has lost none of its Norman thrift or its sense of values. The market is both price-conscious and quality-conscious. Due to their lower incomes and bigger families, French Canadians have to keep a tight control over their purse strings. But this does not mean being penny-wise and pound-foolish. What they buy must be good. They prefer to spend a little more to acquire a product with greater durability or serviceability. If they are satisfied with the brand, they remain loyal to it for a long time. Québec is thus less prey than most areas of Canada to the vagaries that render good products obsolete because of the flash-in-the-pan competition.

On account of this loyalty to existing brands, there is a widespread belief in marketing circles that new products have not much chance of success in Québec. This is not completely true, as can be seen from the following table. It is based on a special research undertaken in 1964 by International Surveys Limited for the French Network of Dailies. The sample consisted of 200 French-speaking housewives, proportionately divided between urban and rural areas.

NEW PRODUCT ACCEPTANCE

New products of general interest marketed within last 2 or 3 years	Total	% buying in first month	% buying after first month but within a year	% who did not buy or bought a year later
Cleaning and polishing floor wax (one application)	100%	16%	29%	55%
Foundation garments	100%	29	36	35
Stretch fabric outer garments	100%	24	40	36
Dry soups	100%	39	41	20
Average	100%	27%	36%	37%

* *Canadian Markets,* May, 1963.

Says International Surveys Limited: "Approximately 27% of Québec house-wives will try a new product within a month of its introduction on the market, another 36% will try it within a year, and 37% will wait a year or more before venturing to get their feet wet. This may not be the fastest consumer market in the world, but it certainly cannot be accused of being the slowest. It must be remembered, too, that if a new product is in a field which is of particular interest to the Québec housewife, her acceptance rate is very much accelerated. Dry soups are a case in point. Here 39% of all Québec housewives tried out this particular product within a month of its introduction, and a year later only 20% had not yet sampled it. This alone would dispel any doubts about Québec having an ingrained dislike of new products."

CDNPA SURVEY

So much for the broad picture of the behavior of the French-Canadian consumer. If one wants to get a detailed account of the differences between French and English Canada in purchasing patterns, shopping habits, and ownership of durable goods, a wealth of information is available from the *1963 Canadian Consumer Survey*. It was conducted by the Canadian Daily Newspaper Publishers Association (CDNPA) in various towns and cities across Canada. The report covers over 250 types of consumer products, and from the mass of data, special tables have been prepared to facilitate comparisons between French households in Québec and English households in Québec and Ontario. (See tables on pages 290 to 300.)

Here are a few broad generalizations from these tables, supplemented where necessary by research from other sources:

FOOD

The Québecers are noted for their "joie de vivre." Despite their lower economic level, they spend more per capita on products related to the satisfactions of the palate. For example, a DBS survey shows that the annual food budget of a typical urban family in Québec is $177 higher than the Canadian average. French cuisine is an art, and a household consumes more gourmet items than elsewhere. The housewife devotes a lot of time to cooking her meals and is proud of the recipes which have been passed down from generation to generation.

French Canadians do not worry so much about calories as the English do. Their addiction to "sweet tooth" items is well known. A Québec woman likes fancy cakes and sweet desserts to a degree where even if she envies the slimness of her English counterpart, she is seldom willing to accept the necessary sacrifices to acquire it.

The CDNPA survey points out the following differences in food purchases between the French and the English:

French Preference	English Preference
Baby food, canned meat	Baby food, canned vegetables
Cake flour, in boxes	Baking chocolate
Biscuits, domestic	Biscuit mix
Coffee, decaffeinated	Pancake mix
Coffee, instant	Margarine
Tea, packaged	Potato chips
Meat sauces	Coffee, in packages or cans
Molasses	Tea, bags
Salad or cooking oil	Jellies
Maple syrup	Salad dressing, liquid
Canned peas	Canned milk, evaporated
Sandwich spread, meat or fish	Canned fruit cocktail
Smoked ham, packaged	Canned corn
Chocolate in boxes	Canned green or wax beans
Macaroni, canned	Macaroni, prepared dinners
Macaroni, packaged	Fresh frozen fruits
Spaghetti, packaged	Frozen fruit juices
	Fresh frozen vegetables
	Frozen fish sticks
	Frozen meat pies
	Frozen prepared dinners
	Sliced cooked meats, packaged
	Wieners, packaged
	Breakfast cereals
	Flavored jelly powders

CLOTHING AND TOILETRIES

In addition to food, Québec provides an above-average market for many items of clothing and toilet preparations. According to a DBS report on urban consumer expenditures, a typical Canadian family spends $626 per year on clothing and personal care, while the expenditure in Québec is as high as $719. Compared to the English, French women more frequently buy foundation garments, hand creams, colognes, and perfumes. Both men and women in French Canada are careful about hair grooming. In proportion to population, the beauty parlors and barber shops do more business in Québec than in any other province. In all these respects, the French Canadians are very Latin, and they remain true to their origin even in the North American environment.

The Latin spirit is also evident in the way they dress. The English-Canadian woman, excepting the unmarried, dresses for other women. Even when she gets older, she continues to buy costly but uncomfortable clothes, rather than have it appear to other women that she "is letting herself go." The French-Canadian woman dresses primarily for the man in her life — or the one she would like to have. On getting older, she simply gives up and changes to inexpensive garments which are comfortable even though dowdy. She does not bother to keep up appearances once her essential reason for dressing up is gone.

HEALTH

Even the attitudes towards health are different. The English-Canadian is mainly concerned with nutrition — with having the protein and vitamin content higher and the fat and carbohydrate content lower. The French Canadian is primarily interested in food items noted for their digestive value.

Also, French Canada provides a good market for patent medicines. The CDNPA survey reveals that a substantially larger proportion of Gallic than Anglo-Saxon households buy:

cold tablets
cough drops
cough syrups
effervescent salts
indigestion remedies
laxatives for adults
nose drops
nose sprays
remedies, external and internal, for muscular aches and pains

SHOPPING HABITS

The same survey also throws some interesting light on the differences in shopping habits. In food buying, only 49% of French-Canadian housewives buy in chain supermarkets, while the corresponding figure for Anglo-Saxon women, both in Québec and Ontario, is over 84%. Similarly for drug products, the Gallic shopper patronises the independent drug store, while the English counterpart purchases mainly from supermarkets and chain drug stores. For cosmetics and toilet preparations, the same pattern is repeated, with one extra touch: house-to-house selling is considerably more popular in French Canada.

When it comes to automotive purchases, such as anti-freeze, batteries, and tires, four out of ten French Canadians go to garages. This ratio is in many cases three times higher than that for English Canadians. The latter rely more on service stations. The purchase patterns are even more drastically different for cigarettes. The restaurant is the chief place for buying cigarettes among the French, while it is negligible among the English. On the other hand, the chain grocery store is relatively unimportant for French people (about 15%), but a key outlet for the English.

The major role of independents in Québec's retail structure is of great significance to businessmen. It means to them that they are not at the mercy of the handful of all-powerful corporate chains. They do not have to resort to uneconomic profit margins to win shelf space. But at the same time their selling job is more complicated. It is not enough to have their product accepted by a few purchasing committees. They have to get the merchandise on the shelves of thousands of small retail outlets all across the province.

COMPARISONS OF PURCHASES BETWEEN FRENCH-SPEAKING HOUSEWIVES IN QUEBEC AND ENGLISH-SPEAKING HOUSEWIVES IN QUEBEC AND ONTARIO, 1963

Consumer products	% of housewives normally buying			French significantly above (+) or below (−)
	French Québec	English Québec	English Ontario	
FOOD PRODUCTS				
Baby foods				
Cereals—packaged	59.7%	63.2%	71.2%	
Fruits and desserts, canned	75.9	75.1	83.4	
Meat, canned	78.0	71.6	70.1	(+)
Vegetables, canned	60.9	90.0	90.1	(−)
Baking products				
Baking chocolate	40.3	59.9	54.9	(−)
Flour				
All purpose	93.5	89.9	96.6	
Cake and pastry, in bags	20.9	21.4	36.1	
Cake, in boxes	24.1	16.8	14.1	(+)
Mixes				
Biscuit	12.8	24.3	26.4	(−)
Cake	65.8	56.6	66.3	
Pancake	40.3	58.6	67.3	(−)
Pie crust	24.7	25.8	19.8	
Shortening				
Lard, packaged	26.5	27.2	30.8	
Margarine	54.2	64.5	65.5	(−)
Shortening, packaged	75.4	82.8	77.7	
Bakery products				
Biscuits, domestic	67.3	48.5	37.6	(+)
Biscuits, imported	18.1	33.7	21.8	
Potato chips	21.6	68.0	73.5	(−)
Beverages				
Cocoa	68.9	66.2	65.2	
Coffee, decaffeinated	27.6	9.2	6.4	(+)
Coffee, instant	84.0	78.5	74.6	(+)
Coffee, in packages or cans	52.9	68.2	71.8	(−)
Food drinks	52.2	46.6	50.6	
Soft drinks, for use at home	81.9	92.9	91.0	(−)
Soft drinks, taken outside home	59.8	62.7	58.1	
Tea, bags	74.6	81.7	90.4	(−)
Tea, instant	9.1	6.9	7.3	
Tea, packaged	41.8	28.2	19.5	(+)

Consumer products	% of housewives normally buying			French significantly above (+) or below (−)
	French Québec	English Québec	English Ontario	
Condiments				
Catsup (Ketchup)	92.0%	92.9%	92.7%	
Jams	82.3	87.9	80.2	
Jellies	28.8	44.1	37.8	(−)
Marmalade	67.5	70.2	57.2	
Meat sauces	43.6	27.5	25.8	(+)
Molasses	73.6	48.7	46.2	(+)
Peanut butter	87.9	85.3	85.5	
Pickles	80.5	84.2	86.2	
Salad or cooking oil	76.5	64.4	63.0	(+)
Salad dressing, liquid	36.8	42.4	47.0	(−)
Salad dressing or mayonnaise	86.9	90.7	89.5	
Sandwich spread, mayonnaise type	21.2	24.7	21.9	
Syrup, corn	77.2	66.4	85.4	
Syrup, maple	48.1	33.9	40.0	(+)
Syrup, table	57.2	47.2	70.6	
Dairy products				
Canned milk, evaporated	47.1	58.3	64.1	(−)
Cheese in packages, jars or glasses	87.7	91.1	92.2	
Dry milk powder	32.8	28.6	28.9	
Fruits and vegetables, canned				
Fruits				
Fruit cocktail	64.9	77.1	73.5	(−)
Peaches	77.5	87.0	74.1	
Pears	66.2	75.7	57.9	
Pineapple	72.2	75.5	71.3	
Vegetables				
Baked beans	74.6	82.5	79.5	
Corn, creamed	60.8	67.4	67.1	(−)
Corn, whole kernel	42.5	61.9	64.2	(−)
Green or wax beans	49.3	68.8	56.0	(−)
Peas	91.8	76.6	77.2	(+)
Tomatoes	78.4	67.1	75.2	
Tomato juice	91.1	88.9	85.7	
Fruits and vegetables—frozen				
Fruits (fresh, frozen)	15.5	25.8	31.8	(−)
Fruit juices (concentrated)	23.7	49.9	57.3	(−)
Fruit pies	7.1	9.0	9.2	
Vegetables (fresh, frozen)	13.4	47.4	58.8	(−)

COMPARISONS OF PURCHASES BETWEEN FRENCH-SPEAKING HOUSEWIVES IN QUEBEC AND ENGLISH-SPEAKING HOUSEWIVES IN QUEBEC AND ONTARIO 1963 (continued)

Consumer products	% of housewives normally buying			French significantly above (+) or below (−)
	French Québec	English Québec	English Ontario	
Meat and fish products				
Canned				
Processed meats	34.9%	37.8%	44.0%	
Salmon	72.4	80.0	83.2	(−)
Sandwich spread, meat or fish	35.9	26.1	13.5	(+)
Frozen				
Fish and chips	8.7	12.9	12.3	
Fish fillets	32.4	33.0	35.8	
Fish sticks	4.7	22.2	15.2	(−)
Meat pies	10.2	18.2	24.0	(−)
Prepared dinners	9.5	15.0	16.4	(−)
Packaged				
Sliced bacon	80.6	82.4	88.6	
Sliced cooked meats	32.2	47.7	60.7	(−)
Sausages	59.4	59.3	57.9	
Smoked hams	58.5	48.9	49.7	(+)
Wieners	64.7	71.5	85.4	(−)
Pet foods				
Canned cat food	8.3	12.5	13.5	
Canned or wet dog food	12.8	24.3	26.4	(−)
Dog biscuits or kibble	24.7	25.8	19.8	
Dog food, meal	19.2	25.8	21.3	
Other groceries				
Breakfast cereals, to be cooked	55.5	77.3	91.2	(−)
Breakfast cereals, ready to eat	84.8	95.5	91.8	(−)
Chocolate bars	73.0	68.9	61.1	
Chocolates in boxes	59.0	50.5	43.8	(+)
Flavored jelly powders	59.1	85.4	91.5	(−)
Instant potatoes	19.2	25.8	21.3	
Macaroni, canned	27.2	15.7	14.5	(+)
Macaroni, packaged	82.3	63.0	60.0	(+)
Macaroni, prepared dinners	27.4	36.9	34.7	(−)
Spaghetti, packaged	88.5	65.1	56.3	(+)
Soup, canned	93.3	93.9	99.5	
Soup, dry mixes	54.9	54.4	63.8	

Consumer products	% of housewives normally buying			French significantly above (+) or below (−)
	French Québec	English Québec	English Ontario	
TOBACCO PRODUCTS				
Cigarettes, men	65.8%	54.2%	57.8%	(+)
Breakdown of these purchases by type:	(100.0)	(100.0)	(100.0)	
Plain	(8.4)	(25.2)	(23.8)	(−)
Regular	(45.6)	(32.9)	(31.8)	(+)
Filter	(31.3)	(34.0)	(33.1)	
King-size	(9.9)	(7.3)	(11.3)	
Other	(4.8)	(0.6)	—	
Cigarettes, women	53.8	43.4	47.9	
Breakdown of these purchases by type:	(100.0)	(100.0)	(100.0)	
Plain	(24.9)	(16.9)	(18.9)	
Regular	(7.0)	(28.7)	(25.3)	(−)
Filter	(55.2)	(41.7)	(41.0)	(+)
King-size	(11.1)	(12.7)	(14.8)	
Other	(1.8)	—	—	
Cigars	22.5	14.7	15.7	
Pipe tobacco	13.8	16.5	14.3	
Cigarette-lighter, men*	32.7	21.4	22.5	(+)
Cigarette-lighter, women*	32.1	21.5	17.5	(+)
CLOTHING				
Men				
Hats	49.7	45.2	46.8	
Raincoats	20.1	24.6	22.3	
Shirts	76.2	78.6	88.3	(−)
Sport shirts	61.8	59.4	74.9	
Sweaters	46.9	41.9	51.5	
Underwear	70.9	72.8	82.6	
Women				
Brassieres	83.0	90.6	86.8	
Corselettes	18.1	7.1	7.5	(+)
Corsets	32.3	14.4	8.5	(+)
Girdles	57.0	66.0	66.4	(−)
Hosiery	85.0	92.2	90.5	
Lingerie	78.8	73.4	82.9	
Raincoats	27.9	27.2	22.4	
Sweaters	66.7	58.9	72.4	

* Figures on cigarette-lighter refer to purchases or presents received during the past three years·

COMPARISONS OF PURCHASES BETWEEN FRENCH-SPEAKING HOUSEWIVES IN QUEBEC AND ENGLISH-SPEAKING HOUSEWIVES IN QUEBEC AND ONTARIO, 1963 (continued)

Consumer products	% of housewives normally buying			French significantly above (+) or below (−)
	French Québec	English Québec	English Ontario	
DRUG PRODUCTS				
Antiseptic ointment	47.0%	43.8%	43.4%	
Bandages, plastic or adhesive	69.1	87.8	85.8	(−)
Chest rubs	74.0	71.6	71.7	
Cold tablets	55.2	34.7	30.5	(+)
Cough drops	74.7	52.2	54.8	(+)
Cough syrups	78.8	52.7	53.4	(+)
Effervescent salts	61.9	50.2	40.2	(+)
Foot remedies	35.0	32.0	27.9	
Indigestion remedies	81.9	49.5	61.4	(+)
Laxatives for adults	62.7	48.5	55.9	(+)
Laxatives for children	43.6	51.5	47.9	
Muscular aches and pains remedies				
External	57.4	44.8	40.6	(+)
Internal	24.1	16.1	15.7	(+)
Mouth wash	60.3	58.8	61.4	
Nose drops	64.4	38.8	31.1	(+)
Nose sprays	36.7	26.2	21.3	(+)
Vitamins	41.5	43.0	45.9	
TOILETRIES				
Men				
After shave lotion	47.7	49.2	58.4	
Brushless shaving cream	7.1	8.7	11.6	
Hair dressings	35.6	54.4	63.6	(−)
Personal deodorants				
Cream	7.6	7.9	7.2	
Liquid	18.7	6.1	6.2	(+)
Roll-on	11.2	22.1	25.1	(−)
Spray	8.2	12.4	13.3	
Stick	9.6	13.1	14.7	
Pre-electric shave lotions	28.5	18.4	24.0	
Shampoo	52.2	39.7	45.1	(+)
Shaving cream, aerosol or pressure can	10.1	12.9	14.2	
Shaving cream, applied with brush	21.4	25.1	26.9	

Consumer products	% of housewives normally buying			French significantly above (+) or below (−)
	French Québec	English Québec	English Ontario	
Women				
Cologne or toilet water	77.7%	68.9%	64.9%	(+)
Face cream				
Foundation	20.0	15.8	21.2	
Cleansing	27.7	27.3	26.7	
Night	12.5	11.9	8.9	
Special and medicated	5.0	11.0	15.2	(−)
Face powder	63.2	58.7	65.9	
Hair dressings	14.5	28.3	33.9	(−)
Hair sprays	52.7	47.7	49.6	
Hand creams	67.9	47.8	54.0	(+)
Hand lotions	42.7	55.8	60.6	(−)
Home permanents	35.4	31.9	27.4	
Make-up or foundation bases				
Cake	13.6	13.8	13.1	
Cream	19.8	19.4	22.4	
Liquid	21.3	26.9	33.4	
Stick	2.5	2.7	1.4	
Nail polish	59.4	52.6	46.9	
Nail polish remover	50.6	49.5	47.5	
Perfume	67.2	60.8	60.2	(+)
Personal deodorants				
Cream	29.9	22.9	26.7	
Liquid	10.1	4.9	6.2	
Roll-on	28.9	43.2	49.2	(−)
Spray	6.0	7.7	2.5	
Stick	8.4	4.6	7.4	
Rouge, cream	15.8	21.7	20.7	
Rouge, dry	15.7	12.7	14.4	
Shampoo				
Cream	10.5	12.2	14.9	
Clear, liquid	70.8	64.1	55.5	(+)
Lotion	6.1	9.6	11.8	
Baby products				
Baby oil	56.0	67.2	88.6	(−)
Baby powder	57.2	59.9	67.1	
Baby soap	55.1	61.7	71.6	(−)

Consumer products	% of housewives normally buying			French significantly above (+) or below (−)
	French Québec	English Québec	English Ontario	
HOUSEHOLD PRODUCTS				
Air-fresheners	64.6%	52.0%	62.5%	
Cleansers				
Drain cleansers	64.4	67.0	68.9	
Oven cleansers	41.8	64.5	67.4	(−)
Pot scourers	61.8	70.6	73.2	(−)
Scouring cleansers	60.4	81.2	84.9	(−)
Wall and floor cleansers, all purpose	79.5	76.1	79.9	
Window cleansers	72.1	67.6	72.4	
Detergents, liquid				
For dishes	91.8	76.6	77.2	(+)
For clothes	28.5	18.4	24.0	
For hosiery and lingerie	19.2	25.7	21.3	
Detergents, powdered or soaps				
For dishes	59.4	59.3	57.9	
For clothes	96.4	96.5	96.0	
For hosiery and lingerie	21.6	68.0	73.5	(−)
Floor polishes and waxes				
Liquid, buffing	27.7	9.6	17.8	(+)
Liquid, self-polishing	54.5	64.7	63.1	(−)
Paste	61.7	67.5	71.5	(−)
Furniture polishes				
Cream	57.4	44.8	40.6	(+)
Oil	12.8	24.3	26.4	(−)
Spray	54.5	49.5	56.3	
AUTOMOTIVE PRODUCTS				
Antifreeze	44.3	52.3	72.2	(−)
Battery	14.7	16.7	19.9	
Car polish	29.3	31.0	47.4	
Gasoline, regular	26.0	43.3	64.1	(−)
Gasoline, premium	19.8	18.7	21.1	
Motor oil	45.0	51.1	72.4	
Tires	26.7	24.3	35.8	
Snow tires	23.1	24.6	27.9	

COMPARISON OF THE STANDARD OF LIVING, AS MEASURED BY THE OWNERSHIP OF CERTAIN DURABLE GOODS, BETWEEN FRENCH-SPEAKING HOUSEHOLDS IN QUEBEC AND ENGLISH-SPEAKING HOUSEHOLDS IN QUEBEC AND ONTARIO, 1963

Durable goods	% of households owning			French significantly above (+) or below (−)
	French Québec	English Québec	English Ontario	
Automotive				
Passenger car	58.1%	61.4%	83.9%	
Second car	6.1	6.9	11.9	
Distribution of the principal car owned by year of the model	(100.0)	(100.0)	(100.0)	
Current year	(13.0)	(8.0)	(8.9)	
One year old	(13.0)	(13.9)	(14.0)	
Two years old	(10.9)	(14.1)	(11.9)	
Three years old	(11.8)	(13.4)	(15.1)	
Four years old	(10.2)	(8.6)	(12.1)	
Five years old	(9.6)	(5.0)	(7.3)	
Six years old	(9.9)	(7.5)	(11.2)	
Seven years old	(5.5)	(6.9)	(8.3)	
Eight years old	(4.5)	(8.2)	(5.8)	
Nine years old	(2.7)	(5.5)	(2.8)	
Ten or more years old	(8.9)	(8.9)	(2.6)	(+)
Major appliances				
Clothes washer, electric				
Automatic	30.1	26.5	28.5	
Conventional washer with wringer	62.5	54.6	64.7	
Clothes dryer, electric	28.4	23.6	37.0	
Cooking range, electric	71.0	77.5	78.6	
Cooking range, gas	9.3	18.7	14.3	
Dish washer, automatic	6.9	6.1	2.6	
Home freezer (separate from refrigerator)	8.8	10.9	24.8	
Phonograph or record player	31.6	33.5	37.6	
Phonograph-radio combination	28.7	30.0	31.3	
Phonograph-radio-TV combination	8.5	6.6	6.9	
Radio, FM	15.9	17.5	16.7	
Television set	92.4	82.5	89.4	
Minor electric appliances				
Can opener	16.9	9.1	8.6	(+)
Coffee percolator	33.5	34.9	38.8	
Floor polisher	45.3	65.5	71.3	(−)

COMPARISON OF THE STANDARD OF LIVING, AS MEASURED BY THE OWNERSHIP OF CERTAIN DURABLE GOODS, BETWEEN FRENCH-SPEAKING HOUSEHOLDS IN QUEBEC AND ENGLISH-SPEAKING HOUSEHOLDS IN QUEBEC AND ONTARIO, 1963 (continued)

Durable goods	% of households owning			French significantly above (+) or below (−)
	French Québec	English Québec	English Ontario	
Food mixer, table	39.0	33.5	31.4	(+)
Food mixer, portable	32.2	39.6	47.8	(−)
Frying pan	32.6	57.8	62.1	(−)
Hair dryer	39.4	35.9	38.6	
Kettle	63.6	69.8	87.0	(−)
Sewing machine	81.8	69.1	72.3	(+)
Toaster	92.5	88.6	94.5	
Vacuum cleaner, upright	36.7	31.4	28.8	(+)
Vacuum cleaner, canister	33.7	61.8	62.6	(−)
Other durable goods				
Camera, still	46.0%	59.5%	69.0%	(−)
Camera, movie	12.6	15.2	17.3	
Power lawn mower	13.7	26.8	35.1	(−)
Outboard motor	10.2	9.7	14.2	
Razor, electric	51.8	54.4	69.8	
Typewriter	24.5	36.2	30.3	(−)

SHOPPING HABITS OF THE FRENCH-SPEAKING HOUSEWIVES IN QUEBEC VERSUS ENGLISH-SPEAKING HOUSEWIVES IN QUEBEC AND ONTARIO, 1963

Retail outlets	% normally buying at different types of stores			French significantly above (+) or below (−)
	French Québec	English Québec	English Ontario	
Most groceries				
Chain grocery store (supermarket)	48.6%	84.4%	86.8%	(−)
Independent grocery store	47.4	14.8	12.2	(+)
Department store	4.0	0.8	1.0	
Total	100.0	100.0	100.0	

Retail outlets	% normally buying at different types of stores			French significantly above (+) or below (−)
	French Québec	English Québec	English Ontario	
Most drug products				
Department store	3.4	3.5	4.0	
Variety store	0.8	0.7	0.9	
Grocery store or supermarket	16.5	26.3	36.2	(−)
Discount store	1.2	2.6	5.3	
Independent drug store	61.3	55.4	33.9	(+)
Chain drug store	13.2	11.0	19.7	
House-to-house salesman	3.6	0.5	—	
Total	100.0	100.0	100.0	
Most cosmetics and toilet preparations				
Department store	12.5	19.8	13.6	
Variety store	3.7	1.7	2.1	
Grocery store or supermarket	9.3	14.5	13.1	
Independent drug store	32.4	35.2	30.3	
Chain drug store	7.8	8.3	14.3	
House-to-house salesman	27.9	15.4	18.4	(+)
Other source	6.4	5.1	8.2	
Total	100.0	100.0	100.0	
Cigarettes, men				
Restaurant	47.4	21.7	7.2	(+)
Tobacco store	13.4	19.6	25.3	(−)
Chain grocery store	14.8	32.7	31.8	(−)
Independent grocery store	21.4	3.6	5.3	(+)
Drug store	1.1	9.9	14.6	(−)
Discount store	—	3.8	7.2	(−)
Other source	1.9	8.7	8.6	(−)
Total	100.0	100.0	100.0	
Cigarettes, women				
Restaurant	40.5%	12.2%	10.0%	(+)
Tobacco store	8.3	11.0	7.6	
Chain grocery store	16.9	50.9	44.8	(−)
Independent grocery store	15.9	15.4	17.5	
Drug store	4.2	7.2	9.6	
Discount store	2.1	3.3	10.5	
Other source	12.1	—	—	(+)
Total	100.0	100.0	100.0	

SHOPPING HABITS OF THE FRENCH-SPEAKING HOUSEWIVES IN QUEBEC VERSUS ENGLISH-SPEAKING HOUSEWIVES IN QUEBEC AND ONTARIO, 1963 (continued)

Retail outlets	% normally buying at different types of stores			French significantly above (+) or below (−)
	French Québec	English Québec	English Ontario	
Antifreeze				
Car dealer	8.0	7.9	9.0	
Discount store	2.5	9.8	16.6	(−)
Service station	34.8	53.4	42.0	(−)
Garage	41.7	11.4	13.5	(+)
Department store	1.5	2.8	7.2	
Accessory store	11.5	14.7	11.7	
Total	100.0	100.0	100.0	
Battery				
Car dealer	11.3	8.2	9.8	
Discount store	6.9	9.9	6.7	
Service station	17.3	32.8	29.0	(−)
Garage	40.3	5.6	17.4	(+)
Department store	2.4	9.5	1.0	
Accessory store	21.8	34.0	36.1	(−)
Total	100.0	100.0	100.0	
Tires				
Car dealer	12.4	8.3	9.0	
Discount store	4.1	9.0	10.8	
Service station	19.4	32.1	32.5	(−)
Garage	38.2	13.2	12.7	(+)
Department store	1.0	7.6	1.9	
Accessory store	24.9	29.8	33.1	
Total	100.0	100.0	100.0	

(Source: Canadian Daily Newspaper Publishers Association, *1963 Canadian Consumer Survey*. Figures refer to urban families only. Results for French Québec are based on a sample of slightly over 2,100 readers of French newspapers in the cities of Granby, Montréal, Québec, Sherbrooke, Three Rivers, and Ottawa-Hull. The size of the sample of English newspaper readers in Québec is about 1,450 and covers the cities of Montréal, Québec, Sherbrooke, and Ottawa-Hull. Ontario includes the top 36 cities, except Ottawa, with a sample size of about 8,100 English newspaper readers.)

HOW TO REACH THE FRENCH-CANADIAN MARKET

In reaching the French-Canadian market, mere awareness of ethnic characteristics is not enough. What is involved also is a grasp of the basic tool — language.

One should not be misled by the fact that a large number of Canadians are bilingual. When these people get home, they think in French, talk in French, read in French, and listen to French. Hence, to sell any product, one should approach them in their own mother tongue.

French-Canadian French, in its popular form, is as different from the French of France as colloquial American English is from Oxford English. Both exhibit less correctness, more careless enunciation, and a certain unbridled freedom in adopting newly coined expressions. However, a movement is now under way to promote pure French. A book written by a teaching priest condemning "joual" was a spectacular success and had a record sale of nearly 100,000 copies (Pierre Jérôme's *Les insolences du Frère Untel*). The author mentioned that by far the majority of the letters he received were from relatively uneducated people who were glad that someone at last had taken a stand against the degeneration of the French tongue.

The provincial government's Department of Cultural Affairs has joined now in the battle to improve French. In one of its bulletins, *Mieux Dire,* it advised against the use of such anglicized expressions as "hot dog," "king-size," "élévateur," "gadget," and "goal." It also suggested that "assignment" should be translated as "tâche assignée," not "assignation"; "chain stores" as "grands magasins à succursales," not "magasins à chaînes"; and "dime novel" as "roman à quatre sous," not "roman à dix sous."

Any communication directed to Québec should be in good French and avoid colloquial expressions built on anglicized syntax and vocabulary. Though he may speak carelessly himself, a French Canadian is easily offended by the use of poor French when it originates from outsiders. He suspects either an attempt to ridicule his everyday speech, or an implication that he is not capable of understanding academic French.

ADVERTISING

Many non-French-owned Québec companies — and several others operating in Québec but with headquarters elsewhere — simply translate their advertisements from English into French and let it go at that. This results not only in bad French but also in grotesque expressions, with meanings twisted and idioms tortured. In translating from English to French, the words themselves often have to be changed, because the emphasis is different. Literary accuracy is not enough. One has to consider the nuances of the language as well.

As one French marketing expert remarks: "If you don't get inside the skeleton and make the bones jerk to the tune it likes, the arm won't bend into the pocket. It is always difficult to know what makes people 'tick.' And crossing the invisible borders of cultural and linguistic differences is particularly tough. The need is for advertising thought out for French Canada and written for and by French Canadians."

What type of advertising approach, then, is needed in French Canada? The French Canadian is a combination of Latin and Norman. As a Latin, he is noted for imagination, volubility, quickness of mind, warmth of feeling, and his artistic temperament. Being a Norman makes him practical, logical, thrifty, slightly cynical, and sometimes suspicious. He is allergic to advertising that talks down to him, shouts at him, tells him the product is good because it is modern and all America loves it. High-faluting superlatives, smart-aleck pitches, captious arguments, and provocative "off color" art or copy — all these tend to arouse his resentment, or worse, sarcastic laughter. He does not care if the product is simply new. He is interested in a clear statement of benefits and advantages along with the newness. A repetitious overstatement of the "new" or "improved" theme only bores him. What will win his patronage is the "soft sell," and solid, practical, and honest reasoning which pays due respect to his judgment and takes into consideration his emotional likes and dislikes.

People tend to project themselves when looking at pictures in advertisements. That is why one has to be careful about the situations portrayed in art work. For example, a French Canadian may have difficulty in identifying himself with an illustration that shows townsmen going to a football game or taking part in curling, golfing, or "throwing the pigskin." The popular sports in Québec are hockey, baseball, hunting, and fishing. The "Canadiens" are not enthusiastic about pets either; consequently, photos of cats and dogs will not evoke the same warm emotions as in the Anglo-Saxon world.

Since the Québecer is proud of his colorful history, especially when it concerns the adventure of the early explorers, advertisements tied in with incidents from the past will get the message across more effectively. On radio and television the approach can be slightly modified through the use of folk music of which there is an ample supply. (*Alouette* is not the only folk song to come out of French Canada.)

Parisian movies and recordings are extremely popular in Québec. The presence of a Parisian or a French-Canadian star can be a direct and powerful appeal in a radio or a TV commercial, far stronger than the dubbed translation of a Hollywood or Broadway personality who is conspicuously unknown in Québec, excepting Montréal.

One can give numerous instances of many products which have been a spectacular success in English Canada but have flopped in Québec because advertising violated certain French-Canadian taboos. One well-known example is the ad for a canned fish where a woman in shorts was shown playing golf with her husband. The caption read that the woman could stay on the links all day and still prepare a delicious dinner that evening if she used the product. Every element in the advertisement represented a violation of some underlying theme of

French-Canadian life: the wife would not be playing golf with her husband; she would not wear shorts; she would not like to shirk her household responsibilities; and she would not be serving the particular kind of fish as a main course.

CONSUMER SALES PROMOTIONS

Another effective method of moving a product in French Canada is through consumer sales promotions, like coupons, off-label deals, special offers, under-pricing, premiums, contests, and extra trading stamps. Such buying incentives are very well accepted in Québec, as revealed by the 1964 survey of the French Network of Dailies conducted by MRC Limited. The results, based on a sample of 200 French-speaking housewives, show that within the previous two months more than three-quarters of the respondents had taken advantage of coupons, off-label deals, special offers, and underpricing. The least popular of all promotions was the contest, but even here only 38% of the housewives mentioned never having entered one at any time.

As may be expected, the preferences for different incentives vary by age groups, city size, and social classes. Couponing is the first choice for women over 30, but it has considerably less appeal for younger housewives. In small cities, under-pricing is the most popular promotion, while it ranks fifth in metropolitan areas. The upper classes are mainly attracted by special offers, the middle and lower by coupons.

All these and other data are shown in detail in the following two tables. They can be valuable to a firm planning to use sales promotion, either as a long-term, franchise-building measure in French Canada, or as a palliative device for tactical purposes, such as checking aggressive competition.

BIBLIOGRAPHY ON FRENCH CANADA

Canadian Daily Newspaper Publishers Association: *1963 Consumer Survey.*
Dominion Bureau of Statistics: *Urban Family Expenditure, 1959,* Catalog No. 62-521.
Elkin, Frederick: "Advertising in French Canada," published in *Marketing: Canada,* edited by Isaiah A. Litvak and Bruce E. Mallen, McGraw-Hill Company of Canada Limited, 1964.
French Network of Dailies: *The French-Speaking Consumer: A Continuing Series of Reports on Attitudes, Motivations and Buying Patterns.* (First report issued in April 1964.) The French Network of Dailies, 1500 St. Catherine Street West, Montréal.
Gzowski, Peter: "Separatism," *Maclean's,* November 2, 1963.
Marketing: "The French Market" (special report appearing annually in the first or second week of June).
Myers, Huge B.: *The Quebec Revolution,* Harvest House, Montréal, 1964.
Rioux, Marcel and Yves Martin (editors): *French-Canadian Society,* Vol. I, McCelland and Stewart Limited, Toronto, 1964.
Scott, Frank and Michael Oliver (editors): *Québec States Her Case,* Macmillan of Canada Limited, Toronto, 1964.
Wade, Mason: *The French-Canadian Outlook,* McCelland and Stewart Limited, Toronto, 1964.
Wade, Mason (editor): *Canadian Dualism: Studies of French-English Relations,* University of Toronto Press, Toronto, 1960.

ATTITUDES OF FRENCH-SPEAKING HOUSEWIVES TO
CONSUMER SALES PROMOTIONS

	Coupon-ing	Off label deals	Special offers	Under-pricing	Extra trading stamps	Pre-miums	Con-tests
Extent to which incentives were acted upon							
When encountered last time	79%	81%	80%	78%	76%	65%	49%
When encountered at some time in the past	7	4	4	7	8	11	13
Never acted upon	14	15	16	15	16	24	38
Total	100%	100%	100%	100%	100%	100%	100%
Average length of time elapsed since the last incentive was acted upon							
Number of months	0.8	0.7	1.3	1.6	2.3	2.4	4.4
Order of preference for the whole sample							
Most likely to buy	21%	17%	17%	26%	14%	4%	2%
Second choice	18	27	21	16	3	12	3
Third choice	28	15	21	6	12	11	2
Fourth, fifth and sixth choice	28	40	33	45	51	51	62
Last choice	5	1	8	7	20	22	31
Total	100%	100%	100%	100%	100%	100%	100%
Indices (range 0–100)	64	63	60	58	42	38	27
Ranking of promotions by age groups							
Under 30	4	1	3	2	5	6	7
30–45	1	2	4	3	5	6	7
Over 45	1	2	2	4	5	6	7
Ranking of promotions by city-size							
100,000 or more	1	1	3	5	4	6	7
Less than 100,000	2	3	4	1	5	6	7

ATTITUDES OF FRENCH-SPEAKING HOUSEWIVES TO
CONSUMER SALES PROMOTIONS (continued)

	Coupon- ing	Off label deals	Special offers	Under- pricing	Extra trading stamps	Pre- miums	Con- tests
Ranking of promotions by							
social classes							
Upper	3	4	1	2	5	5	7
Middle	1	2	3	3	5	6	7
Lower	1	2	3	4	5	6	7

(Source: "Attitudes of the French-Speaking Housewife towards Buying Incentives", prepared by MRC Limited under the supervision of Richard Gelfand. The three-part report is published in *The French-Speaking Consumer* brought out by the French Network of Dailies.)

ATTITUDES OF FRENCH-SPEAKING HOUSEWIVES TO DIFFERENT
TYPES OF COUPONING, SPECIAL OFFERS AND PREMIUMS

	Would buy the product %	Might buy the product %	Would not buy the product %	Total %
Couponing				
"Loose" coupon	70	30	—	100
"In pack" coupon	35	54	11	100
Special offers				
Getting a second package for just a few cents more	79	21	—	100
Getting a large package (e.g. 1/3 more) at regular price	59	38	3	100
Sending away a box top or label to get a voucher for a full package	12	16	72	100
Premiums				
Packed inside the package	30	40	30	100
Attached to the outside of the package	15	63	22	100
Mail a box top or label	11	30	59	100
Cut-outs on the package (mainly toys)	24	35	41	100

(Source: The French Network of Dailies: *Attitudes of the French-Speaking Housewife Towards Buying Incentives*. Survey by MRC Limited under the supervision of Richard Gelfand.)

English Canada

On the basis of the 1961 Census, 58.5% of the inhabitants of Canada have English as their mother tongue. Since persons of British origin account for only 43.8% of the population, the remaining 14.7% are obviously members of other nationalities who in the course of a few generations have become anglicized.

COMPARISON WITH THE U.S.A.

When speaking of English Canada, the first question which immediately comes to mind is: Does it constitute a separate entity with a distinct personality of its own, or is it simply a part of the larger North American society, shaped by the same forces, motivated by the same factors, and espousing the same economic philosophy and political beliefs as the United States? As in most cases, the truth lies somewhere between the two.

That the development of English Canada owes much to the British heritage goes without saying. Yet the suggestion that this country is but a variant of the United Kingdom is hardly acceptable. Canada is essentially a part of the North American milieu. History occasionally loses sight of this fact, but at every step geography imperiously recalls it. Neither the intimacy between France and Belgium nor the one between West Germany and Austria can compare with the affinity that exists between English Canada and the United States. The political boundary may stretch from east to west, but all the physiographic features which give distinct characteristics to a nation run north and south. As a result, English Canadians often have closer cultural ties with their next-door U.S. neighbors than with their fellow citizens in other provinces hundreds of miles away.

A Maritimer usually takes his vacation in New England, whose Gothic churches and little fishing villages evoke more the pleasant feeling of oneness than the Norman spires and the strip farms of neighboring Québec. The inhabitants of Southern Ontario are closer in behavior and manner of living to the residents of upstate New York than to those of Northern Ontario. The Prairies have more in common with the adjacent wheat states of Montana and North Dakota than with the industrialized Lower Great Lakes–St. Lawrence region. Many special features of British Columbia — style of architecture, type of outdoor casual living — follow the pattern of the Pacific Coast states, quite distinct from any other province in Canada. In short, life runs on a natural north-south axis across the border, rather than in the east-west direction across the country.

In economic matters, the two neighbors are very much dependent on each other. Canada is not only the United States' principal supplier, it is also the United States' largest customer. In 1964 Canada bought over $4 billion worth of goods, more than the whole of Latin America combined.

The method of doing business is the same on both sides of the border. This is not surprising since the United States controls 95% of Canada's automotive industry, 90% of the rubber industry, and almost three-fourths of the natural gas and petroleum industry. American investments are also large in electrical apparatus, chemicals, pulp and paper, and mining and smelting.

The corporate links between U.S. and Canadian firms are paralleled by the affiliations between trade unions on both sides of the border. More than seven out of ten workers in Canada belong to international unions with headquarters in the United States. Indeed, the only Canadian unions of any size without American ties are the Canadian Brotherhood of Railway, Transport and General Workers, the Canadian Union of Public Employees, and the Catholic syndicates in the province of Québec.

The magnetic field of the southern neighbor is not confined just to economic matters. It is even more powerful in the realm of communications. The tremendous expansion of media in the United States has given that country the world's most penetrating and effective apparatus for the transmission of ideas. English Canada is wide open to that force. American words, images, and jingles — the good, the bad, the indifferent — batter unrelentingly at Canadian eyes and ears. Over 150 million copies of U.S. consumer magazines are sold annually in Canada against 46 million Canadian consumer magazines. By erecting tall antennas, about 45% of the population can pick up the U.S. television stations that line the border. Even those living farther away are not deprived of their share of American shows, because nearly half the programs on the CBC television network originate in the United States. Nor do the newspapers provide an effective counterbalance. The Canadian dailies are local in character, and most of them depend inordinately for their editorial material on the well-known U.S. columnists and the U.S. wire services.

As a result, English Canadians are well versed about the United States — its social problems, its local politics, and its foreign policy. They follow American sporting events, cheer American heroes, enjoy American movies, and adopt American trends, fads, and fashions. What is even more important is that the mass onslaught of American media makes English Canadians inadvertently and often unknowingly look at their own country through U.S. eyes and interpret behavior by U.S. standards. There is nothing one can do to check this incessant one-way inflow of ideas and culture. Those who feel that Canada, by legislative action, can hold back the American influence are not much different from the advisers who told King Canute that he could sweep back the tide with a broom.

DIFFERENCES

Despite all this, it would be wrong to assume that English Canada is merely a northern extension of the United States. There are some fundamental areas of difference, which seem to get lost in the outer semblance of similarity.

In the first place, the British influence is noticeable everywhere. Most cities have their King and Queen streets. The sovereign's picture is on the stamps, the coins, and the currency notes. The country's military services — the army, the navy, the air force — are all prefixed "royal." The courts are the Queen's courts, the main arteries are the King's highways, the public land is Crown land, and the federal statistical department is the Dominion Bureau of Statistics. Many English-speaking Canadians like fish and chips, wear British tweeds and woolens, religiously observe the afternoon tea ritual, and fondly refer to the United Kingdom as the "Old Country." They are also, like the British, reserved by nature and slow to take newcomers to their bosom. The casual acquaintanship, the easy use of first names, come awkwardly to them. But when they do strike a friendship, it is not likely to be fickle.

Furthermore, while an American is noted for his aggressiveness, the distinguishing trait of a Canadian is restraint, even humility. Distracted by the mossy grandeur of the old world across the Atlantic and the power and wealth of the new world to the south, the English Canadians are the first to deny and the last to realize their own significant achievements. Sometimes this humility degenerates into an exercise in national self-depreciation. Most well-known Canadians tend to accentuate the negative aspect of Canadian character.

"It would be overstatement to say that Canada consists entirely of second rate people, but by no means overstatement to say that it has never been oversupplied with first." (Arthur Lower)*

"Canada is a country as big as Paul Bunyan, but the inhabitants have the personality of a Tom Thumb." (President of a big corporation who chooses to remain anonymous.)

"We've had access to American know-how, British political wisdom, and French culture. Somehow we've managed to end up with British know-how, French political wisdom, and American culture." (Senior government official in a speech to visiting British journalists.)**

Thus, while the Americans talk in terms of superlatives, the Canadians indulge in Calvinistic masochism and torment themselves with ceaseless self-examination.

Another distinctive national trait is conservatism. One does not expect from Canadians unorthodox ideas, radical experiments, vivid imagination, nor a desire to shoot for the stars. But one does look to them for solid dependability, a realistic approach, an ability to get things done as the need arises. True, it is not rare to come across individuals in Toronto and Montréal who are ready to place a bet at the racetrack or gamble on the stock exchange. But in general Canadians are not too responsive to "something for nothing" or the "get rich quickly" philosophy.

This can be clearly seen in the monetary field. Canada's half dozen chartered banks are Gibraltars of financial solidity. Failures are virtually unknown, but venture capital for new and speculative enterprises is more difficult to get than

* Arthur Lower, "Are We Really a Second-Rate People?" *Maclean's,* August 2, 1958.
** Mervin Jones, *Toronto Daily Star,* December 11, 1965.

in the United States. The inhabitants, too, display a careful, frugal attitude toward money. Canadians take out more insurance per capita than any other nation in the world. They invest their savings in government bonds and gilt-edged securities, leaving the American investors to put their money in uncertain, but potentially profitable, new projects in mining and manufacturing fields.

The same note of caution and restraint is apparent in management-employee relations. A labor leader recently remarked: "Canadian unionists tend to be more conservative and accept authority more easily. They don't seek recourse to strike as fast as their American brothers. They are less aggressive, lower-keyed, more patient, more persevering. They are reluctant at the early stages of the crisis to do anything against management. In the United States there is animosity against authority that seems to be inbred."*

Geography has to a great extent shaped Canadian temperament. Although the main areas of settlement still amount to a long thin strip glued to the U.S. frontier, one cannot overlook the mystic appeal of the vast northland on the Canadian temperament. Everywhere the huge hinterland hangs like an immense backdrop behind a narrow stage, a window out onto the infinite. The North is always in people's minds. The line which marks off the frontier from the farmstead, the bush from the baseland, the wilderness from the metropolis, runs through every Canadian psyche. Canadian life to this day is marked by the northern qualities of sobriety, orderliness, and lack of exuberance.

Furthermore, while the United States has emerged into the rule of the organization man, Canada still remains in the opening-up period of development. As a result, a Canadian is apt to be more individualistic than the American; at any rate, the feeling for uniformity is far less pronounced. This is clearly noticeable in the strongly different lines taken by the various provinces. It is also evident in letting the minorities go their separate ways, in not interfering with their customs, traditions and religion. There is no indoctrination — at least, none compared to the process of Americanization in the United States. In Canada the varied folklore of the immigrants is often publicized as indication of the richness and diversity of the country's culture; in the United States the retaining of Old World habits is often stigmatized as refusal to become good Americans or to appreciate adequately the superiority of the "American way of life."

History, too, explains many of the traits in Canadian temperament. At no time in the past have the people been required to turn their backs on Europe or isolate themselves from it. Unlike their southern neighbor, Canadians achieved their autonomy without any violent rupture, without any inhibitions and resentments. Whereas the United States was the product of the revolutionary spirit, Canada grew mainly out of forces counter-revolutionary in character. The lack of such emotional experience has affected in many aspects the development of the English-Canadian society. It cannot boast of any great heroes or notorious

* Shirley Mair: "What Americans Really Think About Us," *Maclean's,* April 20, 1963.

villains, of epic victories or tragic defeats. It has no Washington or Lincoln, nor anything equivalent to Gettysburg or the Boston Tea Party. Placed next to the glowing preamble of the Declaration of Independence, the British North America Act is a cold and lifeless document. It is not, therefore, surprising that English Canada has no national song which the inhabitants can sing with pride, nor any national myth which they can pass on to their children and grandchildren.

Religion has also played a more important role in the development of Canada than of the United States. The political insecurity of the country, the rapid expansion of the neighbor to the south, and the deeply embedded ethnic dissensions among the population led to a considerable dependence upon religion as a force in maintaining community solidarity. Even today the principal churches own great properties and hold real power. The clergy take a strong stand on many public questions, try faithfully to guide the people, and influence the direction of education. The message offered is a rather conservative one, for Canada has not been deeply infiltrated by the comforting, semi-psychiatric, peace-of-mind doctrines popular in the United States. The ministers themselves stick to the traditional Gospel teaching. There is no fanaticism, but also little encouragement given to too liberal interpretation of religious tenets.

Because of all these differences, an English Canadian, despite an all but identical economy and the same mass media of communications, finds himself not an American. He does not react to problems in the same way. He is the product of the pragmatic nineteenth century rather than of the ideological eighteenth. What counts most in Canada is not life, liberty, and the pursuit of happiness, but peace, order and good government. As their history has made Americans primarily absolutists, so a different history has made Canadians primarily relativists in national and international politics.

For example, socialism worries Canadians far less than it does Americans. The controversy over TVA, which persists even today in the United States, puzzles Canadians. Ever since the efforts of John A. MacDonald in the last century to establish a transcontinental railway for the Dominion, the role of the state has always been positive and initiating. The Canadian government now operates the national broadcasting system, an international airline, and a national railroad. The provinces are taking over the ownership of hydro-electric power. Saskatchewan has a National Health Service.

PROSPECTS FOR POLITICAL UNION WITH THE U.S.

Are these differences strong enough to encourage Canadians to remain independent of the United States? In 1964, *Maclean's* engaged Montréal's *Groupe de Recherche Sociale* to undertake a depth survey to find out how many Canadians would be willing to merge with the United States. A sufficiently large sample of 1,042 adults was chosen at random from people living in non-farm areas. The age, income, occupational, geographic, and educational breakdown of the sample closely resembled the distribution of these characteristics in the Canadian population.

OPINIONS OF ADULT CANADIANS TO POLITICAL UNION
WITH THE U.S.A.

1. Percentage for and against merger

For
Strongly favor union	12%
Favor union	17

Neutral
Don't know	9

Against
Oppose union	21
Strongly oppose union	41

Total	100%

2. Percentage of people in each category who are for political union

By education
Primary school	42%
High school	30
University	20
Average	29%

By occupation
Employees	35%
Self-employed	26
Housewives	27
Students	25
Retired	17
Unemployed	47
Average	29%

By annual income
Below $3,000	43%
$3,000–$3,999	40
$4,000–$6,999	28
$7,000–$8,999	24
$9,000 and over	32
Average	29%

By regions
Maritimes	39%
Québec	33
Ontario	24
Prairies and B.C.	29
Average	29%

(Source: Maclean's, June 6, 1964.)

The highlights of the results are shown in the preceding table. The most significant fact to come out of the survey is that over two-thirds of adult Canadians are not prepared to become Americans. Among those who favor the merger, we find an above-average concentration of non-influentials: the under-educated, the unemployed, and the low-incomed. By regions, the highest percentage of would-be Americans are in the Maritimes, the lowest percentage in Ontario. While not shown in the table, the detailed tabulations also reveal that patriotic feeling seems to have little relation to the size of the community in which a Canadian lives, to his sex or age, or, surprisingly enough, to the number of generations his family has been in this country.

In judging the over-all significance of the findings, it is essential to remember that the survey was taken at a time when union with the United States was not a live political issue. The "Groupe de Recherche Sociale" scientists are quick to point out that if one of the major political parties were to adopt a strong pro or anti line in an election campaign, the percentages could swing violently. Another important fact the survey did not touch upon — and it is a question that many are secretly afraid to ask — is how English Canada would consider union with the United States if ever Québec should decide to secede and establish a separate state.

BIBLIOGRAPHY OF ENGLISH CANADA

Berton, Pierre: "Canada: The Land and the People," in *Britannica Book of the Year, 1956,* Encyclopedia Britannica Inc., Chicago.

Chapin, Miriam: *Contemporary Canada,* Oxford University Press, New York, 1959.

Clark, S. D.: *The Developing Canadian Community,* The University of Toronto Press, Toronto, 1962.

Holiday, April 1964. An entire issue on Canada. Especially the article by V. S. Pritchett: "Across the Vast Land."

Horne, Alistair: *Canada and the Canadians,* The Macmillan Company of Canada, Limited, Toronto, 1961.

Hutchinson, Bruce: "The Canadian Personality," in Malcom Ross (ed.): *Our Sense of Identity,* The Ryerson Press, Toronto, 1954.

Laskin, Richard (editor): *Social Problems: a Canadian Profile,* McGraw-Hill Company of Canada, Limited, Toronto, 1964.

Lower, Arthur: *Canadians in the Making,* Longmans, Green and Company, Toronto, 1958.

Mair, Shirley: "What Americans Really Think About Us", *Maclean's,* April 20, 1963.

Morton, W. L.: *The Canadian Identity,* The University of Toronto Press, Toronto, 1961.

Newman, Peter C.: "The U.S. and Us", *Maclean's,* June, 1964.

Chapter 13

MOSAIC BY URBAN-RURAL RESIDENTS

Characteristics of Urban and Rural Living

The place of residence affects to a considerable extent an individual's personality and his outlook towards life. Few who study the characteristics of rural and urban areas can fail to notice the influence of environmental factors in molding the character of the residents. Some outstanding features of rural society are: a preponderance of workers in primary industries (farming, fishing, lumbering), a low man-to-land ratio, small population aggregates or communities, and a high degree of ethnic homogeneity. The rural inhabitant has relatively few outside contacts, and those he does have are restricted to limited geographical and social spheres. Besides, nature in all its benevolent and its malevolent aspects impinges directly upon him, whereas the urban resident has a thick shield of manmade culture between him and nature.

Both cities and villages have their strong and weak points. Urbanism brings congestion, noise, nervous strains, psychological isolation, and other adverse environmental influences. But urban living also implies numerous cultural contacts, opportunities to specialize, the possibility of being selective of associates.

For country residents, the low density of population has many advantages. It means that fresh air is abundant — air that has not been contaminated by soot and smoke nor by the fumes from the exhausts of automobiles. Rural life likewise is conducive to intimate social ties; people are regarded as individuals, not as pawns to be manipulated for personal ends. Furthermore, there are fewer extremes of wealth and poverty; the rural social pyramid neither sinks so low nor rises so high as the urban one.

However, there is also the other side of the coin. Small communities cannot support up-to-date schools, churches and hospitals. Cultural exchanges are rare and modern conveniences costly. The class system, too, is much more rigid than in cities. Intimate social contacts make a person's antecedents well known to all members of the community. Hence, movement from one class to another is not easy, and an individual's position is largely determined by the status of his immediate ancestors.

URBAN-RURAL DICHOTOMY

Typical metropolitan life	*Typical village life*
1. Families operate as democratic units, with authority shared collectively by husband and wife.	1. A patriarchal system is generally prevalent, though not as rigid as before.

Typical metropolitan life

2. The family is not an economic unit. Specialized agencies (schools, clubs, restaurants, laundries) have taken over many of the former family functions.

3. Family members have different occupations and belong to diverse outside groups. There is a transitory attitude towards one's job.

4. The ties between family and relatives are weak, as witnessed by the absence of the spare bedroom in new city apartments.

5. Cities are centers of learning, invention, art, and culture. The "city mentality" is characterized by sophistication, utilitarianism, and rationalism. Sacred beliefs and practices are secularized; fashions and tastes are democratized; new opportunities are open for man to shape his destiny.

6. Urban living resembles a swiftly moving river whose water churns about incessantly. Mobility is the watchword. City residents are not rooted to their ancestral nests and quite easily pick up stakes to follow opportunity elsewhere.

7. The freedom, diversity, anonymity, and excitement of urban life tend to encourage hedonism.

8. Culturally, most big cities are a babel of all types of political, occupational, educational, and religious groups. The population includes a sprinkling of peoples from all corners of the earth, often speaking different languages, following different customs, habituated to different modes and standards of living, and sharing only in a limited way the tastes, beliefs and ideals of native-born citizens.

Typical village life

2. The family produces most of its own food, fuel, and even clothing. The specialized agencies are not yet fully effective.

3. All members work on the same farm throughout their life, and they participate in outside groups on a family basis.

4. Kinship is the basic bond. Relatives stick together closely, even though not living under the same roof.

5. The country is the preserver of tradition, the conservative part of the nation that clings tenaciously to the customary ways of doing things. Rural society has a long memory and is so fully engrossed in the "traditions of our forefathers" that it can hardly refrain from respecting them.

6. A rural community may be likened to a quiet pond with tiny streams meandering in and out of it. Stability is the basic trait. The inhabitants are not mobile—either horizontally from one place to another, or vertically from one social class to the next.

7. The rural pattern of living, with its stress on hard work, is conducive to self-denial and restraint.

8. Rural life is based on similarities, the sameness that results from common traits and experience, the type of cohesion which sociologists call "consciousness of kind." The individual sees mostly those who live in close proximity to him—persons of much the same economic and cultural attainments, whose mores, religious beliefs, and general behavior patterns are very similar to his own.

9. Despite its heterogeneity and complexity, a metropolis is noted for its high degree of integration and co-ordination. Through division of labor and specialization, each part is mutually interdependent with every other. The downtown business area, the industrial districts, the slums, the better located residential sections, and even the suburban fringes are all part of a functioning whole.

10. Cities set a premium upon innovation and change; hence they are ideal for introduction of new products or new methods of retailing, such as self-service and self-selection.

9. Rural society is made up of numerous small, relatively independent units—families, neighborhoods, communities. It does not function as a single entity. Any unity that it has is based mainly on similarities and not on mutual interdependence brought about by the division of labor. As a result, it is often difficult to secure concerted action on the part of the rural population.

10. New products are not readily accepted, and changes in distribution are slow. The general store is the most important retail outlet as well as the major social center.

INDICATIONS OF POVERTY AND GENERAL STANDARD OF LIVING, 1965

	Canada (%)	Urban			Rural		
		Total urban (%)	Large urban (%)	Small urban (%)	Total rural (%)	Non-farm (%)	Farm (%)
Indications of poverty							
% of total households in the area living in dwellings that are:							
With no water piped inside	6.1	1.7	0.3	4.8	18.8	13.5	28.3
Without installed bath facilities	12.8	5.4	2.4	12.5	33.6	27.0	45.5
Without flush toilet facilities	9.5	2.8	0.8	7.7	28.2	21.1	41.1
General standard of living							
% of total households in the area with:							
Electric stoves	69.0	72.8	74.4	68.9	58.3	62.6	50.5
Piped gas stoves	14.1	17.8	20.6	11.2	3.7	4.6	2.0
Electric refrigerators	95.8	97.8	98.5	96.3	90.0	91.0	87.9
Home freezers	22.6	16.8	14.0	23.5	39.1	28.9	57.6
Automatic washers	23.1	26.3	28.0	22.1	14.0	17.9	7.0
Other electric washers	63.2	58.4	53.9	69.2	76.6	72.7	83.7
Electric clothes dryers	25.2	25.3	24.8	26.6	25.0	27.5	20.4
One telephone	76.2	77.5	77.1	78.4	72.6	71.3	75.0
Two or more telephones	13.2	15.5	17.6	10.5	6.7	8.7	3.2
TV sets	92.6	94.5	95.3	92.5	87.4	89.1	84.2
One automobile	62.5	60.9	59.2	64.9	67.1	65.1	70.6
Two or more automobiles	12.4	12.0	13.0	9.5	13.7	13.6	14.0

Note: "Large urban" includes cities of 30,000 population and over and their satellite communities. "Small urban" includes incorporated urban centers of under 30,000 population.

(Source: DBS, *Household Facilities and Equipment, May, 1965*. Special tabulations, catalogue no. 64-202.)

SOCIO-ECONOMIC CHARACTERISTICS OF URBAN-RURAL INHABITANTS

	Canada	Urban					Rural		
		Total urban	100,000 & over	30,000–99,999	10,000–29,999	1,000–9,999	Total rural	Non-farm	Farm
Sex									
Male	50.5%	49.5%	49.4%	49.6%	49.7%	50.0%	52.9%	52.2%	54.0%
Female	49.5	50.5	50.6	50.4	50.3	50.0	47.1	47.8	46.0
Total	100.0%	100.0%	100.0%	100.0%	100.0%	100.0%	100.0%	100.0%	100.0%
Number of persons (000)	18,238	12,700	7,924	1,705	1,049	2,022	5,538	3,465	2,073
Age groups									
Under 15	34.0%	32.2%	30.8%	33.7%	34.4%	35.3%	38.0%	38.5%	37.3%
15–24	14.3	14.2	13.8	14.9	15.1	14.6	14.7	14.1	15.7
25–44	26.7	28.3	29.6	27.3	26.4	25.1	23.0	23.9	21.4
45–64	17.4	17.7	18.3	17.1	16.7	16.4	16.7	15.2	19.1
Over 64	7.6	7.6	7.5	7.0	7.4	8.6	7.6	8.3	6.5
Total	100.0%	100.0%	100.0%	100.0%	100.0%	100.0%	100.0%	100.0%	100.0%
Number of persons (000)	18,238	12,700	7,924	1,705	1,049	2,022	5,538	3,465	2,073

(Source: DBS, *Census of Canada, 1961*. Bulletin 92-542.)

	Canada	Total urban	100,000 & over	30,000–99,999	10,000–29,999	1,000–9,999	Total rural	Non-farm	Farm
Size of household									
Very small (1)	9.3%	9.2%	9.4%	7.8%	8.7%	9.6%	9.7%	11.5%	6.2%
Small (2)	22.2	23.0	23.5	22.0	22.1	22.7	20.1	21.8	17.0
Medium (3–4)	36.2	37.8	38.5	38.4	37.2	34.8	31.8	31.2	32.8
Large (5–8)	28.7	27.4	26.4	29.1	28.9	29.2	32.1	29.9	36.3
Very large (over 8)	3.6	2.6	2.2	2.7	3.1	3.7	6.3	5.6	7.7
Total	100.0%	100.0%	100.0%	100.0%	100.0%	100.0%	100.0%	100.0%	100.0%
Number of households (000)	4,554	3,280	2,089	428	262	501	1,274	824	450
Average size of household	3.9	3.7	3.7	3.8	3.8	3.9	4.2	4.0	4.6
Average number of children	1.9	1.7	1.6	1.8	1.9	2.0	2.3	2.2	2.4

(Source: DBS, *Census of Canada, 1961*. Bulletin 93-510.)

Fertility ratio

(Number of children 0–4 to 1,000 women in the age group of 15–44)								
606	556	527	572	595	645	748	785	681

(Source: DBS, *Census of Canada, 1961*. Bulletin 92-542.)

Educational level of adults

No schooling	5.7%	4.4%	3.9%	4.5%	5.3%	6.0%	8.8%	9.5%	7.6%
Elementary: below 5	7.7	6.3	5.8	6.5	6.8	8.1	11.2	11.6	10.3
over 5	35.9	32.9	31.2	35.6	33.8	37.0	43.4	40.1	49.0
Secondary: 1–2	20.7	21.6	21.6	21.9	22.5	21.0	18.6	19.0	17.9
3–4	17.9	20.2	21.0	19.8	20.2	17.3	12.1	13.0	10.7
5	6.3	7.6	8.5	6.2	6.2	5.5	3.2	3.5	2.7
University: 1–2	2.2	2.5	2.8	2.0	2.1	2.0	1.4	1.6	1.2
3–4	0.8	0.9	1.0	0.7	0.7	0.7	0.4	0.5	0.2
degree	2.8	3.6	4.2	2.8	2.4	2.4	0.9	1.2	0.4
Total	100.0%	100.0%	100.0%	100.0%	100.0%	100.0%	100.0%	100.0%	100.0%
Number of persons (000)	11,615	8,256	5,263	1,072	661	1,260	3,359	2,111	1,248

(Source: DBS, *Census of Canada, 1961*. Bulletin 92-550.)

Native and foreign born

Immigrants								
Before 1946	7.3%	7.9%	9.0%	6.8%	6.4%	5.9%	5.9%	5.4%	6.7%
1946–1955	4.8	5.8	7.1	4.6	3.3	2.8	2.5	2.4	2.5
1956–1961	3.5	4.5	5.8	2.8	2.0	1.8	1.2	1.5	0.8
Born in Canada	84.4	81.8	78.1	85.8	88.3	89.5	90.4	90.7	90.0
Total	100.0%	100.0%	100.0%	100.0%	100.0%	100.0%	100.0%	100.0%	100.0%
Number of persons (000)	18,238	12,700	7,924	1,705	1,049	2,022	5,538	3,465	2,073

(Source: DBS, *Census of Canada, 1961*. Bulletins 92-547 and 92-548.)

HOUSING CHARACTERISTICS OF URBAN-RURAL INHABITANTS

| | Canada | Urban | | | | | Rural | | |
		Total urban	100,000 & over	30,000 -99,999	10,000 -29,999	1,000 -9,999	Total rural	Non-farm	Farm
Housing status									
Own home	66.0	59.3	56.4	61.1	63.0	68.2	83.1	77.8	93.0
Pay rent	34.0	40.7	43.6	38.9	37.0	31.8	16.9	22.2	7.0
Total	100.0%	100.0%	100.0%	100.0%	100.0%	100.0%	100.0%	100.0%	100.0%
Number of households (000)	4,554	3,280	2,089	428	262	501	1,274	824	450
Median value of non-farm home ($)	11,021	12,864	14,818	11,679	10,280	8,527	5,495	5,495	—
Average monthly rent, non-farm ($)	65	68	75	56	54	48	35	35	—

(Source: DBS, *Census of Canada, 1961.* Bulletin 93-523.)

	Canada	Total urban	100,000 & over	30,000 -99,999	10,000 -29,999	1,000 -9,999	Total rural	Non-farm	Farm
Length of occupancy									
Less than one year	15.3	17.2	18.0	16.3	16.7	15.3	10.4	13.6	4.4
1–2 years	16.8	18.8	19.9	17.5	17.3	16.0	11.5	14.4	6.1
3–5 years	19.9	21.5	22.3	20.6	20.1	19.8	15.9	18.9	10.3
6–10 years	16.6	17.0	17.1	17.5	16.4	16.5	15.6	16.6	13.9
More than 10 years	31.4	25.5	22.7	28.1	29.5	32.4	46.6	36.5	65.3
Total	100.0%	100.0%	100.0%	100.0%	100.0%	100.0%	100.0%	100.0%	100.0%
Number of households (000)	4,554	3,280	2,089	428	262	501	1,274	824	450

(Source: DBS, *Census of Canada, 1961.* Bulletin 93-523.)

	Canada	Total urban	100,000 & over	30,000 -99,999	10,000 -29,999	1,000 -9,999	Total rural	Non-farm	Farm
Period of construction									
Before 1920	30.6	27.7	25.3	28.5	31.3	35.0	38.0	30.3	52.1
1920–1945	25.2	25.2	25.2	28.0	25.2	23.2	25.1	24.4	26.4
1946–1959	40.5	43.3	45.4	40.3	40.3	38.4	33.5	40.8	19.9
1960–1961	3.7	3.8	4.1	3.2	3.2	3.4	3.4	4.5	1.6
Total	100.0%	100.0%	100.0%	100.0%	100.0%	100.0%	100.0%	100.0%	100.0%
Number of households (000)	4,554	3,280	2,089	428	262	501	1,274	824	450

(Source: DBS, *Census of Canada, 1961.* Bulletin 93-523.)

Metropolitan Areas

At the beginning of this century, the rural way of life set the pattern for practically the whole of the country. Today, it is confined to a few isolated hamlets and villages situated hundreds of miles away from the hustle and bustle of big cities. Canada is fast becoming a predominantly urban community, and it is the city that in a majority of cases sets the tune. In fact, with the rapid development of transportation and communications, the metropolitan area is able to dominate the life and culture of "rural" localities 50 to 75 miles around. Such communities are merely satellite areas and follow the lead of the big cities. Their inhabitants watch the same TV shows as city folks, read the same newspapers and magazines, shop downtown for the same goods and services, and send their sons and daughters to the same universities.

Throughout the last two decades, there has been a steady movement of population into metropolitan areas, a phenomenon associated with the increasing industrialization of the country and the relative decline in the importance of agriculture in the nation's economy. Even in the once quiet prairie farmlands, the big cities are making rapid headway. In Saskatchewan, the leading agricultural province, 89% of the population gain, between 1951 and 1964, came from Regina and Saskatoon. Calgary and Edmonton together accounted for 74% of Alberta's growth during the same period, while Winnipeg was responsible for 72% of Manitoba's upsurge. In fact, the big cities now constitute the basic milieu of Canadian life. This is where the destiny of the nation is decided for better or for worse.

The metropolis is not static. There is always some change going on. In recent years, the greatest growth has been in the peripheral zones. For example, Toronto's central city population in the 1951-61 period showed an actual decline of 1%, while the adjoining communities boasted a 114% gain. The pattern was roughly the same in other big metropolitan areas. The suburban population around Montréal soared 91%, while the central city trailed behind with only a 17% increase. Vancouver's satellite area outpaced the city's core with a population gain of 87% vs. 12%; Winnipeg's suburbs increased 75% vs. 13%; Hamilton's, 131% vs. 19%.

Suburbia

The outward migration from the city had already started in the Thirties, but since the Fifties it has practically turned into a stampede. Freed by the automobile and the highways, the burgeoning middle-income families have burst out of the concrete jungle to find homes where land is greener and cheaper. New settlements have spread across acre upon acre, straddling the rocky hillocks, dipping into ravines and woodlands, and inundating the flatlands that were once farms and pastures. Here the nation's young families are staking out their claims across the landscape, prospecting on a trial-and-error basis for the good way of life for themselves and their children. The decentralization of industry has further accelerated the trend. Many factories have moved from downtown congestion to fringe locations where they can obtain more land at a lower rate for efficient one-story building layouts. This has forced the blue-collar workers to migrate to suburbs in order to remain closer to their jobs. In fact, so great has been the exodus from the city that one sociologist has even stated: "There is very little 'sub' about this new urbia; it's the prototype of the urban form which will dominate the life of our children. Eventually the big cities would become empty holes surrounded by vast suburban doughnuts."

The influences of suburbia have been far reaching, many with important implications for marketing. The suburbs have made ranch houses popular, kept whole factories busy making lawn and garden furniture, widened the market for station wagons, and promoted the concept of two cars in every garage. It is the suburbanites, not the city dwellers, who have started the current trends in mass fashion — casual dresses, vodka martinis, outdoor barbecues, functional furniture, and picture windows. By virtue of his location, the suburban dweller finds it inconvenient to buy in downtown areas. This has led to the development of shopping centers and branch stores, as retailers have tended to move closer to their customers. In turn, the wholesalers have started to leave the dilapidated warehousing areas in the central cities and to relocate in the outlying zones, especially near fast expressways. Hence, it would not be an exaggeration to say that suburbia is the focus of most of the forces that are remaking Canadian life today.

Suburban society is neither urban nor rural but possesses the characteristics of both. One basic trait that colors its other preferences and habits is its propensity for having children. In 1961, the census shows quite striking differences in fertility ratio between the central and fringe city areas. (See p. 325, last line.) As a result, the children set much of the pattern of life. Their wants are the family's wants, and even their friendships are the family's friendships. "The kids are the only ones who are organized here," says a resident of a suburb near Toronto. "We older people sort of tag along after them." This child-oriented life affects marketing in many ways. Not only does it increase the demand for toys, tricycles, infant foods, and other items used by children, but it also calls for sturdy furniture and furnishings that would stand hard beating from the youngsters. Concern for the offspring is also one of the main reasons why most dwellings are single units rather than apartments, and why suburbanites generally prefer an informal mode of living with emphasis on the outdoors.

Not all suburbs are alike, but they are more alike than different, and certain neighborhoods are remarkably homogeneous. They seem to encourage birds-of-a-feather flocking, screening out equal elements from the urban population, so that social peers — that is, those whose occupations, income, tastes, and life styles are quite similar — come to be attracted to the same niche. This homology has allowed, indeed encouraged, an emphasis on status that is not possible in the city with its juxtaposed settlement of divergent social strata in the same residential area.

Group uniformity is the rule in the suburbs. Social pressures determine when a luxury becomes a necessity. The process works somewhat as follows. First, a few families in the block who have established themselves as "leaders" acquire, say, a new stereophonic set and start talking about its advantages. In the course of time, more and more families follow their example. Eventually it becomes almost an unsocial act not to own one, a sort of unspoken aspersion on others' good judgment and taste. Under such circumstances, only the resolute individualists can hold out. Item by item, this process is constantly repeated. As soon as a certain range of products becomes standard in the neighborhood, the leaders start again the cycle of creating a new necessity.

No picture of suburbia would be complete without a mention of the dominant role played by the housewife. She is the thread that weaves between the family and the community. In the absence of her commuting husband, she is first of all the manager of home and children. In addition, she is an active civic participant with a penchant for keeping the community kettle whistling. She fills her spare time with church meetings, PTA projects and study groups, and takes every opportunity to prod her husband to participate in charity drives or local committees campaigning for better schools, hospitals and roads.

One should not, of course, overlook the many drawbacks of suburban life: the fatiguing and expensive daily trip to and from work; the onerous burden of mortgage payments and mounting property taxes; the loneliness of subdivision life; and, above all, the trials and tribulations of "keeping up the place" — from repairing the leaking basement and patching up the roof to shoveling the sidewalks and plucking the crabgrass. However, to most families with young children, the advantages which suburbia offers by far offset its drawbacks. Hence, the exodus from the core of the city continues.

The Inner City

In view of the outflow into the suburbs, the inner city is becoming more and more a place of residence for mainly the following types of people:

• The cosmopolites, such as students, artists, writers, musicians, entertainers, as well as other intellectuals and professionals, who live near the downtown area in order to be near the cultural attractions.

• Single persons as well as childless couples who rent apartments in order to be close to job or entertainment opportunities.

• The affluent who want to live comfortably in luxurious apartments rather than put up with the chores of home ownership.

- The ethnic groups, especially the newly-arrived immigrants, who stick close to their fellow countrymen so that the adjustment to a new life is psychologically less severe.

- The underprivileged, the very poor, the widowed mothers with small children, the elderly living out their existence on small fortunes — all of whom are forced to reside in the dilapidated dwellings and blighted neighborhoods found mostly in the inner core of the cities.

Despite the urban renewal projects and the drastic surgery going on to put new life into the dying central districts, it is doubtful that the city proper will be able to regain its past pre-eminence. To more and more families, the downtown spells dirt, dust and noise, instead of culture and opportunity. Driving is particularly frustrating. (In 1906, a horse and buggy could move up Yonge Street in Toronto at a rate of 11 m.p.h. Sixty years later, during the rush hours, the average car makes the same trip at 10 m.p.h.) Consequently, while some people will still escape from the small town to the city, even more people may be expected to migrate from the city to the suburbs. The reasons for their going are far too basic to be erased by a slum clearance program or a plan for the beautification of a downtown area. In the case of industry seeking land for horizontal layout and plant expansion, these reasons proceed from physical necessity; in the case of families searching for fresh air, green grass, and the relatively open spaces, these reasons reflect the inherent desire of all parents to rear their children in pleasant surroundings; in the case of retail outlets moving into shopping centers on the city's periphery, these reasons make good economics — to seek a market where the consumer is.

The Megalopolis

Not only is the population spilling out from the cities, but the areas between previously distinct and separate metropolitan centers are being filled in to form a lacy chain of closely related units. Just as the inner cities and the ring communities in the Fifties became socially and economically integrated into metropolitan markets, so the expanding metro areas themselves are starting to form huge urban complexes. For this new type of phenomenon, the name "megalopolis" has been popularized by Professor Jean Gottman of the University of Paris, whose highly influential study, entitled *Megalopolis,* was published in 1961 by the Twentieth Century Fund. The ancient Greeks had given that name to a community in the Peloponnesus that they had intended to build into a giant city-state. Their hopes died, but in North America that dream has come true now.

The megalopolis, sometimes also called interurbia, is seen at its best in the United States. The finest example is the 500-mile area stretching unbroken from Boston to Washington. Other such urban complexes are along the California coast from San Francisco to the Mexican border, and around Lower Lake

Michigan, from southern Wisconsin to northern Indiana. In Canada, the trend is in its infancy, but outlines of urban clusters are already visible, albeit sketchily, from Québec City to Windsor.* This 700-mile strip embraces eight bustling metropolitan centers and is a modern-day Mecca for a goodly number of migrants from abroad as well as from other parts of the country. Already it accounts for more than half of the nation's population, nearly two-thirds of the households with annual incomes of over $10,000, and over seven-tenths of the value of manufacturing shipments.

The counters of this megalopolis will become more clearly etched as Canada marches towards its urban destiny. Many of the same factors which first spawned then spurred metropolitan area growth, will carry these markets further into the age of interurbia. Here are some of the most obvious and potent thrusts behind the gestation:

• The growing ownership of automobiles and the completion or extension of major highways will make it possible for more and more families to live in communities scattered over a wide area.

• Along with people, industry will trek to the suburbs and beyond. Automation, especially, will accelerate decentralization, since the need for central city's vast unskilled and semiskilled labor pools will be reduced.

• As older suburbs get congested and start reeling under mounting tax rates, those who yearn for "breathing space" and lower priced homes will tend to move farther away, filling the less densely populated counties that lie athwart the way of expanding metros.

In short, the trend is toward an urban culture spreading amoebalike over open land, seemingly shapeless in its form, fluid at its boundaries, and in its cellular structure capable of infinite reproduction. This means that one will have to abandon the idea of the metropolitan center as a tightly settled and organized unit in which people, wealth and activities are crowded into a very small area clearly separated from nonurban surroundings. In the interurbia of the future, the city and the country will be inextricably intertwined; but the predominant

---

* This huge Québec City-Windsor megalopolis may be divided into three parts:

1) *Montréal-Québec Interurbia,* comprising the following economic regions: Metro Québec-Eastern Laurentides; Trois Rivières-St. Maurice Valley; Sherbrooke-Eastern Townships; and Metro Montréal and its Environs.

2) *Ottawa-Eastern Ontario Interurbia,* comprising the following economic regions: Ottawa-Ottawa Valley + Hull-Western Laurentides (in Québec Province); and Kingston-Upper St. Lawrence.

3) *Southwestern Ontario Interurbia,* comprising the following economic regions: Peterborough-Central Lake Ontario; Metro Toronto and its Environs; Hamilton/St. Catharines-Niagara; London-Lake Erie; Windsor/Sarnia-Lake St. Clair; and Kitchener-Midlands.

For the counties included in each of these economic regions see page 336 in Part III.

atmosphere will be urban rather than rural. The people will live and think like city people, not like farmers, fishermen or lumbermen. No doubt, farming will be prevalent in the megalopolis to feed the cities and provide raw materials for their factories. Yet agriculture will be only a part of the integrated whole. A large portion of the land now in fields and woodlands will also be used for urban activities — parks, playgrounds, golf courses, reservations surrounding water reservoirs, and landscaped areas around luxurious homes.

BIBLIOGRAPHY

Dakin, A. J.: "The Megalopolitan Monster," *The Globe Magazine, The Globe and Mail,* Toronto, September 11, 1965.

Elias Jr., C. E.; James Gillies; Svend Riemer (editors): *Metropolis: Values in Conflict,* Wadsworth Publishing, Inc., Belmont, California, 1964.

Eriksen, Gordon E.: *Urban Behavior,* Macmillan Company, New York, 1954.

Hauser, Philip M.: *Population Perspectives,* Rutgers University Press, New Brunswick, New Jersey, 1960.

Sales Management: "Interurbia," November 10, 1964.

Time: "Americana," June 20, 1960.

Time: "Cities," March 23, 1962 and November 6, 1964.

Smith, Lynn T.; C. A. McMahan: *The Sociology of Urban Life,* The Dryden Press, New York.

Whyte, William H.: *The Organization Man,* Simon and Schuster, Inc., 1956.

SOCIO-ECONOMIC CHARACTERISTICS OF SELECTED CITIES AND SUBURBS

	Canadian Average	Montréal City	Montréal Suburbs	Toronto City	Toronto Suburbs	Vancouver City	Vancouver Suburbs	Winnipeg City	Winnipeg Suburbs
Families by age of head									
Under 25	4.5%	4.3%	3.8%	4.4%	4.0%	3.6%	3.9%	5.5%	3.6%
25–34	23.1	24.3	27.2	23.3	26.0	18.5	23.8	20.7	25.1
35–44	25.4	24.3	29.3	23.2	28.9	22.3	27.8	22.4	28.7
45–54	20.9	21.5	20.6	19.7	21.1	22.9	21.0	20.7	20.8
55–64	13.6	14.9	11.3	15.2	11.8	15.1	11.2	14.7	11.4
65 and over	12.5	10.7	7.8	14.2	8.2	17.6	12.3	16.0	10.4
Total	100.0%	100.0%	100.0%	100.0%	100.0%	100.0%	100.0%	100.0%	100.0%
Number of families (000)	4,147	282	209	163	304	96	101	66	52

(Source: DBS, *Census of Canada, 1961.* Bulletin 93-515.)

	Canadian Average	Montréal City	Montréal Suburbs	Toronto City	Toronto Suburbs	Vancouver City	Vancouver Suburbs	Winnipeg City	Winnipeg Suburbs
Size of household									
Very small (1)	9.3%	11.7%	4.7%	13.8%	5.4%	17.2%	8.8%	12.6%	5.4%
Small (2)	22.2	24.8	18.7	25.5	23.3	30.3	24.4	26.8	21.3
Medium (3–4)	36.2	38.2	41.5	31.2	43.7	33.5	39.8	36.1	42.8
Large (5–8)	28.7	23.4	30.1	24.6	26.3	18.0	26.1	22.5	29.3
Very large (over 8)	3.6	1.9	5.0	4.9	1.3	1.0	0.9	2.0	1.2
Total	100.0%	100.0%	100.0%	100.0%	100.0%	100.0%	100.0%	100.0%	100.0%
Number of households (000)	4,555	330	220	173	310	118	110	74	54
Average size of household	3.9	3.5	4.0	3.7	3.7	3.1	3.6	3.4	3.8
Average no. of children in families	1.9	1.5	1.9	1.2	1.5	1.2	1.6	1.4	1.8
Fertility ratio	606	434	615	423	550	405	610	442	606

(Source: DBS, *Census of Canada, 1961.* Bulletins 93-510, 93-514 and 92-542.)

SOCIO-ECONOMIC CHARACTERISTICS OF SELECTED CITIES AND SUBURBS (continued)

	Canadian Average	Montréal City	Montréal Suburbs	Toronto City	Toronto Suburbs	Vancouver City	Vancouver Suburbs	Winnipeg City	Winnipeg Suburbs
Income of family households (non-farm)									
Under $2,000	11.7%	8.5%	5.6%	9.9%	3.8%	10.3%	9.5%	9.1%	5.3%
$2,000–$2,999	10.2	9.8	6.3	9.4	4.2	8.5	6.7	8.8	5.6
$3,000–$3,999	15.0	17.8	13.9	15.1	8.7	12.4	10.3	15.8	11.8
$4,000–$4,999	16.7	17.8	16.6	16.5	13.8	15.7	16.1	18.6	19.6
$5,000–$5,999	14.0	13.6	14.8	13.2	16.2	14.2	16.9	14.6	17.6
$6,000–$6,999	9.9	9.1	10.5	10.0	13.5	11.3	13.3	10.2	12.9
$7,000–$9,999	14.3	14.3	17.8	15.5	24.8	17.4	18.4	13.8	18.4
$10,000–$14,999	5.5	6.3	8.8	6.6	10.2	6.7	6.1	5.8	6.1
$15,000 and over	2.7	2.8	5.7	3.8	4.8	3.5	2.7	3.3	2.7
Total	100.0%	100.0%	100.0%	100.0%	100.0%	100.0%	100.0%	100.0%	100.0%
Number of households (000)	3,505	265	199	128	279	90	95	59	49
Average income per household	5,559	5,647	6,910	6,035	7,267	6,084	5,979	5,863	6,167

(Source: DBS, *Census of Canada, 1961.* Bulletin 98-506.)

	Canadian Average	Montréal City	Montréal Suburbs	Toronto City	Toronto Suburbs	Vancouver City	Vancouver Suburbs	Winnipeg City	Winnipeg Suburbs
Educational level									
No schooling	5.7%	4.2%	5.7%	2.8%	2.6%	3.2%	5.4%	3.6%	5.3%
Elementary	43.6	47.1	38.0	45.9	31.2	30.9	26.2	32.8	25.7
Secondary	44.9	42.2	47.3	43.8	57.6	56.3	59.6	55.2	60.7
Some university	3.0	3.2	4.1	3.3	3.6	5.4	5.2	4.7	4.8
University degree	2.8	3.3	4.9	4.2	5.0	4.2	3.6	3.7	3.5
Total	100.0%	100.0%	100.0%	100.0%	100.0%	100.0%	100.0%	100.0%	100.0%
No. of persons 5 years of age and over not attending school (000)	11,615	850	579	495	740	279	259	185	131

(Source: DBS, *Census of Canada, 1961.* Bulletin 92-550.)

SOCIO-ECONOMIC CHARACTERISTICS OF SELECTED CITIES AND SUBURBS (continued)

	Canadian Average	Montréal		Toronto		Vancouver		Winnipeg	
		City	Suburbs	City	Suburbs	City	Suburbs	City	Suburbs
Occupation									
White collar									
Managerial	8.3%	7.4%	11.7%	6.2%	12.7%	9.6%	11.5%	7.3%	10.6%
Professional and technical	9.7	10.3	13.0	9.8	12.0	10.8	11.1	9.9	10.7
Clerical	12.9	17.8	16.6	20.6	20.7	18.4	13.9	19.9	19.5
Sales	6.3	6.6	7.3	5.9	8.8	8.4	9.2	7.0	9.1
Blue collar									
Craftsmen, production process, etc	24.1	30.1	27.4	26.9	25.6	22.3	25.4	24.2	22.9
Unskilled laborers	4.9	5.0	3.6	5.5	3.1	3.8	4.3	5.4	3.8
Other occupations									
Service and recreation	12.3	12.5	10.0	15.8	8.7	15.2	10.9	16.4	12.7
Transport and communications	6.1	6.9	6.5	5.5	5.4	6.2	6.7	6.5	7.1
Farmers and gardeners	10.0	0.4	1.0	0.6	1.3	0.9	2.4	0.7	1.6
Other primary industries	2.8	0.1	0.1	0.1	0.1	1.3	1.8	0.1	0.1
Not stated	2.6	2.9	2.8	3.1	1.6	3.1	2.8	2.6	1.9
Total	100.0%	100.0%	100.0%	100.0%	100.0%	100.0%	100.0%	100.0%	100.0%
No. of persons in labor force (000)	6,472	495	312	320	469	159	136	116	78

(Source: DBS, *Census of Canada, 1961.* Bulletin 94-504.)

PART THREE

REGIONAL ANALYSIS

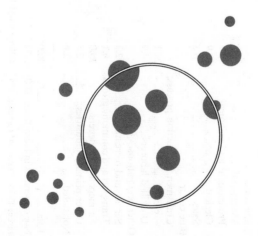

INTRODUCTION: THE NEED AND
VALUE OF REGIONAL ANALYSIS

"Know your country better" is the slogan of the federal and provincial tourist bureaux. Every year thousands of Canadian families spend their vacation driving through different regions of the country. Often when looking out of the car window, they wish they knew more about the basic characteristics of the localities they are passing. How do the inhabitants earn their living? What products do the leading factories make? Are the employment opportunities good, or is the economy sliding downhill?

These questions are also the kind of queries that plague many businessmen in their daily tasks. Take, for example, a sales manager in the head office in Montréal or Toronto. On any typical day, his in-coming basket is piled up with memos and correspondence awaiting his attention. Possibly one of the letters is from the Pacific regional manager. He recommends a raise for his salesman in Prince George because of his exceptional performance in the period just ended.

How does one know that the raise is justified? Was the quota realistically set, taking into account the sharp increase in population of the area? Did that district receive its normal share of advertising and promotion, or did the company overspend there in relation to the potential?

Another letter may be from the Atlantic Provinces regional manager. It seems that in Sydney a local competitor, long dormant, has suddenly come to life. Can an extra salesman be hired quickly to meet this competition?

Once again the questions start bubbling up to the surface. What is the size of the market in Cape Breton Island? Is it worthwhile to increase sales pressure there? Or would it be better to cultivate more intensively some other area of greater potential?

Marketing men are not the only ones interested in regional problems. An economist likes to ascertain the reason for city-by-city variations in per capita cheques cashed against savings accounts. A school superintendent wants to find out why there are fluctuations in high school registrations from one district to another. A demographer is eager to know what causes the differences in birth, death, and migration rates among various places. A banker advancing a loan for the construction of a new plant needs to be assured that the site selected really represents an optimum combination of all factors and is not merely an outgrowth of old business habits.

The interest in, and usefulness of, regional analysis is too well established to need further documentation. However, one of the unpleasant discoveries that immediately confronts a person desiring precise information about a region is that the prevailing statistical system is against him. Most of the data are published either for the 10 provinces or for the multitudinous counties, towns, and cities.

The Canadian provinces are far too big to provide a coherent view. To rely solely on them for regional analysis is very much like trying to color a landscape picture with a brush intended for painting houses. Take for example, Ontario. It covers 333,835 square miles — 30 times the size of Belgium, four times as large as the United Kingdom, and almost equal to Texas and California combined. In such a huge land mass, economic patterns are bound to differ. The area covered by the "Golden Horseshoe" is highly industrialized, with dense population, big cities, and the busy life of a modern American society. On the other hand, Northwestern Ontario is a vast sprawling region of lakes, forests, and mines, still in the early stages of development, with only a sparse population concentrated mainly round the twin Lakehead cities.

The same variation is also found in the Atlantic Provinces, considered by many marketers to be a homogeneous community. There is a big difference between the Avalon Peninsula and Labrador, between the Annapolis Valley and Cape Breton Island, or between the Upper St. John Valley and the New Brunswick woodlands. Only Prince Edward Island, small and compact, is homogeneous in landscape and personality. And the Island is as distinct from the other Atlantic Provinces as from the rest of Canada.

Although the provincial breakdown is not satisfactory, it is not practical to go to the other extreme and try to collect statistics for each of the numerous towns and cities across the country. There are distinct disadvantages in this method:

• A complete analysis by urban places requires the tabulation of data for about 850 towns and cities. The result is embroilment in unnecessary, lengthy, and tedious detail work.

• City boundaries frequently change and it is difficult to study trends over a period of time.

• No data are generally available for unincorporated places, some of which, like Kirkland Lake, Ontario, may be quite large.

• By law, the Dominion Bureau of Statistics cannot publish figures for any city, where the release of such information would disclose the operations of an individual establishment or business organization. Hence, there are many gaps in the statistics collected.

• The customary grouping of urban centers by population size fails to distinguish between independent and satellite towns or between places of equal size but different purchasing power.

But the most serious objection against the city-concept is that it does not fit in with the realities of today's fast-changing urban life. Modern methods of transportation and communications have generated centrifugal forces which are not held in restraint by municipal boundaries. Newspapers, radio, and television are able to carry the messages of the advertisers at least 50 to 70 miles beyond the limits of a city. The increasing ownership of automobiles, the stepping up of highway programs, and the decentralization of industries are causing more and more families to settle beyond the metropolitan zones as defined by the Dominion Bureau of Statistics. Although much of suburbia's bloom has been rubbed off by over-crowding, mounting tax rates, and clogged highways, the urge to live farther and farther away from municipal boundaries has not been dampened.

As a result, the emphasis is gradually shifting from the city to the region. The latter is an aggregation of adjacent localities forming a functionally and structurally related unit, generally within the immediate environs of a dominating urban center. A good region should, as far as it is reasonably possible, have evidence of internal cohesiveness — the cohesion of common interests, common life, common influences, common social and economic characteristics.

The most scientific division of Canada into socio-economic regions is the one prepared a few years ago by the Economics and Statistics Branch of the Department of Defence Production, Ottawa. The results of their pioneering work were released in two reports: *Economic Zoning of Canada and the D.D.P. Geographic Code* brought out in August 1953, and its sequel *Economic Administrative Zoning of Canada* issued in June 1954. The latest version now available is the one published in 1964 by Messrs. Camu, Weeks, and Sametz in *Economic Geography of Canada*. This regional breakdown has been officially accepted by the governments of Québec, Ontario, and Manitoba, and the other provinces too have shown considerable interest in it. The Dominion Bureau of Statistics has accepted the responsibility for a further development of the system, and it is expected that in future more and more information will be available on a regional basis.

Admittedly, no single classification can satisfy all requirements, and it would be presumptuous to assume that the provincial economic regions used in this book would be a perfect substitute for all marketing or trading zones. The latter are tailor-made to fit particular situations, and differ radically from industry to industry and even from one company to another. But when the time comes to realign sales territories, it would be worthwhile to adopt the official classification, since it represents the best possible combination of structural, functional, production, and marketing factors, such as:

> physiographic layout;
> population distribution;
> location of key natural resources (e.g. minerals, forests, water-power);
> transportation and communications network;
> integration of industrial activity (e.g. pulp mill with its forest hinterland);
> unitary labor market, as reflected in the area covered by the local office of the National Employment Service;
> occupational and employment pattern;
> commuting areas;
> marketing requirements;
> availability of statistics.

The last factor is perhaps the most relevant. Since statistics are published by counties or census divisions, the boundaries of the regions have to be so arranged as not to cut across the existing political lines. True, at times counties or census divisions are awkward and even artificial, combining very dissimilar parcels of territory. However, these special cases are few and far between. In Canada, more than in many other countries, there are well-recognized regional entities, and the spatial separation between significant areas makes the delineation of zonal units a not very difficult task.

The ensuing discussion of regional markets in the book is broken into two sections, *A* and *B*. *A* deals with the 64 regions separately. The intention is to give a bird's-eye view of each of the different zones into which Canada can be divided. Such detailed, but readily digestible, information can help a person to make sound decisions on facts rather than on hunch.

In *B*, an aggregative rather than an atomistic approach is taken. Instead of one region with statistics on many topics, each topic is treated separately, and statistics on it are presented by 64 regions. In this way it is easy to compare one region with another on such basic items as population, income, education, occupation, and the like.

Both approaches are useful. One may picture Canada as a necklace of pearls. The regions are the pearls and the necklace the country as a whole. Some are interested in individual pearls, others in the entire necklace. It all depends upon one's primary concern. Each has its own legitimate place, its own conceptual frame of reference, yet the ultimate progress depends upon both the factors being studied side by side.

Marketing Applications

Statistics by economic regions may be employed in many ways for marketing operations. While the following discussion is not all-inclusive, it indicates the common applications of regional data to various phases of business management.

DETERMINING NEW PLANT LOCATION

Although the selection of a site for a plant is highly specialized, depending on the product to be manufactured, regional statistics may often prove quite valuable. By providing data on population, labor conditions, and likely consumer sales, they help to narrow down the choice to a few suitable localities.

DETERMINING TRADE CHANNELS

Different types of territories necessitate different methods of distribution. Many firms rely on outside agents in thinly-populated zones with large traveling distances and employ their own salesmen in concentrated areas of high market potential.

DETERMINING SALES QUOTAS

Regional statistics, by disclosing the sales potential for the product, can suggest the number of active salesmen each territory can support, along with sales quotas and other work load assignments. Such planning is required to assure proper coverage at a minimum cost.

DETERMINING EFFECTIVENESS OF SALES FORCE

By converting the market potential data as well as the actual sales for each area into percentages of total Canada, one may measure readily the performance of different salesmen. The management can see who are above their territory "par" and who are not providing a sales volume consistent with the business possibilities of their area.

DETERMINING THE ALLOCATION OF PROMOTIONAL EFFORT

The regional concept is a valuable tool for ensuring a balanced advertising coverage throughout the country. The media plan is so devised that the advertising messages are distributed in proportion to the likely consumption of the product in each region. Also, comparison of market potential statistics and actual sales indicate the areas of strength and weakness and so help to determine how special advertising and sales promotion funds should be allocated among various markets. Some firms prefer to capitalize on their strength, others to concentrate efforts in areas where they are weak.

DETERMINING MARKET ENTRY AND CONCENTRATING SALES EFFORTS

Many companies, when introducing a new product, adopt a zonal method of sales expansion. The policy is based on the principle of establishing a beachhead in the most profitable territory first, then gradually expanding into the general market. This strategy can be particularly effective in Canada because of the high concentration of consumers in a relatively few localities. The following eight regions account for half of the country's population and two-thirds of the non-farm families earning over $10,000 a year:

Metro Montréal and its Environs
Metro Toronto and its Environs
Vancouver-Lower Fraser
Hamilton/St. Catharines-Niagara
Ottawa-Western Laurentides and Ottawa Valley
Metro Winnipeg and its Environs
Metro Québec-Eastern Laurentides
Edmonton-Parklands.

A small firm selling only in these markets may be able to compete quite effectively with a large manufacturer whose efforts are thinly spread out all across Canada. There are obvious savings in selling costs as a result of this cultivation of concentrated potential.

DETERMINING PROSPECTS OF FUTURE GROWTH

After careful examination of the past trends one can, within reasonable limits of accuracy, project the statistics to the next decade. From these forecasts it is possible to pick out those areas likely to experience above-average rates of growth. These estimates may then become the basis for sales budgets, plant expansion, and other aspects of business planning.

Non-Marketing Applications

The zonal system is also valuable for areas other than marketing. It can be used to advantage by persons in many walks of life — geographers, economists, research sociologists, planners in governmental organizations — in short, by any one interested in finding out how the pattern of livelihood differs from one region to another. Here are a few examples.

GEOGRAPHERS

Except for the pioneering work of a few scholars, economic geography, unlike other social sciences, has not been so far subject to the rigid discipline of statistical measurement and analysis. Now, with scientifically-established regions available, a geographer need no longer rely on informal observation or educated insight. By choosing only those territories where a particular problem exists, he can limit the area of investigation to the right sector. Then the solution may be obtained by collecting and assessing all types of data which have a direct relevance to the problem.

GOVERNMENTAL ORGANIZATIONS AND CROWN CORPORATIONS

Already the Central Mortgage and Housing Corporation has adopted the zoning system, with only minor changes, for co-ordinating and controlling the work of its local offices. Other government bodies too have found in the regional classification a valuable tool for conducting special studies on zones that are:

deficient in manufacturing;

dependent on a declining industry (e.g. coal or cotton textiles);

subject to prolonged migration;

having a concentration of low-income farm families.

ECONOMISTS

Ever since the Keynesian revolution in the Thirties, emphasis has been on "macro economics", with development of such over-all statistics as the gross national product and the indices of industrial production. However, many economists now feel that this policy of condensing basic data has been carried too far. The aggregates not only do not tell the whole tale, but often obliterate the main points of the tale by arithmetically cancelling out too many opposing elements. Very often it is the shifts within the aggregates that matter. It is quite conceivable to have a general state of prosperity in the nation with a high level of unemployment in certain areas. "Two per cent of the labor force unemployed" may seem trivial at the national level, but if all of this unemployment is concentrated in a handful of regions, the situation appears in a different light. Despite the attempt to create a uniform economic climate in the country through national economic and fiscal policies, the structural peculiarities of different areas are so great that regional studies are necessary to minimize the effects of business cycles.

PROVINCIAL ECONOMIC REGIONS

PROVINCE, REGION AND COMPONENT COUNTIES OR CENSUS DIVISIONS

(Based largely on the classification developed by
the Department of Defence Production, Ottawa)

Newfoundland

ST. JOHN'S—SOUTHEASTERN NEWFOUNDLAND—Census Divisions: 1, 2, 3, 7.
CENTRAL NEWFOUNDLAND: Census Divisions: 6, 8.
WESTERN NEWFOUNDLAND—Census Divisions: 4, 5, 9.
LABRADOR—Census Division: 10.

Prince Edward Island

PRINCE EDWARD ISLAND—Counties: Kings, Prince, Queens (whole province).

Nova Scotia

SYDNEY—CAPE BRETON—Counties: Cape Breton, Inverness, Richmond, Victoria.

NORTHERN NOVA SCOTIA—Counties: Antigonish, Colchester, Cumberland, Guysborough, Pictou.

HALIFAX—SOUTH SHORE—Counties: Digby, Halifax, Lunenburg, Queen's, Shelburne, Yarmouth.

ANNAPOLIS VALLEY—Counties: Annapolis, Hants, Kings.

New Brunswick

MONCTON—SOUTHEASTERN NEW BRUNSWICK—Counties: Albert, Kent, Westmorland.

SAINT JOHN—SOUTHERN NEW BRUNSWICK—Counties: Charlotte, Kings, Queens, Saint John.

UPPER ST. JOHN VALLEY—Counties: Carleton, Madawaska, Sunbury, Victoria, York.

NORTHEASTERN NEW BRUNSWICK—Counties: Gloucester, Northumberland, Restigouche.

Québec

NORTH SHORE—NEW QUEBEC—County: Saguenay.

GASPE PENINSULA—SOUTH SHORE—Counties: Bonaventure, Gaspé, Kamouraska, L'Islet, Matane, Montmagny, Rimouski, Témiscouata.

SAGUENAY VALLEY—LAKE ST. JOHN—Counties: Chicoutimi, Lac St. Jean.

METRO QUEBEC—EASTERN LAURENTIDES—Counties: Beauce, Bellechasse, Charlevoix, Dorchester, Lévis, Lotbinière, Montmorency, Portneuf, Québec.

TROIS RIVIERES—ST. MAURICE VALLEY—Counties: Berthier, Champlain, Maskinongé, Nicolet, St. Maurice.

SHERBROOKE—EASTERN TOWNSHIPS—Counties: Arthabaska, Brome, Compton, Drummond, Frontenac, Mégantic, Richmond, Shefford, Sherbrooke, Stanstead, Wolfe.

METRO MONTREAL AND ITS ENVIRONS—Counties: Argenteuil, Bagot, Beauharnois, Chambly, Châteauguay, Deux Montagnes, Huntingdon, Iberville, Joliette, Labelle, Laprairie, L'Assomption, Missisquoi, Montcalm, Iles de Montréal et Jésus, Napierville, Richelieu, Rouville, St. Hyacinthe, St. Jean, Soulanges, Terrebonne, Vaudreuil, Verchères, Yamaska.

WESTERN QUEBEC—Counties: Abitibi, Témiscamingue.

HULL—WESTERN LAURENTIDES—Counties: Hull, Papineau, Pontiac.

Ontario

OTTAWA—OTTAWA VALLEY—Counties: Carleton, Lanark, Prescott, Renfrew, Russell.

KINGSTON—UPPER ST. LAWRENCE—Counties: Dundas, Frontenac, Glengarry, Grenville, Leeds, Stormont.

PETERBOROUGH—CENTRAL LAKE ONTARIO—Counties: Durham, Haliburton, Hastings, Lennox and Addington, Northumberland, Peterborough, Prince Edward, Victoria.

METRO TORONTO AND ITS ENVIRONS—Counties: Halton, Ontario, Peel, York.

HAMILTON/ST. CATHARINES—NIAGARA—Counties: Brant, Haldimand, Lincoln, Welland, Wentworth.

LONDON—LAKE ERIE—Counties: Elgin, Middlesex, Norfolk, Oxford.

WINDSOR/SARNIA—LAKE ST. CLAIR—Counties: Essex, Kent, Lambton.

KITCHENER—MIDLANDS—Counties: Huron, Perth, Waterloo, Wellington.

LAKE HURON—GEORGIAN BAY—Counties: Bruce, Dufferin, Grey, Muskoka, Parry Sound, Simcoe.
NORTHEASTERN ONTARIO: CLAY BELT—Counties: Cochrane, Nipissing, Timiskaming.
NORTHEASTERN ONTARIO: NICKEL RANGE—Counties: Manitoulin, Sudbury.
NORTHEASTERN ONTARIO: SAULT—County: Algoma.
LAKEHEAD—NORTHWESTERN ONTARIO—Counties: Kenora, Rainy River, Thunder Bay.

Manitoba

METRO WINNIPEG AND ITS ENVIRONS—Census Divisions: 1, 2, 5, 6, 9, 12, 19, 20.
SOUTHWESTERN MANITOBA PRAIRIE—Census Divisions: 3, 4, 7, 8, 10, 11, 13.
WEST-CENTRAL MANITOBA PARKLANDS—Census Divisions: 14, 15, 17, 18.
NORTHERN MANITOBA—Census Division: 16.

Saskatchewan

REGINA—SOUTHEASTERN PLAINS—Census Divisions: 1, 2, 6.
SASKATCHEWAN PALLISER—Census Divisions: 3, 4, 7, 8.
SASKATOON—CENTRAL PLAINS—Census Divisions: 11, 12, 13.
SASKATCHEWAN—SOUTHEASTERN PARKLANDS—Census Divisions: 5, 9, 10.
CENTRAL SASKATCHEWAN PARKLANDS—Census Divisions: 14, 15, 16, 17.
NORTHERN SASKATCHEWAN—Census Division: 18.

Alberta

MEDICINE HAT—PALLISER—Census Division: 1.
LETHBRIDGE PRAIRIE—Census Divisions: 2, 3.
ALBERTA ROCKY MOUNTAINS—FOOTHILLS—Census Division: 9.
CALGARY—SOUTH-CENTRAL ALBERTA—Census Divisions: 4, 5, 6.
RED DEER ENVIRONS—Census Division: 8.
EAST-CENTRAL ALBERTA PRAIRIE—Census Divisions: 7, 10.
EDMONTON—PARKLANDS—Census Divisions: 11, 13.
NORTHEASTERN ALBERTA—Census Division: 12.
NORTHWESTERN ALBERTA—PEACE RIVER—Census Divisions: 14, 15.

British Columbia

EAST KOOTENAY—Census Division: 1.
WEST KOOTENAY—Census Division: 2.
OKANAGAN VALLEY—Census Division: 3.
SOUTH-CENTRAL BRITISH COLUMBIA—Census Division: 6.
VANCOUVER—LOWER FRASER—Census Division: 4.
VICTORIA—VANCOUVER ISLAND—Census Division: 5.
NORTHWESTERN BRITISH COLUMBIA—Census Divisions: 7, 9.
NORTH-CENTRAL BRITISH COLUMBIA—Census Division: 8.
NORTHEASTERN BRITISH COLUMBIA—Census Division: 10.

Yukon and Northwest Territories

YUKON AND NORTHWEST TERRITORIES—whole area.

A. ANALYSIS OF EACH ECONOMIC REGION OF CANADA

Introduction

The 64 regions in this section are arranged from east to west, with south to north excursions within each province, where necessary. This presentation coincides to a large extent with the order in which the historical development took place within the country. For persons who want to have a telescopic rather than a microscopic view, a brief description is also given for each of the six broad sectors into which Canada is usually divided: Atlantic Provinces, Québec, Ontario, Prairies, British Columbia, and the Yukon and Northwest Territories. The text on each province is followed by tables showing the various facets of the economic life.

The following model is adopted for each region:

ECONOMIC CAPSULE

The intention here is to feature the main highlights of the region.

AREA COVERED

This clarifies the boundaries and shows the extent of the territory covered

COMPOSITION OF THE MARKET

The population is broken down by urban and rural areas, and all urban places (i.e., those having over 1,000 inhabitants) are listed.

The statistical data for each region and the major city (or cities) are presented under the following headings:

IMPORTANCE OF THE MARKET

Three standard yardsticks are employed to assess the importance of the region: population, households and disposable income. The 1964 estimates of population and households were prepared by the author, while those for disposable income were obtained from the Financial Post's *1965/66 Survey of Markets and Business Year Book.*

GROWTH OF THE MARKET

The rapidity of the growth of the region in the early Sixties can be judged by the percentage increase between 1961 and 1964 of population and disposable income. Figures for households are not given because they follow closely, though not exactly, the population pattern.

CHARACTERISTICS OF THE POPULATION

Considered here are the two major socio-economic characteristics of the population in the region; mother tongue and official language spoken. Only the percentages are given, but the actual numbers can be calculated by applying the percentages to the total 1964 population of the region or the city.

AVERAGE INCOME

Here a quick picture can be obtained about the quality of the market. Rather than having a single general average, like per capita disposable income, which may hide many variations within its parts, the "spending units" are broken down into three categories: non-farm families; persons not in families, non-farm; and farm households.

POVERTY AND AFFLUENCE

A further opportunity for assessing the quality of the region is provided by analyzing the extent of poverty and affluence prevailing in the area. Several yardsticks are used to ascertain poverty and affluence, the choice being obviously limited by the statistics available on a regional basis.

Poverty is judged by the following factors:
- Families earning below $3,000 a year (non-farm).
- Persons not in families earning below $1,500 a year.
- Farms with gross income of less than $2,500 a year.
- Persons not in school with grade 4 or less education.
- Doubled-up households (i.e., more than one family per household).
- Households living in dilapidated dwellings.
- Households without facilities of running water.
- Households without facilities of installed bath or shower.

The criteria used for determining affluence are:
- Families earning over $10,000 a year (non-farm).
- Persons not in families earning over $6,000 a year (non-farm).
- Farms with gross income over $15,000 a year.
- Persons with university degree.
- Households with two or more television sets.
- Households with two or more cars.

In each case, the statistics show the actual number, the percentage it represents of the region's (or city's) total, and the extent to which that percentage is above or below the Canadian average. In this way one can position the region (or city) vis-a-vis the nation as a whole on the poverty or affluence index.

MEANS OF LIVELIHOOD

The figures here deal with the distribution of the labor force in 1961 by industry. This completes the picture by focusing the attention on the resources of the region and the type of employment opportunities available.

Chapter 14

ATLANTIC PROVINCES

Introduction

"Maritimes" is the name given to the three eastern provinces of Prince Edward Island, Nova Scotia, and New Brunswick. When these are considered along with Newfoundland, the term used is "Atlantic Provinces" or "Atlantic Canada."

Their isolated location has promoted a strong feeling of parochialism. Cut off from the rest of English-speaking Canada by the vast bulk of Québec, they have been forced to fall back upon themselves and work out their own destiny.

Down in Newfoundland, thousands still speak of "going abroad" when crossing the Cabot Strait. To many, the continental mainland remains a mystery, and they feel themselves no part of it. The inhabitants, especially those living in the outposts, are too proud, too independent, and too settled in their ways to be changed by a mere constitutional act of union with Canada.

In a slightly different way, the residents of Prince Edward Island are even more provincial. This may be gleaned very well from the remark of a young man who turned up in a Montréal recruiting center during the last war. When the sergeant questioned him as to where he came from, he replied proudly: "From the Island." "What Island?" the sergeant, a mere inlander, asked impatiently. "Why, but Prince Edward Island," replied the dismayed recruit. "What other islands are there?"

The Island is a Lilliputian continent physically and mentally, and it is quite unimpressed by the larger continent beside it. One is reminded of Lord Dufferin's famous observation in 1871: "The Islanders have entered Confederation gladly under the impression that the Dominion has been annexed to Prince Edward Island."

Although the total population of 100,000 is exceeded by even single suburbs in Toronto or Montréal, the Island clings tenaciously to its unique system of representative government. The legislature meets in Charlottetown, which, though a provincial capital, has the air of a comfortable market town. The government is engrossed with problems that would be dealt with elsewhere by county or municipal councils, but here are given full parliamentary treatment.

Across the Northumberland Strait from Prince Edward Island lies Nova Scotia. Its name is Jacobean lawyers' Latin for New Scotland, and the Scottishness of the province is obvious, especially in Pictou county and Cape Breton Island. Many small towns and villages have Scottish names, Gaelic is still the mother tongue in some of the homes, and each July Antigonish celebrates its Highland games.

More fundamental is the Scots' fierce belief in the value of education. Although the total population of Nova Scotia is only half that of Toronto, it maintains no less than seven recognized universities, and has provided a reservoir of talent from which the rest of Canada has freely drawn. Nova Scotia's proud boast is that its greatest export is brains. Proportionately more Nova Scotians find their way into the Canadian "Who's Who" than do people born in other parts of the country.

The sister province of New Brunswick is bi-cultural. The most important group is formed of the descendants of United Empire Loyalists — the Tories who refused to accept the American flag after the Revolution and migrated to these harsh shores in 1783. They brought with them certain traits that have never been completely lost — respect for law and order, reverence for the mother country, and conservatism in manners, politics, and ways of doing business.

The other group in New Brunswick consists of French-speaking Acadians, whose expulsion by the British two centuries ago inspired Longfellow's celebrated poem "Evangeline". With great tenacity, they traced their way back into the homeland, and through *la revanche des berceaux* (the revenge of the cradles), they have made the province over 35% French-speaking. The two races now live harmoniously side by side, and the past bitterness is mostly forgotten.

Agriculture

Apart from Prince Edward Island, agriculture has not made much headway in the Atlantic Provinces. The climate is too humid, the soil too acid, and the land too rough and rocky to permit extensive cultivation of field crops. In Newfoundland farming is so insignificant that national estimates of agricultural production usually exclude that province's share as being too small to measure with a sufficient degree of statistical accuracy. In fact, out of the total land area of 143,000 square miles, only 32 square miles consist of improved farmland.

In Nova Scotia and New Brunswick, too, except for areas of local specialties, like apples in the Annapolis region and potatoes in the Upper St. John Valley, agriculture is not very profitable. Over half the farms fall into the non-commercial category, comprising for the most part small, widely scattered holdings.

The situation is different in Prince Edward Island. Agriculture here is the main industry. Mixed farming prevails, with major emphasis on the production of potatoes, dairy products, and hogs.

Fisheries

From the very beginning fishing has predominated in the life of the Atlantic

Provinces. Since much of the land is unsuitable for agriculture, the inhabitants have turned to the sea for their livelihood. The indented coastline is admirably suited for fishing ports. Offshore lie the famous "banks", some 200,000 square miles of shallow water, constituting one of the greatest fishing grounds in the world. All types of fish are found — cod, herring, haddock, pollock, lobsters, oysters, flounders and soles, not to mention sinister sharks, frolicsome porpoises, and the 25-foot-long whales. In terms of volume, cod is most important, amounting to between 35% to 45% of the total catch, but lobster is the best money-maker, contributing about 30% of the total landed value.

The fishing industry is slowly being mechanized. Trawlers and draggers are replacing traditional schooners. More emphasis is given to marketing fresh fillets than salted catch. Some of the fish freezing plants built recently are quite large. The one at Lunenburg, N.S., can handle 80 million pounds of fish yearly, while the other at Canso, also in Nova Scotia, has an annual capacity of 30 million pounds. Extremely large catches are required to supply these plants, and as a result the fishing fleets are being expanded and modernized and the fishermen trained in scientific methods of augmenting the harvest from the sea.

Mining

In recent years, iron ore has occupied the center of the stage. All the mines are in Newfoundland. Production, because of the developments in Labrador, rose three and a half times from 3,758,526 tons in 1954 to 13,094,240 tons in 1964.

New Brunswick, whose performance till lately had been insignificant, has now been able to join the major league due to important discoveries of base metals in the Bathurst-Newcastle areas. Operations started on a big scale in 1964, and by the end of the year the total value of output of metallic minerals amounted to $30.4 million, compared to only $9.3 million in 1963. Vast development projects currently underway promise to usher into the province a new era of prosperity.

In Nova Scotia, the mineral industry is dependent mainly on gypsum and coal. Gypsum hopes for expansion, but the future of coal is as dark as the galleries it comes from, far beneath the ocean. Plagued by high costs and faced with increasing competition from other fuels, production has dropped by a quarter within a decade, from 5.8 million tons in 1954 to 4.3 million tons in 1964. Despite the federal government's transportation subventions, very little Nova Scotian coal finds its way into the rich industrial market of Southern Ontario. Failing a technological revolution in its use, it is doubtful that coal will ever again enjoy the position of pre-eminence it held in the early part of this century.

Forestry

All the Atlantic Provinces, with the exception of Prince Edward Island, are thickly wooded. The cool, moist climate, and the thin, leached soils, are generally better fitted for forests than farms. Pulp and paper mills are significant props in the economy, especially in Newfoundland and New Brunswick. Enough wood is available to support the establishment of several new mills, if markets for finished products can be developed.

Timber of saw-log size is not abundant, and the value of sawn lumber currently amounts to only one-fifth of that of the pulp and paper production. There are over a thousand sawmills, but many of these are quite small, capable of being moved from one place to another.

Secondary manufacturing

The Atlantic Provinces are highly deficient in secondary manufacturing. They have a very slender industrial base made up of three roughly equal parts: the food-processing group; the Dosco group of steel-making and heavy engineering establishments; and a miscellaneous group of textiles, clothing, tanning, printing, and a number of other plants, none of them very large. On account of its remote peripheral location, the region cannot form part of any of the major industrial areas, while its own resources (material and human) are not sufficiently great to enable it to develop into a major industrial center in its own right.

This does not mean that there is no room for secondary manufacturing of any kind; but the obstacles to be surmounted are high. One firm in the light engineering field has calculated that its present location in Nova Scotia involves a transportation handicap equivalent to 3½ % to 4% of the value of sales in comparison with a location in the Montréal-Toronto area.

Even worse than the direct burden of extra freight charges are the indirect costs of distance. Among these must be reckoned the necessity to carry larger inventories; the need to make use of intermediaries instead of going direct to the supplier or consumer; the difficulty of obtaining spare parts or bottleneck items quickly; and the delays in transit, with all the inefficiency and loss of goodwill that such delays can produce.

Apart from industries based on the regional market, the type of secondary manufacturing that may succeed is one where raw materials are obtainable cheaply and the finished goods are high in value in relation to bulk. In such a case the transportation costs would not be a great hindrance to competing in Central Canada or perhaps even in foreign markets. Products that have tackled the freight-rate bogey with conspicuous success include candy, brushes, clothing, and high-quality shoes.

General observations

The four Atlantic Provinces have many things in common. They have a higher percentage of native-born than any other part of Canada. Except among the Acadians, the British traditions have remained exceptionally strong, and there is a staunch loyalty to the Crown and the mother country. Food, clothing, and furniture are more English and less American than in other provinces.

As regards the market for goods and services, the whole area suffers from many deficiencies. It has been cut off from the main currents of economic progress and left slumping into a backwater. Per capita income is the lowest, per capita production the smallest, and per capita retail trade the least among all the provinces in Canada. This is the result of a combination of several adverse factors.

Fewer persons of working age are in the labor force in the Atlantic Provinces. In 1965, only 48% of the total non-institutional population 14 years of age and over participated in gainful employment. For the rest of the nation the figure was up to 55%.

Even for those in the labor force, the unemployment rate is higher in the Atlantic Provinces — 7.4% in 1965 versus 3.7% elsewhere in the country. The main reason is the relatively greater dependence on seasonal industries, such as agriculture, fishery, forestry, construction, and food processing. In 1965, the difference between the first and third quarter unemployment rates in the Atlantic Provinces was 7.9%, more than twice the national average of 3.0%.

Capital expenditures in the area are also far less than in other parts of Canada. During the decade of 1955 to 1964, not only did the per capita investment average merely 66% of the Canadian average, but a larger proportion of this investment was of non-business nature, a fact which does not normally generate continuing employment.

The average weekly wages and salaries in the Atlantic Provinces are equally low, $72.34 in 1964 compared to an all-Canada figure of $86.65. This is mainly because a large proportion of the labor force is engaged in low-productivity occupations, like subsistence farming and part-time fishing and logging. Also, the regional market is not sufficiently big to have large-scale manufacturing plants, where workers as a rule are well paid.

The economy is faced with a vicious circle. The lack of concentrated population discourages industry, and the lack of industry discourages concentrated population. If the Atlantic Provinces had one large compact market, as Manitoba has in Winnipeg and British Columbia in Vancouver, they would be able to attract both the capital to finance new factories and the experienced manpower to operate them. As it is, many manufactured products, including even basic necessities, have to be brought from outside, involving high transportation costs.

Thus, while the per capita income is 32% below the nation's average, the inhabitants of the Atlantic Provinces have to pay more than other Canadians for the things they eat, wear, and use. Freight rates are burdensome, but the situation is worsened by the fact that they are often used to cover a multitude of unwarranted overcharges by merchants. There is a saying down in the east that "all freight travels first class to the Maritimes".

But hard as the life may be, many of the residents would not exchange it for the noise, the bustle, and the unnerving relentlessness of Toronto and Montréal. To these people, the Atlantic seaboard is the only place that has so far escaped the rat race on this harassed continent. Indeed, no visitor can help feeling an atmosphere of leisurely pleasantness in the environment — a mood of unhurried composure, of being content with things as they are and long have been. There is none of that pressure, that sense of urgency, that singleminded concentration on work that one finds in Central Canada. The inhabitants have kept the flavor of the older, gentler period of yesteryear. They value leisure, natural beauty, and the simple amenities of life. They don't like their time to be ticked off in minutes and seconds. There is efficiency in Atlantic Canada, but it is slow and subdued rather than brisk.

Companies selling their products and services in the Atlantic Provinces must remember that it is not possible to hustle the people into a purchase. Their rural environment and small budget have conditioned them to be cautious, loyal to the known products proven satisfactory, and slow to accept innovations. Lucy Maud Montgomery, a native Maritimer and the author of the famous novel, *Anne of Green Gables,* expressed well the character of her people when she said: "We are not hidebound or overly conservative, but we do not rush madly after new fads and fashions just because they are new. We wait calmly until other parts have tried them out for us, and then, if they have stood the test, we adopt them."

How do these traits of conservatism affect advertising and selling? It is unrealistic to expect a new product to sweep Atlantic Canada. A razzle-dazzle Upper Canadian promotion simply does not whip up the same enthusiasm among the Maritimers. This does not mean that emotional appeals will not work, because a Maritimes housewife is still every bit a woman. But more than other Canadian women she needs a sound logical reason to justify her purchase.

Although the Atlantic Provinces are lagging behind other parts of Canada, it would be a gross error to assume that they are stagnant. The last few years have witnessed a substantial improvement in economic tempo. The provincial governments, by financial and other inducements, have succeeded in attracting many new industries. Personal disposal income and retail sales have shown healthy increases. What is even more significant, the inhabitants have stopped turning to the federal government as a kind of "deus ex machina" that will set everything right. They now realize that their salvation lies in self-help rather than in subventions from Ottawa. There is a mood of optimism in the air, a desire to change, to innovate, to develop, to invest — in short, to pull oneself up by the bootstrap toward a better future.

Place	Provincial region	Population 1961	% of the Atlantic Provinces
Halifax (metro)	Halifax—South Shore	183,946	9.69
Sydney—Glace Bay (urbanized area)	Sydney—Cape Breton	106,114	5.59
Saint John (metro)	Saint John—Southern New Brunswick	95,563	5.04
St. John's (metro)	St. John's—Southeastern Newfoundland	90,838	4.79
Moncton (urbanized area)	Moncton—Southeastern New Brunswick	55,768	2.94
Corner Brook	Western Newfoundland	25,185	1.33
Fredericton (urbanized area)	Upper St. John Valley	24,836	1.31
New Glasgow (urbanized area including Trenton)	Northern Nova Scotia	22,408	1.18
Charlottetown	Prince Edward Island	18,318	0.96
Truro (urbanized area)	Northern Nova Scotia	15,869	0.84
Edmunston	Upper St. John Valley	12,791	0.67
Oromocto	Upper St. John Valley	12,170	0.64
Windsor (urbanized area)	Central Newfoundland	12,110	0.64
Campbellton (urbanized area)	Northeastern New Brunswick	12,018	0.63
Wabana (urbanized area)	St. John's—Southeastern Newfoundland	10,919	0.58
Amherst	Northern Nova Scotia	10,788	0.57
Summerside	Prince Edward Island	8,611	0.45
Yarmouth	Halifax—South Shore	8,636	0.46
Chatham	Northeastern New Brunswick	7,109	0.37
Stephenville	Western Newfoundland	6,043	0.32
Dalhousie	Northeastern New Brunswick	5,856	0.31
Springhill	Northern Nova Scotia	5,836	0.31
Gander	Central Newfoundland	5,725	0.30
Bathurst	Northeastern New Brunswick	5,494	0.29
Newcastle	Northeastern New Brunswick	5,236	0.27
Total of towns over 5,000		768,187	40.48
107 Towns between 1,000 and 5,000		211,109	11.13
Total urban		979,296	51.61
Rural non-farm		755,441	39.81
Rural farm		162,688	8.58
Total population		1,897,425	100.00

IMPORTANCE OF THE MARKET (1964 ESTIMATES)

	Number	% of Canada
Population	1,975,000	10.27
Households	433,000	9.01
Disposable income ($ million)	2,302.0	7.30

GROWTH OF THE MARKET

	Percentage growth 1961 to 1964	% points above or below Canadian average
Population	+ 4.09	−1.38
Disposable income	+19.21	−2.32

CHARACTERISTICS OF THE POPULATION

	% of the total population of the provinces	% points above or below Canadian average
Mother tongue (1961 census)		
English	84.6	+26.2
French	13.8	− 14.3
German	0.2	− 2.9
Native Indian dialects	0.3	− 0.6
Italian	0.1	− 1.8
Dutch	0.2	− 0.7
Polish	0.1	− 0.8
Ukrainian	0.1	− 1.9
Other	0.6	− 3.2
Total	100.0	—
Official language spoken (1961 census)		
English only	84.4	+17.0
French only	6.3	−12.8
Both English and French	9.1	− 3.1
Neither English nor French	0.2	− 1.1
Total	100.0	—

STANDARD OF LIVING BASED ON OWNERSHIP OF
APPLIANCES AND EQUIPMENT, 1965

	Number of households	% of total households in Atlantic Provinces	% points above or below Canadian average
Cooking equipment			
Electric stoves	152,000	34.8	−34.2
Wood or coal cookstoves or ranges	141,000	32.3	+23.1
Piped gas stoves	5,000	1.1	−13.0
Refrigeration			
Electric refrigerators	360,000	82.4	−13.4
Home freezers	49,000	11.2	−11.4
Electric washing machines			
Automatic	47,000	10.8	−12.3
Other	330,000	75.5	+12.3
Clothes dryers			
Electric	52,000	11.9	−13.3
Gas	1,000	0.2	− 2.0
Sewing machines			
Electric	127,000	29.1	−23.3
Non-electric	127,000	29.1	+10.9
Phonographs and record players			
Cabinet model	68,000	15.6	−17.3
Table model	27,000	6.2	+ 1.0
Portable model	93,000	21.3	+ 0.3
Telephones			
One	288,000	65.9	−10.3
Two or more	36,000	8.2	− 5.0
Television sets			
One	353,000	80.8	− 1.0
Two or more	23,000	5.3	− 5.6
Automobiles			
One	254,000	58.1	− 4.4
Two or more	32,000	7.3	− 5.1
Other appliances			
Automatic dishwashers	5,000	1.1	− 1.6
Vacuum cleaners	239,000	54.7	−20.2
Window-type air conditioners	1,000	0.2	− 2.0
FM radio receivers	37,000	8.5	−14.4

(Source: DBS, *Household Facilities and Equipment, May 1965.* Catalogue no. 64-202.)

MEANS OF LIVELIHOOD—DISTRIBUTION OF
LABOR FORCE BY INDUSTRY

Industry	Persons 1961 census	% of the total	% points above or below Canadian average
Agriculture	35,356	6.3	−3.6
Forestry	21,809	3.9	+2.2
Fishing and trapping	21,625	3.9	+3.4
Mines, quarries, oil wells	16,030	2.9	+1.0
Manufacturing	77,771	13.8	−7.9
Construction	38,203	6.8	+0.1
Transportation, communications, and other utilities	64,632	11.5	+2.2
Wholesale trade	23,685	4.2	−0.3
Retail trade	66,012	11.8	+1.0
Finance, insurance, and real estate	11,515	2.0	−1.5
Community and business services	67,390	12.0	−0.8
Personal services	35,568	6.3	−0.5
Public administration and defence	69,841	12.4	+4.9
Miscellaneous	12,195	2.2	−0.2
Total labor force	561,632	100.0	—

POVERTY AND AFFLUENCE (1961 CENSUS)

	Number	% of provinces' total	% points above or below Canadian average
Extent of poverty			
Families earning below $3,000 a year (non-farm)	148,767	41.5	+18.2
Persons not in families earning below $1,500 a year (non-farm)	84,635	64.8	+15.9
Farms with gross income of less than $2,500 a year	24,135	72.3	+26.2
Persons not in school with grade 4 or less education	201,981	17.7	+ 4.3
Doubled-up households (more than one family per household)	22,209	5.3	+ 1.6
Households living in dilapidated dwellings	37,275	8.9	+ 3.3
Households without facilities of running water	98,278	23.4	+12.5
Households without facilities of installed bath or shower	176,229	42.0	+22.3

	Number	% of provinces' total	% points above or below Canadian average
Extent of affluence			
Families earning over $10,000 a year (non-farm)......	13,382	3.7	− 4.1
Persons not in families earning over $6,000 a year (non-farm)........	2,534	1.9	− 1.9
Farms with gross income over $15,000 a year..........	867	2.6	− 2.4
Persons with university degree....................	19,183	1.7	− 1.1
Households with two or more television sets.............	7,774	1.8	− 2.4
Households with two or more cars........................	15,385	3.4	− 3.4

AVERAGE INCOME (1961 CENSUS)

	Dollars	% above or below Canadian average
Income per family (non-farm)...........................	4,072	−25.27
Income per person not in family (non-farm).................	1,535	−28.17
Income per farm (net).........................	1,537	−52.78

St. John's — Southeastern Newfoundland

ECONOMIC CAPSULE

Over six out of 10 people in Newfoundland live in this region. From the very beginning the sea has had a predominant influence on the life of the inhabitants. One of the richest deep-sea fishing grounds in the world — the Grand Banks — lies practically at the doorstep. The region accounts for two-thirds of the provincial fish landings. Redfish, halibut, haddock, flounder, and sole are caught, in addition to the major species, cod.

Since most of the land is barren — unsuited even for a small garden, leaving aside agriculture — fishing is the sole occupation in many of the small settlements dotted along the coast. Communication facilities are scanty, except by sea, and in hundreds of tiny outports the inhabitants still live in seclusion, their way of life very little altered in the centuries that have passed by. The provincial government is anxious to raise their standard of living. Since it is cheaper to bring people to civilization than to extend modern facilities to remote and inaccessible areas, attempts are being made, through grants and subsidies, to induce the villagers to leave their homes and reside in some of the fair-sized fishing settlements such as Carbonear, Bonavista, Grand Bank, and Harbour Grace. Here the establishment of quick freezing, cold storage, and packing facilities tends to place the fishing industry on a remunerative basis. Besides, these towns have other small manufacturing plants which create additional job opportunities.

So far the government has met with considerable success in its task of transplanting the population. But the job is by no means complete. Many fishermen still cling to their little coves where they can continue their rugged, but very independent, lives. Social inertia is obviously at loggerheads with economic geography. As a result, fishing in many parts tends to be an eighteenth century affair in a twentieth century situation.

Minerals provide another source of wealth. St. Lawrence, on the south coast of Burin peninsula, is one of the principal centers in the world for fluorspar, the raw material used as a flux in smelting iron ore and bauxite. However, the mainstay of the mining industry is iron. Under the floor of Conception Bay lies one of the greatest iron ore deposits in the world. It outcrops at Wabana on Bell Island, where long, inclined tunnels have been constructed to permit mining operations two or three miles out under the bay. Unfortunately, the ores have a high phosphorus content which make them unattractive to the American iron and steel industry. They are also too costly to concentrate or pelletize. The output is used mostly in the Sydney steel mills of the parent company, Dosco Industries Limited. But the latter, in recent years, has been forced more and more to obtain high-grade ore from other sources in order to remain competitive in today's steel market. The Wabana mines are no longer profitable and a decision has been made to close them soon.

The economic life of the whole region is dominated by St. John's, one of the oldest cities in Canada. It is the administrative center of the province and the chief commercial depot. Its manufacturing industries include fish processing, shipbuilding and repair, printing and publishing, cordage and twine making, and the building of machinery and equipment. Since its earliest days it has served primarily as a port and a fishing station, supplying all the basic requirements of the fishing industry.

St. John's has certain distinct advantages. It is located in the most settled area of the Island, close to the major fishing grounds; it possesses an unexcelled harbor, substantially ice-free; and it is situated at a point nearest to the United Kingdom, the mother country to which it was inextricably tied for many centuries.

However, the economic geography has changed since Newfoundland joined Canada in 1949. Lying now on the "wrong" side of the Island, St. John's has outlived some of its usefulness. The bulk of the trade is at present in the westerly direction, and the city's role as a dominating wholesale distributing center thus suffers from severe handicaps. Supplies from the mainland must first be shipped to the most easterly point of the Island and then westward again to their final destination. However, it is unlikely that in the near future any community with a better location will grow fast enough to challenge the economic supremacy of St. John's.

ST. JOHN'S—SOUTHEASTERN NEWFOUNDLAND

Area covered: 15,918 square miles. *Census divisions:* 1, 2, 3, 7

COMPOSITION OF THE MARKET

Place	Census Division	Population 1961	% of the region
St. John's (metro)	1	90,838	32.84
Wabana (urbanized area)	1	10,919	3.95
Carbonear	1	4,234	1.53
Bonavista	7	4,186	1.51
Channel-Port aux Basques	3	4,141	1.50
Grand Bank	2	2,703	0.98
Harbour Grace	1	2,650	0.96
St. Lawrence	2	2,095	0.76
Marystown	2	1,691	0.61
Upper Island Cove	1	1,668	0.60
Placentia	1	1,610	0.58
St. Alban's	3	1,547	0.56
Clarenville	7	1,541	0.56
Victoria	1	1,506	0.54
Hare Bay	7	1,467	0.53
Burgeo	3	1,454	0.53
Torbay	1	1,445	0.52
Freshwater	1	1,396	0.50
Fortune	2	1,360	0.49
Bay Roberts	1	1,328	0.48
Pouch Cove	1	1,324	0.48
Spaniard's Bay	1	1,289	0.47
Wesleyville	7	1,285	0.46
Glovertown	7	1,197	0.43
Burin	2	1,144	0.41
Portugal Cove	1	1,141	0.41
Dunville	1	1,121	0.41
Catalina	7	1,110	0.40
Whitbourne	1	1,085	0.39
Harbour Breton	3	1,076	0.39
Total urban	—	151,551	54.78
Rural non-farm	—	119,363	43.15
Rural farm	—	5,720	2.07
Total Population		276,634	100.00

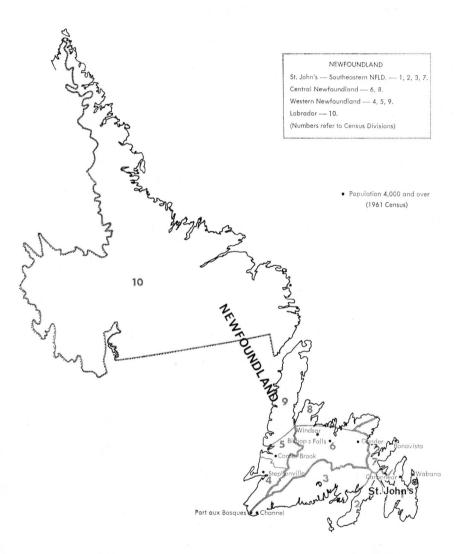

• Population 4,000 and over
(1961 Census)

10

NEWFOUNDLAND

9

8

Windsor

5 Bishop's Falls 6 • Gander

• Bonavista

• Corner Brook

• Stephenville

4

3

Carbonear

• Wabana

St. John's

Port aux Basques • Channel

IMPORTANCE OF THE MARKET (1964 ESTIMATES)

	Region		St. John's	
	Number	% of Canada	Number	% of Canada
Population	293,600	1.53	92,000	0.48
Households	58,500	1.22	19,200	0.40
Disposable income ($ million)	279.5	0.89	122.0	0.39

GROWTH OF THE MARKET

	Region		St. John's	
	Percentage growth 1961 to 1964	% points above or below Canadian average	Percentage growth 1961 to 1964	% points above or below Canadian average
Population	+ 6.13	+0.66	+ 1.28	−4.19
Disposable income	+25.17	+3.64	+19.37	−2.16

CHARACTERISTICS OF THE POPULATION

	Region		St. John's
	% of the total population of the region	% points above or below Canadian average	% of the total population of the city
Mother tongue (1961 census)			
English	99.5	+41.1	99.2
French	0.1	−28.0	0.2
German	0.1	− 3.0	0.2
Native Indian dialects	—	− 0.9	—
Italian	—	− 1.9	—
Dutch	0.1	− 0.8	0.1
Polish	—	− 0.9	—
Ukrainian	—	− 2.0	—
Other	0.2	− 3.6	0.3
Total	100.0	—	100.0
Official language spoken (1961 census)			
English only	99.4	+32.0	98.7
French only	—	−19.1	—
Both English and French	0.6	−11.6	1.2
Neither English nor French	—	− 1.3	0.1
Total	100.0	—	100.0

MEANS OF LIVELIHOOD—DISTRIBUTION OF LABOR FORCE BY INDUSTRY

Industry	Region			St. John's	
	Persons 1961 census	% of the total	% points above or below Canadian average	Persons 1961 census	% of the total
Agriculture	1,124	1.6	− 8.3	386	1.3
Forestry	1,873	2.7	+ 1.0	25	0.1
Fishing and trapping	4,855	7.0	+ 6.5	79	0.3
Mines, quarries, oil wells	2,622	3.8	+ 1.9	90	0.3
Manufacturing	7,182	10.4	−11.3	2,693	9.2
Construction	6,352	9.2	+ 2.5	2,001	6.8
Transportation, communications, and other utilities	9,915	14.3	+ 5.0	4,095	13.9
Wholesale trade	3,203	4.6	+ 0.1	2,218	7.5
Retail trade	9,546	13.8	+ 3.0	4,817	16.4
Finance, insurance, and real estate	1,054	1.5	− 2.0	882	3.0
Community and business services	8,347	12.1	− 0.7	5,075	17.3
Personal services	3,527	5.1	− 1.7	1,942	6.6
Public administration and defence	7,359	10.7	+ 3.2	4,342	14.8
Miscellaneous	2,203	3.2	+ 0.8	721	2.5
Total labor force	69,162	100.0	—	29,366	100.0

POVERTY AND AFFLUENCE (1961 CENSUS)

	Region			St. John's	
	Number	% of region's total	% points above or below Canadian average	Number	% of city's total
Extent of poverty					
Families earning below $3,000 a year (non-farm)	28,120	52.6	+29.3	5,029	28.6
Persons not in families earning below $1,500 a year (non-farm)	12,190	75.1	+26.2	3,811	59.5
Farms with gross income of less than $2,500 a year	1,020	83.8	+37.7	—	—
Persons not in school with grade 4 or less education	43,082	27.0	+13.6	7,643	13.9

	Region			St. John's	
	Number	% of region's total	% points above or below Canadian average	Number	% of city's total
Extent of poverty (continued)					
Doubled-up households (more than one family per household)	4,158	7.5	+ 3.8	1,372	7.7
Households living in dilapidated dwellings	2,722	5.0	− 0.6	1,152	6.4
Households without facilities of running water	18,855	34.3	+23.4	1,558	8.7
Households without facilities of installed bath or shower	33,318	60.6	+40.9	4,424	24.7
Extent of affluence					
Families earning over $10,000 a year (non-farm)	1,663	3.2	− 4.6	1,171	6.6
Persons not in families earning over $6,000 a year (non-farm)	217	1.2	− 2.6	154	2.4
Farms with gross income over $15,000 a year	54	4.5	− 0.5	—	—
Persons with university degree	1,294	0.8	− 2.0	1,006	1.8
Households with two or more television sets	853	1.6	− 2.6	734	4.1
Households with two or more cars	1,823	3.3	− 3.5	1,335	7.5

AVERAGE INCOME (1961 CENSUS)

	Region		St. John's	
	Dollars	% above or below Canadian average	Dollars	% above or below Canadian average
Income per family (non-farm)	3,513	−35.53	4,921	− 9.69
Income per person not in family (non-farm)	1,229	−42.49	1,670	−21.85
Income per farm (net)	1,342	−58.77	—	—

Central Newfoundland

Area covered: 12,700 square miles. *Census divisions:* 6, 8

COMPOSITION OF THE MARKET

Place	Census Division	Population 1961	% of the region
Windsor (urbanized area incl. Grand Falls)	6	12,110	14.64
Gander	6	5,725	6.92
Bishop's Falls	6	4,307	5.21
Botwood	6	3,680	4.45
Lewisporte	8	2,702	3.27
Buchans	6	2,463	2.98
Springdale	8	2,174	2.63
Fogo	8	1,152	1.39
Durrell's Arm	8	1,107	1.34
Joe Batt's Arm	8	1,058	1.28
Badger	6	1,036	1.25
Total urban	—	37,514	45.36
Rural non-farm	—	44,588	53.91
Rural farm	—	602	0.73
Total population		82,704	100.00

ECONOMIC CAPSULE

The three main towns, Windsor-Grand Falls, Bishop's Falls, and Botwood, all within 25 miles of one another, are primarily concerned with the production and shipment of newsprint. The major paper mill of the Anglo-Newfoundland Development Company is located at Grand Falls, and a subsidiary pulp mill is at Bishop's Falls, while Botwood serves as a port of export. To satisfy the demand of the mills, nearly 3,000 people are engaged in logging operations in the neighboring pulpwood forests.

Another important town is Gander, with its large modern airport. It stands by itself in the wilderness, designed primarily to serve the needs of international air transport. However, in recent years, its importance has somewhat diminished, since, with the advent of long-distance jets, refuelling is not so frequently required.

Neither the climate nor the soils are suitable for agriculture, but the waters around the coast are teeming with fish, and for over 7% of the labor force fishing is the sole means of livelihood.

The region is fairly rich in minerals, with a silver-lead-zinc mine at Buchans, a copper-zinc mine at Little Bay, a copper-gold mine at Tilt Cove, and an asbestos mine at Baie Verte. Preliminary figures on the value of production in 1964 show shipments worth $705,000 for gold, $1,874,000 for silver, $9,690,-000 for copper, $6,550,000 for lead, $11,760,000 for zinc, and $8,296,000 for asbestos.

CENTRAL NEWFOUNDLAND
IMPORTANCE OF THE MARKET (1964 ESTIMATES)

	Number	% of Canada
Population	88,900	0.46
Households	16,400	0.34
Disposable income ($ million)	93.0	0.29

CHARACTERISTICS OF THE POPULATION

	% of the total population of the region	% points above or below Canadian average
Mother tongue (1961 census)		
English	99.5	+41.1
French	0.2	−27.9
German	0.1	− 3.0
Native Indian dialects	—	− 0.9
Italian	—	− 1.9
Dutch	—	− 0.9
Polish	—	− 0.9
Ukrainian	0.1	− 1.9
Other	0.1	− 3.7
Total	100.0	—
Official language spoken (1961 census)		
English only	99.4	+32.0
French only	—	−19.1
Both English and French	0.6	−11.6
Neither English nor French	—	− 1.3
Total	100.0	—

GROWTH OF THE MARKET

	Percentage growth 1961 to 1964	% points above or below Canadian average
Population	+ 7.49	+2.02
Disposable income	+25.85	+4.32

AVERAGE INCOME (1961 CENSUS)

	Dollars	% above or below Canadian average
Income per family (non-farm)	3,635	−33.29
Income per person not in family (non-farm)	1,249	−41.55
Income per farm (net)	1,655	−49.16

POVERTY AND AFFLUENCE (1961 CENSUS)

	Number	% of region's total	% points above or below Canadian average
Extent of poverty			
Families earning below $3,000 a year (non-farm)	8,240	52.1	+28.8
Persons not in families earning below $1,500 a year (non-farm)	2,917	76.7	+27.8
Farms with gross income of less than $2,500 a year	84	74.4	+28.3
Persons not in school with grade 4 or less education	14,251	31.2	+17.8
Doubled-up households (more than one family per household)	1,206	7.8	+ 4.1
Households living in dilapidated dwellings	527	3.4	− 2.2
Households without facilities of running water	7,360	47.8	+36.9
Households without facilities of installed bath or shower	9,847	64.0	+44.3
Extent of affluence			
Families earning over $10,000 a year (non-farm)	576	3.7	− 4.1
Persons not in families earning over $6,000 a year (non-farm)	59	1.6	− 2.2
Farms with gross income over $15,000 a year	7	6.1	+ 1.1
Persons with university degree	255	0.6	− 2.2
Households with two or more television sets	100	0.7	− 3.5
Households with two or more cars	360	2.3	− 4.5

MEANS OF LIVELIHOOD—DISTRIBUTION OF
LABOR FORCE BY INDUSTRY

Industry	Persons 1961 census	% of the total	% points above or below Canadian average
Agriculture	156	0.8	− 9.1
Forestry	2,877	15.1	+13.4
Fishing and trapping	1,398	7.3	+ 6.8
Mines, quarries, oil wells	1,170	6.1	+ 4.2
Manufacturing	2,146	11.3	−10.4
Construction	1,201	6.3	− 0.4
Transportation, communications, and other utilities	2,667	14.0	+ 4.7
Wholesale trade	503	2.6	− 1.9
Retail trade	2,398	12.6	+ 1.8
Finance, insurance, and real estate	132	0.7	− 2.8
Community and business services	1,547	8.1	− 4.7
Personal services	940	4.9	− 1.9
Public administration and defence	1,247	6.5	− 1.0
Miscellaneous	703	3.7	+ 1.3
Total labor force	19,085	100.0	—

Western Newfoundland

ECONOMIC CAPSULE

The forest industries play a dominant role in the economy of the region. Corner Brook, a port on the south side of the Humber Fiord, has one of the world's largest paper mills, Newfoundland Pulp and Paper Mills, Ltd., owned by Bowaters. Production capacity is over a thousand tons of newsprint a day. The company employs about 2,000 in the mill, and about the same number work in logging operations in the vast pulpwood forests nearby. The factory employees enjoy a higher standard of living than most Newfoundlanders, but for those out in the woods, hours are long, pay is low, and employment uncertain and seasonal.

The only mineral found in the region is gypsum. Production in 1964 amounted to 350,000 tons. Some is exported to the United States and the remainder processed at a plant in Corner Brook. As in the other parts of Newfoundland, agriculture is of little economic significance, except for some mixed farming near St. George's Bay. On the other hand, fishing is very important — Corner Brook is situated near one of Newfoundland's finest salmon runs.

WESTERN NEWFOUNDLAND

Area covered: 11,941 square miles. *Census divisions:* 4, 5, 9

COMPOSITION OF THE MARKET

Place	Census Division	Population 1961	% of the region
Corner Brook	5	25,185	29.64
Stephenville	4	6,043	7.11
Deer Lake	5	3,998	4.70
Stephenville Crossing	4	2,209	2.60
St. Anthony	9	1,820	2.14
Roddickton	9	1,185	1.39
St. George's	4	1,181	1.39
Kippens	4	1,079	1.27
Total urban	—	42,700	50.24
Rural non-farm	—	39,564	46.56
Rural farm	—	2,717	3.20
Total population		84,981	100.00

MEANS OF LIVELIHOOD—DISTRIBUTION OF LABOR FORCE BY INDUSTRY

Industry	Persons 1961 census	% of the total	% points above or below Canadian average
Agriculture	361	1.8	− 8.1
Forestry	2,082	10.3	+ 8.6
Fishing and trapping	2,129	10.5	+10.0
Mines, quarries, oil wells	104	0.5	− 1.4
Manufacturing	2,820	14.0	− 7.7
Construction	1,556	7.7	+ 1.0
Transportation, communications, and other utilities	2,349	11.6	+ 2.3
Wholesale trade	555	2.7	− 1.8
Retail trade	2,497	12.4	+ 1.6
Finance, insurance, and real estate	216	1.1	− 2.4
Community and business services	1,844	9.1	− 3.7
Personal services	1,118	5.5	− 1.3
Public administration and defence	2,044	10.1	+ 2.6
Miscellaneous	542	2.7	+ 0.3
Total labor force	20,217	100.0	—

IMPORTANCE OF THE MARKET (1964 ESTIMATES)

	Number	% of Canada
Population	92,800	0.48
Households	16,500	0.34
Disposable income ($ million)	93.5	0.30

GROWTH OF THE MARKET

	Percentage growth 1961 to 1964	% points above or below Canadian average
Population	+9.20	+ 3.73
Disposable income	+4.70	−16.83

CHARACTERISTICS OF THE POPULATION

	% of the total population of the region	% points above or below Canadian average
Mother tongue (1961 census)		
English	97.5	+39.1
French	2.0	−26.1
German	0.1	− 3.0
Native Indian dialects	—	− 0.9
Italian	—	− 1.9
Dutch	—	− 0.9
Polish	—	− 0.9
Ukrainian	0.1	− 1.9
Other	0.3	− 3.5
Total	100.0	—
Official language spoken (1961 census)		
English only	97.0	+29.6
French only	0.2	−18.9
Both English and French	2.7	− 9.5
Neither English nor French	0.1	− 1.2
Total	100.0	—

AVERAGE INCOME (1961 CENSUS)

	Dollars	% above or below Canadian average
Income per family (non-farm)	3,876	−28.87
Income per person not in family (non-farm)	1,333	−37.62
Income per farm (net)	1,003	−69.19

POVERTY AND AFFLUENCE (1961 CENSUS)

	Number	% of region's total	% points above or below Canadian average
Extent of poverty			
Families earning below $3,000 a year (non-farm)	6,985	46.8	+23.5
Persons not in families earning below $1,500 a year (non-farm)	2,764	70.5	+21.6
Farms with gross income of less than $2,500 a year	1,367	87.1	+41.0
Persons not in school with grade 4 or less education	14,709	32.0	+18.6
Doubled-up households (more than one family per household)	1,066	7.0	+ 3.3
Households living in dilapidated dwellings	1,193	7.9	+ 2.3
Households without facilities of running water	5,819	38.3	+27.4
Households without facilities of installed bath or shower	9,255	60.9	+41.2
Extent of affluence			
Families earning over $10,000 a year (non-farm)	578	3.9	− 3.9
Persons not in families earning over $6,000 a year (non-farm)	53	1.3	− 2.5
Farms with gross income over $15,000 a year	3	0.7	− 4.3
Persons with university degree	262	0.6	− 2.2
Households with two or more television sets	75	0.5	− 3.7
Households with two or more cars	226	1.5	− 5.3

Labrador

ECONOMIC CAPSULE

This region, which Jacques Cartier referred to as the land God gave to Cain, is now proving to be the greatest storehouse of natural wealth left on this continent. Some of the world's largest reserves of high-grade hematite deposits lie buried in the areas surrounding Wabush Lake and Knob Lake (the latter extending into Québec territory). Although these iron beds were noted in the geological reports of the 19th century, it was only during the last decade that the American steel industry, frightened by the depletion of the Mesabi Range, thought fit to develop them. Production in 1964, on the Newfoundland side, was in the neighborhood of 10 million long tons, and it will go up still higher as more mines are brought into operation. New multi-million dollar beneficiation plants have also been set up to produce the rich concentrates required by the steel industry.

Most of the other natural resources of Labrador are still awaiting development. The Melville Lake area (near the international airport of Goose Bay) has about 40 million cords of accessible pulpwood — more than enough to build a large pulp and paper mill. The only obstacle is the short shipping season of only four to six months.

A major project about to materialize is the harnessing of the mighty Churchill Falls. It will be capable of producing six million horsepower — an amount equal to the combined electrical energy output of the Grand Coulee Dam in the United States, the Aswan Dam in Egypt, plus both the U.S. and the Canadian power dams at Niagara Falls. Engineers estimate the entire Churchill watershed potential at ten million horsepower, an output so huge that if fully harnessed the nation's installed capacity would increase by about 25%. It is not unrealistic to assume that, in the not too distant future, electricity from the wilderness of Labrador may power Manhattan subways and light up the marquees of Broadway — and in return earn badly needed foreign exchange.

Area covered: 102,486 square miles. *Census division:* 10

COMPOSITION OF THE MARKET

Place	Census Division	Population 1961	% of the region
Goose Bay	10	3,040	22.46
Happy Valley	10	2,861	21.14
Total urban	—	5,901	43.60
Rural non-farm	—	7,595	56.12
Rural farm	—	38	0.28
Total population		13,534	100.00

IMPORTANCE OF THE MARKET (1964 ESTIMATES)

	Number	% of Canada
Population	15,700	0.08
Households	2,600	0.06
Disposable income ($ million)	26.0	0.08

GROWTH OF THE MARKET

	Percentage growth 1961 to 1964	% points above or below Canadian average
Population	+16.00	+10.53
Disposable income	+33.33	+11.80

CHARACTERISTICS OF THE POPULATION

	% of the total population of the region	% points above or below Canadian average
Mother tongue (1961 census)		
English	82.4	+24.0
French	7.1	−21.0
German	0.9	− 2.2
Native Indian and Eskimo dialects	8.6	+ 7.7
Italian	0.1	− 1.8
Dutch	0.2	− 0.7
Polish	0.1	− 0.8
Ukrainian	0.1	− 1.9
Other	0.5	− 3.3
Total	100.0	—
Official language spoken (1961 census)		
English only	84.6	+17.2
French only	2.3	−16.8
Both English and French	7.2	− 5.0
Neither English nor French	5.9	+ 4.6
Total	100.0	—

MEANS OF LIVELIHOOD—DISTRIBUTION OF LABOR FORCE BY INDUSTRY

Industry	Persons 1961 census	% of the total	% points above or below Canadian average
Agriculture	—	—	− 9.9
Forestry	59	1.5	− 0.2
Fishing and trapping	7	0.2	− 0.3
Mines, quarries, oil wells	397	10.3	+ 8.4
Manufacturing	20	0.5	−21.2
Construction	416	10.8	+ 4.1
Transportation, communications, and other utilities	282	7.3	− 2.0
Wholesale trade	26	0.7	− 3.8
Retail trade	200	5.2	− 5.6
Finance, insurance, and real estate	30	0.8	− 2.7
Community and business services	248	6.5	− 6.3
Personal services	192	5.0	− 1.8
Public administration and defence	1,929	50.2	+42.7
Miscellaneous	40	1.0	− 1.4
Total labor force	3,846	100.0	—

POVERTY AND AFFLUENCE (1961 CENSUS)

	Number	% of region's total	% points above or below Canadian average
Extent of poverty			
Families earning below $3,000 a year (non-farm)	928	40.2	+16.9
Persons not in families earning below $1,500 a year (non-farm)	342	49.9	+ 1.0
Farms with gross income of less than $2,500 a year	—	—	—
Persons not in school with grade 4 or less education.	2,881	33.7	+20.3
Doubled-up households (more than one family per household)	128	5.6	+ 1.9
Households living in dilapidated dwellings	341	14.8	+ 9.2
Households without facilities of running water	1,355	58.9	+48.0
Households without facilities of installed bath or shower	1,447	62.9	+43.2

Extent of affluence

Families earning over $10,000 a year (non-farm).......	92	4.0	— 3.8
Persons not in families earning over $6,000 a year (non-farm)..	14	2.1	— 1.7
Farms with gross income over $15,000 a year...........	—	—	— 5.0
Persons with university degree.......................................	135	1.6	— 1.2
Households with two or more television sets............	—	—	— 4.2
Households with two or more cars..............................	5	0.2	— 6.6

AVERAGE INCOME (1961 CENSUS)

	Dollars	% above or below Canadian average
Income per family (non-farm).....................................	4,452	−18.30
Income per person not in family (non-farm)................	1,929	— 9.73
Income per farm (net)...	—	—

Prince Edward Island

ECONOMIC CAPSULE

Often referred to as "the Million-Acre Farm", "the Garden of the Gulf", or "the Denmark of Canada", Prince Edward Island is the most cultivated region in the Atlantic Provinces. It has 16% more improved agricultural land than the whole of Nova Scotia. The climate and soil conditions are admirably suited to mixed farming; yields are high in both quantity and quality. Prince Edward Island potatoes are prized throughout the continent; both seed and table varieties are staple exports. The province is equally noted for its hogs and dairy products. Tobacco growing is increasing in popularity.

Fishing is another important industry. Local lobsters and oysters enjoy a wide reputation. Codfish, halibut, mackerel, haddock, and herring are also caught in quantity. The industry may move soon into high gear. At Georgetown a fully integrated fish plant is being established, along with a shipyard for building a fleet of draggers.

During the summer months, the province caters to a large influx of tourists. Few who have felt its comfortable charm would wish to argue against the boast of Anne of Green Gables that Prince Edward Island is "the prettiest place in the world". The Island is renowned for its pastoral serenity. The beautiful rolling sweep and color of the land, the neatly painted farm buildings, the dark-green potato fields, the long sandy beaches, the mustard-colored Lunenburg dories in blue coves, the red roads and winding tidal inlets — all these combine to give

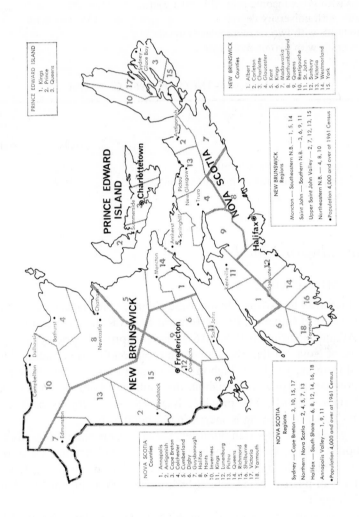

PRINCE EDWARD ISLAND

1. Kings
2. Prince
3. Queens

NEW BRUNSWICK
Counties

1. Albert
2. Carleton
3. Charlotte
4. Gloucester
5. Kent
6. Kings
7. Madawaska
8. Northumberland
9. Queens
10. Restigouche
11. St. John
12. Sunbury
13. Victoria
14. Westmorland
15. York

NEW BRUNSWICK
Regions

Moncton — Southeastern N.B. — 1, 5, 14
Saint John — Southern N.B. — 3, 6, 9, 11
Upper Saint John Valley — 2, 7, 12, 13, 15
Northeastern N.B. — 4, 8, 10

● Population 4,000 and over at 1961 Census

NOVA SCOTIA
Counties

1. Annapolis
2. Antigonish
3. Cape Breton
4. Colchester
5. Cumberland
6. Digby
7. Guysborough
8. Halifax
9. Hants
10. Inverness
11. Kings
12. Lunenburg
13. Pictou
14. Queens
15. Richmond
16. Shelburne
17. Victoria
18. Yarmouth

NOVA SCOTIA
Regions

Sydney — Cape Breton — 3, 10, 15, 17
Northern Nova Scotia — 2, 4, 5, 7, 13
Halifax — South Shore — 6, 8, 12, 14, 16, 18
Annapolis Valley — 1, 9, 11

● Population 4,000 and over at 1961 Census

the landscape a unique, quaint charm. Jacques Cartier, its discoverer, was not exaggerating when he said of the Island: "It needs only a nightingale."

No mines of any kind are found in the province, and the low hills and short, broad rivers make it difficult to develop hydro-electric power. Manufacturing enterprises are small and confined to processing the produce of the land and sea. There are also no large stands of timber for lumbering purposes. The land is too valuable to be left in forest.

The Islanders feel very strongly that they will become prosperous only when Ottawa completes in 1971 the $148 million causeway across the choppy nine miles of Northumberland strait to New Brunswick. The present CNR ferry run, in their opinion, is highly unsatisfactory. They want faster access to markets for their perishable products, as well as a more dependable form of transportation from the mainland for most of their basic necessities. In addition, they contend, the causeway will double the tourist trade, lure new industries to the province, and, during the construction period, alleviate the chronic problem of unemployment. As one PEI cabinet minister remarked: "The causeway will move the Island ahead 50 years in one leap."

Area covered: Whole province, 2,184 square miles. *Counties:* Kings, Prince, Queens

COMPOSITION OF THE MARKET

Place	County	Population 1961	% of the region
Charlottetown	Queens	18,318	17.51
Summerside	Prince	8,611	8.23
Parkdale	Queens	1,735	1.66
Sherwood	Queens	1,580	1.51
Souris	Kings	1,537	1.47
Montague	Kings	1,126	1.07
St. Eleanors	Prince	1,002	0.96
Total urban	—	33,909	32.41
Rural non-farm	—	36,206	34.60
Rural farm	—	34,514	32.99
Total population		104,629	100.00

IMPORTANCE OF THE MARKET (1964 ESTIMATES)

	Number	% of Canada
Population	107,000	0.56
Households	24,000	0.50
Disposable income ($ million)	125.0	0.40

	Percentage growth 1961 to 1964	% points above or below Canadian average
Population	+ 2.27	− 3.20
Disposable income	+30.21	+8.68

CHARACTERISTICS OF THE POPULATION

	% of the total population of the region	% points above or below Canadian average
Mother tongue (1961 census)		
English	91.3	+32.9
French	7.6	−20.5
German	0.1	− 3.0
Native Indian dialects	0.1	− 0.8
Italian	—	− 1.9
Dutch	0.4	− 0.5
Polish	0.1	− 0.8
Ukrainian	0.1	− 1.9
Other	0.3	− 3.5
Total	100.0	—
Official language spoken (1961 census)		
English only	91.1	+23.7
French only	1.1	−18.0
Both English and French	7.6	− 4.6
Neither English nor French	0.2	− 1.1
Total	100.0	—

AVERAGE INCOME (1961 CENSUS)

	Dollars	% above or below Canadian average
Income per family (non-farm)	3,919	−28.08
Income per person not in family (non-farm)	1,470	−31.21
Income per farm (net)	2,172	−33.27

POVERTY AND AFFLUENCE (1961 CENSUS)

	Number	% of region's total	% points above or below Canadian average
Extent of poverty			
Families earning below $3,000 a year (non-farm)	6,447	44.8	+21.5
Persons not in families earning below $1,500 a year (non-farm)	4,414	67.1	+18.2
Farms with gross income of less than $2,500 a year	4,449	60.6	+14.5
Persons not in school with grade 4 or less education	8,033	12.3	− 1.1
Doubled-up households (more than one family per household)	1,204	5.0	+ 1.3
Households living in dilapidated dwellings	1,357	5.7	+ 0.1
Households without facilities of running water	8,267	34.5	+23.6
Households without facilities of installed bath or shower	11,451	47.8	+28.1
Extent of affluence			
Families earning over $10,000 a year (non-farm)	537	3.7	− 4.1
Persons not in families earning over $6,000 a year (non-farm)	82	1.3	− 2.5
Farms with gross income over $15,000 a year	131	1.8	− 3.2
Persons with university degree	908	1.4	− 1.4
Households with two or more television sets	187	0.8	− 3.4
Households with two or more cars	898	3.8	− 3.0

MEANS OF LIVELIHOOD—DISTRIBUTION OF LABOR FORCE BY INDUSTRY

Industry	Persons 1961 census	% of the total	% points above or below Canadian average
Agriculture	9,175	26.9	+17.0
Forestry	142	0.4	− 1.3
Fishing and trapping	2,088	6.1	+ 5.6
Mines, quarries, oil wells	4	—	− 1.9
Manufacturing	3,014	8.8	−12.9
Construction	2,215	6.5	− 0.2
Transportation, communications, and other utilities	2,779	8.2	− 1.1
Wholesale trade	1,292	3.8	− 0.7
Retail trade	3,495	10.2	− 0.6

Industry	Persons 1961 census	% of the total	% points above or below Canadian average
Finance, insurance, and real estate	556	1.6	− 1.9
Community and business services	3,696	10.8	− 2.0
Personal services	1,981	5.8	− 1.0
Public administration and defence	2,981	8.7	+ 1.2
Miscellaneous	730	2.2	− 0.2
Total labor force	34,148	100.0	—

Sydney — Cape Breton

ECONOMIC CAPSULE

Coal and steel play a major role in the economic life of Cape Breton Island. The coal basin at Sydney is the largest in the Atlantic Provinces, stretching for 30 miles along the Atlantic coast. Only a small part of the coal seams outcrop on land, and this necessitates undersea workings which extend as much as two and a half miles from shore. In recent years, the collieries have been highly mechanized to bring the costs down, but marketing problems still remain. In spite of the transportation subventions from the federal government, it is very difficult for Cape Breton to compete with American coal in Southern Ontario. Even in the Maritimes, the marketing outlook is not too bright. Oil is rapidly replacing coal, both on the railways and for domestic heating.

Efforts are being continuously made to prevent the mines from closing. A contract has been signed with Ontario Hydro for the delivery of 2.8 million tons of coal over a five-year period, 1963-1967. It is also anticipated that 100,000 tons of coal will be required annually when the heavy water plant for nuclear energy, now being constructed at Glace Bay, is completed. Recently, the federal government, too, has agreed in principle to provide $25 million in aid to keep the industry alive and healthy. The National Energy Board has been asked to study and report on the best means of using coal on a substantial scale for the Maritime Provinces' power grid. There will, of course, always be some demand for coking coal in the blast furnaces at Sydney. Here, right in the heart of the coal basin, is one of the most important primary iron and steel plants in the country, operated by the Dominion Steel and Coal Corporation, Limited. Recently modernized, it is capable of producing over a million tons of steel ingots per year. Cheap transportation allows for competitive marketing as far west as Montréal.

While steel and coal dominate the picture, various other industries are also important — a pulp mill at Port Hawkesbury, gypsum mining in Inverness and Victoria counties, deep sea fishing along the coast. Soon they will be joined by an automobile industry. Canadian Motor Industries Ltd., in co-operation with the Japanese manufacturers, are planning to build a plant that will assemble 200 Toyota and Isuzu cars a week. This will be the Japanese auto industry's first production beachhead in the North American market.

Tourism too is fast growing. The island is blessed with some of the most beautiful natural scenery in Canada, resembling in austere grandeur the Highlands of Scotland. The Cabot Trail, winding in part through Cape Breton National Park, has made accessible many vistas of breath-taking splendor. Of equal interest to the tourists is the historic French fortress of Louisburg (recently restored) as well as the Gaelic culture preserved among many of the inhabitants.

SYDNEY—CAPE BRETON

Area covered: 3,975 square miles. *Counties:* Cape Breton, Inverness, Richmond, Victoria

COMPOSITION OF THE MARKET

Place	County	Population 1961	% of the region
Sydney—Glace Bay (urbanized area)	Cape Breton	106,114	62.47
Inverness	Inverness	2,109	1.24
Louisburg	Cape Breton	1,417	0.83
Port Hawkesbury	Inverness	1,346	0.79
Donkin	Cape Breton	1,010	0.60
Total urban	—	111,996	65.93
Rural non-farm	—	47,739	28.11
Rural farm	—	10,130	5.96
Total population		169,865	100.00

IMPORTANCE OF THE MARKET (1964 ESTIMATES)

	Region		Sydney–Glace Bay	
	Number	% of Canada	Number	% of Canada
Population	173,300	0.90	109,900	0.57
Households	36,800	0.76	23,900	0.50
Disposable income ($ million)	233.3	0.74	162.8	0.52

GROWTH OF THE MARKET

	Region		Sydney–Glace Bay	
	Percentage growth 1961 to 1964	% points above or below Canadian average	Percentage growth 1961 to 1964	% points above or below Canadian average
Population	+ 2.02	−3.45	+ 3.57	−1.90
Disposable income	+17.83	−3.70	+16.29	−5.24

AVERAGE INCOME (1961 CENSUS)

	Region		Sydney–Glace Bay	
	Dollars	% above or below Canadian average	Dollars	% above or below Canadian average
Income per family (non-farm)	4,156	−23.73	4,442	−18.48
Income per person not in family (non-farm)	1,448	−32.24	1,646	−22.98
Income per farm (net)	822	−74.75	—	—

LABOR FORCE BY INDUSTRY

Industry	Region			Sydney–Glace Bay	
	Persons 1961 census	% of the total	% points above or below Canadian average	Persons 1961 census	% of the total
Agriculture	1,698	3.5	− 6.4	106	0.3
Forestry	809	1.7	—	25	0.1
Fishing and trapping	1,629	3.4	+ 2.9	107	0.3
Mines, quarries, oil wells	8,151	16.9	+15.0	7,138	23.1
Manufacturing	7,348	15.2	− 6.5	5,064	16.4
Construction	2,839	5.9	− 0.8	1,155	3.7
Transportation, communications, and other utilities	5,353	11.1	+ 1.8	3,263	10.5
Wholesale trade	1,489	3.1	− 1.4	1,065	3.4
Retail trade	5,388	11.1	+ 0.3	3,833	12.4
Finance, insurance, and real estate	780	1.6	− 1.9	606	2.0
Community and business services	5,725	11.8	− 1.0	4,014	13.0
Personal services	3,076	6.4	− 0.4	2,009	6.5
Public administration and defence	3,205	6.6	− 0.9	2,131	6.9
Miscellaneous	812	1.7	− 0.7	429	1.4
Total labor force	48,302	100.0	—	30,945	100.0

CHARACTERISTICS OF THE POPULATION

	Region		Sydney–Glace Bay
	% of the total population of the region	% points above or below Canadian average	% of the total population of the city
Mother tongue (1961 census)			
English	87.7	+29.3	94.3
French	7.4	−20.7	2.2
German	0.1	− 3.0	0.2
Native Indian dialects	1.0	+ 0.1	0.2
Italian	0.3	− 1.6	0.4
Dutch	0.2	− 0.7	0.1
Polish	0.4	− 0.5	0.5
Ukrainian	0.3	− 1.7	0.4
Other	2.6	− 1.2	1.7
Total	100.0	—	100.0
Official language spoken (1961 census)			
English only	91.2	+23.8	96.8
French only	1.5	−17.6	0.1
Both English and French	7.0	− 5.2	3.0
Neither English nor French	0.3	− 1.0	0.1
Total	100.0	—	100.0

POVERTY AND AFFLUENCE (1961 CENSUS)

	Region			Sydney–Glace Bay	
	Number	% of region's total	% points above or below Canadian average	Number	% of city's total
Extent of poverty					
Families earning below $3,000 a year (non-farm)	11,641	35.7	+12.4	6,554	29.9
Persons not in families earning below $1,500 a year (non-farm)	8,169	69.8	+20.9	4,751	64.4
Farms with gross income of less than $2,500 a year	1,640	83.0	+36.9	—	—
Persons not in school with grade 4 or less education	14,184	14.2	+ 0.8	7,672	12.2

	Region			Sydney–Glace Bay	
	Number	% of region's total	% points above or below Canadian average	Number	% of city's total
Doubled-up households (more than one family per household)	2,221	6.1	+ 2.4	1,452	6.4
Households living in dilapidated dwellings	3,607	9.9	+ 4.3	2,485	10.9
Households without facilities of running water	4,993	13.7	+ 2.8	490	2.2
Households without facilities of installed bath or shower	14,527	39.8	+20.1	6,464	28.4
Extent of affluence					
Families earning over $10,000 a year (non-farm)	982	3.0	− 4.8	754	3.4
Persons not in families earning over $6,000 a year (non-farm)	211	1.8	− 2.0	166	2.3
Farms with gross income over $15,000 a year	25	1.3	− 3.7	—	—
Persons with university degree	1,379	1.4	− 1.4	968	1.5
Households with two or more television sets	515	1.4	− 2.8	425	1.9
Households with two or more cars	1,056	2.9	− 3.9	668	2.9

Northern Nova Scotia

ECONOMIC CAPSULE

Manufacturing is the key industry in the region. New Glasgow-Trenton and the surrounding areas have factories for shoes, textiles, and fabricated structural steel. They will be soon joined by a kraft pulp mill of Scott Paper Ltd. and a plant for hi-fi and stereo equipment of Clairtone Sound Corporation. Truro, "the hub of Nova Scotia", has large condenseries and creameries, knitting mills, a carpet factory, and wood-working establishments. Amherst, at the gateway to the province, is renowned for its machine shops, which produce all the components for railway carriages.

Other important industries are mining (coal, salt, and gypsum) and fishing. Agriculture is limited. The short growing season is suited chiefly for hay, and farming is confined mostly to dairying and cattle raising.

Antigonish, a Scottish Roman Catholic county and cathedral town, has gained world renown for the Antigonish Movement started in the Thirties by the professors of St. Francis Xavier University. The aim is to foster a co-operative educational program for group action through university extension courses, library service, credit unions, study clubs, and the like. The success of the movement in the Maritimes during the first quarter century of its existence is evident from the following statistics: 419 credit unions with membership of 168,200 and assets of about $46,459,000; co-operative insurance totaling over $5,500,-000; and wholesale organizations with a turnover of $26,000,000. The techniques of this movement have been exported with beneficial results to Mexico, Dominican Republic, Jamaica, British Honduras, and parts of South America.

NORTHERN NOVA SCOTIA

Area covered: 6,410 square miles. *Counties:* Antigonish, Colchester, Cumberland, Guysborough, Pictou

COMPOSITION OF THE MARKET

Place	County	Population 1961	% of the region
New Glasgow (urbanized area including Trenton)	Pictou	22,408	15.60
Truro (urbanized area)	Colchester	15,869	11.05
Amherst	Cumberland	10,788	7.51
Springhill	Cumberland	5,836	4.06
Pictou	Pictou	4,534	3.16
Antigonish	Antigonish	4,344	3.02
Parrsboro	Cumberland	1,834	1.28
Oxford	Cumberland	1,471	1.02
Canso	Guysborough	1,151	0.80
Mulgrave	Guysborough	1,145	0.80
Stewiacke	Colchester	1,042	0.73
Total urban	—	70,422	49.03
Rural non-farm	—	53,692	37.39
Rural farm	—	19,502	13.58
Total population		143,616	100.00

IMPORTANCE OF THE MARKET (1964 ESTIMATES)

	Number	% of Canada
Population	141,400	0.73
Households	34,500	0.72
Disposable income ($ million)	143.1	0.45

GROWTH OF THE MARKET

	Percentage change 1961 to 1964	% points above or below Canadian average
Population	−1.54	− 7.01
Disposable income	+4.22	−17.31

CHARACTERISTICS OF THE POPULATION

	% of the total population of the region	% points above or below Canadian average
Mother tongue (1961 census)		
English	95.9	+37.5
French	2.5	−25.6
German	0.2	− 2.9
Native Indian dialects	0.3	− 0.6
Italian	—	− 1.9
Dutch	0.5	− 0.4
Polish	0.1	− 0.8
Ukrainian	—	− 2.0
Other	0.5	− 3.3
Total	100.0	—
Official language spoken (1961 census)		
English only	96.3	+28.9
French only	0.2	−18.9
Both English and French	3.4	− 8.8
Neither English nor French	0.1	− 1.2
Total	100.0	—

AVERAGE INCOME (1961 CENSUS)

	Dollars	% above or below Canadian average
Income per family (non-farm)	3,514	−35.51
Income per person not in family (non-farm)	1,328	−37.86
Income per farm (net)	1,042	−67.99

MEANS OF LIVELIHOOD—DISTRIBUTION OF LABOR FORCE BY INDUSTRY

Industry	Persons 1961 census	% of the total	% points above or below Canadian average
Agriculture	4,068	9.4	−0.5
Forestry	1,378	3.2	+1.5
Fishing and trapping	1,557	3.6	+3.1
Mines, quarries, oil wells	1,153	2.7	+0.8
Manufacturing	7,429	17.3	−4.4
Construction	3,112	7.2	+0.5
Transportation, communications, and other utilities	4,925	11.4	+2.1
Wholesale trade	1,587	3.7	−0.8
Retail trade	5,241	12.2	+1.4
Finance, insurance, and real estate	874	2.0	−1.5
Community and business services	5,284	12.3	−0.5
Personal services	3,315	7.7	+0.9
Public administration and defence	2,185	5.1	−2.4
Miscellaneous	936	2.2	−0.2
Total labor force	43,044	100.0	—

POVERTY AND AFFLUENCE (1961 CENSUS)

	Number	% of region's total	% points above or below Canadian average
Extent of poverty			
Families earning below $3,000 a year (non-farm)	13,264	49.0	+25.7
Persons not in families earning below $1,500 a year (non-farm)	8,581	69.7	+20.8

	Number	% of region's total	% points above or below Canadian average
Farms with gross income of less than $2,500 a year....	3,560	77.4	+31.3
Persons not in school with grade 4 or less education.	9,270	10.4	− 3.0
Doubled-up households (more than one family per household)..	1,396	3.9	+ 0.2
Households living in dilapidated dwellings...............	3,184	8.8	+ 3.2
Households without facilities of running water...........	7,372	20.5	+ 9.6
Households without facilities of installed bath or shower..	14,619	40.6	+20.9
Extent of affluence			
Families earning over $10,000 a year (non-farm)........	682	2.5	− 5.3
Persons not in families earning over $6,000 a year (non-farm)...	165	1.3	− 2.5
Farms with gross income over $15,000 a year..............	62	1.4	− 3.6
Persons with university degree.....................................	1,584	1.8	− 1.0
Households with two or more television sets............	401	1.1	− 3.1
Households with two or more cars.............................	1,196	3.3	− 3.5

Halifax — South Shore

ECONOMIC CAPSULE

Halifax, without question, is the metropolis of the east, being a major manufacturing, commercial, and administrative center. Its motto "E Mari Merces" is particularly apt: the sea affects its economic life in practically every sphere. It is a base for the Canadian navy; its magnificent harbor handles yearly about 8 to 9 million tons of cargo; its shipyards can build destroyers and other vessels of over 10,000 tons.

Most of the manufacturing industries are dependent on imported raw materials and fuels. Thanks to her sea contacts, Metropolitan Halifax can economically refine oil shipped from Venezuela; brew beer using British hops; produce sugar from Caribbean and Latin American sugarcane; assemble cars with parts from Sweden; make chocolates with cocoa from West Africa; and cure and can fish from the Banks nearby.

Outside Halifax, fishing is the main occupation. Lunenburg has still preserved its century-old tradition of fine boat building. Its economy since 1964 has been further strengthened by a large, ultra-modern plant capable of processing about 80 million pounds of raw fish annually.

HALIFAX—SOUTH SHORE

Area covered: 7,002 square miles. *Counties:* Digby, Halifax, Lunenburg, Queens, Shelburne, Yarmouth

COMPOSITION OF THE MARKET

Place	County	Population 1961	% of the region
Halifax (metro)	Halifax	183,946	55.30
Yarmouth	Yarmouth	8,636	2.60
Bridgewater	Lunenburg	4,497	1.35
Liverpool	Queens	3,712	1.12
Lunenburg	Lunenburg	3,056	0.92
Shelburne	Shelburne	2,408	0.72
Digby	Digby	2,308	0.69
Lockeport	Shelburne	1,231	0.37
New Road	Halifax	1,109	0.33
Mahone Bay	Lunenburg	1,103	0.33
Total urban	—	212,006	63.73
Rural non-farm	—	107,655	32.36
Rural farm	—	13,025	3.91
Total population		332,686	100.00

IMPORTANCE OF THE MARKET (1964 ESTIMATES)

	Region		*Halifax*	
	Number	% of Canada	Number	% of Canada
Population	351,100	1.83	184,000	0.96
Households	83,700	1.74	46,000	0.96
Disposable income ($ million)	485.1	1.54	329.9	1.05

GROWTH OF THE MARKET

	Region		*Halifax*	
	Percentage growth 1961 to 1964	% points above or below Canadian average	Percentage growth 1961 to 1964	% points above or below Canadian average
Population	+ 5.53	+0.06	+ 0.03	−5.44
Disposable income	+19.72	−1.81	+18.33	−3.20

LABOR FORCE BY INDUSTRY

Industry	Region Persons 1961 census	% of the total	% points above or below Canadian average	Halifax Persons 1961 census	% of the total
Agriculture	2,367	2.0	− 7.9	141	0.2
Forestry	1,471	1.3	− 0.4	25	—
Fishing and trapping	4,072	3.5	+ 3.0	150	0.2
Mines, quarries, oil wells	206	0.2	− 1.7	66	0.1
Manufacturing	16,046	13.8	− 7.9	7,472	10.3
Construction	7,206	6.2	− 0.5	3,373	4.6
Transportation, communications, and other utilities	12,434	10.7	+ 1.4	7,667	10.5
Wholesale trade	5,587	4.8	+ 0.3	4,088	5.6
Retail trade	13,399	11.5	+ 0.7	8,344	11.4
Finance, insurance, and real estate	3,573	3.1	− 0.4	2,988	4.1
Community and business services	14,679	12.6	− 0.2	10,858	14.9
Personal services	7,951	6.8	—	4,657	6.4
Public administration and defence	25,562	21.9	+14.4	21,981	30.1
Miscellaneous	1,929	1.6	− 0.8	1,143	1.6
Total labor force	116,482	100.0	—	72,953	100.0

CHARACTERISTICS OF THE POPULATION

	Region % of the total population of the region	% points above or below Canadian average	Halifax % of the total population of the city
Mother tongue (1961 census)			
English	91.8	+33.4	94.6
French	6.7	−21.4	3.2
German	0.3	− 2.8	0.5
Native Indian dialects	—	− 0.9	—
Italian	0.1	− 1.8	0.2
Dutch	0.2	− 0.7	0.3
Polish	0.1	− 0.8	0.1
Ukrainian	0.1	− 1.9	0.1
Other	0.7	− 3.1	1.0
Total	100.0	—	100.0

Official language spoken (1961 census)

English only	91.1	+23.7	94.1
French only	0.9	−18.2	0.2
Both English and French	7.8	− 4.4	5.5
Neither English nor French	0.2	− 1.1	0.2
Total	100.0	—	100.0

AVERAGE INCOME (1961 CENSUS)

	Region		*Halifax*	
	Dollars	% above or below Canadian average	Dollars	% above or below Canadian average
Income per family (non-farm)	4,688	−13.97	5,685	+4.33
Income per person not in family (non-farm)	1,861	−12.92	2,309	+8.05
Income per farm (net)	905	−72.20	—	—

POVERTY AND AFFLUENCE (1961 CENSUS)

	Region			*Halifax*	
	Number	% of region's total	% points above or below Canadian average	Number	% of city's total
Extent of poverty					
Families earning below $3,000 a year (non-farm)	22,688	32.3	+ 9.0	6,457	16.4
Persons not in families earning below $1,500 a year (non-farm)	16,016	55.1	+ 6.2	7,193	41.6
Farms with gross income of less than $2,500 a year	2,331	81.9	+35.8	—	—
Persons not in school with grade 4 or less education	21,509	10.2	− 3.2	8,169	7.0
Doubled-up households (more than one family per household)	4,023	5.0	+ 1.3	2,312	5.5
Households living in dilapidated dwellings	6,074	7.6	+ 2.0	2,661	6.3
Households without facilities of running water	12,616	15.7	+ 4.8	1,453	3.4
Households without facilities of installed bath or shower	23,199	28.9	+ 9.2	4,049	9.6

	Region			Halifax	
	Number	% of region's total	% points above or below Canadian average	Number	% of city's total
Extent of affluence					
Families earning over $10,000 a year (non-farm)	3,779	5.4	− 2.4	3,130	8.0
Persons not in families earning over $6,000 a year (non-farm)	827	2.8	− 1.0	726	4.2
Farms with gross income over $15,000 a year	57	2.0	− 3.0	—	—
Persons with university degree..	5,985	2.8	—	4,870	4.2
Households with two or more television sets	3,195	4.0	− 0.2	2,784	6.6
Households with two or more cars	3,985	5.0	− 1.8	2,550	6.0

Annapolis Valley

ECONOMIC CAPSULE

This is one of the best known agricultural districts in the Maritimes. For decades apple growing was the dominant occupation, but in the postwar era, with the partial loss of the United Kingdom market, many farmers have shifted over to dairying and livestock raising as well.

About 80% of the gypsum mined in Canada comes from Hants county. It is mostly exported to New England where it is used in the plaster, insulation, and paint industries. Barite is obtained at Wolton, also in Hants county.

The region is highly rural. The largest town, Kentville, has a population of only 4,600. Manufacturing is negligible, being for the most part related to agriculture and consisting of such industries as canning and production of fertilizers.

IMPORTANCE OF THE MARKET (1964 ESTIMATES)

	Number	% of Canada
Population	94,200	0.49
Households	23,000	0.48
Disposable income ($ million)	105.5	0.33

Area covered: 3,356 square miles. *Counties:* Annapolis, Hants, Kings

COMPOSITION OF THE MARKET

Place	County	Population 1961	% of the region
Kentville	Kings	4,612	5.08
Windsor	Hants	3,823	4.21
Wolfville	Kings	2,413	2.66
Aldershot	Kings	2,179	2.40
Middleton	Annapolis	1,921	2.11
Hantsport	Hants	1,381	1.52
Berwick	Kings	1,282	1.41
Kingston	Kings	1,210	1.33
Bridgetown	Annapolis	1,043	1.15
Total urban	—	19,864	21.87
Rural non-farm	—	56,801	62.53
Rural farm	—	14,175	15.60
Total population		90,840	100.00

CHARACTERISTICS OF THE POPULATION

	% of the total population of the region	% points above or below Canadian average
Mother tongue (1961 census)		
English	97.0	+38.6
French	1.3	−26.8
German	0.2	− 2.9
Native Indian dialects	0.2	− 0.7
Italian	0.1	− 1.8
Dutch	0.7	− 0.2
Polish	0.1	− 0.8
Ukrainian	0.1	− 1.9
Other	0.3	− 3.5
Total	100.0	—
Official language spoken (1961 census)		
English only	97.4	+30.0
French only	0.1	−19.0
Both English and French	2.4	− 9.8
Neither English nor French	0.1	− 1.2
Total	100.0	—

GROWTH OF THE MARKET

	Percentage growth 1961 to 1964	% points above or below Canadian average
Population	+ 3.70	−1.77
Disposable income	+15.30	−6.23

AVERAGE INCOME (1961 CENSUS)

	Dollars	% above or below Canadian average
Income per family (non-farm)	3,867	−29.03
Income per person not in family (non-farm)	1,474	−31.02
Income per farm (net)	2,732	−16.07

MEANS OF LIVELIHOOD—DISTRIBUTION OF LABOR FORCE BY INDUSTRY

Industry	Persons 1961 census	% of the total	% points above or below Canadian average
Agriculture	3,905	13.5	+ 3.6
Forestry	638	2.2	+ 0.5
Fishing and trapping	235	0.8	+ 0.3
Mines, quarries, oil wells	595	2.0	+ 0.1
Manufacturing	3,258	11.2	−10.5
Construction	2,367	8.2	+ 1.5
Transportation, communications, and other utilities	2,250	7.8	− 1.5
Wholesale trade	940	3.2	− 1.3
Retail trade	3,132	10.8	—
Finance, insurance, and real estate	425	1.5	− 2.0
Community and business services	3,151	10.9	− 1.9
Personal services	1,772	6.1	− 0.7
Public administration and defence	5,864	20.2	+12.7
Miscellaneous	459	1.6	− 0.8
Total labor force	28,991	100.0	—

POVERTY AND AFFLUENCE (1961 CENSUS)

	Number	% of region's total	% points above or below Canadian average
Extent of poverty			
Families earning below $3,000 a year (non-farm)	7,336	43.8	+20.5
Persons not in families earning below $1,500 a year (non-farm)	4,481	67.3	+18.4
Farms with gross income of less than $2,500 a year	1,971	63.6	+17.5
Persons not in school with grade 4 or less education.	5,131	9.1	− 4.3
Doubled-up households (more than one family per household)	738	3.3	− 0.4
Households living in dilapidated dwellings	2,293	10.2	+ 4.6
Households without facilities of running water	4,472	19.8	+ 8.9
Households without facilities of installed bath or shower	8,567	37.9	+18.2
Extent of affluence			
Families earning over $10,000 a year (non-farm)	417	2.5	− 5.3
Persons not in families earning over $6,000 a year (non-farm)	127	1.9	− 1.9
Farms with gross income over $15,000 a year	207	6.7	+ 1.7
Persons with university degree	1,215	2.1	− 0.7
Households with two or more television sets	293	1.3	− 2.9
Households with two or more cars	949	4.2	− 2.6

Moncton — Southeastern New Brunswick

ECONOMIC CAPSULE

Forestry and agriculture are the principal primary industries. Most farms are of small size, specializing in dairying and livestock raising to satisfy the demands of the local markets.

At Dorchester, in Westmorland county, the provincial government recently has created an industrial park, with facilities tailored to suit the needs of chemical manufacturers. Its aim is to attract new factories so that all the chemical requirements of eastern Canada can be met from one central location.

Moncton functions as a transportation node and a distribution center with roads and railways radiating in all directions. It is the headquarters of the Atlantic division of the Canadian National Railways and has a large railroad rolling stock industry. It has also many food manufacturing plants.

MONCTON—SOUTHEASTERN NEW BRUNSWICK

Area covered: 3,845 square miles. *Counties:* Albert, Kent, Westmorland

COMPOSITION OF THE MARKET

Place	County	Population 1961	% of the region
Moncton (urbanized area)	Albert, Westmorland	55,768	41.98
Sackville	Westmorland	3,038	2.29
Shediac	Westmorland	2,159	1.63
Buctouche	Kent	1,537	1.16
Richibucto	Kent	1,375	1.03
Total urban	—	63,877	48.09
Rural non-farm	—	53,918	40.59
Rural farm	—	15,036	11.32
Total population		132,831	100.00

CHARACTERISTICS OF THE POPULATION

	Region		Moncton
	% of the total population of the region	% points above or below Canadian average	% of the total population of the city
Mother tongue (1961 census)			
English	53.5	− 4.9	66.2
French	45.1	+17.0	32.5
German	0.1	− 3.0	0.2
Native Indian dialects	0.6	− 0.3	—
Italian	0.1	− 1.8	0.2
Dutch	0.1	− 0.8	0.2
Polish	0.1	− 0.8	0.1
Ukrainian	0.1	− 1.9	0.1
Other	0.3	− 3.5	0.5
Total	100.0	—	100.0
Official language spoken (1961 census)			
English only	51.7	−15.7	63.2
French only	16.9	− 2.2	4.5
Both English and French	31.1	+18.9	32.0
Neither English nor French	0.3	− 1.0	0.3
Total	100.0	—	100.0

IMPORTANCE OF THE MARKET (1964 ESTIMATES)

	Region		Moncton	
	Number	% of Canada	Number	% of Canada
Population	136,300	0.71	59,600	0.31
Households	30,400	0.63	14,500	0.30
Disposable income ($ million)	169.8	0.54	102.2	0.32

GROWTH OF THE MARKET

	Region		Moncton	
	Percentage growth 1961 to 1964	% points above or below Canadian average	Percentage growth 1961 to 1964	% points above or below Canadian average
Population	+ 2.61	−2.86	+ 6.87	+ 1.40
Disposable income	+16.06	−5.47	+10.01	−11.52

MEANS OF LIVELIHOOD—DISTRIBUTION OF LABOR FORCE BY INDUSTRY

Industry	Region			Moncton	
	Persons 1961 census	% of the total	% points above or below Canadian average	Persons 1961 census	% of the total
Agriculture	2,827	6.9	−3.0	104	0.5
Forestry	1,055	2.6	+0.9	29	0.1
Fishing and trapping	761	1.9	+1.4	4	—
Mines, quarries, oil wells	63	0.1	−1.8	13	0.1
Manufacturing	5,893	14.4	−7.3	2,288	11.5
Construction	2,962	7.2	+0.5	1,042	5.2
Transportation, communications, and other utilities	6,492	15.8	+6.5	3,923	19.7
Wholesale trade	2,507	6.1	+1.6	1,696	8.5
Retail trade	5,841	14.2	+3.4	3,586	18.0
Finance, insurance, and real estate	1,043	2.5	−1.0	794	4.0
Community and business services	4,947	12.1	−0.7	2,784	13.9
Personal services	2,740	6.7	−0.1	1,452	7.3
Public administration and defence	3,112	7.6	+0.1	1,830	9.2
Miscellaneous	794	1.9	−0.5	399	2.0
Total labor force	41,037	100.0	—	19,944	100.0

AVERAGE INCOME (1961 CENSUS)

	Region		Moncton	
	Dollars	% above or below Canadian average	Dollars	% above or below Canadian average
Income per family (non-farm)............................	4,334	−20.46	5,218	− 4.24
Income per person not in family (non-farm)..	1,613	−24.52	1,876	−12.21
Income per farm (net)....................................	952	−70.75	—	—

POVERTY AND AFFLUENCE (1961 CENSUS)

	Region			Moncton	
	Number	% of region's total	% points above or below Canadian average	Number	% of city's total
Extent of poverty					
Families earning below $3,000 a year (non-farm)...................	8,988	36.0	+12.7	2,645	21.2
Persons not in families earning below $1,500 a year (non-farm)......................	5,570	60.6	+11.7	2,533	49.7
Farms with gross income of less than $2,500 a year.................	2,271	81.4	+35.3	—	—
Persons not in school with grade 4 or less education........	14,396	17.7	+ 4.3	3,825	10.9
Doubled-up households (more than one family per household)...	1,600	5.4	+ 1.7	576	4.3
Households living in dilapidated dwellings.......................	3,398	11.6	+ 6.0	1,057	8.0
Households without facilities of running water..........................	4,962	16.9	+ 6.0	351	2.6
Households without facilities of installed bath or shower..........	9,584	32.6	+12.9	1,010	7.6
Extent of affluence					
Families earning over $10,000 a year (non-farm).....................	1,022	4.1	− 3.7	751	6.0
Persons not in families earning over $6,000 a year (non-farm)...	167	1.9	− 1.9	102	2.0

Farms with gross income over $15,000 a year	47	1.7	− 3.3	—	—
Persons with university degree	1,523	1.9	− 0.9	966	2.7
Households with two or more television sets	733	2.5	− 1.7	555	4.2
Households with two or more cars	1,405	4.8	− 2.0	792	6.0

Saint John — Southern New Brunswick

Area covered: 4,601 square miles. *Counties:* Charlotte, Kings, Queens, Saint John

COMPOSITION OF THE MARKET

Place	County	Population 1961	% of the region
Saint John (metro)	Kings, St. John	95,563	63.67
Sussex	Kings	3,457	2.30
St. Stephen	Charlotte	3,380	2.25
Milltown	Charlotte	1,892	1.26
St. Andrews	Charlotte	1,531	1.02
Rothwell	Queens	1,357	0.91
St. George	Charlotte	1,133	0.76
Total urban	—	108,313	72.17
Rural non-farm	—	32,374	21.57
Rural farm	—	9,397	6.26
Total population		150,084	100.00

ECONOMIC CAPSULE

The region has a diversified economy. There is fishing (Charlotte county), dairy farming (Kings county), coal mining (Minto), forestry (pulp mill at St. George), and tourism (Lower St. John Valley and the Reversing Falls at Saint John).

Saint John is a close rival to Halifax as the industrial center of the Maritimes. However, unlike the capital of Nova Scotia, it has no universities, no naval base, no provincial seat of government. It earns its way through its manufacturing and commercial activities. Being an open-water port at the eastern terminal of the Canadian Pacific Railway, its large harbor is always bustling with activity. In 1964, 5.8 million tons of cargo were handled. Winter is the busiest season, when there is no competition from Montréal.

The manufacturing industries of Saint John are quite varied. They include sawmilling, pulp and paper making, metal fabricating, petroleum refining, shipbuilding and repair, and the processing or packing of imported products (e.g., tea, coffee, spices, and cane sugar). The city is also the focus of the wholesale and retail trade for southern New Brunswick.

POVERTY AND AFFLUENCE (1961 CENSUS)

	Region			Saint John	
	Number	% of region's total	% points above or below Canadian average	Number	% of city's total
Extent of poverty					
Families earning below $3,000 a year (non-farm)	10,322	32.8	+ 9.5	4,920	23.6
Persons not in families earning below $1,500 a year (non-farm)	7,855	57.9	+ 9.0	4,572	50.3
Farms with gross income of less than $2,500 a year	1,540	69.6	+23.5	—	—
Persons not in school with grade 4 or less education	10,845	11.1	− 2.3	6,611	10.6
Doubled-up households (more than one family per household)	1,154	3.0	− 0.7	682	2.8
Households living in dilapidated dwellings	4,677	12.0	+ 6.4	2,887	12.0
Households without facilities of running water	5,267	13.6	+ 2.7	1,241	5.1
Households without facilities of installed bath or shower	11,995	30.9	+11.2	5,153	21.3
Extent of affluence					
Families earning over $10,000 a year (non-farm)	1,444	4.6	− 3.2	1,171	5.6
Persons not in families earning over $6,000 a year (non-farm)	322	2.5	− 1.3	248	2.7
Farms with gross income over $15,000 a year	48	2.2	− 2.8	—	—
Persons with university degree	1,824	1.9	− 0.9	1,417	2.3
Households with two or more television sets	943	2.4	− 1.8	775	3.2
Households with two or more cars	1,827	4.7	− 2.1	1,146	4.7

IMPORTANCE OF THE MARKET (1964 ESTIMATES)

	Region		Saint John	
	Number	% of Canada	Number	% of Canada
Population	152,400	0.79	100,000	0.52
Households	39,300	0.82	26,300	0.55
Disposable income ($ million)	194.5	0.62	148.0	0.47

GROWTH OF THE MARKET

	Region		Saint John	
	Percentage growth 1961 to 1964	% points above or below Canadian average	Percentage growth 1961 to 1964	% points above or below Canadian average
Population	+ 1.54	−3.93	+ 4.64	−0.83
Disposable income	+17.59	−3.94	+22.11	+0.58

CHARACTERISTICS OF THE POPULATION

	Region		Saint John
	% of the total population of the region	% points above or below Canadian average	% of the total population of the city
Mother tongue (1961 census)			
English	93.7	+35.3	92.1
French	4.9	−23.2	6.3
German	0.3	− 2.8	0.4
Native Indian dialects	—	− 0.9	—
Italian	0.1	− 1.8	0.1
Dutch	0.2	− 0.7	0.2
Polish	0.1	− 0.8	0.1
Ukrainian	0.1	− 1.9	0.1
Other	0.6	− 3.2	0.7
Total	100.0	—	100.0
Official language spoken (1961 census)			
English only	93.2	+25.8	91.4
French only	0.5	−18.6	0.7
Both English and French	6.2	− 6.0	7.8
Neither English nor French	0.1	− 1.2	0.1
Total	100.0	—	100.0

AVERAGE INCOME (1961 CENSUS)

	Region		Saint John	
	Dollars	% above or below Canadian average	Dollars	% above or below Canadian average
Income per family (non-farm)	4,637	−14.90	5,067	− 7.01
Income per person not in family (non-farm)	1,726	−19.23	1,905	−10.86
Income per farm (net)	1,258	−61.35	—	—

MEANS OF LIVELIHOOD—DISTRIBUTION OF LABOR FORCE BY INDUSTRY

Industry	Region			Saint John	
	Persons 1961 census	% of the total	% points above or below Canadian average	Persons 1961 census	% of the total
Agriculture	2,294	4.6	−5.3	199	0.6
Forestry	1,127	2.3	+0.6	73	0.2
Fishing and trapping	827	1.7	+1.2	87	0.3
Mines, quarries, oil wells	523	1.0	−0.9	12	—
Manufacturing	10,091	20.1	−1.6	6,744	20.2
Construction	3,210	6.4	−0.3	2,206	6.6
Transportation, communications, and other utilities	6,564	13.1	+3.8	4,716	14.1
Wholesale trade	3,313	6.6	+2.1	2,873	8.6
Retail trade	5,934	11.8	+1.0	4,317	12.9
Finance, insurance, and real estate	1,584	3.2	−0.3	1,377	4.1
Community and business services	6,885	13.7	+0.9	5,454	16.3
Personal services	3,436	6.9	+0.1	2,284	6.9
Public administration and defence	3,275	6.5	−1.0	2,364	7.1
Miscellaneous	1,031	2.1	−0.3	702	2.1
Total labor force	50,094	100.0	—	33,408	100.0

Upper St. John Valley

ECONOMIC CAPSULE

A rich agricultural valley, the area between Woodstock and Grand Falls is one of the most important potato-growing districts in Canada. It is particularly noted for its seed stock, much of which finds its way into the export market.

The rest of the region is highly forested and derives most of its wealth from lumber and pulpwood. A very large pulp and paper mill is located at Edmundston.

Work has started on the proposed $110 million Mactaquac hydro-electric project. When fully operational in 1976, it will have an output of 500,000 kilowatts, doubling the province's present generating capacity and probably reducing the cost of electricity by more than a third.

Fredericton, the capital of New Brunswick, is strictly an administrative and educational center, with very few manufacturing industries. Oromocto is the site of Camp Gagetown, the largest army training area in the country. Its economy is tied completely to military spending. Its population between 1956 and 1961 censuses rose from 661 to 12,170, making it the fifth largest community in the province.

Area covered: 9,260 square miles. *Counties:* Carleton, Madawaska, Sunbury, Victoria, York

COMPOSITION OF THE MARKET

Place	County	Population 1961	% of the region
Fredericton (urbanized area)	York	24,836	15.75
Edmundston	Madawaska	12,791	8.11
Oromocto	Sunbury	12,170	7.72
Woodstock	Carleton	4,305	2.73
Grand Falls	Victoria	3,983	2.53
Marysville	York	3,233	2.05
McAdam	York	2,472	1.57
St. Basil	Madawaska	1,733	1.10
St. Leonard	Madawaska	1,666	1.06
Minto	Sunbury	1,319	0.84
Plaster Rock	Victoria	1,267	0.80
Ste. Anne de Madawaska	Madawaska	1,122	0.71
Hartland	Carleton	1,025	0.65
Total urban	—	71,922	45.62
Rural non-farm	—	62,111	39.39
Rural farm	—	23,637	14.99
Total population		157,670	100.00

IMPORTANCE OF THE MARKET (1964 ESTIMATES)

	Number	% of Canada
Population	169,700	0.88
Households	37,800	0.79
Disposable income ($ million)	197.3	0.62

GROWTH OF THE MARKET

	Percentage growth 1961 to 1964	% points above or below Canadian average
Population	+ 7.63	+2.16
Disposable income	+30.15	+8.62

POVERTY AND AFFLUENCE (1961 CENSUS)

	Number	% of region's total	% points above or below Canadian average
Extent of poverty			
Families earning below $3,000 a year (non-farm)	10,579	38.0	+14.7
Persons not in families earning below $1,500 a year (non-farm)	5,931	63.7	+14.8
Farms with gross income of less than $2,500 a year	2,658	61.8	+15.7
Persons not in school with grade 4 or less education	16,713	17.8	+ 4.4
Doubled-up households (more than one family per household)	1,381	3.9	+ 0.2
Households living in dilapidated dwellings	3,437	9.8	+ 4.2
Households without facilities of running water	6,526	18.6	+ 7.7
Households without facilities of installed bath or shower	13,045	37.2	+17.5
Extent of affluence			
Families earning over $10,000 a year (non-farm)	974	3.4	− 4.4
Persons not in families earning over $6,000 a year (non-farm)	213	2.3	− 1.5
Farms with gross income over $15,000 a year	208	4.8	− 0.2
Persons with university degree	1,859	2.0	− 0.8
Households with two or more television sets	356	1.0	− 3.2
Households with two or more cars	1,134	3.2	− 3.6

MEANS OF LIVELIHOOD—DISTRIBUTION OF

LABOR FORCE BY INDUSTRY

Industry	Persons 1961 census	% of the total	% points above or below Canadian average
Agriculture	5,554	11.5	+ 1.6
Forestry	3,807	7.9	+ 6.2
Fishing and trapping	75	0.2	− 0.3
Mines, quarries, oil wells	480	1.0	− 0.9
Manufacturing	5,171	10.8	−10.9
Construction	2,644	5.5	− 1.2
Transportation, communications, and other utilities	5,301	11.0	+ 1.7
Wholesale trade	1,623	3.4	− 1.1
Retail trade	4,983	10.4	− 0.4
Finance, insurance, and real estate	803	1.7	− 1.8
Community and business services	5,746	11.9	− 0.9
Personal services	2,937	6.1	− 0.7
Public administration and defence	8,000	16.6	+ 9.1
Miscellaneous	984	2.0	− 0.4
Total labor force	48,108	100.0	—

CHARACTERISTICS OF THE POPULATION

	% of the total population of the region	% points above or below Canadian average
Mother tongue (1961 census)		
English	67.3	+ 8.9
French	30.6	+ 2.5
German	0.2	− 2.9
Native Indian dialects	0.6	− 0.3
Italian	0.1	− 1.8
Dutch	0.3	− 0.6
Polish	0.1	− 0.8
Ukrainian	0.1	− 1.9
Other	0.7	− 3.1
Total	100.0	—

CHARACTERISTICS OF THE POPULATION (continued)

	% of the total population of the region	% points above or below Canadian average
Official language spoken (1961 census)		
English only	67.2	− 0.2
French only	19.0	− 0.1
Both English and French	13.7	+ 1.5
Neither English nor French	0.1	− 1.2
Total	100.0	—

AVERAGE INCOME (1961 CENSUS)

	Dollars	% above or below Canadian average
Income per family (non-farm)	4,073	−25.25
Income per person not in family (non-farm)	1,539	−27.98
Income per farm (net)	2,111	−35.15

Northeastern New Brunswick

ECONOMIC CAPSULE

The economy revolves around exploiting the wealth of the forests, the sea, and the mines. Agriculture in most cases provides only a part-time occupation for those whose chief means of livelihood is either lumbering or fishing.

Manufacturing rests mainly on forest resources. There are over a hundred sawmills across the region, and pulp and paper mills at Campbellton, Dalhousie, Bathurst, Newcastle, and South Nelson.

Over a decade ago extremely rich deposits of lead, copper, and zinc were discovered in the Newcastle-Bathurst zone, and the mines have already started producing at the rate of 4,500 tons per day. Recently, Brunswick Mining and Smelting Corporation Limited announced plans to undertake in this area a huge investment program which when completed may well total $200 million. The project includes the opening of two lead-zinc mines, the building of two new ore concentrators, the construction of a 250,000 ton-per-year steel mill, the erection of plants for manufacturing sulphuric acid and chemical fertilizers, and the creation of a new harbor complete with shipping and handling facilities at Belledune Point. The project will be completed in stages between 1965 and 1969 and will be the biggest single investment in the history of New Brunswick, creating well over a thousand new jobs.

COMPOSITION OF THE MARKET

Area covered: 9,767 square miles. *Counties:* Gloucester, Northumberland, Restigouche

Place	County	Population 1961	% of the region
Campbellton (urbanized area)	Restigouche	12,018	7.64
Chatham	Northumberland	7,109	4.52
Dalhousie	Restigouche	5,856	3.72
Bathurst	Gloucester	5,494	3.49
Newcastle	Northumberland	5,236	3.33
St. Quentin	Restigouche	2,089	1.33
East Bathurst	Gloucester	1,876	1.19
Tracadie	Gloucester	1,651	1.05
Shippegan	Gloucester	1,631	1.04
Chatham Head	Northumberland	1,610	1.02
South Bathurst	Gloucester	1,390	0.88
West Bathurst	Gloucester	1,183	0.75
Kedgwick	Restigouche	1,095	0.70
Rogersville	Northumberland	1,083	0.69
Total urban	—	49,321	31.35
Rural non-farm	—	93,835	59.63
Rural farm	—	14,195	9.02
Total population		157,351	100.00

IMPORTANCE OF THE MARKET (1964 ESTIMATES)

	Number	% of Canada
Population	158,600	0.83
Households	29,500	0.61
Disposable income ($ million)	156.4	0.50

GROWTH OF THE MARKET

	Percentage growth 1961 to 1964	% points above or below Canadian average
Population	+ 0.79	−4.68
Disposable income	+16.98	−4.55

MEANS OF LIVELIHOOD—DISTRIBUTION OF
LABOR FORCE BY INDUSTRY

Industry	Persons 1961 census	% of the total	% points above or below Canadian average
Agriculture	1,827	4.7	−5.2
Forestry	4,491	11.5	+9.8
Fishing and trapping	1,992	5.1	+4.6
Mines, quarries, oil wells	562	1.4	−0.5
Manufacturing	7,353	18.8	−2.9
Construction	2,123	5.4	−1.3
Transportation, communications, and other utilities	3,321	8.5	−0.8
Wholesale trade	1,060	2.7	−1.8
Retail trade	3,958	10.1	−0.7
Finance, insurance, and real estate	445	1.1	−2.4
Community and business services	5,291	13.5	+0.7
Personal services	2,583	6.6	−0.2
Public administration and defence	3,078	7.9	+0.4
Miscellaneous	1,032	2.7	+0.3
Total labor force	39,116	100.0	—

CHARACTERISTICS OF THE POPULATION

	% of the total population of the region	% points above or below Canadian average
Mother tongue (1961 census)		
English	38.6	−19.8
French	60.3	+32.2
German	0.1	− 3.0
Native Indian dialects	0.5	− 0.4
Italian	0.1	− 1.8
Dutch	0.1	− 0.8
Polish	—	− 0.9
Ukrainian	0.1	− 1.9
Other	0.2	− 3.6
Total	100.0	—

English only	35.9	−31.5
French only	37.5	+18.4
Both English and French	26.3	+14.1
Neither English nor French	0.3	− 1.0
Total	100.0	—

AVERAGE INCOME (1961 CENSUS)

	Dollars	% above or below Canadian average
Income per family (non-farm)	3,467	−36.37
Income per person not in family (non-farm)	1,298	−39.26
Income per farm (net)	478	−85.31

POVERTY AND AFFLUENCE (1961 CENSUS)

	Number	% of region's total	% points above or below Canadian average
Extent of poverty			
Families earning below $3,000 a year (non-farm)	13,229	50.3	+27.0
Persons not in families earning below $1,500 a year (non-farm)	5,405	70.5	+21.6
Farms with gross income of less than $2,500 a year	2,244	90.3	+44.2
Persons not in school with grade 4 or less education	26,977	30.3	+16.9
Doubled-up households (more than one family per household)	1,934	6.6	+ 2.9
Households living in dilapidated dwellings	4,465	15.2	+ 9.6
Households without facilities of running water	10,414	35.4	+24.5
Households without facilities of installed bath or shower	15,375	52.3	+32.6
Extent of affluence			
Families earning over $10,000 a year (non-farm)	636	2.4	− 5.4
Persons not in families earning over $6,000 a year (non-farm)	77	1.0	− 2.8
Farms with gross income over $15,000 a year	18	0.7	− 4.3
Persons with university degree	960	1.1	− 1.7
Households with two or more television sets	123	0.4	− 3.8
Households with two or more cars	521	1.8	− 5.0

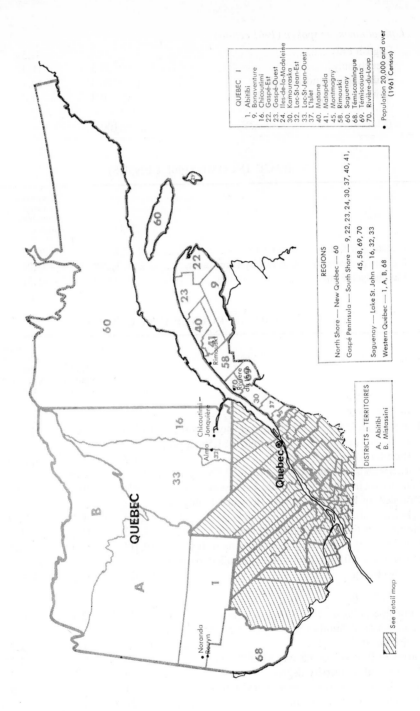

QUEBEC I

1. Abitibi
9. Bonaventure
16. Chicoutimi
22. Gaspé-Est
23. Gaspé-Ouest
24. Îles-de-la-Madeleine
30. Kamouraska
32. Lac-St-Jean-Est
33. Lac-St-Jean-Ouest
37. L'Islet
40. Matane
41. Matapédia
45. Montmagny
58. Rimouski
60. Saguenay
68. Témiscamingue
69. Témiscouata
70. Rivière-du-Loup

• Population 20,000 and over
  (1961 Census)

REGIONS

North Shore — New Québec — 60
Gaspé Peninsula — South Shore — 9, 22, 23, 24, 30, 37, 40, 41,
                                45, 58, 69, 70
Saguenay — Lake St. John — 16, 32, 33
Western Québec — 1, A, B, 68

DISTRICTS — TERRITOIRES

A. Abitibi
B. Mistassini

See detail map

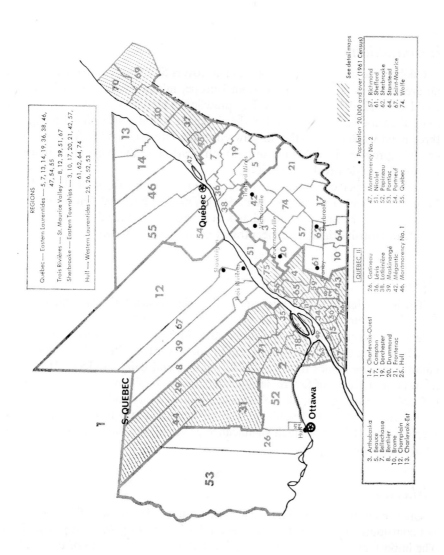

S-QUEBEC

Ottawa

Québec

REGIONS

Québec — Eastern Laurentides — 5, 7, 13, 14, 19, 36, 38, 46,
47, 54, 55
Trois Rivières — St. Maurice Valley — 8, 12, 39, 51, 67
Sherbrooke — Eastern Townships — 3, 10, 17, 20, 21, 42, 57,
61, 62, 64, 74
Hull — Western Laurentides — 25, 26, 52, 53

• Population 20 000 and over (1961 Census)

See detail maps

3. Arthabaska
5. Beauce
7. Bellechasse
10. Berthier
12. Brome
13. Champlain
. Charlevoix-Est

14. Charlevoix-Ouest
17. Compton
19. Dorchester
20. Drummond
21. Frontenac
25. Hull

26. Gatineau
36. Lévis
38. Lotbinière
39. Maskinongé
42. Mégantic
46. Montmorency No. 1

47. Montmorency No. 2
51. Nicolet
52. Papineau
53. Pontiac
54. Portneuf
55. Québec

57. Richmond
61. Shefford
62. Sherbrooke
64. Stanstead
67. Saint-Maurice
74. Wolfe

QUEBEC, II

403

Chapter 15

QUEBEC

Introduction

Québec, the largest province in Canada, covers 523,860 square miles of land, an area so vast that most of Western Europe, minus the European U.S.S.R., could be tucked between its wide, sprawling boundaries. Settlement started more than four centuries ago, but development is still concentrated along the three main waterways — the St. Lawrence, the Ottawa, and the Saguenay rivers. The province is highly urbanized with nearly half the population living in Metropolitan Montréal and Québec.

Eighty-one per cent of the population is of French origin; of these three-fourths speak only French. Another 25% claim to be bilingual, but the majority of them, it may be safely presumed, talk in French most of the time at home. The people of British origin are concentrated mainly in Greater Montréal.

Agriculture

The love of land has long been one of the prime characteristics of the French-Canadian culture. Although in recent years the industrial revolution has dislodged agriculture from its top position, the old farming traditions are still honored here more than anywhere else in Canada. Over four-fifths of the total agricultural income comes from livestock, poultry, and dairy products. However, a few areas, because of favorable soil and climatic conditions, have become specialized in certain crops, like tobacco in Joliette county and sugar beets in the Richelieu Valley. One traditional feature of agriculture is the collection of maple syrup. It has not much significance economically, but adds color to the rural scene in early spring.

Fisheries

Québec has both sea and inland fisheries, but the size of the entire catch does not contribute more than 0.1% to the total net value of provincial production. The important fishing settlements are located on the north shore of the Gulf of St. Lawrence, around Gaspé Peninsula, and on the Magdalen Islands. Cod, herring, redfish, lobster, mackerel, flounder, and sole are the most valuable species. The provincial government assists the fishermen by providing cold storage facilities, so that the fish may be marketed fresh instead of salted.

Mining

Topographically, most of Québec is covered by the Canadian Shield, one of the world's largest treasure-troves of minerals. The first area to be developed was around Noranda-Rouyn, noted for copper, zinc, lead, gold, and silver. Later the continuing demand for copper resulted in the opening up of new mines in Chibougamau. At present, the main attention is on the Labrador border where huge deposits of iron ore are located. Production on a big scale began in 1954, but exploration is still going on and new discoveries are likely.

The Shield is not the only source of minerals. Copper is mined at Murdochville in Gaspé, while the Eastern Townships are extremely rich in asbestos, supplying nearly two-thirds of the non-communist world's output.

In 1964, Québec accounted for 55% of Canada's nonmetallic mineral production. The province was the sole producer in the country of feldspar, graphite, iron oxides, lithia, magnesitic-dolomite, brucite, and titanium dioxide.

To process the ores from the mines, an extensive smelting and refining industry has been set up, with plants at Noranda, Murdochville, Sorel, Val d'Or, Valleyfield, and Montréal Est. In addition, Québec is also the world's leading producer of aluminum and has five of the six reduction plants in Canada. The abundance of water power gives the province a distinct advantage, although bauxite, the ore from which the metal is extracted, has to come from abroad.

Forestry

The forest industries play a key role in the economy of Québec. Productive woodlands cover 141,200 square miles, almost equivalent to the combined area of England and France. The annual cut averages about a billion cubic feet, most of it being absorbed by the pulp and paper industry. It has been estimated that Québec provides newsprint for two out of every five newspaper pages printed in the United States, and one out of every four throughout the world. The city of Trois Rivières is the world's newsprint capital, its mills producing over 2,500 tons of paper per day. The lumbering industry, too, is well established in Québec, but the annual production from sawmills averages only one-eighth of the value of shipments from pulp and paper mills.

Secondary manufacturing

Québec is second only to Ontario in the size of the secondary manufacturing industry. Cheap water power, abundant raw materials, relatively low labor costs, and dense concentration of population in the St. Lawrence Lowlands — all these have encouraged numerous firms during the last two decades to locate their plants in Québec.

The food and beverage industry is the largest cash earner. It is built on a solid base, since most of the products are sold domestically. The province also has several textile and clothing mills, most of them concentrated in the Eastern Townships, particularly in Sherbrooke, Drummondville, and Magog. Lately the industry has been hurt by strong competition from U.S. synthetic fabrics and Japanese cotton goods.

Metropolitan Montréal region constitutes the foremost industrial area. With over 5,000 plants, it accounts for 60% of Québec's manufacturing output. It is a leading producer for aircraft and aircraft parts, railway locomotives, leather footwear, chemicals, and pharmaceutical supplies. Other industries are flour milling, brewing and distilling, and the manufacture of tobacco and cigarettes. Montréal also has big oil refineries which supply nearly one-third of the petroleum requirements of Canada.

General observations

Many English-speaking Canadians still think of Québec as an agrarian, inward-looking community, dominated by a small group of landed gentry and Roman Catholic priests. The inhabitants are supposed to be poor but honest, reliable and hard-working, but unsuited for managerial position, considerably advanced in liberal culture, but unprepared for and hostile to business life.

This picture is now completely out of date. Only about 6% of the labor force is engaged in agriculture, and three out of four Québecers live in urban areas where the influence of priests is less dominant. Nor are French Canadians unfit for top executive posts: the problem is not lack of talents but the want of opportunity.

Also, far from being passive and stagnant, Québec society is the most dynamic in Canada today. The province is in the throes of a revolution or, more accurately still, two revolutions. The first, which strikes at the whole concept of federal government, aims to win for Québec a new place in the dominion structure — as a nation within a nation rather than simply as one out of ten provinces. The second revolution, having as its watchword "maîtres chez nous", is directed at getting the control of big business in the hands of French Canadians.

In over-all development, Québec has lagged sadly behind Ontario. Its per capita income in 1964 was only $1,608, compared to Ontario's $2,125, while its unemployment rate of 6.4% was double that of its neighbor. Moreover, Québec's economic growth has not benefited the "Canadiens". Montréal, Canada's largest city, is bursting with activity on all sides, but at the vital centers of authority, French Canadians are conspicuous by their absence. Within the major corporations and banks, few French-speaking employees have risen to the top. The paths to promotion have been blocked, even in the nationally-owned CNR and Air Canada, both headquartered in Montréal.

In the backwaters of the province, much of the rural population ekes out a meager living by cultivating small farms in summer and cutting wood on a contract basis in winter. Where industrialization has come in, it is of a variety that bestows comparatively little benefit on the French Canadians. The primary industries connected with the mines and forests are generally owned by English Canadians or Americans. The French firms in the secondary industry field are mostly small family affairs, lacking funds for expansion.

The provincial government is determined to remedy the situation. Impressed by France's example in economic planning, it has set up an Economic Advisory Council, whose aim is to promote maximum industrial growth with a distinct French seasoning. The government's first move, on the suggestion of the Council, was the nationalization of electric power. To spur industrialization, electricity is now offered at vastly reduced rates to investors willing to install new factories in depressed zones or remote areas of the province.

Another major step has been the establishment of the General Investment Corporation, authorized to supply expansion capital to Québec firms, to act as a marriage broker in the amalgamation of small companies, and to loan money to start new industries. The Corporation has already prevented many medium-sized French-Canadian firms from falling into the hands of outsiders. It has also put up all the money for an automobile plant which will assemble under license 8,000 Renault and Peugeot cars a year. Its most ambitious project is the $225 million integrated steel mill at Bécancourt, intended to promote a measure of self-sufficiency in a product that symbolizes industrial progress.

In order to make sure that the French Canadians will be ready to run the vast industrial empire which G.I.C. is slowly building up, the Québec government has drastically overhauled the province's archaic educational system. New high schools are being built and the emphasis is being shifted from liberal arts to vocational and technical training. If all goes as planned, by 1967 the secondary-school enrollment will have increased by 36% over 1964, and the number of students receiving vocational or technical training will have tripled.

IMPORTANCE OF THE MARKET (1964 ESTIMATES)

	Number	% of Canada
Population	5,562,000	28.92
Households	1,262,000	26.26
Disposable income ($ million)	8,124.0	25.76

GROWTH OF THE MARKET

	Percentage growth 1961 to 1964	% points above or below Canadian average
Population	+ 5.76	+0.29
Disposable income	+21.45	−0.08

Place	Provincial region	Population 1961	% of Québec
Montréal (metro)	Metro Montréal and its Environs	2,109,509	40.11
Québec (metro)	Metro Québec—Eastern Laurentides	357,568	6.80
Chicoutimi–Jonquière*	Saguenay Valley—Lake St. John	105,009	2.00
Hull (Québec sector of Metro Ottawa)	Hull—Western Laurentides	96,851	1.84
Trois Rivières*	Trois Rivières—St. Maurice Valley	83,659	1.59
Sherbrooke*	Sherbrooke—Eastern Townships	70,253	1.34
Shawinigan*	Trois Rivières—St. Maurice Valley	63,518	1.21
Drummondville*	Sherbrooke—Eastern Townships	39,307	0.75
St. Jean*	Metro Montréal and its Environs	34,576	0.66
St. Hyacinthe	Metro Montréal and its Environs	31,659	0.60
Granby	Sherbrooke—Eastern Townships	31,463	0.60
Noranda-Rouyn*	Western Québec	30,193	0.57
Valleyfield*	Metro Montréal and its Environs	29,849	0.57
St. Jérôme	Metro Montréal and its Environs	29,107	0.55
Sorel*	Metro Montréal and its Environs	28,906	0.55
Thetford Mines*	Sherbrooke—Eastern Townships	25,798	0.49
Rimouski*	Gaspé Peninsula—South Shore	22,443	0.43
Joliette*	Metro Montréal and its Environs	22,198	0.42
Victoriaville	Sherbrooke—Eastern Townships	21,697	0.41
Alma*	Saguenay Valley—Lake St. John	19,854	0.38
Val-d'Or*	Western Québec	14,327	0.27
Magog*	Sherbrooke—Eastern Townships	14,233	0.27
Sept Iles	North Shore—New Québec	14,196	0.27
La Tuque	Trois Rivières—St. Maurice Valley	13,023	0.25
Asbestos	Sherbrooke—Eastern Townships	11,083	0.21
Rivière du Loup	Gaspé Peninsula—South Shore	10,835	0.21
Matane	Gaspé Peninsula—South Shore	9,190	0.17
Port Alfred	Saguenay Valley—Lake St. John	9,066	0.17
Beauharnois	Metro Montréal and its Environs	8,704	0.17
Baie Comeau	North Shore—New Québec	7,956	0.15
Roberval	Saguenay Valley—Lake St. John	7,739	0.15
Lachute	Metro Montréal and its Environs	7,560	0.14
Buckingham	Hull—Western Laurentides	7,421	0.14
Cowansville	Metro Montréal and its Environs	7,050	0.13
Lac Mégantic	Sherbrooke—Eastern Townships	7,015	0.13
Malartic	Western Québec	6,998	0.13
Coaticook	Sherbrooke—Eastern Townships	6,906	0.13
Montmagny	Gaspé Peninsula—South Shore	6,850	0.13
Windsor	Sherbrooke—Eastern Townships	6,589	0.13
Plessisville	Sherbrooke—Eastern Townships	6,570	0.12

* (Urbanized area)

Farnham	Metro Montréal and its Environs	6,354	0.12
Maniwaki	Hull—Western Laurentides	6,349	0.12
Beloeil	Metro Montréal and its Environs	6,283	0.12
Terrebonne	Metro Montréal and its Environs	6,207	0.12
Mont Joli	Gaspé Peninsula—South Shore	6,178	0.12
Amos	Western Québec	6,080	0.12
Dolbeau	Saguenay Valley—Lake St. John	6,052	0.11
Hauterive	North Shore—New Québec	5,980	0.11
Mont Laurier	Metro Montréal and its Environs	5,859	0.11
Ste. Agathe des Monts	Metro Montréal and its Environs	5,725	0.11
Bagotville	Saguenay Valley—Lake St. John	5,629	0.11
St. Félicien	Saguenay Valley—Lake St. John	5,133	0.10
Total of towns over 5,000		3,508,557	66.71
218 towns between 1,000 and 5,000		428,912	8.16
Total urban		3,937,469	74.87
Rural non-farm		756,916	14.39
Rural farm		564,826	10.74
Total population		5,259,211	100.00

CHARACTERISTICS OF THE POPULATION

	% of the total population of the region	% points above or below Canadian average
Mother tongue (1961 census)		
English	13.3	−45.1
French	81.2	+53.1
German	0.6	− 2.5
Native Indian and Eskimo dialects	0.3	− 0.6
Italian	1.7	− 0.2
Dutch	0.1	− 0.8
Polish	0.4	− 0.5
Ukrainian	0.2	− 1.8
Other	2.2	− 1.6
Total	100.0	—
Official language spoken (1961 census)		
English only	11.6	−55.8
French only	61.9	+42.8
Both English and French	25.4	+13.2
Neither English nor French	1.1	− 0.2
Total	100.0	—

STANDARD OF LIVING BASED ON OWNERSHIP OF
APPLIANCES AND EQUIPMENT, 1965

	Number of households	% of total households in Québec	% points above or below Canadian average
Cooking equipment			
Electric stoves	881,000	68.8	− 0.2
Wood or coal cookstoves or ranges	134,000	10.5	+ 1.3
Piped gas stoves	190,000	14.8	+ 0.7
Refrigeration			
Electric refrigerators	1,248,000	97.5	+ 1.7
Home freezers	122,000	9.5	−13.1
Electric washing machines			
Automatic	314,000	24.5	+ 1.4
Other	792,000	61.9	− 1.3
Clothes dryers			
Electric	257,000	20.1	− 5.1
Gas	2,000	0.2	− 2.0
Sewing machines			
Electric	748,000	58.4	+ 6.0
Non-electric	216,000	16.9	− 1.3
Phonographs and record players			
Cabinet model	374,000	29.2	− 3.7
Table model	83,000	6.5	+ 1.3
Portable model	284,000	22.2	+ 1.2
Telephones			
One	974,000	76.1	− 0.1
Two or more	171,000	13.4	+ 0.2
Television sets			
One	1,068,000	83.4	+ 1.6
Two or more	155,000	12.1	+ 1.2
Automobiles			
One	762,000	59.5	− 3.0
Two or more	84,000	6.6	− 5.8
Other appliances			
Automatic dishwashers	48,000	3.8	+ 1.1
Vacuum cleaners	833,000	65.1	− 9.8
Window-type air conditioners	27,000	2.1	− 0.1
FM radio receivers	308,000	24.1	+ 1.2

(Source: DBS, *Household Facilities and Equipment, May 1965.* Catalogue no. 64-202.)

LABOR FORCE BY INDUSTRY

Industry	Persons 1961 census	% of the total	% points above or below Canadian average
Agriculture	131,197	7.4	−2.5
Forestry	42,441	2.4	+0.7
Fishing and trapping	3,029	0.2	−0.3
Mines, quarries, oil wells	25,854	1.5	−0.4
Manufacturing	466,443	26.4	+4.7
Construction	126,361	7.2	+0.5
Transportation, communications, and other utilities	161,268	9.1	−0.2
Wholesale trade	69,334	3.9	−0.6
Retail trade	178,704	10.1	−0.7
Finance, insurance, and real estate	62,163	3.5	—
Community and business services	228,160	12.9	+0.1
Personal services	122,704	6.9	+0.1
Public administration and defence	99,194	5.6	−1.9
Miscellaneous	51,267	2.9	+0.5
Total labor force	1,768,119	100.0	—

AVERAGE INCOME (1961 CENSUS)

	Dollars	% above or below Canadian average
Income per family (non-farm)	5,387	− 1.14
Income per person not in family (non-farm)	2,018	− 5.57
Income per farm (net)	1,501	−53.89

POVERTY AND AFFLUENCE (1961 CENSUS)

	Number	% of province's total	% points above or below Canadian average
Extent of poverty			
Families earning below $3,000 a year (non-farm)	241,552	24.3	+ 1.0
Persons not in families earning below $1,500 a year (non-farm)	178,627	49.7	+ 0.8
Farms with gross income of less than $2,500 a year	56,850	59.3	+13.2
Persons not in school with grade 4 or less education	596,083	17.9	+ 4.5
Doubled-up households (more than one family per household)	39,229	3.3	− 0.4

	Number	% of province's total	% points above or below Canadian average
Households living in dilapidated dwellings	49,392	4.2	− 1.4
Households without facilities of running water	32,945	2.8	− 8.1
Households without facilities of installed bath or shower	217,054	18.3	− 1.4
Extent of affluence			
Families earning over $10,000 a year (non-farm)	84,032	8.5	+ 0.7
Persons not in families earning over $6,000 a year (non-farm)	12,237	3.4	− 0.4
Farms with gross income over $15,000 a year	1,502	1.6	− 3.4
Persons with university degree	90,703	2.7	− 0.1
Households with two or more television sets	43,678	3.7	− 0.5
Households with two or more cars	33,228	2.8	− 4.0

North Shore — New Québec

ECONOMIC CAPSULE

For nearly four centuries this huge region, covering about 60% of the province's area, was considered unfit for human settlement. But during the last two decades a complete metamorphosis has occurred, the change being triggered by the never ending thirst of the blast furnaces in the United States for steady supplies of iron ore. Since the deposits here are extremly large as well as rich in iron content, the steel industry has decided to develop them, despite their remote location. Over a billion dollars have been invested to open the mines, to build railways and harbors, and to provide a host of ancillary services. New towns, like Schefferville and Gagnon, have sprung up almost overnight in what was once a bleak, inhospitable wilderness. The total population of the region jumped by 92% from 42,700 in 1951 to 81,900 in 1961.

The two major mining sites are at Knob Lake and Lac Jeannine. Since the operations began in 1954 at Knob Lake over 100 million tons of ore have been shipped from both Québec and the Newfoundland side of Labrador. Reserves are more than ample, and annual production may reach 30 million by 1970. The ore is sent by rail to St. Lawrence ports like Sept Iles, from where it is moved directly by ships to the steel centers of the United States.

So far, only the surface of the huge land mass has been scratched. Further north, bordering on Ungava Bay, preliminary surveys have revealed the presence of important reserves of iron ore, copper, nickel, and asbestos. Prospecting is, indeed, just beginning and promises more sensational discoveries. The provincial government envisages an eventual large-scale development of this area, based to some extent on the training of the Eskimos. It is, therefore, anxious to regain jurisdiction over these people, which it relinquished to Ottawa in 1939.

While mining has sparked the boom, other manufacturing plants have come into the region and accelerated the pace of industrialization. Baie Comeau, a year-round port, is the site of a large pulp and paper mill of Québec North Shore Paper Company Limited. It also has an aluminum smelter of Canadian British Aluminum Company Limited with eventual capacity planned at 180,000 tons per year, twice the current level.

Nearby on the Manicouagan and the Outardes rivers, Hydro-Québec is now in the process of erecting six generating stations. This gigantic power complex is regarded by many as the most significant showpiece of the newly resurgent French Canada. It involves a capital investment of nearly $2 billion, practically double the cost of the St. Lawrence Seaway. When completed within a decade, it will provide 6,000,000 kilowatts of installed capacity, enabling Québec to maintain unchallenged its position as the province with more hydro power per capita than anywhere else in the world.

NORTH SHORE—NEW QUEBEC

Area covered: 315,176 square miles. *County:* Saguenay.

IMPORTANCE OF THE MARKET (1964 ESTIMATES)

	Number	% of Canada
Population	100,100	0.52
Households	17,700	0.37
Disposable income ($ million)	183.3	0.58

GROWTH OF THE MARKET

	Percentage growth 1961 to 1964	% points above or below Canadian average
Population	+12.22	+ 6.75
Disposable income	+71.31	+49.78

COMPOSITION OF THE MARKET

Place	County	Population 1961	% of the region
Sept Iles	Saguenay	14,196	17.33
Baie Comeau	Saguenay	7,956	9.72
Hauterive	Saguenay	5,980	7.30
Port Cartier	Saguenay	3,458	4.22
Schefferville	Saguenay	3,178	3.88
Havre St. Pierre	Saguenay	2,407	2.94
Gagnon	Saguenay	1,900	2.32
Escoumins	Saguenay	1,607	1.96
Forestville	Saguenay	1,529	1.87
Chute-aux-Outardes	Saguenay	1,336	1.63
Sacré-Coeur-de-Jésus	Saguenay	1,108	1.35
Tadoussac	Saguenay	1,083	1.32
Total urban		45,738	55.84
Rural non-farm		34,691	42.36
Rural farm		1,471	1.80
Total population		81,900	100.00

MEANS OF LIVELIHOOD—DISTRIBUTION OF LABOR FORCE BY INDUSTRY

Industry	Persons 1961 census	% of the total	% points above or below Canadian average
Agriculture	234	0.9	− 9.0
Forestry	2,774	11.0	+ 9.3
Fishing and trapping	638	2.5	+ 2.0
Mines, quarries, oil wells	3,420	13.6	+11.7
Manufacturing	2,705	10.8	−10.9
Construction	3,072	12.2	+ 5.5
Transportation, communications, and other utilities	2,982	11.9	+ 2.6
Wholesale trade	570	2.3	− 2.2
Retail trade	1,880	7.5	− 3.3
Finance, insurance, and real estate	341	1.4	− 2.1
Community and business services	2,225	8.8	− 4.0
Personal services	1,966	7.8	+ 1.0
Public administration and defence	1,148	4.6	− 2.9
Miscellaneous	1,175	4.7	+ 2.3
Total labor force	25,130	100.0	—

CHARACTERISTICS OF THE POPULATION

	% of the total population of the region	% points above or below Canadian average
Mother tongue (1961 census)		
English	10.6	−47.8
French	79.0	+50.9
German	0.3	− 2.8
Native Indian and Eskimo dialects	8.7	+ 7.8
Italian	0.6	− 1.3
Dutch	0.1	− 0.8
Polish	—	− 0.9
Ukrainian	—	− 2.0
Other	0.7	− 3.1
Total	100.0	—
Official language spoken (1961 census)		
English only	9.4	−58.0
French only	68.5	+49.4
Both English and French	16.1	+ 3.9
Neither English nor French	6.0	+ 4.7
Total	100.0	—

POVERTY AND AFFLUENCE (1961 CENSUS)

	Number	% of region's total	% points above or below Canadian average
Extent of poverty			
Families earning below $3,000 a year (non-farm)	4,003	27.1	+ 3.8
Persons not in families earning below $1,500 a year (non-farm)	1,909	39.3	− 9.6
Farms with gross income of less than $2,500 a year	181	82.6	+36.5
Persons not in school with grade 4 or less education	14,418	29.5	+16.1
Doubled-up households (more than one family per household)	1,430	10.2	+ 6.5
Households living in dilapidated dwellings	1,032	7.4	+ 1.8
Households without facilities of running water	2,464	17.5	+ 6.6
Households without facilities of installed bath or shower	4,643	33.0	+13.3

	Number	% of region's total	% points above or below Canadian average
Extent of affluence			
Families earning over $10,000 a year (non-farm)	1,266	8.6	+ 0.8
Persons not in families earning over $6,000 a year (non-farm)	254	5.2	+ 1.4
Farms with gross income over $15,000 a year	1	0.5	− 4.5
Persons with university degree	837	1.7	− 1.1
Households with two or more television sets	142	1.0	− 3.2
Households with two or more cars	275	2.0	− 4.8

AVERAGE INCOME (1961 CENSUS)

	Dollars	% above or below Canadian average
Income per family (non-farm)	5,574	+ 2.29
Income per person not in family (non-farm)	2,505	+17.22
Income per farm (net)	692	−78.74

Gaspé Peninsula — South Shore

ECONOMIC CAPSULE

This is the poorest and least urbanized region of the province. Despite the inferior quality of the soil, 19% of the people earn their living through agriculture, which is mainly confined to dairying and livestock raising. The climate is too cold for any type of field crops except potatoes. The farms, as a rule, are non-commercial, only 5% having an annual cash income of more than $5,000 from the sale of their products.

The forests provide another means of livelihood. Nearly 14,000 work in the woods to collect raw material for over 250 sawmills and two pulp mills located in the region.

Fishing is also important. About three-quarters of the province's fishermen live here. Cod, lobster, mackerel, herring, and salmon are the most valuable species caught. As a result of government assistance in providing cold storage facilities, the fish can be marketed fresh instead of salted.

In the summer months, tourism becomes a major source of revenue. The wild rocks of Gaspé, though inimical to agriculture, present scenery of the most awe-inspiring kind. The coast around Percé and the sea-bird sanctuary on Bonaventure Isle rank among the most extraordinarily beautiful places on earth. The fact that the old way of life of the French Canadians is still preserved in its pristine purity adds considerably to touristic charm. Some of the parishes date back to the pre-conquest days, and have hardly changed in the last 200 years.

But Gaspésia will not escape for long the onrush of industrial civilization. Already at Murdochville the copper mines have turned sleepy villages into an industrial center of primary importance. Mining operations have commenced on a large scale, and a smelter has been established, capable of producing 300,000 tons of copper anodes per year. The region is also believed to have large deposits of oil. If they prove feasible for commercial exploitation, their development will further upset the tranquillity of the countryside.

GASPE PENINSULA—SOUTH SHORE

Area covered: 17,898 square miles. *Counties:* Bonaventure, Gaspé (Gaspé Est, Gaspé Ouest, Iles de la Madeleine), Kamouraska, L'Islet, Matane (Matane, Matapédia), Montmagny, Rimouski, Témiscouata (Rivière du Loup, Témiscouata).

COMPOSITION OF THE MARKET

Place	County	Population 1961	% of the region
Rimouski (urbanized area)	Rimouski	22,443	5.60
Rivière du Loup	Rivière du Loup	10,835	2.70
Matane	Matane	9,190	2.29
Montmagny	Montmagny	6,850	1.71
Mont Joli	Rimouski	6,178	1.54
Trois Pistoles	Rivière du Loup	4,349	1.09
Amqui	Matapédia	3,659	0.91
Causapscal	Matapédia	3,463	0.86
Chandler	Gaspé Est	3,406	0.85
Price	Matane	3,094	0.77
Ste. Anne de la Pocatière	Kamouraska	3,086	0.77
Murdochville	Gaspé Ouest	2,951	0.74
Cabano	Témiscouata	2,695	0.67
Gaspé	Gaspé Est	2,603	0.65
Sayabec	Matapédia	2,314	0.58
St. Pascal	Kamouraska	2,144	0.54
Cap Chat	Gaspé Ouest	2,035	0.51
Ste. Rose du Dégelé	Témiscouata	1,943	0.48

COMPOSITION OF THE MARKET (continued)

Place	County	Population 1961	% of the region
Ste. Anne des Monts	Gaspé Ouest	1,906	0.48
St. Pamphile	L'Islet	1,839	0.46
Rivière au Renard	Gaspé Est	1,722	0.43
Notre Dame du Lac	Témiscouata	1,695	0.42
St. Jean Port Joli	L'Islet	1,615	0.40
Lac au Saumon	Matapédia	1,548	0.39
St. Joseph de la Rivière Bleue	Témiscouata	1,540	0.38
L'Isle Verte	Rivière du Loup	1,517	0.38
St. Fabien	Rimouski	1,466	0.37
Luceville	Rimouski	1,419	0.35
New Carlisle	Bonaventure	1,333	0.33
St. Thomas de la Pointe à la Caille	Montmagny	1,319	0.33
Cap St. Ignace	Montmagny	1,247	0.31
St. Pacôme	Kamouraska	1,242	0.31
Estcourt et Village Blier	Témiscouata	1,230	0.31
L'Isletville	L'Islet	1,184	0.30
St. Jean de Dieu	Rivière du Loup	1,177	0.29
Bic	Rimouski	1,177	0.29
Grande Rivière	Gaspé Est	1,176	0.29
Mont Albert	Gaspé Ouest	1,153	0.29
St. Noël	Matapédia	1,124	0.28
Squatec	Témiscouata	1,088	0.27
St. Joachim de Tourelle	Gaspé Ouest	1,068	0.27
Ste. Félicité	Matane	1,057	0.26
St. Ulric	Matane	1,021	0.25
St. Eleuthère	Kamouraska	1,014	0.25
Total urban		128,115	31.95
Rural non-farm		163,389	40.75
Rural farm		109,462	27.30
Total population		400,966	100.00

IMPORTANCE OF THE MARKET (1964 ESTIMATES)

	Number	% of Canada
Population	394,900	2.05
Households	68,200	1.42
Disposable income ($ million)	336.8	1.07

CHARACTERISTICS OF THE POPULATION

	% of the total population of the region	% points above or below Canadian average
Mother tongue (1961 census)		
English	3.9	−54.5
French	95.6	+67.5
German	—	− 3.1
Native Indian dialects	0.2	− 0.7
Italian	0.1	− 1.8
Dutch	—	− 0.9
Polish	—	− 0.9
Ukrainian	—	− 2.0
Other	0.2	− 3.6
Total	100.0	—
Official language spoken (1961 census)		
English only	2.9	−64.5
French only	87.9	+68.8
Both English and French	9.0	− 3.2
Neither English nor French	0.2	− 1.1
Total	100.0	—

POVERTY AND AFFLUENCE (1961 CENSUS)

	Number	% of region's total	% points above or below Canadian average
Extent of poverty			
Families earning below $3,000 a year (non-farm)	26,342	50.1	+26.8
Persons not in families earning below $1,500 a year (non-farm)	10,957	71.4	+22.5
Farms with gross income of less than $2,500 a year	12,154	76.4	+30.3
Persons not in school with grade 4 or less education	66,887	29.0	+15.6
Doubled-up households (more than one family per household)	4,737	6.8	+ 3.1
Households living in dilapidated dwellings	5,502	7.9	+ 2.3
Households without facilities of running water	9,595	13.8	+ 2.9
Households without facilities of installed bath or shower	37,533	53.9	+34.2

	Number	% of region's total	% points above or below Canadian average
Extent of affluence			
Families earning over $10,000 a year (non-farm)	1,921	3.7	− 4.1
Persons not in families earning over $6,000 a year (non-farm)	153	0.9	− 2.9
Farms with gross income over $15,000 a year	37	0.3	− 4.7
Persons with university degree	2,052	0.9	− 1.9
Households with two or more television sets	482	0.7	− 3.5
Households with two or more cars	1,419	2.0	− 4.8

GROWTH OF THE MARKET

	Percentage change 1961 to 1964	% points above or below Canadian average
Population	− 1.51	−6.98
Disposable income	+25.86	+4.33

LABOR FORCE BY INDUSTRY

Industry	Persons 1961 census	% of the total	% points above or below Canadian average
Agriculture	19,745	18.7	+ 8.8
Forestry	13,868	13.1	+11.4
Fishing and trapping	1,894	1.8	+ 1.3
Mines, quarries, oil wells	1,768	1.7	− 0.2
Manufacturing	11,504	10.9	−10.8
Construction	6,421	6.1	− 0.6
Transportation, communications, and other utilities	9,288	8.8	− 0.5
Wholesale trade	2,553	2.4	− 2.1
Retail trade	9,174	8.7	− 2.1
Finance, insurance, and real estate	1,369	1.3	− 2.2
Community and business services	12,215	11.6	− 1.2
Personal services	8,018	7.6	+ 0.8
Public administration and defence	3,025	2.8	− 4.7
Miscellaneous	4,759	4.5	+ 2.1
Total labor force	105,601	100.0	—

AVERAGE INCOME (1961 CENSUS)

	Dollars	% above or below Canadian average
Income per family (non-farm)	3,473	−36.26
Income per person not in family (non-farm)	1,254	−41.32
Income per farm (net)	944	−71.00

Saguenay Valley — Lake St. John

ECONOMIC CAPSULE

This pioneer region is the most prosperous agricultural area in the entire Canadian Shield. The best land lies around Lake St. John, particularly along its southeastern shore. Mixed farming is the rule, with the emphasis on raising milk cattle.

However, the chief wealth of the region comes not from agriculture, but from the woods and hydro-electric power. The extensive forests of spruce and fir promise an ever-renewed supply of raw material to the newsprint industry. The pulp and paper mills of Chicoutimi-Jonquière, Desbiens, Alma, Port Alfred, and Dolbeau are second in importance only to those of the Trois Rivières region.

The waters of the Saguenay and its tributaries have tremendous power potential—more than 3,000,000 horsepower. This has enabled Arvida (in Chicoutimi-Jonquière urbanized area) to become one of the greatest aluminum producing centers in the world. The huge smelter, owned by Aluminum Company of Canada Limited, has an annual capacity of 373,000 tons. Another smaller smelter, with a capacity of 115,000 tons per year, is operated by the same company at Alma.

Most of the newsprint and aluminum produced is exported. The provincial government, anxious to reduce the over-dependence of the economy on foreign markets is encouraging more secondary industries to locate in this area. It was partly for this reason that the decision was made to establish a Peugeot-Renault car assembly plant at St. Bruno.

IMPORTANCE OF THE MARKET (1964 ESTIMATES)

	Region		Chicoutimi-Jonquière	
	Number	% of Canada	Number	% of Canada
Population	272,500	1.42	112,800	0.59
Households	46,700	0.97	21,300	0.44
Disposable income ($ million)	387.8	1.23	198.0	0.63

SAGUENAY VALLEY—LAKE ST. JOHN

Area covered: 41,523 square miles. *Counties:* Chicoutimi, Lac St. Jean
(Lac St. Jean Est, Lac St. Jean Ouest).

COMPOSITION OF THE MARKET

Place	County	Population 1961	% of the region
Chicoutimi-Jonquière (urbanized area)	Chicoutimi	105,009	40.01
Alma (urbanized area)	Lac St. Jean Est	19,854	7.57
Port Alfred	Chicoutimi	9,066	3.45
Roberval	Lac St. Jean Ouest	7,739	2.95
Dolbeau	Lac St. Jean Ouest	6,052	2.31
Bagotville	Chicoutimi	5,629	2.14
St. Félicien	Lac St. Jean Ouest	5,133	1.96
Mistassini	Lac St. Jean Ouest	3,461	1.32
Desbiens	Lac St. Jean Est	1,970	0.75
St. Jérôme	Lac St. Jean Est	1,962	0.75
Normandin	Lac St. Jean Ouest	1,838	0.70
Notre Dame d'Hébertville	Lac St. Jean Est	1,604	0.61
St. Ambroise	Chicoutimi	1,576	0.60
St. Coeur de Marie	Lac St. Jean Est	1,302	0.50
Hébertville Station	Lac St. Jean Est	1,257	0.48
L'Ascension	Lac St. Jean Est	1,197	0.46
Chambord	Lac St. Jean Ouest	1,188	0.45
St. Bruno	Lac St. Jean Est	1,158	0.44
St. Fulgence	Chicoutimi	1,094	0.42
St. Honoré	Chicoutimi	1,009	0.38
Girardville	Lac St. Jean Ouest	1,004	0.38
Total urban		180,102	68.63
Rural non-farm		50,712	19.32
Rural farm		31,612	12.05
Total population		262,426	100.00

GROWTH OF THE MARKET

	Region		Chicoutimi-Jonquière	
	Percentage growth 1961 to 1964	% points above or below Canadian average	Percentage growth 1961 to 1964	% points above or below Canadian average
Population	+ 3.84	− 1.63	+ 7.42	+ 1.95
Disposable income	+41.43	+19.90	+48.43	+26.90

POVERTY AND AFFLUENCE (1961 CENSUS)

	Region			Chicoutimi-Jonquière	
	Number	% of region's total	% points above or below Canadian average	Number	% of city's total
Extent of poverty					
Families earning below $3,000 a year (non-farm)	10,145	25.1	+ 1.8	3,410	17.6
Persons not in families earning below $1,500 a year (non-farm)	4,836	64.2	+15.3	2,117	58.5
Farms with gross income of less than $2,500 a year	2,617	60.2	+14.1	—	—
Persons not in school with grade 4 or less education	27,087	18.6	+ 5.2	9,267	15.8
Doubled-up households (more than one family per household)	2,108	4.7	+ 1.0	760	4.0
Households living in dilapidated dwellings	2,288	5.1	− 0.5	601	3.1
Households without facilities of running water	774	1.7	− 9.2	32	0.2
Households without facilities of installed bath or shower	14,399	32.2	+12.5	3,270	17.0
Extent of affluence					
Families earning over $10,000 a year (non-farm)	3,061	7.5	− 0.3	1,824	9.4
Persons not in families earning over $6,000 a year (non-farm)	177	2.4	− 1.4	116	3.2
Farms with gross income over $15,000 a year	31	0.8	− 4.2	—	—
Persons with university degree	2,824	1.9	− 0.9	1,724	2.9
Households with two or more television sets	661	1.5	− 2.7	498	2.6
Households with two or more cars	1,140	2.6	− 4.2	507	2.6

LABOR FORCE BY INDUSTRY

	Region			Chic.-Jon.	
Industry	Persons 1961 census	% of the total	% points above or below Canadian average	Persons 1961 census	% of the total
Agriculture	6,009	8.5	− 1.4	146	0.5
Forestry	6,676	9.5	+ 7.8	850	2.9
Fishing and trapping	31	—	− 0.5	1	—
Mines, quarries, oil wells	271	0.4	− 1.5	52	0.2
Manufacturing	15,688	22.2	+ 0.5	9,536	32.4
Construction	5,256	7.4	+ 0.7	2,451	8.3
Transportation, communications, and other utilities	5,364	7.6	− 1.7	1,951	6.6
Wholesale trade	1,552	2.2	− 2.3	825	2.8
Retail trade	7,542	10.7	− 0.1	3,696	12.6
Finance, insurance, and real estate	1,386	2.0	− 1.5	768	2.6
Community and business services.	9,807	13.9	+ 1.1	5,077	17.3
Personal services	4,912	7.0	+ 0.2	1,906	6.5
Public administration and defence	3,658	5.2	− 2.3	1,325	4.5
Miscellaneous	2,365	3.4	+ 1.0	838	2.8
Total labor force	70,517	100.0	—	29,422	100.0

CHARACTERISTICS OF THE POPULATION

	Region		Chicoutimi-Jonquière
	% of the total population of the region	% points above or below Canadian average	% of the total population of the city
Mother tongue (1961 census)			
English	2.2	−56.2	2.8
French	97.2	+69.1	96.5
German	—	− 3.1	0.1
Native Indian dialects	0.2	− 0.7	—
Italian	0.1	− 1.8	0.1
Dutch	—	− 0.9	—
Polish	0.1	− 0.8	0.1
Ukrainian	—	− 2.0	—
Other	0.2	− 3.6	0.4
Total	100.0	—	100.0

Official language spoken (*1961 census*)

English only	1.3	−66.1	1.4
French only	89.2	+70.1	84.3
Both English and French	9.4	− 2.8	14.2
Neither English nor French	0.1	− 1.2	0.1
Total	100.0	—	100.0

AVERAGE INCOME (1961 CENSUS)

	Region		Chicoutimi-Jonquière	
	Dollars	% above or below Canadian average	Dollars	% above or below Canadian average
Income per family (non-farm)	5,176	− 5.01	5,763	+ 5.76
Income per person not in family (non-farm)	1,625	−23.96	1,826	−14.55
Income per farm (net)	1,407	−56.77	—	—

Metro Québec — Eastern Laurentides

ECONOMIC CAPSULE

The region is completely dominated by Québec, "the Cradle of New France". Jacques Cartier was the first mariner to be impressed by the commanding position of the rock at the head of the Gulf of St. Lawrence. Later Champlain, who had a discerning eye, chose the site for the foundation of his colony, nine years before the landing of the Pilgrim Fathers at Plymouth in 1617. At the height of France's power, the governor of Québec ruled over a vast territory extending from the Gulf of Mexico to Hudson Bay and from the St. Lawrence to the Rocky Mountains.

Perhaps no other city in North America has had such a stormy history. Québec has been subjected to sieges, bombardments, and capitulations. It has been burned and pillaged, rebuilt and burned again. Here Wolfe gave a crushing blow to the aspirations of France in the New World; Carleton saved Canada from the American revolutionists; and during the last war Churchill and Roosevelt met to plan the grand strategy for the defeat of Hitler.

Québec is a city of many facets. It is an important port and a distribution point, the headquarters of the provincial government, the primatial see of the Roman Catholic Church in Canada, and a center of higher learning (being the site of old Laval University, noted for its theology faculty and law school). Its strategic location, which earned it the title of the "Gibraltar of North America", has lost most of its meaning in the nuclear age. It still, however, has a garrison quartered in the massive citadel, as well as an arsenal making munitions for the armed forces.

Québec acts as a magnet on tourists. People from far and near are drawn to this "only walled city in North America," with its historic buildings, old churches, and narrow, winding streets — all of which provide a distinct European touch. Among the visitors are also pilgrims en route to the famous shrine of Ste. Anne de Beaupré, called the Lourdes of the North, in recognition of the miraculous cure of the lame, the deaf, and the blind.

Like other places in the province, Québec has not been left untouched by the onrush of industrialization. Manufacturing now provides employment to 19% of the labor force. Some of the major items produced are food products, cigarettes, shoes and other leather goods, cotton yarn and cloth, foundation garments, and pulp and paper. A large drydock and shipyards are located across the river at Lauzon. The port of Québec handled in 1964 six million tons of cargo.

Outside Metropolitan Québec, agriculture is most important. The farmers specialize mainly in dairying and the rearing of livestock for beef. There is also some poultry raising and market gardening, to satisfy the requirements of the large urban center.

METRO QUEBEC—EASTERN LAURENTIDES

Area covered: 12,219 square miles. *Counties:* Beauce, Bellechasse, Charlevoix (Charlevoix Est, Charlevoix Ouest), Dorchester, Lévis, Lotbinière, Montmorency (Montmorency No. 1, Montmorency No. 2 and Ile d'Orléans), Portneuf, Québec.

COMPOSITION OF THE MARKET

Place	County	Population 1961	% of the region
Québec (metro)	Lévis and Québec	357,568	55.54
Donnacona	Portneuf	4,812	0.75
St. Georges Ouest	Beauce	4,755	0.74
Baie St. Paul	Charlevoix Ouest	4,674	0.73
St. Georges	Beauce	4,082	0.63
St. Raymond	Portneuf	3,931	0.61
Ste. Marie	Beauce	3,662	0.57
Clermont	Charlevoix Est	3,114	0.48

COMPOSITION OF THE MARKET (continued)

Place	County	Population 1961	% of the region
Pont Rouge	Port Neuf	2,988	0.46
St. Marc des Carrières	Port Neuf	2,622	0.41
Beaupré	Montmorency No. 1	2,587	0.40
La Malbaie	Charlevoix Est	2,580	0.40
St. Joseph	Beauce	2,484	0.39
Lac Etchemin	Dorchester	2,297	0.36
Beauceville Est	Beauce	1,920	0.30
Ste. Anne de Beaupré	Montmorency No. 1	1,878	0.29
Château Richer	Montmorency No. 1	1,837	0.28
St. Basile	Portneuf	1,709	0.26
Beauceville	Beauce	1,645	0.26
St. Jean de Boischatel	Montmorency No. 1	1,576	0.24
L'Ange Gardien	Montmorency No. 1	1,543	0.24
Vallée Jonction	Beauce	1,405	0.22
St. Casimir	Portneuf	1,386	0.21
Notre Dame de Portneuf	Portneuf	1,380	0.21
Ste. Croix	Lotbinière	1,363	0.21
St. Zacharie	Beauce	1,361	0.21
St. Prosper	Dorchester	1,357	0.21
Portneuf Station	Portneuf	1,353	0.21
Ste. Claire	Dorchester	1,338	0.21
Pointe au Pic	Charlevoix Est	1,333	0.21
Val St. Michel	Québec	1,290	0.20
St. Martin de Tours	Beauce	1,290	0.20
Deschaillons sur St. Laurent	Lotbinière	1,283	0.20
Linière	Beauce	1,269	0.20
Tring-Jonction	Beauce	1,214	0.19
Ste. Hélène de Breakeyville	Lévis	1,213	0.19
St. Siméon	Charlevoix Est	1,197	0.19
East Broughton Station	Beauce	1,136	0.18
St. Raphaël	Bellechasse	1,134	0.18
St. Anselme	Dorchester	1,131	0.18
St. Agapitville	Lotbinière	1,117	0.17
Deschambault	Portneuf	1,056	0.16
St. Rédempteur	Lévis	1,035	0.16
Total urban		441,905	68.64
Rural non-farm		104,066	16.16
Rural farm		97,872	15.20
Total population		643,843	100.00

IMPORTANCE OF THE MARKET (1964 ESTIMATES)

	Region		Québec	
	Number	% of Canada	Number	% of Canada
Population	667,500	3.47	384,000	2.00
Households	138,800	2.89	91,400	1.90
Disposable income ($ million)	869.2	2.76	612.8	1.94

GROWTH OF THE MARKET

	Region		Québec	
	Percentage growth 1961 to 1964	% points above or below Canadian average	Percentage growth 1961 to 1964	% points above or below Canadian average
Population	+ 3.67	−1.80	+ 7.39	+ 1.92
Disposable income	+28.66	+7.13	+33.95	+12.42

MEANS OF LIVELIHOOD—DISTRIBUTION OF LABOR FORCE BY INDUSTRY

Industry	Region			Québec	
	Persons 1961 census	% of the total	% points above or below Canadian average	Persons 1961 census	% of the total
Agriculture	24,166	11.4	+1.5	1,111	0.9
Forestry	5,734	2.7	+1.0	488	0.4
Fishing and trapping	133	0.1	−0.4	91	0.1
Mines, quarries, oil wells	990	0.5	−1.4	152	0.1
Manufacturing	37,420	17.7	−4.0	23,749	18.8
Construction	14,843	7.0	+0.3	9,074	7.2
Transportation, communications, and other utilities	16,948	8.0	−1.3	10,976	8.7
Wholesale trade	8,114	3.8	−0.7	6,628	5.2
Retail trade	22,305	10.5	−0.3	15,173	12.0
Finance, insurance, and real estate	6,243	2.9	−0.6	5,127	4.0
Community and business services	31,714	15.0	+2.2	23,525	18.6
Personal services	14,528	6.8	—	9,194	7.3
Public administration and defence	22,828	10.8	+3.3	17,819	14.1
Miscellaneous	5,875	2.8	+0.4	3,304	2.6
Total labor force	211,841	100.0	—	126,411	100.0

CHARACTERISTICS OF THE POPULATION

	Region		Québec
	% of the total population of the region	% points above or below Canadian average	% of the total population of the city
Mother tongue (1961 census)			
English	3.0	− 55.4	3.8
French	96.4	+68.3	95.4
German	0.1	− 3.0	0.1
Native Indian dialects	—	− 0.9	—
Italian	0.1	− 1.8	0.2
Dutch	—	− 0.9	—
Polish	—	− 0.9	—
Ukrainian	—	− 2.0	—
Other	0.4	− 3.4	0.5
Total	100.0	—	100.0
Official language spoken (1961 census)			
English only	1.3	− 66.1	1.4
French only	81.8	+62.7	74.2
Both English and French	16.8	+ 4.6	24.3
Neither English nor French	0.1	− 1.2	0.1
Total	100.0	—	100.0

POVERTY AND AFFLUENCE (1961 CENSUS)

		Region		Québec	
	Number	% of region's total	% points above or below Canadian average	Number	% of city's total
Extent of poverty					
Families earning below $3,000 a year (non-farm)	28,417	26.5	+ 3.2	13,609	19.2
Persons not in families earning below $1,500 a year (non-farm)	20,286	56.6	+ 7.7	13,156	51.0
Farms with gross income of less than $2,500 a year	9,970	61.4	+15.3	—	—
Persons not in school with grade 4 or less education	75,701	18.7	+ 5.3	31,123	13.3

	Number	Region % of region's total	% points above or below Canadian average	Québec Number	% of city's total
Doubled-up households (more than one family per household)	3,772	2.8	− 0.9	1,957	2.5
Households living in dilapidated dwellings	5,003	3.7	− 1.9	2,475	3.1
Households without facilities of running water	1,855	1.4	− 9.5	128	0.2
Households without facilities of installed bath or shower	35,587	26.6	+ 6.9	10,664	13.5
Extent of affluence					
Families earning over $10,000 a year (non-farm)	8,774	8.2	+ 0.4	7,195	10.2
Persons not in families earning over $6,000 a year (non-farm)	780	2.2	− 1.6	651	2.5
Farms with gross income over $15,000 a year	173	1.1	− 3.9	—	—
Persons with university degree	10,522	2.6	− 0.2	8,715	3.7
Households with two or more television sets	4,058	3.0	− 1.2	3,769	4.8
Households with two or more cars	3,673	2.7	− 4.1	2,476	3.1

AVERAGE INCOME (1961 CENSUS)

	Region Dollars	% above or below Canadian average	Québec Dollars	% above or below Canadian average
Income per family (non-farm)	5,245	− 3.74	5,801	+ 6.46
Income per person not in family (non-farm)	1,716	−19.70	1,878	−12.12
Income per farm (net)	1,217	−62.61	—	—

Trois Rivières — St. Maurice Valley

Area covered: 15,226 square miles. *Counties:* Berthier, Champlain, Maskinongé, Nicolet, St. Maurice.

COMPOSITION OF THE MARKET

Place	County	Population 1961	% of the region
Trois Rivières (urbanized area)	Champlain, St. Maurice	83,659	27.77
Shawinigan (urbanized area)	Champlain, St. Maurice	63,518	21.09
La Tuque	Champlain	13,023	4.32
Nicolet	Nicolet	4,441	1.47
Louiseville	Maskinongé	4,138	1.37
Berthierville	Berthier	3,708	1.23
St. Gabriel de Brandon	Berthier	3,425	1.14
St. Tite	Champlain	3,250	1.08
Ste. Thècle	Champlain	2,009	0.67
St. Alexis des Monts	Maskinongé	1,991	0.66
St. Michel des Saints	Berthier	1,763	0.59
Parent	Champlain	1,298	0.43
Yamachiche	St. Maurice	1,186	0.39
La Pérade	Champlain	1,184	0.39
La Visitation de la Pointe du Lac	St. Maurice	1,074	0.36
St. Joseph de Lanoraie	Berthier	1,060	0.35
Alençon	Berthier	1,039	0.35
Lavaltrie	Berthier	1,034	0.34
Total urban		192,800	64.00
Rural non-farm		61,650	20.46
Rural farm		46,802	15.54
Total population		301,252	100.00

ECONOMIC CAPSULE

The region lies on both banks of the St. Lawrence. Agriculture (mainly dairying) predominates on the southern side. In the north a little pioneer farming is carried on, but the soil is too acid and the climate too severe for successful cultivation.

However, the northern part is richly endowed with two other natural resources: dense coniferous forests and ample water power. Industrialization has made rapid strides, and the area has become the newsprint capital of the world. Over half a dozen giant mills provide paper for one out of every six newspapers printed throughout the globe. Other enterprises include chemical plants and textile mills, iron foundries, and an aluminum smelter (at Shawinigan). One third of the labor force is engaged in manufacturing, the highest proportion for any region in the province. Industrialization will proceed still further when the Québec government's first integrated steel complex at Bécancourt is completed at a cost of $225,000,000.

Trois Rivières, the biggest city, is strategically located half-way between Montréal and Québec, with excellent road, railway, and river communications. It has a good deepwater port with large grain elevators, and in some years it handles more freight than Québec. It has still retained its early religious fervor, and every year tens of thousands of the faithful make a pilgrimage to the Marial sanctuary of Cap de la Madeleine.

IMPORTANCE OF THE MARKET (1964 ESTIMATES)

	Region		Trois Rivières		Shawinigan	
	Number	% of Canada	Number	% of Canada	Number	% of Canada
Population	305,900	1.59	87,700	0.46	66,200	0.34
Households	65,600	1.36	20,400	0.42	14,700	0.31
Disposable income ($ million)	403.4	1.28	133.0	0.42	111.1	0.35

GROWTH OF THE MARKET

	Region		Trois Rivières		Shawinigan	
	Percentage growth 1961 to 1964	% points above or below Canadian average	Percentage growth 1961 to 1964	% points above or below Canadian average	Percentage growth 1961 to 1964	% points above or below Canadian average
Population	+ 1.54	−3.93	+ 4.83	−0.64	+ 4.22	−1.25
Disposable income	+28.31	+6.78	+31.16	+9.63	+31.17	+9.64

AVERAGE INCOME (1961 CENSUS)

	Region		Trois Rivières		Shawinigan	
	Dollars	% above or below Canadian average	Dollars	% above or below Canadian average	Dollars	% above or below Canadian average
Income per family (non-farm)	4,636	−14.92	4,970	− 8.79	5,231	− 4.00
Income per person not in family (non-farm)	1,498	−29.90	1,737	−18.72	1,666	−22.04
Income per farm (net)	1,593	−51.06	—	—	—	—

POVERTY AND AFFLUENCE (1961 CENSUS)

	Region			Trois Rivières		Shawinigan	
	Number	% of region's total	% points above or below Canadian average	Number	% of city's total	Number	% of city's total
Extent of poverty							
Families earning below $3,000 a year (non-farm)	16,276	31.5	+ 8.2	4,237	24.5	2,935	22.5
Persons not in families earning below $1,500 a year (non-farm)	8,737	63.4	+14.5	2,808	57.3	1,731	62.9
Farms with gross income of less than $2,500 a year	4,601	56.1	+10.0	—	—	—	—
Persons not in school with grade 4 or less education	32,553	17.7	+ 4.3	7,486	14.0	5,963	16.0
Doubled-up households (more than one family per household)	1,952	3.1	− 0.6	434	2.3	245	1.8
Households living in dilapidated dwellings	2,718	4.3	− 1.3	572	3.0	406	2.9
Households without facilities of running water	1,151	1.8	− 9.1	15	0.1	15	0.1
Households without facilities of installed bath or shower	15,725	24.7	+ 5.0	1,880	10.0	1,493	10.7
Extent of affluence							
Families earning over $10,000 a year (non-farm)	2,884	5.6	− 2.2	1,160	6.7	882	6.8
Persons not in families earning over $6,000 a year (non-farm)	236	1.6	− 2.2	93	1.9	64	2.3
Farms with gross income over $15,000 a year	161	1.9	− 3.1	—	—	—	—
Persons with university degree	3,115	1.7	− 1.1	1,086	2.0	918	2.5
Households with two or more television sets	895	1.4	− 2.8	417	2.2	161	1.2
Households with two or more cars	1,099	1.7	− 5.1	290	1.5	272	2.0

MEANS OF LIVELIHOOD—DISTRIBUTION OF
LABOR FORCE BY INDUSTRY

Industry	Region Persons 1961 census	% of the total	% points above or below Canadian average	Trois Rivières Persons 1961 census	% of the total	Shawinigan Persons 1961 census	% of the total
Agriculture	11,672	12.6	+2.7	107	0.4	79	0.4
Forestry	3,455	3.7	+2.0	88	0.3	255	1.4
Fishing and trapping	38	—	−0.5	1	—	1	—
Mines, quarries, oil wells	163	0.2	−1.7	22	0.1	32	0.2
Manufacturing	29,051	31.2	+9.5	10,216	37.3	7,930	43.4
Construction	6,161	6.6	−0.1	1,992	7.3	1,143	6.2
Transportation, communications, and other utilities	6,601	7.1	−2.2	2,198	8.0	1,349	7.4
Wholesale trade	1,885	2.0	−2.5	839	3.1	359	2.0
Retail trade	9,095	9.8	−1.0	3,195	11.7	2,085	11.4
Finance, insurance, and real estate	1,731	1.9	−1.6	715	2.6	414	2.3
Community and business services	11,557	12.4	−0.4	4,346	15.9	2,115	11.6
Personal services	5,607	6.0	−0.8	1,773	6.5	1,071	5.9
Public administration and defence	3,331	3.6	−3.9	1,219	4.4	922	5.0
Miscellaneous	2,661	2.9	+0.5	647	2.4	511	2.8
Total labor force	93,008	100.0	—	27,358	100.0	18,266	100.0

CHARACTERISTICS OF THE POPULATION

	Region % of the total population of the region	% points above or below Canadian average	Trois Rivières % of the total population of the city	Shawinigan % of the total population of the city
Mother tongue (1961 census)				
English	2.4	−56.0	3.3	3.4
French	96.9	+68.8	96.2	96.1
German	—	−3.1	—	0.1
Native Indian dialects	0.3	−0.6	—	—
Italian	0.1	−1.8	0.1	0.1

	Region		Trois Rivières	Shawinigan
	% of the total population of the region	% points above or below Canadian average	% of the total population of the city	% of the total population of the city
Dutch	—	− 0.9	—	—
Polish	—	− 0.9	—	—
Ukrainian	—	− 2.0	—	—
Other	0.3	− 3.5	0.4	0.3
Total	100.0	—	100.0	100.0
Official language spoken (1961 census)				
English only	1.1	−66.3	1.3	1.6
French only	83.2	+64.1	75.9	78.6
Both English and French	15.5	+ 3.3	22.6	19.7
Neither English nor French	0.2	− 1.1	0.2	0.1
Total	100.0	—	100.0	100.0

Sherbrooke — Eastern Townships

ECONOMIC CAPSULE

The Eastern Townships, as the name implies, cover a cluster of municipalities east of Montréal. Agriculture is important, nearly two-thirds of the area being covered by farmland. Sixty-eight per cent of the commercial farms specialize in dairying and 13% in livestock raising. The region is also renowned for its maple trees, whose sap is condensed to syrup or made into a brown, slightly pungent sugar prized by gourmets. The festival of the spring syrup is one of the gayest and most picturesque in French Canada.

The area of the Serpentine Belt produces three-quarters of the free world's supply of asbestos. Mining began as far back as 1878, but reserves are still ample to meet the growing demand. Current production is at the rate of 1,200,000 tons per year. Thetford Mines, Asbestos, Danville, Coleraine, and Robertsonville are some of the several towns and villages dependent on the asbestos mines. About 90% of the raw material is exported, mainly to the United States. The remainder is processed in Canada and used in a wide variety of products ranging from brake linings and electrical insulation to fire-proofing materials, textiles, plastics, and floor tiles.

The Eastern Townships have about a dozen thriving manufacturing centers. Sherbrooke is noted for its textile and hosiery mills, boiler and plate works, and machinery-making plants. Drummondville, Granby, and Magog are textile towns. Pulp and paper mills are located at Windsor, East Angus, Danville, and Bromptonville. Victoriaville specializes in furniture making, while Plessisville is the headquarters of maple sugar producers. Although Sherbrooke is the largest city, its influence is not all-dominating because of the presence of numerous small towns, each of which acts as a nucleus of marketing activity for the immediate neighborhood.

SHERBROOKE—EASTERN TOWNSHIPS

Area covered: 7,230 square miles. *Counties:* Arthabaska, Brome, Compton, Drummond, Frontenac, Mégantic, Richmond, Shefford, Sherbrooke, Stanstead, Wolfe.

IMPORTANCE OF THE MARKET (1964 ESTIMATES)

	Region		Sherbrooke	
	Number	% of Canada	Number	% of Canada
Population	467,200	2.43	74,100	0.39
Households	102,200	2.13	18,500	0.39
Disposable income ($ million)	539.6	1.71	102.6	0.33

GROWTH OF THE MARKET

	Region		Sherbrooke	
	Percentage growth 1961 to 1964	% points above or below Canadian average	Percentage growth 1961 to 1964	% points above or below Canadia averagen
Population	+ 1.18	−4.29	+5.48	+ 0.01
Disposable income	+13.62	−7.91	+6.65	−14.88

AVERAGE INCOME (1961 CENSUS)

	Region		Sherbrooke	
	Dollars	% above or below Canadian average	Dollars	% above or below Canadian average
Income per family (non-farm)	4,523	−16.99	4,900	−10.08
Income per person not in family (non-farm)	1,664	−22.13	1,742	−18.48
Income per farm (net)	1,581	−51.43	—	—

COMPOSITION OF THE MARKET

Place	County	Population 1961	% of the region
Sherbrooke (urbanized area)	Sherbrooke	70,253	15.21
Drummondville (urbanized area)	Drummond	39,307	8.51
Granby	Shefford	31,463	6.81
Thetford Mines (urbanized area)	Mégantic	25,798	5.59
Victoriaville (urbanized area)	Arthabaska	21,697	4.70
Magog (urbanized area)	Stanstead	14,233	3.08
Asbestos	Richmond	11,083	2.40
Lac Mégantic	Frontenac	7,015	1.52
Coaticook	Stanstead	6,906	1.50
Windsor	Richmond	6,589	1.43
Plessisville	Mégantic	6,570	1.42
East Angus	Compton	4,756	1.03
Waterloo	Shefford	4,543	0.98
Richmond	Richmond	4,072	0.88
Princeville	Arthabaska	3,174	0.69
Disraëli	Wolfe	3,079	0.67
Bromptonville	Richmond	2,726	0.59
Bernierville	Mégantic	2,706	0.59
Danville	Richmond	2,562	0.55
Warwick	Arthabaska	2,487	0.54
Sutton	Brome	1,755	0.38
La Guadeloupe	Frontenac	1,728	0.37
Rock Island	Stanstead	1,608	0.35
Weedon Centre	Wolfe	1,426	0.31
Cookshire	Compton	1,412	0.31
Knowlton	Brome	1,396	0.30
Beebe Plain	Stanstead	1,363	0.30
Waterville	Compton	1,330	0.29
Coleraine	Mégantic	1,205	0.26
Robertsonville	Mégantic	1,156	0.25
St. Cyrille	Drummond	1,138	0.25
Stanstead Plain	Stanstead	1,116	0.24
Scotstown	Compton	1,038	0.22
St. Germain de Grantham	Drummond	1,015	0.22
Total urban		289,705	62.74
Rural non-farm		78,334	16.97
Rural farm		93,698	20.29
Total population		461,737	100.00

LABOR FORCE BY INDUSTRY

Industry	Region			Sherbrooke	
	Persons 1961 census	% of the total	% points above or below Canadian average	Persons 1961 census	% of the total
Agriculture	22,526	15.6	+5.7	118	0.5
Forestry	1,502	1.0	−0.7	62	0.2
Fishing and trapping	30	—	−0.5	1	—
Mines, quarries, oil wells	6,238	4.3	+2.4	31	0.1
Manufacturing	44,155	30.6	+8.9	7,060	29.0
Construction	8,667	6.0	−0.7	1,767	7.3
Transportation, communications, and other utilities	8,119	5.6	−3.7	1,547	6.3
Wholesale trade	3,575	2.5	−2.0	1,231	5.1
Retail trade	13,912	9.6	−1.2	2,865	11.8
Finance, insurance, and real estate	2,765	1.9	−1.6	866	3.6
Community and business services	16,496	11.4	−1.4	5,052	20.8
Personal services	8,764	6.1	−0.7	1,749	7.2
Public administration and defence	3,974	2.8	−4.7	1,339	5.5
Miscellaneous	3,815	2.6	+0.2	642	2.6
Total labor force	144,538	100.0	—	24,330	100.0

CHARACTERISTICS OF THE POPULATION

	Region		Sherbrooke
	% of the total population of the region	% points above or below Canadian average	% of the total population of the city
Mother tongue (1961 census)			
English	10.2	−48.2	13.7
French	89.0	+60.9	85.0
German	0.1	− 3.0	0.2
Native Indian dialects	—	− 0.9	—
Italian	0.1	− 1.8	0.2
Dutch	0.1	− 0.8	0.1
Polish	0.1	− 0.8	0.1
Ukrainian	—	− 2.0	—
Other	0.4	− 3.4	0.7
Total	100.0	—	100.0

English only	7.1	− 60.3	9.1
French only	72.1	+53.0	56.5
Both English and French	20.7	+ 8.5	34.3
Neither English nor French	0.1	− 1.2	0.1
Total	100.0	—	100.0

POVERTY AND AFFLUENCE (1961 CENSUS)

	Region			*Sherbrooke*	
	Number	% of region's total	% points above or below Canadian average	Number	% of city's total
Families earning below $3,000 a year (non-farm)	23,355	31.0	+ 7.7	3,793	25.6
Persons not in families earning below $1,500 a year (non-farm)	13,601	59.0	+10.1	2,798	55.5
Farms with gross income of less than $2,500 a year	8,524	51.4	+ 5.3	—	—
Persons not in school with grade 4 or less education	58,772	21.1	+ 7.7	7,287	16.4
Doubled-up households (more than one family per household)	1,953	2.0	− 1.7	271	1.6
Households living in dilapidated dwellings	5,279	5.3	− 0.3	580	3.5
Households without facilities of running water	2,335	2.3	− 8.6	25	0.1
Households without facilities of installed bath or shower	20,945	21.0	+ 1.3	829	4.9
Families earning over $10,000 a year (non-farm)	3,619	4.8	− 3.0	975	6.6
Persons not in families earning over $6,000 a year (non-farm)	597	2.6	− 1.2	130	2.6
Farms with gross income over $15,000 a year	341	2.1	− 2.9	—	—
Persons with university degree	4,245	1.5	− 1.3	1,278	2.9
Households with two or more television sets	1,125	1.1	− 3.1	395	2.4
Households with two or more cars	2,400	2.4	− 4.4	464	2.8

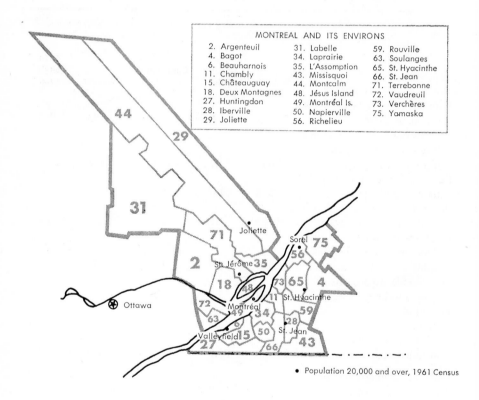

MONTREAL AND ITS ENVIRONS

2. Argenteuil	31. Labelle	59. Rouville
4. Bagot	34. Laprairie	63. Soulanges
6. Beauharnois	35. L'Assomption	65. St. Hyacinthe
11. Chambly	43. Missisquoi	66. St. Jean
15. Châteauguay	44. Montcalm	71. Terrebonne
18. Deux Montagnes	48. Jésus Island	72. Vaudreuil
27. Huntingdon	49. Montréal Is.	73. Verchères
28. Iberville	50. Napierville	75. Yamaska
29. Joliette	56. Richelieu	

• Population 20,000 and over, 1961 Census

Metro Montréal and Its Environs

Area covered: 15,174 square miles. *Counties:* Argenteuil, Bagot, Beauharnois, Chambly, Châteauguay, Deux Montagnes, Huntingdon, Iberville, Joliette, Labelle, Laprairie, L'Assomption, Missisquoi, Montcalm, Iles de Montréal et Jésus, Napierville, Richelieu, Rouville, St. Hyacinthe, St. Jean, Soulanges, Terrebonne, Vaudreuil, Verchères, Yamaska.

ECONOMIC CAPSULE

In terms of population concentration, this region is unrivalled. Nearly one out of every six persons in Canada lives in Metropolitan Montréal and its surrounding zone.

Founded in 1642 by Maisonneuve as an outpost in the wilderness, Montréal in three centuries has risen to a position of pre-eminence on the North American continent. Not only is it the biggest city in the country; it is also the largest center of French culture outside of Metropolitan France. The 1961 census shows that of its 2,110,000 inhabitants, 1,366,000 or nearly two-thirds of the population, speak French. Other groups, on the basis of mother tongue, are 495,000 English, 85,300 Italians, 33,400 Jews, 26,500 Germans, 17,200 Poles, 13,100 Hungarians, and 12,000 Ukrainians.

Being at the crossroads of two civilizations and influenced by so many other small ethnic groups, Montréal has an interesting cosmopolitan touch. Westmount has the air of an exclusive London suburb, whereas the old harbor area reminds one very strongly of Marseilles. St. Laurent Boulevard, with its stalls of Kosher meat, has the distinctive atmosphere of a Jewish quarter, while not far away are more or less compact colonies of Hungarians, Germans, Italians, Poles, Greeks, and Syrians, with their own churches, stores, restaurants, and folklore clubs. Montréal has been able to maintain its diversity thanks to the French Canadians. They have refused to become part of the North American melting pot and expect no others to melt with them.

Montréal has all the earmarks of a great metropolis — vitality, frenzied activity, grace, culture, and charm. It has two large universities (McGill and University of Montréal); a magnificent concert hall at Place des Arts; several museums, libraries, and art galleries; and about half a dozen professional drama groups, like Le Théâtre du Nouveau Monde, La Comédie Canadienne, and Le Rideau Vert.

Montréal is equally famous for its night life. Its cabarets are among the most colorful on the continent and its big restaurants are known for their cuisine well beyond the borders of the province. However, the true spirit of French Canada, in all its sparkling gaiety, is seen not in the American-style night clubs and hotel dining-rooms, but in the small restaurants and the "clubs de diseurs et de chansonniers", some of which compare favorably with the best in Paris.

However, Montréal is not merely a city of arts and amusements. It has many other claims to distinction. In normal years it is the busiest port in Canada, despite its location a thousand miles away from the sea. It is regarded as the aviation capital of the world, being the headquarters of the International Civil Aviation Organization and the International Air Transport Association. It ranks as one of the biggest centers on the globe for the production of live TV shows. In addition, it is a major wholesale market, the place of "haute couture", and the home of two large stock exchanges. When a decision was made to celebrate Canada's centenary with a world's fair, Montréal became a logical choice for the site.

Nor is that all. The metropolis is the hub and keystone of Québec's industrial revolution. It has over 5,000 plants whose output, running annually into billions of dollars, accounts for one-fifth of Canada's gross value of manufacturing production. Montréal in 1961 made 42% of the country's tobacco products, 44% of its railway rolling stock, 42% of its men's clothing, 29% of its shoes, 58% of its furs, 31% of its refined petroleum products, and 44% of its pharmaceutical and medical supplies. Such a concentration of manufacturing activity is really phenomenal, and brings out forcefully the major role the city plays in the growth and material well-being of the nation.

In the Sixties, Montréal has been in the midst of a building boom, unparalleled in its history. The major new developments are:

• Place Ville-Marie, the 619-foot-high skyscraper which, with its elegant offices, shopping promenades, cinemas and restaurants surpasses Rockefeller Plaza of New York. It is joined by underground passageways to CNR's Central Station and the Queen Elizabeth Hotel.

• Place Victoria, the 624-foot tower sheathed in brown-toned aluminum curtain walls, is the world's tallest reinforced concrete building. The square is also home for the Montréal and Canadian Exchanges, houses five restaurants and an arcade of 35 shops, and by 1970 the owners plan to add a twin tower and a direct link to Place Ville-Marie.

• Place Bonaventure, a $75 million marketplace modeled on Chicago's Merchandise Mart, will have a ground-level concourse of 70 shops and a convention hall seating 17,000, topped by a 17-story hotel and a roof garden with summer waterfalls and winter skating rinks.

• Mace Development Ltd.'s $125 million project, sponsored by the T. Eaton Company Ltd. and associated developers, will result in a 115-foot-wide elegant boulevard, from McGill University's gates to Place Ville-Marie. Twin 34-story office towers will flank the boulevard at Avenue du President Kennedy, and tree-shaded malls and a glass-roofed shopping arcade will connect the new buildings with Eaton's own store, and an underground passage with Simpson's and Morgan's too.

Surrounding Metropolitan Montréal are several small towns which have thriving industries of their own. Among them may be mentioned St. Jean (sewing machines, synthetic textiles, tires, and miscellaneous electrical products); St. Hyacinthe (textiles, knitting, and clothing, as well as the celebrated Casavant organ factory); Valleyfield (cotton yarn and cloth, beverages, chemicals, and tires); St. Jérôme (rubber goods, knitting, pulp and paper); Sorel (synthetic textiles, iron and steel, smelting and refining, shipbuilding and repair); and Joliette (clothing, pulp and paper, tobacco, iron and steel).

Despite the highly industrialized nature of the region, agriculture is important. In the low-lying lands of the St. Lawrence are to be found some of the richest and best equipped farms in the province. The market gardens of Laprairie, L'Assomption, and Napierville counties supply the metropolis with a plentiful variety of fresh vegetables; flue-cured cigarette tobacco is cultivated on the sandy plains in the counties of Joliette, L'Assomption, and Montcalm; sugar beets are grown in the counties of Bagot, Napierville, and St. Hyacinthe; while the counties of Deux Montagnes, Huntingdon, and Rouville are noted for their fruit orchards.

IMPORTANCE OF THE MARKET (1964 ESTIMATES)

	Region		Montréal	
	Number	% of Canada	Number	% of Canada
Population	2,992,400	15.56	2,260,000	11.75
Households	749,600	15.60	610,800	12.71
Disposable income ($ million)	4,938.3	15.66	4,051.4	12.85

GROWTH OF THE MARKET

	Region		Montréal	
	Percentage growth 1961 to 1964	% points above or below Canadian average	Percentage growth 1961 to 1964	% points above or below Canadian average
Population	+8.55	+3.08	+ 7.13	+1.66
Disposable income	+18.12	−3.41	+13.19	−8.34

AVERAGE INCOME (1961 CENSUS)

	Region		Montréal	
	Dollars	% above or below Canadian average	Dollars	% above or below Canadian average
Income per family (non-farm)	5,787	+ 6.20	6,046	+10.96
Income per person not in family (non-farm)	2,188	+ 2.39	2,282	+ 6.79
Income per farm (net)	2,146	−34.07	—	—

COMPOSITION OF THE MARKET

Place	County	Population 1961	% of the region
Montréal (metro)	Chambly, Châteauguay, Deux Montagnes, La Prairie, L'Assomption, Iles de Montréal et Jésus, Terrebonne, Vaudreuil	2,109,509	76.52
St. Jean (urbanized area)	Iberville, St. Jean	34,576	1.25
St. Hyacinthe	Bagot, St. Hyacinthe	31,659	1.15
Valleyfield (urbanized area)	Beauharnois	29,849	1.08
St. Jérôme (urbanized area)	Terrebonne	29,107	1.06
Sorel (urbanized area)	Richelieu	28,906	1.05
Joliette (urbanized area)	Joliette	22,198	0.80
Beauharnois	Beauharnois	8,704	0.32
Lachute	Argenteuil	7,560	0.27
Cowansville	Missisquoi	7,050	0.26
Farnham	Missisquoi	6,354	0.23
Beloeil	Verchères	6,283	0.23
Terrebonne	Terrebonne	6,207	0.22
Mont Laurier	Labelle	5,859	0.21
Ste. Agathe des Monts	Terrebonne	5,725	0.21
L'Assomption	L'Assomption	4,448	0.16
Acton Vale	Bagot	3,957	0.14
Marieville	Rouville	3,809	0.14
Chambly	Chambly	3,737	0.14
Brownsburg	Argenteuil	3,617	0.13
Huntingdon	Huntingdon	3,134	0.11
Ayersville	Argenteuil	2,957	0.11
St. Paul l'Ermite	L'Assomption	2,930	0.11
St. Hilaire	Rouville	2,911	0.11
Bedford	Missisquoi	2,855	0.10
St. Jovite	Terrebonne	2,692	0.10
L'Epiphanie	L'Assomption	2,663	0.10
Otterburn Park	Rouville	2,627	0.10
Bois des Filion	Terrebonne	2,499	0.09
Rawdon	Montcalm	2,388	0.09
St. Rémi	Napierville	2,276	0.08
Varennes	Verchères	2,240	0.08
St. Césaire	Rouville	2,097	0.08
McMasterville	Verchères	2,075	0.07
St. Jacques	Montcalm	2,038	0.07
Contrecoeur	Verchères	2,007	0.07
Rigaud	Vaudreuil	1,990	0.07

COMPOSITION OF THE MARKET (continued)

Place	County	Population 1961	% of the region
Fort Chambly	Chambly	1,987	0.07
Ferme Neuve	Labelle	1,971	0.07
Napierville	Napierville	1,812	0.07
St. Janvier de Blainville	Terrebonne	1,811	0.07
Verchères	Verchères	1,768	0.06
St. Sauveur des Monts	Terrebonne	1,702	0.06
Laurentides	L'Assomption	1,698	0.06
Ste. Martine	Châteauguay	1,695	0.06
Hudson	Vaudreuil	1,671	0.06
Melocheville	Beauharnois	1,666	0.06
Richelieu	Rouville	1,612	0.06
Pierreville	Yamaska	1,559	0.06
Hudson Heights	Vaudreuil	1,540	0.06
Ormstown	Châteauguay	1,527	0.06
Mont Rolland	Terrebonne	1,457	0.05
St. Pie	Bagot	1,434	0.05
St. Donat de Montcalm	Montcalm	1,414	0.05
Maple Grove	Beauharnois	1,412	0.05
St. Félix de Valois	Joliette	1,399	0.05
Oka	Deux Montagnes	1,375	0.05
Ste. Adèle	Terrebonne	1,331	0.05
Grenville	Argenteuil	1,330	0.05
Crabtree	Joliette	1,313	0.05
Ste. Anne des Plaines	Terrebonne	1,256	0.05
Labelle	Labelle	1,224	0.04
Terrebonne Heights	L'Assomption	1,215	0.04
St. Basile le Grand	Chambly	1,210	0.04
Lacolle	St. Jean	1,187	0.04
St. André Est	Argenteuil	1,183	0.04
Val David	Terrebonne	1,118	0.04
St. Denis	St. Hyacinthe	1,063	0.04
L'Annonciation	Labelle	1,042	0.04
Shawbridge	Terrebonne	1,034	0.04
La Station du Coteau	Soulanges	1,032	0.04
St. Timothée	Beauharnois	1,003	0.04
Total urban		2,451,544	88.93
Rural non-farm		176,107	6.39
Rural farm		129,080	4.68
Total population		2,756,731	100.00

MEANS OF LIVELIHOOD—DISTRIBUTION OF LABOR FORCE BY INDUSTRY

Industry	Region			Montréal	
	Persons 1961 census	% of the total	% points above or below Canadian average	Persons 1961 census	% of the total
Agriculture	37,242	3.7	−6.2	3,970	0.5
Forestry	2,129	0.2	−1.5	217	—
Fishing and trapping	142	—	−0.5	41	—
Mines, quarries, oil wells	1,962	0.2	−1.7	1,052	0.1
Manufacturing	311,788	30.8	+9.1	255,381	31.7
Construction	73,980	7.3	+0.6	56,310	7.0
Transportation, communications, and other utilities	104,286	10.3	+1.0	88,634	11.0
Wholesale trade	48,388	4.8	+0.3	43,394	5.4
Retail trade	104,658	10.3	−0.5	85,029	10.5
Finance, insurance, and real estate	46,337	4.6	+1.1	41,984	5.2
Community and business services	133,296	13.2	+0.4	110,376	13.7
Personal services	70,464	7.0	+0.2	56,574	7.0
Public administration and defence	50,162	4.9	−2.6	42,050	5.2
Miscellaneous	27,054	2.7	+0.3	21,961	2.7
Total labor force	1,011,888	100.0	—	806,973	100.0

CHARACTERISTICS OF THE POPULATION

	Region		Montréal
	% of the total population of the region	% points above or below Canadian average	% of the total population of the city
Mother tongue (1961 census)			
English	19.8	−38.6	23.4
French	70.8	+42.7	64.8
German	1.0	− 2.1	1.3
Native Indian dialects	0.1	− 0.8	0.1
Italian	3.1	+ 1.2	4.0
Dutch	0.2	− 0.7	0.2
Polish	0.7	− 0.2	0.8

CHARACTERISTICS OF THE POPULATION (continued)

	Region		Montréal
	% of the total population of the region	% points above or below Canadian average	% of the total population of the city
Ukrainian	0.5	− 1.5	0.6
Other	3.8	—	4.8
Total	100.0	—	100.0
Official language spoken (1961 census)			
English only	8.0	−59.4	21.9
French only	69.6	+50.5	39.2
Both English and French	22.2	+10.0	36.8
Neither English nor French	0.2	− 1.1	2.1
Total	100.0	—	100.0

POVERTY AND AFFLUENCE (1961 CENSUS)

		Region		Montréal	
	Number	% of region's total	% points above or below Canadian average	Number	% of city's total
Extent of poverty					
Families earning below $3,000 a year (non-farm)	116,935	19.7	− 3.6	82,969	17.2
Persons not in families earning below $1,500 a year (non-farm)	108,794	45.0	− 3.9	88,643	42.5
Farms with gross income of less than $2,500 a year	11,675	46.8	+ 0.7	—	—
Persons not in school with grade 4 or less education	268,155	14.7	+ 1.3	190,127	13.3
Doubled-up households (more than one family per household)	20,832	3.0	− 0.7	17,643	3.2
Households living in dilapidated dwellings	21,513	3.1	− 2.5	15,401	2.8
Households without facilities of running water	7,284	1.1	− 9.8	1,568	0.3
Households without facilities of installed bath or shower	63,166	9.2	−10.5	28,458	5.2

		Region		Montréal	
	Number	% of region's total	% points above or below Canadian average	Number	% of city's total

Extent of affluence

Families earning over $10,000 a year (non-farm)	59,096	10.0	+ 2.2	52,875	10.9
Persons not in families earning over $6,000 a year (non-farm)	9,607	4.0	+ 0.2	8,987	4.3
Farms with gross income over $15,000 a year	723	2.9	− 2.1	—	—
Persons with university degree	63,688	3.5	+ 0.7	56,934	4.0
Households with two or more television sets	35,014	5.0	+ 0.8	32,258	5.9
Households with two or more cars	21,468	3.1	− 3.7	17,806	3.2

Western Québec

ECONOMIC CAPSULE

Western Québec is extremely rich in minerals. Lying in the same geological belt as the rich mines of Kirkland Lake in Ontario, this region is the principal producer in the province of copper, lead, zinc, gold, and silver. Other minerals include bismuth, molybdenum, selenium, tellurium, lithium, and pyrites. Around the mining camps many modern towns have sprung up, like Noranda-Rouyn, Val d'Or, Malartic, Amos, Sullivan, and Cadillac. At Noranda, in the heart of the mining area, there is a huge smelter operated by Noranda Mines Limited, capable of producing 1,700,000 tons of copper anodes a year. The latest development is around Chibougamau, the Indian word for "a land of promise". Located in the northeast, it remained untouched for lack of transportation till an all-weather road and railway line were constructed a few years ago. Now several copper mines are in operation.

Although this is a pioneer region, it is much more developed than its counterpart in Ontario because of the efforts of the provincial government to establish well-organized rural communities. Mixed farming is carried on in most of the Clay Belt, with emphasis on the raising of dairy and beef cattle. In the northern part of the belt, most farmers work as part-time loggers; a few operate trap lines or seek temporary employment in the mines.

WESTERN QUEBEC

Area covered: 85,702 square miles. *Counties:* Abitibi, Témiscamingue.

COMPOSITION OF THE MARKET

Place	County	Population 1961	% of the region
Noranda-Rouyn (urbanized area)	Témiscamingue	30,193	17.91
Val-d'Or (urbanized area)	Abitibi	14,327	8.50
Malartic	Abitibi	6,998	4.15
Amos	Abitibi	6,080	3.61
Chibougamau	Abitibi	4,765	2.83
La Sarre	Abitibi	3,944	2.34
Senneterre	Abitibi	3,246	1.92
Temiscaming	Témiscamingue	2,517	1.49
Chapais	Abitibi	2,363	1.40
Normétal	Abitibi	2,284	1.35
Ville Marie	Témiscamingue	1,710	1.01
Macamic	Abitibi	1,614	0.96
Barraute	Abitibi	1,199	0.71
Sullivan	Abitibi	1,146	0.68
Cadillac	Abitibi	1,077	0.64
Total urban		83,463	49.50
Rural non-farm		51,364	30.47
Rural farm		33,774	20.03
Total population		168,601	100.00

IMPORTANCE OF THE MARKET (1964 ESTIMATES)

	Number	% of Canada
Population	172,400	0.90
Households	32,800	0.68
Disposable income ($ million)	205.6	0.65

GROWTH OF THE MARKET

	Percentage growth 1961 to 1964	% points above or below Canadian average
Population	+2.25	− 3.22
Disposable income	+9.77	−11.76

CHARACTERISTICS OF THE POPULATION

	% of the total population of the region	% points above or below Canadian average
Mother tongue (1961 census)		
English	6.4	−52.0
French	88.4	+60.3
German	0.4	− 2.7
Native Indian dialects	2.1	+ 1.2
Italian	0.5	− 1.4
Dutch	0.1	− 0.8
Polish	0.6	− 0.3
Ukrainian	0.3	− 1.7
Other	1.2	− 2.6
Total	100.0	—
Official language spoken (1961 census)		
English only	6.3	−61.1
French only	72.7	+53.6
Both English and French	19.2	+ 7.0
Neither English nor French	1.8	+ 0.5
Total	100.0	—

AVERAGE INCOME (1961 CENSUS)

	Dollars	% above or below Canadian average
Income per family (non-farm)	4,601	−15.56
Income per person not in family (non-farm)	1,984	− 7.16
Income per farm (net)	870	−73.27

MEANS OF LIVELIHOOD—DISTRIBUTION OF

LABOR FORCE BY INDUSTRY

Industry	Persons 1961 census	% of the total	% points above or below Canadian average
Agriculture	4,703	9.9	—
Forestry	4,046	8.5	+ 6.8
Fishing and trapping	115	0.2	− 0.3
Mines, quarries, oil wells	10,389	21.8	+19.9
Manufacturing	3,467	7.3	−14.4
Construction	2,564	5.4	− 1.3
Transportation, communications, and other utilities	3,651	7.7	− 1.6
Wholesale trade	1,206	2.5	− 2.0
Retail trade	4,178	8.8	− 2.0
Finance, insurance, and real estate	743	1.6	− 1.9
Community and business services	4,865	10.2	− 2.6
Personal services	3,451	7.2	+ 0.4
Public administration and defence	2,470	5.2	− 2.3
Miscellaneous	1,782	3.7	+ 1.3
Total labor force	47,630	100.0	—

POVERTY AND AFFLUENCE (1961 CENSUS)

	Number	% of region's total	% points above or below Canadian average
Extent of poverty			
Families earning below $3,000 a year (non-farm)	7,187	28.4	+ 5.1
Persons not in families earning below $1,500 a year (non-farm)	3,749	49.3	+ 0.4
Farms with gross income of less than $2,500 a year	4,254	81.3	+35.2
Persons not in school with grade 4 or less education	25,920	27.2	+13.8
Doubled-up households (more than one family per household)	906	2.8	− 0.9
Households living in dilapidated dwellings	2,874	9.0	+ 3.4
Households without facilities of running water	3,391	10.6	− 0.3
Households without facilities of installed bath or shower	12,092	37.9	+18.2

	Number	% of region's total	% points above or below Canadian average
Extent of affluence			
Families earning over $10,000 a year (non-farm)	1,312	5.2	− 2.6
Persons not in families earning over $6,000 a year (non-farm)	214	2.8	− 1.0
Farms with gross income over $15,000 a year	2	—	− 5.0
Persons with university degree	1,277	1.3	− 1.5
Households with two or more television sets	161	0.5	− 3.7
Households with two or more cars	383	1.2	− 5.6

Hull — Western Laurentides

Area covered: 13,712 square miles. *Counties:* Hull (Gatineau, Hull), Papineau, Pontiac.

COMPOSITION OF THE MARKET

Place	County	Population 1961	% of the region
Hull (urbanized area)	Gatineau, Hull	96,851*	53.29
Buckingham	Papineau	7,421	4.08
Maniwaki	Gatineau	6,349	3.49
Thurso	Papineau	3,310	1.82
Masson	Papineau	1,933	1.06
Fort Coulonge	Pontiac	1,823	1.00
Shawville	Pontiac	1,534	0.85
Montebello	Papineau	1,486	0.82
Papineauville	Papineau	1,300	0.72
St. André Avellin	Papineau	1,066	0.59
Campbell's Bay	Pontiac	1,024	0.56
Total urban		124,097	68.28
Rural non-farm		36,603	20.14
Rural farm		21,055	11.58
Total population		181,755	100.00

* Part of Metropolitan Ottawa.

ECONOMIC CAPSULE

This is the Québec section of the region which also includes Ottawa-Ottawa Valley in Ontario. Hull, the chief city, is a part of Metropolitan Ottawa and is considerably affected by all the activities in the capital. The following statistics refer only to the Québec sector. A more detailed account of the whole region is given in the next chapter.

HULL—WESTERN LAURENTIDES

IMPORTANCE OF THE MARKET (1964 ESTIMATES)

	Number	% of Canada
Population	189,100	0.98
Households	40,400	0.84
Disposable income ($ million)	260.0	0.82

POVERTY AND AFFLUENCE (1961 CENSUS)

	Number	% of region's total	% points above or below Canadian average
Extent of poverty			
Families earning below $3,000 a year (non-farm)	8,892	26.5	+ 3.2
Persons not in families earning below $1,500 a year (non-farm)	5,758	57.7	+ 8.8
Farms with gross income of less than $2,500 a year	2,874	69.6	+23.5
Persons not in school with grade 4 or less education	26,590	24.1	+10.7
Doubled-up households (more than one family per household)	1,539	3.9	+ 0.2
Households living in dilapidated dwellings	3,183	8.0	+ 2.4
Households without facilities of running water	4,096	10.3	− 0.6
Households without facilities of installed bath or shower	12,964	32.5	+12.8
Extent of affluence			
Families earning over $10,000 a year (non-farm)	2,099	6.2	− 1.6
Persons not in families earning over $6,000 a year (non-farm)	219	2.2	− 1.6
Farms with gross income over $15,000 a year	33	0.8	− 4.2
Persons with university degree	2,143	2.0	− 0.8
Households with two or more television sets	1,140	2.9	− 1.3
Households with two or more cars	1,371	3.4	− 3.4

GROWTH OF THE MARKET

	Percentage growth 1961 to 1964	% points above or below Canadian average
Population	+ 4.04	−1.43
Disposable income	+25.36	+3.83

CHARACTERISTICS OF THE POPULATION

	% of the total population of the region	% points above or below Canadian average
Mother tongue (1961 census)		
English	19.8	−38.6
French	78.4	+50.3
German	0.4	− 2.7
Native Indian dialects	0.4	− 0.5
Italian	0.1	− 1.8
Dutch	0.1	− 0.8
Polish	0.1	− 0.8
Ukrainian	0.1	− 1.9
Other	0.6	− 3.2
Total	100.0	—
Official language spoken (1961 census)		
English only	16.2	−51.2
French only	45.7	+26.6
Both English and French	37.7	+25.5
Neither English nor French	0.4	− 0.9
Total	100.0	—

AVERAGE INCOME (1961 CENSUS)

	Dollars	% above or below Canadian average
Income per family (non-farm)	5,070	− 6.96
Income per person not in family (non-farm)	1,716	−19.70
Income per farm (net)	1,316	−59.57

MEANS OF LIVELIHOOD—DISTRIBUTION OF
LABOR FORCE BY INDUSTRY

Industry	Persons 1961 census	% of the total	% points above or below Canadian average
Agriculture	4,900	8.5	−1.4
Forestry	2,257	3.9	+2.2
Fishing and trapping	8	—	−0.5
Mines, quarries, oil wells	653	1.1	−0.8
Manufacturing	10,665	18.4	−3.3
Construction	5,397	9.3	+2.6
Transportation, communications, and other utilities	4,029	6.9	−2.4
Wholesale trade	1,491	2.6	−1.9
Retail trade	5,960	10.3	−0.5
Finance, insurance, and real estate	1,248	2.2	−1.3
Community and business services	5,985	10.3	−2.5
Personal services	4,994	8.6	+1.8
Public administration and defence	8,598	14.8	+7.3
Miscellaneous	1,781	3.1	+0.7
Total labor force	57,966	100.0	—

Chapter 16

ONTARIO

Introduction

Although the huge land mass of Ontario is located in the heart of the continent, it is by no means completely an inland province. It possesses a salt water shoreline of about 700 miles on Hudson Bay and James Bay. In the south, the four Great Lakes, together with the interconnecting rivers, form one of the most important navigable bodies of fresh water in the world. The St. Lawrence Seaway permits ocean liners to go as far inland as Fort William-Port Arthur.

Agriculture

Ontario ranks first in Canada in agricultural production. Although it has only one-quarter of the nation's farms, it accounts for about a third of the total farm cash income. The Great Lakes-St. Lawrence Lowlands have some of the best agricultural lands in the country. Mixed farming is the rule, and cattle are raised for meat and milk. Hay and feed grains to meet the needs of livestock are the dominant crops. However, favorable climate and soil conditions have encouraged specialization in certain areas, as for example, tobacco in Norfolk county, corn in Essex and Kent counties, and fruits in the Niagara Peninsula.

More than 95% of the total farm production comes from Southern Ontario. In the north there is very little farming, except in the region of the Clay Belts. Low temperatures, shortness of the growing season, and poor quality of the soil put definite limits on the scope of agricultural development.

Mining

What the north lacks in agriculture it more than makes up by its tremendous mineral wealth. It is a veritable treasure house of rich metallic ores, and practically every year new discoveries are made. As a result, Ontario is by far the first province in Canada in mineral production. The five top ranking minerals are nickel, copper, uranium, iron ore, and gold. Over half the output comes from the Sudbury district.

The effect of mining on the economy of Northern Ontario cannot be over-estimated. It has sparked roads and railways which otherwise would never have been constructed and led to the establishment of such towns as Sudbury, Timmins, Porcupine, Kirkland Lake, and Elliot Lake, in areas which would otherwise have remained a barren wilderness.

Forestry

The forest industry too has helped in the development of Northern Ontario. While the lowlands of the Great Lakes and the St. Lawrence basin have been cleared for agriculture, almost the whole of the north is still thickly forested. Billions of cubic feet of merchantable timber are accessible for cutting, and they help to support several hundred sawmills and nearly two dozen pulp and paper mills. Spruce is the principal species used for pulpwood, while the lumber industry relies mainly on white and jack pines.

The provincial government has given increased attention to building access roads in order to open up more timber stands. At the same time, it limits the annual cut of each tree species to an amount which will not upset the proper "age distribution". In this way, a steady supply of good quality timber is ensured for the future.

Secondary manufacturing

Ontario is the workshop of Canada and from its factories come half of the goods produced in the country. The province is favored by many factors which encourage the establishment and expansion of secondary manufacturing industries. The concentration of three-fifths of Canada's population in the Lower Great Lakes-St. Lawrence Lowlands is of primary importance, since it provides a ready market for the products of local industries. Ontario also has excellent transportation facilities. A network of both rail lines and highways permits fast shipment of raw materials and finished goods throughout the nation. Other assets are cheap water power, skilled labor force, favorable climate, and location along the St. Lawrence Seaway. In short, the net sum of advantages for the establishment of a manufacturing plant is greater here than in other parts of the country. As a result certain industries are carried on almost exclusively in this province. These include production of motor vehicle parts, heavy electrical machinery, agricultural implements, machine tools, bicycles, and soaps.

By far the greater part of manufacturing production takes place in Southern Ontario. The region bordering western Lake Ontario gives promise of becoming one of the world's greatest industrial areas, like the Midlands of England or the Ruhr of Germany. The nine counties in this "golden horseshoe" (Ontario, York, Peel, Halton, Wentworth, Lincoln, Welland, Haldimand, and Brant) produce about 60 per cent of Ontario's and 30 per cent of Canada's manufactured output. The heart of this area is Metropolitan Toronto, a focal point of industry and finance and one of the fastest growing cities in North America. A few miles on either side are Oshawa and Oakville, twin automobile manufacturing centers. Forty miles to the west is Hamilton, which makes most of Canada's steel. Other important cities are St. Catharines, Niagara Falls, Welland, and Brantford, all noted for wide diversity of manufactured products, ranging from farm machinery and stainless sheet steel to canned fruits and flour. Three other industrial

cities, which lie just outside this region, are Windsor, another center of the automotive industry, Sarnia, the leading producer of chemicals in Canada, and London, noted for its food and beverage products.

General observations

Just as New York is called the Empire State, Ontario deserves to be known as
the Empire Province. With almost seven million people and more arriving every
day by birth and immigration, with booming industry and boundless wealth of
forests, farms, and mines, the province is fully sufficient unto itself. As Peter
Newman graphically remarks: "No province places as few limitations on its citizens as Ontario. You can cultivate rice stalks there in the subtropical summer —
or hunt polar bear in the subarctic winter. You can strike gold, capitalize on
Shakespeare, make a million in real estate, or earn a dusty living in the contem-
plation of the Ming dynasty's monochromatic porcelain."*

Ontario has only 34% of Canada's population, but it accounts for 37% of
retail sales, 39% disposable income and 50% of manufacturing production.
(1964 statistics) Metropolitan Toronto alone contains more people than the
four Atlantic Provinces put together and more disposable income than Manitoba plus Saskatchewan.

Since economic opportunities are plentiful, the province regularly skims the
cream off the Canadian population. Every year thousands of young men and women from other parts of Canada come to Ontario in order to improve their prospects. Their ranks are considerably reinforced by immigrants from Europe. The
1961 census showed that there were 833,300 New Canadians in Ontario, a number almost equal to the combined population of Nova Scotia and Prince Edward
Island. As a result of this influx, the bulk of the labor force is concentrated in the
young and energetic age bracket of 25 to 44. Another point to note is that not
only are the average earnings per worker high, but many families have more
than one bread-earner. Because of the proliferation of service industries, the proportion of married women working outside the home is greater in Ontario than
anywhere else in the country.

The most important market by far is southwestern Ontario covering the following regions: Peterborough – Central Lake Ontario; Metro Toronto and its
environs; Hamilton/St. Catharines – Niagara; London – Lake Erie; Windsor/
Sarnia – Lake St. Clair; and Kitchener – Midlands. It is the biggest, the richest,
the most sophisticated, and at the same time the most competitive zone in Canada. Its inhabitants pay more income tax, cash more cheques, and buy more
goods than the people of any other area of similar size in the country. Here, too,
one sees all the characteristics that have led to the "interurbia" agglomerations
in the United States. Rich farmlands are disappearing, industry is moving into
the countryside, and the market is growing in broad ribbons and corridors, with

---

* "Ontario in the Sixties", *Maclean's Magazine,* June 4, 1960.

cities at different intersections reaching out toward each other with inexorable gravitational pull. The urban growth has spilled over municipal boundaries, confused local allegiances, and edged impatiently toward the link-up of neighboring areas into a single, sprawling megalopolis.

The whole market is also innovation oriented. Better education, higher incomes, and greater contacts with outsiders have made the inhabitants progressive and forward-looking, ready to accept new types of stores, new ways of selling, new methods of distribution. There is a saying in the marketing circles "As Southern Ontario goes, so goes the nation." This area was the pioneer in Canada for such postwar retailing trends as self-service stores, shopping centres, discount houses, automatic vending machines, and wholesalers' cooperative chains. Actually, these trends started in the United States; but since this region is highly Americanized, having the largest collection of subsidiaries of U.S. companies, it is very quick to adopt innovations from the south.

ONTARIO

IMPORTANCE OF THE MARKET (1964 ESTIMATES)

	Number	% of Canada
Population	6,586,000	34.24
Households	1,737,000	36.15
Disposable income ($ million)	12,423.0	39.39

GROWTH OF THE MARKET

	Percentage growth 1961 to 1964	% points above or below Canadian average
Population	+ 5.61	+0.14
Disposable income	+20.47	−1.06

AVERAGE INCOME (1961 CENSUS)

	Dollars	% above or below Canadian average
Income per family (non-farm)	5,868	+ 7.69
Income per person not in family (non-farm)	2,352	+10.06
Income per farm (net)	3,913	+20.22

COMPOSITION OF THE MARKET

Place	Provincial region	Population 1961	% of Ontario
Toronto (metro)..........Metro Toronto and its Environs................		1,824,481	29.26
Hamilton (metro).......Hamilton /St. Catharines—Niagara...........		395,189	6.34
Ottawa (Ontario sector of Metro Ottawa)....Ottawa—Ottawa Valley............................		332,899	5.34
Windsor (metro).........Windsor /Sarnia—Lake St. Clair................		193,365	3.10
London (metro).........London—Lake Erie................................		181,283	2.91
Kitchener (metro).......Kitchener—Midlands..............................		154,864	2.48
Sudbury (metro).........Northeastern Ontario: Nickel Range........		110,694	1.77
St. Catharines*...........Hamilton /St. Catharines—Niagara.........		95,577	1.53
Fort William-Port Arthur*....................Lakehead—Northwestern Ontario..		93,251	1.50
Oshawa*......................Metro Toronto and its Environs................		80,918	1.30
Kingston*...................Kingston—Upper St. Lawrence................		63,419	1.02
Sarnia*.......................Windsor /Sarnia—Lake St. Clair................		61,293	0.98
Sault Ste. Marie*.......Northeastern Ontario: Sault......................		58,460	0.94
Brantford*..................Hamilton /St. Catharines—Niagara...........		56,741	0.91
Niagara Falls*............Hamilton /St. Catharines—Niagara...........		54,649	0.88
Peterborough*...........Peterborough—Central Lake Ontario......		49,902	0.80
Cornwall...................Kingston—Upper St. Lawrence................		43,639	0.70
Guelph*.....................Kitchener—Midlands..............................		41,767	0.67
Timmins*....................Northeastern Ontario: Clay Belt.............		40,121	0.64
Welland.....................Hamilton /St. Catharines—Niagara...........		36,079	0.58
North Bay*.................Northeastern Ontario: Clay Belt.............		33,545	0.54
Belleville....................Peterborough—Central Lake Ontario......		30,655	0.49
Chatham....................Windsor /Sarnia—Lake St. Clair................		29,826	0.48
St. Thomas................London—Lake Erie................................		22,469	0.36
Barrie........................Lake Huron—Georgian Bay....................		21,169	0.34
Woodstock.................London—Lake Erie................................		20,486	0.33
Stratford....................Kitchener—Midlands..............................		20,467	0.33
Pembroke*.................Ottawa—Ottawa Valley...........................		18,811	0.30
Brampton...................Metro Toronto and its Environs................		18,467	0.30
Orillia*......................Lake Huron—Georgian Bay....................		18,246	0.29
Brockville..................Kingston—Upper St. Lawrence................		17,744	0.28
Owen Sound...............Lake Huron—Georgian Bay....................		17,421	0.28
Port Colborne*...........Hamilton /St. Catharines—Niagara...........		16,717	0.27
Kirkland Lake*..........Northeastern Ontario: Clay Belt...............		16,510	0.26
Trenton.....................Peterborough—Central Lake Ontario......		13,183	0.21
Kenora*......................Lakehead—Northwestern Ontario.............		13,101	0.21
Lindsay.....................Peterborough—Central Lake Ontario......		11,399	0.18
Georgetown*.............Metro Toronto and its Environs................		11,172	0.18
Cobourg....................Peterborough—Central Lake Ontario......		10,646	0.17
Elliot Lake.................Northeastern Ontario: Sault......................		9,950	0.16

* Urbanized area.

Place	Provincial region	Population 1961	% of Ontario
Smith Falls	Ottawa—Ottawa Valley	9,603	0.15
Fort Frances	Lakehead—Northwestern Ontario	9,481	0.15
Leamington	Windsor/Sarnia—Lake St. Clair	9,030	0.14
Fort Erie	Hamilton/St. Catharines—Niagara	9,027	0.14
Renfrew	Ottawa—Ottawa Valley	8,935	0.14
Newmarket	Metro Toronto and its Environs	8,932	0.14
Aurora	Metro Toronto and its Environs	8,791	0.14
Simcoe	London—Lake Erie	8,754	0.14
Hawkesbury	Ottawa—Ottawa Valley	8,661	0.14
Midland	Lake Huron—Georgian Bay	8,656	0.14
Collingwood	Lake Huron—Georgian Bay	8,385	0.13
Port Hope	Peterborough—Central Lake Ontario	8,091	0.13
Wallaceburg	Windsor/Sarnia—Lake St. Clair	7,881	0.13
Bowmanville	Peterborough—Central Lake Ontario	7,397	0.12
Ingersoll	London—Lake Erie	6,874	0.11
Kapuskasing	Northeastern Ontario: Clay Belt	6,870	0.11
Atikokan	Lakehead—Northwestern Ontario	6,674	0.11
Tillsonburg	London—Lake Erie	6,600	0.11
Goderich	Kitchener—Midlands	6,411	0.10
Sturgeon Falls	Northeastern Ontario: Clay Belt	6,288	0.10
Parry Sound	Lake Huron—Georgian Bay	6,004	0.10
Paris	Hamilton/St. Catharines—Niagara	5,820	0.09
Dryden	Lakehead—Northwestern Ontario	5,728	0.09
Milton	Metro Toronto and its Environs	5,629	0.09
Arnprior	Ottawa—Ottawa Valley	5,474	0.09
Deep River	Ottawa—Ottawa Valley	5,377	0.09
Prescott	Kingston—Upper St. Lawrence	5,366	0.09
Perth	Ottawa—Ottawa Valley	5,360	0.09
Espanola	Northeastern Ontario: Nickel Range	5,353	0.09
Penetanguishene	Lake Huron—Georgian Bay	5,340	0.09
Dunnville	Hamilton/St. Catharines—Niagara	5,181	0.08
Strathroy	London—Lake Erie	5,150	0.08
Grimsby	Hamilton/St. Catharines—Niagara	5,148	0.08
Gananoque	Kingston—Upper St. Lawrence	5,096	0.08
Total of towns over 5,000		4,577,942	73.41
178 towns between 1,000 and 5,000		384,553	6.17
Total urban		4,962,495	79.58
Rural non-farm		767,898	12.31
Rural farm		505,699	8.11
Total population		6,236,092	100.00

MEANS OF LIVELIHOOD—DISTRIBUTION OF
LABOR FORCE BY INDUSTRY

Industry	Persons 1961 census	% of the total	% points above or below Canadian average
Agriculture	168,775	7.0	−2.9
Forestry	17,935	0.7	−1.0
Fishing and trapping	2,185	0.1	−0.4
Mines, quarries, oil wells	42,660	1.8	−0.1
Manufacturing	643,284	26.9	+5.2
Construction	153,866	6.4	−0.3
Transportation, communications, and other utilities	195,223	8.2	−1.1
Wholesale trade	102,733	4.3	−0.2
Retail trade	267,807	11.2	+0.4
Finance, insurance, and real estate	98,454	4.1	+0.6
Community and business services	303,074	12.7	−0.1
Personal services	164,053	6.8	—
Public administration and defence	181,263	7.6	+0.1
Miscellaneous	51,703	2.2	−0.2
Total labor force	2,393,015	100.0	—

CHARACTERISTICS OF THE POPULATION

	% of the total population of the province	% points above or below Canadian average
Mother tongue (1961 census)		
English	77.5	+19.1
French	6.8	−21.3
German	3.0	− 0.1
Native Indian dialects	0.4	− 0.5
Italian	3.4	+ 1.5
Dutch	1.5	+ 0.6
Polish	1.3	+ 0.4
Ukrainian	1.4	− 0.6
Other	4.7	+ 0.9
Total	100.0	—

CHARACTERISTICS OF THE POPULATION (continued)

	% of the total population of the province	% points above or below Canadian average
Official language spoken (1961 census)		
English only	89.0	+21.6
French only	1.5	−17.6
Both English and French	7.9	− 4.3
Neither English nor French	1.6	+ 0.3
Total	100.0	—

POVERTY AND AFFLUENCE (1961 CENSUS)

	Number	% of province's total	% points above or below Canadian average
Extent of poverty			
Families earning below $3,000 a year (non-farm)	245,396	17.8	−5.5
Persons not in families earning below $1,500 a year (non-farm)	240,077	44.9	−4.0
Farms with gross income of less than $2,500 a year	51,666	42.5	−3.6
Persons not in school with grade 4 or less education	363,416	9.0	−4.4
Doubled-up households (more than one family per household)	76,015	4.6	+0.9
Households living in dilapidated dwellings	74,127	4.5	−1.1
Households without facilities of running water	97,382	5.9	−5.0
Households without facilities of installed bath or shower	178,964	10.9	−8.8
Extent of affluence			
Families earning over $10,000 a year (non-farm)	121,470	8.9	+1.1
Persons not in families earning over $6,000 a year (non-farm)	25,806	4.7	+0.9
Farms with gross income over $15,000 a year	10,592	8.8	+3.8
Persons with university degree	132,904	3.3	+0.5
Households with two or more television sets	106,141	6.5	+2.3
Households with two or more cars	161,307	9.8	+3.0

STANDARD OF LIVING BASED ON OWNERSHIP OF
APPLIANCES AND EQUIPMENT, 1965

	Number of households	% of total households in Ontario	% points above or below Canadian average
Cooking equipment			
Electric stoves	1,435,000	81.3	+12.3
Wood or coal cookstoves or ranges	38,000	2.2	− 7.0
Piped gas stoves	253,000	14.3	+ 0.2
Refrigeration			
Electric refrigerators	1,743,000	98.7	+ 2.9
Home freezers	413,000	23.4	+ 0.8
Electric washing machines			
Automatic	409,000	23.2	+ 0.1
Other	1,103,000	62.5	− 0.7
Clothes dryers			
Electric	550,000	31.1	+ 5.9
Gas	55,000	3.1	+ 0.9
Sewing machines			
Electric	946,000	53.6	+ 1.2
Non-electric	245,000	13.9	− 4.3
Phonographs and record players			
Cabinet model	662,000	37.5	+ 4.6
Table model	93,000	5.3	+ 0.1
Portable model	371,000	21.0	—
Telephones			
One	1,392,000	78.8	+ 2.6
Two or more	288,000	16.3	+ 3.1
Television sets			
One	1,442,000	81.7	− 0.1
Two or more	248,000	14.0	+ 3.1
Automobiles			
One	1,156,000	65.5	+ 3.0
Two or more	275,000	15.6	+ 3.2
Other appliances			
Automatic dishwashers	44,000	2.5	− 0.2
Vacuum cleaners	1,475,000	83.5	+ 8.6
Window-type air conditioners	64,000	3.6	+ 1.4
FM radio receivers	535,000	30.3	+ 7.4

(Source: DBS, *Household Facilities and Equipment, May 1965.* Catalogue no. 64-202.)

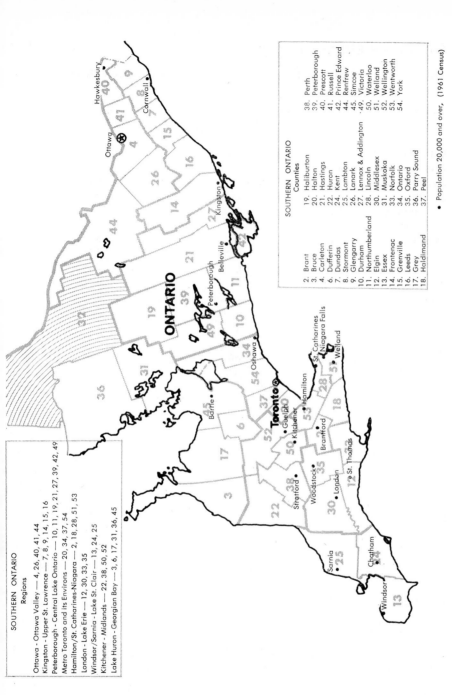

SOUTHERN ONTARIO
Regions

Ottawa - Ottawa Valley — 4, 26, 40, 41, 44
Kingston - Upper St. Lawrence — 7, 8, 9, 14, 15, 16
Peterborough - Central Lake Ontario — 10, 11, 19, 21, 27, 39, 42, 49
Metro Toronto and its Environs — 20, 34, 37, 54
Hamilton/St. Catharines-Niagara — 2, 18, 28, 51, 53
London - Lake Erie — 12, 30, 33, 35
Windsor / Sarnia - Lake St. Clair — 13, 24, 25
Kitchener - Midlands — 22, 38, 50, 52
Lake Huron - Georgian Bay — 3, 6, 17, 31, 36, 45

SOUTHERN ONTARIO
Counties

2. Brant	19. Haliburton	38. Perth
3. Bruce	20. Halton	39. Peterborough
4. Carleton	21. Hastings	40. Prescott
6. Dufferin	22. Huron	41. Russell
7. Dundas	24. Kent	42. Prince Edward
8. Stormont	25. Lambton	44. Renfrew
9. Glengarry	26. Lanark	45. Simcoe
10. Durham	27. Lennox & Addington	49. Victoria
11. Northumberland	28. Lincoln	50. Waterloo
12. Elgin	30. Middlesex	51. Welland
13. Essex	31. Muskoka	52. Wellington
14. Frontenac	33. Norfolk	53. Wentworth
15. Grenville	34. Ontario	54. York
16. Leeds	35. Oxford	
17. Grey	36. Parry Sound	
18. Haldimand	37. Peel	

• Population 20,000 and over, (1961 Census)

ONTARIO

465

Ottawa — Ottawa Valley

Area covered: 5,995 square miles. *Counties:* Carleton, Lanark, Prescott, Renfrew, Russell.

COMPOSITION OF THE MARKET

Place	County	Population 1961	% of the region
Ottawa (metro)	Carleton	332,899*	62.69
Pembroke (urbanized area)	Renfrew	18,811	3.54
Smiths Falls	Lanark	9,603	1.81
Renfrew	Renfrew	8,935	1.68
Hawkesbury	Prescott	8,661	1.63
Arnprior	Renfrew	5,474	1.03
Deep River	Renfrew	5,377	1.01
Perth	Lanark	5,360	1.01
Carleton Place	Lanark	4,796	0.90
Petawawa	Renfrew	4,509	0.85
Almonte	Lanark	3,267	0.62
Rockland	Russell	3,037	0.57
Vankleek Hill	Prescott	1,735	0.33
Eganville	Renfrew	1,549	0.29
Stittsville	Carleton	1,508	0.29
Barry's Bay	Renfrew	1,439	0.27
Casselman	Russell	1,277	0.24
Richmond	Carleton	1,215	0.23
Alfred	Prescott	1,195	0.23
L'Orignal	Prescott	1,189	0.22
Chalk River	Renfrew	1,135	0.21
Embrun	Russell	1,112	0.21
Total urban		424,083	79.86
Rural non-farm		61,995	11.68
Rural farm		44,920	8.46
Total population		530,998	100.00

* Total population of Metro Ottawa is 429,750, of which 332,899 is in Ontario and 96,851 is in Hull county of Québec.

ECONOMIC CAPSULE

This is the Ontario section of the region which includes also Hull-Western Laurentides in Québec. Canada has never been able to establish a federal district for its capital as the United States has done for Washington. Québec will not surrender its sovereignty over Hull, an industrial town across the river from Ottawa. Any plans for a federal district must include it, since the two cities are so closely linked as to be practically one. Here political geography is at loggerheads with economic reality. The following statistics refer only to the Ontario portion of the region. The whole area is analyzed in greater detail in the next section.

IMPORTANCE OF THE MARKET (1964 ESTIMATES)

	Number	% of Canada
Population	573,000	2.98
Households	144,200	3.00
Disposable income ($ million)	1,149.8	3.65

GROWTH OF THE MARKET

	Percentage growth 1961 to 1964	% points above or below Canadian average
Population	+ 7.91	+ 2.44
Disposable income	+34.34	+12.81

CHARACTERISTICS OF THE POPULATION

	% of the total population of the region	% points above or below Canadian average
Mother tongue (1961 census)		
English	68.9	+10.5
French	23.7	− 4.4
German	2.0	− 1.1
Native Indian dialects	—	− 0.9
Italian	1.3	− 0.6
Dutch	0.7	− 0.2
Polish	1.2	+ 0.3
Ukrainian	0.4	− 1.6
Other	1.8	− 2.0
Total	100.0	—
Official language spoken (1961 census)		
English only	70.0	+ 2.6
French only	6.8	−12.3
Both English and French	22.3	+10.1
Neither English nor French	0.9	− 0.4
Total	100.0	—

MEANS OF LIVELIHOOD—DISTRIBUTION OF
LABOR FORCE BY INDUSTRY

Industry	Persons 1961 census	% of the total	% points above or below Canadian average
Agriculture	13,199	6.6	− 3.3
Forestry	1,070	0.5	− 1.2
Fishing and trapping	37	—	− 0.5
Mines, quarries, oil wells	263	0.1	− 1.8
Manufacturing	21,646	10.8	−10.9
Construction	13,523	6.7	—
Transportation, communications, and other utilities	14,084	7.0	− 2.3
Wholesale trade	6,295	3.1	− 1.4
Retrail trade	19,408	9.6	− 1.2
Finance, insurance, and real estate	7,782	3.9	+ 0.4
Community and business services	26,658	13.2	+ 0.4
Personal services	12,229	6.1	− 0.7
Public administration and defence	59,972	29.8	+22.3
Miscellaneous	5,211	2.6	+ 0.2
Total labor force	201,377	100.0	—

POVERTY AND AFFLUENCE (1961 CENSUS)

	Number	% of region's total	% points above or below Canadian average
Extent of poverty			
Families earning below $3,000 a year (non-farm)	17,442	16.1	−7.2
Persons not in families earning below $1,500 a year (non-farm)	18,351	39.5	−9.4
Farms with gross income of less than $2,500 a year	5,190	51.5	+5.4
Persons not in school with grade 4 or less education	31,493	9.4	−4.0
Doubled-up households (more than one family per household)	4,555	3.4	−0.3
Households living in dilapidated dwellings	5,468	4.1	−1.5
Households without facilities of running water	9,858	7.4	−3.5
Households without facilities of installed bath or shower	17,824	13.4	−6.3

Families earning over $10,000 a year (non-farm)	12,841	11.9	+4.1
Persons not in families earning over $6,000 a year (non-farm)	2,894	6.2	+2.4
Farms with gross income over $15,000 a year	296	2.9	−2.1
Persons with university degree	18,610	5.6	+2.8
Households with two or more television sets	8,378	6.3	+2.1
Households with two or more cars	11,482	8.6	+1.8

AVERAGE INCOME (1961 CENSUS)

	Dollars	% above or below Canadian average
Income per family (non-farm)	6,310	+15.80
Income per person not in family (non-farm)	2,678	+25.32
Income per farm (net)	2,335	−28.26

Ottawa — Western Laurentides and Ottawa Valley

ECONOMIC CAPSULE

Although public administration and defence account for 26.4% of the labor force, the economy has other props to rely on, like forestry, agriculture, mining, and manufacturing.

The timber from the nearby forests is sawn into dressed lumber or crushed into pulp. There are over 200 sawmills in the region as well as large pulp and paper mills in Metropolitan Ottawa, Buckingham, and Masson.

The short growing season and the rather poor soil limit cultivation mainly to fodder crops. Mixed farming is the rule, and cattle are raised for both milk and beef to satisfy the urban market requirements not only of Ottawa but in some cases of Montréal as well. Many farmers obtain supplementary revenue from their woodlots, selling their timber to pulp and paper mills and other wood-using enterprises. This is particularly so in Russell County, where large tracts of sandy soil are not suitable for general farming.

Among the minerals, magnesium is the most important, the only operating mine in Canada being located at Haley. The total value of shipments in 1964 was 18,042,000 lbs., worth $5,593,000. Other minerals are feldspar and mica, plus structural materials like limestone, clay products, sand, and gravel.

The region is also the center of nuclear research. Atomic Energy of Canada Limited's plant at Chalk River produces radioactive isotopes used in medical and industrial laboratories all over the world. Rolphton is the site of Canada's first atomic power station. It is mainly experimental, the primary purpose being to demonstrate the feasibility of generating electricity from nuclear power.

Ottawa is a city of charm and dignity, befitting the nation's capital. Confederation Square, with its War Memorial, the giant viaducts over the canal, the impressive Château Laurier and Union Station, all combine with the majestic Parliament Buildings in the background to make the capital a showpiece for the nation.

The process of beautifying the city is a continuous one. At work constantly is the National Capital Commission, an enlightened body concerned, among other things, with urban renewal, decentralization, and preservation of vast open spaces. Its major project is a cultural center which will include a concert hall seating 1,500 and sumptuous new homes for the National Gallery and the National Library, the whole impressive complex to be surrounded by terraced gardens. The vast wilderness of Gatineau Park, 75,000 acres of woods and lakes on the doorstep of the capital, has been acquired by the Commission as a part of its plans to make Ottawa green as well as pleasant.

The presence of the civil service and crown corporations ensures a high degree of stability to the market. But Ottawa is not merely an administrative center. Immense reserves of forests in the north, extensive areas of dairy farms in the south, plus an ample power supply from the Chaudière and Gatineau falls, help to provide a healthy manufacturing base. Major industries are food processing, printing and publishing, metal fabricating, furniture designing, and manufacturing of pulp and paper, textiles, clothing, cosmetics, and pharmaceuticals. In recent years, a number of highly specialized firms, like those producing electronic devices for the defence department, have located in Ottawa to take advantage of the technical services provided by the National Research Council and the Defence Research Board. In future, with the increasing complexities of governmental requirements, one may expect more firms of this type to be established in or near the metropolis.

IMPORTANCE OF THE MARKET (1964 ESTIMATES)

| | Region | | Ottawa | |
	Number	% of Canada	Number	% of Canada
Population	762,100	3.96	468,000	2.43
Households	184,600	3.84	120,000	2.50
Disposable income ($ million)	1,409.8	4.47	1,036.0	3.29

Area covered: 19,707 square miles. *Counties in Québec:* Hull (Gatineau, Hull), Papineau, Pontiac; *in Ontario:* Carleton, Lanark, Prescott, Renfrew, Russell.

COMPOSITION OF THE MARKET

Place	County	Population 1961	% of the region
Ottawa (metro)	Carleton, Gatineau, Hull	429,750	60.29
Pembroke (urbanized area)	Renfrew	18,811	2.64
Smiths Falls	Lanark	9,603	1.35
Renfrew	Renfrew	8,935	1.25
Hawkesbury	Prescott	8,661	1.22
Buckingham	Papineau	7,421	1.04
Maniwaki	Gatineau	6,349	0.89
Arnprior	Renfrew	5,474	0.77
Deep River	Renfrew	5,377	0.75
Perth	Lanark	5,360	0.75
Carleton Place	Lanark	4,796	0.67
Petawawa	Renfrew	4,509	0.63
Thurso	Papineau	3,310	0.46
Almonte	Lanark	3,267	0.46
Rockland	Russell	3,037	0.43
Masson	Papineau	1,933	0.27
Fort Coulonge	Pontiac	1,823	0.26
Vankleek Hill	Prescott	1,735	0.24
Eganville	Renfrew	1,549	0.22
Shawville	Pontiac	1,534	0.22
Stittsville	Carleton	1,508	0.21
Montebello	Papineau	1,486	0.21
Barry's Bay	Renfrew	1,439	0.20
Papineauville	Papineau	1,300	0.18
Casselman	Russell	1,277	0.18
Richmond	Carleton	1,215	0.17
Alfred	Prescott	1,195	0.17
L'Orignal	Prescott	1,189	0.17
Chalk River	Renfrew	1,135	0.16
Embrun	Russell	1,112	0.16
St. André Avellin	Papineau	1,066	0.15
Campbell's Bay	Pontiac	1,024	0.14
Total urban		548,180	76.91
Rural non-farm		98,598	13.83
Rural farm		65,975	9.26
Total population		712,753	100.00

GROWTH OF THE MARKET

	Region		Ottawa	
	Percentage growth 1961 to 1964	% points above or below Canadian average	Percentage growth 1961 to 1964	% points above or below Canadian average
Population	+ 6.92	+ 1.45	+ 8.90	+ 3.43
Disposable income	+32.59	+11.06	+42.07	+20.54

CHARACTERISTICS OF THE POPULATION

	Region		Ottawa
	% of the total population of the region	% points above or below Canadian average	% of the total population of the city
Mother tongue (1961 census)			
English	56.4	− 2.0	55.7
French	37.7	+ 9.6	37.7
German	1.5	− 1.6	1.4
Native Indian dialects	0.1	− 0.8	—
Italian	1.0	− 0.9	1.6
Dutch	0.6	− 0.3	0.6
Polish	0.9	—	0.5
Ukrainian	0.3	− 1.7	0.4
Other	1.5	− 2.3	2.1
Total	100.0	—	100.0
Official language spoken (1961 census)			
English only	56.3	−11.1	55.0
French only	16.8	− 2.3	13.2
Both English and French	26.2	+14.0	30.8
Neither English nor French	0.7	− 0.6	1.0
Total	100.0	—	100.0

POVERTY AND AFFLUENCE (1961 CENSUS)

		Region		Ottawa	
	Number	% of region's total	% points above or below Canadian average	Number	% of city's total
Extent of poverty					
Families earning below $3,000 a year (non-farm)	26,334	18.6	− 4.7	11,939	12.6
Persons not in families earning below $1,500 a year (non-farm)	24,109	42.7	− 6.2	14,264	35.3
Farms with gross income of less than $2,500 a year	8,064	56.8	+10.7	—	—
Persons not in school with grade 4 or less education	58,083	13.1	− 0.3	22,648	8.4
Doubled-up households (more than one family per household)	6,094	3.5	− 0.2	3,829	3.6
Households living in dilapidated dwellings	8,651	5.0	− 0.6	3,892	3.6
Households without facilities of running water	13,954	8.0	− 2.9	959	0.9
Households without facilities of installed bath or shower	30,788	17.8	− 1.9	6,459	6.0
Extent of affluence					
Families earning over $10,000 a year (non-farm)	14,940	10.5	+ 2.7	12,368	13.0
Persons not in families earning over $6,000 a year (non-farm)	3,113	5.5	+ 1.7	2,747	6.8
Farms with gross income over $15,000 a year	329	2.3	− 2.7	—	—
Persons with university degree	20,753	4.7	+ 1.9	17,548	6.5
Households with two or more television sets	9,518	5.5	+ 1.3	8,548	7.9
Households with two or more cars	12,853	7.4	+ 0.6	9,318	8.7

AVERAGE INCOME (1961 CENSUS)

| | Region | | Ottawa | |
	Dollars	% above or below Canadian average	Dollars	% above or below Canadian average
Income per family (non-farm)	6,017	+10.42	6,643	+21.91
Income per person not in family (non-farm)	2,508	+17.36	2,845	+33.13
Income per farm (net)	2,039	−37.36	—	—

LABOR FORCE BY INDUSTRY

| | Region | | | Ottawa | |
Industry	Persons 1961 census	% of the total	% points above or below Canadian average	Persons 1961 census	% of the total
Agriculture	18,099	7.0	− 2.9	1,345	0.8
Forestry	3,327	1.3	− 0.4	220	0.1
Fishing and trapping	45	—	− 0.5	28	—
Mines, quarries, oil wells	916	0.3	− 1.6	166	0.1
Manufacturing	32,311	12.5	− 9.2	17,766	10.6
Construction	18,920	7.3	+ 0.6	11,809	7.0
Transportation, communications, and other utilities	18,113	7.0	− 2.3	11,396	6.8
Wholesale trade	7,786	3.0	− 1.5	5,993	3.6
Retail trade	25,368	9.8	− 1.0	16,798	10.0
Finance, insurance, and real estate	9,030	3.5	—	7,480	4.5
Community and business services	32,643	12.6	− 0.2	23,388	13.9
Personal services	17,223	6.6	− 0.2	11,152	6.7
Public administration and defence	68,570	26.4	+18.9	55,835	33.3
Miscellaneous	6,992	2.7	+ 0.3	4,336	2.6
Total labor force	259,343	100.0	—	167,712	100.0

Kingston — Upper St. Lawrence

ECONOMIC CAPSULE

Ideally situated between Toronto and Montréal, favored by good transportation facilities, and having at its disposal ample supplies of low-cost electric power, this region has been attracting an increasing number of new manufacturing firms every year.

The three major urban centers are Kingston, Cornwall, and Brockville. Kingston, besides being the site of two renowned educational institutions — the Royal Military College and Queen's University — is also a growing industrial town having locomotive shops, shipyards, aluminum plants, chemical works, and woolen and synthetic textile mills. Cornwall has firms producing all types of chemicals, as well as pulp and paper, cotton yarn and cloth, synthetic textiles, men's clothing, and construction materials. Brockville is noted for the manufacture of telephone equipment, wire and cable, pharmaceutical supplies, power tools, felt hats, and milk products.

The region is not rich in forests or minerals. However, the soil is fertile and farming plays a major role. Four out of five farms specialize in dairying, and the bulk of the fluid milk is converted into cheese, butter, and other dairy products. About a third of the cheddar cheese produced in the province comes from here. The field crops consist mainly of hay and oats required to feed the large cattle population. Beef and dairy herds are often exported to the United States for breeding or slaughter.

KINGSTON—UPPER ST. LAWRENCE

Area covered: 4,236 square miles. *Counties:* Dundas, Frontenac, Glengarry, Grenville, Leeds, Stormont.

COMPOSITION OF THE MARKET

Place	County	Population 1961	% of the region
Kingston (urbanized area)	Frontenac	63,419	25.21
Cornwall	Stormont	43,639	17.35
Brockville	Leeds	17,744	7.06
Prescott	Grenville	5,366	2.13
Gananoque	Leeds	5,096	2.02
Alexandria	Glengarry	2,597	1.03
Kemptville	Grenville	1,959	0.78
Cardinal	Grenville	1,944	0.77
Morrisburg	Dundas	1,820	0.73
Winchester	Dundas	1,429	0.57
Chesterville	Dundas	1,248	0.50
Iroquois	Dundas	1,136	0.45
Athens	Leeds	1,015	0.40
Total urban		148,412	59.00
Rural non-farm		62,967	25.03
Rural farm		40,154	15.97
Total population		251,533	100.00

IMPORTANCE OF THE MARKET (1964 ESTIMATES)

	Region		Kingston	
	Number	% of Canada	Number	% of Canada
Population	256,900	1.34	65,600	0.34
Households	66,000	1.37	18,200	0.38
Disposable income ($ million)	407.6	1.29	130.7	0.41

GROWTH OF THE MARKET

	Region		Kingston	
	Percentage growth 1961 to 1964	% points above or below Canadian average	Percentage growth 1961 to 1964	% points above or below Canadian average
Population	+ 2.13	−3.34	+ 3.44	−2.03
Disposable income	+23.52	+1.99	+26.89	+5.36

LABOR FORCE BY INDUSTRY

Industry	Region			Kingston	
	Persons 1961 census	% of the total	% points above or below Canadian average	Persons 1961 census	% of the total
Agriculture	11,908	13.5	+3.6	70	0.3
Forestry	276	0.3	−1.4	1	—
Fishing and trapping	27	—	−0.5	3	—
Mines, quarries, oil wells	109	0.1	−1.8	24	0.1
Manufacturing	20,610	23.3	+1.6	4,886	20.0
Construction	5,980	6.8	+0.1	1,322	5.4
Transportation, communications, and other utilities	6,769	7.7	−1.6	1,307	5.4
Wholesale trade	2,365	2.7	−1.8	617	2.5
Retail trade	8,944	10.1	−0.7	2,572	10.5
Finance, insurance, and real estate	1,950	2.2	−1.3	758	3.1
Community and business services	13,120	14.8	+2.0	5,576	22.8
Personal services	5,923	6.7	−0.1	1,586	6.5
Public administration and defence	8,012	9.1	+1.6	5,024	20.6
Miscellaneous	2,379	2.7	+0.3	687	2.8
Total labor force	88,372	100.0	—	24,433	100.0

CHARACTERISTICS OF THE POPULATION

	Region		Kingston
	% of the total population of the region	% points above or below Canadian average	% of the total population of the city
Mother tongue (1961 census)			
English	81.0	+22.6	91.1
French	13.8	− 14.3	2.5
German	0.9	− 2.2	1.2
Native Indian dialects	0.2	− 0.7	—
Italian	0.4	− 1.5	0.8
Dutch	1.9	+ 1.0	1.1
Polish	0.4	− 0.5	0.6
Ukrainian	0.2	− 1.8	0.3
Other	1.2	− 2.6	2.4
Total	100.0	—	100.0
Official language spoken (1961 census)			
English only	82.1	+14.7	94.0
French only	2.9	− 16.2	0.3
Both English and French	14.6	+ 2.4	5.2
Neither English nor French	0.4	− 0.9	0.5
Total	100.0	—	100.0

POVERTY AND AFFLUENCE (1961 CENSUS)

	Region			Kingston	
	Number	% of region's total	% points above or below Canadian average	Number	% of city's total
Extent of poverty					
Families earning below $3,000 a year (non-farm)	11,478	24.0	+0.7	2,035	14.8
Persons not in families earning below $1,500 a year (non-farm)	9,450	51.3	+2.4	2,477	40.1
Farms with gross income of less than $2,500 a year	4,753	51.5	+5.4	—	—
Persons not in school with grade 4 or less education	16,629	10.3	−3.1	3,157	7.6

POVERTY AND AFFLUENCE (continued)

	Region			Kingston	
	Number	% of region's total	% points above or below Canadian average	Number	% of city's total
Doubled-up households (more than one family per household)......	1,860	2.9	−0.8	468	3.0
Households living in dilapidated dwellings......	4,185	6.5	+0.9	707	4.5
Households without facilities of running water......	9,998	15.7	+4.8	103	0.7
Households without facilities of installed bath or shower......	15,402	24.2	+4.5	597	3.8
Extent of affluence					
Families earning over $10,000 a year (non-farm)......	2,920	6.1	−1.7	1,278	9.3
Persons not in families earning over $6,000 a year (non-farm)......	694	3.8	—	286	4.6
Farms with gross income over $15,000 a year......	200	2.2	−2.8	—	—
Persons with university degree..	4,691	2.9	+0.1	2,221	5.3
Households with two or more television sets......	1,984	3.1	−1.1	866	5.5
Households with two or more cars......	4,387	6.9	+0.1	1,358	8.6

AVERAGE INCOME (1961 CENSUS)

	Region		Kingston	
	Dollars	% above or below Canadian average	Dollars	% above or below Canadian average
Income per family (non-farm)......	5,147	− 5.54	5,959	+9.36
Income per person not in family (non-farm)..	2,054	− 3.88	2,324	+8.75
Income per farm (net)......	2,143	−34.16	—	—

Peterborough — Central Lake Ontario

Area covered: 9,495 square miles. *Counties:* Durham, Haliburton, Hastings, Lennox and Addington, Northumberland, Peterborough, Prince Edward, Victoria.

COMPOSITION OF THE MARKET

Place	County	Population 1961	% of the region
Peterborough (urbanized area)	Peterborough	49,902	14.89
Belleville	Hastings	30,655	9.15
Trenton	Hastings	13,183	3.93
Lindsay	Victoria	11,399	3.40
Cobourg	Northumberland	10,646	3.18
Port Hope	Durham	8,091	2.41
Bowmanville	Durham	7,397	2.21
Picton	Prince Edward	4,862	1.45
Napanee	Lennox & Addington	4,500	1.34
Campbellford	Northumberland	3,478	1.04
Bancroft	Hastings	2,615	0.78
Brighton	Northumberland	2,403	0.72
Lakefield	Peterborough	2,167	0.65
Darlington Township	Durham	1,857*	0.55
Deseronto	Hastings	1,797	0.54
Tweed	Hastings	1,791	0.53
Frankford	Hastings	1,642	0.49
Marmora	Hastings	1,381	0.41
Fenelon Falls	Victoria	1,359	0.41
Madoc	Hastings	1,347	0.40
Colborne	Northumberland	1,336	0.40
Stirling	Hastings	1,315	0.39
Newcastle	Durham	1,272	0.38
Havelock	Peterborough	1,260	0.38
Bobcaygeon	Victoria	1,210	0.36
Wellington	Prince Edward	1,064	0.32
Bridgenorth and Chemong Park Area	Peterborough	1,061	0.32
Norwood	Peterborough	1,060	0.32
Total urban		172,050	51.35
Rural non-farm		106,106	31.67
Rural farm		56,907	16.98
Total population		335,063	100.00

* Part of the urbanized area of Oshawa.

ECONOMIC CAPSULE

The region has a wide and diversified economic base: agriculture, mining, manufacturing, and tourism.

The raising of beef and dairy herds is the prime feature of agriculture, and the products derived — beef, milk, butter, and cheese — make a significant contribution to the income of the area. Field crops for the most part consist of hay and oats, used for feeding livestock and poultry. In recent years, the cultivation of tobacco as a cash crop has expanded in the sandy plains of the southern part bordering Lake Ontario. Apples, raspberries, strawberries, tomatoes, peas, and other fruits and vegetables are also grown in this belt and are used by the local canning industry.

The region is equally rich in minerals. Iron ore is mined at Marmora in Hastings county. Annual production capacity is 450,000 long tons of pellets, containing about 65% iron. Nepheline syenite, utilized in the glassware and ceramic industries, is obtained from two mines at Blue Mountain north of Havelock in Peterborough county. Production in 1964 amounted to 292,000 tons worth $3.4 million. There are also large reserves of uranium at Bancroft, and, though the mines have suspended operations, they can be readily reopened when the demand picks up.

The region is a top vacation land, visited every year by thousands of persons interested in camping, fishing, hunting, boating, sailing, and other recreational activities. In many areas, particularly in the scenic highlands of Haliburton and Hastings, tourism is the mainstay of the economy.

The two large urban communities are Peterborough and Belleville. The former is an industrial city with plants of several large companies like Canadian General Electric Company Limited (electrical machines and equipment); Outboard Marine Corporation of Canada Limited (outboard motors, power lawn mowers, chain saws); Westclox Canada Limited (watches and clocks); Quaker Oats Company of Canada Limited (breakfast cereals); and De Laval Company Limited (farm dairy equipment). Other manufacturing activities include meat packing, preparation of feeds for livestock, rug making, and manufacture of paper products. The proximity of the Kawartha Lakes attracts many tourists in summer.

In Belleville, the largest single employer is the Canadian National Railway repair shop, followed by the Northern Electric Company Limited which manufactures fire alarms, traffic signals, defence equipment (radar), and office intercommunication systems. Close by at Batawa is the Bata Shoe Company of Canada, not only turning out several kinds of footwear but also producing complicated shoe-making machinery.

Manufacturing in the whole region is growing and at the same time becoming increasingly diversified. During the last decade, well over 100 firms have established new plants, opened new branches, or made additions to existing production capacities. As settlement and industry fan out along the lakeshore, it may be anticipated that the area will assume more and more the role of one of the extended arms of the "Golden Horseshoe," which currently encircles the western end of Lake Ontario.

IMPORTANCE OF THE MARKET (1964 ESTIMATES)

| | Region | | Peterborough | |
	Number	% of Canada	Number	% of Canada
Population	342,500	1.78	53,000	0.28
Households	93,800	1.95	14,700	0.31
Disposable income ($ million)	556.3	1.76	107.1	0.34

CHARACTERISTICS OF THE POPULATION

| | Region | | Peterborough |
	% of the total population of the region	% points above or below Canadian average	% of the total population of the city
Mother tongue (1961 census)			
English	94.8	+36.4	95.7
French	1.1	−27.0	0.7
German	0.7	− 2.4	0.8
Native Indian dialects	0.1	− 0.8	—
Italian	0.3	− 1.6	0.7
Dutch	1.6	+ 0.7	0.7
Polish	0.3	− 0.6	0.3
Ukrainian	0.2	− 1.8	0.1
Other	0.9	− 2.9	1.0
Total	100.0	—	100.0
Official language spoken (1961 census)			
English only	97.3	+29.9	97.2
French only	0.1	−19.0	—
Both English and French	2.4	− 9.8	2.6
Neither English nor French	0.2	− 1.1	0.2
Total	100.0	—	100.0

GROWTH OF THE MARKET

	Region		Peterborough	
	Percentage growth 1961 to 1964	% points above or below Canadian average	Percentage growth 1961 to 1964	% points above or below Canadian average
Population	+ 2.22	−3.25	+ 6.21	+0.74
Disposable income	+22.61	+1.08	+18.34	−3.19

AVERAGE INCOME (1961 CENSUS)

	Region		Peterborough	
	Dollars	% above or below Canadian average	Dollars	% above or below Canadian average
Income per family (non-farm)	5,036	− 7.58	5,799	+6.42
Income per person not in family (non-farm)	1,860	−12.96	2,229	+4.31
Income per farm (net)	2,654	−18.46	—	—

LABOR FORCE BY INDUSTRY

Industry	Region			Peterborough	
	Persons 1961 census	% of the total	% points above or below Canadian average	Persons 1961 census	% of the total
Agriculture	15,112	13.2	+3.3	73	0.4
Forestry	789	0.7	−1.0	7	—
Fishing and trapping	132	0.1	−0.4	3	—
Mines, quarries, oil wells	1,596	1.4	−0.5	18	0.1
Manufacturing	29,892	26.0	+4.3	7,279	40.1
Construction	7,395	6.4	−0.3	933	5.1
Transportation, communications, and other utilities	8,628	7.5	−1.8	1,024	5.7
Wholesale trade	3,322	2.9	−1.6	641	3.5
Retail trade	12,537	10.9	+0.1	2,358	13.0
Finance, insurance, and real estate	2,487	2.2	−1.3	620	3.4
Community and business services	12,198	10.6	−2.2	2,769	15.3
Personal services	7,837	6.8	—	1,316	7.3
Public administration and defence	10,535	9.2	+1.7	769	4.2
Miscellaneous	2,364	2.1	−0.3	347	1.9
Total labor force	114,824	100.0	—	18,157	100.0

POVERTY AND AFFLUENCE (1961 CENSUS)

	Region			Peterborough	
	Number	% of region's total	% points above or below Canadian average	Number	% of city's total
Extent of poverty					
Families earning below $3,000 a year (non-farm)	16,097	24.3	+1.0	2,074	17.4
Persons not in families earning below $1,500 a year (non-farm)	13,708	58.3	+9.4	2,236	49.4
Farms with gross income of less than $2,500 a year	7,214	52.8	+6.7	—	—
Persons not in school with grade 4 or less education	18,582	8.8	−4.6	1,983	6.3
Doubled-up households (more than one family per household)	2,216	2.5	−1.2	388	2.9
Households living in dilapidated dwellings	5,922	6.5	+0.9	446	3.3
Households without facilities of running water	16,490	18.2	+7.3	46	0.3
Households without facilities of installed bath or shower	24,091	26.6	+6.9	421	3.1
Extent of affluence					
Families earning over $10,000 a year (non-farm)	3,477	5.3	−2.5	973	8.1
Persons not in families earning over $6,000 a year (non-farm)	660	2.8	−1.0	166	3.7
Farms with gross income over $15,000 a year	518	3.8	−1.2	—	—
Persons with university degree	4,423	2.1	−0.7	1,176	3.7
Households with two or more television sets	2,293	2.5	−1.7	773	5.7
Households with two or more cars	6,982	7.7	+0.9	1,215	9.0

Metro Toronto and Its Environs

Area covered: 2,567 square miles. *Counties:* Halton, Ontario, Peel, York.

COMPOSITION OF THE MARKET

Place	County	Population 1961	% of the region
Toronto (metro)	Halton, Ontario, Peel, York	1,860,833*	89.13
Oshawa (urbanized area)	Ontario	79,061†	3.79
Brampton	Peel	18,467	0.88
Georgetown (urbanized area)	Halton	11,172	0.54
Newmarket	York	8,932	0.43
Aurora	York	8,791	0.42
Milton	Halton	5,629	0.27
Markham	York	4,294	0.21
Acton	Halton	4,144	0.20
Gwillimbury E.	York	3,920	0.19
Stouffville	York	3,188	0.15
Uxbridge	Ontario	2,316	0.11
Port Perry	Ontario	2,262	0.11
Bolton	Peel	2,104	0.10
Wilcox Lake	York	1,957	0.09
King City	York	1,864	0.09
Brooklin	Ontario	1,531	0.07
Sutton	York	1,470	0.07
Beaverton	Ontario	1,217	0.06
Cannington	Ontario	1,024	0.05
Oak Ridges	York	1,006	0.05
Total urban		2,025,182	97.01
Rural non-farm		30,776	1.48
Rural farm		31,587	1.51
Total population		2,087,545	100.00

* Population of Metro Toronto, 1,824,481, plus 36,352 portion of Burlington area in Halton county which forms part actually of Metro Hamilton, but added here to Toronto.

† Total population of urbanized area of Oshawa is 80,918, of which 1,857 is in Durham county of Lake Ontario region.

ECONOMIC CAPSULE

This is Canada's foremost industrial and commercial center and an extremely important market that no businessman can afford to ignore. As one economist aptly remarks: "Cut Toronto area out of Canada, and the nation's heart stops beating; it suffocates and collapses."

The Queen City of Canada is second to Montréal in size, but surpasses its rival in retail sales and disposable income. In economic power, in money, in marketing opportunities, and in concentration of industry, Toronto constitutes the very core and hub of the nation. It is a boom town par excellence. Few cities on earth can match it for prosperity, for opportunity, for sheer thrust and dynamism in every field of human endeavor.

"Toronto" in the Indian language means "the meeting place", and the name is still very much to the point. Reaching into and out of Toronto are 10 railway lines and 12 major highways. Five scheduled airlines (Air Canada, CPA, BOAC, American, Mohawk) serve Toronto International airport. With the completion of the St. Lawrence Seaway, the city has acquired the status of an international seaport. Just as Toronto was in a bygone era meeting place for the Indian tribes, it is today the meeting place for all Canada — the rendez-vous for people who want to do business. In fact, its influence as a financial, industrial, transportation, and commercial center is so great that mere distance from Toronto has become a major fact in the economic geography of the country.

Time was when, not too long ago, Toronto was known all across Canada for being stubbornly traditional, strongly puritanical, and solidly Anglo-Saxon and Protestant — part Methodist, part Family Compact Anglican, part United Empire Loyalist, part Orange Lodge. It used to be a common joke among outsiders that Toronto was perhaps the finest city in the world in which to die on a Sunday afternoon, since the transition between the living and the dead would be so gradual as to be almost imperceptible.

All that is over. During the last two decades Toronto has undergone the most sweeping and rapid change in its 175-year history. Within the city limits proper, largely because of postwar immigration, every second Torontonian is at present a Roman Catholic. Half of all the immigrants arriving in Canada come to Ontario, and about 50% of these settle down in Toronto. The outlanders whose mother tongue is Italian, Slavic, or German can by themselves constitute medium-sized cities. As a result the old Toronto is now largely a piece of the past. This town of quiet homes and quiet Sundays, this primary outpost of Victorian culture, has somehow exploded into something dramatically different.

The new Toronto is a much more lively and interesting city. It has its Bohemia, its poets and artists, and even satirists — a true sign of maturity. The city is also getting a touch of European sophistication. Already the bars and coffee houses and foreign restaurants are blossoming, and one may even come across a few sidewalk cafés in summer. The downtown newsstands are full of foreign language papers, many of which are published locally. In the immigrant areas, grocery stores sell exotic imported foods, while druggists advertise their medicines in half a dozen tongues. The "Hogtown" now has avant-garde plays, Broadway musicals, ragtime bands, Italian song festivals, pizza carnivals, motoramas, stripper-amas, and attic and cellar clubs where the patrons listen to poetry, jazz, and folk songs late into the night.

On the basis of 3.3% annual increase in population, Toronto's rate of growth is much more rapid than Montréal's 2.5%. With a booming birth rate, a flood of immigrants, and a rush of fortune hunters from all parts of Canada and the United States, the population of Metro Toronto is expanding at the rate of nearly 70,000 people a year — the equivalent of another Kingston or Sarnia. Very few cities in North America can match this performance. In fact, compared to it, the similar-sized cities in the United States — Buffalo, Baltimore, Cleveland, St. Louis, Minneapolis-St. Paul — appear almost stagnant. Already in the last few years, an almost entirely new Toronto has grown around the core of the old town. In the three outlying municipalities, North York, Etobicoke, and Scarborough, the population between the years 1951 and 1965 increased by about 630,000. It is as if the entire cities of Calgary and Edmonton went to Toronto for the Grey Cup game and stayed there.

"Toronto has become a boom town glutted with prosperity" says a U.S. reporter. "With only a tenth of Canada's population, it pays more than a fifth in income taxes. Here the talk is in millions of dollars and hundreds of millions of tons of ore. In the downtown area are concentrated the country's top executives, whose one word can set men blasting mountains, clearing forests, boring oil wells, and building dams in the wilderness. If it weren't for the difference in accents, an American would think he was in Texas."

In many respects Toronto is even ahead. Texas, and especially Houston, has been riding an oil boom. But Toronto has several booms working for it. It is half a dozen major American cities rolled into one. It is like New York with its tremendous stock market activity (the Toronto Stock Exchange is second only to Wall Street in the volume of shares traded, and has the largest transaction of mining shares in the world). It is like Detroit with its auto industry (General Motors at nearby Oshawa and Ford at Oakville on the other flank are the largest automotive plants in Canada). It is like Chicago as a distributing center (over two-thirds of Ontario's wholesale business originates from firms located in Toronto or its vicinity). It is like Los Angeles in its endless construction activity (the city bears all the marks of uncompleted growth — bare forests of structural steel, the shells of gutted buildings, the rubble of demolition).

Here are some more impressive statistics: "Every day Metro Toronto makes 6,000,000 telephone calls, trades 3,000,000 shares on the stock exchange, cashes $500,000,000 in cheques; buys $8,000,000 worth of goods off store counters, and drives to work or pleasure in its 500,000 cars." (Toronto Daily Star's booklet: *Boom Town Metro*.) Its Canadian National Exhibition, described as the "Show Window of the Nation," is the world's greatest annual exposition, and during its 16-day duration approximately three million visitors pass through its gates.

What makes the Toronto region so dynamic? It is a manufacturing center of the first category. Cheap and abundant electric power, low-cost water transportation, good rail, road, and air connections, a big pool of skilled labor, and proximity to the thickly populated areas of Canada and the United States — all these have lured numerous manufacturers to set up their plants in this area. The Metropolitan Toronto Industrial Commission points out that within a 100-mile radius of King and Bay Streets may be found one-fifth of Canada's people and one-third of Canada's purchasing power.

Practically everything that a consumer needs is manufactured in or around Toronto — food and beverage products, toilet preparations, household goods, clothing, furniture, automobiles, and appliances. However, manufacturing is not confined to consumer goods only. Equally important are industrial products like trucks, aircraft, machine tools, refined petroleum, farm machinery, and office equipment.

Of the 5,000 manufacturing establishments, a bare 20 have more than 1,000 workers. The average factory employs fewer than 50 persons. This proliferation of small plants makes for buoyancy and stability in the region's economy. If one plant goes broke, few people are affected. If one goes on strike, little damage is done to the community at large. No single industry or union dominates the city and sets the wage level. Toronto is a good-wage community without being a high-wage one.

METRO TORONTO AND ITS ENVIRONS

IMPORTANCE OF THE MARKET (1964 ESTIMATES)

	Region		Toronto		Oshawa	
	Number	% of Canada	Number	% of Canada	Number	% of Canada
Population	2,291,900	11.91	1,989,000	10.34	88,000	0.46
Households	604,500	12.58	537,600	11.19	24,400	0.51
Disposable income ($ million)	4,754.2	15.07	4,106.3	13.02	193.0	0.61

GROWTH OF THE MARKET

	Region		Toronto		Oshawa	
	Percentage growth 1961 to 1964	% points above or below Canadian average	Percentage growth 1961 to 1964	% points above or below Canadian average	Percentage growth 1961 to 1964	% points above or below Canadian average
Population	+ 9.79	+4.32	+ 9.02	+3.55	+ 8.75	+ 3.28
Disposable income	+22.94	+1.41	+17.14	−4.39	+39.15	+17.62

POVERTY AND AFFLUENCE (1961 CENSUS)

	Region			Toronto		Oshawa	
	Num-ber	% of region's total	% points above or below Cdn. average	Num-ber	% of city's total	Num-ber	% of city's total
Extent of poverty							
Families earning below $3,000 a year (non-farm)	73,503	14.3	− 9.0	64,893	14.1	2,199	11.1
Persons not in families earning below $1,500 a year (non-farm)	86,053	39.0	− 9.9	78,214	38.4	2,484	41.0
Farms with gross income of less than $2,500 a year	3,609	42.9	− 3.2	—	—	—	—
Persons not in school with grade 4 or less education	105,486	7.5	− 5.9	94,205	7.6	3,586	6.9
Doubled-up households (more than one family per household)	43,340	7.9	+ 4.2	41,405	8.6	691	3.2
Households living in di-lapidated dwellings	13,302	2.4	− 3.2	10,747	2.2	704	3.3
Households without fa-cilities of running water	6,423	1.2	− 9.7	2,105	0.4	153	0.7
Households without fa-cilities of installed bath or shower	13,853	2.6	−17.1	5,999	1.2	555	2.6
Extent of affluence							
Families earning over $10,000 a year (non-farm)	59,781	11.6	+ 3.8	55,534	12.1	1,366	6.9
Persons not in families earning over $6,000 a year (non-farm)	12,360	5.6	+ 1.8	11,676	5.7	265	4.4
Farms with gross income over $15,000 a year	897	10.7	+ 5.7	—	—	—	—
Persons with university degree	61,788	4.4	+ 1.6	57,257	4.6	1,077	2.1
Households with two or more television sets	57,329	10.4	+ 6.2	53,821	11.2	1,012	4.7
Households with two or more cars	66,706	12.1	+ 5.3	58,349	12.1	2,058	9.6

MEANS OF LIVELIHOOD—DISTRIBUTION OF
LABOR FORCE BY INDUSTRY

Industry	*Region*			*Toronto*		*Oshawa*	
	Persons 1961 census	% of the total	% points above or below Cdn. average	Persons 1961 census	% of the total	Persons 1961 census	% of the total
Agriculture	15,505	1.8	−8.1	6,524	0.8	199	0.7
Forestry	348	—	−1.7	277	—	10	—
Fishing and trapping	97	—	−0.5	82	—	1	—
Mines, quarries, oil wells	2,123	0.3	−1.6	1,737	0.2	19	0.1
Manufacturing	269,650	30.5	+8.8	234,511	29.7	14,923	49.6
Construction	56,834	6.4	−0.3	51,055	6.5	1,484	4.9
Transportation, communications, and other utilities	75,184	8.5	−0.8	68,701	8.7	1,711	5.7
Wholesale trade	53,359	6.0	+1.5	49,594	6.3	723	2.4
Retail trade	106,927	12.1	+1.3	96,902	12.3	3,407	11.3
Finance, insurance, and real estate	54,990	6.2	+2.7	52,338	6.6	753	2.5
Community and business services	120,643	13.7	+0.9	109,854	13.9	3,772	12.5
Personal services	62,851	7.1	+0.3	57,868	7.3	1,534	5.1
Public administration and defence	46,761	5.3	−2.2	42,958	5.5	1,164	3.9
Miscellaneous	18,787	2.1	−0.3	17,250	2.2	409	1.3
Total labor force	884,059	100.0	—	789,651	100.0	30,109	100.0

CHARACTERISTICS OF THE POPULATION

	Region		*Toronto*	*Oshawa*
	% of the total population of the region	% points above or below Canadian average	% of the total population of the city	% of the total population of the city
Official language spoken (1961 census)				
English only	93.1	+25.7	92.6	95.6
French only	0.2	−18.9	0.2	0.2
Both English and French	4.1	− 8.1	4.3	3.4
Neither English nor French	2.6	+ 1.3	2.9	0.8
Total	100.0	—	100.0	100.0

CHARACTERISTICS OF THE POPULATION (continued)

	Region		Toronto	Oshawa
	% of the total population of the region	% points above or below Canadian average	% of the total population of the city	% of the total population of the city
Mother tongue (1961 census)				
English	78.0	+19.6	76.6	82.0
French	1.4	−26.7	1.4	1.9
German	3.2	+ 0.1	3.4	2.3
Native Indian dialects	—	− 0.9	—	—
Italian	5.7	+ 3.8	6.4	1.4
Dutch	1.1	+ 0.2	0.8	2.4
Polish	1.7	+ 0.8	1.8	2.8
Ukrainian	1.9	− 0.1	1.9	3.6
Other	7.0	+ 3.2	7.7	3.6
Total	100.0	—	100.0	100.0

AVERAGE INCOME (1961 CENSUS)

	Region		Toronto		Oshawa	
	Dollars	% above or below Cdn. average	Dollars	% above or below Cdn. average	Dollars	% above or below Cdn. average
Income per family (non-farm)	6,456	+18.48	6,542	+20.06	5,852	+ 7.40
Income per person not in family (non-farm)	2,572	+20.36	2,594	+21.39	2,592	+21.29
Income per farm (net)	4,807	+47.68	—	—	—	—

Hamilton/St. Catharines-Niagara

ECONOMIC CAPSULE

Manufacturing is the kingpin of the economy of the region. Embracing the southern arm of the "Golden Horseshoe", the Niagara, with only 4% of Canadian population, accounts for roughly 9% of the aggregate value of the nation's factory shipments. Suitable climatic conditions, cheap water transport, good rail and road connections, abundant low-cost electric power, and proximity to the large urban concentrations of Central Canada and the United States — all these have enabled the area to rise to a position of industrial pre-eminence. It has a higher percentage of its labor force engaged in manufacturing than any other region in the country.

Agriculture is noted for its specialization. The Niagara Peninsula has been nicknamed "the fruit basket of Canada" and "the blossom bouquet of Ontario". Here the natural advantages of soil and climate permit the growth of "tender" and other types of fruits. Estimates prepared by the Ontario Department of Economics and Development show that in a normal year the area produces almost all of Canada's grapes, over three-quarters of its sour cherries, 67% of its peaches, 44% of its pears, and 36% of its sweet cherries. The annual value of shipment of all fruits amounts to about $14 million, representing 56% of Ontario and 27% of Canadian production. In addition, the Niagara fruit crop supports the wine and the fruit processing industries, whose annual factory shipments run to over $60 million a year.

Because of the onward rush of industrialization and urbanization, it is feared that the Fruit Belt may one day completely disappear. But this is by no means inevitable. Unfortunately, so far the pattern of urbanization has been to a large extent of the haphazard, low-density type. This kind of "urban sprawl" can be channelled into an orderly and compact urban development, which would not only save the valuable fruit land but also permit industry to expand. What is needed is some kind of planning body with statutory authority to devise and implement a regional land-use program on a long-term basis.

Outside of the Fruit Belt, the raising of cattle for beef and milk dominates the agricultural scene. Tobacco is cultivated on a large scale in Brant county. The soil is suitable for all types of vegetables, but only asparagus, tomatoes, and mushrooms are grown extensively.

Hamilton, a big port on the western extremity of Lake Ontario, is Canada's third leading manufacturing city, outranked only by Montréal and Toronto. It is sometimes called the "Pittsburgh of Canada", since it produces more than one-half of the nation's primary iron and steel. The raw material for the blast furnaces can be assembled quite readily — coal from the Appalachian region, iron ore from Lake Superior ports, and limestone from the Niagara Escarpment. The Steel Company of Canada and Dominion Foundries together provide work for about 19,000 persons.

Hamilton has other big manufacturers as well, like Canadian Westinghouse Company Limited, International Harvester Company of Canada Limited, American Can Company of Canada Limited, Otis Elevator Company Limited, Canadian Canners, Proctor and Gamble Company of Canada Limited, National Steel Car Corporation Limited.

St. Catharines, the "Garden City", is located in the heart of the famous fruit orchards of the Niagara Peninsula. Each year, the colorful Blossom Festival in the spring and the Grape Festival in the fall attract large numbers of tourists. However, the rapid growth of St. Catharines is due mainly to its numerous industries. The biggest employer is McKinnon Industries Limited, North Amer-

HAMILTON /ST. CATHARINES—NIAGARA

Area covered: 2,086 square miles. *Counties:* Brant, Haldimand, Lincoln, Welland, Wentworth.

COMPOSITION OF THE MARKET

Place	County	Population 1961	% of the region
Hamilton (metro)	Wentworth	358,837*	47.07
St. Catharines (urbanized area)	Welland and Lincoln	95,577	12.54
Brantford (urbanized area)	Brant	56,741	7.44
Niagara Falls (urbanized area)	Welland	54,649	7.17
Welland	Welland	36,079	4.73
Port Colborne (urbanized area)	Welland	16,717	2.19
Fort Erie	Welland	9,027	1.18
Paris	Brant	5,820	0.76
Dunnville	Haldimand	5,181	0.68
Grimsby	Lincoln	5,148	0.68
Niagara	Lincoln	2,712	0.36
Beamsville	Lincoln	2,537	0.33
Fonthill	Welland	2,324	0.31
Caledonia	Haldimand	2,198	0.29
Hagersville	Haldimand	2,075	0.27
Crystal Beach	Welland	1,886	0.25
Ridgeway	Welland	1,871	0.25
Burford	Brant	1,074	0.14
Total urban		660,453	86.64
Rural non-farm		57,604	7.56
Rural farm		44,231	5.80
Total population		762,288	100.00

* Total population of Metro Hamilton is 395,189 of which 36,352 is in Halton county of Toronto Environs region.

ica's most diversified automotive parts producer. Other products manufactured in the city are pulp and paper, boilers and furnaces, hardware tools, and fabricated structural metals. The facilities provided by the Welland Canal have contributed greatly to the industrialization of St. Catharines, and the $180 million federal government project of twinning the locks may be expected to bring still more prosperity.

Brantford is another city with diversified industry. It has plants making frozen foods, textiles (particularly carpets, and twine and cordage), clothing, agricultural implements, heavy machinery, commercial refrigeration equipment, truck bodies and trailers, paints and varnishes, and sporting goods. Other major places are: Niagara Falls, the world-famous tourist mecca; Welland, Canada's foremost producer of specialty steels; and Port Colborne, the home of the world's biggest nickel refinery.

HAMILTON/ST. CATHARINES—NIAGARA

CHARACTERISTICS OF THE POPULATION

	Region		% of the total population of the city			
	% of the total population of the region	% points above or below Canadian average	Hamilton	St. Catharines	Brantford	Niagara Falls
Mother tongue *(1961 census)*						
English	78.7	+20.3	79.9	76.7	87.8	78.3
French	2.5	−25.6	1.5	2.5	1.1	2.7
German	3.0	− 0.1	2.7	4.4	1.2	2.4
Native Indian dialects	0.1	− 0.8	0.1	—	0.1	—
Italian	4.5	+ 2.6	4.6	4.4	1.7	9.2
Dutch	2.2	+ 1.3	2.1	2.0	1.0	0.6
Polish	2.1	+ 1.2	2.2	2.7	2.3	1.1
Ukrainian	2.1	+ 0.1	1.9	3.5	1.5	1.5
Other	4.8	+ 1.0	5.0	3.8	3.3	4.2
Total	100.0	—	100.0	100.0	100.0	100.0
Official language spoken *(1961 census)*						
English only	94.3	+26.9	95.0	94.3	96.4	93.4
French only	0.3	−18.8	0.1	0.2	0.1	0.2
Both English and French	4.1	− 8.1	3.4	4.5	2.8	4.6
Neither English nor French	1.3	—	1.5	1.0	0.7	1.8
Total	100.0	—	100.0	100.0	100.0	100.0

IMPORTANCE OF THE MARKET (1964 ESTIMATES)

	Region		Hamilton		St. Catharines		Brantford		Niagara Falls	
	Number	% of Canada	Number	% of Canada	Number	% of Canada	Number	% of Canada	Number	% of Canada
Population	783,700	4.08	418,000	2.17	98,000	0.51	57,200	0.30	56,300	0.29
Households	211,900	4.41	113,000	2.35	27,200	0.57	16,800	0.35	15,600	0.32
Disposable income ($ million)	1,506.5	4.78	863.1	2.74	202.3	0.64	104.0	0.33	115.7	0.37

GROWTH OF THE MARKET

	Region		Hamilton		St. Catharines		Brantford		Niagara Falls	
	Percentage growth 1961 to 1964	% points above or below Canadian average	Percentage growth 1961 to 1964	% points above or below Canadian average	Percentage growth 1961 to 1964	% points above or below Canadian average	Percentage growth 1961 to 1964	% points above or below Canadian average	Percentage growth 1961 to 1964	% points above or below Canadian average
Population	+ 2.81	− 2.66	+ 5.77	+0.30	+ 2.54	− 2.93	+ 0.81	−4.66	+3.02	− 2.45
Disposable income	+11.52	−10.01	+12.35	−9.18	+13.72	−7.81	+13.41	−8.12	+6.73	−14.80

AVERAGE INCOME (1961 CENSUS)

	Region		Hamilton		St. Catharines		Brantford		Niagara Falls	
	Dollars	% above or below Canadian average	Dollars	% above or below Canadian average	Dollars	% above or below Canadian average	Dollars	% above or below Canadian average	Dollars	% above or below Canadian average
Income per family (non-farm)	5,702	+ 4.64	6,030	+10.66	5,722	+5.01	5,346	−1.89	5,658	+3.84
Income per person not in family (non-farm)	2,253	+ 5.43	2,378	+11.28	2,219	+3.84	2,336	+9.31	2,165	+1.31
Income per farm (net)	3,959	+21.63	—	—	—	—	—	—	—	—

MEANS OF LIVELIHOOD—DISTRIBUTION OF LABOR FORCE BY INDUSTRY

Industry	Region			Hamilton		St. Catharines		Brantford		Niagara Falls	
	Persons 1961 census	% of the total	% points above or below Canadian average	Persons 1961 census	% of the total	Persons 1961 census	% of the total	Persons 1961 census	% of the total	Persons 1961 census	% of the total
Agriculture	14,754	5.2	− 4.7	4,116	2.7	427	1.2	320	1.4	92	0.5
Forestry	67	—	− 1.7	36	—	4	—	3	—	1	—
Fishing and trapping	129	—	− 0.5	62	—	3	—	—	—	1	—
Mines, quarries, oil wells	931	0.3	− 1.6	287	0.2	60	0.2	31	0.1	100	0.5
Manufacturing	110,408	38.8	+17.1	61,090	40.3	14,898	42.6	9,567	43.2	6,746	32.7
Construction	18,768	6.6	− 0.1	10,585	7.0	2,225	6.4	1,063	4.8	1,300	6.3
Transportation, communications and other utilities	19,438	6.8	− 2.5	9,374	6.2	2,376	6.8	1,159	5.2	2,192	10.6
Wholesale trade	9,917	3.5	− 1.0	6,429	4.2	988	2.8	786	3.6	619	3.0
Retail trade	31,893	11.2	+ 0.4	17,599	11.6	4,105	11.8	2,567	11.6	2,355	11.4
Finance, insurance, and real estate	7,977	2.8	− 0.7	4,969	3.3	1,028	2.9	640	2.9	531	2.6
Community and business services	35,008	12.3	− 0.5	19,145	12.6	4,558	13.0	3,306	14.9	2,665	12.9
Personal services	18,947	6.7	− 0.1	9,685	6.4	2,321	6.6	1,399	6.3	2,211	10.7
Public administration and defence	11,141	3.9	− 3.6	5,438	3.6	1,273	3.7	893	4.0	1,307	6.4
Miscellaneous	5,369	1.9	− 0.5	2,822	1.9	687	2.0	438	2.0	484	2.4
Total labor force	284,747	100.0	—	151,637	100.0	34,953	100.0	22,172	100.0	20,604	100.0

HAMILTON/ST. CATHARINES—NIAGARA

POVERTY AND AFFLUENCE (1961 CENSUS)

	Region			Hamilton		St. Catharines		Brantford		Niagara Falls	
	Number	% of region's total	% points above or below Canadian average	Number	% of city's total	Number	% of city's total	Number	% of city's total	Number	% of city's total
Extent of poverty											
Families earning below $3,000 a year (non-farm)	29,821	16.9	− 6.4	13,993	14.7	3,497	14.8	2,588	18.2	2,372	17.1
Persons not in families earning below $1,500 a year (non-farm)	28,828	48.0	− 0.9	15,125	45.5	3,396	47.2	2,393	46.8	2,165	48.2
Farms with gross income of less than $2,500 a year	5,267	48.2	+ 2.1	—	—	—	—	—	—	—	—
Persons not in school with grade 4 or less education	40,399	8.2	− 5.2	20,058	7.8	4,519	7.5	2,359	6.3	2,909	8.3
Doubled-up households (more than one family per household)	8,431	4.1	+ 0.4	5,343	5.1	750	2.9	410	2.5	643	4.3
Households living in dilapidated dwellings	8,330	4.1	− 1.5	3,305	3.1	855	3.3	752	4.6	453	3.0
Households without facilities of running water	6,230	3.0	− 7.9	1,556	1.5	74	0.3	70	0.4	5	—
Households without facilities of installed bath or shower	11,482	5.6	−14.1	3,546	3.4	479	1.8	528	3.2	137	0.9

POVERTY AND AFFLUENCE (1961 CENSUS) (continued)

	Region			Hamilton		St. Catharines		Brantford		Niagara Falls	
	Number	% of region's total	% points above or below Canadian average	Number	% of city's total	Number	% of city's total	Number	% of city's total	Number	% of city's total
Extent of affluence											
Families earning over $10,000 a year (non-farm)	12,727	7.2	− 0.6	8,048	8.5	1,751	7.4	779	5.5	979	7.1
Persons not in families earning over $6,000 a year (non-farm)	2,746	4.6	+ 0.8	1,721	5.2	315	4.4	198	3.9	213	4.7
Farms with gross income over $15,000 a year	1,107	10.1	+ 5.1	—	—	—	—	—	—	—	—
Persons with university degree	12,157	2.5	− 0.3	7,530	2.9	1,575	2.6	859	2.3	1,011	2.9
Households with two or more television sets	12,880	6.3	+ 2.1	8,121	7.7	1,517	5.8	971	6.0	1,023	6.9
Households with two or more cars	23,023	11.2	+ 4.4	12,415	11.8	2,796	10.7	1,427	8.7	1,705	11.5

London —Lake Erie

ECONOMIC CAPSULE

The sustained economic growth of this region over the past few decades has been due mainly to its rich agricultural resources. Eighty-eight per cent of the total land area is cleared and used mainly for farm operations. Various types of crops are grown. Oxford and Middlesex counties have the highest oats production in the province, while the sandy soils of Norfolk and Elgin account for nearly 80% of Canada's tobacco crop. Livestock also contributes much to farm income.

Commercial fishing is fairly significant. Lake Erie, a shallow lake, supplies between half and two-thirds of the volume of the total provincial catch. The main species are perch, smelt, white bass, and yellow pickerel.

London, the major urban center of the region, is the home of many large industrial enterprises. Most of the desirable attributes which attract new plants to a city are found here — central location, rich regional market, superior rail and trucking services, outstanding industrial training facilities, and pleasant living conditions. All types of goods are manufactured — dairy products, biscuits, breakfast cereals, shoes, hosiery, clothing, furniture, telephone sets, household appliances, heavy machinery, pharmaceuticals, glassware, commercial fertilizers — to mention a few. This diversity has contributed to economic stability and encouraged steady, if not spectacular, growth.

However, London (aptly named the "Forest City" because of its tree-lined streets and its lovely parks) is far more than an industrial town. It is a transportation hub, a commercial center, a major retail trading zone, and the headquarters of several large national insurance firms and trust companies. The University of Western Ontario is also located here on a high hill overlooking the winding Thames.

London is regarded by many national manufacturers as an ideal place for testing new products or merchandising ideas. It is a fairly typical community, representing to some extent in microcosm the urban life in English Canada. The market is big enough to have a metropolitan attitude, yet small enough to permit the researchers to collect the necessary data economically.

Two other urban centers in the region are St. Thomas and Woodstock. The former, at the junction of six Canadian and U.S. railroads, is a thriving industrial town with several big plants manufacturing construction equipment, automotive parts and accessories, shoes, toys, and pet supplies. The latter, situated in the heart of the productive Oxford dairy region, specializes in the making of cheese, livestock feeds, and agricultural implements. It has also textile and knitting mills and primary metal industries.

LONDON—LAKE ERIE

Area covered: 3,359 square miles. *Counties:* Elgin, Middlesex, Norfolk, Oxford.

COMPOSITION OF THE MARKET

Place	County	Population 1961	% of the region
London (metro)	Middlesex	181,283	44.73
St. Thomas	Elgin	22,469	5.54
Woodstock	Oxford	20,486	5.05
Simcoe	Norfolk	8,754	2.16
Ingersoll	Oxford	6,874	1.70
Tillsonburg	Oxford	6,600	1.63
Strathroy	Middlesex	5,150	1.27
Aylmer	Elgin	4,705	1.16
Delhi	Norfolk	3,427	0.85
Port Dover	Norfolk	3,064	0.76
Waterford	Norfolk	2,221	0.55
Norwich	Oxford	1,703	0.42
Port Stanley	Elgin	1,460	0.36
Dorchester Station and Village	Middlesex	1,183	0.29
Parkhill	Middlesex	1,169	0.29
Glencoe	Middlesex	1,156	0.29
West Lorne	Elgin	1,070	0.26
Rodney	Elgin	1,041	0.26
Mount Brydges	Middlesex	1,016	0.25
Total urban		274,831	67.82
Rural non-farm		67,359	16.62
Rural farm		63,068	15.56
Total population		405,258	100.00

IMPORTANCE OF THE MARKET (1964 ESTIMATES)

	Region		London	
	Number	% of Canada	Number	% of Canada
Population	421,500	2.19	192,000	1.00
Households	118,100	2.46	56,500	1.18
Disposable income ($ million)	689.6	2.19	370.8	1.18

GROWTH OF THE MARKET

	Region		London	
	Percentage growth 1961 to 1964	% points above or below Canadian average	Percentage growth 1961 to 1964	% points above or below Canadian average
Population	+ 4.01	− 1.46	+ 5.91	+0.44
Disposable income	+11.46	−10.07	+18.35	−3.18

AVERAGE INCOME (1961 CENSUS)

	Region		London	
	Dollars	% above or below Canadian average	Dollars	% above or below Canadian average
Income per family (non-farm)	5,447	− 0.04	5,985	+ 9.84
Income per person not in family (non-farm)	2,146	+ 0.42	2,398	+12.21
Income per farm (net)	6,870	+111.06	—	—

LABOR FORCE BY INDUSTRY

Industry	Region			London	
	Persons 1961 census	% of the total	% points above or below Canadian average	Persons 1961 census	% of the total
Agriculture	27,313	17.4	+7.5	1,575	2.1
Forestry	138	0.1	−1.6	11	—
Fishing and trapping	146	0.1	−0.4	21	—
Mines, quarries, oil wells	275	0.2	−1.7	69	0.1
Manufacturing	34,400	21.9	+0.2	18,416	25.0
Construction	9,229	5.9	−0.8	4,383	5.9
Transportation, communications, and other utilities	11,574	7.3	−2.0	5,915	8.0
Wholesale trade	6,811	4.3	−0.2	4,140	5.6
Retail trade	17,277	11.0	+0.2	9,094	12.3
Finance, insurance, and real estate	6,555	4.2	+0.7	4,580	6.2
Community and business services	22,117	14.0	+1.2	13,275	18.0
Personal services	9,080	5.8	−1.0	4,779	6.5
Public administration and defence	9,466	6.0	−1.5	6,075	8.2
Miscellaneous	2,864	1.8	−0.6	1,507	2.1
Total labor force	157,245	100.0	—	73,840	100.0

CHARACTERISTICS OF THE POPULATION

	Region		London
	% of the total population of the region	% points above or below Canadian average	% of the total population of the city
Mother tongue (1961 census)			
English	86.4	+28.0	88.6
French	0.8	−27.3	1.0
German	2.7	− 0.4	2.2
Native Indian dialects	0.2	− 0.7	—
Italian	0.7	− 1.2	1.2
Dutch	3.2	+ 2.3	2.1
Polish	0.9	—	1.0
Ukrainian	0.7	− 1.3	0.6
Other	4.4	+ 0.6	3.3
Total	100.0	—	100.0
Official language spoken (1961 census)			
English only	96.7	+29.3	95.9
French only	0.1	−19.0	0.1
Both English and French	2.5	− 9.7	3.4
Neither English nor French	0.7	− 0.6	0.6
Total	100.0	—	100.0

POVERTY AND AFFLUENCE (1961 CENSUS)

		Region		London	
	Number	% of region's total	% points above or below Canadian average	Number	% of city's total
Extent of poverty					
Families earning below $3,000 a year (non-farm)	16,243	19.8	− 3.5	6,098	14.4
Persons not in families earning below $1,500 a year (non-farm)	15,541	47.2	− 1.7	7,123	39.9
Farms with gross income of less than $2,500 a year	4,319	28.6	−17.5	—	—
Persons not in school with grade 4 or less education	18,696	7.0	− 6.4	6,284	5.3

	Region			London	
	Number	% of region's total	% points above or below Canadian average	Number	% of city's total
Doubled-up households (more than one family per household)	2,648	2.4	− 1.3	1,304	2.6
Households living in dilapidated dwellings	5,932	5.3	− 0.3	1,559	3.1
Households without facilities of running water	5,969	5.3	− 5.6	329	0.7
Households without facilities of installed bath or shower	11,307	10.1	− 9.6	1,032	2.0
Extent of affluence					
Families earning over $10,000 a year (non-farm)	5,596	6.9	− 0.9	3,584	8.5
Persons not in families earning over $6,000 a year (non-farm)	1,203	3.7	− 0.1	802	4.5
Farms with gross income over $15,000 a year	3,711	24.6	+19.6	—	—
Persons with university degree	7,294	2.7	− 0.1	4,948	4.2
Households with two or more television sets	5,127	4.6	+ 0.4	3,461	6.9
Households with two or more cars	11,537	10.3	+ 3.5	5,964	11.8

Windsor/Sarnia — Lake St. Clair

ECONOMIC CAPSULE

This region is noted as the "Corn Belt" of Ontario. The statistics for 1963 show that though it has only 13% of the provincial field crop acreage, yet it accounts for 92% of the production of sugar beets, 87% of soy beans, 52% of husking corn, 42% of dry beans, and 38% of winter wheat. It is also Ontario's second major fruit growing belt, the leading species being peaches, apples, and cantaloupes. Because of the early spring, the Leamington district in the extreme south specializes in truck gardening. Its lettuce, radishes, cucumbers, cabbages, tomatoes, and cauliflowers reach the urban markets weeks before those from any other area.

The principal minerals are salt, petroleum, and natural gas. An estimated two-thirds of the nation's salt is produced near Windsor. The output of oil and natural gas is the highest for Ontario, but is insignificant when compared to the heavy local requirements.

Sarnia, the "Chemical Valley", has the greatest concentration of petro-chemical industries in Canada. Here are located the country's biggest oil refineries, the largest fiberglass plant, the only synthetic rubber plant, and the first glycol plant. Other local products include caustic soda, fabricated and structural steel, automotive equipment, builders' supplies, and hardware specialties. Labor is highly skilled and average weekly wages are among the highest in the country.

Windsor was for many years strictly an automobile city. The Detroit automotive manufacturers found it convenient to establish their plants here in order to enter the Canadian market as well as to take advantage of British Commonwealth tariff rates. But too much dependence on a single industry was not very healthy, and Windsor passed through many bad years when Ford's assembly plant and several other feeder companies moved out of the community in the early Fifties.

Lately the city has succeeded to a considerable extent in diversifying its industrial potential. At present, eight of the fifteen largest industrial taxpayers are non-automotive. Plants now turn out a wide variety of goods ranging all the way from buttons, Chinese food, fishing tackle, and playing cards to chemicals, alcoholic beverages, and fire extinguishers. Although the automotive industry is still of prime importance, any sharp decline in motor vehicle sales is not likely to affect the solidarity of the economy as much as it did in the past.

Many believe that Windsor has pulled out of its industrial doldrums and is back on the road to solid growth. This can be clearly seen from the following statistics: Between 1962 and 1965 the employment index in Windsor rose by 32% compared to only 12% in Ontario as a whole. During the same period the increase in capital expenditures was even more dramatic — 224% for Windsor to 42% average for the whole province.

The city's renaissance is mainly due to the fact that it offers several almost unique advantages:

- It came under Ottawa's first "designated area" plan of governmental assistance. As a result the newly established manufacturing firms are exempted from federal and provincial corporate income tax for the first three years. In addition businessmen can get a quick 100% write-off in two years for new machinery and equipment and in five years for new buildings and extensions.

- Windsor is considered by the U.S. Interstate Commerce Commission as a "contiguous community". This means substantial freight rate savings as a part of the Detroit commercial zone.

- Skilled and productive labor is readily available. Long established as a center of the metal-working and tool-and-die industries, Windsor has a reputation for engineering skills based on working to close tolerances. Another facet of the city's new image is a more mature spirit of co-operation and understanding in labor-management relations. The old stigma of being a labor-strife city has gone.

• Last but not least, Windsor provides the opportunity to set up a manufacturing plant right on the doorstep of the huge automotive market of Detroit. This location has assumed added significance in view of the new Canadian-U.S. auto-tariff agreement. Windsor is both geographically and industrially in the best position of any Canadian city to benefit from this arrangement.

WINDSOR/SARNIA—LAKE ST. CLAIR

Area covered: 2,749 square miles. *Counties:* Essex, Kent, Lambton.

COMPOSITION OF THE MARKET

Place	County	Population 1961	% of the region
Windsor (metro)	Essex	193,365	42.99
Sarnia (urbanized area)	Lambton	61,293	13.63
Chatham	Kent	29,826	6.63
Leamington	Essex	9,030	2.01
Wallaceburg	Kent	7,881	1.75
Amherstburg	Essex	4,452	0.99
Petrolia	Lambton	3,708	0.83
Essex	Essex	3,428	0.76
Blenheim	Kent	3,151	0.70
Kingsville	Essex	3,041	0.68
Tilbury	Essex & Kent	3,030	0.67
Ridgetown	Kent	2,603	0.58
Dresden	Kent	2,346	0.52
Forest	Lambton	2,188	0.49
Belle River	Essex	1,854	0.41
Harrow	Essex	1,787	0.40
Wheatley	Kent	1,362	0.30
Watford	Lambton	1,293	0.29
Puce-Emeryville	Essex	1,275	0.28
Thamesville	Kent	1,054	0.23
Chatham Twp. (urban)	Kent	1,007	0.22
Total urban		338,974	75.36
Rural non-farm		57,009	12.68
Rural farm		53,793	11.96
Total population		449,776	100.00

POVERTY AND AFFLUENCE (1961 CENSUS)

	Region			Windsor		Sarnia	
	Number	% of region's total	% points above or below Cdn. average	Number	% of city's total	Number	% of city's total
Extent of poverty							
Families earning below $3,000 a year (non-farm)	20,640	21.6	− 1.7	9,573	20.6	1,801	12.2
Persons not in families earning below $1,500 a year (non-farm)	17,414	53.9	+ 5.0	8,193	51.9	2,080	46.7
Farms with gross income of less than $2,500 a year	4,908	35.5	−10.6	—	—	—	—
Persons not in school with grade 4 or less education	25,681	9.1	− 4.3	11,823	9.7	2,512	6.8
Doubled-up households (more than one family per household)	2,953	2.4	− 1.3	1,455	2.7	374	2.3
Households living in dilapidated dwellings	6,560	5.3	− 0.3	2,379	4.5	599	3.7
Households without facilities of running water	4,778	3.9	− 7.0	269	0.5	81	0.5
Households without facilities of installed bath or shower	10,368	8.4	−11.3	1,118	2.1	369	2.3
Extent of affluence							
Families earning over $10,000 a year (non-farm)	6,401	6.7	− 1.1	3,133	6.7	1,348	9.1
Persons not in families earning over $6,000 a year (non-farm)	1,332	4.1	+ 0.3	689	4.4	259	5.8
Farms with gross income over $15,000 a year	1,245	9.0	+ 4.0	—	—	—	—
Persons with university degree	7,158	2.6	− 0.2	3,381	2.8	1,814	4.9
Households with two or more television sets	8,021	6.5	+ 2.3	5,149	9.7	972	5.9
Households with two or more cars	11,837	9.6	+ 2.8	4,984	9.3	1,872	11.4

IMPORTANCE OF THE MARKET (1964 ESTIMATES)

	Region		Windsor		Sarnia	
	Number	% of Canada	Number	% of Canada	Number	% of Canada
Population..........	447,900	2.33	200,000	1.04	62,700	0.33
Households.........	125,100	2.60	55,600	1.16	16,900	0.35
Disposable income ($ million)........	843.2	2.67	392.2	1.24	149.8	0.48

GROWTH OF THE MARKET

	Region		Windsor		Sarnia	
	Percentage change 1961 to 1964	% points above or below Canadian average	Percentage growth 1961 to 1964	% points above or below Canadian average	Percentage growth 1961 to 1964	% points above or below Canadian average
Population..........	− 0.42	−5.89	+ 3.43	− 2.04	+ 2.30	−3.17
Disposable income.............	+15.18	−6.35	+10.45	−11.08	+22.99	+1.46

CHARACTERISTICS OF THE POPULATION

	Region		Windsor	Sarnia
	% of the total population of the region	% points above or below Canadian average	% of the total population of the city	% of the total population of the city
Mother tongue (1961 census)				
English..	77.1	+18.7	72.0	85.5
French...	8.0	−20.1	10.3	4.8
German...	2.6	− 0.5	2.8	1.1
Native Indian dialects....................	0.2	− 0.7	—	0.2
Italian...	2.8	+ 0.9	4.7	1.8
Dutch...	2.1	+ 1.2	0.4	2.2
Polish..	1.1	+ 0.2	1.7	1.0
Ukrainian..	1.3	− 0.7	2.1	0.8
Other...	4.8	+ 1.0	6.0	2.6
Total...	100.0	—	100.0	100.0

English only	89.1	+21.7	86.3	92.3
French only	0.6	−18.5	0.7	0.5
Both English and French	9.4	− 2.8	12.0	6.5
Neither English nor French	0.9	− 0.4	1.0	0.7
Total	100.0	—	100.0	100.0

AVERAGE INCOME (1961 CENSUS)

	Region		*Windsor*		*Sarnia*	
	Dollars	% above or below Cdn. average	Dollars	% above or below Cdn. average	Dollars	% above or below Cdn. average
Income per family (non-farm)	5,361	− 1.61	5,384	−1.19	6,409	+17.62
Income per person not in family (non-farm)	2,043	− 4.40	2,115	−1.03	2,415	+13.01
Income per farm (net)	4,411	+35.51	—	—	—	—

LABOR FORCE BY INDUSTRY

Industry	*Region*			*Windsor*		*Sarnia*	
	Persons 1961 census	% of the total	% points above or below Cdn. average	Persons 1961 census	% of the total	Persons 1961 census	% of the total
Agriculture	20,145	12.5	+2.6	905	1.3	109	0.5
Forestry	64	—	−1.7	5	—	4	—
Fishing and trapping	377	0.2	−0.3	12	—	10	—
Mines, quarries, oil wells	717	0.5	−1.4	303	0.5	68	0.3
Manufacturing	47,934	29.8	+8.1	24,602	35.8	8,013	36.7
Construction	10,189	6.3	−0.4	4,047	5.9	2,141	9.8
Transportation, communications, and other utilities	11,962	7.4	−1.9	5,345	7.8	1,840	8.4
Wholesale trade	5,754	3.6	−0.9	2,501	3.7	523	2.4
Retail trade	18,135	11.3	+0.5	8,333	12.1	2,643	12.1
Finance, insurance, and real estate	4,863	3.0	−0.5	2,690	3.9	683	3.1
Community and business services	19,440	12.1	−0.7	9,685	14.1	2,983	13.7
Personal services	11,503	7.1	+0.3	5,666	8.3	1,531	7.0
Public administration and defence	6,742	4.2	−3.3	2,975	4.3	875	4.0
Miscellaneous	3,180	2.0	−0.4	1,590	2.3	436	2.0
Total labor force	161,005	100.0	—	68,659	100.0	21,859	100.0

Kitchener — Midlands

Area covered: 3,670 square miles. *Counties:* Huron, Perth, Waterloo, Wellington.

COMPOSITION OF THE MARKET

Place	County	Population 1961	% of the region
Kitchener (metro)	Waterloo	154,864	41.55
Guelph (urbanized area)	Wellington	41,767	11.21
Stratford	Perth	20,467	5.49
Goderich	Huron	6,411	1.72
St. Mary's	Perth	4,482	1.20
Listowel	Perth	4,002	1.07
Fergus	Wellington	3,831	1.03
Clinton	Huron	3,491	0.94
Elmira	Waterloo	3,337	0.90
Exeter	Huron	3,047	0.82
Wingham	Huron	2,922	0.78
Mount Forest	Wellington	2,623	0.70
Seaforth	Huron	2,255	0.60
Mitchell	Perth	2,247	0.60
New Hamburg	Waterloo	2,181	0.58
Harriston	Wellington	1,631	0.44
Palmerston	Wellington	1,554	0.42
Elora	Wellington	1,486	0.40
Tavistock	Perth	1,232*	0.33
Arthur	Wellington	1,200	0.32
Milverton	Perth	1,111	0.30
Erin	Wellington	1,005	0.27
Total urban		267,146	71.67
Rural non-farm		40,202	10.79
Rural farm		65,365	17.54
Total population		372,713	100.00

* Actually only 670 is in Perth; 562 is in Oxford.

ECONOMIC CAPSULE

This is a rich agricultural zone specializing in livestock raising. It has one of the largest hog populations in the province and also ranks first in the production of creamery butter. Poultry breeding is equally important. Field crops are grown chiefly for feed rather than for sale, with a few exceptions like potatoes, turnips, and flax.

Metropolitan Kitchener, a leading manufacturing city, turns out a wide variety of items — tires and other rubber goods, dairy products, alcoholic beverages, shoes, textiles, furniture, hardware tools, electrical appliances, and motor vehicle parts. In addition, the presence of the head offices of about half a dozen nationally known insurance and trust companies makes this city one of Canada's leading financial centers and lends an unusual degree of stability to the whole area.

Guelph, 15 miles from Kitchener, has factories producing stoves, boiler machinery, electrical apparatus, leather goods, textiles, clothing, and dairy products. Just south of the city is located the Ontario Agricultural College, founded in 1874. This institution has trained several generations of noted Canadian scientists.

Stratford, on the Avon River, has gained international fame as a cultural center. The Stratford Shakespearean Festival is Canada's most exciting and widely-known venture in the theater and attracts thousands of tourists every summer. As one writer remarks: "One corner at least of Ontario has escaped the economic revolution and felt instead a revolution of culture. Stratford has become an independent city-state of poetry, drama, and imagination. The Festival has done more to give Canada pride and sense of nationhood than a dozen gold mines could."

KITCHENER—MIDLANDS

IMPORTANCE OF THE MARKET (1964 ESTIMATES)

	Region		Kitchener	
	Number	% of Canada	Number	% of Canada
Population	388,600	2.02	163,000	0.85
Households	105,900	2.21	45,300	0.94
Disposable income ($ million)	664.1	2.11	314.6	1.00

GROWTH OF THE MARKET

	Region		Kitchener	
	Percentage growth 1961 to 1964	% points above or below Canadian average	Percentage growth 1961 to 1964	% points above or below Canadian average
Population	+ 4.26	−1.21	+ 5.25	−0.22
Disposable income	+17.08	−4.45	+15.20	−6.33

CHARACTERISTICS OF THE POPULATION

	Region		Kitchener
	% of the total population of the region	% points above or below Canadian average	% of the total population of the city
Mother tongue (1961 census)			
English	82.9	+24.5	79.0
French	0.9	−27.2	1.1
German	10.0	+ 6.9	13.3
Native Indian dialects	—	− 0.9	—
Italian	1.1	− 0.8	0.5
Dutch	2.0	+ 1.1	1.0
Polish	0.9	—	1.6
Ukrainian	0.5	− 1.5	0.9
Other	1.7	− 2.1	2.6
Total	100.0	—	100.0
Official language spoken (1961 census)			
English only	97.0	+29.6	96.3
French only	0.1	−19.0	0.1
Both English and French	2.1	−10.1	2.6
Neither English nor French	0.8	− 0.5	1.0
Total	100.0	—	100.0

AVERAGE INCOME (1961 CENSUS)

	Region		Kitchener	
	Dollars	% above or below Canadian average	Dollars	% above or below Canadian average
Income per family (non-farm)	5,478	+ 0.53	5,911	+8.48
Income per person not in family (non-farm)	2,074	− 2.95	2,339	+9.45
Income per farm (net)	5,014	+54.04	—	—

POVERTY AND AFFLUENCE (1961 CENSUS)

	Region			Kitchener	
	Number	% of region's total	% points above or below Canadian average	Number	% of city's total
Extent of poverty					
Families earning below $3,000 a year (non-farm)	13,899	18.5	− 4.8	4,718	12.6
Persons not in families earning below $1,500 a year (non-farm)	13,868	48.4	− 0.5	5,471	40.4
Farms with gross income of less than $2,500 a year	4,115	26.4	−19.7	—	—
Persons not in school with grade 4 or less education	16,031	6.6	− 6.8	5,910	5.9
Doubled-up households (more than one family per household)	3,111	3.1	− 0.6	1,478	3.5
Households living in dilapidated dwellings	4,304	4.3	− 1.3	1,807	4.3
Households without facilities of running water	4,450	4.4	− 6.5	413	1.0
Households without facilities of installed bath or shower	11,231	11.1	− 8.6	1,579	3.7
Extent of affluence					
Families earning over $10,000 a year (non-farm)	5,126	6.9	− 0.9	2,914	7.8
Persons not in families earning over $6,000 a year (non-farm)	890	3.1	− 0.7	457	3.4
Farms with gross income over $15,000 a year	1,725	11.0	+ 6.0	—	—
Persons with university degree	5,805	2.4	− 0.4	2,752	2.7
Households with two or more television sets	4,114	4.1	− 0.1	2,603	6.2
Households with two or more cars	10,125	10.0	+ 3.2	4,986	11.8

MEANS OF LIVELIHOOD—DISTRIBUTION OF
LABOR FORCE BY INDUSTRY

Industry	Region			Kitchener	
	Persons 1961 census	% of the total	% points above or below Canadian average	Persons 1961 census	% of the total
Agriculture	21,376	14.6	+ 4.7	1,426	2.2
Forestry	59	—	− 1.7	15	—
Fishing and trapping	43	—	− 0.5	—	—
Mines, quarries, oil wells	348	0.2	− 1.7	55	0.1
Manufacturing	49,122	33.6	+11.9	29,294	45.3
Construction	8,874	6.1	− 0.6	4,274	6.6
Transportation, communications, and other utilities	8,120	5.5	− 3.8	3,107	4.8
Wholesale trade	4,816	3.3	− 1.2	2,360	3.7
Retail trade	15,398	10.5	− 0.3	7,485	11.6
Finance, insurance, and real estate	4,957	3.4	− 0.1	3,152	4.9
Community and business services	15,925	10.9	− 1.9	6,799	10.5
Personal services	7,849	5.4	− 1.4	3,661	5.7
Public administration and defence	7,110	4.9	− 2.6	2,027	3.1
Miscellaneous	2,292	1.6	− 0.8	956	1.5
Total labor force	146,289	100.0	—	64,611	100.0

Lake Huron — Georgian Bay

ECONOMIC CAPSULE

This region is a vital link between the highly industrialized part of southern Ontario and the resource-rich treasure house of the north. Agriculture constitutes the backbone of the economy, the area having the largest sheep population and the highest number of beef cattle for any region in the province. The Holland Marsh is one of the best known market gardens in Canada. It produces a wide variety of vegetables — beets, cabbages, carrots, cauliflower, celery, lettuce, onions, and radishes — some of which are even exported to the United States.

In several sectors the economic activity revolves round catering to the wants and needs of the tourists. Georgian Bay itself is a fisherman's paradise, and the numerous lakes and rivers are well-stocked with nearly every type of game fish known in Ontario, including trout, pike, pickerel, bass, and, in Parry Sound, the famous maskinonge or "mighty muskie". The hunter, too, can have his choice: deer, bear, duck, and partridge. Some of North America's finest fresh water beaches are to be found along the shores of Lake Huron and Georgian Bay, most popular being Sauble Beach near Southampton and Wasaga Beach, east of Collingwood. Winter, too, has its own special charms, and every year more and more people come for skiing, ice fishing, and tobogganing.

Manufacturing is dependent largely on agriculture, e.g. slaughtering and meat packing, leather tanning, flour milling, and processing of fruits and vegetables. The thick forest cover that envelops the Highlands sub-region has encouraged the development of wood-using industries. These include sawmills, furniture factories, veneer and plywood plants, and sash, door, and planing mills. The region also specializes in the construction of cargo vessels, tugs, sailboats, and cruisers.

Canada's first large-scale nuclear-electric power station is located at Douglas Point on the shore of Lake Huron. Built by Atomic Energy of Canada Limited, with the co-operation of Ontario Hydro, the plant has an initial installed capacity of 200,000 kilowatts in one unit. It uses a nuclear reactor known as the CANDU type (Canadian Deuterium Uranium), with natural uranium as fuel and heavy water as a coolant and moderator.

Camp Borden, a large Canadian Army and Air Force base, a few miles north of Alliston, exerts a considerable impact on the surrounding area through the trade generated by the presence of some 5,500 military personnel. Approximately 2,750 civilians work at the camp, thus making the Defence Department the largest employer in the region. Civilian payrolls exceed six million dollars annually.

LAKE HURON—GEORGIAN BAY

Area covered: 11,499 square miles. *Counties:* Bruce, Dufferin, Grey, Muskoka, Parry Sound, Simcoe.

IMPORTANCE OF THE MARKET (1964 ESTIMATES)

	Number	% of Canada
Population	316,100	1.64
Households	85,100	1.77
Disposable income ($ million)	445.1	1.41

COMPOSITION OF THE MARKET

Place	County	Population 1961	% of the region
Barrie	Simcoe	21,169	6.64
Orillia (urbanized area)	Simcoe	18,246	5.72
Owen Sound	Grey	17,421	5.47
Midland	Simcoe	8,656	2.72
Collingwood	Simcoe	8,385	2.63
Parry Sound	Parry Sound	6,004	1.88
Penetanguishene	Simcoe	5,340	1.68
Orangeville	Dufferin	4,593	1.44
Hanover	Grey	4,401	1.38
Walkerton	Bruce	3,851	1.21
Meaford	Grey	3,834	1.20
Huntsville	Muskoka	3,189	1.00
Gravenhurst	Muskoka	3,077	0.97
Bracebridge	Muskoka	2,927	0.92
Alliston	Simcoe	2,884	0.91
Kincardine	Bruce	2,841	0.89
Bradford	Simcoe	2,342	0.74
Durham	Grey	2,180	0.68
Wiarton	Bruce	2,138	0.67
Southampton	Bruce	1,818	0.57
Chesley	Bruce	1,697	0.53
Stayner	Simcoe	1,671	0.52
Port Elgin	Bruce	1,632	0.51
Shelburne	Dufferin	1,239	0.39
Callander	Parry Sound	1,236	0.39
Angus	Simcoe	1,180	0.37
Thornbury	Grey	1,097	0.34
Markdale	Grey	1,090	0.34
Victoria Harbour	Simcoe	1,066	0.34
Powassan	Parry Sound	1,064	0.33
Port McNicoll	Simcoe	1,053	0.33
South River	Parry Sound	1,044	0.33
Lucknow	Bruce	1,031	0.32
Total urban		141,396	44.36
Rural non-farm		108,438	34.02
Rural farm		68,910	21.62
Total population		318,744	100.00

GROWTH OF THE MARKET

	Percentage change 1961 to 1964	% points above or below Canadian average
Population	− 0.83	−6.30
Disposable income	+19.91	−1.62

AVERAGE INCOME (1961 CENSUS)

	Dollars	% above or below Canadian average
Income per family (non-farm)	4,576	−16.02
Income per person not in family (non-farm)	1,710	−19.98
Income per farm (net)	3,234	− 0.65

CHARACTERISTICS OF THE POPULATION

	% of the total population of the region	% points above or below Canadian average
Mother tongue (1961 census)		
English	91.6	+33.2
French	2.9	−25.2
German	1.8	− 1.3
Native Indian dialects	0.5	− 0.4
Italian	0.3	− 1.6
Dutch	1.2	+ 0.3
Polish	0.3	− 0.6
Ukrainian	0.3	− 1.7
Other	1.1	− 2.7
Total	100.0	—
Official language spoken (1961 census)		
English only	95.5	+28.1
French only	0.3	−18.8
Both English and French	3.9	− 8.3
Neither English nor French	0.3	− 1.0
Total	100.0	—

POVERTY AND AFFLUENCE (1961 CENSUS)

	Number	% of region's total	% points above or below Canadian average
Extent of poverty			
Families earning below $3,000 a year (non-farm)	18,369	31.7	+ 8.4
Persons not in families earning below $1,500 a year (non-farm)	14,098	60.9	+12.0
Farms with gross income of less than $2,500 a year	7,593	43.2	− 2.9
Persons not in school with grade 4 or less education	22,531	10.9	− 2.5
Doubled-up households (more than one family per household)	1,963	2.3	− 1.4
Households living in dilapidated dwellings	5,975	6.9	+ 1.3
Households without facilities of running water	10,823	12.5	+ 1.6
Households without facilities of installed bath or shower	20,916	24.2	+ 4.5
Extent of affluence			
Families earning over $10,000 a year (non-farm)	2,508	4.3	− 3.5
Persons not in families earning over $6,000 a year (non-farm)	611	2.7	− 1.1
Farms with gross income over $15,000 a year	814	4.7	− 0.3
Persons with university degree	3,286	1.6	− 1.2
Households with two or more television sets	1,826	2.1	− 2.1
Households with two or more cars	5,481	6.3	− 0.5

MEANS OF LIVELIHOOD—DISTRIBUTION OF LABOR FORCE BY INDUSTRY

Industry	Persons 1961 census	% of the total	% points above or below Canadian average
Agriculture	22,486	20.2	+10.3
Forestry	843	0.8	− 0.9
Fishing and trapping	129	0.1	− 0.4
Mines, quarries, oil wells	242	0.2	− 1.7
Manufacturing	19,675	17.6	− 4.1
Construction	7,797	7.0	+ 0.3
Transportation, communications, and other utilities	9,901	8.9	− 0.4
Wholesale trade	2,990	2.7	− 1.8
Retail trade	12,166	10.9	+ 0.1

Finance, insurance, and real estate	2,254	2.0	− 1.5
Community and business services	11,873	10.6	− 2.2
Personal services	8,831	7.9	+ 1.1
Public administration and defence	10,015	9.0	+ 1.5
Miscellaneous	2,361	2.1	− 0.3
Total labor force	111,563	100.0	—

Northeastern Ontario — Clay Belt

ECONOMIC CAPSULE

Mining operations are of major importance in this area. Principal minerals are gold, silver, and cobalt. The gold mining industry is in a cost-price squeeze. The bullion price has remained fixed since 1934 at $35 (U.S.) per ounce, while the costs of mining, especially since the end of World War II, have spiraled rapidly upwards. The federal government, in order to maintain the existing gold mining communities, has been paying a subsidy since 1948 under the Emergency Gold Mining Assistance Act. But despite this, as well as the devaluation of the Canadian dollar (which added about $4 per oz. to the price of gold), the production trends have been steadily downwards. Several once-prolific mines near Timmins have been closed, and those that have survived are finding it harder and harder to operate profitably.

Despite this gloomy outlook for gold, the Timmins area sees a new ray of hope in the spectacular discovery of base metals made in 1964 by Texas Gulf Sulphur Company. Preliminary estimates place the size of the orebody at about 55 million tons averaging 1.33% copper, 7.08% zinc, and 4.85 oz. silver. This has revitalized interest in prospecting in the area and raised visions of an entirely new base metal camp expanding over the perimeter of a plucky but dying gold camp.

In Kirkland Lake, another declining gold mining town, the new source of prosperity is iron ore. Geologists have long been aware of the existence of vast low-grade iron deposits, but it was only after the development of the pelletizing process that the ore became attractive to the steel companies. Since 1965, Jones and Laughlin Steel Corporation has commenced mining in the area, and erected a concentrator and a pelletizing plant to boost up the iron content of the ore from 23% to 66%. Annual capacity is 1.25 million tons of pellets, which are shipped by rail to the parent company's steel plants near Cleveland and Pittsburgh.

Forest-based industries also play a major role. The region has numerous sawmills as well as pulp and paper mills at Kapuskasing, North Bay, Sturgeon Falls, Iroquois Falls, and Smooth Rock Falls. Agriculture is insignificant. Low temperatures, shortness of the growing season, and unfavorable harvest weather vigorously limit the choice of crops. Most of the food consumed in the towns has to be brought from distant places.

NORTHEASTERN ONTARIO—CLAY BELT

Area covered: 65,693 square miles. *Counties:* Cochrane, Nipissing, Timiskaming.

COMPOSITION OF THE MARKET

Place	County	Population 1961	% of the region
Timmins (urbanized area)	Cochrane	40,121	18.47
North Bay (urbanized area)	Nipissing	33,545	15.44
Kirkland Lake (urbanized area)	Timiskaming	16,510	7.60
Kapuskasing	Cochrane	6,870	3.16
Sturgeon Falls	Nipissing	6,288	2.90
New Liskeard	Timiskaming	4,896	2.25
Cochrane	Cochrane	4,521	2.08
Mattawa	Nipissing	3,314	1.53
Ansonville	Cochrane	3,080	1.42
Haileybury	Timiskaming	2,638	1.22
Hearst	Cochrane	2,373	1.09
Cobalt	Timiskaming	2,209	1.02
Larder Lake	Timiskaming	2,030	0.94
Val Albert	Cochrane	2,018	0.93
Virginiatown	Timiskaming	2,009	0.93
Englehart	Timiskaming	1,786	0.82
Iroquois Falls	Cochrane	1,681	0.77
Brunetville	Cochrane	1,550	0.71
North Cobalt	Timiskaming	1,133	0.52
Smooth Rock Falls	Cochrane	1,131	0.52
Total urban		139,703	64.32
Rural non-farm		61,575	28.35
Rural farm		15,927	7.33
Total population		217,205	100.00

IMPORTANCE OF THE MARKET (1964 ESTIMATES)

	Number	% of Canada
Population	223,900	1.16
Households	52,100	1.09
Disposable income ($ million)	377.2	1.20

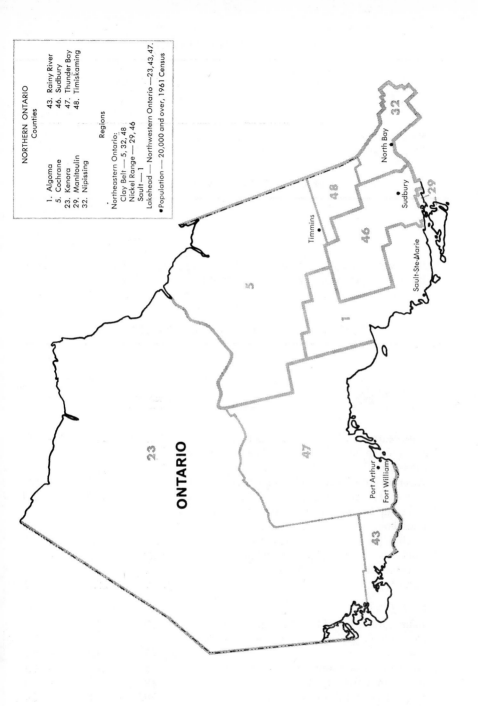

NORTHERN ONTARIO
Counties

1. Algoma   43. Rainy River
5. Cochrane   46. Sudbury
23. Kenora   47. Thunder Bay
29. Manitoulin   48. Timiskaming
32. Nipissing

Regions

Northeastern Ontario:
Clay Belt — 5, 32, 48
Nickel Range — 29, 46
Sault — 1
Lakehead — Northwestern Ontario — 23, 43, 47.
●Population — 20,000 and over, 1961 Census

ONTARIO

North Bay

Sudbury

Sault-Ste-Marie

Timmins

Port Arthur
Fort William

	Percentage growth 1961 to 1964	% points above or below Canadian average
Population	+ 3.08	− 2.39
Disposable income	+17.99	− 3.54

AVERAGE INCOME (1961 CENSUS)

	Dollars	% above or below Canadian average
Income per family (non-farm)	5,217	− 4.26
Income per person not in family (non-farm)	2,013	− 5.80
Income per farm (net)	1,516	−53.43

POVERTY AND AFFLUENCE (1961 CENSUS)

	Number	% of region's total	% points above or below Canadian average
Extent of poverty			
Families earning below $3,000 a year (non-farm)	9,220	21.1	− 2.2
Persons not in families earning below $1,500 a year (non-farm)	7,067	52.5	+ 3.6
Farms with gross income of less than $2,500 a year	1,973	70.9	+24.8
Persons not in school with grade 4 or less education	21,039	16.2	+ 2.8
Doubled-up households (more than one family per household)	1,241	2.4	− 1.3
Households living in dilapidated dwellings	5,252	10.3	+ 4.7
Households without facilities of running water	6,201	12.2	+ 1.3
Households without facilities of installed bath or shower	12,721	25.0	+ 5.3
Extent of affluence			
Families earning over $10,000 a year (non-farm)	2,398	5.6	− 2.2
Persons not in families earning over $6,000 a year (non-farm)	459	3.4	− 0.4
Farms with gross income over $15,000 a year	30	1.1	− 3.9
Persons with university degree	2,191	1.7	− 1.1
Households with two or more television sets	892	1.8	− 2.4
Households with two or more cars	2,045	4.0	− 2.8

MEANS OF LIVELIHOOD—DISTRIBUTION OF
LABOR FORCE BY INDUSTRY

Industry	Persons 1961 census	% of the total	% points above or below Canadian average
Agriculture	2,771	4.0	− 5.9
Forestry	5,024	7.2	+ 5.5
Fishing and trapping	40	0.1	− 0.4
Mines, quarries, oil wells	10,847	15.5	+13.6
Manufacturing	9,012	12.9	− 8.8
Construction	4,376	6.3	− 0.4
Transportation, communications, and other utilities	8,111	11.6	+ 2.3
Wholesale trade	2,129	3.0	− 1.5
Retail trade	7,308	10.4	− 0.4
Finance, insurance, and real estate	1,338	1.9	− 1.6
Community and business services	7,589	10.8	− 2.0
Personal services	5,073	7.2	+ 0.4
Public administration and defence	4,031	5.8	− 1.7
Miscellaneous	2,297	3.3	+ 0.9
Total labor force	69,946	100.0	—

CHARACTERISTICS OF THE POPULATION

	% of the total population of the region	% points above or below Canadian average
Mother tongue (1961 census)		
English	50.9	− 7.5
French	38.3	+10.2
German	1.1	− 2.0
Native Indian dialects	1.3	+ 0.4
Italian	2.0	+ 0.1
Dutch	0.3	− 0.6
Polish	1.2	+ 0.3
Ukrainian	1.1	− 0.9
Other	3.8	—
Total	100.0	—

	% of the total population of the region	% points above or below Canadian average
Official language spoken (1961 census)		
English only	56.4	−11.0
French only	11.8	− 7.3
Both English and French	30.5	+18.3
Neither English nor French	1.3	—
Total	100.0	—

Northeastern Ontario — Nickel Range

ECONOMIC CAPSULE

The economy of the region hinges almost entirely on mining. The Sudbury basin is the greatest single source of mineral wealth. It supplies over 75% of the free world's nickel and almost half of the nation's output of copper, as well as a large proportion of its cobalt. It is also the world's principal source of the platinum group of metals.

Low grade iron ore is obtained by open pit mining from the Moose Mountain area. Annual production capacity is 625,000 long tons of pellets. Even more iron, about 900,000 long tons of pellets, is derived as a by-product from nickel-bearing pyrrhotite deposits of the Sudbury basin.

Agriculture is negligible. Much of the land is suitable only for bare subsistence or part-time farming, except on Manitoulin Island where a large number of young beef cattle are raised for finishing elsewhere. The forests, covering approximately four-fifths of the total land area, supply the raw material for pulp and lumbering industries. At Espanola, a large mill operated by the Kalamazoo Vegetable Parchment Company manufactures wood pulp and a variety of paper goods.

Sudbury is the biggest urban center in Northern Ontario and a commercial and distributing node for a large area. Its economic activity is heavily dependent on two big corporations: the International Nickel Company of Canada Limited, and Falconbridge Nickel Mines Limited. A large portion of its labor force is engaged in the smelting and refining plants and in other allied industries. The city thus has all its eggs in one basket. Fortunately, there is ample demand for nickel throughout the world. In September 1965, INCO announced plans to spend $79 million in the next few years to carry out an expansion program which would include the development of one mine, the extension of another, the construction of a 22,500-ton-a-day concentrator, and improvements to the smelter at Copper Cliff.

NORTHEASTERN ONTARIO—NICKEL RANGE
Area covered: 19,646 square miles. *Counties:* Manitoulin, Sudbury.
COMPOSITION OF THE MARKET

Place	County	Population 1961	% of the region
Sudbury (metro)	Sudbury	110,694	62.53
Espanola	Sudbury	5,353	3.02
Chapleau	Sudbury	3,785	2.14
Lively	Sudbury	3,211	1.81
Levack	Sudbury	3,178	1.79
Capreol	Sudbury	3,003	1.70
Chelmsford	Sudbury	2,559	1.45
Little Current	Manitoulin	1,527	0.86
Massey	Sudbury	1,324	0.75
Falconbridge	Sudbury	1,138	0.64
Total urban		135,772	76.69
Rural non-farm		33,911	19.16
Rural farm		7,355	4.15
Total population		177,038	100.00

IMPORTANCE OF THE MARKET (1964 ESTIMATES)

	Region		Sudbury	
	Number	% of Canada	Number	% of Canada
Population	184,400	0.96	110,000	0.57
Households	43,400	0.90	26,800	0.56
Disposable income ($ million)	368.7	1.17	243.6	0.77

GROWTH OF THE MARKET

	Region		Sudbury	
	Percentage growth 1961 to 1964	% points above or below Canadian average	Percentage change 1961 to 1964	% points above or below Canadian average
Population	+ 4.16	−1.31	− 0.63	−6.10
Disposable income	+19.17	−2.36	+20.12	−1.41

POVERTY AND AFFLUENCE (1961 CENSUS)

		Region		Sudbury	
	Number	% of region's total	% points above or below Canadian average	Number	% of city's total
Extent of poverty					
Families earning below $3,000 a year (non-farm)	5,419	14.8	− 8.5	2,500	10.2
Persons not in families earning below $1,500 a year (non-farm)	4,734	43.3	− 5.6	2,695	36.5
Farms with gross income of less than $2,500 a year	1,043	66.5	+20.4	—	—
Persons not in school with grade 4 or less education	15,105	14.5	+ 1.1	8,293	12.6
Doubled-up households (more than one family per household)	1,012	2.5	− 1.2	694	2.6
Households living in dilapidated dwellings	2,928	7.1	+ 1.5	1,371	5.2
Households without facilities of running water	3,857	9.4	− 1.5	452	1.7
Households without facilities of installed bath or shower	10,579	25.7	+ 6.0	4,308	16.4
Extent of affluence					
Families earning over $10,000 a year (non-farm)	2,714	7.4	− 0.4	2,151	8.8
Persons not in families earning over $6,000 a year (non-farm)	535	4.9	+ 1.1	396	5.4
Farms with gross income over $15,000 a year	17	1.1	− 3.9	—	—
Persons with university degree	1,893	1.8	− 1.0	1,439	2.2
Households with two or more television sets	1,020	2.5	− 1.7	837	3.2
Households with two or more cars	1,881	4.6	− 2.2	1,402	5.3

CHARACTERISTICS OF THE POPULATION

	Region		Sudbury
	% of the total population of the region	% points above or below Canadian average	% of the total population of the city
Mother tongue (1961 census)			
English	51.3	− 7.1	49.7
French	31.1	+ 3.0	30.7
German	1.9	− 1.2	2.1
Native Indian dialects	1.8	+ 0.9	0.1
Italian	3.8	+ 1.9	5.6
Dutch	0.3	− 0.6	0.3
Polish	1.2	+ 0.3	1.6
Ukrainian	2.5	+ 0.5	3.2
Other	6.1	+ 2.3	6.7
Total	100.0	—	100.0
Official language spoken (1961 census)			
English only	63.9	− 3.5	63.8
French only	6.2	−12.9	5.1
Both English and French	28.2	+16.0	29.1
Neither English nor French	1.7	+ 0.4	2.0
Total	100.0	—	100.0

AVERAGE INCOME (1961 CENSUS)

	Region		Sudbury	
	Dollars	% above or below Canadian average	Dollars	% above or below Canadian average
Income per family (non-farm)	5,870	+ 7.73	6,219	+14.13
Income per person not in family (non-farm)	2,511	+17.50	2,773	+29.76
Income per farm (net)	1,654	−49.19	—	—

MEANS OF LIVELIHOOD—DISTRIBUTION OF
LABOR FORCE BY INDUSTRY

Industry	Region			Sudbury	
	Persons 1961 census	% of the total	% points above or below Canadian average	Persons 1961 census	% of the total
Agriculture	1,638	2.8	− 7.1	134	0.3
Forestry	1,768	3.0	+ 1.3	134	0.3
Fishing and trapping	57	0.1	− 0.4	3	—
Mines, quarries, oil wells	16,350	28.0	+26.1	12,450	32.0
Manufacturing	7,402	12.6	− 9.1	4,998	12.9
Construction	3,258	5.6	− 1.1	2,317	6.0
Transportation, communications, and other utilities	5,221	8.9	− 0.4	2,488	6.4
Wholesale trade	1,449	2.5	− 2.0	1,185	3.1
Retail trade	5,944	10.2	− 0.6	4,391	11.3
Finance, insurance, and real estate	1,175	2.0	− 1.5	994	2.6
Community and business services	5,949	10.2	− 2.6	4,678	12.0
Personal services	3,997	6.8	—	2,451	6.3
Public administration and defence	2,672	4.6	− 2.9	1,657	4.3
Miscellaneous	1,597	2.7	+ 0.3	989	2.5
Total labor force	58,477	100.0	—	38,869	100.0

Northeastern Ontario — Sault

ECONOMIC CAPSULE

This region is rich in minerals, though mining does not play such a predominant role as in other parts of Northeastern Ontario. In the Michipicoten area, iron is obtained by underground and open pit mining. The annual output is about two million long tons of sinter, most of which is used in the steel mills at Sault Ste. Marie. Some of the world's richest deposits of uranium are found near Blind River and Elliot Lake. This area enjoyed a fantastic boom in the Fifties, but lately, because of the lack of demand, many mines have suspended operations. Elliot Lake, a model pioneering community planned in the wilderness as a symbol of progress, is now a sick town slowly dying away. The prospect of mines being reopened depends on foreign demand and this in turn hinges on the speed with which nuclear energy becomes a commercial source of power among the leading industrialized countries.

In sharp contrast to Elliot Lake, Sault Ste. Marie, the chief city in the region, is passing through a period of healthy growth. Situated on the St. Mary's River, which connects Lake Superior and Lake Huron, "the Soo" is an industrial "island" at the center of the world's busiest waterway. Its canals accommodate more waterborne freight each year than the combined tonnage of the Suez and Panama Canals. It is a "twin city", not uncommon on an international boundary, but for once the Canadian city is much larger than its American counterpart.

About 40% of the labor force at Sault Ste. Marie is engaged in manufacturing. The chief industries are iron and steel (Algoma Steel Corporation Limited), pulp and paper (Abitibi Power and Paper Company Limited), wood products (Weyerheuser Canada Limited) and steel tubing (Mannesman Tube Company Limited). Workers are highly skilled and very well paid. During the last few years, income tax statistics have consistently shown the city to rank first or second in Canada for average income per taxpayer.

NORTHEASTERN ONTARIO—SAULT

Area covered: 19,320 square miles. *County:* Algoma.

COMPOSITION OF THE MARKET

Place	County	Population 1961	% of the region
Sault Ste. Marie (urbanized area)	Algoma	58,460	52.47
Elliot Lake	Algoma	9,950	8.93
Blind River	Algoma	4,093	3.67
Jamestown (Wawa)	Algoma	4,040	3.63
Thessalon	Algoma	1,725	1.55
Hornepayne	Algoma	1,692	1.52
Spanish	Algoma	1,536	1.38
Total urban		81,496	73.15
Rural non-farm		24,620	22.10
Rural farm		5,292	4.75
Total population		111,408	100.00

IMPORTANCE OF THE MARKET (1964 ESTIMATES)

	Region		Sault Ste. Marie*	
	Number	% of Canada	Number	% of Canada
Population	131,700	0.69	62,000	0.32
Households	31,300	0.65	15,900	0.33
Disposable income ($ million)	249.8	0.79	209.5	0.66

* The territory covered is the old major urban area as defined by the 1961 census.

GROWTH OF THE MARKET

	Region		Sault Ste. Marie	
	Percentage growth 1961 to 1964	% points above or below Canadian average	Percentage growth 1961 to 1964	% points above or below Canadian average
Population	+18.21	+12.74	+ 6.06	+0.59
Disposable income	+27.51	+ 5.98	+24.85	+3.32

AVERAGE INCOME (1961 CENSUS)

	Region		Sault Ste. Marie	
	Dollars	% above or below Canadian average	Dollars	% above or below Canadian average
Income per family (non-farm)	6,020	+10.48	6,439	+18.17
Income per person not in family (non-farm)	2,770	+29.62	2,807	+31.35
Income per farm (net)	1,859	−42.89	—	—

LABOR FORCE BY INDUSTRY

Industry	Region			Sault Ste. Marie	
	Persons 1961 census	% of the total	% points above or below Canadian average	Persons 1961 census	% of the total
Agriculture	731	1.9	− 8.0	51	0.2
Forestry	1,148	3.0	+ 1.3	175	0.8
Fishing and trapping	60	0.1	− 0.4	8	—
Mines, quarries, oil wells	4,592	11.9	+10.0	75	0.4
Manufacturing	10,768	27.9	+ 6.2	8,545	40.1
Construction	2,528	6.5	− 0.2	1,620	7.6
Transportation, communications, and other utilities	3,828	9.9	+ 0.6	1,731	8.1
Wholesale trade	1,059	2.7	− 1.8	717	3.4
Retail trade	3,936	10.2	− 0.6	2,479	11.6
Finance, insurance, and real estate	726	1.9	− 1.6	530	2.5
Community and business services	3,701	9.6	− 3.2	2,399	11.3
Personal services	2,997	7.8	+ 1.0	1,509	7.1
Public administration and defence	1,515	3.9	− 3.6	964	4.5
Miscellaneous	1,026	2.7	+ 0.3	517	2.4
Total labor force	38,615	100.0	—	21,320	100.0

POVERTY AND AFFLUENCE (1961 CENSUS)

	Number	Region % of region's total	% points above or below Canadian average	Sault Ste. Marie Number	% of city's total
Extent of poverty					
Families earning below $3,000 a year (non-farm)	3,713	15.7	− 7.6	1,705	12.4
Persons not in families earning below $1,500 a year (non-farm)	2,992	37.3	−11.6	1,644	36.6
Farms with gross income of less than $2,500 a year	474	66.9	+20.8	—	—
Persons not in school with grade 4 or less education	8,548	12.7	− 0.7	4,080	11.3
Doubled-up households (more than one family per household)	959	3.6	− 0.1	583	4.0
Households living in dilapidated dwellings	2,008	7.5	+ 1.9	906	6.3
Households without facilities of running water	2,508	9.4	− 1.5	71	0.5
Households without facilities of installed bath or shower	4,841	18.1	− 1.6	806	5.6
Extent of affluence					
Families earning over $10,000 a year (non-farm)	2,083	8.7	+ 0.9	1,462	10.7
Persons not in families earning over $6,000 a year (non-farm)	627	7.8	+ 4.0	297	6.6
Farms with gross income over $15,000 a year	9	1.3	− 3.7	—	—
Persons with university degree	1,334	2.0	− 0.8	903	2.5
Households with two or more television sets	1,019	3.8	− 0.4	863	5.9
Households with two or more cars	2,196	8.2	+ 1.4	1,535	10.6

CHARACTERISTICS OF THE POPULATION

	Region		Sault Ste. Marie
	% of the total population of the region	% points above or below Canadian average	% of the total population of the city
Mother tongue (1961 census)			
English	69.2	+10.8	71.1
French	11.9	−16.2	5.8
German	2.5	− 0.6	1.9
Native Indian dialects	1.3	+ 0.4	—
Italian	6.8	+ 4.9	11.7
Dutch	0.4	− 0.5	0.4
Polish	1.2	+ 0.3	1.5
Ukrainian	1.5	− 0.5	1.8
Other	5.2	+ 1.4	5.8
Total	100.0	—	100.0
Official language spoken (1961 census)			
English only	83.0	+15.6	89.1
French only	2.3	−16.8	0.5
Both English and French	12.4	+ 0.2	7.4
Neither English nor French	2.3	+ 1.0	3.0
Total	100.0	—	100.0

Lakehead — Northwestern Ontario

ECONOMIC CAPSULE

Endowed with an abundance of minerals, timber, and water power, this huge and challenging territory, although rich in actual development, is richer still in potential. Economic activity ranges from trapping and fishing to modern, highly mechanized manufacturing.

It has been estimated that two-thirds of the population derives its livelihood, directly or indirectly, from the forests or the processing of forest products. Pulp and paper is the pillar of the economy. The following eight companies employ about 7,000 in their mills and another 6,000 in wood operations.

Abitibi Power and Paper Company Limited (mill in Fort William and another in Port Arthur)

Domtar Newsprint Limited (Red Rock)

Dryden Paper Company Limited (Dryden)

Great Lakes Paper Company Limited (Fort William)

Kimberly-Clark Pulp and Paper Company Limited (Terrace Bay)

Marathon Corporation of Canada (Marathon)

Ontario-Minnesota Pulp and Paper Company Limited (Kenora and Fort Frances)

Provincial Paper Limited (Port Arthur)

Numerous sawmills are also scattered throughout the southern portion of the region, especially in the Thunder Bay district. They produce in the neighbor-

LAKEHEAD—NORTHWESTERN ONTARIO

Area covered: 183,520 square miles. *Counties:* Kenora, Rainy River, Thunder Bay.

COMPOSITION OF THE MARKET

Place	County	Population 1961	% of the region
Fort William-Port Arthur (urbanized area)	Thunder Bay	93,251	43.07
Kenora (urbanized area)	Kenora	13,101	6.05
Fort Frances	Rainy River	9,481	4.38
Atikokan	Rainy River	6,674	3.08
Dryden	Kenora	5,728	2.64
Geraldton	Thunder Bay	3,375	1.56
Marathon	Thunder Bay	2,568	1.18
Sioux Lookout	Kenora	2,453	1.13
Schreiber	Thunder Bay	2,230	1.03
Nipigon	Thunder Bay	2,105	0.97
Red Lake	Kenora	2,051	0.95
Manitouwadge Lake	Thunder Bay	2,006	0.93
Terrace Bay	Thunder Bay	1,901	0.88
Balmertown-Cochenour	Kenora	1,421	0.66
Red Rock	Thunder Bay	1,316	0.61
Rainy River	Rainy River	1,168	0.54
Longlac	Thunder Bay	1,125	0.52
Beardmore	Thunder Bay	1,043	0.48
Total urban		152,997	70.66
Rural non-farm		55,336	25.56
Rural farm		8,190	3.78
Total population		216,523	100.00

hood of 125 million board feet of lumber each year. Lately, the industry has had to face mounting competition from such substitutes as metals and plastics.

As regards minerals, gold is mined in the Red Lake area, copper and zinc at Manitouwadge, and iron ore at Steep Rock. Prospecting has led to the discovery of numerous other minerals, like manganese, lithium, cobalt, asbestos, and nickel, which may one day be developed.

Northwestern Ontario is also a veritable paradise for the vacationist. Its scenic splendor, healthy climate, and abundant fish and wildlife lure thousands of tourists from Canada and the United States. The Ontario government has established more than 20 Provincial Parks, the largest being Quetico Provincial Park. It covers 1,750 square miles of woodland, lakes, and streams, representing one of the few remaining areas of great wilderness on the continent.

The main concentration of population is at the Lakehead. Fort William-Port Arthur account for 43% of the region's population. Transportation and trade are the major economic activities, the twin cities constituting the world's largest grain storage and shipping center. Situated at the head of the Great Lakes System, they serve as the transfer point between western and central Canada. In 1964, their port handled over 14 million tons of freight, making it the third busiest in Canada after Montréal and Vancouver. A huge new terminal has been opened since 1962, and many ocean vessels ("salties") now come here regularly to pick up grain and general cargo.

Although primary industries — flour milling and pulp and paper — still predominate, secondary manufacturing is assuming growing importance in the Lakehead cities. Production is quite diversified, including ships, pleasure craft, subway cars, prefab houses, aircraft parts, chemicals, petroleum products, pulp and paper machinery, and specialized goods demanded by prospectors, miners, loggers, and construction workers. Labor is skilled and well paid, and working-class families enjoy a standard of living not much different from those in southern urban centers.

LAKEHEAD—NORTHWESTERN ONTARIO

IMPORTANCE OF THE MARKET (1964 ESTIMATES)

	Region		Fort William-Port Arthur	
	Number	% of Canada	Number	% of Canada
Population	223,900	1.16	97,000	0.50
Households	55,600	1.16	26,200	0.55
Disposable income ($ million)	410.9	1.30	181.5	0.58

GROWTH OF THE MARKET

	Region		Fort William-Port Arthur	
	Percentage growth 1961 to 1964	% points above or below Canadian average	Percentage growth 1961 to 1964	% points above or below Canadian average
Population	+ 3.41	− 2.06	+ 4.02	− 1.45
Disposable income	+ 20.75	− 0.78	+ 14.95	− 6.58

AVERAGE INCOME (1961 CENSUS)

	Region		Fort William-Port Arthur	
	Dollars	% above or below Canadian average	Dollars	% above or below Canadian average
Income per family (non-farm)	5,321	− 2.35	5,565	+2.13
Income per person not in family (non-farm)	2,261	+ 5.80	2,174	+1.73
Income per farm (net)	1,881	−42.21	—	—

CHARACTERISTICS OF THE POPULATION

	Region		Fort William-Port Arthur
	% of the total population of the region	% points above or below Canadian average	% of the total population of the city
Mother tongue (1961 census)			
English	65.4	+ 7.0	67.8
French	4.4	−23.7	2.1
German	2.5	− 0.6	2.0
Native Indian dialects	6.2	+ 5.3	0.2
Italian	3.5	+ 1.6	5.7
Dutch	0.8	− 0.1	0.4
Polish	2.0	+ 1.1	2.6
Ukrainian	5.3	+ 3.3	7.0
Other	9.9	+ 6.1	12.2
Total	100.0	—	100.0

	Region		Fort William-Port Arthur
	% of the total population of the region	% points above or below Canadian average	% of the total population of the city
Official language spoken (1961 census)			
English only	89.6	+22.2	93.9
French only	0.6	−18.5	0.2
Both English and French	5.3	− 6.9	3.4
Neither English nor French	4.5	+ 3.2	2.5
Total	100.0	—	100.0

MEANS OF LIVELIHOOD—DISTRIBUTION OF

LABOR FORCE BY INDUSTRY

Industry	Region			Fort William-Port Arthur	
	Persons 1961 census	% of the total	% points above or below Canadian average	Persons 1961 census	% of the total
Agriculture	1,837	2.4	−7.5	88	0.3
Forestry	6,341	8.3	+6.6	1,279	3.7
Fishing and trapping	911	1.2	+0.7	30	0.1
Mines, quarries, oil wells	4,267	5.6	+3.7	221	0.6
Manufacturing	12,765	16.7	−5.0	6,027	17.3
Construction	5,115	6.7	—	2,980	8.6
Transportation, communications, and other utilities	12,403	16.2	+6.9	6,515	18.7
Wholesale trade	2,467	3.2	−1.3	1,792	5.1
Retail trade	7,934	10.4	−0.4	4,248	12.2
Finance, insurance, and real estate	1,400	1.8	−1.7	917	2.6
Community and business services	8,853	11.6	−1.2	5,264	15.1
Personal services	6,936	9.0	+2.2	2,633	7.6
Public administration and defence	3,291	4.3	−3.2	1,799	5.2
Miscellaneous	1,976	2.6	+0.2	994	2.9
Total labor force	76,496	100.0	—	34,787	100.0

POVERTY AND AFFLUENCE (1961 CENSUS)

	Number	Region % of region's total	% points above or below Canadian average	Fort William-Port Arthur Number	% of city's total
Extent of poverty					
Families earning below $3,000 a year (non-farm)	9,552	20.6	− 2.7	3,834	17.3
Persons not in families earning below $1,500 a year (non-farm)	7,973	48.0	− 0.9	4,158	50.3
Farms with gross income of less than $2,500 a year	1,208	64.7	+18.6	—	—
Persons not in school with grade 4 or less education	23,196	17.2	+ 3.8	7,451	12.5
Doubled-up households (more than one family per household)	1,726	3.2	− 0.5	991	4.1
Households living in dilapidated dwellings	3,961	7.4	+ 1.8	1,286	5.4
Households without facilities of running water	9,797	18.3	+ 7.4	376	1.6
Households without facilities of installed bath or shower	14,349	26.8	+ 7.1	1,572	6.6
Extent of affluence					
Families earning over $10,000 a year (non-farm)	2,898	6.2	− 1.6	1,605	7.2
Persons not in families earning over $6,000 a year (non-farm)	795	4.8	+ 1.0	378	4.6
Farms with gross income over $15,000 a year	23	1.3	− 3.7	—	—
Persons with university degree	2,274	1.7	− 1.1	1,209	2.0
Households with two or more television sets	1,258	2.3	− 1.9	1,133	4.7
Households with two or more cars	3,625	6.8	—	2,209	9.2

Chapter 17

PRAIRIE PROVINCES

Introduction

Because of the term "prairies," one often imagines the three mid-west provinces as a vast, level tract of treeless land, stretching mile after mile with little variety in scenery and topography. This conception is not strictly accurate, for less than 30% of the area consists of grassland. This, however, is the portion which is most thickly populated and provides the major source of wealth.

Agriculture

Wheat dominates the production pattern on the majority of the farms. The three Prairie Provinces are the "bread basket of Canada," producing over 90% of all wheat grown in the country. Number One Northern has become synonymous with the finest, protein-full bread-flour grain in world markets. The soils, with their high content of nitrates and phosphates, are extremely fertile, and generally the weather, too, in most areas, helps the farmer to get a good crop.

Technological improvements have been going on continuously since the first settlers started to plough. Research has developed new, richer, hardier, and more rust-resistant varieties of grain. Science has produced new chemicals for control of weeds, insects, and many plant diseases. Farm equipment manufacturers have brought out bigger and more efficient machinery. Farm operators have increased the size of their holdings in order to reap the full benefit of mechanization. As a result, the index of the physical volume of agricultural production has risen considerably since the prewar era (1935-1939 = 100). It averaged during the 1962-1964 period 144.6 for Manitoba, 178.9 for Saskatchewan, and 172.9 for Alberta.

The Prairie Provinces can go far toward feeding the hungry world. Yet very often the wheat piles up in elevators and fields for lack of overseas buyers with cash to pay. In a glut year, 900,000 bushels of wheat have been known to be on hand after the harvest, half of it carry-over. Lately, the big sales to Communist countries have eased the situation considerably, but this is only a temporary relief.

The long-term prospects are not too promising. Per capita wheat consumption is declining in Britain and Western Europe, as increased affluence permits more people to switch over to meat and vegetables. The underdeveloped countries can use a lot of Prairie wheat, but unfortunately the majority of them do not have the wherewithal to pay for their purchases in dollars. They depend for the most part on giveaway programs, which usually means relying on the United States. To make matters worse, wheat production is rising in many importing countries. In some cases this is due to more efficient farming methods, but generally it is the result of government policy to attain self-sufficiency even though it may be more economical to buy from outside.

Because of this uncertain international situation, it seems probable that the Prairie farmer will in future reduce his dependence on wheat and try to diversify his output. The growing domestic demand for meat will encourage cattle and hog raising. As a result one may expect considerable changes in the pattern of farming. Intensive rather than extensive cultivation will become more prominent. The emphasis will turn toward increasing the carrying capacity of grazing pastures, producing more fodder crops, and modifying the practice of summer fallowing to make available more land for coarse grains and hay. Though wheat will continue to be the leading cash crop, the acreage will be reduced, and the farmer will be less at the mercy of uncontrollable forces far outside his own country. The mainstay of the agricultural economy, particularly in the black soil zone, will be grain-fed animals, with a tendency for specialization in hog production.

Mining

Mines are slowly elbowing farms off the center of the stage. In 1951, agriculture accounted for 58% of the net value of commodity production and mining 9%. In 1961, agriculture's share was only 22%, while mining had gone up to 21%. Oil and natural gas have been mainly responsible for this dramatic change. A never-to-be-forgotten event occurred at Leduc near Edmonton in February 1947, when Atlantic Number Three literally went wild. With a terrible rumbling and fearful bubbling the great well suddenly erupted, tossing its stream of oil and mud like a gigantic geyser high into the air. Since then thousands of new wells have been developed, and several millions of dollars have been expended to build pipelines for delivering surplus oil and natural gas to British Columbia, Eastern Canada, and even to the United States. More discoveries are continuously being made, but even with current availabilities the industry can stay healthy for many years to come. As of December 31, 1964, the proved remaining reserves were conservatively estimated at:

	Crude oil (000 barrels)	Natural gas (million cu. ft.)
Alberta	5,279,146	35,198,661
Saskatchewan	602,352	1,040,669
Manitoba	33,637	3,473

These figures do not include the fantastically vast potential reservoir of oil locked in the bituminous sand deposits along the Athabaska river. Estimates place the recoverable reserves at 300 billion barrels, as much as the world's entire known conventional oil reserves.

The cretaceous rocks of the Prairie Provinces also have one of the largest deposits of coal on earth — about 72 billion tons, enough to supply the requirements of the whole country for more than a thousand years. The coal of Alberta is largely bituminous, though there is some anthracite in the foothill areas. In Saskatchewan the coal is almost all lignite. Because of the fall in demand, production declined by almost 33% within a decade, from 6,976,000 tons in 1954 to 4,683,000 tons in 1964. However, the situation is gradually improving. New markets have been found in Japan, and more coal is needed by the thermal power plants in the Prairies.

The metallic minerals are obtained from the sector covered by the Canadian Shield. Flin Flon, on the Manitoba-Saskatchewan border, is a major producer not only of copper, zinc, gold, and silver, but also of such relatively unknown metals as cadmium, selenium, and tellurium. Thompson, in northern Manitoba, is second to Sudbury in the free world's production of nickel. There are vast deposits of uranium within a 30-mile radius of Beaverlodge Lake.

Among non-metallics, potash is by far the most important. Saskatchewan has the biggest and purest deposits on the American continent, reputed to be over 6.5 billion tons — enough to enrich all the world's arable land for the next 500 years. According to the Department of Mines and Technical Surveys, Ottawa, the annual production capacity is expected to increase from 1.6 million tons in 1965 to 5.5 million tons in 1970. By that year, Canada would be by far the top producer, accounting for 27% of the world's production of 20.3 million tons. In view of the population pressures on agricultural lands in underdeveloped countries, one can safely predict a high demand for chemical fertilizers for many years to come. Thus potash will be to Saskatchewan what oil has been to Alberta — a unique opportunity to diversify an economy that has been tied to the highs and lows of international wheat demand.

Forestry

The forest reserves of the Prairie Provinces are quite extensive, but lack of large local markets and high transportation costs hamper regular tree farming. The annual output is about 5% of the Canadian total. Enough timber is cut to meet the needs of the cities and farms for sawn lumber, but no significant forest industry exists. Nevertheless, the potential cannot be discounted. Recent surveys have shown that the forests can supply sufficient wood on a sustained yield basis to support several pulp and paper mills.

Manufacturing

The Prairie Provinces are not highly industrialized. Manufacturing is based largely on processing the raw material resources of the area. Food items, petroleum products, and refining of local minerals account for a large proportion of the value of manufactured goods. Most plants are small and serve only the Prairies or a provincial market. There is an urgent need for greater and more varied industrialization to ensure full employment of the labor force and to keep the economy stable during the bad farm years. As a result, the governments in each of the provinces are stepping up considerably their aid-to-industry programs.

Marketing characteristics

The Prairie Provinces have had hardly more than half a century to acquire a distinct personality, but already they are easily differentiated from the rest of the country. If the eastern Canadians seem sometimes to be starchy, hidebound, and conservative, the prairie inhabitants appear just the opposite. Here is a society where "Western hospitality" really means something. A deep spirit of "help-your-neighbor" and a fundamental sincerity that goes with it are the characteristics prevalent in full measure across the Prairies.

The people are also well informed about the world at large, in notable contrast to their counterparts in the American Midwest. The U.S. farmers can sell most of their produce at home, so they do not have to worry about what is going on overseas. In Canada, about 80% of the wheat crop has to be sold abroad, and the man who grows it cannot help being concerned about what the rest of the world is doing. Hence, there is more internationalism here than anywhere else in the country, and less rancorous dispute about Anglicism on the one hand and Americanism on the other.

During the last two decades, the Prairies have passed through many changes that have altered their character considerably. Developments in mining and secondary industries have enabled the economy to have more substantial props to rely upon. Concomitantly, improvements in agricultural technology, in marketing arrangements, and in credit facilities have brought increased stability to farm incomes. This, of course, does not mean that the Mid-West has become as stable a market as the East. Weather is still a big factor, and a one- or two-year drought can reverberate through the economy and cause retail sales to fall off somewhat. But the boom or bust atmosphere is certainly not as sharp as it used to be.

As a result of this diversification, population is drifting away from farms and small rural communities to large urban centers. Winnipeg has more than half of the people of Manitoba, while Calgary and Edmonton together make up about 48% of Alberta's population. Even in predominantly rural Saskatchewan, the two top cities account for nearly a quarter of the province's population.

The rural areas do not differ sharply from the urban. The farmers are not self-sustaining. Many of them buy food, clothes, and other necessities from near-by towns. Thanks to the automobile and an excellent network of highways, a farm family thinks nothing of driving 30 miles or more to town for normal purchases. Local country store patronage and mail-order buying are changing toward city shopping. Thus, even though a portion of the population is still scattered across the Prairies, retail sales are becoming more and more concentrated in a score of strategically located urban centers. This means a considerable saving in distribution costs for the manufacturer.

PRAIRIE PROVINCES

COMPOSITION OF THE MARKET

Place	Provincial region	Population 1961	% of Prairie Provinces
Winnipeg	Metro Winnipeg and its Environs	473,498	14.89
Edmonton (metro)	Edmonton—Parklands	337,568	10.62
Calgary (metro)	Calgary—South Central Alberta	279,062	8.78
Regina	Regina—Southeastern Plains	112,141	3.53
Saskatoon	Saskatoon—Central Plains	95,526	3.00
Lethbridge	Lethbridge Prairie	35,454	1.12
Moose Jaw	Saskatchewan Palliser	33,206	1.04
Brandon	Southwestern Manitoba Prairie	28,166	0.89
Medicine Hat	Medicine Hat—Palliser	24,484	0.77
Prince Albert	Central Saskatchewan Parklands	24,168	0.76
Red Deer	Red Deer Environs	19,612	0.62
Portage la Prairie	Metro Winnipeg and its Environs	12,388	0.40
Swift Current	Saskatchewan Palliser	12,186	0.38
North Battleford	Central Saskatchewan Parklands	11,230	0.35
Flin Flon	Northern Manitoba and Northern Saskatchewan	11,104	0.35
Yorkton	Saskatchewan—Southeastern Parklands	9,995	0.31
Weyburn	Regina—Southeastern Plains	9,101	0.29
Selkirk	Metro Winnipeg and its Environs	8,576	0.27
Grande Prairie	Northwestern Alberta—Peace River	8,352	0.26
Estevan	Regina—Southeastern Plains	7,728	0.24
Dauphin	West—Central Manitoba Parklands	7,374	0.23
Camrose	East—Central Alberta Prairie	6,939	0.22
Wetaskiwin	Edmonton — Parklands	5,300	0.17
Melville	Saskatchewan—Southeastern Parklands	5,191	0.16
Total of towns over 5,000		1,578,349	49.65
134 towns between 1,000 and 5,000		270,834	8.52
Total urban		1,849,183	58.17
Rural non-farm		567,661	17.86
Rural farm		761,967	23.97
Total population		3,178,811	100.00

The rising level of education is also obliterating the sharp disparity between urban and rural life. Today's prairie farmer is no rube, bound by conventions and unwilling to try something new. He is more likely to be a graduate of an agricultural college, with a wide range of interests, and well informed on many things besides farming. He is no longer impressed by the traditional rural values of frugality and austere existence. He wants to attain the same high standard of living as the urban resident, and his rising income makes him a good prospect for many luxury items that were once considered saleable only to city dwellers.

The changes in rural life are also noticeable in the different concepts about the duties of a farmer's wife. Not too long ago her efficiency was measured by the number of jobs she could do by hand—sewing clothes, baking bread, churning butter. Today she gains more status by having her kitchen filled with modern appliances and buying the basic necessities from outside. The old days when the condition of the barn was more important than the comforts at home are fast vanishing.

PRAIRIE PROVINCES

IMPORTANCE OF THE MARKET (1964 ESTIMATES)

	Number	% of Canada
Population	3,333,000	17.32
Households	875,000	18.21
Disposable income ($ million)	5,376.0	17.05

GROWTH OF THE MARKET

	Percentage growth 1961 to 1964	% points above or below Canadian average
Population	+ 4.85	−0.62
Disposable income	+25.72	+4.19

AVERAGE INCOME (1961 CENSUS)

	Dollars	% above or below Canadian average
Income per family (non-farm)	5,290	− 2.92
Income per person not in family (non-farm)	2,108	− 1.36
Income per farm (net)	3,999	+22.86

POVERTY AND AFFLUENCE (1961 CENSUS)

	Number	% of provinces' total	% points above or below Canadian average
Extent of poverty			
Families earning below $3,000 a year (non-farm)	136,114	24.4	+ 1.1
Persons not in families earning below $1,500 a year (non-farm)	110,027	48.1	− 0.8
Farms with gross income of less than $2,500 a year	77,407	36.8	− 9.3
Persons not in school with grade 4 or less education	282,578	14.0	+ 0.6
Doubled-up households (more than one family per household)	19,558	2.3	− 1.4
Households living in dilapidated dwellings	67,738	8.1	+ 2.5
Households without facilities of running water	240,591	28.8	+17.9
Households without facilities of installed bath or shower	279,474	33.5	+13.8
Extent of affluence			
Families earning over $10,000 a year (non-farm)	39,639	7.1	− 0.7
Persons not in families earning over $6,000 a year (non-farm)	8,097	3.5	− 0.3
Farms with gross income over $15,000 a year	9,368	4.5	− 0.5
Persons with university degree	49,710	2.5	− 0.3
Households with two or more television sets	21,727	2.6	− 1.6
Households with two or more cars	55,287	6.6	− 0.2

CHARACTERISTICS OF THE POPULATION

	% of the total population of the provinces	% points above or below Canadian average
Official language spoken (1961 census)		
English only	92.7	+25.3
French only	0.5	−18.6
Both English and French	5.3	− 6.9
Neither English nor French	1.5	+ 0.2
Total	100.0	—

CHARACTERISTICS OF THE POPULATION (continued)

	% of the total population of the provinces	% points above or below Canadian average
Mother tongue (1961 census)		
English	68.7	+10.3
French	4.4	−23.7
German	8.5	+ 5.4
Native Indian dialects	2.6	+ 1.7
Italian	0.5	− 1.4
Dutch	1.5	+ 0.6
Polish	1.5	+ 0.6
Ukrainian	7.4	+ 5.4
Other	4.9	+ 1.1
Total	100.0	—

MEANS OF LIVELIHOOD—DISTRIBUTION OF LABOR FORCE BY INDUSTRY

Industry	Persons 1961 census	% of the total	% points above or below Canadian average
Agriculture	282,111	24.4	+14.5
Forestry	5,244	0.5	− 1.2
Fishing and trapping	3,259	0.3	− 0.2
Mines, quarries, oil wells	26,977	2.3	+ 0.4
Manufacturing	104,107	9.0	−12.7
Construction	75,598	6.5	− 0.2
Transportation, communications, and other utilities.	117,486	10.1	+ 0.8
Wholesale trade	61,948	5.4	+ 0.9
Retail trade	121,097	10.5	− 0.3
Finance, insurance, and real estate	34,037	2.9	− 0.6
Community and business services	145,081	12.5	− 0.3
Personal services	71,147	6.1	− 0.7
Public administration and defence	83,409	7.2	− 0.3
Miscellaneous	26,241	2.3	− 0.1
Total labor force	1,157,742	100.0	—

STANDARD OF LIVING BASED ON OWNERSHIP OF
APPLIANCES AND EQUIPMENT, 1965

	Number of households	% of total households in Prairie Provinces	% points above or below Canadian average
Cooking equipment			
Electric stoves	544,000	62.5	− 6.5
Wood or coal cookstoves or ranges	112,000	12.9	+ 3.7
Piped gas stoves	155,000	17.8	+ 3.7
Refrigeration			
Electric refrigerators	808,000	92.8	− 3.0
Home freezers	376,000	43.2	+20.6
Electric washing machines			
Automatic	170,000	19.5	− 3.6
Other	589,000	67.6	+ 4.4
Clothes dryers			
Electric	229,000	26.3	+ 1.1
Gas	43,000	4.9	+ 2.7
Sewing machines			
Electric	438,000	50.3	− 2.1
Non-electric	220,000	25.3	+ 7.1
Phonographs and record players			
Cabinet model	286,000	32.8	− 0.1
Table model	26,000	3.0	− 2.2
Portable model	183,000	21.0	—
Telephones			
One	645,000	74.1	− 2.1
Two or more	85,000	9.8	− 3.4
Television sets			
One	688,000	79.0	− 2.8
Two or more	63,000	7.2	− 3.7
Automobiles			
One	560,000	64.3	+ 1.8
Two or more	117,000	13.4	+ 1.0
Other appliances			
Automatic dishwashers	20,000	2.3	− 0.4
Vacuum cleaners	669,000	76.8	+ 1.9
Window-type air conditioners	10,000	1.1	− 1.1
FM radio receivers	130,000	14.9	− 8.0

(Source: DBS, *Household Facilities and Equipment, May 1965*. Catalogue no. 64-202.)

MANITOBA

Metro Winnipeg and its Environs — 1, 2, 5, 6, 9, 12, 19, 20

Southwestern Manitoba — Prairie — 3, 4, 7, 8, 10, 11, 13

West-Central Manitoba — Parklands — 14, 15, 17, 18

Northern Manitoba — 16

(Numbers refer to Census Divisions)

Thompson

MANITOBA

16

Flin Flon

The Pas

Swan River

15

18

14

1 Dauphin

12

13 11 Neepawa

Minnedosa 10

St. James 5 Selkirk

Virden Winnipeg ⊗ 19

8 7 St. Boniface

Brandon Portage la Prairie Steinbach

Winkler

4 3 Morden 2

Altona

20

1

● Population 2,000 and over
(1961 Census)

Metro Winnipeg and Its Environs

Area covered: 24,181 square miles. *Census Divisions:* 1, 2, 5, 6, 9, 12, 19, and 20.

COMPOSITION OF THE MARKET

Place	Census Division	Population 1961	% of the region
Winnipeg	20	473,498	71.35
Portage la Prairie	6	12,388	1.87
Selkirk	5	8,576	1.29
Steinbach	1	3,739	0.56
Morden	2	2,793	0.42
Winkler	2	2,529	0.38
Altona	2	2,026	0.30
Carman	2	1,930	0.29
Gimli	12	1,841	0.28
Beauséjour	5	1,770	0.27
Stonewall	9	1,420	0.21
Morris	2	1,370	0.21
Pine Falls	19	1,244	0.19
Total urban	—	515,124	77.62
Rural non-farm	—	65,428	9.86
Rural farm	—	83,046	12.52
Total population		663,598	100.00

ECONOMIC CAPSULE

It is customary to divide this region into four parts: Winnipeg Metro (Census Division 20), Southeastern Manitoba (Census Divisions 1, 5 and 19), Manitoba Interlake (Census Divisions 9 and 12), and South-Central Manitoba Prairie (Census Divisions 2 and 6). Outside Metro Winnipeg, farming provides the chief means of livelihood, though in northern parts the forest-based industries play a significant role. (There is a large pulp and paper mill at Pine Falls.) The type of agriculture varies from one sub-region to another. Dairying is fairly important in Southeastern Manitoba, raising of beef cattle in Manitoba Interlake, and growing of wheat and other cereal crops in South-Central Manitoba Prairie.

Winnipeg is the nerve center of Manitoba, having more than half the population of the province. It is the Gateway City, a point where all routes through or around the Canadian Shield meet and then fan out across the prairies. No one can travel from east to west in Canada without passing through it.

The city is very cosmopolitan with various ethnic groups — Ukrainian, German, Italian, Polish, Hungarian, and Jewish — all of them with their own organizations, parochial schools, grocery stores, butcher shops, doctors, and law-

POVERTY AND AFFLUENCE (1961 CENSUS)

	Region			Winnipeg	
	Number	% of region's total	% points above or below Canadian average	Number	% of city's total
Extent of poverty					
Families earning below $3,000 a year (non-farm)	27,388	19.8	−3.5	18,468	16.1
Persons not in families earning below $1,500 a year (non-farm)	26,550	46.7	−2.2	21,075	43.4
Farms with gross income of less than $2,500 a year	10,155	51.8	+5.7	—	—
Persons not in school with grade 4 or less education	56,356	9.7	−3.7	30,830	9.7
Doubled-up households (more than one family per household)	6,102	3.5	−0.2	5,243	4.1
Households living in dilapidated dwellings	11,329	6.5	+0.9	6,421	5.0
Households without facilities of running water	26,741	15.4	+4.5	2,551	2.0
Households without facilities of installed bath or shower	33,944	19.6	−0.1	5,580	4.3
Extent of affluence					
Families earning over $10,000 a year (non-farm)	10,533	7.6	−0.2	9,814	8.5
Persons not in families earning over $6,000 a year (non-farm)	1,691	3.0	−0.8	1,563	3.2
Farms with gross income over $15,000 a year	747	3.9	−1.1	—	—
Persons with university degree	12,555	2.9	+0.1	11,483	3.6
Households with two or more television sets	8,429	4.9	+0.7	8,149	6.3
Households with two or more cars	11,735	6.8	—	9,667	7.5

yers. Across the Red River is St. Boniface, a very strong outpost of French Canadians. All the different nationalities have played a prominent part in enriching the life of the city by their cultural contribution. Good examples are the Winnipeg Symphony Orchestra, the Royal Winnipeg Ballet, and the Winnipeg Musical Festival.

Commerce and communications have made Winnipeg grow to its present size. The city is the nucleus of wholesale trade, its merchants selling their wares to a wide market throughout the province and even beyond. The once mighty Hudson's Bay Company still has its headquarters here. Of late, Winnipeg has become a manufacturing center as well. Its industries include slaughtering and meat packing, petroleum refining, metal fabricating, flour and feed milling, printing and publishing, and the manufacture of railroad rolling stock. There are also plants making dairy products, textiles, clothing, furniture, structural steel, and paper bags and boxes. Manufacturing, however, is on a small scale intended to serve the local or provincial rather than a national market. Almost 70% of the factories have fewer than 25 employees, while just over 7% have more than 100.

Winnipeg's growth in recent years has been fairly slow. Between 1961 and 1965, the population increased by only 2.9% compared to Canada's average of 7.3%. This is mainly due to a high rate of emigration. A mean temperature chart tells why. The average of January is 1 °F. Even at Whitehorse in the Yukon Territory it is 5 °F. It is not unusual in winter to have days at a stretch with the mercury dipping to 30 or 40 degrees below zero. Also, Winnipeg's dominant role as a wholesale center for the Prairies is declining. Many companies are dealing directly with the retailer instead of through wholesalers, and certain jobbers are decentralizing by setting up branch offices all over the west. In order to regain its past eminence, Winnipeg will have to switch its emphasis from commerce to manufacturing, and establish some major industrial enterprise which can serve as a nucleus around which small satellite plants may grow.

METRO WINNIPEG AND ITS ENVIRONS

IMPORTANCE OF THE MARKET (1964 ESTIMATES)

	Region		Winnipeg	
	Number	% of Canada	Number	% of Canada
Population	699,400	3.64	487,000	2.53
Households	182,500	3.80	135,300	2.82
Disposable income ($ million)	1,148.5	3.64	901.9	2.86

GROWTH OF THE MARKET

	Region		Winnipeg	
	Percentage growth 1961 to 1964	% points above or below Canadian average	Percentage growth 1961 to 1964	% points above or below Canadian average
Population	+ 5.40	−0.07	+ 2.31	−3.16
Disposable income	+19.66	−1.87	+17.96	−3.57

AVERAGE INCOME (1961 CENSUS)

	Region		Winnipeg	
	Dollars	% above or below Canadian average	Dollars	% above or below Canadian average
Income per family (non-farm)	5,569	+2.20	5,874	+7.80
Income per person not in family (non-farm)	2,068	−3.23	2,165	+1.31
Income per farm (net)	3,036	−6.73	—	—

LABOR FORCE BY INDUSTRY

Industry	Region			Winnipeg	
	Persons 1961 census	% of the total	% points above or below Canadian average	Persons 1961 census	% of the total
Agriculture	26,868	10.5	+0.6	1,553	0.8
Forestry	687	0.3	−1.4	87	—
Fishing and trapping	359	0.1	−0.4	40	—
Mines, quarries, oil wells	983	0.4	−1.5	414	0.2
Manufacturing	43,362	17.0	−4.7	38,537	19.8
Construction	16,423	6.4	−0.3	12,629	6.5
Transportation, communications, and other utilities	31,461	12.4	+3.1	26,812	13.8
Wholesale trade	17,771	7.0	+2.5	16,055	8.3
Retail trade	29,795	11.7	+0.9	25,229	13.0
Finance, insurance, and real estate	10,973	4.3	+0.8	10,252	5.3
Community and business services	33,399	13.1	+0.3	27,820	14.3
Personal services	16,895	6.6	−0.2	14,356	7.4
Public administration and defence	20,054	7.9	+0.4	16,156	8.3
Miscellaneous	5,804	2.3	−0.1	4,380	2.3
Total labor force	254,834	100.0	—	194,320	100.0

	Region		Winnipeg
	% of the total population of the region	% points above or below Canadian average	% of the total population of the city
Mother tongue (1961 census)			
English	61.6	+ 3.2	67.9
French	7.4	− 20.7	5.9
German	11.3	+ 8.2	7.5
Native Indian dialects	0.9	—	0.1
Italian	0.6	− 1.3	0.8
Dutch	1.7	+ 0.8	1.3
Polish	2.6	+ 1.7	2.6
Ukrainian	8.8	+ 6.8	8.3
Other	5.1	+ 1.3	5.6
Total	100.0	—	100.0
Official language spoken (1961 census)			
English only	89.0	+21.6	90.9
French only	1.0	−18.1	0.6
Both English and French	8.3	− 3.9	7.4
Neither English nor French	1.7	+ 0.4	1.1
Total	100.0	—	100.0

Southwestern Manitoba Prairie

ECONOMIC CAPSULE

The region is primarily agricultural, specializing in the cultivation of wheat and other cereals. Farms are quite large, averaging 534 acres, and highly mechanized. Ninety-four per cent have tractors and 65% grain combines.

Virtually all the known provincial petroleum resources are found near Virden. Production in 1964 amounted to 4.4 million barrels worth $10.6 million. This represented 6% of Manitoba's total value of mineral output.

Brandon, the largest city after Winnipeg, is fairly industrialized with flour milling, meat packing, oil refining, tanning, and electrical equipment manufacturing. Brandon College and a Dominion Experimental Farm Station make it a regional center for education and research.

SOUTHWESTERN MANITOBA PRAIRIE

Area covered: 16,071 square miles. *Census divisions:* 3, 4, 7, 8, 10, 11, 13.

COMPOSITION OF THE MARKET

Place	Census Division	Population 1961	% of the region
Brandon	7	28,166	18.41
Neepawa	10	3,197	2.09
Virden	8	2,708	1.77
Minnedosa	10	2,211	1.45
Souris	8	1,841	1.20
Killarney	3	1,729	1.13
Rivers	8	1,574	1.03
Boissevain	4	1,303	0.85
Russell	13	1,263	0.83
Carberry	7	1,113	0.73
Melita	4	1,038	0.68
Total urban	—	46,143	30.17
Rural non-farm	—	46,264	30.24
Rural farm	—	60,566	39.59
Total population		152,973	100.00

IMPORTANCE OF THE MARKET (1964 ESTIMATES)

	Number	% of Canada
Population	150,400	0.78
Households	40,400	0.84
Disposable income ($ million)	240.9	0.76

GROWTH OF THE MARKET

	Percentage change 1961 to 1964	% points above or below Canadian average
Population	− 1.68	− 7.15
Disposable income	+36.10	+14.57

POVERTY AND AFFLUENCE (1961 CENSUS)

	Number	% of region's total	% points above or below Canadian average
Extent of poverty			
Families earning below $3,000 a year (non-farm)	7,924	36.4	+13.1
Persons not in families earning below $1,500 a year (non-farm)	5,506	59.9	+11.0
Farms with gross income of less than $2,500 a year	4,559	28.3	− 17.8
Persons not in school with grade 4 or less education	12,975	13.1	− 0.3
Doubled-up households (more than one family per household)	710	1.7	− 2.0
Households living in dilapidated dwellings	3,600	8.7	+ 3.1
Households without facilities of running water	17,746	43.1	+32.2
Households without facilities of installed bath or shower	20,578	50.0	+30.3
Extent of affluence			
Families earning over $10,000 a year (non-farm)	725	3.4	− 4.4
Persons not in families earning over $6,000 a year (non-farm)	214	2.3	− 1.5
Farms with gross income over $15,000 a year	448	2.8	− 2.2
Persons with university degree	1,326	1.3	− 1.5
Households with two or more television sets	481	1.2	− 3.0
Households with two or more cars	2,099	5.1	− 1.7

CHARACTERISTICS OF THE POPULATION

	% of the total population of the region	% points above or below Canadian average
Mother tongue (1961 census)		
English	79.1	+20.7
French	4.3	−23.8
German	3.4	+ 0.3
Native Indian dialects	1.7	+ 0.8
Italian	0.1	− 1.8
Dutch	1.2	+ 0.3
Polish	1.3	+ 0.4
Ukrainian	6.3	+ 4.3
Other	2.6	− 1.2
Total	100.0	—

CHARACTERISTICS OF THE POPULATION (continued)

	% of the total population of the region	% points above or below Canadian average
Official language spoken (1961 census)		
English only	93.7	+26.3
French only	0.6	−18.5
Both English and French	4.9	− 7.3
Neither English nor French	0.8	− 0.5
Total	100.0	—

AVERAGE INCOME (1961 CENSUS)

	Dollars	% above or below Canadian average
Income per family (non-farm)	4,161	−23.64
Income per person not in family (non-farm)	1,716	−19.70
Income per farm (net)	3,933	+20.83

LABOR FORCE BY INDUSTRY

Industry	Persons 1961 census	% of the total	% points above or below Canadian average
Agriculture	22,442	41.8	+31.9
Forestry	35	0.1	− 1.6
Fishing and trapping	5	—	− 0.5
Mines, quarries, oil wells	273	0.5	− 1.4
Manufacturing	2,189	4.1	−17.6
Construction	2,332	4.3	− 2.4
Transportation, communications, and other utilities	5,073	9.4	+ 0.1
Wholesale trade	1,717	3.2	− 1.3
Retail trade	4,836	9.0	− 1.8
Finance, insurance, and real estate	932	1.7	− 1.8
Community and business services	5,747	10.7	− 2.1
Personal services	3,014	5.6	− 1.2
Public administration and defence	4,135	7.7	+ 0.2
Miscellaneous	1,004	1.9	− 0.5
Total labor force	53,734	100.0	—

West-Central Manitoba Parklands

ECONOMIC CAPSULE

This Park Belt forms a transition between the plains and the forest. Over half the population is engaged in agriculture, though only 5% of the total area can be used as farmland. 51% of the commercial farms specialize in field crops, and 22% raise beef cattle, while the rest practise mixed farming. Manufacturing is negligible. Dauphin is the chief retail and distributing center for the surrounding farm settlements.

WEST-CENTRAL MANITOBA PARKLANDS

Area covered: 9,625 square miles. *Census divisions:* 14, 15, 17, and 18.

COMPOSITION OF THE MARKET

Place	Census Division	Population 1961	% of the region
Dauphin	17	7,374	12.64
Swan River	15	3,163	5.42
Roblin	14	1,368	2.35
Grandview	17	1,057	1.81
Total urban	—	12,962	22.22
Rural non-farm	—	17,928	30.73
Rural farm	—	27,444	47.05
Total population		58,334	100.00

IMPORTANCE OF THE MARKET (1964 ESTIMATES)

	Number	% of Canada
Population	56,500	0.29
Households	14,700	0.30
Disposable income ($ million)	69.1	0.22

GROWTH OF THE MARKET

	Percentage change 1961 to 1964	% points above or below Canadian average
Population	− 3.14	−8.61
Disposable income	+26.33	+4.80

POVERTY AND AFFLUENCE (1961 CENSUS)

	Number	% of region's total	% points above or below Canadian average
Extent of poverty			
Families earning below $3,000 a year (non-farm)	3,582	50.6	+27.3
Persons not in families earning below $1,500 a year (non-farm)	2,020	68.8	+19.9
Farms with gross income of less than $2,500 a year	4,227	56.5	+10.4
Persons not in school with grade 4 or less education.	9,569	26.2	+12.8
Doubled-up households (more than one family per household)	327	2.1	− 1.6
Households living in dilapidated dwellings	2,234	14.6	+ 9.0
Households without facilities of running water	10,667	69.5	+58.6
Households without facilities of installed bath or shower	11,089	72.3	+52.6
Extent of affluence			
Families earning over $10,000 a year (non-farm)	207	2.9	− 4.9
Persons not in families earning over $6,000 a year (non-farm)	19	0.7	− 3.1
Farms with gross income over $15,000 a year	55	0.8	− 4.2
Persons with university degree	278	0.8	− 2.0
Households with two or more television sets	25	0.2	− 4.0
Households with two or more cars	442	2.9	− 3.9

CHARACTERISTICS OF THE POPULATION

	% of the total population of the region	% points above or below Canadian average
Mother tongue (1961 census)		
English	53.3	− 5.1
French	5.4	−22.7
German	4.6	+ 1.5
Native Indian dialects	4.7	+ 3.8
Italian	—	− 1.9
Dutch	0.3	− 0.6
Polish	1.9	+ 1.0
Ukrainian	26.5	+24.5
Other	3.3	− 0.5
Total	100.0	—

CHARACTERISTICS OF THE POPULATION (continued)

	% of the total population of the region	% points above or below Canadian average
Official language spoken (1961 census)		
English only	91.2	+23.8
French only	0.7	−18.4
Both English and French	5.9	− 6.3
Neither English nor French	2.2	+ 0.9
Total	100.0	—

AVERAGE INCOME (1961 CENSUS)

	Dollars	% above or below Canadian average
Income per family (non-farm)	3,541	−35.02
Income per person not in family (non-farm)	1,400	−34.49
Income per farm (net)	2,230	−31.49

LABOR FORCE BY INDUSTRY

Industry	Persons 1961 census	% of the total	% points above or below Canadian average
Agriculture	9,841	51.4	+41.5
Forestry	275	1.4	− 0.3
Fishing and trapping	105	0.5	—
Mines, quarries, oil wells	85	0.4	− 1.5
Manufacturing	539	2.8	−18.9
Construction	970	5.1	− 1.6
Transportation, communications, and other utilities	1,565	8.2	− 1.1
Wholesale trade	495	2.6	− 1.9
Retail trade	1,540	8.1	− 2.7
Finance, insurance, and real estate	188	1.0	− 2.5
Community and business services	1,580	8.3	− 4.5
Personal services	898	4.7	− 2.1
Public administration and defence	565	3.0	− 4.5
Miscellaneous	486	2.5	+ 0.1
Total labor force	19,132	100.0	—

Northern Manitoba

Area covered: 161,898 square miles. *Census division:* 16.

COMPOSITION OF THE MARKET

Place	Census Division	Population 1961	% of the region
Flin Flon	16	10,546*	22.54
The Pas	16	4,671	9.99
Thompson	16	3,418	7.31
Churchill	16	1,878	4.01
Lynn Lake	16	1,851	3.96
Total urban	—	22,364	47.81
Rural non-farm	—	24,001	51.30
Rural farm	—	416	0.89
Total population		46,781	100.00

* Total population of Flin Flon is 11,104, of which 10,546 is in Manitoba and 558 is in Census Division 18 of Saskatchewan.

ECONOMIC CAPSULE

This area is the principal source of Manitoba's metallic mineral wealth. Most of the substantial growth in recent years has been due to expansion in the mining of nickel. One of the largest known nickel deposits in the world is located at Thompson, 400 miles north of Winnipeg, where the International Nickel Company of Canada Limited invested about $200 million in establishing a nickel mine, smelter, refining plant, and town site. Operations commenced in 1961 and by 1964 production had reached 127 million pounds, valued at $107 million.

Flin Flon is the intriguing name of a comparatively old mining community, where copper and zinc are extracted and smelted by the Hudson Bay Mining and Smelting Company Limited. About 150 miles north of Flin Flon, at Lynn Lake, Sherritt Gordon Mines Limited operates copper and nickel mines. The ore is concentrated and then shipped out of the province for refining.

Far up in the north is the Hudson Bay port of Churchill. It has, unfortunately, not lived up to its expectations of moving grain out in large quantities to Europe. It is true that the distance from Saskatoon to Liverpool via Churchill is only 4,073 miles compared to 5,224 miles through the Great Lakes. But the port's short season — usually late July to mid-October — plus a failure to get a real saving on transportation costs have hampered the development of the Hudson Bay route. So far the history of Churchill has been one of heavy government subsidies and dreamy visions.

The Pas is the center of wholesale and retail trade for a greater part of the region. It is the most important transportation node in northern Manitoba, well served by railway, highway, and airplane. Its major industry is sawmilling. The logs come not only from the surrounding district, but also from the forests of eastern Saskatchewan.

Climatic conditions throughout the region are somewhat unfavorable to settlement. Winters are long and severe, lasting from October to June. The frost-free period ranges from 90-100 days in The Pas to only 60 days at Churchill. However, as past experience has shown, the weather will not hinder new communities from being established if the resources to be exploited are sufficiently rich.

IMPORTANCE OF THE MARKET (1964 ESTIMATES)

	Number	% of Canada
Population	51,700	0.27
Households	10,400	0.22
Disposable income ($ million)	106.5	0.34

CHARACTERISTICS OF THE POPULATION

	% of the total population of the region	% points above or below Canadian average
Mother tongue (1961 census)		
English	51.1	− 7.3
French	3.6	−24.5
German	1.8	− 1.3
Native Indian dialects	34.7	+33.8
Italian	0.3	− 1.6
Dutch	0.5	− 0.4
Polish	0.7	− 0.2
Ukrainian	3.7	+ 1.7
Other	3.6	− 0.2
Total	100.0	—
Official language spoken (1961 census)		
English only	83.5	+16.1
French only	0.4	−18.7
Both English and French	4.6	− 7.6
Neither English nor French	11.5	+10.2
Total	100.0	—

GROWTH OF THE MARKET

	Percentage growth 1961 to 1964	% points above or below Canadian average
Population	+10.51	+5.04
Disposable income	+30.67	+9.14

AVERAGE INCOME (1961 CENSUS)

	Dollars	% above or below Canadian average
Income per family (non-farm)	4,518	−17.09
Income per person not in family (non-farm)	2,276	+ 6.50
Income per farm (net)	1,553	−52.29

POVERTY AND AFFLUENCE (1961 CENSUS)

	Number	% of region's total	% points above or below Canadian average
Extent of poverty			
Families earning below $3,000 a year (non-farm)	2,737	31.1	+ 7.8
Persons not in families earning below $1,500 a year (non-farm)	1,272	46.7	− 2.2
Farms with gross income of less than $2,500 a year	79	65.9	+19.8
Persons not in school with grade 4 or less education	8,129	28.9	+15.5
Doubled-up households (more than one family per household)	387	4.1	+ 0.4
Households living in dilapidated dwellings	1,342	14.0	+ 8.4
Households without facilities of running water	4,205	44.0	+33.1
Households without facilities of installed bath or shower	4,419	46.2	+26.5
Extent of affluence			
Families earning over $10,000 a year (non-farm)	309	3.5	− 4.3
Persons not in families earning over $6,000 a year (non-farm)	109	4.0	+ 0.2
Farms with gross income over $15,000 a year	4	3.3	− 1.7
Persons with university degree	477	1.7	− 1.1
Households with two or more television sets	5	0.1	− 4.1
Households with two or more cars	148	1.6	− 5.2

LABOR FORCE BY INDUSTRY

Industry	Persons 1961 census	% of the total	% points above or below Canadian average
Agriculture	150	1.0	− 8.9
Forestry	331	2.2	+ 0.5
Fishing and trapping	815	5.5	+ 5.0
Mines, quarries, oil wells	4,279	28.6	+26.7
Manufacturing	623	4.2	−17.5
Construction	1,175	7.9	+ 1.2
Transportation, communications, and other utilities	1,636	10.9	+ 1.6
Wholesale trade	225	1.5	− 3.0
Retail trade	969	6.5	− 4.3
Finance, insurance, and real estate	133	0.9	− 2.6
Community and business services	1,545	10.3	− 2.5
Personal services	964	6.5	− 0.3
Public administration and defence	1,769	11.8	+ 4.3
Miscellaneous	328	2.2	− 0.2
Total labor force	14,942	100.0	—

Regina — Southeastern Plains

Area covered: 19,417 square miles. *Census divisions:* 1, 2, and 6.

COMPOSITION OF THE MARKET

Place	Census Division	Population 1961	% of the region
Regina	6	112,141	49.39
Weyburn	2	9,101	4.01
Estevan	1	7,728	3.41
Indian Head	6	1,802	0.79
Fort Qu'Appelle	6	1,521	0.67
Oxbow	1	1,359	0.60
Radville	2	1,067	0.47
Total urban	—	134,719	59.34
Rural non-farm	—	42,133	18.56
Rural farm	—	50,183	22.10
Total population		227,035	100.00

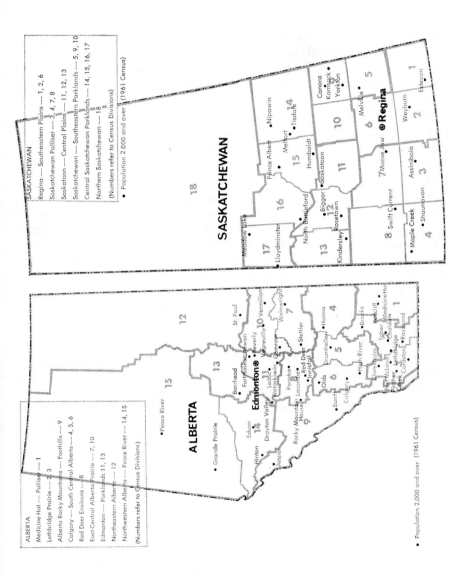

ECONOMIC CAPSULE

This is the southern part of the mixed-grass, dark-brown-soil prairie, plus the Oxbow portion of the black-soil belt. The land is very well suited for wheat, and agriculture is by far the most important means of livelihood.

Estevan is the center of a lignite coal field. The recoverable reserves are very high — over 10 billion tons. Though at first worked by conventional underground methods, the coal is now obtained almost entirely by strip-mining. Annual production has remained almost constant at about two million tons. A large amount is sold to the public utility company which supplies electricity to many parts of southeastern Saskatchewan.

Another valuable mineral is potash. At Belle Plaine a mine has already started operation with annual production capacity of 600,000 tons, likely to be doubled by 1975. Oil is found in large quantities at Weyburn, Midale, and Steelman. These and other wells in the vicinity accounted for more than half of Saskatchewan's oil production of 81 million barrels in 1964.

Regina, "the Queen of the Plains", is a city that demands admiration. Its growth has been a dogged triumph of man over nature. Originally it was the camping site of Indian buffalo hunters on the trackless prairie, with insufficient water, poor drainage, no sheltering hills, and no trees for fuel or timber. When it was selected as the capital, the *Winnipeg Free Press* snootily predicted that it "would never amount to more than a country village." Regina has defied its detractors and grown into a striving and spirited city of over 100,000 souls. Its stagnant creek has been miraculously transformed into a beautiful lake which reflects, like a mirror, the impressive Legislative Buildings.

The greater part of the city's population is employed in servicing occupations, transportation, and trade. Only about 10% are engaged in manufacturing. However, in recent years, stimulated by nearby oil and gas discoveries, Regina has attracted a considerable number of small industries. Its manufacturing activities include steel fabricating, oil refining, brewing, slaughtering and meat-packing, printing and publishing. In addition there are plants for fertilizers, cement, concrete products, and scientific instruments.

REGINA—SOUTHEASTERN PLAINS

IMPORTANCE OF THE MARKET (1964 ESTIMATES)

	Region		Regina	
	Number	% of Canada	Number	% of Canada
Population	239,500	1.24	122,000	0.63
Households	63,000	1.31	33,900	0.71
Disposable income ($ million)	403.9	1.28	231.3	0.73

GROWTH OF THE MARKET

	Region		Regina	
	Percentage growth 1961 to 1964	% points above or below Canadian average	Percentage growth 1961 to 1964	% points above or below Canadian average
Population	+ 5.49	+ 0.02	+ 8.79	+3.32
Disposable income	+32.99	+11.46	+28.71	+7.18

AVERAGE INCOME (1961 CENSUS)

	Region		Regina	
	Dollars	% above or below Canadian average	Dollars	% above or below Canadian average
Income per family (non-farm)	5,463	+ 0.26	6,010	+10.30
Income per person not in family (non-farm)	2,171	+ 1.59	2,332	+ 9.13
Income per farm (net)	4,021	+23.53	—	—

LABOR FORCE BY INDUSTRY

	Region			Regina	
Industry	Persons 1961 census	% of the total	% points above or below Canadian average	Persons 1961 census	% of the total
Agriculture	19,585	23.0	+13.1	499	1.1
Forestry	112	0.1	− 1.6	5	—
Fishing and trapping	13	—	− 0.5	2	—
Mines, quarries, oil wells	1,497	1.8	− 0.1	310	0.7
Manufacturing	5,391	6.3	−15.4	4,681	10.0
Construction	5,179	6.1	− 0.6	3,682	7.9
Transportation, communications, and other utilities	9,126	10.7	+ 1.4	5,805	12.4
Wholesale trade	5,056	5.9	+ 1.4	4,123	8.8
Retail trade	9,739	11.4	+ 0.6	6,666	14.3
Finance, insurance, and real estate	2,979	3.5	—	2,530	5.4
Community and business services	11,621	13.6	+ 0.8	7,261	15.6
Personal services	5,581	6.5	− 0.3	3,728	8.0
Public administration and defence	7,472	8.8	+ 1.3	6,245	13.4
Miscellaneous	1,949	2.3	− 0.1	1,135	2.4
Total labor force	85,300	100.0	—	46,672	100.0

CHARACTERISTICS OF THE POPULATION

	Region		Regina
	% of the total population of the region	% points above or below Canadian average	% of the total population of the city
Mother tongue (1961 census)			
English	77.4	+19.0	77.4
French	3.0	−25.1	1.7
German	10.0	+ 6.9	10.9
Native Indian dialects	0.7	− 0.2	0.1
Italian	0.2	− 1.7	0.4
Dutch	0.5	− 0.4	0.6
Polish	1.0	+ 0.1	0.9
Ukrainian	2.6	+ 0.6	3.2
Other	4.6	+ 0.8	4.8
Total	100.0	—	100.0
Official language spoken (1961 census)			
English only	95.5	+28.1	96.5
French only	0.2	−18.9	0.1
Both English and French	3.9	− 8.3	2.9
Neither English nor French	0.4	− 0.9	0.5
Total	100.0	—	100.0

POVERTY AND AFFLUENCE (1961 CENSUS)

	Region			Regina	
	Number	% of region's total	% points above or below Canadian average	Number	% of city's total
Extent of poverty					
Families earning below $3,000 a year (non-farm)	9,334	22.6	− 0.7	3,989	15.0
Persons not in families earning below $1,500 a year (non-farm)	8,408	46.2	− 2.7	4,963	40.5
Farms with gross income of less than $2,500 a year	4,008	25.2	−20.9	—	—
Persons not in school with grade 4 or less education	16,191	11.1	− 2.3	6,036	8.3

		Region		*Regina*	
	Number	% of region's total	% points above or below Canadian average	Number	% of city's total
Doubled-up households (more than one family per household)	1,286	2.1	− 1.6	909	3.0
Households living in dilapidated dwellings	4,017	6.6	+ 1.0	1,446	4.8
Households without facilities of running water	17,032	28.1	+17.2	1,449	4.8
Households without facilities of installed bath or shower	20,021	33.0	+13.3	2,168	7.2
Extent of affluence					
Families earning over $10,000 a year (non-farm)	3,231	7.9	+ 0.1	2,475	9.3
Persons not in families earning over $6,000 a year (non-farm)	716	3.9	+ 0.1	498	4.1
Farms with gross income over $15,000 a year	480	3.0	− 2.0	—	—
Persons with university degree	3,956	2.7	− 0.1	3,126	4.3
Households with two or more television sets	1,700	2.8	− 1.4	1,493	5.0
Households with two or more cars	4,607	7.6	+ 0.8	2,916	9.7

Saskatchewan Palliser

ECONOMIC CAPSULE

This dry belt of short grass and light brown soil is the Saskatchewan section of the Palliser Triangle. Agriculture is all important, 94% of the area consisting of farmland. Wheat is the dominant crop. Farms are extremely large, averaging 1,042 acres, and almost completely mechanized. On the hilly tracts near the Alberta border, ranching is more common.

Some oil has been found in the vicinity of Swift Current. The major wells are located at Battrum, Fosterton, Instow, Dollard, and Rapdan. Annual production is estimated at about 15 million barrels. Also near this area are Canada's only wells of helium, a rare gas used in space exploration and low-temperature experiments. Production started for the first time in 1964.

Moose Jaw, the largest urban center, is the most industrialized city in Saskatchewan. The biggest employers are the yards of the Canadian Pacific Railway, the flour mills of Robin Hood, and the petroleum refineries of British American Oil and Canadian Husky. Other industries are meat packing, foundry casting, garment making, jute-bag manufacturing, and production of various types of greases and transmission oils.

Swift Current is the main business center for southwestern Saskatchewan. Nearby is an important experimental station operated by the federal government's Department of Agriculture for the study of the soil and crop problems in semi-arid areas.

SASKATCHEWAN PALLISER

Area covered: 31,960 square miles. *Census divisions:* 3, 4, 7, and 8

COMPOSITION OF THE MARKET

Place	Census Division	Population 1961	% of the region
Moose Jaw	7	33,206	22.31
Swift Current	8	12,186	8.19
Assiniboia	3	2,491	1.67
Maple Creek	4	2,291	1.54
Shaunavon	4	2,154	1.45
Eston	8	1,695	1.14
Gravelbourg	3	1,499	1.00
Leader	8	1,211	0.81
Gull Lake	8	1,038	0.70
Herbert	7	1,008	0.68
Total urban	—	58,779	39.49
Rural non-farm	—	36,594	24.59
Rural farm	—	53,465	35.92
Total population		148,838	100.00

IMPORTANCE OF THE MARKET (1964 ESTIMATES)

	Number	% of Canada
Population	149,000	0.77
Households	41,200	0.86
Disposable income ($ million)	260.1	0.82

GROWTH OF THE MARKET

	Percentage growth 1961 to 1964	% points above or below Canadian average
Population	+ 0.11	− 5.36
Disposable income	+65.67	+44.14

AVERAGE INCOME (1961 CENSUS)

	Dollars	% above or below Canadian average
Income per family (non-farm)	4,559	−16.33
Income per person not in family (non-farm)	1,861	−12.92
Income per farm (net)	5,369	+64.95

POVERTY AND AFFLUENCE (1961 CENSUS)

	Number	% of region's total	% points above or below Canadian average
Extent of poverty			
Families earning below $3,000 a year (non-farm)	7,186	32.3	+ 9.0
Persons not in families earning below $1,500 a year (non-farm)	5,130	55.0	+ 6.1
Farms with gross income of less than $2,500 a year	3,513	19.0	−27.1
Persons not in school with grade 4 or less education	11,745	12.4	− 1.0
Doubled-up households (more than one family per household)	486	1.2	− 2.5
Households living in dilapidated dwellings	3,483	8.5	+ 2.9
Households without facilities of running water	14,965	36.6	+25.7
Households without facilities of installed bath or shower	18,191	44.5	+24.8
Extent of affluence			
Families earning over $10,000 a year (non-farm)	1,154	5.3	− 2.5
Persons not in families earning over $6,000 a year (non-farm)	243	2.6	− 1.2
Farms with gross income over $15,000 a year	1,181	6.4	+ 1.4
Persons with university degree	1,233	1.3	− 1.5
Households with two or more television sets	366	0.9	− 3.3
Households with two or more cars	2,366	5.8	− 1.0

MEANS OF LIVELIHOOD—DISTRIBUTION OF

LABOR FORCE BY INDUSTRY

Industry	Persons 1961 census	% of the total	% points above or below Canadian average
Agriculture	21,122	41.1	+31.2
Forestry	33	0.1	− 1.6
Fishing and trapping	2	—	− 0.5
Mines, quarries, oil wells	214	0.4	− 1.5
Manufacturing	2,123	4.1	−17.6
Construction	2,170	4.2	− 2.5
Transportation, communications, and other utilities	5,002	9.8	+ 0.5
Wholesale trade	1,628	3.2	− 1.3
Retail trade	5,044	9.8	− 1.0
Finance, insurance, and real estate	910	1.8	− 1.7
Community and business services	6,070	11.8	− 1.0
Personal services	2,990	5.8	− 1.0
Public administration and defence	2,807	5.5	− 2.0
Miscellaneous	1,231	2.4	—
Total labor force	51,346	100.0	—

CHARACTERISTICS OF THE POPULATION

	% of the total population of the region	% points above or below Canadian average
Mother tongue (1961 census)		
English	75.4	+17.0
French	5.3	−22.8
German	10.2	+ 7.1
Native Indian dialects	0.1	− 0.8
Italian	0.1	− 1.8
Dutch	1.9	+ 1.0
Polish	0.5	− 0.4
Ukrainian	1.6	− 0.4
Other	4.9	+ 1.1
Total	100.0	—

	% of the total population of the region	% points above or below Canadian average
Official language spoken (1961 census)		
English only	93.2	+25.8
French only	0.6	−18.5
Both English and French	5.7	− 6.5
Neither English nor French	0.5	− 0.8
Total	100.0	—

Saskatoon — Central Plains

ECONOMIC CAPSULE

This region constitutes the northern portion of the mixed-grass, dark-brown-soil prairie. Agriculture provides the chief prop to the economy. Four out of five commercial farms specialize in the cultivation of wheat. The area stands to benefit considerably when the multi-million-dollar irrigation and power project on the South Saskatchewan River is completed.

The economy is getting an additional boost from the fast development of potash mining. Three big companies have started operations and, by 1970, production may reach three million tons, with a value at current prices of almost $107 million.

Saskatoon, the "Hub City of the West", is a noted medical and educational center. It is the site of the University of Saskatchewan with its famous University Hospital, where for the first time in the world the cobalt bomb was employed for the treatment of cancer. Saskatoon is also a busy railway junction and a major wholesale and retail center for Central Saskatchewan. Manufacturing is concerned with processing the various farm products raised in the surrounding territory. There are flour mills, flax and oil seed mills, meat-packing establishments, bakeries, and the like. The effects of the potash boom are already being felt. Two new chemical plants have recently been established: one to produce fertilizers and the other to make materials used in refining potash ores. The cement industry too is expanding its operations. As a result of all these activities, the population of Saskatoon, according to city officials, is expected to increase rapidly from 102,000 in 1964 to 180,000 in 1975.

SASKATOON—CENTRAL PLAINS

Area covered: 18,809 square miles. *Census divisions:* 11, 12, and 13.

COMPOSITION OF THE MARKET

Place	Census Division	Population 1961	% of the region
Saskatoon	11	95,526	51.05
Kindersley	13	2,990	1.60
Biggar	12	2,702	1.44
Rosetown	12	2,450	1.31
Unity	13	1,902	1.02
Battleford	12	1,627	0.87
Wilkie	13	1,612	0.86
Watrous	11	1,461	0.78
Outlook	11	1,340	0.72
Kerrobert	13	1,220	0.65
Total urban	—	112,830	60.30
Rural non-farm	—	30,173	16.12
Rural farm	—	44,120	23.58
Total population		187,123	100.00

IMPORTANCE OF THE MARKET (1964 ESTIMATES)

	Region		Saskatoon	
	Number	% of Canada	Number	% of Canada
Population	199,900	1.04	102,000	0.53
Households	54,000	1.12	29,100	0.61
Disposable income ($ million)	332.7	1.06	185.8	0.59

GROWTH OF THE MARKET

	Region		Saskatoon	
	Percentage growth 1961 to 1964	% points above or below Canadian average	Percentage growth 1961 to 1964	% points above or below Canadian average
Population	+ 6.83	+ 1.36	+ 6.78	+1.31
Disposable income	+37.31	+15.78	+29.03	+7.50

AVERAGE INCOME (1961 CENSUS)

	Region		Saskatoon	
	Dollars	% above or below Canadian average	Dollars	% above or below Canadian average
Income per family (non-farm)	5,274	− 3.21	5,797	+6.39
Income per person not in family (non-farm)	2,184	+ 2.20	2,254	+5.48
Income per farm (net)	4,640	+42.55	—	—

POVERTY AND AFFLUENCE (1961 CENSUS)

	Region			Saskatoon	
	Number	% of region's total	% points above or below Canadian average	Number	% of city's total
Extent of poverty					
Families earning below $3,000 a year (non-farm)	8,307	25.1	+ 1.8	4,285	19.2
Persons not in families earning below $1,500 a year (non-farm)	7,022	46.8	− 2.1	4,501	43.5
Farms with gross income of less than $2,500 a year	3,166	22.5	−23.6	—	—
Persons not in school with grade 4 or less education	13,584	11.6	− 1.8	6,066	10.0
Doubled-up households (more than one family per household)	956	1.9	− 1.8	663	2.6
Households living in dilapidated dwellings	3,386	6.8	+ 1.2	1,160	4.5
Households without facilities of running water	12,745	25.5	+14.6	480	1.9
Households without facilities of installed bath or shower	15,715	31.4	+11.7	1,121	4.3
Extent of affluence					
Families earning over $10,000 a year (non-farm)	2,128	6.4	− 1.4	1,708	7.7
Persons not in families earning over $6,000 a year (non-farm)	571	3.8	—	370	3.6

POVERTY AND AFFLUENCE (continued)

	Region			Saskatoon	
	Number	% of region's total	% points above or below Canadian average	Number	% of city's total
Farms with gross income over $15,000 a year	642	4.6	− 0.4	—	—
Persons with university degree	3,501	3.0	+ 0.2	2,865	4.7
Households with two or more television sets	920	1.8	− 2.4	843	3.3
Households with two or more cars	3,011	6.0	− 0.8	1,931	7.5

CHARACTERISTICS OF THE POPULATION

	Region		Saskatoon
	% of the total population of the region	% points above or below Canadian average	% of the total population of the city
Mother tongue (1961 census)			
English	76.5	+18.1	76.8
French	1.8	−26.3	1.8
German	9.9	+ 6.8	7.5
Native Indian dialects	1.0	+ 0.1	0.1
Italian	0.2	− 1.7	0.3
Dutch	0.8	− 0.1	1.3
Polish	0.6	− 0.3	0.8
Ukrainian	4.9	+ 2.9	7.1
Other	4.3	+ 0.5	4.3
Total	100.0	—	100.0
Official language spoken (1961 census)			
English only	96.5	+29.1	96.1
French only	0.2	−18.9	0.2
Both English and French	2.8	− 9.4	3.3
Neither English nor French	0.5	− 0.8	0.4
Total	100.0	—	100.0

LABOR FORCE BY INDUSTRY

	Region			Saskatoon	
Industry	Persons 1961 census	% of the total	% points above or below Canadian average	Persons 1961 census	% of the total
Agriculture	17,089	25.8	+15.9	584	1.6
Forestry	68	0.1	− 1.6	33	0.1
Fishing and trapping	6	—	− 0.5	3	—
Mines, quarries, oil wells	329	0.5	− 1.4	92	0.3
Manufacturing	4,079	6.2	−15.5	3,755	10.6
Construction	4,272	6.4	− 0.3	2,879	8.1
Transportation, communications, and other utilities	7,128	10.8	+ 1.5	4,308	12.1
Wholesale trade	4,077	6.2	+ 1.7	3,326	9.3
Retail trade	6,994	10.6	− 0.2	4,612	13.0
Finance, insurance, and real estate	1,816	2.7	− 0.8	1,471	4.1
Community and business services	10,302	15.6	+ 2.8	7,686	21.6
Personal services	4,253	6.4	− 0.4	2,816	7.9
Public administration and defence	4,200	6.3	− 1.2	2,966	8.3
Miscellaneous	1,616	2.4	—	1,062	3.0
Total labor force	66,229	100.0	—	35,593	100.0

Saskatchewan — Southeastern Parklands

ECONOMIC CAPSULE

This region of fertile black soil is the richly cultivated portion of the Saskatchewan Parkland Belt. Moisture conditions allow greater diversification than in the brown-soil zone, and the farmers have taken advantage of this adaptability to grow, in addition to wheat, coarse grains and fodder crops for a thriving livestock industry.

Recently at Esterhazy, a potash mine of International Minerals and Chemical Corporation (Canada) Limited has been brought into operation, with an annual capacity of 1.6 million tons. At Gerald, another mine of the same company is expected to be ready for production by 1967. The annual capacity here is expected to be 2.5 million tons.

Yorkton is the chief urban center, but its grip on the surrounding area is limited. In fact, the whole region is functionally tied to Manitoba in the east, and serviced mainly from Winnipeg, Brandon, and Dauphin.

SASKATCHEWAN—SOUTHEASTERN PARKLANDS

Area covered: 15,630 square miles. *Census divisions:* 5, 9, and 10.

COMPOSITION OF THE MARKET

Place	Census Division	Population 1961	% of the region
Yorkton	9	9,995	7.72
Melville	5	5,191	4.01
Kamsack	9	2,968	2.29
Canora	9	2,117	1.64
Moosomin	5	1,781	1.38
Wynyard	10	1,686	1.30
Wadena	10	1,311	1.01
Grenfell	5	1,256	0.97
Esterhazy	5	1,114	0.86
Wolseley	5	1,031	0.80
Broadview	5	1,008	0.78
Total urban	—	29,458	22.76
Rural non-farm	—	35,786	27.66
Rural farm	—	64,150	49.58
Total population		129,394	100.00

LABOR FORCE BY INDUSTRY

Industry	Persons 1961 census	% of the total	% points above or below Canadian average
Agriculture	26,484	57.7	+47.8
Forestry	88	0.2	− 1.5
Fishing and trapping	—	—	− 0.5
Mines, quarries, oil wells	249	0.5	− 1.4
Manufacturing	1,215	2.6	−19.1
Construction	1,646	3.6	− 3.1
Transportation, communications, and other utilities	3,485	7.6	− 1.7
Wholesale trade	1,149	2.5	− 2.0
Retail trade	3,332	7.3	− 3.5
Finance, insurance, and real estate	484	1.1	− 2.4
Community and business services	3,916	8.5	− 4.3
Personal services	1,885	4.1	− 2.7
Public administration and defence	1,025	2.2	− 5.3
Miscellaneous	976	2.1	− 0.3
Total labor force	45,934	100.0	—

IMPORTANCE OF THE MARKET (1964 ESTIMATES)

	Number	% of Canada
Population	124,500	0.65
Households	33,700	0.70
Disposable income ($ million)	159.8	0.51

GROWTH OF THE MARKET

	Percentage change 1961 to 1964	% points above or below Canadian average
Population	− 3.78	− 9.25
Disposable income	+34.74	+13.21

CHARACTERISTICS OF THE POPULATION

	% of the total population of the region	% points above or below Canadian average
Mother tongue (1961 census)		
English	53.8	− 4.6
French	1.1	−27.0
German	9.3	+ 6.2
Native Indian dialects	2.6	+ 1.7
Italian	—	− 1.9
Dutch	0.2	− 0.7
Polish	2.4	+ 1.5
Ukrainian	22.1	+20.1
Other	8.5	+ 4.7
Total	100.0	—
Official language spoken (1961 census)		
English only	96.2	+28.8
French only	0.1	−19.0
Both English and French	1.6	−10.6
Neither English nor French	2.1	+ 0.8
Total	100.0	—

POVERTY AND AFFLUENCE (1961 CENSUS)

	Number	% of region's total	% points above or below Canadian average
Extent of poverty			
Families earning below $3,000 a year (non-farm)	7,044	45.4	+22.1
Persons not in families earning below $1,500 a year (non-farm)	4,438	66.8	+17.9
Farms with gross income of less than $2,500 a year	7,933	42.0	− 4.1
Persons not in school with grade 4 or less education	18,604	22.3	+ 8.9
Doubled-up households (more than one family per household)	667	1.9	− 1.8
Households living in dilapidated dwellings	3,802	10.8	+ 5.2
Households without facilities of running water	23,968	68.1	+57.2
Households without facilities of installed bath or shower	25,435	72.3	+52.6
Extent of affluence			
Families earning over $10,000 a year (non-farm)	514	3.4	− 4.4
Persons not in families earning over $6,000 a year (non-farm)	159	2.3	− 1.5
Farms with gross income over $15,000 a year	213	1.1	− 3.9
Persons with university degree	752	0.9	− 1.9
Households with two or more television sets	117	0.3	− 3.9
Households with two or more cars	1,079	3.1	− 3.7

AVERAGE INCOME (1961 CENSUS)

	Dollars	% above or below Canadian average
Income per family (non-farm)	3,863	−29.11
Income per person not in family (non-farm)	1,496	−30.00
Income per farm (net)	2,895	−11.06

Central Saskatchewan Parklands

ECONOMIC CAPSULE

The parkland here is covered with aspen groves and mixed woods. Despite the northern latitudes, over half the area has been cleared for cultivation. As one moves farther north, agriculture gradually changes from wheat growing to cattle raising and then to pioneer farming. A good potential for forest industries exists on the northern fringe.

Prince Albert is an important distribution point and a gateway to Northern Saskatchewan. It is also a tourist outfitting center, being not far from Prince Albert National Park, a scenic 1,500 square miles of lakes, forests, and game preserve.

Area covered: 36,624 square miles. *Census divisions:* 14, 15, 16, and 17.

COMPOSITION OF THE MARKET

Place	Census Division	Population 1961	% of the region
Prince Albert	15	24,168	11.40
North Battleford	16	11,230	5.30
Melfort	14	4,039	1.90
Nipawin	14	3,836	1.81
Humboldt	15	3,245	1.53
Meadow Lake	17	2,803	1.32
Lloydminster	17	2,723*	1.28
Tisdale	14	2,402	1.13
Hudson Bay	14	1,601	0.76
Rosthern	15	1,264	0.60
Shellbrook	16	1,042	0.49
Total urban	—	58,353	27.52
Rural non-farm	—	62,253	29.35
Rural farm	—	91,477	43.13
Total population		212,083	100.00

* Total population of Lloydminster is 5,667 of which 2,723 is in Saskatchewan and 2,944 is in Census Division 10 of Alberta.

IMPORTANCE OF THE MARKET (1964 ESTIMATES)

	Number	% of Canada
Population	209,400	1.09
Households	53,800	1.12
Disposable income ($ million)	258.5	0.82

GROWTH OF THE MARKET

	Percentage change 1961 to 1964	% points above or below Canadian average
Population	− 1.27	− 6.74
Disposable income	+35.06	+13.53

POVERTY AND AFFLUENCE (1961 CENSUS)

	Number	% of region's total	% points above or below Canadian average
Extent of poverty			
Families earning below $3,000 a year (non-farm)	11,039	41.4	+18.1
Persons not in families earning below $1,500 a year (non-farm)	7,106	62.2	+13.3
Farms with gross income of less than $2,500 a year	11,541	43.9	− 2.2
Persons not in school with grade 4 or less education	25,676	19.3	+ 5.9
Doubled-up households (more than one family per household)	1,015	1.8	− 1.9
Households living in dilapidated dwellings	6,618	12.1	+ 6.5
Households without facilities of running water	34,512	63.3	+52.4
Households without facilities of installed bath or shower	37,116	68.1	+48.4
Extent of affluence			
Families earning over $10,000 a year (non-farm)	1,239	4.7	− 3.1
Persons not in families earning over $6,000 a year (non-farm)	289	2.5	− 1.3
Farms with gross income over $15,000 a year	463	1.8	− 3.2
Persons with university degree	1,436	1.1	− 1.7
Households with two or more television sets	192	0.4	− 3.8
Households with two or more cars	1,793	3.3	− 3.5

CHARACTERISTICS OF THE POPULATION

	% of the total population of the region	% points above or below Canadian average
Mother tongue (1961 census)		
English	61.4	+ 3.0
French	7.5	−20.6
German	9.5	+ 6.4
Native Indian dialects	4.0	+ 3.1
Italian	0.1	− 1.8
Dutch	1.0	+ 0.1
Polish	1.5	+ 0.6
Ukrainian	9.8	+ 7.8
Other	5.2	+ 1.4
Total	100.0	—

CHARACTERISTICS OF THE POPULATION (continued)

	% of the total population of the region	% points above or below Canadian average
Official language spoken (1961 census)		
English only	89.6	+22.2
French only	0.9	−18.2
Both English and French	7.8	− 4.4
Neither English nor French	1.7	+ 0.4
Total	100.0	—

AVERAGE INCOME (1961 CENSUS)

	Dollars	% above or below Canadian average
Income per family (non-farm)	4,092	−24.90
Income per person not in family (non-farm)	1,660	−22.32
Income per farm (net)	3,094	− 4.95

LABOR FORCE BY INDUSTRY

Industry	Persons 1961 census	% of the total	% points above or below Canadian average
Agriculture	34,411	48.4	+38.5
Forestry	608	0.9	− 0.8
Fishing and trapping	62	0.1	− 0.4
Mines, quarries, oil wells	205	0.3	− 1.6
Manufacturing	2,293	3.2	−18.5
Construction	3,930	5.5	− 1.2
Transportation, communications, and other utilities	5,244	7.4	− 1.9
Wholesale trade	2,205	3.1	− 1.4
Retail trade	5,932	8.3	− 2.5
Finance, insurance, and real estate	895	1.3	− 2.2
Community and business services	7,828	11.0	− 1.8
Personal services	3,397	4.8	− 2.0
Public administration and defence	2,544	3.6	− 3.9
Miscellaneous	1,507	2.1	− 0.3
Total labor force	71,061	100.0	—

Northern Saskatchewan

ECONOMIC CAPSULE

This huge disjointed region is Saskatchewan's portion of the Canadian Shield. The vast coniferous forests that blanket the terrain are not as yet commercially exploited. They serve merely as a conserve for game, where white and Indian trappers make their living by hunting and fishing. At present, most of the income is derived from mining operations: base metals in the Flin Flon area and uranium near Beaverlodge Lake. There is no special marketing center covering the whole region. Most supplies for the area come from Prince Albert, North Battleford, Flin Flon, and Edmonton.

Area covered: 97,742 square miles. *Census division:* 18.

COMPOSITION OF THE MARKET

Place	Census Division	Population 1961	% of the region
Creighton	18	1,729	8.35
Uranium City	18	1,665	8.04
Total urban	—	3,394	16.39
Rural non-farm	—	16,037	77.44
Rural farm	—	1,277	6.17
Total population		20,708	100.00

IMPORTANCE OF THE MARKET (1964 ESTIMATES)

	Number	% of Canada
Population	20,700	0.11
Households	4,300	0.09
Disposable income ($ million)	41.0	0.13

GROWTH OF THE MARKET

	Percentage change 1961 to 1964	% points above or below Canadian average
Population	− 0.04	− 5.51
Disposable income	+51.85	+30.32

POVERTY AND AFFLUENCE (1961 CENSUS)

	Number	% of region's total	% points above or below Canadian average
Extent of poverty			
Families earning below $3,000 a year (non-farm)	2,013	56.7	+33.4
Persons not in families earning below $1,500 a year (non-farm)	690	62.5	+13.6
Farms with gross income of less than $2,500 a year	217	63.8	+17.7
Persons not in school with grade 4 or less education	5,448	44.1	+30.7
Doubled-up households (more than one family per household)	156	3.7	—
Households living in dilapidated dwellings	811	19.1	+13.5
Households without facilities of running water	3,138	73.8	+62.9
Households without facilities of installed bath or shower	3,290	77.4	+57.7
Extent of affluence			
Families earning over $10,000 a year (non-farm)	163	4.6	− 3.2
Persons not in families earning over $6,000 a year (non-farm)	42	3.8	—
Farms with gross income over $15,000 a year	1	0.3	− 4.7
Persons with university degree	129	1.1	− 1.7
Households with two or more television sets	10	0.2	− 4.0
Households with two or more cars	72	1.7	− 5.1

CHARACTERISTICS OF THE POPULATION

	% of the total population of the region	% points above or below Canadian average
Mother tongue (1961 census)		
English	35.9	−22.5
French	2.4	−25.7
German	5.2	+ 2.1
Native Indian dialects	50.6	+49.7
Italian	0.3	− 1.6
Dutch	0.4	− 0.5
Polish	0.7	− 0.2
Ukrainian	1.9	− 0.1
Other	2.6	− 1.2
Total	100.0	—

CHARACTERISTICS OF THE POPULATION (continued)

	% of the total population of the region	% points above or below Canadian average
Official language spoken (1961 census)		
English only	74.3	+ 6.9
French only	0.5	−18.6
Both English and French	4.2	− 8.0
Neither English nor French	21.0	+19.7
Total	100.0	—

AVERAGE INCOME (1961 CENSUS)

	Dollars	% above or below Canadian average
Income per family (non-farm)	3,734	−31.47
Income per person not in family (non-farm)	1,820	−14.83
Income per farm (net)	1,984	−39.05

LABOR FORCE BY INDUSTRY

Industry	Persons 1961 census	% of the total	% points above or below Canadian average
Agriculture	546	9.5	− 0.4
Forestry	223	3.9	+ 2.2
Fishing and trapping	1,053	18.4	+17.9
Mines, quarries, oil wells	1,513	26.5	+24.6
Manufacturing	76	1.3	−20.4
Construction	141	2.5	− 4.2
Transportation, communications, and other utilities	331	5.8	− 3.5
Wholesale trade	142	2.5	− 2.0
Retail trade	303	5.3	− 5.5
Finance, insurance, and real estate	32	0.6	− 2.9
Community and business services	510	8.9	− 3.9
Personal services	409	7.1	+ 0.3
Public administration and defence	211	3.7	− 3.8
Miscellaneous	229	4.0	+ 1.6
Total labor force	5,719	100.0	—

Medicine Hat — Palliser

ECONOMIC CAPSULE

This small belt of semi-arid, sage-brush vegetation and light-brown soils is the Alberta sector of the Palliser Triangle. During the last few years, hundreds of thousands of acres have been brought under irrigation, and the land, once too dry for crops, now produces wheat, coarse grains, flaxseed, mustard seed, and sugar beets. In the non-irrigated areas, ranching is still prevalent. The average size of the farm, 1,950 acres, is the largest for any region in Canada. Mechanization has reached its apex, with the value of machinery and equipment per farm amounting to $11,815, which is 2.2 times higher than the Canadian average. The region is also rich in coal and natural gas.

Medicine Hat is situated on the banks of the South Saskatchewan River, almost midway between Moose Jaw and Calgary. Based on some legend long forgotten, the Indians named this site after a hat worn by a medicine man, and the name was adopted by the white settlers. Nearby is a very large reservoir of natural gas, which prompted Rudyard Kipling's celebrated remark: "the place has all Hell for a basement."

Major industries in Medicine Hat and in the neighboring municipality of Redcliff just nine miles away, include glassware (Dominion Glass), rubber tires (Goodyear Tire and Rubber Company of Canada), chemicals (Northwest Nitro-chemicals), and pipes (Canadian Johns-Manville). The city is equally renowned for its pottery. The food industry is well represented, with mills producing flour, breakfast cereals, and animal feeds. Medicine Hat has also some of the largest greenhouses in Canada. Flowers in season and hothouse vegetables are shipped as far east as the Lakehead and as far west as Vancouver.

MEDICINE HAT—PALLISER

Area covered: 8,079 square miles. *Census division:* 1.

COMPOSITION OF THE MARKET

Place	Census Division	Population 1961	% of the region
Medicine Hat	1	24,484	62.55
Redcliff	1	2,221	5.68
Bow Island	1	1,122	2.87
Total urban	—	27,827	71.10
Rural non-farm	—	4,064	10.38
Rural farm	—	7,249	18.52
Total population		39,140	100.00

IMPORTANCE OF THE MARKET (1964 ESTIMATES)

	Number	% of Canada
Population	41,500	0.22
Households	11,300	0.24
Disposable income ($ million)	69.7	0.22

GROWTH OF THE MARKET

	Percentage growth 1961 to 1964	% points above or below Canadian average
Population	+ 6.03	+0.56
Disposable income	+31.51	+9.98

POVERTY AND AFFLUENCE (1961 CENSUS)

	Number	% of region's total	% points above or below Canadian average
Extent of poverty			
Families earning below $3,000 a year (non-farm)	2,079	26.9	+ 3.6
Persons not in families earning below $1,500 a year (non-farm)	1,302	51.1	+ 2.2
Farms with gross income of less than $2,500 a year	315	14.6	−31.5
Persons not in school with grade 4 or less education	3,614	14.4	+ 1.0
Doubled-up households (more than one family per household)	223	2.1	− 1.6
Households living in dilapidated dwellings	717	6.6	+ 1.0
Households without facilities of running water	1,209	11.2	+ 0.3
Households without facilities of installed bath or shower	1,748	16.2	− 3.5
Extent of affluence			
Families earning over $10,000 a year (non-farm)	389	5.0	− 2.8
Persons not in families earning over $6,000 a year (non-farm)	63	2.4	− 1.4
Farms with gross income over $15,000 a year	350	16.1	+11.1
Persons with university degree	426	1.7	− 1.1
Households with two or more television sets	202	1.9	− 2.3
Households with two or more cars	772	7.1	+ 0.3

MEANS OF LIVELIHOOD—DISTRIBUTION OF

LABOR FORCE BY INDUSTRY

Industry	Persons 1961 census	% of the total	% points above or below Canadian average
Agriculture	3,033	22.4	+12.5
Forestry	4	—	− 1.7
Fishing and trapping	1	—	− 0.5
Mines, quarries, oil wells	107	0.8	− 1.1
Manufacturing	2,138	15.8	− 5.9
Construction	858	6.3	− 0.4
Transportation, communications, and other utilities	1,393	10.3	+ 1.0
Wholesale trade	392	2.9	− 1.6
Retail trade	1,551	11.4	+ 0.6
Finance, insurance, and real estate	295	2.2	− 1.3
Community and business services	1,566	11.6	− 1.2
Personal services	863	6.4	− 0.4
Public administration and defence	1,040	7.7	+ 0.2
Miscellaneous	299	2.2	− 0.2
Total labor force	13,540	100.0	—

CHARACTERISTICS OF THE POPULATION

	% of the total population of the region	% points above or below Canadian average
Mother tongue (1961 census)		
English	68.4	+10.0
French	0.6	−27.5
German	23.8	+20.7
Native Indian dialects	0.1	− 0.8
Italian	0.4	− 1.5
Dutch	1.6	+ 0.7
Polish	0.6	− 0.3
Ukrainian	1.0	− 1.0
Other	3.5	− 0.3
Total	100.0	—

CHARACTERISTICS OF THE POPULATION (continued)

	% of the total population of the region	% points above or below Canadian average
Official language spoken (1961 census)		
English only	97.9	+30.5
French only	0.1	−19.0
Both English and French	1.3	−10.9
Neither English nor French	0.7	− 0.6
Total	100.0	—

AVERAGE INCOME (1961 CENSUS)

	Dollars	% above or below Canadian average
Income per family (non-farm)	4,740	− 13.01
Income per person not in family (non-farm)	2,061	− 3.56
Income per farm (net)	8,296	+154.87

Lethbridge Prairie

ECONOMIC CAPSULE

This is the zone of fertile mid-grass prairie. A third of the labor force is engaged in agriculture. On the irrigated lands, in addition to wheat and other cereals, specialty crops like flaxseed, rape-seed, mustard seed, sugar beets, corn, peas, and beans are grown. In the drier areas, towards the foothills, cattle ranching is still common. The region is also rich in coal, oil, and natural gas.

Lethbridge, "the Irrigation Capital of Canada", 140 miles southeast of Calgary, is the third most populous city in Alberta. Originally known as Coal Bank, it still operates a few coal mines, but it is becoming more and more a marketing center for the surrounding ranching and grain growing districts. Its manufacturing industries are based mainly on the raw materials indigenous to the area — slaughtering and meat packing, feed and flour milling, sugar refining, vegetable canning and freezing, brewing, oil-seed processing, making of butter and cheese, and preparation of macaroni, spaghetti, and other Italian foods. Of the total labor force in manufacturing, nearly 60% is employed in food and beverage industries.

LETHBRIDGE PRAIRIE

Area covered: 11,785 square miles. *Census divisions:* 2, and 3.

COMPOSITION OF THE MARKET

Place	Census Division	Population 1961	% of the region
Lethbridge	2	35,454	31.03
Taber	2	3,951	3.46
Pincher Creek	3	2,961	2.59
Brooks	2	2,827	2.47
Cardston	3	2,801	2.45
Coaldale	2	2,592	2.27
Fort Macleod	3	2,490	2.18
Raymond	2	2,362	2.07
Claresholm	3	2,143	1.87
Magrath	3	1,338	1.17
Nanton	3	1,054	0.92
Total urban	—	59,973	52.48
Rural non-farm	—	20,055	17.55
Rural farm	—	34,245	29.97
Total population		114,273	100.00

IMPORTANCE OF THE MARKET (1964 ESTIMATES)

	Number	% of Canada
Population	116,000	0.60
Households	29,000	0.60
Disposable income ($ million)	175.1	0.56

GROWTH OF THE MARKET

	Percentage growth 1961 to 1964	% points above or below Canadian average
Population	+ 1.51	−3.96
Disposable income	+17.36	−4.17

MEANS OF LIVELIHOOD—DISTRIBUTION OF

LABOR FORCE BY INDUSTRY

Industry	Persons 1961 census	% of the total	% points above or below Canadian average
Agriculture	13,000	32.6	+22.7
Forestry	17	—	− 1.7
Fishing and trapping	5	—	− 0.5
Mines, quarries, oil wells	576	1.5	− 0.4
Manufacturing	2,641	6.6	−15.1
Construction	2,698	6.8	+ 0.1
Transportation, communications, and other utilities	3,530	8.9	− 0.4
Wholesale trade	1,906	4.8	+ 0.3
Retail trade	4,360	10.9	+ 0.1
Finance, insurance, and real estate	877	2.2	− 1.3
Community and business services	4,914	12.3	− 0.5
Personal services	2,370	5.9	− 0.9
Public administration and defence	2,070	5.2	− 2.3
Miscellaneous	907	2.3	− 0.1
Total labor force	39,871	100.0	—

CHARACTERISTICS OF THE POPULATION

	% of the total population of the region	% points above or below Canadian average
Mother tongue (1961 census)		
English	70.1	+11.7
French	0.8	−27.3
German	9.8	+ 6.7
Native Indian dialects	3.7	+ 2.8
Italian	0.8	− 1.1
Dutch	3.5	+ 2.6
Polish	1.1	+ 0.2
Ukrainian	1.6	− 0.4
Other	8.6	+ 4.8
Total	100.0	—

Official language spoken (1961 census)

English only	96.9	+29.5
French only	0.1	−19.0
Both English and French	1.6	−10.6
Neither English nor French	1.4	+ 0.1
Total	100.0	—

AVERAGE INCOME (1961 CENSUS)

	Dollars	% above or below Canadian average
Income per family (non-farm)	5,076	− 6.85
Income per person not in family (non-farm)	2,106	− 1.45
Income per farm (net)	8,492	+160.89

POVERTY AND AFFLUENCE (1961 CENSUS)

	Number	% of region's total	% points above or below Canadian average
Extent of poverty			
Families earning below $3,000 a year (non-farm)	4,645	25.6	+ 2.3
Persons not in families earning below $1,500 a year (non-farm)	3,257	49.5	+ 0.6
Farms with gross income of less than $2,500 a year	1,481	20.1	−26.0
Persons not in school with grade 4 or less education	8,749	12.5	− 0.9
Doubled-up households (more than one family per household)	575	2.0	− 1.7
Households living in dilapidated dwellings	2,457	8.5	+ 2.9
Households without facilities of running water	5,032	17.5	+ 6.6
Households without facilities of installed bath or shower	7,190	25.0	+ 5.3
Extent of affluence			
Families earning over $10,000 a year (non-farm)	1,190	6.6	− 1.2
Persons not in families earning over $6,000 a year (non-farm)	283	4.4	+ 0.6
Farms with gross income over $15,000 a year	1,380	18.7	+13.7
Persons with university degree	1,373	2.0	− 0.8
Households with two or more television sets	673	2.3	− 1.9
Households with two or more cars	2,208	7.7	+ 0.9

Alberta Rocky Mountains — Foothills

ECONOMIC CAPSULE

This region lies in the majestic Rocky Mountains. Located here are the two world-famous national parks, Banff and Jasper, where thousands of tourists come every year to ski, hike, ride, or just admire nature's awe-inspiring grandeur. The recently completed Banff-Jasper Highway is one of the continent's most scenic motor routes. The Banff School of Fine Arts, operated in the summer by the extension department of the University of Alberta, draws students from all parts of the continent.

In addition to tourism, the chief economic activities are forestry, mining, and cattle ranching. Coal is the major mineral; it is extracted chiefly at Blairmore, Canmore, and Coleman.

As a marketing area, the region is heterogeneous, with no town acting as a nucleus of distribution. Blairmore serves the main Crowsnest zone, Calgary dominates the central or Banff zone, Red Deer caters to the northeastern zone along the Red Deer spur, while the Jasper zone is tied to Edson.

Area covered: 17,775 square miles. *Census division:* 9.

COMPOSITION OF THE MARKET

Place	Census Division	Population 1961	% of the region
Banff	9	3,429	16.91
Jasper	9	2,360	11.64
Blairmore	9	1,980	9.77
Canmore	9	1,736	8.56
Coleman	9	1,713	8.45
Bellevue	9	1,323	6.53
Total urban	—	12,541	61.86
Rural non-farm	—	7,013	34.59
Rural farm	—	720	3.55
Total population		20,274	100.00

IMPORTANCE OF THE MARKET (1964 ESTIMATES)

	Number	% of Canada
Population	21,500	0.11
Households	5,700	0.12
Disposable income ($ million)	31.8	0.10

POVERTY AND AFFLUENCE (1961 CENSUS)

	Number	% of region's total	% points above or below Canadian average
Extent of poverty			
Families earning below $3,000 a year (non-farm).......	948	22.6	− 0.7
Persons not in families earning below $1,500 a year (non-farm)...	874	43.8	− 5.1
Farms with gross income of less than $2,500 a year....	101	57.7	+11.6
Persons not in school with grade 4 or less education..	1,901	14.1	+ 0.7
Doubled-up households (more than one family per household)...	112	2.1	− 1.6
Households living in dilapidated dwellings..............	615	11.6	+ 6.0
Households without facilities of running water........	771	14.6	+ 3.7
Households without facilities of installed bath or shower..	1,473	27.9	+ 8.2
Extent of affluence			
Families earning over $10,000 a year (non-farm)........	225	5.4	− 2.4
Persons not in families earning over $6,000 a year (non-farm)...	87	4.4	+ 0.6
Farms with gross income over $15,000 a year..........	16	9.2	+ 4.2
Persons with university degree.................................	209	1.6	− 1.2
Households with two or more television sets...........	24	0.5	− 3.7
Households with two or more cars............................	292	5.5	− 1.3

CHARACTERISTICS OF THE POPULATION

	% of the total population of the region	% points above or below Canadian average
Mother tongue (1961 census)		
English..	69.9	+11.5
French...	1.8	−26.3
German..	3.4	+ 0.3
Native Indian dialects......................................	6.7	+ 5.8
Italian..	3.9	+ 2.0
Dutch...	1.1	+ 0.2
Polish..	2.7	+ 1.8
Ukrainian...	2.6	+ 0.6
Other...	7.9	+ 4.1
Total...	100.0	—

CHARACTERISTICS OF THE POPULATION (continued)

	% of the total population of the region	% points above or below Canadian average
Official language spoken (1961 census)		
English only	93.8	+26.4
French only	0.2	−18.9
Both English and French	4.2	− 8.0
Neither English nor French	1.8	+ 0.5
Total	100.0	—

GROWTH OF THE MARKET

	Percentage change 1961 to 1964	% points above or below Canadian average
Population	+6.05	+ 0.58
Disposable income	−4.79	−26.32

LABOR FORCE BY INDUSTRY

Industry	Persons 1961 census	% of the total	% points above or below Canadian average
Agriculture	299	3.6	− 6.3
Forestry	308	3.7	+ 2.0
Fishing and trapping	3	—	− 0.5
Mines, quarries, oil wells	809	9.7	+ 7.8
Manufacturing	494	6.0	−15.7
Construction	900	10.8	+ 4.1
Transportation, communications, and other utilities	992	12.0	+ 2.7
Wholesale trade	82	1.0	− 3.5
Retail trade	653	7.9	− 2.9
Finance, insurance, and real estate	73	0.9	− 2.6
Community and business services	735	8.9	− 3.9
Personal services	1,650	19.9	+13.1
Public administration and defence	1,103	13.3	+ 5.8
Miscellaneous	190	2.3	− 0.1
Total labor force	8,291	100.0	—

AVERAGE INCOME (1961 CENSUS)

	Dollars	% above or below Canadian average
Income per family (non-farm)	4,940	− 9.34
Income per person not in family (non-farm)	2,434	+13.90
Income per farm (net)	4,656	+43.04

Calgary — South Central Alberta

ECONOMIC CAPSULE

This is largely a mid-grass prairie zone. At the western end it merges slowly with the foothills of the Rocky Mountains. Agriculture (livestock and mixed farming) is the major primary industry, followed by mining (coal, oil, and natural gas).

Calgary, the "biggest" city in Canada in terms of land area, is often referred to as "the Sunshine City of the Foothills". Not only does it have as a backdrop the majestic snow-capped Rockies, but it is fortunate in enjoying a dry climate with an impressive 2,200 hours of sunshine yearly, more than most other places in the west. A Gaelic word, Calgary means "clear, running water". That well describes its picturesque location at the junction of the Bow and the Elbow rivers.

Calgary has two unassailable claims to fame: the chinook and the Stampede, and there is a pleasant sort of madness associated with each. The chinook is a warm, dry wind blowing from the Pacific, and it can, in a matter of hours, raise the mercury by as much as 50 degrees. It is not rare to hear almost incredible stories of inhabitants playing tennis in midwinter when only a few hours ago the ground was covered with snow. Of course, not all chinooks cause the temperatures to soar so high, but the contrast between the weather of one day and the next can be often very exhilarating.

The Stampede is a combination of rodeo, carnival, and Royal Agricultural Fair. To half a million visitors who come to watch "the Biggest Outdoor Show on Earth", it provides the nearest thing to a fiesta in North America. For a week in July, Calgary deliberately submerges the present and tries exuberantly to revive its pioneer "cow-town" days. Thousands of citizens don cowboy costumes and white ten-gallon hats. Feed stalls are set up along the main streets, and cowboys and cowgirls toss out sourdough flapjacks from the chuckwagons where they are cooked. The program includes all types of activities, such as dancing in the streets, thrilling chuckwagon races, colorful parades of Indians in their ceremonial dresses, climaxed by a grand cowboy ball finale.

When the excitement of the Stampede has died down and Calgary returns to its normal self, it is very much like a U.S. mid-west town. One finds the same conglomeration of towering steel office buildings, sprawling suburbs, large shopping centers, and other earmarks of American life — motels, drive-ins, outdoor movievilles, and used-car lots. The city has been under strong U.S. influence. Three separate waves of American immigration have rolled up here to pause at the foothills. The first came on horseback some seventy years ago. The second came by rail during the real estate boom of 1912. The third came in Cadillacs and Lincolns after the last war, to bore for oil.

Calgary disputes with Edmonton the title of the petroleum capital of Canada. The majority of the large Canadian and American companies have selected Calgary for their head offices, and from here they direct exploratory and drilling operations over wide areas of the western plains. The employees of these firms earn well, which fact explains the city's very high per capita income. The 1961 census shows that one out of five households made more than $8,000 a year. It is small wonder, then, that Calgary leads the nation in per capita motor vehicle registration, and is way up on the list of per capita housing construction and per capita retail trade, particularly for luxury and recreational goods. Oil has spelt growth and expansion for the city.

But though oil overshadows cattle as Calgary's biggest industry, the latter still provides the catalyst for much of the business activity. Nearly $100 million worth of livestock passes through the stockyards annually. The city holds the largest bull sale in the world, in terms of total number of critters auctioned, at mid-March every year.

Manufacturing is quite varied, though most of it is directly or indirectly tied to oil and agriculture, e.g. petroleum refineries, chemical firms, flour and feed mills, meat-packing establishments, breweries, fertilizer plants, and factories producing farm machinery and equipment. Other industries include metal fabricating, printing and publishing, and the manufacture of railroad rolling stock, batteries, tires, paper boxes, furniture, and gypsum products.

Calgary wholesalers supply a very extensive area of southern Alberta and eastern British Columbia, and the city is an important financial center. Its banking transactions place it in fifth position behind Toronto, Montréal, Winnipeg, and Vancouver, by far outstripping many big eastern cities.

Farm families still come to Calgary for much of their shopping, as they have done over the years. For them now the days of depression and grasshoppers and drought are dim memories. They have benefited from Calgary's prosperity, and find in the city an ideal outlet to sell their varied crops and high quality livestock. The market will continue to expand, since, according to the estimates prepared by the City Planning Department, Calgary's population is likely to reach 645,-500 by 1981.

CALGARY—SOUTH CENTRAL ALBERTA

Area covered: 19,896 square miles. *Census divisions:* 4, 5, and 6.

COMPOSITION OF THE MARKET

Place	Census Division	Population 1961	% of the region
Calgary (metro)	6	279,062	75.19
Drumheller	5	2,931	0.79
Hanna	4	2,645	0.71
Olds	6	2,433	0.66
High River	6	2,276	0.62
Three Hills	5	1,491	0.40
Vulcan	5	1,310	0.35
Didsbury	6	1,254	0.34
Black Diamond	6	1,043	0.28
Okotoks	6	1,043	0.28
Total urban	—	295,488	79.62
Rural non-farm	—	32,018	8.63
Rural farm	—	43,618	11.75
Total population		371,124	100.00

IMPORTANCE OF THE MARKET (1964 ESTIMATES)

	Region		Calgary	
	Number	% of Canada	Number	% of Canada
Population	416,700	2.17	310,000	1.61
Households	115,400	2.40	91,200	1.90
Disposable income ($ million)	763.0	2.42	605.4	1.92

GROWTH OF THE MARKET

	Region		Calgary	
	Percentage growth 1961 to 1964	% points above or below Canadian average	Percentage growth 1961 to 1964	% points above or below Canadian average
Population	+12.28	+6.81	+11.09	+5.62
Disposable income	+25.39	+3.86	+21.88	+0.35

LABOR FORCE BY INDUSTRY

Industry	Region Persons 1961 census	Region % of the total	Region % points above or below Canadian average	Calgary Persons 1961 census	Calgary % of the total
Agriculture	16,456	11.7	+ 1.8	998	0.9
Forestry	115	0.1	− 1.6	76	0.1
Fishing and trapping	12	—	− 0.5	12	—
Mines, quarries, oil wells	8,395	6.0	+ 4.1	6,942	6.3
Manufacturing	13,706	9.7	−12.0	13,064	12.0
Construction	12,014	8.5	+ 1.8	10,613	9.7
Transportation, communications, and other utilities	15,035	10.7	+ 1.4	12,202	11.2
Wholesale trade	10,383	7.4	+ 2.9	9,529	8.7
Retail trade	16,857	12.0	+ 1.2	14,317	13.1
Finance, insurance, and real estate	5,984	4.2	+ 0.7	5,566	5.1
Community and business services.	18,471	13.1	+ 0.3	15,373	14.1
Personal services	9,506	6.7	− 0.1	8,081	7.4
Public administration and defence	10,589	7.5	—	9,786	8.9
Miscellaneous	3,313	2.4	—	2,697	2.5
Total labor force	140,836	100.0	—	109,256	100.0

CHARACTERISTICS OF THE POPULATION

	Region % of the total population of the region	Region % points above or below Canadian average	Calgary % of the total population of the city
Mother tongue (1961 census)			
English	81.8	+23.4	82.1
French	1.2	−26.9	1.3
German	6.2	+ 3.1	5.8
Native Indian dialects	0.6	− 0.3	—
Italian	1.0	− 0.9	1.2
Dutch	1.8	+ 0.9	1.9
Polish	0.8	− 0.1	0.8
Ukrainian	1.5	− 0.5	1.6
Other	5.1	+ 1.3	5.3
Total	100.0	—	100.0

CHARACTERISTICS OF THE POPULATION (continued)

	Region		Calgary
	% of the total population of the region	% points above or below Canadian average	% of the total population of the city
Official language spoken (1961 census)			
English only	96.3	+28.9	95.9
French only	0.1	−19.0	0.1
Both English and French	2.9	− 9.3	3.3
Neither English nor French	0.7	− 0.6	0.7
Total	100.0	—	100.0

AVERAGE INCOME (1961 CENSUS)

	Region		Calgary	
	Dollars	% above or below Canadian average	Dollars	% above or below Canadian average
Income per family (non-farm)	6,093	+ 11.82	6,351	+16.55
Income per person not in family (non-farm)	2,497	+ 16.85	2,563	+19.94
Income per farm (net)	7,616	+133.98	—	—

POVERTY AND AFFLUENCE (1961 CENSUS)

	Region			Calgary	
	Number	% of region's total	% points above or below Canadian average	Number	% of city's total
Extent of poverty					
Families earning below $3,000 a year (non-farm)	12,638	16.2	− 7.1	9,132	13.8
Persons not in families earning below $1,500 a year (non-farm)	12,770	39.1	− 9.8	10,283	36.7
Farms with gross income of less than $2,500 a year	2,301	20.4	−25.7	—	—
Persons not in school with grade 4 or less education	18,889	8.0	− 5.4	12,776	7.1
Doubled-up households (more than one family per household)	1,957	1.9	− 1.8	1,647	2.1

	Region			Calgary	
	Number	% of region's total	% points above or below Canadian average	Number	% of city's total
Households living in dilapidated dwellings	5,048	4.9	− 0.7	2,774	3.5
Households without facilities of running water	8,532	8.3	− 2.6	1,118	1.4
Households without facilities of installed bath or shower	11,746	11.4	− 8.3	1,841	2.4
Extent of affluence					
Families earning over $10,000 a year (non-farm)	7,581	9.8	+ 2.0	6,942	10.5
Persons not in families earning over $6,000 a year (non-farm)	1,593	4.9	+ 1.1	1,385	4.9
Farms with gross income over $15,000 a year	1,888	16.7	+11.7	—	—
Persons with university degree	9,476	4.0	+ 1.2	8,782	4.9
Households with two or more television sets	4,158	4.0	− 0.2	3,873	4.9
Households with two or more cars	10,351	10.1	+ 3.3	9,043	11.5

Red Deer Environs

ECONOMIC CAPSULE

The deep valley of the Red Deer River — "the little Grand Canyon of Canada" — cuts through soft rock which tells dramatically the geological story of the land. Numerous fossils have been found which indicate that dinosaurs and other prehistoric animals once roamed in this terrain. On the area adjacent to these "badlands", mixed farming is the rule, with special emphasis on the raising of beef cattle.

The whole region is a "watershed" between the Calgary and Edmonton areas of influence. Red Deer serves as the chief marketing center. The largest single manufacturing establishment here is the plant of the Central Alberta Dairy Pool, producing butter, milk powders and condensed milk. Other industries include a seed-cleaning mill, a poultry processing plant, and a brewery.

Area covered: 5,655 square miles. *Census division:* 8.

COMPOSITION OF THE MARKET

Place	Census Division	Population 1961	% of the region
Red Deer	8	19,612	25.63
Ponoka	8	3,938	5.15
Lacombe	8	3,029	3.96
Rocky Mountain House	8	2,360	3.08
Innisfail	8	2,270	2.97
Sylvan Lake	8	1,381	1.80
Rimbey	8	1,266	1.65
Total urban	—	33,856	44.24
Rural non-farm	—	16,205	21.17
Rural farm	—	26,472	34.59
Total population		76,533	100.00

CHARACTERISTICS OF THE POPULATION

	% of the total population of the region	% points above or below Canadian average
Mother tongue (1961 census)		
English	84.1	+25.7
French	1.0	−27.1
German	3.9	+ 0.8
Native Indian dialects	1.8	+ 0.9
Italian	0.2	− 1.7
Dutch	2.2	+ 1.3
Polish	0.4	− 0.5
Ukrainian	1.0	− 1.0
Other	5.4	+ 1.6
Total	100.0	—
Official language spoken (1961 census)		
English only	97.6	+30.2
French only	0.1	−19.0
Both English and French	1.7	−10.5
Neither English nor French	0.6	− 0.7
Total	100.0	—

IMPORTANCE OF THE MARKET (1964 ESTIMATES)

	Number	% of Canada
Population	81,600	0.42
Households	20,400	0.42
Disposable income ($ million)	119.4	0.38

GROWTH OF THE MARKET

	Percentage growth 1961 to 1964	% points above or below Canadian average
Population	+ 6.62	+1.15
Disposable income	+21.71	+0.18

POVERTY AND AFFLUENCE (1961 CENSUS)

	Number	% of region's total	% points above or below Canadian average
Extent of poverty			
Families earning below $3,000 a year (non-farm)	2,698	25.2	+ 1.9
Persons not in families earning below $1,500 a year (non-farm)	1,852	46.8	− 2.1
Farms with gross income of less than $2,500 a year	2,479	37.9	− 8.2
Persons not in school with grade 4 or less education	6,486	13.5	+ 0.1
Doubled-up households (more than one family per household)	311	1.6	− 2.1
Households living in dilapidated dwellings	1,781	9.3	+ 3.7
Households without facilities of running water	6,044	31.4	+20.5
Households without facilities of installed bath or shower	7,522	39.1	+19.4
Extent of affluence			
Families earning over $10,000 a year (non-farm)	858	8.0	+ 0.2
Persons not in families earning over $6,000 a year (non-farm)	141	3.5	− 0.3
Farms with gross income over $15,000 a year	386	5.9	+ 0.9
Persons with university degree	732	1.5	− 1.3
Households with two or more television sets	206	1.1	− 3.1
Households with two or more cars	1,195	6.2	− 0.6

AVERAGE INCOME (1961 CENSUS)

	Dollars	% above or below Canadian average
Income per family (non-farm)	5,429	− 0.37
Income per person not in family (non-farm)	2,130	− 0.33
Income per farm (net)	4,334	+33.15

LABOR FORCE BY INDUSTRY

Industry	Persons 1961 census	% of the total	% points above or below Canadian average
Agriculture	8,634	33.1	+23.2
Forestry	85	0.3	− 1.4
Fishing and trapping	4	—	− 0.5
Mines, quarries, oil wells	914	3.5	+ 1.6
Manufacturing	1,127	4.3	−17.4
Construction	2,015	7.7	+ 1.0
Transportation, communications, and other utilities	1,784	6.8	− 2.5
Wholesale trade	871	3.3	− 1.2
Retail trade	2,518	9.6	− 1.2
Finance, insurance, and real estate	509	2.0	− 1.5
Community and business services	3,864	14.8	+ 2.0
Personal services	1,532	5.9	− 0.9
Public administration and defence	1,749	6.7	− 0.8
Miscellaneous	519	2.0	− 0.4
Total labor force	26,125	100.0	—

East-Central Alberta Prairie

ECONOMIC CAPSULE

This region comprises the northern portion of the Alberta Prairie and the adjacent fringe of the Park Belt. The economy revolves around agriculture. The growing season is sufficiently long for certain crops, but the danger of frost is ever present. This has compelled the farmers to rely on early maturing wheats, or to go in for mixed farming. There is no major marketing center. The region is dominated by Edmonton from the west, except Stettler, which has economic ties with Red Deer.

EAST-CENTRAL ALBERTA PRAIRIE

Area covered: 15,748 square miles. *Census divisions:* 7 and 10.

COMPOSITION OF THE MARKET

Place	Census Division	Population 1961	% of the region
Camrose	10	6,939	6.25
Stettler	7	3,638	3.28
Wainwright	7	3,351	3.02
Lloydminster	10	2,944*	2.65
Vegreville	10	2,908	2.62
Vermilion	10	2,449	2.21
Viking	10	1,043	0.94
Castor	7	1,025	0.92
Provost	7	1,022	0.92
Total urban	—	25,319	22.81
Rural non-farm	—	29,579	26.64
Rural farm	—	56,116	50.55
Total population		111,014	100.00

* Total population of Lloydminster is 5,667 of which 2,944 is in Alberta and 2,723 is in Census Division 17 of Saskatchewan.

LABOR FORCE BY INDUSTRY

Industry	Persons 1961 census	% of the total	% points above or below Canadian average
Agriculture	21,167	52.9	+43.0
Forestry	12	—	− 1.7
Fishing and trapping	—	—	− 0.5
Mines, quarries, oil wells	554	1.4	− 0.5
Manufacturing	1,067	2.7	−19.0
Construction	1,478	3.7	− 3.0
Transportation, communications, and other utilities	2,878	7.2	− 2.1
Wholesale trade	1,050	2.6	− 1.9
Retail trade	3,353	8.4	− 2.4
Finance, insurance, and real estate	546	1.4	− 2.1
Community and business services	3,920	9.8	− 3.0
Personal services	1,716	4.3	− 2.5
Public administration and defence	1,594	4.0	− 3.5
Miscellaneous	666	1.6	− 0.8
Total labor force	40,001	100.0	—

IMPORTANCE OF THE MARKET (1964 ESTIMATES)

	Number	% of Canada
Population	106,000	0.55
Households	28,600	0.60
Disposable income ($ million)	154.9	0.49

GROWTH OF THE MARKET

	Percentage change 1961 to 1964	% points above or below Canadian average
Population	− 4.52	−9.99
Disposable income	+16.03	−5.50

CHARACTERISTICS OF THE POPULATION

	% of the total population of the region	% points above or below Canadian average
Mother tongue (1961 census)		
English	66.8	+ 8.4
French	1.4	−26.7
German	5.9	+ 2.8
Native Indian dialects	0.1	− 0.8
Italian	0.1	− 1.8
Dutch	0.5	− 0.4
Polish	1.4	+ 0.5
Ukrainian	18.4	+16.4
Other	5.4	+ 1.6
Total	100.0	—
Official language spoken (1961 census)		
English only	96.7	+29.3
French only	0.2	−18.9
Both English and French	1.8	−10.4
Neither English nor French	1.3	—
Total	100.0	—

AVERAGE INCOME (1961 CENSUS)

	Dollars	% above or below Canadian average
Income per family (non-farm)	4,481	−17.76
Income per person not in family (non-farm)	1,760	−17.64
Income per farm (net)	3,975	+22.12

POVERTY AND AFFLUENCE (1961 CENSUS)

	Number	% of region's total	% points above or below Canadian average
Extent of poverty			
Families earning below $3,000 a year (non-farm)	4,423	35.0	+11.7
Persons not in families earning below $1,500 a year (non-farm)	3,069	57.6	+ 8.7
Farms with gross income of less than $2,500 a year	5,139	33.4	−12.7
Persons not in school with grade 4 or less education	10,769	15.4	+ 2.0
Doubled-up households (more than one family per household)	488	1.6	− 2.1
Households living in dilapidated dwellings	3,006	10.1	+ 4.5
Households without facilities of running water	13,880	46.9	+36.0
Households without facilities of installed bath or shower	15,673	53.0	+33.3
Extent of affluence			
Families earning over $10,000 a year (non-farm)	619	4.8	− 3.0
Persons not in families earning over $6,000 a year (non-farm)	121	2.3	− 1.5
Farms with gross income over $15,000 a year	569	3.7	− 1.3
Persons with university degree	862	1.2	− 1.6
Households with two or more television sets	78	0.3	− 3.9
Households with two or more cars	1,362	4.6	− 2.2

Edmonton — Parklands

ECONOMIC CAPSULE

This is a rich farming area covering the northern portion of the Prairie zone and the cultivated Park Belt. The economy is diversified, based upon agriculture (mixed farming), mining (oil, gas, and coal), and forestry along the northern fringe.

The whole region is dominated by Metropolitan Edmonton, the capital of Alberta and the West's boom market par excellence. As one writer aptly remarks: "Take the wealth of oil and petrochemical industries; mix it with one of Canada's most productive agricultural zones; add to it the unlimited prospects of being the gateway to the treasure-house of the North; stir it with some dose of civic spirit as evidenced by the ultra-modern, highly sophisticated city center; allow these ingredients to harmonize under the sunny skies of Alberta, and the result is Edmonton, one of the fastest growing cities on the continent."

In all Canada, no other city is so pleasantly egocentric, so certain of Providence's special dispensation, so eager to quote statistics of progress. It is, as Bruce Hutchison says, "the self-worshipping Narcissus of the nation." Nothing seems to matter here if it represents growth; for growth is Edmonton's pride and joy. The population has more than doubled itself in the last 15 years and the City Fathers confidently expect it to reach 660,000 by 1980.

Edmonton has been a center of many booms. In the days of the Hudson's Bay Company it was the greatest fur metropolis on the continent. Another boom occurred in 1898 when it became a base of supplies for the Klondike's gold rush. When that fever died down, many disillusioned miners and prospectors settled permanently in the city. Later on there were mining booms and land-grabbing sprees. During the depression and drought years the pace slowed down practically to a halt, but the Second World War brought another burst of activity. In 1942 Edmonton became the base for building the Alaska Highway and the Canol pipeline linking Norman Wells with Whitehorse, Yukon. The current boom started in the wake of the oil discovery at Leduc in 1947. Since then new fields have been opened up in quick succession, and most of the benefits have accrued to Edmonton, because 60% of Alberta's producing oil wells are within a 50-mile radius of the city.

Before the effects of the oil development peter out (and there is no sign of that as yet on the horizon) a new boom is budding that may outstrip oil in importance. Canada's north is bustling with activity, and Edmonton is sure to benefit, being the natural gateway to the continent's last great frontier. It is not only an entrepôt to the rapidly growing Peace River Country, but also a "rear base" for the gigantic mining operation at Pine Point, as well as a distribution center for the supplies shipped to McMurray, where the work has just started on extracting oil from the tar sands.

Edmonton's industries are based upon its rich hinterland. The products of farm, forest, coal mines, oil fields, and gas wells, from Central Alberta all the way to the Arctic, are sucked into the city by rail, road, air, and pipeline. Meat packing is the major industry, Edmonton being, after Toronto, the largest processor of beef in Canada. Northern fisheries sell yearly more than $1,000,000 worth of fish through this market. About the same amount of business is done annually in furs from northern traplines and from fur farms. The forests to the northwest supply lumber for plywood and other wood product industries.

For many years coal mining was carried on in the vicinity of Edmonton and even within the city limits, but now natural gas and petroleum products have replaced coal as the chief sources of fuel. The discovery of oil has led to the building of several petroleum refineries. Edmonton is the starting point of the Interprovincial Pipe Line to Ontario and Trans-Mountain Oil Pipe Line to British Columbia. The city lately has become the nucleus of a multi-million dollar petro-chemical complex. Modern chemical plants extract and convert several components of natural gas — butane, propane, ethane, and many others — into a wide range of valuable industrial chemicals and plastics. Secondary

EDMONTON—PARKLANDS

Area covered: 14,956 square miles. *Census divisions:* 11 and 13.

COMPOSITION OF THE MARKET

Place	Census Division	Population 1961	% of the region
Edmonton (metro)	11	337,568	74.01
Wetaskiwin	11	5,300	1.16
Drayton Valley	11	3,854	0.84
Fort Saskatchewan	11	2,972	0.65
Strathcona	11	2,923	0.64
Leduc	11	2,356	0.52
Barrhead	13	2,286	0.50
Westlock	13	1,838	0.40
Athabasca	13	1,487	0.33
Devon	11	1,418	0.31
Stony Plain	11	1,311	0.29
Redwater	13	1,135	0.25
Total urban	—	364,448	79.90
Rural non-farm	—	28,644	6.28
Rural farm	—	63,018	13.82
Total population		456,110	100.00

manufacturing plants using some of these materials are already in production, and future expansion in this direction seems limitless.

The exploration and growth of the Northland have led to the establishment in Edmonton of companies manufacturing such items as geophysical instruments, prospecting equipment, and mining machinery. Other industries include aircraft maintenance and repair, structural steel fabrication, steel rolling mills, cement production, and nickel refining (at nearby Fort Saskatchewan). The gross value of manufacturing more than quadrupled from $119,448,000 in 1950 to more than $492,000,000 in 1964.

With each new basic industrial development—prospecting, processing, manufacturing, distributing, and servicing — more and more workers and their families are attracted to Edmonton. The economic foundation rests on a firm base, and many experts believe that if Edmonton is able to maintain its current pace of growth, it may within a generation overtake Winnipeg as Canada's most populous city and largest industrial center between the Great Lakes and the Rockies.

CHARACTERISTICS OF THE POPULATION

	Region		Edmonton
	% of the total population of the region	% points above or below Canadian average	% of the total population of the city
Mother tongue (1961 census)			
English	70.0	+11.6	71.9
French	3.7	−24.4	3.3
German	8.1	+ 5.0	7.0
Native Indian dialects	0.9	—	0.3
Italian	0.8	− 1.1	1.1
Dutch	2.1	+ 1.2	2.3
Polish	1.7	+ 0.8	1.6
Ukrainian	8.5	+ 6.5	8.3
Other	4.2	+ 0.4	4.2
Total	100.0	—	100.0
Official language spoken (1961 census)			
English only	93.6	+26.2	93.8
French only	0.3	−18.8	0.3
Both English and French	5.1	− 7.1	5.0
Neither English nor French	1.0	− 0.3	0.9
Total	100.0	—	100.0

IMPORTANCE OF THE MARKET (1964 ESTIMATES)

	Region		Edmonton	
	Number	% of Canada	Number	% of Canada
Population	502,600	2.61	372,000	1.93
Households	131,900	2.75	100,500	2.09
Disposable income ($ million)	851.5	2.70	689.7	2.19

GROWTH OF THE MARKET

	Region		Edmonton	
	Percentage growth 1961 to 1964	% points above or below Canadian average	Percentage growth 1961 to 1964	% points above or below Canadian average
Population	+10.19	+4.72	+10.20	+4.73
Disposable income	+17.87	−3.66	+19.97	−1.56

LABOR FORCE BY INDUSTRY

	Region			Edmonton	
Industry	Persons 1961 census	% of the total	% points above or below Canadian average	Persons 1961 census	% of the total
Agriculture	22,430	12.9	+ 3.0	1,346	1.0
Forestry	334	0.2	− 1.5	129	0.1
Fishing and trapping	59	—	− 0.5	23	—
Mines, quarries, oil wells	4,844	2.8	+ 0.9	2,839	2.2
Manufacturing	18,929	10.9	−10.8	17,477	13.3
Construction	14,930	8.6	+ 1.9	12,442	9.5
Transportation, communications, and other utilities	17,662	10.2	+ 0.9	14,649	11.1
Wholesale trade	11,624	6.7	+ 2.2	10,648	8.1
Retail trade	19,952	11.5	+ 0.7	17,062	13.0
Finance, insurance, and real estate	5,881	3.4	− 0.1	5,467	4.1
Community and business services	24,796	14.3	+ 1.5	21,819	16.6
Personal services	10,870	6.3	− 0.5	9,248	7.0
Public administration and defence	17,089	9.9	+ 2.4	15,211	11.6
Miscellaneous	3,953	2.3	− 0.1	3,216	2.4
Total labor force	173,353	100.0	—	131,576	100.0

AVERAGE INCOME (1961 CENSUS)

	Region		Edmonton	
	Dollars	% above or below Canadian average	Dollars	% above or below Canadian average
Income per family (non-farm)	5,825	+6.90	5,998	+10.08
Income per person not in family (non-farm)	2,325	+8.80	2,384	+11.56
Income per farm (net)	2,997	−7.93	—	—

POVERTY AND AFFLUENCE (1961 CENSUS)

	Region			Edmonton	
	Number	% of region's total	% points above or below Canadian average	Number	% of city's total
Extent of poverty					
Families earning below $3,000 a year (non-farm)	15,536	17.1	−6.2	11,651	14.9
Persons not in families earning below $1,500 a year (non-farm)	14,490	41.6	−7.3	11,747	39.0
Farms with gross income of less than $2,500 a year	7,898	49.9	+3.8	—	—
Persons not in school with grade 4 or less education	34,473	12.1	−1.3	21,768	10.3
Doubled-up households (more than one family per household)	3,071	2.6	−1.1	2,507	2.8
Households living in dilapidated dwellings	7,669	6.4	+0.8	4,000	4.5
Households without facilities of running water	17,762	14.9	+4.0	1,793	2.0
Households without facilities of installed bath or shower	20,827	17.5	−2.2	2,860	3.2
Extent of affluence					
Families earning over $10,000 a year (non-farm)	7,820	8.6	+0.8	7,116	9.1
Persons not in families earning over $6,000 a year (non-farm)	1,523	4.5	+0.7	1,295	4.3

	Region			Edmonton	
	Number	% of region's total	% points above or below Canadian average	Number	% of city's total
Farms with gross income over $15,000 a year	425	2.7	−2.3	—	—
Persons with university degree	10,018	3.5	+0.7	9,181	4.3
Households with two or more television sets	4,106	3.5	−0.7	3,947	4.4
Households with two or more cars	10,714	9.0	+2.2	9,223	10.4

Northeastern Alberta

ECONOMIC CAPSULE

The population here is very sparse. The majority of the inhabitants live in the south where agriculture (mixed farming and livestock raising) provides the chief means of livelihood. In the north, lumbering, fishing, and trapping are the main occupations. The whole region depends mainly on Edmonton for distribution.

The Athabaska area contains a vast reservoir of oil imprisoned in the tar-sands. The deposit, covering about 20,700 square miles, has long been known as one of the world's greatest untapped sources of petroleum. The Alberta Gas and Conservation Board estimates the reserves at 626 billion barrels of the "black gold". Experts believe that at least half of these can be recovered economically — enough to supply Canada and the United States, at current consumption rates, for over 100 years.

These fabulous deposits have lured oil men for decades. Now at last they are being opened and mined. Great Canadian Oil Sands, Ltd., backed by the Sun Oil Company, is investing $191 million to build at McMurray a plant which by 1967 will be capable of extracting (by a special hot water recovery process) about 45,000 barrels of oil daily. The high-grade synthetic crude will be piped 270 miles to Interprovincial Pipe Lines' hookup near Edmonton. In the course of the refining process, the company will also produce large quantities of petroleum coke which will be used for generating electricity for the town. Meanwhile, as the plant devours mountains of black oil sands, it will spew out other mountains of gleaming white sand as fine and clean as any on an ocean beach. Much thought is being given to disposal of this by-product; there is even talk of a local glass industry based on it.

So far, Great Canadian is the only company authorized by the Alberta Government to tap the oil-sand treasure. Several other firms, including Cities Service, Shell, and Imperial Oil, have leases in the area and are ready to commence large-scale commercial operations once they get the green light from the provincial officials. Ironically, the Athabaska reserves are so vast that once oil can be extracted economically, the government fears the companies may cease development of traditional oil wells.

NORTHEASTERN ALBERTA

Area covered: 50,242 square miles. *Census division:* 12.

COMPOSITION OF THE MARKET

Place	Census Division	Population 1961	% of the region
St. Paul	12	2,823	5.97
Bonnyville	12	1,736	3.67
Grand Centre	12	1,493	3.15
Lac La Biche	12	1,314	2.78
Cold Lake	12	1,307	2.76
McMurray	12	1,186	2.51
Total urban	—	9,859	20.84
Rural non-farm	—	18,837	39.82
Rural farm	—	18,614	39.34
Total population		47,310	100.00

IMPORTANCE OF THE MARKET (1964 ESTIMATES)

	Number	% of Canada
Population	47,300	0.25
Households	10,600	0.22
Disposable income ($ million)	57.5	0.18

GROWTH OF THE MARKET

	Percentage change 1961 to 1964	% points above or below Canadian average
Population	−0.02	− 5.49
Disposable income	+4.55	−16.98

POVERTY AND AFFLUENCE (1961 CENSUS)

	Number	% of region's total	% points above or below Canadian average
Extent of poverty			
Families earning below $3,000 a year (non-farm)........	2,455	43.4	+20.1
Persons not in families earning below $1,500 a year (non-farm)................	1,462	69.3	+20.4
Farms with gross income of less than $2,500 a year....	2,589	57.6	+11.5
Persons not in school with grade 4 or less education..	7,485	27.3	+13.9
Doubled-up households (more than one family per household)................	300	2.8	− 0.9
Households living in dilapidated dwellings................	2,078	19.4	+13.8
Households without facilities of running water........	7,285	67.9	+57.0
Households without facilities of installed bath or shower................	7,727	72.0	+52.3
Extent of affluence			
Families earning over $10,000 a year (non-farm)........	137	2.4	− 5.4
Persons not in families earning over $6,000 a year (non-farm)................	45	2.1	− 1.7
Farms with gross income over $15,000 a year.........	23	0.6	− 4.4
Persons with university degree....	291	1.1	− 1.7
Households with two or more television sets...........	15	0.1	− 4.1
Households with two or more cars............	253	2.4	− 4.4

CHARACTERISTICS OF THE POPULATION

	% of the total population of the region	% points above or below Canadian average
Official language spoken (1961 census)		
English only................	74.5	+ 7.1
French only................	2.8	−16.3
Both English and French................	17.7	+ 5.5
Neither English nor French................	5.0	+ 3.7
Total................	100.0	—

Mother tongue (1961 census)

English	40.9	−17.5
French	18.1	−10.0
German	1.3	− 1.8
Native Indian dialects	13.3	+12.4
Italian	0.3	− 1.6
Dutch	0.2	− 0.7
Polish	2.0	+ 1.1
Ukrainian	21.2	+19.2
Other	2.7	− 1.1
Total	100.0	—

AVERAGE INCOME (1961 CENSUS)

	Dollars	% above or below Canadian average
Income per family (non-farm)	3,752	−31.14
Income per person not in family (non-farm)	1,442	−32.52
Income per farm (net)	2,030	−37.63

LABOR FORCE BY INDUSTRY

Industry	Persons 1961 census	% of the total	% points above or below Canadian average
Agriculture	7,274	46.3	+36.4
Forestry	161	1.0	− 0.7
Fishing and trapping	259	1.7	+ 1.2
Mines, quarries, oil wells	106	0.7	− 1.2
Manufacturing	304	1.9	−19.8
Construction	494	3.1	− 3.6
Transportation, communications, and other utilities	1,020	6.5	− 2.8
Wholesale trade	227	1.4	− 3.1
Retail trade	875	5.6	− 5.2
Finance, insurance, and real estate	122	0.8	− 2.7
Community and business services	1,398	8.9	− 3.9
Personal services	617	3.9	− 2.9
Public administration and defence	2,425	15.4	+ 7.9
Miscellaneous	446	2.8	+ 0.4
Total labor force	15,728	100.0	—

Northwestern Alberta — Peace River

ECONOMIC CAPSULE

The Peace River District represents the fringe of agricultural settlement in Western Canada. This is the isolated northern extension of the Great Plains Belt and the Park Belt. Summer temperatures are but slightly below those of Edmonton, although midwinter is considerably colder. Precipitation figures, too, resemble those of Central Alberta, with the same summer concentration of rainfall.

The generalized wheat farming that characterized the early pioneer wave (1906-1914) has given way to emphasis on barley and oats grown in support of livestock raising, or else to a specialization in seed oats, seed hay, and seed alfalfa. These last do particularly well because the region is still free from many of the weeds and pests that damage the crops farther south.

However, the economy is not dependent solely on agriculture. The river valley is extensively wooded, and lumbering is an important industry in many places, especially on the grey soils beyond the better farming area. The extraction of oil and natural gas is rapidly expanding, though distance from the market still keeps the cost of transportation high.

Grande Prairie is the unacknowledged capital of the Peace River Country, and the regional headquarters of banks and insurance companies, as well as of provincial government agencies. A new highway provides a fast short-cut to Edmonton.

Area covered: 104,664 square miles. *Census divisions:* 14 and 15.

COMPOSITION OF THE MARKET

Place	Census Division	Population 1961	% of the region
Grande Prairie	15	8,352	8.68
Hinton	14	3,529	3.67
Edson	14	3,198	3.32
Peace River	15	2,543	2.64
High Prairie	15	1,756	1.83
Fairview	15	1,506	1.57
Grimshaw	15	1,095	1.14
McLennan	15	1,078	1.12
Valleyview	15	1,077	1.12
Whitecourt	14	1,054	1.10
Total urban	—	25,188	26.19
Rural non-farm	—	35,207	36.61
Rural farm	—	35,771	37.20
Total population		96,166	100.00

IMPORTANCE OF THE MARKET (1964 ESTIMATES)

	Number	% of Canada
Population	98,800	0.51
Households	24,100	0.50
Disposable income ($ million)	132.1	0.42

GROWTH OF THE MARKET

	Percentage growth 1961 to 1964	% points above or below Canadian average
Population	+ 2.74	−2.73
Disposable income	+20.20	−1.33

POVERTY AND AFFLUENCE (1961 CENSUS)

	Number	% of region's total	% points above or below Canadian average
Extent of poverty			
Families earning below $3,000 a year (non-farm)	4,138	33.7	+10.4
Persons not in families earning below $1,500 a year (non-farm)	2,809	51.9	+ 3.0
Farms with gross income of less than $2,500 a year	5,706	57.5	+11.4
Persons not in school with grade 4 or less education	11,935	20.7	+ 7.3
Doubled-up households (more than one family per household)	429	1.8	− 1.9
Households living in dilapidated dwellings	3,745	15.9	+10.3
Households without facilities of running water	14,357	61.1	+50.2
Households without facilities of installed bath or shower	15,770	67.1	+47.4
Extent of affluence			
Families earning over $10,000 a year (non-farm)	617	5.0	− 2.8
Persons not in families earning over $6,000 a year (non-farm)	188	3.4	− 0.4
Farms with gross income over $15,000 a year	97	0.9	− 4.1
Persons with university degree	680	1.2	− 1.6
Households with two or more television sets	20	0.1	− 4.1
Households with two or more cars	788	3.4	− 3.4

MEANS OF LIVELIHOOD—DISTRIBUTION OF

LABOR FORCE BY INDUSTRY

Industry	Persons 1961 census	% of the total	% points above or below Canadian average
Agriculture	11,280	35.5	+25.6
Forestry	1,748	5.5	+ 3.8
Fishing and trapping	496	1.6	+ 1.1
Mines, quarries, oil wells	1,045	3.3	+ 1.4
Manufacturing	1,811	5.7	−16.0
Construction	1,973	6.2	− 0.5
Transportation, communications, and other utilities	3,141	9.9	+ 0.6
Wholesale trade	948	3.0	− 1.5
Retail trade	2,494	7.8	− 3.0
Finance, insurance, and real estate	408	1.3	− 2.2
Community and business services	2,899	9.1	− 3.7
Personal services	1,737	5.5	− 1.3
Public administration and defence	968	3.0	− 4.5
Miscellaneous	818	2.6	+ 0.2
Total labor force	31,766	100.0	—

CHARACTERISTICS OF THE POPULATION

	% of the total population of the region	% points above or below Canadian average
Mother tongue (1961 census)		
English	63.0	+ 4.6
French	8.6	−19.5
German	6.6	+ 3.5
Native Indian dialects	8.8	+ 7.9
Italian	0.2	− 1.7
Dutch	1.5	+ 0.6
Polish	1.3	+ 0.4
Ukrainian	5.5	+ 3.5
Other	4.5	+ 0.7
Total	100.0	—

CHARACTERISTICS OF THE POPULATION (continued)

	% of the total population of the region	% points above or below Canadian average
Official language spoken (1961 census)		
English only	87.6	+20.2
French only	1.8	−17.3
Both English and French	8.2	− 4.0
Neither English nor French	2.4	+ 1.1
Total	100.0	—

AVERAGE INCOME (1961 CENSUS)

	Dollars	% above or below Canadian average
Income per family (non-farm)	4,557	−16.37
Income per person not in family (non-farm)	1,991	− 6.83
Income per farm (net)	2,340	−28.11

Chapter 18

BRITISH COLUMBIA

Introduction

British Columbia is Canada's third largest province, with an area of 359,279 square miles, yet its population, 1,738,000 (1964), is only three-fourths that of Metropolitan Montréal. About 7 out of 10 people live within 100 miles of Vancouver in the southwestern corner. A vast gulf exists between the varied and balanced economy of the south and the sparsely occupied pioneer settlements of the north, largely engaged in primary production. Although new highways and railroads are cutting into untracked wilderness, most of the northern half is as yet inaccessible. The construction costs in this rugged terrain are often a million dollars a mile or even more.

Agriculture

The mountainous nature of the land sets distinct limits on the development of agriculture. In 1964 net income received by farm operators amounted to only 1.8% of total personal income of the province, compared to 3.9% for the whole of Canada. Agricultural land covers only 4.5 million acres, less than 2% of the provincial land area. Merely 1.3 million acres are cultivated; the remaining 3.2 million acres are classified as "unimproved" and used mostly for grazing of cattle and sheep. Farming is concentrated mainly in the Okanagan Valley, the Fraser Plateau, the Lower Fraser Valley, and the Peace River district. The pattern of agriculture changes constantly to fit local conditions. Cattle and sheep are raised on the hillsides, wheat is cultivated on the heavier black soil, while fruits are grown on irrigated terraces.

Fisheries

The province is first in Canada in the value of fish landed, being responsible during the last decade for about 30% of the nation's catch. The fishing industry is quite diversified — salmon in the long fiords and river mouths, herring in the inner passages and fiords of the inshore, halibut in the deeper seas between the inner and outer isles, and whales and seals in the farther waters, beyond the outer isles. The salmon normally contributes from 60% to 70% to the total value of the fish caught. Of the half dozen species, the sockeye, weighing on the average seven pounds, is the most valuable because of its red-colored tender meat. The catch is taken to the local cannery, situated near the mouth of the salmon run, or to a floating cannery which accompanies the fishing fleet. The finished product is shipped to Vancouver for distribution all over the world.

Mining

Mining also plays an important role in the economic life of the province. The total value of mineral production increased by nearly 70% between 1959 and 1964. British Columbia is by far the biggest producer of lead, zinc, antimony, cadmium, diatomite, tin, and tungsten in Canada, and the second largest for silver and asbestos. Gold, which first attracted settlers to the province in 1858 and 1860 has now lost much of its glamor. In 1964 production was only 132,600 ounces worth $5,000,000. However, the decline in the output of gold has been more than counterbalanced by the major discoveries of oil and natural gas in the Peace River district.

Forestry

Forestry overshadows all the other primary industries. Directly or indirectly the woodlands generate about one-half of all the income earned by British Columbians. Productive forests carpet nearly 60% of the land area. The moist warm climate of the coastal region favors a luxuriant growth of conifers, such as Douglas fir, western hemlock, and western cedar, which provide some of the best timber for construction purposes in the world. The trees grow in dense stands and attain heights of 100 to 200 feet, with diameters of 3 to 8 feet. As a result, not only is the average yield per acre very high (6,000 cubic feet or more), but it is also possible to cut lumber to great lengths and breadths. To the east of the Coast Range the drier climate precludes luxuriant growth, but toward the Rockies the precipitation is heavier and the forests are dense again. A few years ago, the tidewater sawmills on Vancouver Island and along the lower mainland coast dominated B.C.'s lumber industry, but now interior mills have come into their own, and they are producing as much lumber as the coast mills.

Lately, the newsprint industry, too, has been very active. Many existing firms intend to expand their operations, and over half a dozen other companies are planning to erect new pulp or paper mills. If all goes well, more than $800 million dollars will be invested in the paper industry over the next several years, and pulpwood production by 1970 should be about 40% higher than in 1964.

The B.C. forests also support other industries — the manufacture of cellulose, veneers, plywood, sashes, doors, boxes, poles, piles, props, etc. Undoubtedly, as further advances are made in technology, new wood-using industries will spring up. There is no danger of timber depletion to hold back the growth. Forest management is now a scientific business. Careful tree farming and reforestation guarantee steady supplies of wood from the present stands. Today, lumberjacks are harvesting barely half of the allowable annual cut, and the only limit to expansion is the size and availability of markets.

Manufacturing

British Columbia does not have too many secondary manufacturing industries. The local market is, as yet, too small to warrant large-scale production. Most of the plants are concerned with the processing of raw materials found in the province or imported from overseas. Good examples are fish canneries, sawmills, pulp and paper mills, aluminum smelter (Kitimat), base metal smelter (Trail), petroleum refineries (Vancouver). There is thus a heavy concentration on primary exporting industries, but, as population increases, the economy will probably become diversified with the establishment of more secondary manufacturing and service industries.

Marketing characteristics

On the whole, British Columbia is a lucrative market to cultivate. The people are free spending, due to a combination of high wages and comparatively lower living costs. More money is left over for discretionary spending, since less is mopped up by fuel bills and other necessities for winter. Also, because of the government's hospitalization schemes, only a small portion of the family's budget is devoted to medical care. As a result, in normal years, the retail sales per capita are higher here than in any other province. There is a feeling of steady optimism in the air, in fact even of boom psychology, based on solid facts of past developments and future prospects.

However, the market presents some obstacles to national manufacturers whose plants are located in the east. The Rocky Mountain freight rates have forced British Columbia to become more and more economically independent of the rest of Canada. Consequently, many regional brands are well entrenched and cannot be ousted easily. Competition from south of the border is equally severe. The B.C. stores are excessively stocked with U.S. products, since comparable merchandise can be shipped from Oregon and Washington at a cost lower than that incurred by companies in Eastern Canada. Nor should one overlook the common practice of the inhabitants of the Coast of bringing back U.S. goods from their frequent trips to Bellingham, Seattle, and points south.

Another disadvantage of the B.C. market is the high distribution cost, especially in the interior. A salesman has to travel long distances to cover some thinly-populated settlements. The mountainous terrain splits the province into countless minor cells whose separate pockets of human life often have no direct communication with each other.

COMPOSITION OF THE MARKET

Place	Provincial region	Population 1961	% of British Columbia
Vancouver (metro)	Vancouver—Lower Fraser	790,165	48.50
Victoria (metro)	Victoria—Vancouver Island	154,152	9.46
Kamloops*	South Central British Columbia	18,700	1.15
Nanaimo*	Victoria—Vancouver Island	18,031	1.11
Prince George*	North-Central British Columbia	16,458	1.01
Port Alberni*	Victoria—Vancouver Island	16,176	0.99
Kelowna*	Okanagan Valley	14,243	0.87
Penticton	Okanagan Valley	13,859	0.85
Prince Rupert	Northwestern British Columbia	11,987	0.74
Chilliwack	Vancouver—Lower Fraser	11,724	0.72
Trail	West Kootenay	11,580	0.71
Dawson Creek	Northeastern British Columbia	10,946	0.67
Powell River	Northwestern British Columbia	10,748	0.66
Vernon	Okanagan Valley	10,250	0.63
Kitimat	Northwestern British Columbia	8,217	0.51
Nelson	West Kootenay	7,074	0.43
White Rock	Vancouver—Lower Fraser	6,453	0.40
Kimberley	East Kootenay	6,013	0.37
Cranbrook	East Kootenay	5,549	0.34
Total of towns over 5,000		1,142,325	70.12
53 Towns between 1,000 and 5,000		116,226	7.13
Total urban		1,258,551	77.25
Rural non-farm		292,991	17.99
Rural farm		77,540	4.76
Total population		1,629,082	100.00

* Urbanized area.

AVERAGE INCOME (1961 CENSUS)

	Dollars	% above or below Canadian average
Income per family (non-farm)	5,618	+ 3.10
Income per person not in family (non-farm)	2,224	+ 4.07
Income per farm (net)	2,720	− 16.44

IMPORTANCE OF THE MARKET (1964 ESTIMATES)

	Number	% of Canada
Population	1,738,000	9.04
Households	489,000	10.18
Disposable income ($ million)	3,263.0	10.35

GROWTH OF THE MARKET

	Percentage growth 1961 to 1964	% points above or below Canadian average
Population	+ 6.69	+1.22
Disposable income	+20.94	−0.59

POVERTY AND AFFLUENCE (1961 CENSUS)

	Number	% of province's total	% points above or below Canadian average
Extent of poverty			
Families earning below $3,000 a year (non-farm)	75,674	20.6	− 2.7
Persons not in families earning below $1,500 a year (non-farm)	74,052	48.7	− 0.2
Farms with gross income of less than $2,500 a year	11,784	59.1	+13.0
Persons not in school with grade 4 or less education	103,892	9.7	− 3.7
Doubled-up households (more than one family per household)	10,617	2.3	− 1.4
Households living in dilapidated dwellings	25,309	5.5	− 0.1
Households without facilities of running water	22,809	5.0	− 5.9
Households without facilities of installed bath or shower	38,817	8.5	−11.2
Extent of affluence			
Families earning over $10,000 a year (non-farm)	28,249	7.6	− 0.2
Persons not in families earning over $6,000 a year (non-farm)	6,211	4.1	+ 0.3
Farms with gross income over $15,000 a year	1,589	8.0	+ 3.0
Persons with university degree	33,859	3.2	+ 0.4
Households with two or more television sets	12,862	2.8	− 1.4
Households with two or more cars	45,508	9.9	+ 3.1

STANDARD OF LIVING BASED ON OWNERSHIP OF
APPLIANCES AND EQUIPMENT, 1965

	Number of households	% of total households in British Columbia	% points above or below Canadian average
Cooking equipment			
Electric stoves	337,000	67.5	− 1.5
Wood or coal cookstoves or ranges	23,000	4.6	− 4.6
Piped gas stoves	83,000	16.6	+ 2.5
Refrigeration			
Electric refrigerators	489,000	98.0	+ 2.2
Home freezers	139,000	27.9	+ 5.3
Electric washing machines			
Automatic	179,000	35.9	+12.8
Other	251,000	50.3	−12.9
Clothes dryers			
Electric	136,000	27.3	+ 2.1
Gas	6,000	1.2	− 1.0
Sewing machines			
Electric	285,000	57.1	+ 4.7
Non-electric	77,000	15.4	− 2.8
Phonographs and record players			
Cabinet model	206,000	41.3	+ 8.4
Table model	25,000	5.0	− 0.2
Portable model	87,000	17.4	− 3.6
Telephones			
One	401,000	80.4	+ 4.2
Two or more	61,000	12.2	− 1.0
Television sets			
One	417,000	83.6	+ 1.8
Two or more	38,000	7.6	− 3.3
Automobiles			
One	302,000	60.5	− 2.0
Two or more	96,000	19.2	+ 6.8
Other appliances			
Automatic dishwashers	16,000	3.2	+ 0.5
Vacuum cleaners	420,000	84.2	+ 9.3
Window-type air conditioners	6,000	1.2	− 1.0
FM radio receivers	99,000	19.8	− 3.1

(Source: DBS, *Household Facilities and Equipment, May 1965*. Catalogue no. 64-202.)

MEANS OF LIVELIHOOD—DISTRIBUTION OF

LABOR FORCE BY INDUSTRY

Industry	Persons 1961 census	% of the total	% points above or below Canadian average
Agriculture	23,290	4.0	− 5.9
Forestry	21,068	3.6	+ 1.9
Fishing and trapping	4,478	0.8	+ 0.3
Mines, quarries, oil wells	8,179	1.4	− 0.5
Manufacturing	113,019	19.6	− 2.1
Construction	36,338	6.3	− 0.4
Transportation, communications, and other utilities	62,806	10.9	+ 1.6
Wholesale trade	32,074	5.6	+ 1.1
Retail trade	67,204	11.6	+ 0.8
Finance, insurance, and real estate	22,642	3.9	+ 0.4
Community and business services	80,761	14.0	+ 1.2
Personal services	43,021	7.4	+ 0.6
Public administration and defence	46,001	8.0	+ 0.5
Miscellaneous	16,767	2.9	+ 0.5
Total labor force	577,648	100.0	—

CHARACTERISTICS OF THE POPULATION

	% of the total population of the province	% points above or below Canadian average
Mother tongue (1961 census)		
English	80.9	+22.5
French	1.6	−26.5
German	4.5	+ 1.4
Native Indian dialects	1.3	+ 0.4
Italian	1.5	− 0.4
Dutch	1.5	+ 0.6
Polish	0.6	− 0.3
Ukrainian	1.2	− 0.8
Other	6.9	+ 3.1
Total	100.0	—

Official language spoken (1961 census)

English only	95.3	+27.9
French only	0.2	−18.9
Both English and French	3.5	− 8.7
Neither English nor French	1.0	− 0.3
Total	100.0	—

East Kootenay

Area covered: 15,984 square miles. *Census division:* 1.

COMPOSITION OF THE MARKET

Place	Census Division	Population 1961	% of the region
Kimberley	1	6,013	17.56
Cranbrook	1	5,549	16.20
Fernie	1	2,661	7.77
Golden	1	1,776	5.19
Marysville	1	1,057	3.09
Slaterville	1	1,012	2.95
Total urban	—	18,068	52.76
Rural non-farm	—	14,722	42.99
Rural farm	—	1,454	4.25
Total population		34,244	100.00

ECONOMIC CAPSULE

Mining dominates the scene in this mountainous region in the southeastern corner of British Columbia. Half the reserves of coal in the province lie beneath the Crow's Nest Pass field in the Rockies. This coal is of the bituminous type, capable of producing good coke and therefore valuable for smelters. The chief mine is at Fernie, with an annual output of about 870,000 tons.

At Kimberley is located the famous Sullivan base-metal mine, which produces approximately 75% of Canada's lead and about 5% of the world's supply. In addition, the ore contains large amounts of zinc and iron sulphide and a small proportion of gold, silver, copper, and tin. So far the iron-rich waste from the smelter has been allowed to accumulate, but soon it will be put to good use, feeding the furnaces of Western Canada's first primary iron and steel plant, to be constructed near the mine site.

BRITISH COLUMBIA
East Kootenay — 1
West Kootenay — 2
Okanagan Valley — 3
South-Central British Columbia — 6
Vancouver — Lower Fraser — 4
Victoria — Vancouver Island — 5
Northwestern British Columbia — 7, 9
North-Central British Columbia — 8
North Eastern British Columbia — 10
(Numbers refer to Census Divisions)

9

10

• Dawson Creek

• Prince Rupert
• Kitimat

8

• Prince George

BRITISH COLUMBIA

6

1

5

• Powell River

• Kamloops

• Vernon

• Kelowna

2

Kimberley •

• Nelson

• Cranbrook

Port Alberni •

• Nanaimo

4

Vancouver

• Chilliwack

3

• Penticton

• Trail

Victoria •

• Population 5,000 and over
(1961 Census)

The region is also extensively forested, and lumbering is important locally. Some farming is carried on in the valleys, while the lower slopes of the mountains are used for grazing sheep and cattle.

The tourist trade continues to grow. The row of mountains topped by snow-capped peaks, the great longitudinal trenches with their rivers and lakes, the picturesque farming settlements and ranches — all combine to give the landscape a unique and well-differentiated geographic personality.

IMPORTANCE OF THE MARKET (1964 ESTIMATES)

	Number	% of Canada
Population	36,500	0.19
Households	9,800	0.20
Disposable income ($ million)	61.6	0.20

POVERTY AND AFFLUENCE (1961 CENSUS)

	Number	% of region's total	% points above or below Canadian average
Extent of poverty			
Families earning below $3,000 a year (non-farm)	1,282	17.2	− 6.1
Persons not in families earning below $1,500 a year (non-farm)	1,356	49.1	+ 0.2
Farms with gross income of less than $2,500 a year	274	69.0	+22.9
Persons not in school with grade 4 or less education	2,579	12.0	− 1.4
Doubled-up households (more than one family per household)	179	2.0	− 1.7
Households living in dilapidated dwellings	1,024	11.3	+ 5.7
Households without facilities of running water	1,105	12.2	+ 1.3
Households without facilities of installed bath or shower	2,013	22.2	+ 2.5
Extent of affluence			
Families earning over $10,000 a year (non-farm)	384	5.2	− 2.6
Persons not in families earning over $6,000 a year (non-farm)	121	4.4	+ 0.6
Farms with gross income over $15,000 a year	12	3.0	− 2.0
Persons with university degree	403	1.9	− 0.9
Households with two or more television sets	40	0.4	− 3.8
Households with two or more cars	408	4.5	− 2.3

GROWTH OF THE MARKET

	Percentage change 1961 to 1964	% points above or below Canadian average
Population	+6.59	+ 1.12
Disposable income	−8.74	−30.27

AVERAGE INCOME (1961 CENSUS)

	Dollars	% above or below Canadian average
Income per family (non-farm)	5,269	− 3.30
Income per person not in family (non-farm)	2,215	+ 3.65
Income per farm (net)	1,814	−44.27

CHARACTERISTICS OF THE POPULATION

	% of the total population of the region	% points above or below Canadian average
Mother tongue (1961 census)		
English	80.3	+21.9
French	1.7	−26.4
German	3.2	+ 0.1
Native Indian dialects	1.0	+ 0.1
Italian	4.6	+ 2.7
Dutch	0.6	− 0.3
Polish	1.0	+ 0.1
Ukrainian	1.3	− 0.7
Other	6.3	+ 2.5
Total	100.0	—
Official language spoken (1961 census)		
English only	96.3	+28.9
French only	0.1	−19.0
Both English and French	2.9	− 9.3
Neither English nor French	0.7	− 0.6
Total	100.0	—

LABOR FORCE BY INDUSTRY

Industry	Persons 1961 census	% of the total	% points above or below Canadian average
Agriculture	357	2.9	− 7.0
Forestry	524	4.3	+ 2.6
Fishing and trapping	7	0.1	− 0.4
Mines, quarries, oil wells	1,777	14.6	+12.7
Manufacturing	2,361	19.5	− 2.2
Construction	959	7.9	+ 1.2
Transportation, communications, and other utilities	1,399	11.5	+ 2.2
Wholesale trade	242	2.0	− 2.5
Retail trade	1,144	9.4	− 1.4
Finance, insurance, and real estate	183	1.5	− 2.0
Community and business services	1,124	9.3	− 3.5
Personal services	993	8.2	+ 1.4
Public administration and defence	789	6.5	− 1.0
Miscellaneous	275	2.3	− 0.1
Total labor force	12,134	100.0	—

West Kootenay

ECONOMIC CAPSULE

West Kootenay has recently hit the limelight because of the multi-million-dollar project on the Columbia River. Three storage dams are being constructed at Mica Creek, Arrow Lake, and Duncan Lake to control the flow of the river south of the border. British Columbia is paid substantially for the "down-stream power benefits" that the U.S. will enjoy. No large scale hydro-electric developments are planned on the Canadian side, except at the Mica dam (1.8 million kw.). However, it is expected that the different sites on the Columbia River basin will eventually be able to produce 4 million kilowatts of energy for distribution to the southern half of the province.

The region is also rich in minerals. It has silver-lead-zinc mines at Salmo, Riondel, Silverton, Slocan, and Remac. At Trail, the Consolidated Mining and Smelting Company of Canada Limited processes the ores from its Sullivan Mine. The smelter is the largest in Canada, and one of the biggest for nonferrous metals in the world. Besides lead, zinc, silver, and tin, many by-products are recovered, including cadmium, bismuth, antimony, and indium. Sulphur, another by-product, is combined with phosphates, nitrogen, and hydrogen in the production of commercial fertilizers.

Nelson, at the junction of the travelways of the Kootenay district, serves as a financial, administrative, and marketing center. It has grown with the development of forest, farming, and fruit-growing industries in the neighborhood, and has several factories processing local produce. Its attractive setting makes it also a popular tourist spot. Mountains over 5,000 feet virtually rim the settlement.

Near Nelson are the settlements of the Doukhobors. These people have attracted considerable attention because of their strong opposition to public education, birth registration, census-taking, and other routine government activities. Since the protest takes the form of stripping off their clothes in public, burning property that is usually (but not always) their own, and dynamiting railroads and telegraph installations, they gain splendid newspaper headlines all across the nation.

WEST KOOTENAY

Area covered: 13,343 square miles. *Census division:* 2.

COMPOSITION OF THE MARKET

Place	Census Division	Population 1961	% of the region
Trail	2	11,580	16.38
Nelson	2	7,074	10.00
Rossland	2	4,354	6.16
Revelstoke	2	3,624	5.12
Creston	2	2,460	3.48
Castlegar	2	2,253	3.19
Warfield	2	2,212	3.13
Kinnaird	2	2,123	3.00
Fruitvale	2	1,032	1.46
Other unincorporated urban	2	2,105	2.98
Total urban	—	38,817	54.90
Rural non-farm	—	27,895	39.45
Rural farm	—	3,995	5.65
Total population		70,707	100.00

IMPORTANCE OF THE MARKET (1964 ESTIMATES)

	Number	% of Canada
Population	71,300	0.37
Households	20,000	0.42
Disposable income ($ million)	140.3	0.44

GROWTH OF THE MARKET

	Percentage growth 1961 to 1964	% points above or below Canadian average
Population	+0.84	− 4.63
Disposable income	+4.00	−17.53

AVERAGE INCOME (1961 CENSUS)

	Dollars	% above or below Canadian average
Income per family (non-farm)	5,206	− 4.46
Income per person not in family (non-farm)	2,059	− 3.65
Income per farm (net)	1,461	−55.12

MEANS OF LIVELIHOOD—DISTRIBUTION OF
LABOR FORCE BY INDUSTRY

Industry	Persons 1961 census	% of the total	% points above or below Canadian average
Agriculture	523	2.3	−7.6
Forestry	1,003	4.3	+2.6
Fishing and trapping	11	—	−0.5
Mines, quarries, oil wells	1,004	4.3	+2.4
Manufacturing	6,847	29.4	+7.7
Construction	1,445	6.2	−0.5
Transportation, communications, and other utilities	3,118	13.4	+4.1
Wholesale trade	606	2.6	−1.9
Retail trade	2,384	10.3	−0.5
Finance, insurance, and real estate	469	2.0	−1.5
Community and business services	2,598	11.2	−1.6
Personal services	1,417	6.1	−0.7
Public administration and defence	1,161	5.0	−2.5
Miscellaneous	670	2.9	+0.5
Total labor force	23,256	100.0	—

POVERTY AND AFFLUENCE (1961 CENSUS)

	Number	% of region's total	% points above or below Canadian average
Extent of poverty			
Families earning below $3,000 a year (non-farm).......	3,397	21.3	− 2.0
Persons not in families earning below $1,500 a year (non-farm)........	2,676	53.8	+ 4.9
Farms with gross income of less than $2,500 a year....	747	73.8	+27.7
Persons not in school with grade 4 or less education..	6,281	14.0	+ 0.6
Doubled-up households (more than one family per household)........	335	1.7	− 2.0
Households living in dilapidated dwellings...............	1,559	7.9	+ 2.3
Households without facilities of running water........	644	3.3	− 7.6
Households without facilities of installed bath or shower........	2,523	12.8	− 6.9
Extent of affluence			
Families earning over $10,000 a year (non-farm)........	911	5.7	− 2.1
Persons not in families earning over $6,000 a year (non-farm)........	176	3.5	− 0.3
Farms with gross income over $15,000 a year..........	33	3.2	− 1.8
Persons with university degree........	1,133	2.5	− 0.3
Households with two or more television sets...........	80	0.4	− 3.8
Households with two or more cars...........	1,147	5.8	− 1.0

CHARACTERISTICS OF THE POPULATION

	% of the total population of the region	% points above or below Canadian average
Mother tongue (1961 census)		
English........	74.6	+16.2
French........	1.3	−26.8
German........	2.6	− 0.5
Native Indian dialects........	0.1	− 0.8
Italian........	4.8	+ 2.9
Dutch........	0.7	− 0.2
Polish........	0.6	− 0.3
Ukrainian........	1.2	− 0.8
Other........	14.1	+10.3
Total........	100.0	—

	% of the total population of the region	% points above or below Canadian average
Official language spoken (1961 census)		
English only	95.4	+28.0
French only	0.1	−19.0
Both English and French	2.6	− 9.6
Neither English nor French	1.9	+ 0.6
Total	100.0	—

Okanagan Valley

Area covered: 10,729 square miles. *Census division:* 3.

COMPOSITION OF THE MARKET

Place	Census Division	Population 1961	% of the region
Kelowna (urbanized area)	3	14,243	15.05
Penticton	3	13,859	14.64
Vernon	3	10,250	10.83
Grand Forks	3	2,347	2.48
Princeton	3	2,163	2.29
Oliver	3	1,774	1.87
Armstrong	3	1,288	1.36
Enderby	3	1,075	1.14
Osoyoos	3	1,022	1.08
Total urban	—	48,021	50.74
Rural non-farm	—	30,011	31.71
Rural farm	—	16,614	17.55
Total population		94,646	100.00

ECONOMIC CAPSULE

The Okanagan Valley is one of the most important agricultural districts in British Columbia. Climatic and soil conditions favor horticulture. The raising of orchard fruits, especially on irrigated terraces, is the most distinguishing feature of the economy. Two million trees blossom every year: apple, peach, plum, cherry, apricot, and nectarine. The long, hot growing season with lots of sunshine is ideal for fruits and enables them to mature with a high flavor and bright color.

In normal years the valley contributes one quarter of the total value of Canadian fruit production. Thanks to a well-developed co-operative marketing system, the output is sold all over the world. Europeans and Asians, as well as Americans, buy from this valley, and its business today is in the multi-million dollar class. However, the market is highly volatile, and since 1950 there has been some switch-over to dairying and livestock raising, resulting in a more diversified agriculture.

The towns in the valley are intimately connected with the fruit industry. Vernon is the center of apple trade; Penticton and Peachland are in the middle of the peach belt; Oliver and Osoyoos are famous for apricots and cantaloupes. Kelowna, the largest town, is the distribution point for the valley's fruit-packing industry. It is also well known for its international regatta, claimed to be Canada's greatest water show, drawing many foreign competitors each year.

POVERTY AND AFFLUENCE (1961 CENSUS)

	Number	% of region's total	% points above or below Canadian average
Extent of poverty			
Families earning below $3,000 a year (non-farm)	5,461	29.2	+ 5.9
Persons not in families earning below $1,500 a year (non-farm)	4,106	57.5	+ 8.6
Farms with gross income of less than $2,500 a year	2,595	58.2	+12.1
Persons not in school with grade 4 or less education	7,894	12.9	− 0.5
Doubled-up households (more than one family per household)	437	1.6	− 2.1
Households living in dilapidated dwellings	2,104	7.7	+ 2.1
Households without facilities of running water	1,615	5.9	− 5.0
Households without facilities of installed bath or shower	3,434	12.6	− 7.1
Extent of affluence			
Families earning over $10,000 a year (non-farm)	850	4.6	− 3.2
Persons not in families earning over $6,000 a year (non-farm)	154	2.1	− 1.7
Farms with gross income over $15,000 a year	188	4.2	− 0.8
Persons with university degree	1,381	2.2	− 0.6
Households with two or more television sets	296	1.1	− 3.1
Households with two or more cars	2,826	10.3	+ 3.5

IMPORTANCE OF THE MARKET (1964 ESTIMATES)

	Number	% of Canada
Population	97,300	0.51
Households	27,900	0.58
Disposable income ($ million)	156.9	0.50

GROWTH OF THE MARKET

	Percentage growth 1961 to 1964	% points above or below Canadian average
Population	+ 2.80	−2.67
Disposable income	+21.16	−0.37

CHARACTERISTICS OF THE POPULATION

	% of the total population of the region	% points above or below Canadian average
Mother tongue (1961 census)		
English	76.3	+17.9
French	1.2	−26.9
German	7.8	+ 4.7
Native Indian dialects	0.9	—
Italian	0.9	− 1.0
Dutch	1.3	+ 0.4
Polish	0.6	− 0.3
Ukrainian	2.3	+ 0.3
Other	8.7	+ 4.9
Total	100.0	—
Official language spoken (1961 census)		
English only	96.2	+28.8
French only	0.1	−19.0
Both English and French	2.7	− 9.5
Neither English nor French	1.0	− 0.3
Total	100.0	—

AVERAGE INCOME (1961 CENSUS)

	Dollars	% above or below Canadian average
Income per family (non-farm)	4,674	−14.22
Income per person not in family (non-farm)	1,896	−11.28
Income per farm (net)	2,471	−24.09

LABOR FORCE BY INDUSTRY

Industry	Persons 1961 census	% of the total	% points above or below Canadian average
Agriculture	5,022	15.9	+6.0
Forestry	1,222	3.9	+2.2
Fishing and trapping	12	—	−0.5
Mines, quarries, oil wells	355	1.1	−0.8
Manufacturing	4,703	14.9	−6.8
Construction	1,941	6.2	−0.5
Transportation, communications, and other utilities	2,614	8.3	−1.0
Wholesale trade	2,071	6.6	+2.1
Retail trade	3,852	12.2	+1.4
Finance, insurance, and real estate	884	2.8	−0.7
Community and business services	3,703	11.7	−1.1
Personal services	2,680	8.5	+1.7
Public administration and defence	1,660	5.3	−2.2
Miscellaneous	812	2.6	+0.2
Total labor force	31,531	100.0	—

South Central British Columbia

ECONOMIC CAPSULE

This is the northern portion of the Fraser Plateau, the principal range area in British Columbia for beef cattle and sheep. Most farms are extremely large, averaging about 1,000 acres, but, on account of the semi-arid climate, the cultivated area is fairly small. The crops are at a discount compared to natural pasture.

At present, transhumance is practised in many sections. Livestock are driven to alpine pastures in early summer where they graze until late August. Following summer feeding, a large part of the herd is rounded up and marketed. The remainder range in the valleys during winter. Since North American eating habits tend to favor grain-fed steak, the practice is increasing of producing alfalfa to make up nature's scanty fare. Creeks are dammed and valley flats irrigated to grow that crop. This helps to produce better and more saleable beef.

The region is also rich in minerals. Copper is obtained at Merritt (daily mill capacity 5,000 tons) and Ashcroft (daily mill capacity 3,800 tons). Gold was once important and some of it is still mined in the vicinity of Kamloops and Lillooet.

Lumbering provides another source of income. Yellow pine is the chief type available. It is not a good construction timber, because it is easily attacked by the weather, rot, and fungus, but it is quite adequate for packaging the fruit grown in the Okanagan Valley.

SOUTH-CENTRAL BRITISH COLUMBIA

CHARACTERISTICS OF THE POPULATION

	% of the total population of the region	% points above or below Canadian average
Mother tongue (1961 census)		
English	80.8	+22.4
French	1.4	−26.7
German	2.9	− 0.2
Native Indian dialects	5.1	+ 4.2
Italian	1.6	− 0.3
Dutch	1.0	+ 0.1
Polish	0.5	− 0.4
Ukrainian	1.2	− 0.8
Other	5.5	+ 1.7
Total	100.0	—
Official language spoken (1961 census)		
English only	96.0	+28.6
French only	0.2	−18.9
Both English and French	2.7	− 9.5
Neither English nor French	1.1	− 0.2
Total	100.0	—

SOUTH-CENTRAL BRITISH COLUMBIA

Area covered: 31,420 square miles. *Census division:* 6.

COMPOSITION OF THE MARKET

Place	Census Division	Population 1961	% of the region
Kamloops (urbanized area)	6	18,700	28.21
Merritt	6	3,039	4.58
Salmon Arm	6	1,506	2.27
Lillooet	6	1,304	1.97
Total urban	—	24,549	37.03
Rural non-farm	—	33,280	50.20
Rural farm	—	8,461	12.77
Total population		66,290	100.00

POVERTY AND AFFLUENCE (1961 CENSUS)

	Number	% of region's total	% points above or below Canadian average
Extent of poverty			
Families earning below $3,000 a year (non-farm)	3,114	25.0	+ 1.7
Persons not in families earning below $1,500 a year (non-farm)	2,509	47.3	− 1.6
Farms with gross income of less than $2,500 a year	1,176	67.9	+21.8
Persons not in school with grade 4 or less education	6,171	15.0	+ 1.6
Doubled-up households (more than one family per household)	372	2.2	− 1.5
Households living in dilapidated dwellings	1,871	11.0	+ 5.4
Households without facilities of running water	3,353	19.8	+ 8.9
Households without facilities of installed bath or shower	5,007	29.6	+ 9.9
Extent of affluence			
Families earning over $10,000 a year (non-farm)	717	5.7	− 2.1
Persons not in families earning over $6,000 a year (non-farm)	145	2.7	− 1.1
Farms with gross income over $15,000 a year	104	6.1	+ 1.1
Persons with university degree	773	1.9	− 0.9
Households with two or more television sets	111	0.7	− 3.5
Households with two or more cars	969	5.7	− 1.1

SOUTH-CENTRAL BRITISH COLUMBIA

IMPORTANCE OF THE MARKET (1964 ESTIMATES)

	Number	% of Canada
Population	73,000	0.38
Households	18,600	0.39
Disposable income ($ million)	122.6	0.39

GROWTH OF THE MARKET

	Percentage growth 1961 to 1964	% points above or below Canadian average
Population	+10.12	+4.65
Disposable income	+13.62	−7.91

MEANS OF LIVELIHOOD—DISTRIBUTION OF LABOR FORCE BY INDUSTRY

Industry	Persons 1961 census	% of the total	% points above or below Canadian average
Agriculture	2,191	10.0	+0.1
Forestry	1,392	6.4	+4.7
Fishing and trapping	17	0.1	−0.4
Mines, quarries, oil wells	698	3.2	+1.3
Manufacturing	4,199	19.2	−2.5
Construction	1,302	6.0	−0.7
Transportation, communications, and other utilities	3,069	14.0	+4.7
Wholesale trade	526	2.4	−2.1
Retail trade	2,131	9.8	−1.0
Finance, insurance, and real estate	408	1.9	−1.6
Community and business services	2,359	10.8	−2.0
Personal services	1,732	7.9	+1.1
Public administration and defence	1,084	5.0	−2.5
Miscellaneous	713	3.3	+0.9
Total labor force	21,821	100.0	—

AVERAGE INCOME (1961 CENSUS)

	Dollars	% above or below Canadian average
Income per family (non-farm)	5,000	− 8.24
Income per person not in family (non-farm)	2,092	− 2.11
Income per farm (net)	2,927	−10.08

Vancouver — Lower Fraser

ECONOMIC CAPSULE

Over half the population of British Columbia is concentrated in and around Vancouver. It is Canada's third largest metropolis, even though it has not yet reached the age of four score years and ten.

In a very real sense Vancouver is the child of the Canadian Pacific Railway. The historic arrival of the first locomotive in 1887 virtually created the city, which before then was little more than a bush-clearing of 2,000 souls, called by the undignified name of Gastown. The settlement flourished because of the extensive trade between Canada and the Far East, especially in lumber and fish, its basic industries from the start. By 1912 the population had reached the 100,000 mark. The opening of the Panama Canal permitted ships to avoid the long and treacherous journey around Cape Horn, and Vancouver could compete with eastern Canadian ports for trade with Europe and the West Indies. After 1921, an increasing amount of grain from Alberta and western Saskatchewan was shipped to Europe via the Pacific rather than through the traditional route of the Great Lakes and the St. Lawrence River.

As time passed on, Vancouver expanded the trade with the Far East and Oceania, importing items like tea, coffee, spices, palm oil, cocoanut, sugar, and silk. Slowly it began to process many of these products. Large sugar refining, soap making, and oil extracting plants were set up.

With the growth of the city, local needs had to be met, and food manufacturing became important, making use of the produce of the rich farms and market gardens of the Fraser delta. Finally, during and after the Second World War, new establishments were set up, such as pulp and paper mills, iron and steel plants, iron foundries, metal fabricating industries, and factories making machinery and equipment. The piping of oil and gas from Alberta provided badly-needed fuels at low cost and aided considerably in industrial expansion.

Despite the development of manufacturing, commercial interests are still paramount. Vancouver is the wholesale and financial center of the province. It has become the greatest wheat port in the world (thanks to the increased trade with China and Russia) and in a normal year handles more cargo than San Francisco, Portland, and Seattle combined. The city is also the site of an important fair known as the Pacific Exhibition.

However, there is more to life in Vancouver than trade and commerce. The population has grown very rapidly, due largely to the influx from outside — immigrants as well as Canadians from other provinces. These people are lured here not solely on account of the booming economy: the city has other attractions as well. First of all are its magnificent natural surroundings which have earned for it the proud title of "the Constantinople of the West". No metropolis in Canada, and few on the globe, have been planted in such a beautiful setting, surrounded by mountain, sea, and forest. Then there is the famous thousand-acre Stanley Park, where, within walking distance from the bustle and noise of the downtown area, one can wander for miles in the cathedral-like stillness of the mighty forest, surrounded by the majestic columns of Douglas fir and pine.

VANCOUVER—LOWER FRASER

Area covered: 9,764 square miles. *Census division:* 4.

COMPOSITION OF THE MARKET

Place	Census Division	Population 1961	% of the region
Vancouver (metro)	4	790,165	87.07
Chilliwack (urbanized area)	4	11,724	1.29
White Rock	4	6,453	0.71
Maple Ridge (urban part)	4	3,716	0.41
Mission City	4	3,251	0.36
Hope	4	2,751	0.30
Matsqui (urban part)	4	2,479	0.27
Langley	4	2,365	0.26
Surrey (urban part)	4	2,293	0.25
Haney	4	2,117	0.23
Clearbrook	4	1,964	0.22
Squamish	4	1,557	0.17
Port Hammond	4	1,267	0.14
Sumas (urban part)	4	1,244	0.14
Gibson's Landing	4	1,091	0.12
Total urban	—	834,437	91.94
Rural non-farm	—	46,072	5.08
Rural farm	—	27,022	2.98
Total population		907,531	100.00

The climate, too, is highly suitable: summer temperatures in the decent seventies, and a mild winter that rarely goes below freezing. Good fishing, hunting, swimming, and boating are often only a short distance away from home or job. It is possible to do both skiing and skin-diving on the same day, without driving more than a few miles.

Vancouver can chalk up a list of other pluses as well. In the field of arts it is well out in front, with the annual International Festival as its showpiece. Past participants cover a spectrum that ranges from the Comédie Française to Japan's Bunraku puppets. The city has its own Opera Association and its modern municipally-owned Queen Elizabeth Theatre and Playhouse. For the open-air enthusiasts there is the Theatre Under the Stars in Stanley Park.

Scholars are served by the magnificent University of British Columbia, fishing and sailing fans by the accommodating ocean, and the gourmet by an array of restaurants that includes the specialized delights of Chinatown. English immigrants can play cricket at Brockton Oval, while for those who feel that a house is not a home unless you like the look of it, the city has numerous examples of some of the most distinctive architectural styles in Canada. In Vancouver, as elsewhere in the Pacific Northwest, the work may be hard but the living is easy.

In fact, it is the most relaxed city in Canada. As one writer observes: "Québec is inward looking, Montréal is very aware of itself, Toronto is harassed, and Edmonton is thinking of next year. Vancouver is like a man walking to his office on a warm spring morning, in step with a distant military band playing Elgar's 'Pomp and Circumstance' March, and facing a day which he feels will go as planned . . . Vancouver is not a place for those who feel that human beings are

IMPORTANCE OF THE MARKET (1964 ESTIMATES)

	Region		Vancouver	
	Number	% of Canada	Number	% of Canada
Population	975,000	5.07	828,000	4.30
Households	279,200	5.81	250,900	5.22
Disposable income ($ million)	1,845.7	5.85	1,654.2	5.25

GROWTH OF THE MARKET

	Region		Vancouver	
	Percentage growth 1961 to 1964	% points above or below Canadian average	Percentage growth 1961 to 1964	% points above or below Canadian average
Population	+ 7.43	+1.96	+ 4.79	−0.68
Disposable income	+23.04	+1.51	+22.93	+1.40

at their most interesting when they are depressed and frustrated. It sees no glamour in the death-wish, and existentialism is not likely to reach it for some time."*

* By permission from Ernest Watkins, *Prospect of Canada,* Secker and Warburg, London, England, 1954, p. 129.

POVERTY AND AFFLUENCE (1961 CENSUS)

	Region			Vancouver	
	Number	% of region's total	% points above or below Canadian average	Number	% of city's total
Extent of poverty					
Families earning below $3,000 a year (non-farm)	42,071	19.6	− 3.7	35,251	18.4
Persons not in families earning below $1,500 a year (non-farm)	44,739	48.2	− 0.7	39,968	47.1
Farms with gross income of less than $2,500 a year	3,743	50.8	+ 4.7	—	—
Persons not in school with grade 4 or less education	51,840	8.5	− 4.9	43,665	8.1
Doubled-up households (more than one family per household)	6,806	2.6	− 1.1	6,374	2.8
Households living in dilapidated dwellings	10,818	4.1	− 1.5	8,510	3.7
Households without facilities of running water	2,956	1.1	− 9.8	1,120	0.5
Households without facilities of installed bath or shower	7,518	2.8	−16.9	3,730	1.6
Extent of affluence					
Families earning over $10,000 a year (non-farm)	18,475	8.6	+ 0.8	17,497	9.1
Persons not in families earning over $6,000 a year (non-farm)	3,858	4.1	+ 0.3	3,637	4.3
Farms with gross income over $15,000 a year	993	13.5	+ 8.5	—	—
Persons with university degree	22,423	3.7	+ 0.9	20,958	3.9
Households with two or more television sets	10,694	4.1	− 0.1	10,416	4.6
Households with two or more cars	29,399	11.2	+ 4.4	26,871	11.8

To outsiders, Vancouverites seem rather egocentric. They refer to themselves, a trifle grandiloquently, as the inhabitants of "the Coast". Western Canada, to them, ends at Alberta. They feel no particular kinship with the Prairie Provinces and even less with the East. French Canadians scarcely exist for them, except as a troublesome little sect. The Federal Government in Ottawa interests them only when they are directly affected by legislation on some such topic as electric power, salmon fishing, or trade with the Orient.

On the other hand, the U.S. influence is very strong, almost as much as in Windsor. Personal links with Oregon, Washington, and California are as close as they are numerous. The casual approach to living, the informal yet up-to-date clothing styles, the disregard for conventional designs in furniture and furnishings, the outdoor patio complete with barbecue equipment — all these have clear U.S. Pacific Coast overtones.

VANCOUVER—LOWER FRASER

CHARACTERISTICS OF THE POPULATION

	Region		Vancouver
	% of the total population of the region	% points above or below Canadian average	% of the total population of the city
Mother tongue (1961 census)			
English	81.3	+22.9	82.0
French	1.6	−26.5	1.7
German	5.0	+ 1.9	4.0
Native Indian dialects	0.1	− 0.8	0.1
Italian	1.4	− 0.5	1.5
Dutch	1.6	+ 0.7	1.3
Polish	0.6	− 0.3	0.6
Ukrainian	1.3	− 0.7	1.3
Other	7.1	+ 3.3	7.5
Total	100.0	—	100.0
Official language spoken (1961 census)			
English only	95.1	+27.7	94.9
French only	0.2	−18.9	0.2
Both English and French	3.7	− 8.5	3.9
Neither English nor French	1.0	− 0.3	1.0
Total	100.0	—	100.0

Vancouver has about the same proportion of British as many cities in Ontario, but with one major difference. In the east, the British blood goes back several generations and still has the strong strain of ancestral puritanism. The population on the Pacific Coast is composed to a great extent of newcomers from the old country, who have shed their austere religious garb a long time ago. This, coupled with the influence of pagan, informal, easy-going California, has made Vancouver the least puritanic of most English cities. In fact, it holds an unsavory distinction for having a large proportion of illegitimate children, great frequency of divorce, and a high rate of alcoholism and narcotics addiction.

As consumers, Vancouverites show a willingness to experiment and are not hide-bound when it comes to adopting new ideas. The customary caution of Eastern Canada is thrown aside. The appeal to tradition, which strikes the right note elsewhere, often falls on deaf ears here. The retailers, too, by and large, are quick to accept new products, to start new promotions, to experiment with new store layouts. It is not, therefore, surprising that, when introducing new products regionally, many national manufacturers start with the Vancouver market.

MEANS OF LIVELIHOOD—DISTRIBUTION OF

LABOR FORCE BY INDUSTRY

Industry	Region			Vancouver	
	Persons 1961 census	% of the total	% points above or below Canadian average	Persons 1961 census	% of the total
Agriculture	9,629	2.9	−7.0	3,806	1.3
Forestry	5,037	1.5	−0.2	2,518	0.9
Fishing and trapping	2,154	0.7	+0.2	1,836	0.6
Mines, quarries, oil wells	2,182	0.7	−1.2	1,581	0.5
Manufacturing	62,591	18.9	−2.8	57,485	19.5
Construction	22,461	6.8	+0.1	19,897	6.7
Transportation, communications, and other utilities	37,865	11.4	+2.1	34,934	11.9
Wholesale trade	23,842	7.2	+2.7	22,757	7.7
Retail trade	40,817	12.3	+1.5	37,142	12.6
Finance, insurance, and real estate	16,679	5.0	+1.5	15,918	5.4
Community and business services	52,148	15.7	+2.9	47,639	16.2
Personal services	25,062	7.6	+0.8	22,741	7.7
Public administration and defence	21,148	6.4	−1.1	18,003	6.1
Miscellaneous	9,635	2.9	+0.5	8,502	2.9
Total labor force	331,250	100.0	—	294,759	100.0

AVERAGE INCOME (1961 CENSUS)

	Region		Vancouver	
	Dollars	% above or below Canadian average	Dollars	% above or below Canadian average
Income per family (non-farm)	5,816	+6.74	5,934	+8.90
Income per person not in family (non-farm)	2,237	+4.68	2,281	+6.74
Income per farm (net)	3,413	+4.85	—	—

Victoria — Vancouver Island

ECONOMIC CAPSULE

This is by far the largest island on the Pacific coast, nearly six times the size of Prince Edward Island. Its backbone is an almost unbroken ridge of mountains that rise five to seven thousand feet above sea level. There are no navigable rivers, but the coast line is deeply indented with inlets that form good harbors. These are used as shelters for fishing fleets and as bases of operations for forest industries. The island is sparsely populated, except along a narrow strip of the southeast coastline, about 170 miles long, from Victoria to Campbell River. The economy of most small settlements is based primarily on sea and forests — that is, fishing, logging, sawmilling, and, above all, pulp or paper manufacturing (mills at Nanaimo, Port Alberni, and Campbell River). Mining is making a slow come-back since new export markets have been found for coal and iron ore in Japan. Agriculture is confined mainly to the production of fruits, vegetables, bulbs, and flowers. There is also some dairying and poultry-raising.

Victoria is the principal marketing center, though it does not dominate the island's economic life. Vancouver performs a major wholesaling role for much of the island, especially the northern districts. Victoria is essentially the administrative headquarters. Twenty-six per cent of the labor force is engaged in government services compared to only 11% in manufacturing. Industrial activities comprise mainly the production of lumber and wood products and the building of barges and ships.

In the eyes of the rest of Canada, Victoria has acquired a special image, which can be best described in the words of a Québecer who surveyed the local rituals and remarked: "This town is so bloody English that it brings tea to your eyes." Actually, it is quite possible that more crumpets are bought on a Friday evening in the supermarkets of Toronto than are served all week in the teashops of

Victoria. But the image still persists that Victoria is a "little bit of olde England, more British than Britain". This is bringing good tourist money — over $10,-000,000 a year — to a city which industry and transportation have to some extent passed by.

During the summer season, the visitor is taken on a sight-seeing tour in a horsedrawn tallyho, through streets whose lampposts are festooned with baskets of flowers and whose shops are filled with tartans and shortbread, English tweed, and English bone china. However, as the years pass by, Victoria becomes more and more North American, except for the tourist spots. The new generation of inhabitants are skeptical of quaintness, scornful of myth, and determined to discard, for the sake of economic progress, this fuddy-duddy anachronism of vanished Empire.

In the past, Victoria attracted many wealthy Englishmen looking for a suitable spot to settle after retirement. It had many titled Britons, colonial administrators from India and Malaya, and the whole Gilbert and Sullivan group of vice-admirals and major-generals. Now they are a dwindling lot. The reinforce-

VICTORIA—VANCOUVER ISLAND

Area covered: 13,206 square miles. *Census division:* 5.

COMPOSITION OF THE MARKET

Place	Census Division	Population 1961	% of the region
Victoria (metro)	5	154,152	53.00
Nanaimo (urbanized area)	5	18,031	6.20
Port Alberni (urbanized area)	5	16,176	5.56
Campbell River	5	3,737	1.28
Duncan	5	3,726	1.28
Courtenay	5	3,485	1.20
Ladysmith	5	2,173	0.75
Lake Cowichan	5	2,149	0.74
Comox	5	1,756	0.60
Sydney	5	1,558	0.53
Chemainus	5	1,518	0.52
Cumberland	5	1,303	0.45
Parksville	5	1,183	0.41
Youbou	5	1,153	0.40
Port Alice	5	1,065	0.37
Total urban	—	213,165	73.29
Rural non-farm	—	70,080	24.10
Rural farm	—	7,590	2.61
Total population		290,835	100.00

ments from Britain have been cut off. The pound has fallen in value, the Canadian cost of living has risen, and the British Health Service makes it more advantageous to remain at home. Victoria is still a city of retirement. Fifteen per cent of its population is over 65, compared to the national average of 8%. The old couples now are mainly from the Prairies, people who are not rich enough for the Bahamas but whose pensions and savings enable them to buy a home, plant a garden, and live comfortably in the mild climate.

The weather is, indeed, ideal. Victoria has none of the extremes of temperature so common in other parts of Canada. In January it is as warm as Richmond, Virginia, while its summers are as cool as the winters of St. Petersburg, Florida. To quote a few statistics: average annual precipitation, 26.2 inches; average annual sunshine, 2,093 hours; average January temperature, 39°F; average July temperature, 60°F.

VICTORIA—VANCOUVER ISLAND

CHARACTERISTICS OF THE POPULATION

| | Region | | Victoria |
	% of the total population of the region	% points above or below Canadian average	% of the total population of the city
Mother tongue (1961 census)			
English	87.2	+28.8	90.7
French	1.4	−26.7	1.1
German	2.0	− 1.1	1.6
Native Indian dialects	1.4	+ 0.5	0.2
Italian	0.7	− 1.2	0.4
Dutch	1.2	+ 0.3	0.9
Polish	0.3	− 0.6	0.3
Ukrainian	0.6	− 1.4	0.5
Other	5.2	+ 1.4	4.3
Total	100.0	—	100.0
Official language spoken (1961 census)			
English only	95.4	+28.0	95.1
French only	0.1	−19.0	0.1
Both English and French	3.7	− 8.5	4.0
Neither English nor French	0.8	− 0.5	0.8
Total	100.0	—	100.0

Climate is not the sole attraction. The city is a delightful place to live in. It is small and relaxed, and practically everybody seems to have a green thumb. Gardening here is more than a skill, a hobby, or a pictorial art. It is a cult, a philosophy, a passion, in fact, almost a religion.

POVERTY AND AFFLUENCE (1961 CENSUS)

	Region			Victoria	
	Number	% of region's total	% points above or below Canadian average	Number	% of city's total
Extent of poverty					
Families earning below $3,000 a year (non–farm)	13,980	20.6	− 2.7	7,402	19.9
Persons not in families earning below $1,500 a year (non-farm)	13,354	50.7	+ 1.8	8,116	48.9
Farms with gross income of less than $2,500 a year	1,337	64.9	+18.8	—	—
Persons not in school with grade 4 or less education	14,205	7.4	− 6.0	5,690	5.4
Doubled-up households (more than one family per household)	1,372	1.6	− 2.1	742	1.6
Households living in dilapidated dwellings	3,591	4.2	− 1.4	1,372	2.9
Households without facilities of running water	1,599	1.9	− 9.0	207	0.4
Households without facilities of installed bath or shower	3,695	4.4	−15.3	650	1.4
Extent of affluence					
Families earning over $10,000 a year (non-farm)	4,567	6.7	− 1.1	2,709	7.3
Persons not in families earning over $6,000 a year (non-farm)	1,084	4.1	+ 0.3	669	4.0
Farms with gross income over $15,000 a year	201	9.8	+ 4.8	—	—
Persons with university degree	6,056	3.1	+ 0.3	4,143	3.9
Households with two or more television sets	1,563	1.8	− 2.4	1,222	2.6
Households with two or more cars	8,446	9.9	+ 3.1	5,316	11.2

IMPORTANCE OF THE MARKET (1964 ESTIMATES)

	Region		Victoria	
	Number	% of Canada	Number	% of Canada
Population	304,100	1.58	165,000	0.86
Households	89,500	1.86	53,200	1.11
Disposable income ($ million)	604.8	1.92	306.5	0.97

GROWTH OF THE MARKET

	Region		Victoria	
	Percentage growth 1961 to 1964	% points above or below Canadian average	Percentage growth 1961 to 1964	% points above or below Canadian average
Population	+ 4.56	−0.91	+ 7.04	+1.57
Disposable income	+25.24	+3.71	+25.46	+3.93

LABOR FORCE BY INDUSTRY

Industry	Region			Victoria	
	Persons 1961 census	% of the total	% points above or below Canadian average	Persons 1961 census	% of the total
Agriculture	2,343	2.3	− 7.6	1,170	2.1
Forestry	7,424	7.4	+ 5.7	616	1.1
Fishing and trapping	1,319	1.3	+ 0.8	198	0.4
Mines, quarries, oil wells	816	0.8	− 1.1	53	0.1
Manufacturing	16,308	16.2	− 5.5	5,960	10.7
Construction	4,998	5.0	− 1.7	2,830	5.1
Transportation, communications, and other utilities	7,954	7.9	− 1.4	4,272	7.7
Wholesale trade	2,978	3.0	− 1.5	1,926	3.5
Retail trade	11,762	11.7	+ 0.9	7,188	13.0
Finance, insurance, and real estate	3,112	3.1	− 0.4	2,244	4.0
Community and business services	13,441	13.3	+ 0.5	8,608	15.5
Personal services	7,394	7.3	+ 0.5	4,412	8.0
Public administration and defence	17,783	17.7	+10.2	14,316	25.8
Miscellaneous	2,999	3.0	+ 0.6	1,657	3.0
Total labor force	100,631	100.0	—	55,450	100.0

AVERAGE INCOME (1961 CENSUS)

	Region		Victoria	
	Dollars	% above or below Canadian average	Dollars	% above or below Canadian average
Income per family (non-farm)	5,442	− 0.13	5,581	+2.42
Income per person not in family (non-farm)	2,175	+ 1.78	2,225	+4.12
Income per farm (net)	2,521	−22.55	—	—

Northwestern British Columbia

Area covered: 110,315 square miles. *Census divisions:* 7, and 9.

COMPOSITION OF THE MARKET

Place	Census Division	Population 1961	% of the region
Prince Rupert	9	11,987	20.14
Powell River	7	10,748	18.06
Kitimat	9	8,217	13.80
Terrace	9	4,682	7.87
Ocean Falls	7	3,056	5.13
Total urban	—	38,690	65.00
Rural non-farm	—	20,301	34.10
Rural farm	—	537	0.90
Total population		59,528	100.00

ECONOMIC CAPSULE

This region comprises the coastal zone plus the northwestern interior section of the province. Population is very scarce. Only 60,000 people reside in this vast land mass of 110,300 square miles. The scenery along the coast reminds one very much of Norway, with huge tree-covered mountains falling abruptly into countless deep fiords. The vegetation is one wild rain forest of great conifers — Douglas fir, Sitka spruce, red cedar, and western hemlock.

Forestry and fishing dominate the life of the small villages. Thirty years ago many sawmills and salmon canneries were scattered throughout the upcoast area, but modern transportation has changed all that. Fast floating canneries take their catch to Vancouver, while the logs go to the pulpmills or the great sawmills of the Fraser River in the south. As a result many settlements are deserted now. Small logging camps have multiplied, but the majority are temporary, moving from one timber stand to another. Most of their needs are supplied by seaplanes. The once important steamship service that knit the coast together is now only a skeleton.

However, the whole area offers much promise because of its vast hydro-power potentialities. The most spectacular development in the postwar era has been the famous Kitimat project of the Aluminum Company of Canada Limited. Here at the head of a fiord 400 miles north of Vancouver, engineers were lured by the twin attractions of inexpensive power and access to deep sea shipping, both essential to a profitable aluminum industry. Close to half a billion dollars were spent to reverse the flow of a river, to bore a ten-mile tunnel through a mountain, to build an underground power house at Kemano, to establish wharfs and docks for ocean-going freighters, and to set up a smelter at Kitimat capable of producing 192,000 tons of aluminum a year. Today, bauxite from Jamaica comes nearly 5,000 miles by sea to be turned into aluminum ingots. Cheap hydro-power makes the long voyage worthwhile. Kitimat itself has blossomed into an attractive town of 8,000, with neat homes, green lawns, paved streets, good schools, and well-laid-out recreation grounds. It is the product of design, planning, and execution, rather than accident and circumstances — the first completely new, completely modern city to be built in North America in this century.

Prince Rupert, the largest town in the region, is the western terminus of the CNR's northern route from Alberta. It has fish processing plants (specializing mainly in halibut) and a pulp mill, plus a cellulose factory at Watson Island. In 1906, a city plan was designed to accommodate a population of 50,000.

IMPORTANCE OF THE MARKET (1964 ESTIMATES)

	Number	% of Canada
Population	59,100	0.31
Households	14,200	0.30
Disposable income ($ million)	130.0	0.41

GROWTH OF THE MARKET

	Percentage change 1961 to 1964	% points above or below Canadian average
Population	− 0.72	−6.19
Disposable income	+17.54	−3.99

Many expected the port to rival Vancouver, since it is situated closer to Asia on the Great Circle Route. But, despite its few periods of boom, it has not grown up to expectations because of its very limited hinterland.

Powell River, on the other hand, is a thriving community. Its economy is mainly dependent on the pulp and paper mills of MacMillan, Bloedel and Powell River Limited. The company recently announced plans to spend $90 million to increase the newsprint capacity in this area. This is perhaps the largest single industrial expansion ever undertaken in British Columbia. Ocean Falls, to the north, is another center of pulp and paper manufacturing, the mills here being owned by Crown Zellerbach Canada Limited.

AVERAGE INCOME (1961 CENSUS)

	Dollars	% above or below Canadian average
Income per family (non-farm)	5,996	+10.04
Income per person not in family (non-farm)	2,842	+32.99
Income per farm (net)	1,686	−48.20

MEANS OF LIVELIHOOD—DISTRIBUTION OF LABOR FORCE BY INDUSTRY

Industry	Persons 1961 census	% of the total	% points above or below Canadian average
Agriculture	168	0.8	− 9.1
Forestry	2,652	12.1	+10.4
Fishing and trapping	884	4.0	+ 3.5
Mines, quarries, oil wells	585	2.7	+ 0.8
Manufacturing	8,030	36.5	+14.8
Construction	806	3.7	− 3.0
Transportation, communications, and other utilities	1,814	8.2	− 1.1
Wholesale trade	378	1.7	− 2.8
Retail trade	1,635	7.4	− 3.4
Finance, insurance, and real estate	280	1.3	− 2.2
Community and business services	2,101	9.6	− 3.2
Personal services	1,160	5.3	− 1.5
Public administration and defence	875	4.0	− 3.5
Miscellaneous	594	2.7	+ 0.3
Total labor force	21,962	100.0	—

POVERTY AND AFFLUENCE (1961 CENSUS)

	Number	% of region's total	% points above or below Canadian average
Extent of poverty			
Families earning below $3,000 a year (non-farm)........	1,961	15.8	− 7.5
Persons not in families earning below $1,500 a year (non-farm).................	1,840	38.6	−10.3
Farms with gross income of less than $2,500 a year....	96	70.6	+24.5
Persons not in school with grade 4 or less education..	4,888	13.3	− 0.1
Doubled-up households (more than one family per household)................	598	4.2	+ 0.5
Households living in dilapidated dwellings................	993	7.0	+ 1.4
Households without facilities of running water........	1,208	8.6	− 2.3
Households without facilities of installed bath or shower................	2,199	15.6	− 4.1
Extent of affluence			
Families earning over $10,000 a year (non-farm)........	1,161	9.4	+ 1.6
Persons not in families earning over $6,000 a year (non-farm).................	332	6.9	+ 3.1
Farms with gross income over $15,000 a year..........	8	5.8	+ 0.8
Persons with university degree................	787	2.1	− 0.7
Households with two or more television sets...........	15	0.1	− 4.1
Households with two or more cars.............	974	6.9	+ 0.1

CHARACTERISTICS OF THE POPULATION

	% of the total population of the region	% points above or below Canadian average
Mother tongue (1961 census)		
English................	71.1	+12.7
French................	1.5	−26.6
German................	5.4	+ 2.3
Native Indian dialects................	8.1	+ 7.2
Italian................	3.0	+ 1.1
Dutch................	1.6	+ 0.7
Polish................	0.6	− 0.3
Ukrainian................	1.2	− 0.8
Other................	7.5	+ 3.7
Total................	100.0	—

English only	95.4	+28.0
French only	0.1	−19.0
Both English and French	3.3	− 8.9
Neither English nor French	1.2	− 0.1
Total	100.0	—

North-Central British Columbia

Area covered: 71,985 square miles. *Census division:* 8.

COMPOSITION OF THE MARKET

Place	Census Division	Population 1961	% of the region
Prince George (urbanized area)	8	16,458	22.17
Quesnel	8	4,673	6.29
Smithers	8	2,487	3.35
Williams Lake	8	2,120	2.86
Vanderhoof	8	1,460	1.97
Burns Lake	8	1,041	1.40
Total urban	—	28,239	38.04
Rural non-farm	—	39,261	52.88
Rural farm	—	6,740	9.08
Total population		74,240	100.00

ECONOMIC CAPSULE

This is a distinct physiographic area, termed the Nechako Plateau. Most activity is tied to the immediate environs of the two transportation routes, the northern line of the Canadian National Railway and the extension of the Pacific Great Eastern.

Dotted across the land are several pioneer rural settlements where mixed farming and ranching are practised. About 638,000 acres are classified as farm-land. However, occasional summer frosts, heavy autumn rains, infertile soils, and distance from markets impose severe limitations on agricultural expansion. On the other hand, the scope for lumber industries is practically unlimited, since most of the territory is thickly forested. There are more sawmills here than in any other region of Canada.

Prince George, a meeting place of roads and railroads, is the main nucleus of northern development, the headquarters and entrepôt of a virgin empire extending from here to the Yukon. Whatever passes in or out of the north must somehow find its way through this town. As no community of equal size exists within 300 miles, Prince George acts, in addition, as a center of governmental administration and above all as an important shipping point for lumber. It calls itself "the spruce capital of the world" because of the numerous sawmills within its distribution zone. It is also the site of a pulp and paper industry. With the growing demand for wood products, the town has enjoyed a tremendous boom in recent years, its population almost tripling in the course of the last decade. The abundant supplies of relatively inexpensive power that will soon be available from the Peace River Project will help to further stimulate the wave of expansion.

NORTH-CENTRAL BRITISH COLUMBIA

IMPORTANCE OF THE MARKET (1964 ESTIMATES)

	Number	% of Canada
Population	81,700	0.42
Households	20,000	0.42
Disposable income ($ million)	126.5	0.40

LABOR FORCE BY INDUSTRY

Industry	Persons 1961 census	% of the total	% points above or below Canadian average
Agriculture	1,449	5.8	−4.1
Forestry	1,686	6.8	+5.1
Fishing and trapping	57	0.2	−0.3
Mines, quarries, oil wells	240	1.0	−0.9
Manufacturing	7,330	29.5	+7.8
Construction	1,400	5.7	−1.0
Transportation, communications, and other utilities	3,392	13.7	+4.4
Wholesale trade	865	3.5	−1.0
Retail trade	2,332	9.4	−1.4
Finance, insurance, and real estate	429	1.7	−1.8
Community and business services	2,385	9.6	−3.2
Personal services	1,671	6.7	−0.1
Public administration and defence	842	3.4	−4.1
Miscellaneous	752	3.0	+0.6
Total labor force	24,830	100.0	—

GROWTH OF THE MARKET

	Percentage growth 1961 to 1964	% points above or below Canadian average
Population	+10.05	+ 4.58
Disposable income	+ 6.57	−14.96

CHARACTERISTICS OF THE POPULATION

	% of the total population of the region	% points above or below Canadian average
Mother tongue (1961 census)		
English	72.0	+13.6
French	2.6	−25.5
German	6.1	+ 3.0
Native Indian dialects	8.2	+ 7.3
Italian	1.3	− 0.6
Dutch	2.4	+ 1.5
Polish	0.5	− 0.4
Ukrainian	1.6	− 0.4
Other	5.3	+ 1.5
Total	100.0	—
Official language spoken (1961 census)		
English only	94.8	+27.4
French only	0.3	−18.8
Both English and French	3.7	− 8.5
Neither English nor French	1.2	− 0.1
Total	100.0	—

AVERAGE INCOME (1961 CENSUS)

	Dollars	% above or below Canadian average
Income per family (non-farm)	5,251	− 3.63
Income per person not in family (non-farm)	2,349	+ 9.92
Income per farm (net)	1,473	−54.75

	Number	% of region's total	% points above or below Canadian average
Extent of poverty			
Families earning below $3,000 a year (non-farm).......	3,302	23.8	+ 0.5
Persons not in families earning below $1,500 a year (non-farm)...	2,628	42.5	− 6 4
Farms with gross income of less than $2,500 a year....	996	73.1	+27.0
Persons not in school with grade 4 or less education..	7,619	16.9	+ 3.5
Doubled-up households (more than one family per household)...	368	2.0	− 1.7
Households living in dilapidated dwellings................	2,457	13.6	+ 8.0
Households without facilities of running water........	6,553	36.2	+25.3
Households without facilities of installed bath or shower...	8,466	46.8	+27.1
Extent of affluence			
Families earning over $10,000 a year (non-farm)........	825	5.9	− 1.9
Persons not in families earning over $6,000 a year (non-farm)...	249	4.1	+ 0.3
Farms with gross income over $15,000 a year..........	27	2.0	− 3.0
Persons with university degree....................................	599	1.3	− 1.5
Households with two or more television sets	21	0.1	− 4.1
Households with two or more cars..............................	1,046	5.8	− 1.0

Northeastern British Columbia

Area covered: 82,533 square miles. *Census division:* 10.

COMPOSITION OF THE MARKET

Place	Census Division	Population 1961	% of the region
Dawson Creek...	10	10,946	35.24
Fort St. John...	10	3,619	11.65
Total urban...	—	14,565	46.89
Rural non-farm...	—	11,369	36.60
Rural farm...	—	5,127	16.51
Total population...		31,061	100.00

ECONOMIC CAPSULE

Lying east of the Rockies on the Great Plains, the region is physically and economically an extension of the Peace River Country of Alberta. Agriculture is the main occupation, characterized by grain growing and livestock raising. Lately the cultivation of clover seeds has increased in importance. The soil is fertile and the climate reasonably favorable, though the occurrence of frost during the growing season may be expected in one year out of five.

Oil and natural gas in large quantities have been discovered at several places. Most of these fuels are sent by pipelines to Vancouver. They cannot be used locally for industrial development because of the dearth of population (only about 40,000 people) and the remoteness of the area from major markets.

This region is also the site of the giant $800 million hydro-electric project to control the headwaters of the Peace River. At Portage Mountain, a dam a mile and a quarter long will create a reservoir covering 680 square miles — by far the biggest lake in B.C. The power house, when completed in 1968, will have an estimated capacity of 2,300,000 kilowatts. A comparison of this figure with that of 1,500,000 kilowatts at Beauharnois in Québec, at present Canada's largest generating plant, gives some idea of the energy that will be available from the Peace River.

Dawson Creek is a small marketing center which serves the surrounding farming communities and the oil and gas fields. It is also a major rail and road terminus. The grain elevators here have a capacity of about one million bushels, making the town one of the largest initial shipping points for grain in Canada.

NORTHEASTERN BRITISH COLUMBIA

IMPORTANCE OF THE MARKET (1964 ESTIMATES)

	Number	% of Canada
Population	40,000	0.21
Households	9,800	0.20
Disposable income ($ million)	74.6	0.24

GROWTH OF THE MARKET

	Percentage growth 1961 to 1964	% points above or below Canadian average
Population	+28.78	+23.31
Disposable income	+62.53	+41.00

POVERTY AND AFFLUENCE (1961 CENSUS)

	Number	% of region's total	% points above or below Canadian average
Extent of poverty			
Families earning below $3,000 a year (non-farm)	1,106	20.2	− 3.1
Persons not in families earning below $1,500 a year (non-farm)	844	43.8	− 5.1
Farms with gross income of less than $2,500 a year	820	58.3	+12.2
Persons not in school with grade 4 or less education	2,415	13.1	− 0.3
Doubled-up households (more than one family per household)	150	1.9	− 1.8
Households living in dilapidated dwellings	892	11.6	+ 6.0
Households without facilities of running water	3,776	49.1	+38.2
Households without facilities of installed bath or shower	3,962	51.5	+31.8
Extent of affluence			
Families earning over $10,000 a year (non-farm)	359	6.6	− 1.2
Persons not in families earning over $6,000 a year (non-farm)	92	4.8	+ 1.0
Farms with gross income over $15,000 a year	23	1.6	− 3.4
Persons with university degree	304	1.6	− 1.2
Households with two or more television sets	42	0.5	− 3.7
Households with two or more cars	293	3.8	− 3.0

CHARACTERISTICS OF THE POPULATION

	% of the total population of the region	% points above or below Canadian average
Mother tongue (1961 census)		
English	82.3	+23.9
French	2.6	−25.5
German	4.7	+ 1.6
Native Indian dialects	4.0	+ 3.1
Italian	0.3	− 1.6
Dutch	0.8	− 0.1
Polish	0.4	− 0.5
Ukrainian	1.4	− 0.6
Other	3.5	− 0.3
Total	100.0	—

CHARACTERISTICS OF THE POPULATION (continued)

	% of the total population of the region	% points above or below Canadian average
Official language spoken (1961 census)		
English only	94.9	+27.5
French only	0.3	−18.8
Both English and French	3.7	− 8.5
Neither English nor French	1.1	− 0.2
Total	100.0	—

AVERAGE INCOME (1961 CENSUS)

	Dollars	% above or below Canadian average
Income per family (non-farm)	5,594	+ 2.66
Income per person not in family (non-farm)	2,361	+10.48
Income per farm (net)	2,386	−26.70

LABOR FORCE BY INDUSTRY

Industry	Persons 1961 census	% of the total	% points above or below Canadian average
Agriculture	1,608	15.7	+ 5.8
Forestry	128	1.3	− 0.4
Fishing and trapping	17	0.2	− 0.3
Mines, quarries, oil wells	522	5.1	+ 3.2
Manufacturing	650	6.4	−15.3
Construction	1,026	10.0	+ 3.3
Transportation, communications, and other utilities	1,581	15.5	+ 6.2
Wholesale trade	566	5.5	+ 1.0
Retail trade	1,147	11.2	+ 0.4
Finance, insurance, and real estate	198	1.9	− 1.6
Community and business services	902	8.8	− 4.0
Personal services	912	8.9	+ 2.1
Public administration and defence	659	6.4	− 1.1
Miscellaneous	317	3.1	+ 0.7
Total labor force	10,233	100.0	—

Chapter 19

THE YUKON AND NORTHWEST TERRITORIES

The North is a land abounding in poetry and latent hopes. The very word evokes images of ice and snow and brilliant Aurora Borealis, of long winter nights and summer midnight sun, of Eskimos huddled up in their igloos, of Mounties out to get their man, and of lonely trappers winding their way to the distant fur-trading posts. New images have now been added, of military personnel scanning their radar screens and of prospectors searching for new minerals to build the "great land of tomorrow."

However, as is usually the case, the vision and the reality differ sharply. To a small number of Canadians who have actually been there, the Arctic seems more like a "land of yesterday", a land that time forgot. Most of the North is as primitive as it was when Mackenzie found it. One can travel for miles without seeing a soul or a sign of life. An area of 1.5 million square miles, about half the size of the United States, is occupied by a scattering of pioneers, plus a few Indians and Eskimos, all of whom, if assembled in Toronto, would just suffice to fill the Maple Leaf Gardens and the Stadium.

Agriculture

Unlike Northern Russia, where nearly a million acres are already under cultivation, agriculture is practically non-existent in the Yukon and Northwest Territories. Strange as it may seem, low temperatures and long winters do not constitute the chief obstacles to farming. More fundamental are the scarcity of rainfall and the poor quality of the soil. Nevertheless, in small-scale operations, grain has been grown successfully in the Yukon, while in the Mackenzie Valley fine gardens are found as far north as the Arctic Circle. Potatoes, cabbages, carrots, and beans thrive even in places where the permafrost is just a few inches below the surface of the ground. In the long nightless days of summer, growth is practically uninterrupted, and some record-sized vegetables have been produced — carrots over 12 inches long and cabbages about the size of footballs. The federal government's experimental farm at Fort Simpson, on the Mackenzie, claims to have succeeded with every vegetable crop grown in Canada, except corn-on-the-cob. However, all this is on a small, trial basis.

Other Subsidiary Resources

The prospects for developing other resources are equally limited. The fur trade has in recent decades declined considerably in value as a result of changes in women's fashions and the rise of synthetic furs. Commercial fishing is confined to whitefish and lake trout on Great Slave Lake and, around Frobisher Bay, to the catching of arctic char for the Montréal gourmet market. Substantial stands of good timber are found south of the tree line, but their relative remoteness and inaccessibility inhibits the establishment of any type of forest industry. The same reasons also hinder the development of a tourist trade.

Mineral Resources

At present, the main asset of the North is its mineral wealth. The Yukon was the site of the celebrated Klondike gold rush in 1896. The boom lasted for only a short time, but some gold continues to be recovered even now. In the Northwest Territories, the area near Yellowknife has very rich gold mines, the value of production in 1964 amounting to $15 million, slightly over 10% of the Canadian output.

While gold is important, the base metals hold the greatest promise for the future. Lead and zinc are mined in the Mayo district in central Yukon. More lead and zinc are obtained from Pine Point, on the south shore of Great Slave Lake. This deposit is one of the largest and richest of its kind on the North American continent. Much of the high grade ore is so close to the surface that it can be scraped up with a bulldozer.

Other rarer minerals known to be in the same district include tungsten, tantalum, beryllium, and lithium. The chances of making more discoveries are extremely bright. At least two thirds of the area of the Northwest Territories is occupied by the Canadian Shield, which has yielded immense wealth along its more accessible southern fringe. The few scattered sections that have been prospected indicate that the Shield may be just as rich in the minerals further north.

Oil has been extracted at Norman Wells, on the lower Mackenzie, for over 30 years. More oil is known to exist in the Yukon's Eagle Plains and in the general region of Great Slave Lake. Geologists believe that a north-south belt of oil-bearing rock formations may extend from southern Alberta through the Mackenzie Basin to the most northerly islands of the Arctic Archipelago. If this is true (and there is good evidence to support the belief), the Far North may one day become a new Middle East in terms of oil production.

Difficulties in the Development of the North

Notwithstanding this wealth of mineral resources, the rate of development has been painfully slow. The hurdles along the way are still formidable. It has been estimated that, including pay and supplies, it costs $100 a day to maintain one semi-skilled laborer in the North. He requires 16 tons of supplies, most of it fuel, for one season. In addition, it is necessary to bring in every piece of equipment hundreds of miles by rail, road, water, even air, and it is just as expensive sending out the minerals to be sold.

All of this means that a company may easily have to pay double or triple the normal amount to develop and operate a mine in the north. Businessmen are naturally reluctant to risk capital unless the deposits are of such high grade as to more than balance out costs. A professor at the University of Alberta has calculated that the extraction of a northern gold orebody is economical only if it assays at least 0.45 ounces per ton, while in Ontario it is possible to make a profit by working deposits that contain only 0.15 ounces of gold. As a result, the chances that a northern mineral discovery will develop into a producing mine are as low as one in a thousand.

The federal government is trying to reduce these odds by providing more transportation facilities. It has built railway lines as well as a network of "resource roads" to link the mineral-rich areas with the communities in the south. Air transport too has been improved. Bigger aircraft, better navigational methods, and more airfields provide safer lifelines for isolated communities. But, despite this, the water still remains the most economical mode of transport. Each summer, thousands of tons of freight move up and down the Mackenzie and its tributaries, the Slave and the Athabasca. Unfortunately, the navigation season is short, hardly four months in the year. Also, since the mineral deposits are not likely to be close to the rivers, the need for supplementary arteries is extremely urgent if development is to occur at a faster pace.

The difficulties are, no doubt, great, but perhaps not much greater than those surmounted in the past hundred years in opening up other areas of this country. Indeed, the historical development of Canada has been largely a story of response and adaptation to the challenge of geography, and there is no reason why the North cannot be tamed eventually. Perhaps the new vehicle, the Hovercraft, able to skim across muskeg and frozen tundra carrying huge loads economically and rapidly, could finally exorcise the spectre of costly transportation that has perpetually haunted northern development.

The climate, by itself, is not likely to prove a formidable obstacle, as is often imagined. Up in the High Arctic it is certainly cold, but the average January temperature at Whitehorse, capital of the Yukon Territory, is actually 5 degrees warmer than in Winnipeg. The mean summer temperature at Fort Smith, a sub-Arctic community on the Slave River, is just about the same as at Edmonton (62°F.). The main difference between the north and south is the length of the cold season. Winters in the north generally last for eight to nine months. However, they are very dry and hence not unbearable. The annual snowfall in most parts is less than that in Toronto or Montréal.

Also, thanks to the airplane and other technological developments, many settlers moving to the North are now able to take the essential paraphernalia of modern living with them. Citizens of towns such as Yellowknife and Whitehorse live like southern suburbanites, in neat frame houses with central heating, indoor plumbing, and electric refrigerators. Many of them own cars as well. Life on the frontier can still be tough, but it is not as rugged as it once was.

YUKON AND NORTHWEST TERRITORIES

Area covered: Whole of Yukon and Northwest Territories (1,458,784 square miles).

COMPOSITION OF THE MARKET

Place	Territory and District	Population 1961	% of the region
Whitehorse	Yukon	5,031	13.37
Yellowknife	Mackenzie (NWT)	3,245	8.62
Fort Smith	Mackenzie (NWT)	1,681	4.47
Frobisher Bay	Franklin (NWT)	1,426	3.79
Hay River	Mackenzie (NWT)	1,338	3.56
Inuvik	Mackenzie (NWT)	1,248	3.32
Total urban		13,969	37.13
Rural non-farm		23,592	62.70
Rural farm		65	0.17
Total population		37,626	100.00

CHARACTERISTICS OF THE POPULATION

	% of the total population of the region	% points above or below Canadian average
Mother tongue (1961 census)		
English	50.6	− 7.8
French	3.8	−24.3
German	3.0	− 0.1
Native Indian and Eskimo dialects	36.5	+35.6
Italian	0.7	− 1.2
Dutch	0.4	− 0.5
Polish	0.5	− 0.4
Ukrainian	1.1	− 0.9
Other	3.4	− 0.4
Total	100.0	—
Official language spoken (1961 census)		
English only	72.4	+ 5.0
French only	0.4	−18.7
Both English and French	6.5	− 5.7
Neither English nor French	20.7	+19.4
Total	100.0	—

IMPORTANCE OF THE MARKET (1964 ESTIMATES)

	Number	% of Canada
Population	41,000	0.21
Households	9,000	0.19
Disposable income ($ million)	49.0	0.15

GROWTH OF THE MARKET

	Percentage growth 1961 to 1964	% points above or below Canadian average
Population	+ 8.97	+ 3.50
Disposable income	+11.36	−10.17

POVERTY AND AFFLUENCE (1961 CENSUS)

	Number	% of region's total	% points above or below Canadian average
Extent of poverty			
Families earning below $3,000 a year (non-farm)	437	15.5	− 7.8
Persons not in families earning below $1,500 a year (non-farm)	439	36.3	−12.6
Farms with gross income of less than $2,500 a year	24	92.4	+46.3
Persons not in school with grade 4 or less education	9,359	38.4	+25.0
Doubled-up households (more than one family per household)	315	4.0	+ 0.3
Households living in dilapidated dwellings	1,573	19.9	+14.3
Households without facilities of running water	4,175	52.7	+41.8
Households without facilities of installed bath or shower	4,435	56.0	+36.3
Extent of affluence			
Families earning over $10,000 a year (non-farm)	313	11.2	+ 3.4
Persons not in families earning over $6,000 a year (non-farm)	67	5.5	+ 1.7
Farms with gross income over $15,000 a year	—	—	− 5.0
Persons with university degree	544	2.2	− 0.6
Households with two or more television sets	10	0.1	− 4.1
Households with two or more cars	185	2.3	− 4.5

AVERAGE INCOME (1961 CENSUS)

	Dollars	% above or below Canadian average
Income per family (non-farm)	6,473	+18.79
Income per person not in family (non-farm)	2,712	+26.91
Income per farm (net)	—	—

MEANS OF LIVELIHOOD—DISTRIBUTION OF
LABOR FORCE BY INDUSTRY

Industry	Persons 1961 census	% of the total	% points above or below Canadian average
Agriculture	57	0.4	− 9.5
Forestry	83	0.6	− 1.1
Fishing and trapping	1,687	12.3	+11.8
Mines, quarries, oil wells	2,002	14.6	+12.7
Manufacturing	241	1.7	−20.0
Construction	727	5.3	− 1.4
Transportation, communications, and other utilities	1,871	13.7	+ 4.4
Wholesale trade	110	0.8	− 3.7
Retail trade	782	5.7	− 5.1
Finance, insurance, and real estate	94	0.7	− 2.8
Community and business services	1,378	10.1	− 2.7
Personal services	1,025	7.5	+ 0.7
Public administration and defence	3,217	23.5	+16.0
Miscellaneous	420	3.1	+ 0.7
Total labor force	13,694	100.0	—

Chapter 20

CANADA — PROVINCIALISM AND FOREIGN INVESTMENTS

Economic Capsule

Some sixty years ago, Sir Wilfrid Laurier, in a burst of optimism, declared that the twentieth century would belong to Canada. His prophecy has not been proved far wrong. No doubt, the country is still very thinly settled, with hardly three-fifths of 1% of the world population; but it has turned out to be rich in natural resources far beyond anything Laurier ever dreamed of.

Known reserves of a dozen important minerals are huge by any standards and new finds are constantly being reported. There are large deposits of iron ore, nickel, asbestos, lead and zinc, while the oil locked in the Athabaska tar sands is regarded as one of the world's greatest untapped sources of petroleum. Timber, after centuries of felling, presents no problem of replacement, and virgin forests are still awaiting exploitation. Several big hydro-electric projects have been completed since the Second World War; yet enough unharnessed water-power sites are available to easily double or triple the present output.

These natural resources are more than adequately supplemented by human and manmade resources. The inhabitants are well educated; the labor force is skilled and hard-working, the administrative and entrepreneurial talent is of an exceptionally high order. The country has social and private fixed capital facilities that are fairly well developed and substantial in amount. The per capita income is the second highest in the world, providing lucrative markets for many goods and services, despite the low density of population. True, the economy is dependent on foreign markets, but most of the exports are of a kind for which the external demand is expected to remain strong in the future. In short, unlike most countries, there are no critical resource scarcities or bottlenecks which may in some way hamper or hinder economic progress.

In the past decade (1955-1965), Canada's economy burgeoned with a vigor that would have brought cries of jubilation in a less reticent society. Population grew by 25%, personal income by 98%, and corporate profits by 97%. The unemployment level, hovering above 7% a few years ago, was cut down by more than half. The consumers' buoyant spending mood was evident all across the land from Heart's Delight, Newfoundland, to Hope, British Columbia — which, incidentally, became the first province to top $100 in average weekly wages in 1965.

And yet, the essential question of the continued existence of the nation as a political unit is still as much an issue as it was when the Confederation was formed about a hundred years ago. Despite prosperity, Canada continues to be plagued by twin factors that have acted as a deterrent throughout her history:

- The rather weak sense of nationalism among her citizens.
- The powerful tug of the giant United States across the border.

Provincialism

The task of holding the disparate elements of the nation together has always been the prime objective of the federal government since Confederation. Lately, the sectional strains have become more severe. In fact, it would not be too far-fetched to say that the provinces, rather than the Conservatives, form the real opposition to the Liberal government at Ottawa. Québec's "quiet revolution" has led the way to decentralization. Although the main concern of the French Canadians is to achieve true equality in the nation, their means to this end is a strong emphasis on provincial rights. In this respect, Québec has become a rallying point for other provincial premiers who also want to see the financial powers of Ottawa curtailed.

They have good reasons for feeling as they do. During the past fifteen years or so, the growth of governmental functions has been remarkably one-sided. The numerous services of the welfare state are all constitutionally provincial responsibilities; so are highways, roads, education and urban redevelopment. No federal function, calling for such large expenditures of public funds, has grown so rapidly in recent years. This has compelled the provincial premiers to clamor for more autonomy in financial matters. They won a significant victory in the spring of 1965 when Parliament passed the "opting out" bill, letting the provinces pull out of projects administered co-operatively with the federal government and giving them special tax abatements to finance programs of their own.

This is not all. Of late the provinces have thrust themselves into the area that strictly speaking would be considered the preserve of the central government. Typical examples are: Ontario's "trade crusade" to expand exports and reduce imports; the Lesage government's spectacular success in achieving quasi-diplomatic status for Québec House in Paris; and the insistence of some premiers that the provinces should be consulted prior to any major decisions being made on monetary, fiscal and tariff policies.

Thus, paradoxically, while the wind of change seems to lead nations towards greater centralization, Canada is moving in the opposite direction toward a loose federation. One of the fundamental problems of Canadian nationhood is how to provide for different provincial sentiments and observances within a single house without increasing irritations, acrimony and ultimate separation. Perhaps this problem will never be fully solved, but today, for numerous reasons, it has come to the forefront as the leading threat to the continuation of Canada as a unified and independent nation.

U. S. Influence

The second of Canada's two major problems is also one that can never be "solved" in the final sense; it is the question of how to live with the giant neighbor to the south. The old fear of military conquest by the United States has disappeared, but only to be replaced by a deeper and more subtle one of economic domination. Perhaps no country in the world, certainly none as fully developed as Canada, has so much of its industry owned by non-residents.

The latest available figures for 1962 indicate that foreigners, mostly U.S. citizens, control 60% of Canada's manufacturing, 74% of oil and gas production, and 57% of mining and smelting. The pattern of outside domination is strongest in the biggest and most dynamic concerns — the ones which are the pacesetters of the whole economy. Foreign interests control one out of every three companies worth more than one million and two out of three worth more than $25 million. This process of Americanization goes on steadily as more and more Canadian companies are taken over by U.S. firms.

The whole question of foreign ownership is charged with emotion and generates more heat than light. Some paint the whole picture in very dark colors, and stress the following objectionable features:

• The American subsidiaries do not employ enough Canadians, especially in senior posts; nor do they have independent Canadian directors. Also, they tend to buy their components and services from the U.S. rather than from available Canadian sources.

• As foreign control over industries grows, it means that decisions affecting jobs of millions of workers and the survival of whole communities are made not in Canada but in the board rooms of New York and Chicago — and with the U.S., not Canadian, interests chiefly in mind.

• Canada urgently needs foreign trade, but U.S. subsidiaries are unwilling to push their products in overseas markets where they might be in competition with the parent concern. These firms have a sort of a built-in ceiling to their growth. They have been established with a limited horizon and are not free to conquer the world markets.

• Almost all research on new products and processes is conducted at the parent company laboratories in the U.S. This tends to mould the subsidiaries along U.S. lines, inhibiting the desire to strike out in new directions more relevant to the Canadian setting. Furthermore, the absence of research facilities accelerates what has been referred to as the "haemorrhage of Canadian brains" to the United States, a matter of great concern to the whole economy.

• American subsidiaries tend to bring U.S. law with them into Canada. For example, they refuse to sell their products to Cuba or China — although such sales are perfectly legal under Canadian law — for fear of violating Washington's "trading with the enemy" legislation.

• The degree of processing permitted to the subsidiary is relatively small. The bulk of manufacturing activity is concentrated in the U.S., leaving the Canadian plant in the position of a supplier of raw or semi-processed materials. This, combined with the structure of the U.S. tariff, has the effect of keeping the Canadian economy highly resource-oriented, the "hewer of wood and drawer of water" for the American industry.

All these economic disadvantages, point out the critics, lead to one distinct conclusion — jeopardy of the country's political independence. Economic and political freedom, they say, go hand in hand; if the first is lost, Canada cannot help becoming a more or less helpless satellite of the United States. Canadians are frequently warned that the dependence on foreign capital reflects a serious weakness of character — a desire to live beyond one's means, a shortsighted willingness to sell the Canadian birthright for a mess of American pottage, a crass materialism incompatible with the demands of national sacrifice.

On the other side of the fence, it is not difficult to find equally vociferous champions of American investments in Canada. In their opinion, much of the criticism is based on popular polemics, being the syndrome of the old Canadian fear of American expansion. They point out that, considering the enormous variety of situations regarding both direct and portfolio investments in Canada, little can be said that is universally valid. There are no authoritative empirical studies, and the intangibles are simply too complex to permit the passing of sweeping generalizations. Examples are cited of U.S.-controlled companies that make vigorous efforts to export to all countries of the world; that permit Canadians to rise to top positions in management; that sell a reasonable proportion of their common stock to the public; that contribute generously to local charities and are in numerous ways as beneficial to the community as the locally-owned firms.

In short, the supporters of American investments in Canada argue that the disadvantages of American capital are based on flimsy foundations, and do not in any case offset the advantages. Some of the benefits, in their opinion, are extremely important. The parent-subsidiary relationship, for example, vastly simplifies the problems of transmitting the results of new research and technology. Beyond this, the parent company can arrange for training facilities, make capital available at low rates of interest, and provide market contacts which might not otherwise be readily available. In other words, the accumulated experience of the U.S. corporation can inject a high degree of efficiency and viability to the Canadian subsidiary, so that the latter is not forced to undergo the often painful, lengthy and expensive process of trial and error in the early stages of the operation.

The average Canadian is not too concerned with the pros and cons of these arguments. He tends to equate U.S. investments with the ebullient prosperity which the country has enjoyed in the postwar era. Canadian economic growth, he instinctively feels, would have been much slower without the American know-how, capital, and penchant for risk taking. In this, he is not far off the mark. Many experts believe that the booming oil industry would be 15 years behind its current output of 200 million barrels of crude oil a year if the U.S. giants had not invested billions in exploration and production. Similarly, in potash, an industry that is changing the economy of Saskatchewan, the mines would have still not been in operation, were it not for the pioneering work of Potash Company of America in the late 1950's and, especially, the big plunge of International Minerals and Chemical Corporation.

Looked at in objective terms, the U.S. investments may be regarded as a part of a long-run historical trend towards the progressive integration of the North American economy. Already there is pressure for freer trade between Canada and the United States, leading eventually to a customs union under which most goods would move back and forth across the border without restrictions. In a world of discriminatory trading blocs with external tariff structures becoming more rigid in the name of European integration, or some other kind of integration, it is argued that the full development of Canada's manufacturing industries can best be accomplished through access to the American market. With the advantage of a 20% or sometimes even greater differential in the wage rates, many Canadian industries may be able to compete in tariff-free U.S. markets, particularly when they have geographic advantages over competitors. Ontario, for example, has a better location for supplying the American Middle West than many areas in the United States.

Though some form of customs union seems likely, it is not expected to arrive overnight. In view of the opposition from vested interests on both sides of the border, it could at best be achieved step by step. Just as the Schuman Plan for a Coal-Steel Community was the preliminary move in paving the way for a broader European Common Market, so the North American Common Market would require beachheads of free trade for individual industries. The first successful beachhead of this type was set up as far back as 1944 for agricultural equipment and machinery. The second one came in 1965 when Ottawa and Washington signed an agreement covering automobiles and automotive parts. Some of the other candidates for future experiments may be electronics and electrical appliances, chemicals, pulp and paper, aluminum, aircraft parts, processed foods, and industrial machinery.

CANADA

IMPORTANCE OF THE MARKET (1964 ESTIMATES)

	Number
Population	19,235,000
Households	4,805,000
Disposable income ($ million)	31,537.0

COMPOSITION OF THE MARKET

Place	Province	Population 1961	% of Canada
Montréal	Québec	2,109,509	11.57
Toronto	Ontario	1,824,481	10.00
Vancouver	British Columbia	790,165	4.33
Winnipeg	Manitoba	475,989	2.61
Ottawa	Ontario-Québec	429,750	2.36
Hamilton	Ontario	395,189	2.17
Québec	Québec	357,568	1.96
Edmonton	Alberta	337,568	1.85
Calgary	Alberta	279,062	1.53
Windsor	Ontario	193,365	1.06
Halifax	Nova Scotia	183,946	1.01
London	Ontario	181,283	0.99
Kitchener	Ontario	154,864	0.85
Victoria	British Columbia	154,152	0.85
Regina	Saskatchewan	112,141	0.61
Sudbury	Ontario	110,694	0.61
Sydney-Glace Bay	Nova Scotia	106,114	0.58
Chicoutimi-Jonquière	Québec	105,009	0.58
St. Catharines	Ontario	95,577	0.52
Saint John	New Brunswick	95,563	0.52
Saskatoon	Saskatchewan	95,526	0.52
Fort William-Port Arthur	Ontario	93,251	0.51
St. John's	Newfoundland	90,838	0.50
Trois Rivières	Québec	83,659	0.46
Oshawa	Ontario	80,918	0.44
Sherbrooke	Québec	70,253	0.38
Shawinigan	Québec	63,518	0.35
Kingston	Ontario	63,419	0.35
Sarnia	Ontario	61,293	0.34
Sault Ste. Marie	Ontario	58,460	0.32
Brantford	Ontario	56,741	0.31
Moncton	New Brunswick	55,768	0.31
Niagara Falls	Ontario	54,649	0.30
Peterborough	Ontario	49,902	0.27
Sub-total		9,470,184	51.92
Other urban		3,530,221	19.36
Total urban		13,000,405	71.28
Rural non-farm		3,165,057	17.35
Rural farm		2,072,785	11.37
Total population		18,238,247	100.00

GROWTH OF THE MARKET

	Percentage growth 1961 to 1964
Population	+ 5.47
Disposable income	+21.53

AVERAGE INCOME (1961 CENSUS)

	Dollars
Income per family (non-farm)	5,449
Income per person not in family (non-farm)	2,137
Income per farm (net)	3,255

POVERTY AND AFFLUENCE (1961 CENSUS)

	Number	% of the total
Extent of poverty		
Families earning below $3,000 a year (non-farm)	847,940	23.3
Persons not in families earning below $1,500 a year (non-farm)	687,857	48.9
Farms with gross income of less than $2,500 a year	221,866	46.1
Persons not in school with grade 4 or less education	1,557,309	13.4
Doubled-up households (more than one family per household)	167,943	3.7
Households living in dilapidated dwellings	255,414	5.6
Households without facilities of running water	496,180	10.9
Households without facilities of installed bath or shower	894,973	19.7
Extent of affluence		
Families earning over $10,000 a year (non-farm)	287,085	7.8
Persons not in families earning over $6,000 a year (non-farm)	54,952	3.8
Farms with gross income over $15,000 a year	23,918	5.0
Persons with university degree	326,903	2.8
Households with two or more television sets	192,192	4.2
Households with two or more cars	310,900	6.8

CHARACTERISTICS OF THE POPULATION

	% of the total population
Mother tongue (1961 census)	
English	58.4
French	28.1
German	3.1
Native Indian dialects	0.9
Italian	1.9
Dutch	0.9
Polish	0.9
Ukrainian	0.2
Other	3.8
Total	100.0
Official language spoken (1961 census)	
English only	67.4
French only	19.1
Both English and French	12.2
Neither English nor French	1.3
Total	100.0

LABOR FORCE BY INDUSTRY

Industry	Persons 1961 census	% of the total
Agriculture	640,786	9.9
Forestry	108,580	1.7
Fishing and trapping	36,263	0.5
Mines, quarries, oil wells	121,702	1.9
Manufacturing	1,404,865	21.7
Construction	431,093	6.7
Transportation, communications, and other utilities	603,286	9.3
Wholesale trade	289,884	4.5
Retail trade	701,606	10.8
Finance, insurance and real estate	228,905	3.5
Community and business services	825,844	12.8
Personal services	437,518	6.8
Public administration and defence	482,925	7.5
Miscellaneous	158,593	2.4
Total labor force	6,471,850	100.0

STANDARD OF LIVING BASED ON OWNERSHIP OF
APPLIANCES AND EQUIPMENT, 1965

	Number of households	% of total households in Canada
Cooking equipment		
Electric stoves	3,349,000	69.0
Wood or coal cookstoves or ranges	448,000	9.2
Piped gas stoves	686,000	14.1
Refrigeration		
Electric refrigerators	4,648,000	95.8
Home freezers	1,099,000	22.6
Electric washing machines		
Automatic	1,119,000	23.1
Other	3,065,000	63.2
Clothes dryers		
Electric	1,224,000	25.2
Gas	107,000	2.2
Sewing machines		
Electric	2,544,000	52.4
Non-electric	885,000	18.2
Phonographs and record players		
Cabinet model	1,596,000	32.9
Table model	254,000	5.2
Portable model	1,018,000	21.0
Telephones		
One	3,700,000	76.2
Two or more	641,000	13.2
Television sets		
One	3,968,000	81.8
Two or more	527,000	10.9
Automobiles		
One	3,034,000	62.5
Two or more	604,000	12.4
Other appliances		
Automatic dishwashers	133,000	2.7
Vacuum cleaners	3,636,000	74.9
Window-type air conditioners	108,000	2.2
FM radio receivers	1,109,000	22.9

(Source: DBS, *Household Facilities and Equipment, May 1965*. Catalogue no. 64-202.)

BIBLIOGRAPHY

Bennet, C. L., G. Filion, G. Clark, M. W. Campbell, and R. Haig-Brown: *The Face of Canada,* Clarke, Irwin & Company Limited, Toronto, 1959.

Bogue, Donald J. and Calvin L. Beale: *Economic Areas of the United States,* The Free Press of Glencoe, Inc., New York, 1961.

Business Week: "Canada — A Special Report", May 22, 1965.

Chapin, Miriam: *Contemporary Canada,* Oxford University Press, New York, 1959.

Camu, Pierre, E. P. Week, and Z. W. Sametz: *Economic Geography of Canada, with an Introduction to a 68-Region System,* Macmillan of Canada, Toronto, 1964.

Dominion Bureau of Statistics: "Regional Statistics and Regional Statistical Classifications", in *The Canadian Statistical Review,* August, 1961.

Duncan, Otis D., Ray P. Cuzzort, and Beverly Duncan: *Statistical Geography,* The Free Press of Glencoe, Illinois, 1961.

Fortune: "Le Canada Français En Révolte", February, 1965.

Horne, Alistair: *Canada and the Canadians,* The Macmillan Company of Canada Limited, 1961.

Hutchison, Bruce: *Canada: Tomorrow's Giant,* Longmans, Green and Company, Toronto, 1957.

Krueger, Ralph R., Frederick O. Sargent, Anthony Vos, and Norman Pearson (editors): *Regional and Resource Planning in Canada,* Holt, Rinehart and Winston of Canada, Ltd., Toronto, 1963. (A book of readings based primarily on the "Resources for Tomorrow" Conference background papers.)

Putnam, Donald F. and Donald P. Kerr: *A Regional Geography of Canada,* J. M. Dent and Sons (Canada) Limited, Toronto, 1964 (revised).

Smith, Charles W.: *Targeting Sales Effort,* Columbia University Press, New York, 1958.

Watson, Wreford J.: *North America, Its Countries and Regions,* Longmans, Green and Co. Ltd., London, 1963.

Wilson, George W., S. Gordon, and S. Judek: *Canada: An Appraisal of Its Needs and Resources,* The Twentieth Century Fund, New York. University of Toronto Press, Toronto, 1965.

B. REGIONAL ANALYSIS BY SOCIO-ECONOMIC AND MARKETING CHARACTERISTICS

Introduction

So far the 64 economic regions have been treated individually. Now they are grouped together and analyzed by certain major topics, such as population, age groups, income, education, occupation, retail sales, and the like. The purpose is to look at the country as a whole and see how one region (or metropolitan city) differs from another on important marketing and socio-economic characteristics. Most of the statistics published here have not been presented in the previous section.

Wherever necessary, an attempt has been made to project 1961 census figures to 1964 by the use of well-established statistical techniques. No doubt, in any up-dating of this type, some error is likely to creep in. But past experience has shown that new trends, especially in the socio-economic field, emerge rather slowly, and violent statistical fluctuations from one year to another are somewhat rare. Hence, while it would be presumptuous to expect from the 1964 figures the same precision as obtained from a hundred per cent census count in 1961, the estimates given are reasonably accurate and can be used with confidence as long as they are treated as guidelines and not blueprints.

Viewed as pure statistics, the column after column of figures in the tables may seem to bury rather than highlight the profile of the region. But it need not be so. If analyzed with patience and imagination, the data will bring out subtle but critical distinctions between regions or cities. This can be put to good use not only by line sales managers when checking their operations, but also by top executives when formulating long-term plans and policies.

It is impossible to prepare an exhaustive compilation of all the applications of the tables presented in the following pages. The scope is indeed, vast. Below are a few examples of how the data can be used in marketing. (There may be some overlapping in the list; few business problems can be sealed off by themselves.)

MARKET ANALYSIS

- Develop a buying power index geared to specific products.
- Select the prime markets on the basis of population, income, education, retail sales, and the like.
- Make comparative market measurements on specific characteristics.
- Differentiate the market for high-priced goods from the mass markets.
- Break out the best household prospects for particular products in special markets.
- Design samples for consumer surveys . . . pick out test markets.

ADVERTISING AND SALES PROMOTION

• Plan advertising and promotion budgets with maximum effectiveness based on actual size of markets and exact locations of consumers and prospects.

• Relate advertising costs to territorial costs.

• Evaluate media-supplied figures . . . compare media coverage with market size . . . ascertain the best type of media for supporting the sales efforts.

• Prepare special advertising and promotion campaigns to apply pressure badly needed in certain regions.

• Appraise advertising results against potentials and sales.

SALES MANAGEMENT

• Map sales territories to assure coverage of the market in a consistent and organized manner.

• Assign work loads to sales force in each territory based on actual need and potential.

• Develop an equitable sales compensation plan.

• Compare potentials with salesmen's travel time.

• Measure salesman's performance against a territorial yardstick.

• Keep tabs on dealers, wholesalers, and retailers.

• Find and analyze territorial "soft spots".

• Pinpoint most promising locations for a new plant, a branch office, or a warehouse.

THE TOP SIX MARKETING REGIONS

One picture emerges very clearly from the tables: the tremendous concentration of Canada's marketing potential in the following six regions:

Metro Montréal and its Environs,
Metro Toronto and its Environs,
Vancouver-Lower Fraser,
Hamilton/St. Catharines-Niagara,
Ottawa-Ottawa Valley *plus* Hull-Western Laurentides,
Metro Winnipeg and its Environs.

These regions comprise only 2.07% of Canada's land area, but they account for:

44.22% of its population,
46.04% of its households,
47.56% of its retail sales,
49.47% of its personal disposable income,
58.59% of its manufacturing output,
59.01% of its households with a university degree,
60.02% of its households earning over $10,000 a year.

Chapter 21

REGIONAL DATA BY DEMOGRAPHIC CHARACTERISTICS

Population

The starting point for any socio-economic analysis is population. Everything in the fields of economics, politics, government, industry, education, religion, and recreation is done by the people and for the people. Human beings are both the means and the end of all society's endeavors.

At the regional level, population statistics are of fundamental importance in the intelligent shaping of public policies. Questions such as those connected with welfare measures, equalization of educational opportunities, construction of highways, location of hospitals and other health facilities can be studied only in close relation to population facts and trends.

The same is true for marketing. The primary characteristic of a market for any consumer product or service is people, for without people no market can exist. Hence the first step in the process of evaluating the potential of a region is to find out its population and the percentage it constitutes of the whole of Canada.

Rate of growth

Population gains come from two directions, natural increase (excess of births over deaths) and net migration (surplus of inward over outward migration). With the interregional differences in the rates of natural increase being relatively small, migration is now looked upon as the sensitive indicator of local economic health, since it shows whether a region is attracting people from elsewhere or losing its people (especially the young adults) to other areas. In this respect, the net migration ratio may be regarded as an index of metabolism for the region.

Whether an area is able to attract migrants depends not only upon business and employment opportunities but also upon living conditions; for example, the quality of housing and the availability of community facilities and services at reasonable rates. The degree of tolerance prevailing in the locality is equally important. Some welcome newcomers with open arms, while others impose subtle sanctions against "outsiders."

The migrants include all types of people — the hardy pioneers building settlements in the northern wilderness; the persons with special skills or education looking for industries where their services can be best utilized; the immigrants eager to start afresh in the new land of their adoption; the young unmarried abandoning their parental nests to seek fortune in greener pastures elsewhere; the ex-farmhands wanting to learn a more remunerative trade in the big city; the socially disenfranchised hoping to secure a more pleasant life in a different environment. The motives that trigger migration may be complex, but these people, as a rule, have a few things in common: they are daring, ambitious, progressive, ready to respond to new stimulations, eager to experiment with new ways of living.

Age composition

Data on the age composition of the population have widespread uses in many fields of human endeavor; for example, in the planning of educational policies, the execution of social welfare programs, and the preparation of life insurance tables, to cite just a few. For a social scientist, particularly a demographer, such information is of paramount importance. Until differences in the age composition of the population are ironed out, little significance can be attached to seeming contradictions between regions in respect to mortality rates, birth rates, and marriage rates.

In the field of marketing, too, age has an effect on the sales of many products. For example, children consume almost twice as much milk per capita as adults. Hence the dairy industry can put to good use the data on the number of children in each region or city. The same information is also useful to other industries, such as the makers of baby carriages, infant foods, children's toys, school desks, children's clothing, and the like.

In rural cultures, where age is generally respected, a high proportion of people in the older group tends to make social and recreational life institutionalized, routinized, formal, and patronizing. Elderly persons tend to be set in their ways. They have a store of likes and dislikes acquired over the years which they hold tenaciously. As a result, they are often in direct conflict with the younger generations. It is quite conceivable that the predominance of older ages among farmers in the Atlantic Provinces may account for the conservatism in agricultural practices, compared to the radical approaches in the Prairies where the older group is not so heavily represented in the farm population.

Economists generally use the age group statistics for computing the dependency ratio; that is, the number of dependents (0 to 14 plus 65 and over) to 100 people in the working age group (15-64). Obviously, even if two regions had about the same population and income, the different dependency ratio would affect the incidence of saving and investment, as well as the pattern of consumption. The demand for luxuries and semi-luxuries is likely to be curtailed if a small number of workers have to support a large number of children and old people.

On account of internal movement from rural to large urban communities and the concentration of New Canadians in metropolitan centers, marked differences in the dependency ratio exist between various areas. Regions such as Montréal and its Environs and Toronto and its Environs have far less than their pro rata shares of the nation's children and more than their pro rata shares of people in the economically productive ages. On the other hand, most of the regions of the Atlantic Provinces are burdened with fairly excessive dependency ratios because of the high birth rates and the trend among the young adults to pick up stakes in order to seek better opportunities elsewhere.

Sex composition

The breakdown of age statistics by sex is obviously important in the marketing of certain products like lipsticks, foundation garments, shaving creams, and cigars. For a social scientist, too, the data have great significance. A little reflection will make it evident that the proportion of males and females in a region has a direct bearing on the marriage and birth rates. Furthermore, many of the important social and economic relationships are largely dependent upon a balance between the sexes or the lack of it.

Certain northern regions — for example, Labrador, Yukon and Northwest Territories, Northern Manitoba, Northwestern British Columbia, North-Central British Columbia, Northern Saskatchewan — are highly male-dominated communities. This has a rather subtle but profound effect upon the psychological traits and general behavior pattern of the denizens. A carefree spirit of reckless abandon prevails, the community being regarded not as a home but merely as a place for making money. The population is in a continual flux, for the men tire of womanless life, and after they have made their "pile" return to the south to marry and settle down.

In other parts of the country, too, unequal sex ratios have diverse sociological effects. More girls than boys move out from rural to urban areas, resulting in the preponderance of eligible bachelors on the farms. For example, in the three predominantly agricultural regions of Saskatchewan—Palliser, Southeastern Parklands and Central Parklands — there were, in the age group of 15 to 44, 107 males for every 100 females. On the other hand, in the nineteen metropolitan centers, women exceeded males by 3%. Actually, the female ratio here would have been higher still were it not for the fact that a large proportion of postwar immigrants, mostly bachelors, have tended to gravitate towards big cities. Thus, the dynamics of population movements operate in a way that gives the foreign male a comparative advantage over the Canadian-born farmer in securing a mate from among the native women.

Households

The statistics on households and families are often of greater significance than those dealing with population. The sales of appliances, such as refrigerators and vacuum cleaners, are more dependent on the number of households than upon the number of individuals in a community. Also, when analyzing the effectiveness of the broadcast media, it is preferable to know how many homes rather than persons are reached by each station or program.

A household, as defined by the DBS, consists of a person or a group of persons occupying a dwelling unit. A dwelling may be a house, an apartment, or even a room, as long as it is a structurally separate set of living premises with a private entrance from outside the building or from a common hallway or stairway inside. For statistical purposes, the number of households is the same as the number of occupied dwellings.

In popular parlance, a household is often regarded as synonymous with a family, but strictly speaking the two terms are not interchangeable. A family, according to the DBS, consists of a husband or wife, with or without unmarried children, or a parent with one or more unmarried children, living together in the same dwelling. Once a son or daughter marries, he or she ceases to be considered as a member of the parents' family even though continuing to live under the same roof.

Thus, households can be divided into family and non-family households. The family household may be further broken down into those having one family and those with two or more families. Since families double-up generally for monetary reasons, they may be regarded as potential home owners or tenants once their economic conditions improve. Consequently statistics relating to them are of interest to organizations concerned with residential construction.

Data on the *size* of households can be of use to manufacturers who sell their products in packages of varied sizes. One can roughly assess from the statistics what is the potential within a region for each type of package. The size of the household also affects the pattern of consumption. A survey on urban family expenditures conducted by the DBS showed that in a household with two adults and five or more children, food accounted for 31% of the budget, compared to 26% for households with two adults and three children, and 22% for households with two adults only.

ESTIMATES OF POPULATION FOR 1964 AND 1970 AND AVERAGE ANNUAL RATE OF GROWTH

Economic regions	Estimated population, June 1, 1964				Average annual rate of growth (%)*			Estimated population 1970
	Males	Females	Persons	% of Canada	Natural increase	Net migration	Actual increase	
Newfoundland	251,800	239,200	491,000	2.55	+2.9	-0.8	+2.1	545,000
St. John's-Southeastern Nfld.	149,100	144,500	293,600	1.53	+2.5	-0.8	+1.7	319,200
Central Nfld.	46,100	42,800	88,900	0.46	+2.6	-0.4	+2.2	99,200
Western Nfld.	47,800	45,000	92,800	0.48	+4.1	-1.4	+2.7	106,400
Labrador.	8,800	6,900	15,700	0.08	+3.9	+1.1	+5.0	20,200
Prince Edward Island	54,700	52,300	107,000	0.56	+1.8	-0.7	+1.1	109,000
Nova Scotia	385,800	374,200	760,000	3.95	+1.9	-0.7	+1.2	815,000
Sydney-Cape Breton	88,300	85,000	173,300	0.90	+1.9	-1.0	+0.9	182,100
Northern Nova Scotia	71,400	70,000	141,400	0.73	+1.3	-1.6	-0.3	138,500
Halifax-South Shore	177,500	173,600	351,100	1.83	+2.1	-0.1	+2.0	392,000
Annapolis Valley	48,600	45,600	94,200	0.49	+2.0	-0.5	+1.5	102,400
New Brunswick	311,900	305,100	617,000	3.21	+2.2	-0.6	+1.6	663,000
Moncton-Southeastern N.B.	68,300	68,000	136,300	0.71	+2.1	-0.6	+1.5	145,400
Saint John-Southern N.B.	75,800	76,600	152,400	0.79	+1.5	-0.5	+1.0	158,000
Upper Saint John Valley	87,000	82,700	169,700	0.88	+2.4	+0.7	+3.1	197,000
Northeastern N.B.	80,800	77,800	158,600	0.83	+2.6	-1.8	+0.8	162,600
Québec	2,781,500	2,780,500	5,562,000	28.92	+2.2	+0.5	+2.7	6,269,000
North Shore-New Québec	52,800	47,300	100,100	0.52	+4.4	+4.2	+8.6	146,100
Gaspé Peninsula-South Shore	203,100	191,800	394,900	2.05	+2.5	-2.1	+0.4	388,700
Saguenay Valley-Lake St. John.	139,100	133,400	272,500	1.42	+3.3	-0.9	+2.4	299,000
Metro Québec-Eastern Laurentides	331,000	336,500	667,500	3.47	+2.1	-0.2	+1.9	714,000
Trois Rivières-St. Maurice Valley	153,000	152,900	305,900	1.59	+2.1	-0.8	+1.3	316,700
Sherbrooke-Eastern Townships	233,600	233,600	467,200	2.43	+2.2	-0.8	+1.4	486,500
Metro Montréal and its Environs.	1,482,500	1,509,900	2,992,400	15.56	+2.1	+1.7	+3.8	3,528,700
Western Québec	89,000	83,400	172,400	0.90	+3.1	-1.7	+1.4	179,300
Hull-Western Laurentides	97,400	91,700	189,100	0.98	+2.6	—	+2.6	210,000

Ontario	*3,303,000*	*3,283,000*	*6,586,000*	*34.24*	*+1.9*	*+1.2*	*+3.1*	*7,566,000*
Ottawa-Ottawa Valley	284,100	288,900	573,000	2.98	+2.0	+1.9	+3.9	653,700
Kingston-Upper St. Lawrence	128,800	128,100	256,900	1.34	+1.7	−0.1	+1.6	282,200
Peterborough-Central Lake Ontario	171,700	170,800	342,500	1.78	+1.6	+0.4	+2.0	391,200
Metro Toronto and its Environs	1,136,200	1,155,700	2,291,900	11.91	+2.0	+2.5	+4.5	2,583,000
Hamilton/St. Catharines-Niagara	393,100	390,600	783,700	4.08	+1.8	+0.6	+2.4	914,000
London-Lake Erie	208,100	213,400	421,500	2.19	+1.6	+0.8	+2.4	487,200
Windsor/Sarnia-Lake St. Clair	224,600	223,300	447,900	2.33	+1.9	−0.6	+1.3	536,400
Kitchener-Midlands	194,900	193,700	388,600	2.02	+1.7	+0.8	+2.5	443,400
Lake Huron-Georgian Bay	161,800	154,300	316,100	1.64	+1.3	—	+1.3	368,500
Northeastern Ontario: Clay Belt	115,600	108,300	223,900	1.16	+2.5	−0.5	+2.0	233,800
Northeastern Ontario: Nickel Range	95,800	88,600	184,400	0.96	+2.9	+0.2	+3.1	209,600
Northeastern Ontario: Sault	69,400	62,300	131,700	0.69	+3.4	+3.8	+7.2	195,900
Lakehead-Northwestern Ontario	118,900	105,000	223,900	1.16	+2.2	−0.1	+2.1	267,100
Manitoba	*485,100*	*472,900*	*958,000*	*4.98*	*+1.8*	*−0.1*	*+1.7*	*1,039,000*
Metro Winnipeg and its Environs	349,300	350,100	699,400	3.64	+1.8	+0.4	+2.2	774,400
Southwestern Manitoba Prairie	78,100	72,300	150,400	0.78	+1.5	−1.5	—	150,400
West-Central Manitoba Parklands	29,600	26,900	56,500	0.29	+1.5	−2.1	−0.6	54,200
Northern Manitoba	28,100	23,600	51,700	0.27	+3.4	+0.3	+3.7	60,000
Saskatchewan	*485,700*	*457,300*	*943,000*	*4.90*	*+2.0*	*−1.0*	*+1.0*	*989,000*
Regina-Southeastern Plains	121,900	117,600	239,500	1.24	+2.2	+0.1	+2.3	267,500
Saskatchewan Palliser	76,700	72,300	149,000	0.77	+1.8	−1.3	+0.5	150,600
Saskatoon-Central Plains	101,500	98,400	199,900	1.04	+2.2	+0.6	+2.8	229,300
Saskatchewan-Southeastern Parklds	65,100	59,400	124,500	0.65	+1.4	−2.4	−1.0	114,800
Central Saskatchewan Parklands	109,300	100,100	209,400	1.09	+1.7	−1.7	—	205,500
Northern Saskatchewan	11,200	9,500	20,700	0.11	+4.3	−3.5	+0.8	21,300

* From 1956 to 1961.

Economic regions	Estimated population, June 1, 1964				Average annual rate of growth (%)*			Estimated population 1970
	Males	Females	Persons	% of Canada	Natural increase	Net migration	Actual increase	
Alberta	736,900	695,100	1,432,000	7.44	+2.6	+1.1	+3.7	1,662,000
Medicine Hat-Palliser	20,600	20,900	41,500	0.22	+2.0	+0.7	+2.7	45,200
Lethbridge Prairie	59,700	56,300	116,000	0.60	+2.2	-0.5	+1.7	119,700
Alberta Rocky Mountains-Foothills	11,800	9,700	21,500	0.11	+1.7	+1.8	+3.5	24,400
Calgary-South Central Alberta	211,500	205,200	416,700	2.17	+2.7	+2.9	+5.6	514,300
Red Deer Environs	42,700	38,900	81,600	0.42	+2.4	+1.4	+3.8	93,900
East-Central Alberta Prairie	56,000	50,000	106,000	0.55	+1.7	-1.8	-0.1	98,700
Edmonton-Parklands	256,400	246,200	502,600	2.61	+2.9	+1.9	+4.8	606,300
Northeastern Alberta	25,100	22,200	47,300	0.25	+2.9	-1.8	+1.1	54,300
Northwestern Alberta-Peace River	53,100	45,700	98,800	0.51	+2.9	-0.6	+2.3	105,200
British Columbia	879,300	858,700	1,738,000	9.04	+1.8	+1.5	+3.3	2,025,000
East Kootenay	19,300	17,200	36,500	0.19	+2.0	+0.4	+2.4	40,500
West Kootenay	36,900	34,400	71,300	0.37	+1.6	-0.1	+1.5	75,100
Okanagan Valley	48,400	48,900	97,300	0.51	+1.4	+0.9	+2.3	107,100
South-Central British Columbia	38,700	34,300	73,000	0.38	+2.6	+1.8	+4.4	89,300
Vancouver-Lower Fraser	484,500	490,500	975,000	5.07	+1.6	+2.0	+3.6	1,147,800
Victoria-Vancouver Island	153,900	150,200	304,100	1.58	+1.6	+1.1	+2.7	342,200
Northwestern British Columbia	32,500	26,600	59,100	0.31	+2.8	-2.3	+0.5	63,200
North-Central British Columbia	44,000	37,700	81,700	0.42	+3.5	+1.2	+4.7	101,500
Northeastern British Columbia	21,100	18,900	40,000	0.21	+4.5	+5.8	+10.3	58,300
Yukon and Northwest Territories	22,500	18,500	41,000	0.21	+3.5	+0.4	+3.9	47,000
Canada	9,698,200	9,536,800	19,235,000	100.00	+2.1	+0.6	+2.7	21,729,000

* From 1956 to 1961.

ESTIMATES OF POPULATION FOR 1964 AND 1970 AND AVERAGE ANNUAL RATE OF GROWTH (continued)

Metropolitan centers	Estimated population, June 1, 1964				Average annual rate of growth 1956–61 (%)			Estimated population 1970
	Males	Females	Persons	% of Canada	Natural increase	Net migration	Actual increase	
Calgary	155,900	154,100	310,000	1.61	+3.0	+4.7	+7.7	377,000
Edmonton	187,500	184,500	372,000	1.93	+3.3	+2.8	+6.1	434,000
Halifax	92,600	91,400	184,000	0.96	+2.1	+0.3	+2.4	219,000
Hamilton	208,200	209,800	418,000	2.17	+2.1	+1.3	+3.4	477,000
Kitchener	80,800	82,200	163,000	0.85	n.a.*	n.a.	n.a.	197,000
London	94,100	97,900	192,000	1.00	+1.9	+1.6	+3.5	216,000
Montréal	1,111,900	1,148,100	2,260,000	11.75	+1.9	+1.6	+3.5	2,673,000
Ottawa	229,300	238,700	468,000	2.43	+2.2	+2.7	+4.9	561,000
Québec	185,100	198,900	384,000	2.00	+2.0	+1.0	+3.0	440,000
Regina	60,400	61,600	122,000	0.63	n.a.	n.a.	n.a.	143,000
Saint John	49,200	50,800	100,000	0.52	+1.7	+0.5	+2.2	124,000
St. John's	44,900	47,100	92,000	0.48	+2.7	+0.1	+2.8	114,000
Saskatoon	50,000	52,000	102,000	0.53	n.a.	n.a.	n.a.	127,000
Sudbury	57,000	53,000	110,000	0.57	n.a.	n.a.	n.a.	125,000
Toronto	984,600	1,004,400	1,989,000	10.34	+1.9	+1.9	+3.8	2,376,000
Vancouver	412,300	415,700	828,000	4.31	+1.5	+2.2	+3.7	975,000
Victoria	81,200	83,800	165,000	0.86	+1.1	+1.4	+2.5	192,000
Windsor	99,400	100,600	200,000	1.04	+1.8	−1.0	+0.8	218,000
Winnipeg	240,100	246,900	487,000	2.53	+1.7	+1.4	+3.1	567,000
Total of metropolitan cities	4,424,500	4,521,500	8,946,000	46.51	n.a.	n.a.	n.a.	10,555,000
Other urban	2,356,700	2,411,300	4,768,000	24.79	n.a.	n.a.	n.a.	5,597,000
Rural: non-farm	1,863,500	1,706,500	3,570,000	18.56	n.a.	n.a.	n.a.	3,849,000
Rural: farm	1,053,500	897,500	1,951,000	10.14	n.a.	n.a.	n.a.	1,728,000
Canada	9,698,200	9,536,800	19,235,000	100.00	+2.1	+0.6	+2.7	21,729,000

*Note: *n.a.* means not available.

BREAKDOWN OF MALES BY AGE GROUPS, 1964 ESTIMATES

Economic regions	Total (000)	0-4 (000)	5-9 (000)	10-14 (000)	15-19 (000)	20-24 (000)	25-34 (000)	35-44 (000)	45-64 (000)	65+ (000)
Newfoundland	*251.8*	*37.1*	*33.0*	*31.8*	*27.2*	*18.5*	*27.6*	*25.7*	*36.8*	*14.1*
St. John's-Southeastern Nfld.	149.1	20.4	18.8	18.8	16.5	10.3	15.3	15.6	23.7	9.7
Central Nfld.	46.1	7.3	6.3	6.0	5.0	3.4	5.1	4.5	6.2	2.3
Western Nfld.	47.8	8.1	6.9	6.2	5.1	3.7	5.5	4.5	5.9	1.9
Labrador	8.8	1.3	1.0	0.8	0.6	1.1	1.7	1.1	1.0	0.2
Prince Edward Island	*54.7*	*6.9*	*6.2*	*6.2*	*5.5*	*3.8*	*5.6*	*5.4*	*9.7*	*5.4*
Nova Scotia	*385.8*	*46.7*	*44.9*	*42.2*	*37.6*	*28.8*	*43.8*	*42.8*	*67.8*	*31.2*
Sydney-Cape Breton	88.3	11.2	11.3	10.7	8.9	5.8	8.8	9.3	15.5	6.8
Northern Nova Scotia	71.4	7.8	8.3	8.3	7.1	4.1	6.6	7.7	14.0	7.5
Halifax-South Shore	177.5	21.7	19.9	18.1	16.7	15.1	22.7	20.6	30.0	12.7
Annapolis Valley	48.6	6.0	5.4	5.1	4.9	3.8	5.7	5.2	8.3	4.2
New Brunswick	*311.9*	*39.7*	*39.0*	*37.8*	*33.0*	*22.4*	*32.3*	*33.6*	*51.3*	*22.8*
Moncton-Southeastern N.B.	68.3	8.4	8.4	8.3	7.3	4.9	6.9	7.8	11.1	5.2
Saint John-Southern N.B.	75.8	8.6	8.3	8.0	7.2	5.0	7.9	8.8	15.2	6.8
Upper Saint John Valley	87.0	11.3	10.9	10.6	9.4	6.9	9.6	9.3	13.4	5.6
Northeastern N.B.	80.8	11.4	11.4	10.9	9.1	5.6	7.9	7.7	11.6	5.2
Québec	*2,781.5*	*337.4*	*334.4*	*308.8*	*270.2*	*211.2*	*360.8*	*349.6*	*454.6*	*154.5*
North Shore-New Québec	52.8	8.3	6.9	5.6	4.6	5.3	8.8	6.1	5.8	1.4
Gaspé Peninsula-South Shore	203.1	26.4	28.5	27.9	23.4	14.8	20.0	21.3	28.7	12.1
Saguenay Valley-Lake St. John	139.1	20.3	20.1	18.1	16.2	11.7	17.0	14.9	16.1	4.7
Metro Québec-Eastern Laurentides	331.0	38.7	39.5	38.4	35.3	26.5	40.7	40.4	52.9	18.6
Trois Rivières-St. Maurice Valley	153.0	18.1	19.2	18.2	16.5	11.7	17.9	18.2	24.2	9.0
Sherbrooke-Eastern Townships	233.6	29.9	32.1	30.7	26.0	17.2	25.9	27.4	29.7	14.7
Metro Montréal and its Environs	1,482.5	169.6	162.7	147.4	129.1	110.2	207.7	200.1	270.9	84.8
Western Québec	89.0	13.0	12.5	11.1	9.7	6.8	10.5	9.6	12.4	3.4
Hull-Western Laurentides	97.4	13.1	12.9	11.4	9.4	7.0	12.3	11.6	13.9	5.8

Ontario	*3,303.0*	*390.0*	*364.5*	*332.8*	*273.4*	*206.0*	*424.1*	*456.1*	*613.6*	*242.5*
Ottawa-Ottawa Valley	284.1	34.5	32.7	31.1	26.3	19.7	34.8	38.2	48.0	18.8
Kingston-Upper St. Lawrence	128.8	14.7	14.3	13.5	12.3	8.6	14.9	16.4	23.7	10.4
Peterborough-Central Lake Ontario	171.7	20.1	20.1	19.2	15.5	9.7	18.7	21.5	31.7	15.2
Metro Toronto and its Environs	1,136.2	131.3	116.4	103.0	81.2	70.4	167.0	172.5	216.6	77.8
Hamilton/St. Catharines-Niagara	393.1	45.2	43.8	40.7	32.8	22.6	47.6	56.1	75.0	29.3
London-Lake Erie	208.1	23.7	22.1	20.7	18.2	13.4	24.5	27.4	40.3	17.8
Windsor/Sarnia-Lake St. Clair	224.6	27.2	25.9	23.8	19.4	13.0	25.6	28.7	42.9	18.1
Kitchener-Midlands	194.9	22.7	22.0	19.8	17.5	12.4	22.9	24.8	36.3	16.5
Lake Huron-Georgian Bay	161.8	17.7	18.2	17.9	15.7	9.2	16.1	19.1	31.6	16.3
Northeastern Ontario: Clay Belt	115.6	15.3	14.3	12.9	11.0	7.8	14.0	13.5	19.8	7.0
Northeastern Ontario: Nickel Range	95.8	13.4	12.3	10.4	8.2	7.0	12.8	12.7	15.0	4.0
Northeastern Ontario: Sault	69.4	9.6	8.5	7.3	5.8	4.8	10.1	9.4	10.6	3.3
Lakehead-Northwestern Ontario	118.9	14.6	13.9	12.5	9.5	7.4	15.1	15.8	22.1	8.0
Manitoba	*485.1*	*56.2*	*52.9*	*49.8*	*42.1*	*32.4*	*57.8*	*59.6*	*91.4*	*42.9*
Metro Winnipeg and its Environs	349.3	40.7	37.8	35.1	29.6	23.8	42.9	43.8	65.4	30.2
Southwestern Manitoba Prairie	78.1	8.4	8.4	8.3	7.1	4.1	7.9	9.2	15.9	8.8
West-Central Manitoba Parklands	29.6	3.0	3.3	3.5	3.0	1.6	2.8	3.4	6.1	2.9
Northern Manitoba	28.1	4.1	3.4	2.9	2.4	2.9	4.2	3.2	4.0	1.0
Saskatchewan	*485.7*	*57.7*	*55.8*	*51.2*	*42.2*	*30.8*	*53.3*	*57.2*	*90.3*	*47.2*
Regina-Southeastern Plains	121.9	14.8	13.9	12.3	10.2	8.3	14.7	14.7	22.4	10.6
Saskatchewan Palliser	76.7	8.9	8.8	8.2	6.5	4.5	8.4	9.5	13.3	8.6
Saskatoon-Central Plains	101.5	12.8	11.8	10.0	8.2	7.2	12.0	12.1	17.5	9.9
Saskatchewan-Southeastern Parklds	65.1	6.8	7.2	7.1	6.1	3.3	5.9	7.8	14.0	6.9
Central Saskatchewan Parklands	109.3	12.5	12.6	12.3	10.2	6.6	10.8	11.9	21.6	10.8
Northern Saskatchewan	11.2	1.9	1.5	1.3	1.0	0.9	1.5	1.2	1.5	0.4

BREAKDOWN OF MALES BY AGE GROUPS, 1964 ESTIMATES (continued)

Economic regions	Total (000)	0-4 (000)	5-9 (000)	10-14 (000)	15-19 (000)	20-24 (000)	25-34 (000)	35-44 (000)	45-64 (000)	65+ (000)
Alberta	736.9	96.2	88.4	76.5	60.0	47.0	97.9	93.8	124.4	52.7
Medicine Hat-Palliser	20.6	2.6	2.5	2.2	1.7	1.3	2.6	2.7	3.2	1.8
Lethbridge Prairie	59.7	7.5	7.2	6.7	5.7	3.8	6.8	6.8	10.6	4.6
Alberta Rocky Mountains-Foothills	11.8	1.4	1.1	1.0	0.9	1.0	1.8	1.5	2.2	0.9
Calgary-South Central Alberta	211.5	28.1	24.8	20.5	15.4	13.5	30.9	28.7	34.2	15.4
Red Deer Environs	42.7	5.2	5.0	4.7	3.9	2.8	4.9	5.2	7.7	3.3
East-Central Alberta Prairie	56.0	6.1	6.4	6.3	5.3	2.9	5.6	6.8	11.2	5.4
Edmonton-Parklands	256.4	34.4	31.2	26.3	19.9	16.4	35.8	33.5	42.8	16.1
Northeastern Alberta	25.1	3.5	3.4	2.8	2.5	1.7	2.9	2.8	3.8	1.7
Northwestern Alberta-Peace River	53.1	7.4	6.8	6.0	4.7	3.6	6.6	5.8	8.7	3.5
British Columbia	879.3	96.3	93.7	85.9	71.3	54.8	108.6	114.9	170.0	83.8
East Kootenay	19.3	2.2	2.2	2.1	1.6	1.4	2.5	2.5	3.5	1.3
West Kootenay	36.9	4.0	4.1	4.0	3.4	2.4	4.0	4.5	7.7	2.8
Okanagan Valley	48.4	4.8	5.2	5.3	4.6	2.8	4.8	5.5	9.9	5.5
South-Central British Columbia	38.7	5.0	4.5	4.0	3.2	2.7	5.1	4.9	6.7	2.6
Vancouver-Lower Fraser	484.5	50.0	49.3	45.9	37.9	28.3	59.4	65.9	98.0	49.8
Victoria-Vancouver Island	153.9	16.3	16.2	15.0	13.1	10.2	17.6	19.3	28.8	17.4
Northwestern British Columbia	32.5	4.3	3.8	3.0	2.4	2.4	5.2	4.3	5.4	1.7
North-Central British Columbia	44.0	6.4	5.6	4.4	3.5	3.2	6.6	5.5	6.9	1.9
Northeastern British Columbia	21.1	3.3	2.8	2.2	1.6	1.4	3.4	2.5	3.1	0.8
Yukon and Northwest Territories	22.5	3.7	2.8	2.2	1.5	1.5	3.8	3.1	3.1	0.8
Canada	9,698.2	1,167.9	1,115.6	1,025.2	864.0	657.2	1,215.6	1,241.8	1,713.0	697.9

BREAKDOWN OF MALES BY AGE GROUPS, 1964 ESTIMATES (continued)

Metropolitan centers	Total (000)	0–4 (000)	5–9 (000)	10–14 (000)	15–19 (000)	20–24 (000)	25–34 (000)	35–44 (000)	45–64 (000)	65+ (000)
Calgary	155.9	21.6	18.2	14.6	10.2	10.4	25.0	21.9	23.6	10.4
Edmonton	187.5	26.3	22.9	18.4	13.5	12.7	28.3	25.4	29.3	10.7
Halifax	92.6	11.7	10.4	8.5	8.6	9.7	13.6	11.2	14.3	4.6
Hamilton	208.2	24.8	23.0	20.6	16.1	11.9	27.3	31.2	38.8	14.5
Kitchener	80.8	9.7	9.2	8.0	6.4	5.3	10.7	11.4	14.6	5.5
London	94.1	11.1	10.0	9.0	7.4	6.3	12.3	13.6	17.1	7.3
Montréal	1,111.9	124.9	116.9	104.0	91.1	83.5	165.2	156.6	209.0	60.7
Ottawa	229.3	28.9	26.5	24.6	19.9	16.7	30.8	32.5	37.0	12.4
Québec	185.1	21.1	20.3	19.3	18.8	14.7	25.0	24.6	31.7	9.6
Regina	60.4	7.8	6.6	5.7	4.8	5.1	8.5	7.6	9.8	4.5
Saint John	49.2	5.9	5.5	5.0	4.5	3.5	5.6	6.0	9.5	3.7
St. John's	44.9	6.2	5.3	5.0	4.8	3.7	5.4	5.0	7.1	2.4
Saskatoon	50.0	6.7	5.6	4.5	3.5	4.1	7.0	6.1	7.9	4.6
Sudbury	57.0	8.0	7.2	5.9	4.8	4.3	7.9	7.9	9.1	1.9
Toronto	984.6	111.5	98.6	87.5	69.0	61.9	146.5	151.5	190.9	67.2
Vancouver	412.3	42.2	41.0	38.0	31.0	24.2	52.0	57.2	84.4	42.3
Victoria	81.2	8.0	7.9	7.6	6.9	5.5	8.8	10.2	14.8	11.5
Windsor	99.4	12.1	11.5	10.3	7.9	5.3	11.5	13.1	19.8	7.9
Winnipeg	240.1	27.3	24.9	22.7	18.6	17.0	31.8	31.7	45.3	20.8
Total of metropolitan cities	4,424.5	515.8	471.5	419.2	347.8	305.8	623.2	624.7	814.0	302.5
Canada	9,698.2	1,167.9	1,115.6	1,025.2	864.0	657.2	1,215.6	1,241.8	1,713.0	697.9
Metropolitan centers' share of Canada (%)	45.6	44.2	42.3	40.9	40.3	46.5	51.3	50.3	47.5	43.3

BREAKDOWN OF FEMALES BY AGE GROUPS, 1964 ESTIMATES

Economic regions	Total (000)	0-4 (000)	5-9 (000)	10-14 (000)	15-19 (000)	20-24 (000)	25-34 (000)	35-44 (000)	45-64 (000)	65 + (000)
Newfoundland	*239.2*	*35.4*	*32.2*	*31.0*	*26.5*	*18.5*	*25.4*	*23.3*	*32.7*	*14.2*
St. John's-Southeastern Nfld.	144.5	19.6	18.2	18.4	16.1	10.7	14.7	14.6	21.9	10.3
Central Nfld.	42.8	6.8	6.1	5.8	4.7	3.3	4.6	4.0	5.4	2.1
Western Nfld.	45.0	7.7	6.9	6.0	5.1	3.7	5.0	4.1	4.9	1.6
Labrador	6.9	1.3	1.0	0.8	0.6	0.8	1.1	0.6	0.5	0.2
Prince Edward Island	*52.3*	*6.5*	*6.1*	*6.0*	*5.3*	*3.5*	*5.0*	*5.4*	*9.0*	*5.5*
Nova Scotia	*374.2*	*44.7*	*42.6*	*40.2*	*35.7*	*26.5*	*41.5*	*43.7*	*64.6*	*34.7*
Sydney-Cape Breton	85.0	10.5	10.7	10.2	8.8	5.7	8.7	9.6	13.8	7.0
Northern Nova Scotia	70.0	7.5	7.7	7.8	6.8	4.1	6.6	8.0	13.4	8.1
Halifax-South Shore	173.6	21.0	19.0	17.4	16.0	13.7	21.1	21.0	29.6	14.8
Annapolis Valley	45.6	5.7	5.2	4.8	4.1	3.0	5.1	5.1	7.8	4.8
New Brunswick	*305.1*	*38.0*	*37.0*	*36.7*	*31.7*	*21.1*	*31.8*	*34.4*	*49.3*	*25.1*
Moncton-Southeastern N.B.	68.0	8.1	8.0	8.1	7.0	4.6	7.1	8.0	11.2	5.9
Saint John-Southern N.B.	76.6	8.2	7.9	7.8	6.9	5.0	8.0	9.4	15.2	8.2
Upper Saint John Valley	82.7	10.7	10.2	10.1	8.7	6.2	9.2	9.3	12.4	5.9
Northeastern N.B.	77.8	11.0	10.9	10.7	9.1	5.3	7.5	7.7	10.5	5.1
Québec	*2,780.5*	*320.5*	*321.6*	*295.6*	*261.5*	*214.2*	*366.9*	*357.9*	*465.0*	*177.3*
North Shore-New Québec	47.3	7.8	6.9	5.4	4.6	4.8	7.3	5.0	4.4	1.1
Gaspé Peninsula-South Shore	191.8	24.9	27.5	26.8	22.1	13.7	20.0	20.3	25.8	10.7
Saguenay Valley-Lake St. John	133.4	19.5	19.6	17.2	15.4	11.3	17.2	14.2	14.8	4.2
Metro Québec-Eastern Laurentides	336.5	36.8	38.2	36.6	34.5	26.4	43.1	42.2	56.6	22.1
Trois Rivières-St. Maurice Valley	152.9	17.3	18.3	17.5	16.2	11.7	18.8	18.6	24.8	9.7
Sherbrooke-Eastern Townships	233.6	27.7	29.7	28.2	24.6	16.8	26.9	27.5	36.8	15.4
Metro Montréal and its Environs	1,509.9	161.5	157.0	142.1	126.1	116.2	212.1	210.2	278.5	106.2
Western Québec	83.4	12.7	12.6	11.0	9.4	6.7	10.0	8.9	9.7	2.4
Hull-Western Laurentides	91.7	12.3	11.8	10.8	8.6	6.6	11.5	11.0	13.6	5.5

	3,283.0	372.2	347.3	316.4	260.0	206.7	419.4	457.4	607.5	296.1
Ontario										
Ottawa-Ottawa Valley	288.9	33.2	31.2	29.5	24.7	18.9	34.7	40.2	51.6	24.9
Kingston-Upper St. Lawrence	128.1	14.4	14.0	13.4	11.2	7.8	14.5	16.4	23.4	13.0
Peterborough-Central Lake Ontario	170.8	19.3	19.1	18.1	14.2	9.3	19.0	22.4	31.1	18.3
Metro Toronto and its Environs	1,155.7	124.9	111.1	97.9	80.0	76.0	166.6	171.4	223.7	104.1
Hamilton/St. Catharines-Niagara	390.6	42.5	41.2	38.0	31.2	23.3	49.0	56.0	73.6	35.8
London-Lake Erie	213.4	22.8	21.6	20.3	17.5	13.7	25.1	28.5	41.3	22.6
Windsor/Sarnia-Lake St. Clair	223.3	25.8	25.0	22.6	18.8	13.2	26.0	30.1	41.7	20.1
Kitchener-Midlands	193.7	21.4	20.6	19.0	16.3	11.4	22.6	25.4	36.6	20.4
Lake Huron-Georgian Bay	154.3	16.6	17.1	16.6	13.2	7.9	15.6	19.3	30.1	17.9
Northeastern Ontario: Clay Belt	108.3	15.1	13.7	12.7	10.3	7.4	13.0	13.3	16.9	5.9
Northeastern Ontario: Nickel Range	88.6	13.2	12.1	9.9	8.2	6.4	11.8	11.8	11.7	3.5
Northeastern Ontario: Sault	62.3	9.3	7.9	6.8	5.3	4.7	8.6	8.1	8.5	3.1
Lakehead-Northwestern Ontario	105.0	13.7	12.7	11.6	9.1	6.7	12.9	14.5	17.3	6.5
Manitoba	472.9	53.8	50.4	47.6	40.3	31.2	55.1	61.3	89.4	43.8
Metro Winnipeg and its Environs	350.1	38.5	36.1	33.9	29.3	24.4	42.2	46.3	66.9	32.5
Southwestern Manitoba Prairie	72.3	8.0	7.9	7.7	6.1	3.6	7.4	9.2	14.2	8.2
West-Central Manitoba Parklands	26.9	3.1	3.2	3.3	2.7	1.2	2.5	3.3	5.3	2.3
Northern Manitoba	23.6	4.2	3.2	2.7	2.2	2.0	3.0	2.5	3.0	0.8
Saskatchewan	457.3	55.6	53.1	49.3	40.8	29.6	49.8	55.1	83.2	40.8
Regina-Southeastern Plains	117.6	14.2	12.9	11.9	10.2	8.6	13.7	14.5	21.4	10.2
Saskatchewan Palliser	72.3	8.6	8.5	7.6	6.1	4.3	7.8	9.2	13.0	7.2
Saskatoon-Central Plains	98.4	12.3	11.4	9.6	8.6	7.4	11.5	11.6	17.0	9.0
Saskatchewan-Southeastern Parklds.	59.4	6.4	6.9	7.0	5.5	2.8	5.7	7.3	12.2	5.6
Central Saskatchewan Parklands	100.1	12.3	12.0	12.1	9.4	5.7	10.0	11.5	18.6	8.5
Northern Saskatchewan	9.5	1.8	1.4	1.1	1.0	0.8	1.1	1.0	1.0	0.3

BREAKDOWN OF FEMALES BY AGE GROUPS, 1964 ESTIMATES (continued)

Economic regions	Total (000)	0–4 (000)	5–9 (000)	10–14 (000)	15–19 (000)	20–24 (000)	25–34 (000)	35–44 (000)	45–64 (000)	65+ (000)
Alberta..........	*695.1*	*92.3*	*83.4*	*72.7*	*57.5*	*46.9*	*92.8*	*90.1*	*113.0*	*46.4*
Medicine Hat-Palliser..........	20.9	2.5	2.4	2.2	1.8	1.3	2.5	2.8	3.7	1.7
Lethbridge Prairie..........	56.3	7.0	7.0	6.2	5.3	3.4	6.5	6.9	10.0	4.0
Alberta Rocky Mountains-Foothills....	9.7	1.2	1.1	1.0	0.8	0.7	1.3	1.3	1.7	0.6
Calgary-South Central Alberta..........	205.2	27.0	23.1	19.8	15.1	14.3	29.9	28.0	33.2	14.8
Red Deer Environs..........	38.9	5.1	4.7	4.5	3.5	2.5	4.6	5.1	6.0	2.9
East-Central Alberta Prairie..........	50.0	5.7	6.0	5.9	4.6	2.4	5.2	6.4	9.4	4.4
Edmonton-Parklands..........	246.2	33.2	29.5	24.6	20.0	17.9	34.9	32.0	39.4	14.7
Northeastern Alberta..........	22.2	3.5	3.2	2.9	2.1	1.3	2.4	2.5	3.1	1.2
Northwestern Alberta-Peace River....	45.7	7.1	6.4	5.6	4.3	3.1	5.5	5.1	6.5	2.1
British Columbia..........	*858.7*	*93.2*	*89.1*	*81.6*	*68.0*	*54.2*	*103.3*	*117.3*	*165.8*	*86.2*
East Kootenay..........	17.2	2.1	2.1	1.9	1.4	1.1	2.1	2.3	3.3	0.9
West Kootenay..........	34.4	3.9	3.9	3.8	3.0	2.1	3.8	4.6	6.8	2.5
Okanagan Valley..........	48.9	4.8	4.9	5.3	4.5	2.6	4.9	6.4	10.3	5.2
South Central British Columbia..........	34.3	4.8	4.3	3.7	3.1	2.4	4.3	4.3	5.4	2.0
Vancouver-Lower Fraser..........	490.5	48.2	47.1	43.9	37.5	30.8	59.9	69.7	99.3	54.1
Victoria-Vancouver Island..........	150.2	15.7	15.3	13.9	11.7	8.7	16.2	19.8	30.1	18.8
Northwestern British Columbia..........	26.6	4.2	3.4	2.8	2.2	2.0	3.9	3.4	3.8	0.9
North-Central British Columbia..........	37.7	6.1	5.3	4.3	3.2	3.0	5.3	4.6	4.6	1.3
Northeastern British Columbia..........	18.9	3.4	2.8	2.0	1.4	1.5	2.9	2.2	2.2	0.5
Yukon and Northwest Territories..........	*18.5*	*3.5*	*2.7*	*2.1*	*1.5*	*1.3*	*2.8*	*2.1*	*2.1*	*0.4*
Canada..........	*9,536.8*	*1,115.7*	*1,065.5*	*979.2*	*828.8*	*653.7*	*1,193.8*	*1,248.0*	*1,681.6*	*770.5*

BREAKDOWN OF FEMALES BY AGE GROUPS, 1964 ESTIMATES (continued)

Metropolitan centers	Total (000)	0-4 (000)	5-9 (000)	10-14 (000)	15-19 (000)	20-24 (000)	25-34 (000)	35-44 (000)	45-64 (000)	65 + (000)
Calgary	154.1	20.6	16.9	13.9	10.7	11.6	24.2	21.3	23.9	11.0
Edmonton	184.5	25.0	21.4	17.2	14.5	14.9	27.8	24.4	28.4	10.9
Halifax	91.4	11.3	9.8	8.3	8.5	8.4	12.3	11.6	15.0	6.2
Hamilton	209.8	23.5	21.7	19.5	16.1	12.6	28.1	30.9	38.9	18.5
Kitchener	82.2	9.2	8.5	7.6	6.8	5.4	10.7	11.6	15.3	7.1
London	97.9	10.5	9.5	8.7	7.7	7.1	12.6	13.9	18.2	9.7
Montréal	1,148.1	119.1	112.9	100.7	90.5	90.8	169.0	165.8	218.6	80.7
Ottawa	238.7	27.4	25.3	23.4	20.1	17.2	30.6	34.4	42.1	18.2
Québec	198.9	19.8	19.6	18.4	19.0	16.6	27.7	27.3	36.7	13.8
Regina	61.6	7.4	6.1	5.4	5.5	5.9	8.1	7.7	10.7	4.8
Saint John	50.8	5.6	5.1	4.9	4.5	3.6	5.7	6.5	10.0	4.9
St. John's	47.1	5.9	5.2	4.9	5.5	4.4	5.6	5.1	7.4	3.1
Saskatoon	52.0	6.4	5.4	4.3	4.5	5.1	6.8	6.0	8.7	4.8
Sudbury	53.0	7.6	7.0	5.6	5.0	4.2	7.3	7.5	7.0	1.8
Toronto	1,004.4	105.8	93.7	82.8	68.9	67.2	145.9	150.6	198.3	91.2
Vancouver	415.7	40.0	38.7	36.0	31.0	26.7	51.7	59.9	84.9	46.8
Victoria	83.8	7.6	7.5	7.0	6.2	4.7	8.4	10.9	17.7	13.8
Windsor	100.6	11.3	11.0	9.9	8.0	5.9	12.1	14.0	19.7	8.7
Winnipeg	246.9	25.8	23.5	22.0	19.7	18.4	31.4	34.1	48.4	23.6
Total of metropolitan cities	4,521.5	489.8	448.8	400.5	352.7	330.7	626.0	643.5	849.9	379.6
Canada	9,536.8	1,115.7	1,065.5	979.2	828.8	653.7	1,193.8	1,248.0	1,681.6	770.5
Metropolitan centers' share of Canada (%)	47.4	43.9	42.1	40.9	42.6	50.6	52.4	51.6	50.5	49.3

NUMBER OF HOUSEHOLDS AND THEIR BREAKDOWN BY TYPE AND SIZE IN EACH REGION, 1964 ESTIMATES

Economic regions	Households 1964		Type of households in each region (%)			Size of households in each region (%)					No. of persons per hsld.
			Family hslds.		Non-family hslds.	Very small (1)	Small (2)	Medium (3-4)	Large (5-8)	Very large (9+)	
	Number	% of Canada	One family	Over one family							
Newfoundland	94,000	1.96	86.1	7.5	6.4	4.4	14.3	29.9	39.6	11.8	5.0
St. John's-Southeastern Nfld.	58,500	1.22	85.1	7.5	7.4	5.0	15.6	30.7	38.1	10.6	4.9
Central Nfld.	16,400	0.34	87.8	7.8	4.4	3.2	12.7	29.4	41.9	12.8	5.3
Western Nfld.	16,500	0.34	87.5	7.0	5.5	4.0	11.3	27.0	42.4	15.3	5.4
Labrador.	2,600	0.06	89.3	5.6	5.1	3.2	10.3	34.7	41.9	9.9	5.0
Prince Edward Island	24,000	0.50	81.3	5.0	13.7	8.9	20.5	31.7	32.4	6.5	4.2
Nova Scotia	178,000	3.70	82.2	4.8	13.0	8.6	20.7	34.9	31.3	4.5	4.0
Sydney-Cape Breton.	36,800	0.76	83.2	6.1	10.7	6.8	16.4	32.7	36.7	7.4	4.6
Northern Nova Scotia.	34,500	0.72	80.4	3.9	15.7	10.7	23.2	32.8	29.0	4.3	3.9
Halifax-South Shore.	83,700	1.74	82.3	5.0	12.7	8.2	20.9	36.8	30.5	3.6	4.0
Annapolis Valley.	23,000	0.48	83.0	3.3	13.7	9.5	22.7	35.3	29.1	3.4	3.9
New Brunswick.	137,000	2.85	84.2	4.6	11.2	7.4	19.4	33.1	33.0	7.1	4.4
Moncton-Southeastern N.B.	30,400	0.63	84.4	5.4	10.2	6.4	19.0	33.7	34.1	6.8	4.4
Saint John-Southern N.B.	39,300	0.82	81.9	3.0	15.1	10.1	24.3	35.5	26.9	3.2	3.7
Upper Saint John Valley.	37,800	0.79	85.8	3.9	10.3	6.9	19.0	33.8	34.0	6.3	4.3
Northeastern N.B.	29,500	0.61	85.3	6.6	8.1	5.5	13.7	28.5	38.6	13.7	5.2
Québec.	1,262,000	26.26	85.6	3.3	11.1	7.0	19.1	35.7	32.2	6.0	4.2
North Shore-New Québec.	17,700	0.37	85.7	10.2	4.1	2.3	9.9	30.0	42.8	15.0	5.5
Gaspé Peninsula-South Shore.	68,200	1.42	86.8	6.8	6.4	4.0	12.1	26.9	40.0	17.0	5.6
Saguenay Valley-Lake St. John.	46,700	0.97	92.1	4.7	3.2	1.9	9.3	28.7	44.0	16.1	5.7
Metro Québec-Eastern Laurentides.	138,800	2.89	87.3	2.8	9.9	6.0	16.8	34.3	35.1	7.8	4.5
Trois Rivières-St. Maurice Valley.	65,600	1.36	88.7	3.1	8.2	5.1	16.6	34.3	36.6	7.4	4.6
Sherbrooke-Eastern Townships.	102,200	2.13	88.4	2.0	9.6	6.5	18.7	32.9	34.0	7.9	4.5
Metro Montréal and its Environs.	749,600	15.60	83.7	3.0	13.3	8.4	21.7	38.3	28.6	3.0	3.8
Western Québec.	32,800	0.68	89.6	2.8	7.6	5.2	13.1	30.0	39.8	11.9	5.1
Hull-Western Laurentides.	40,400	0.84	87.4	3.9	8.7	5.8	17.3	34.2	36.4	6.3	4.5

Ontario	1,737,000	36.15	82.1	4.6	13.3	9.1	23.9	37.7	26.9	2.4	3.7
Ottawa-Ottawa Valley	144,200	3.00	82.8	3.4	13.8	8.8	22.2	36.9	29.2	2.9	3.9
Kingston-Upper St. Lawrence	66,000	1.37	83.5	2.9	13.6	9.1	23.7	36.8	27.4	3.0	3.8
Peterborough-Central Lake Ontario	93,800	1.95	83.5	2.5	14.0	10.2	25.2	36.0	26.5	2.1	3.6
Metro Toronto and its Environs	604,500	12.58	79.2	7.9	12.9	8.2	24.1	39.3	25.9	2.5	3.7
Hamilton/St. Catharines-Niagara	211,900	4.41	83.8	4.1	12.1	8.5	24.4	38.6	26.8	1.7	3.7
London-Lake Erie	118,100	2.46	82.2	2.4	15.4	10.9	26.2	37.3	24.1	1.5	3.5
Windsor/Sarnia-Lake St. Clair	125,100	2.60	83.6	2.4	14.0	10.5	25.5	36.0	26.1	1.9	3.6
Kitchener-Midlands	105,900	2.21	83.2	3.1	13.7	9.6	24.9	37.4	26.2	1.9	3.6
Lake Huron-Georgian Bay	85,100	1.77	81.8	2.3	15.9	11.9	26.2	34.2	25.4	2.3	3.6
Northeastern Ontario: Clay Belt	52,100	1.09	86.3	2.4	11.3	8.4	20.2	35.1	31.6	4.7	4.1
Northeastern Ontario: Nickel Range	43,400	0.90	88.4	2.5	9.1	6.5	18.2	37.6	33.8	3.9	4.2
Northeastern Ontario: Sault	31,300	0.65	86.1	3.6	10.3	7.0	18.1	38.9	32.7	3.3	4.1
Lakehead-Northwestern Ontario	55,600	1.16	83.8	3.2	13.0	9.8	20.9	36.6	29.8	2.9	3.8
Manitoba	248,000	5.16	82.9	3.1	14.0	10.2	23.6	36.6	27.1	2.5	3.7
Metro Winnipeg and its Environs	182,500	3.80	82.9	3.5	13.6	9.7	23.8	37.4	26.7	2.4	3.7
Southwestern Manitoba Prairie	40,400	0.84	82.9	1.7	15.4	11.9	24.5	35.0	26.8	1.8	3.6
West-Central Manitoba Parklands	14,700	0.30	82.0	2.1	15.9	13.0	22.6	33.2	28.0	3.2	3.7
Northern Manitoba	10,400	0.22	84.8	4.1	11.1	8.2	16.8	33.5	33.8	7.7	4.4
Saskatchewan	250,000	5.20	82.0	1.9	16.1	12.7	23.2	34.3	27.4	2.4	3.6
Regina-Southeastern Plains	63,000	1.31	82.8	2.1	15.1	11.5	23.4	36.1	27.1	1.9	3.6
Saskatchewan Palliser	41,200	0.86	81.5	1.2	17.3	14.0	24.1	34.0	26.3	1.6	3.5
Saskatoon-Central Plains	54,000	1.12	81.9	1.9	16.2	12.1	23.6	34.7	27.5	2.1	3.6
Saskatchewan-Southeastern Parklds	33,700	0.70	82.1	1.9	16.0	13.2	23.2	34.7	26.7	2.2	3.6
Central Saskatchewan Parklands	53,800	1.12	81.4	1.8	16.8	13.7	22.3	32.1	28.6	3.3	3.7
Northern Saskatchewan	4,300	0.09	82.1	3.7	14.2	11.3	14.2	30.1	34.9	9.5	4.6

NUMBER OF HOUSEHOLDS AND THEIR BREAKDOWN BY TYPE AND SIZE IN EACH REGION, 1964 ESTIMATES (continued)

Economic regions	Households 1964		Type of households in each region (%)			Size of households in each region (%)					No. of persons per hsld.
			Family hslds.								
	Number	% of Canada	One family	Over one family	Non-family hslds.	Very small (1)	Small (2)	Me-dium (3-4)	Large (5-8)	Very large (9+)	
Alberta	377,000	7.85	82.3	2.1	15.6	12.0	21.8	36.0	28.1	2.1	3.7
Medicine Hat-Palliser	11,300	0.24	83.2	2.1	14.7	11.9	24.4	35.9	26.7	1.1	3.5
Lethbridge Prairie	29,000	0.60	83.3	2.0	14.7	11.7	21.9	34.6	29.2	2.6	3.7
Alberta Rocky Mountains-Foothills	5,700	0.12	77.9	2.1	20.0	15.6	25.7	33.5	23.3	1.9	3.4
Calgary-South Central Alberta	115,400	2.40	81.4	1.9	16.7	12.5	23.3	37.5	25.5	1.2	3.5
Red Deer Environs	20,400	0.42	84.0	1.6	14.4	11.4	22.1	35.1	29.3	2.1	3.7
East-Central Alberta Prairie	28,600	0.60	82.3	1.6	16.1	13.1	22.7	33.7	28.5	2.0	3.6
Edmonton-Parklands	131,900	2.75	83.3	2.6	14.1	10.8	20.9	37.4	29.0	1.9	3.7
Northeastern Alberta	10,600	0.22	82.7	2.8	14.5	12.2	16.7	31.6	33.1	6.4	4.2
Northwestern Alberta-Peace River	24,100	0.50	79.4	1.8	18.8	15.4	17.9	30.9	30.9	4.9	3.9
British Columbia	489,000	10.18	80.2	2.3	17.5	13.5	26.4	35.2	23.5	1.4	3.4
East Kootenay	9,800	0.20	81.8	2.0	16.2	12.5	22.4	35.4	28.0	1.7	3.6
West Kootenay	20,000	0.42	82.9	1.7	15.4	12.9	24.1	35.8	26.0	1.2	3.5
Okanagan Valley	27,900	0.58	81.4	1.6	17.0	14.1	27.3	33.8	23.6	1.2	3.3
South-Central British Columbia	18,600	0.39	79.9	2.2	17.9	13.9	21.0	33.7	28.6	2.8	3.7
Vancouver-Lower Fraser	279,200	5.81	79.9	2.6	17.5	13.2	27.4	36.0	22.3	1.1	3.3
Victoria-Vancouver Island	89,500	1.86	80.0	1.6	18.4	14.9	28.6	33.9	21.5	1.1	3.2
Northwestern British Columbia	14,200	0.30	81.0	4.2	14.8	11.3	19.8	35.1	30.0	3.8	3.9
North-Central British Columbia	20,000	0.42	80.1	2.0	17.9	13.7	18.0	33.6	30.7	4.0	3.9
Northeastern British Columbia	9,800	0.20	82.4	1.9	15.7	12.3	17.6	34.3	32.6	3.2	3.9
Yukon and Northwest Territories	9,000	0.19	79.7	4.0	16.3	11.9	17.3	32.5	32.6	5.7	4.2
Canada	4,805,000	100.00	83.0	3.7	13.3	9.3	22.2	36.2	28.7	3.6	3.9

NUMBER OF HOUSEHOLDS AND THEIR BREAKDOWN BY TYPE AND SIZE IN EACH METROPOLITAN CITY, 1964 ESTIMATES

| Metropolitan centers | Households 1964 | | Type of households in each region (%) | | | Size of households in each region (%) | | | | | No. of persons per hsld. |
	Number	% of Canada	Family hslds. One family	Over one family	Non-family hslds.	Very small (1)	Small (2)	Medium (3-4)	Large (5-8)	Very large (9+)	
Calgary	91,200	1.90	81.3	2.1	16.6	12.1	23.7	38.6	24.6	1.0	3.4
Edmonton	100,500	2.09	83.3	2.8	13.9	10.2	21.4	38.4	28.5	1.5	3.7
Halifax	46,000	0.96	83.2	5.5	11.3	6.4	19.5	38.9	31.9	3.3	4.0
Hamilton	113,000	2.35	83.3	5.1	11.6	7.9	23.6	39.5	27.4	1.6	3.7
Kitchener	45,300	0.94	84.1	3.5	12.4	8.4	24.2	40.1	25.8	1.5	3.6
London	56,500	1.17	81.3	2.6	16.1	10.9	26.0	38.8	23.1	1.2	3.4
Montréal	610,800	12.71	82.5	3.2	14.3	8.9	22.4	39.5	27.1	2.1	3.7
Ottawa	120,000	2.50	83.4	3.5	13.1	8.1	21.2	38.1	29.7	2.9	3.9
Québec	91,400	1.90	86.2	2.5	11.3	6.7	18.2	37.2	33.1	4.8	4.2
Regina	33,900	0.70	82.4	3.0	14.6	10.6	23.6	38.3	25.8	1.7	3.6
Saint John	26,300	0.55	82.6	2.8	14.6	9.3	23.4	36.6	27.6	3.1	3.8
St. John's	19,200	0.40	85.1	7.7	7.2	3.8	15.4	33.7	38.6	8.5	4.8
Saskatoon	29,100	0.60	81.7	2.5	15.8	11.2	24.5	37.0	25.8	1.5	3.5
Sudbury	26,800	0.56	89.6	2.6	7.8	5.1	18.4	39.9	33.3	3.3	4.1
Toronto	537,600	11.19	78.0	8.6	13.4	8.4	24.1	39.2	25.7	2.6	3.7
Vancouver	250,900	5.22	79.5	2.8	17.7	13.1	27.5	36.5	21.9	1.0	3.3
Victoria	53,200	1.11	77.8	1.6	20.6	16.4	31.2	32.9	18.7	0.8	3.1
Windsor	55,600	1.16	83.3	2.7	14.0	10.3	25.7	36.2	26.0	1.8	3.6
Winnipeg	135,300	2.82	82.1	4.1	13.8	9.5	24.5	38.9	25.4	1.7	3.6
Total metropolitan cities	2,442,600	50.83	81.4	4.4	14.2	9.4	23.6	38.5	26.4	2.1	3.7
Other urban	1,088,300	22.65	84.9	2.8	12.3	8.7	22.0	36.5	29.3	3.5	3.8
Rural: non-farm	850,000	17.69	82.5	2.8	14.7	11.5	21.8	31.2	29.9	5.6	4.0
Rural: farm	424,100	8.83	87.1	3.9	9.0	6.2	17.0	32.8	36.3	7.7	4.6
Canada	4,805,000	100.00	83.0	3.7	13.3	9.3	22.2	36.2	28.7	3.6	3.9

Chapter 22

REGIONAL DATA BY SOCIO-ECONOMIC CHARACTERISTICS

Income

Willingness to purchase is not enough. To be a worthwhile prospect, a consumer must obviously possess some monetary resources. There is no point in creating needs and wants if no buying power exists to satisfy them. Everybody has desires, but it takes money to make a market.

In short, though population is important, breakdown of households by income groups is of even greater significance in evaluating the marketing potential of a region. The demand for practically all goods and services, other than basic necessities, bears some relationship to the financial position of the consumer. Of course, this must not be construed to mean that the $10,000 household would consume twice the amount of the same product as a $5,000 household. Because of the varying "elasticities of demand," the move from a lower to a higher income bracket results in more than a proportionate increase for luxuries and semi-luxuries, and less than a proportionate increase for lower-priced goods.

The latest available DBS survey on urban consumer expenditures shows that a family earning over $10,000 spends 92% more a year than the average for all families, but this percentage differs considerably from item to item.

	The extent to which $10,000 + family spends more than average family
Education	+333%
Non-automobile transportation (e.g. air travel)	+171
Recreation	+144
Automobile	+138
Household operation	+137
Clothing	+125
Furnishings and equipment	+112
Personal care	+ 97
Average of all items	+ 92
Reading	+ 86
Smoking and alcoholic beverages	+ 85
Medical care	+ 71
Food	+ 57
Housing, fuel, light, water	+ 56

Occupation

Breakdown by occupations is a valuable working tool for assessing the social structure of the households in each region. A few decades ago, when economic thinking dominated the social sciences, classes were regarded as synonymous with income groups. Lately, the emphasis has shifted from income to occupation as a major determinant of status. A person in a service occupation (e.g., a boxer, a night-club singer, or a hairdresser) may become tremendously wealthy, yet not improve his social position. Conversely, especially in small towns, an individual may live in genteel poverty and still have entry into the best circles if he is in the high-status category of "professionals." Thus, income provides only a one-dimensional profile. Occupation has to be considered as well in order to lend depth to the picture.

It is frequently asserted in many quarters that the blue-collar class as a socially identifiable segment of the population has all but disappeared, being merged in the generic middle class. In outward appearances this is undoubtedly true. Thanks to the steady rise in wages, blue-collar families now have pleasant homes, bedecked with all the modern appliances, furniture and furnishings. But in the intangible realm of values, the working class is still insulated from middle-class currents of thought.

For example, in the middle-class families the trend is towards "togetherness"; a husband is expected to help with the dishes or to take turns during the night with the baby's bottle. For working-class couples, there is usually no sharing of chores. Both the men and the women accept the traditional division of masculine and feminine tasks, and the wives do not look for assistance from their husbands in everyday activities. Clearly, the hand that rocks the cradle does not rule the roost in a working-class family. At social gatherings, it is not uncommon to see the men filtering off to one side of the room to discuss hunting and fishing and other exclusively male topics, leaving the women apparently happily engaged in feminine chit-chat. Moreover, whereas middle-class women have misgivings about being "just a housewife," very little trace of this attitude appears in the blue-collar class. Attempts to tap feelings about the domestic role would evoke a puzzled reply: "Why, it's natural, isn't it? It can't be anything else."

Education

Education, like occupation, is another important factor in understanding the forces and characteristics behind consumer behavior in the market place. Not that formal schooling necessarily improves everyone's taste; but it does help. In fact, it is probably the most powerful single factor in the upgrading process. Enough evidence exists to show that as educational level rises, numerous bene-

(*Text continues on page 714*)

NUMBER OF HOUSEHOLDS IN DIFFERENT INCOME GROUPS, 1964 ESTIMATES

Economic regions	Total households	Under $2,000	$2,000–$2,999	$3,000–$3,999	$4,000–$4,999	$5,000–$5,999	$6,000–$9,999	$10,000 and over
Newfoundland	94,000	30,600	17,000	12,600	11,700	7,900	10,500	3,700
St. John's-Southeastern Nfld.	58,500	20,900	10,200	7,000	7,400	4,300	6,600	2,100
Central Nfld.	16,400	4,800	3,500	2,300	1,900	1,600	1,800	500
Western Nfld.	16,500	4,300	2,900	3,100	2,100	1,700	1,400	1,000
Labrador	2,600	600	400	200	300	300	700	100
Prince Edward Island	24,000	9,000	4,100	3,800	2,700	1,900	1,900	600
Nova Scotia	178,000	40,100	27,900	27,600	27,300	21,500	26,300	7,300
Sydney-Cape Breton	36,800	4,100	4,700	6,300	7,700	6,500	6,400	1,100
Northern Nova Scotia	34,500	9,300	6,200	7,400	4,600	2,500	3,600	900
Halifax-South Shore	83,700	20,700	12,000	10,300	11,700	10,000	14,500	4,500
Annapolis Valley	23,000	6,000	5,000	3,600	3,300	2,500	1,800	800
New Brunswick	137,000	37,200	22,200	20,100	19,000	14,600	18,700	5,200
Moncton-Southeastern N.B.	30,400	8,900	4,300	4,400	2,900	4,100	4,600	1,200
Saint John-Southern N.B.	39,300	9,000	6,800	4,900	6,800	3,700	6,200	1,900
Upper Saint John Valley	37,800	9,000	5,800	6,000	6,100	4,300	5,200	1,400
Northeastern N.B.	29,500	10,300	5,300	4,800	3,200	2,500	2,700	700
Québec	1,262,000	178,500	152,700	189,300	207,100	170,100	261,500	102,800
North Shore-New Québec	17,700	2,000	1,400	1,300	2,200	2,400	6,700	1,700
Gaspé Peninsula-South Shore	68,200	22,000	15,100	11,700	6,400	4,500	6,300	2,200
Saguenay Valley-Lake St. John	46,700	7,000	6,000	5,400	7,000	7,900	10,200	3,200
Metro Québec-Eastern Laurentides	138,800	15,800	20,200	23,900	22,100	19,700	25,700	11,400
Trois Rivières-St. Maurice Valley	65,600	8,500	11,400	11,600	11,000	6,800	12,800	3,500
Sherbrooke-Eastern Townships	102,200	14,500	19,000	19,600	18,100	12,400	14,300	4,300
Metro Montréal and its Environs	749,600	93,000	69,700	105,700	128,900	107,900	171,700	72,700
Western Québec	32,800	6,800	4,800	5,300	5,400	3,800	5,200	1,500
Hull-Western Laurentides	40,400	8,900	5,100	4,800	6,000	4,700	8,600	2,300

Ontario	*1,737,000*	*240,500*	*141,700*	*190,400*	*264,800*	*274,600*	*471,600*	*153,400*
Ottawa-Ottawa Valley	144,200	17,700	8,900	16,200	23,100	22,800	38,800	16,700
Kingston-Upper St. Lawrence	66,000	13,400	7,300	8,700	11,500	9,400	12,800	2,900
Peterborough-Central Lake Ontario	93,800	20,600	10,100	11,300	15,500	13,300	18,800	4,200
Metro Toronto and its Environs	604,500	62,300	30,200	59,200	82,200	94,900	200,700	75,000
Hamilton/St. Catharines-Niagara	211,900	24,300	19,500	21,200	33,700	39,000	58,500	15,700
London-Lake Erie	118,100	18,900	11,700	14,900	20,400	16,900	26,200	9,100
Windsor/Sarnia-Lake St. Clair	125,100	18,500	14,400	13,400	15,000	22,200	33,500	8,100
Kitchener-Midlands	105,900	13,400	11,000	13,500	20,500	17,200	23,300	7,000
Lake Huron-Georgian Bay	85,100	22,500	12,000	12,200	15,100	9,200	11,200	2,900
Northeastern Ontario:Clay Belt	52,100	9,400	5,100	7,300	9,400	6,800	11,600	2,500
Northeastern Ontario:Nickel Range	43,400	6,700	3,400	4,300	6,300	8,300	11,500	2,900
Northeastern Ontario: Sault	31,300	3,500	2,400	2,200	3,500	5,300	11,300	3,100
Lakehead-Northwestern Ontario	55,600	9,300	5,700	6,000	8,600	9,300	13,400	3,300
Manitoba	*248,000*	*47,600*	*27,700*	*30,400*	*45,600*	*33,000*	*49,500*	*14,200*
Metro Winnipeg and its Environs	182,500	32,500	16,800	20,200	33,400	26,100	40,900	12,600
Southwestern Manitoba Prairie	40,400	7,800	7,800	7,100	8,700	3,800	4,200	1,000
West-Central Manitoba Parklands	14,700	5,200	2,500	2,300	2,200	800	1,400	300
Northern Manitoba	10,400	2,100	600	800	1,300	2,300	3,000	300
Saskatchewan	*250,000*	*56,600*	*31,800*	*31,800*	*48,200*	*26,600*	*42,600*	*12,400*
Regina-Southeastern Plains	63,000	8,600	6,000	9,200	13,200	6,900	14,400	4,700
Saskatchewan Palliser	41,200	10,400	4,100	3,500	9,700	5,300	6,400	1,800
Saskatoon-Central Plains	54,000	9,700	5,900	6,000	11,200	7,500	10,800	2,900
Saskatchewan-Southeastern Parklds	33,700	6,900	8,400	5,000	5,500	3,100	4,000	800
Central Saskatchewan Parklands	53,800	18,800	7,000	7,800	8,300	3,400	6,500	2,000
Northern Saskatchewan	4,300	2,200	400	300	300	400	500	200

Economic regions	Total households	Under $2,000	$2,000–$2,999	$3,000–$3,999	$4,000–$4,999	$5,000–$5,999	$6,000–$9,999	$10,000 and over
Alberta	*377,000*	*81,200*	*35,600*	*42,500*	*58,700*	*48,600*	*82,400*	*28,000*
Medicine Hat-Palliser	11,300	2,400	1,000	1,900	2,700	1,100	1,600	600
Lethbridge Prairie	29,000	6,300	2,700	3,300	4,300	4,900	5,200	2,300
Alberta Rocky Mountains-Foothills	5,700	1,400	300	700	800	800	1,400	300
Calgary-South Central Alberta	115,400	18,800	8,800	13,100	17,700	16,600	30,000	10,400
Red Deer Environs	20,400	4,100	3,200	3,500	3,800	1,800	2,800	1,200
East-Central Alberta Prairie	28,600	7,900	5,300	3,700	5,100	2,800	3,000	800
Edmonton-Parklands	131,900	25,100	10,400	12,700	20,200	17,500	34,700	11,300
Northeastern Alberta	10,600	5,900	1,200	800	1,100	800	600	200
Northwestern Alberta-Peace River	24,100	9,300	2,700	2,800	3,000	2,300	3,100	900
British Columbia	*489,000*	*85,100*	*47,600*	*53,000*	*62,400*	*73,900*	*128,300*	*38,700*
East Kootenay	9,800	1,900	200	1,400	2,000	1,800	2,200	300
West Kootenay	20,000	4,100	1,900	2,200	2,300	3,800	4,600	1,100
Okanagan Valley	27,900	5,400	3,500	5,000	4,500	3,700	4,400	1,400
South Central British Columbia	18,600	4,000	1,800	1,600	2,900	3,000	4,300	1,000
Vancouver-Lower Fraser	279,200	45,500	30,400	29,300	31,000	41,900	75,700	25,400
Victoria-Vancouver Island	89,500	15,900	6,600	10,100	12,400	12,500	25,900	6,100
Northwestern British Columbia	14,200	2,000	700	600	1,200	2,800	5,300	1,600
North-Central British Columbia	20,000	4,100	1,500	1,800	4,100	3,000	4,300	1,200
Northeastern British Columbia	9,800	2,200	1,000	1,000	2,000	1,400	1,600	600
Yukon and Northwest Territories	*9,000*	*800*	*400*	*700*	*900*	*1,600*	*3,700*	*900*
Canada	*4,805,000*	*807,200*	*508,700*	*602,200*	*748,400*	*674,300*	*1,097,000*	*367,200*

NUMBER OF HOUSEHOLDS IN DIFFERENT INCOME GROUPS, 1964 ESTIMATES (continued)

Metropolitan centers	Total households	Under $2,000	$2,000–$2,999	$3,000–$3,999	$4,000–$4,999	$5,000–$5,999	$6,000–$9,999	$10,000 and over
Calgary	91,200	12,200	6,300	10,300	12,700	13,600	27,100	9,000
Edmonton	100,500	12,000	6,700	9,900	15,500	14,800	31,400	10,200
Halifax	46,000	5,000	4,100	5,700	8,000	7,500	11,900	3,800
Hamilton	113,000	9,900	9,100	10,200	16,100	21,700	36,000	10,000
Kitchener	45,300	3,300	3,500	5,400	8,300	8,800	12,500	3,500
London	56,500	5,800	4,700	6,900	9,100	9,300	16,100	4,600
Montréal	610,800	61,600	50,500	83,400	103,600	92,300	153,300	66,100
Ottawa	120,000	10,000	7,300	12,700	19,700	19,600	36,000	14,700
Québec	91,400	5,400	10,000	15,600	14,700	15,100	20,900	9,700
Regina	33,900	2,600	2,000	4,400	5,400	4,500	11,300	3,700
Saint John	26,300	3,700	3,800	3,400	5,200	3,100	5,500	1,600
St. John's	19,200	3,100	2,600	2,600	3,300	2,100	4,000	1,500
Saskatoon	29,100	3,800	2,400	3,000	4,800	4,700	8,100	2,300
Sudbury	26,800	2,300	1,700	2,300	4,200	5,900	8,100	2,300
Toronto	537,600	52,100	26,500	52,500	70,000	83,600	182,400	70,500
Vancouver	250,900	36,700	26,500	25,900	27,300	38,500	71,800	24,200
Victoria	53,200	9,100	4,200	6,200	7,000	7,600	15,200	3,900
Windsor	55,600	6,900	5,500	5,800	6,600	10,500	16,500	3,800
Winnipeg	135,300	15,700	10,800	14,700	25,000	21,800	36,100	11,200
Total of metropolitan cities	2,442,600	261,200	188,200	280,900	366,500	385,000	704,200	256,600
Canada	4,805,000	807,200	508,700	602,200	748,400	674,300	1,097,000	367,200
Metropolitan centers' share of Canada (%)	50.8	32.4	37.0	46.6	49.0	57.1	64.2	69.9

OCCUPATION OF THE HEAD OF THE HOUSEHOLD, 1964 ESTIMATES

Economic regions	Total households (000)	White collar				Blue collar		Other occupations				Hsld. head not in labor force (000)
		Managerial (000)	Professional (000)	Clerical (000)	Sales (000)	Craftsmen, etc. (000)	Laborers (000)	Primary Farmers (000)	Others (000)	Transport (000)	Services (000)	
Newfoundland	*94.0*	*6.7*	*3.5*	*3.4*	*2.2*	*20.0*	*4.9*	*1.0*	*10.7*	*6.2*	*5.3*	*30.1*
St. John's-Southeastern Nfld.	58.5	4.3	2.2	2.3	1.5	12.4	2.9	0.7	5.2	3.9	3.1	20.0
Central Nfld.	16.4	1.1	0.6	0.4	0.3	3.2	0.9	0.1	2.9	1.1	0.9	4.9
Western Nfld.	16.5	1.2	0.5	0.5	0.4	3.7	0.9	0.2	2.5	1.0	0.7	4.9
Labrador	2.6	0.1	0.2	0.2	—	0.7	0.2	—	0.1	0.2	0.6	0.3
Prince Edward Island	*24.0*	*1.9*	*1.0*	*0.8*	*0.7*	*3.7*	*0.7*	*5.2*	*1.5*	*1.3*	*1.9*	*5.3*
Nova Scotia	*178.0*	*15.6*	*9.9*	*8.1*	*6.3*	*38.7*	*7.9*	*7.5*	*13.0*	*11.5*	*21.7*	*37.8*
Sydney-Cape Breton	36.8	2.6	1.6	1.6	1.2	8.7	1.9	1.1	5.9	2.6	1.9	7.7
Northern Nova Scotia	34.5	3.1	1.6	1.2	1.3	7.2	1.6	2.4	2.4	2.3	1.5	9.9
Halifax-South Shore	83.7	8.2	5.7	4.7	3.1	18.4	3.3	1.6	4.0	5.4	14.5	14.8
Annapolis Valley	23.0	1.7	1.0	0.6	0.7	4.4	1.1	2.4	0.7	1.2	3.8	5.4
New Brunswick	*137.0*	*12.1*	*7.3*	*6.6*	*5.3*	*29.4*	*7.2*	*7.5*	*8.5*	*9.5*	*12.4*	*31.2*
Moncton-Southeastern N.B.	30.4	2.9	1.8	2.1	1.5	6.9	1.6	1.7	1.1	2.4	1.8	6.6
Saint John-Southern N.B.	39.3	4.0	2.1	2.3	1.7	9.5	1.9	1.4	1.3	2.8	2.3	10.0
Upper Saint John Valley	37.8	3.1	2.1	1.3	1.2	6.5	1.8	3.3	2.2	2.4	5.7	8.2
Northeastern N.B.	29.5	2.1	1.3	0.9	0.9	6.5	1.9	1.1	3.9	1.9	2.6	6.4
Québec	*1,262.0*	*124.7*	*95.6*	*81.5*	*63.1*	*342.2*	*54.3*	*71.5*	*27.0*	*84.2*	*88.4*	*229.5*
North Shore-New Québec	17.7	1.4	1.2	1.1	0.5	5.7	1.0	0.1	1.8	1.6	1.5	1.8
Gaspé Peninsula-South Shore	68.2	5.4	2.7	2.0	2.2	14.8	4.2	10.7	8.0	4.9	3.0	10.3
Saguenay Valley-Lake St. John	46.7	3.7	3.3	2.2	2.2	15.4	2.8	3.6	2.8	3.3	3.5	3.9
Metro Québec-Eastern Laurentides	138.8	13.4	11.1	9.5	7.8	35.0	5.8	12.5	2.8	10.1	12.5	18.3
Trois Rivières-St. Maurice Valley	65.6	5.4	4.1	2.7	2.7	20.8	3.1	6.3	1.4	4.2	3.6	11.3
Sherbrooke-Eastern Townships	102.2	8.6	5.5	4.0	4.3	30.8	4.5	12.3	2.4	6.0	4.3	19.5
Metro Montréal and its Environs	749.6	80.7	63.5	56.0	40.8	202.0	27.7	20.6	1.5	49.1	55.0	152.7
Western Québec	32.8	2.7	1.7	1.1	1.1	7.1	2.0	2.7	5.2	2.1	1.8	5.3
Hull-Western Laurentides	40.4	3.4	2.5	2.9	1.5	10.6	3.2	2.7	1.1	2.9	3.2	6.4

Ontario	*1,737.0*	*190.9*	*150.4*	*120.0*	*86.9*	*463.8*	*61.9*	*98.0*	*27.7*	*98.1*	*140.3*	*299.0*
Ottawa-Ottawa Valley	144.2	16.7	18.2	12.4	6.1	25.1	4.6	7.9	0.6	7.3	21.5	23.8
Kingston-Upper St. Lawrence	66.0	5.9	5.2	3.0	2.4	16.2	2.8	6.9	0.2	3.7	6.9	12.8
Peterborough-Central Lake Ontario	93.8	8.2	5.9	4.0	3.6	22.7	3.3	9.2	1.1	4.8	8.5	22.5
Metro Toronto and its Environs	604.5	81.5	66.8	57.4	39.3	168.8	19.0	10.3	0.5	34.2	45.4	81.3
Hamilton/St. Catharines-Niagara	211.9	20.3	15.9	13.0	9.9	72.5	8.6	8.5	0.4	11.9	12.9	38.0
London-Lake Erie	118.1	11.4	7.5	6.2	5.9	25.4	3.4	14.3	0.2	6.3	9.4	28.1
Windsor/Sarnia-Lake St. Clair	125.1	12.0	9.2	6.9	5.3	34.3	3.7	11.4	0.5	7.1	7.9	26.8
Kitchener-Midlands	105.9	10.5	6.6	5.7	5.0	30.7	3.2	12.3	0.2	4.9	6.8	20.0
Lake Huron-Georgian Bay	85.1	8.4	3.8	2.9	3.1	18.9	3.2	12.8	0.6	5.3	8.6	17.5
Northeastern Ontario: Clay Belt	52.1	5.0	3.3	2.5	2.1	12.4	2.7	1.7	7.3	3.3	4.0	7.8
Northeastern Ontario: Nickel Range	43.4	3.2	2.6	1.6	1.5	11.1	2.3	1.0	8.2	2.7	2.6	6.6
Northeastern Ontario: Sault	31.3	2.4	1.9	1.4	0.9	9.8	2.0	0.5	2.4	2.0	1.7	6.3
Lakehead-Northwestern Ontario	55.6	5.4	3.5	3.0	1.8	15.9	3.1	1.2	5.5	4.6	4.1	7.5
Manitoba	*248.0*	*23.7*	*16.4*	*15.6*	*11.0*	*50.0*	*9.0*	*34.3*	*3.0*	*14.4*	*22.1*	*48.5*
Metro Winnipeg and its Environs	182.5	18.7	13.5	14.0	9.2	40.2	6.9	15.3	0.8	11.5	16.7	35.7
Southwestern Manitoba Prairie	40.4	3.2	1.5	0.9	1.3	5.4	1.0	13.4	0.1	1.8	3.4	8.4
West-Central Manitoba Parklands	14.7	1.1	0.6	0.3	0.3	1.7	0.4	5.5	0.2	0.5	0.4	3.7
Northern Manitoba	10.4	0.7	0.8	0.4	0.2	2.7	0.7	0.1	1.9	0.6	1.6	0.7
Saskatchewan	*250.0*	*21.2*	*14.8*	*9.6*	*9.0*	*35.3*	*5.5*	*71.8*	*2.7*	*10.8*	*13.9*	*55.4*
Regina-Southeastern Plains	63.0	6.5	5.0	3.9	3.1	10.5	1.6	12.3	0.4	3.1	4.5	12.1
Saskatchewan Palliser	41.2	3.2	1.8	1.2	1.3	5.4	0.7	13.5	0.1	1.8	2.4	9.8
Saskatoon-Central Plains	54.0	4.9	4.0	2.4	2.4	8.2	1.2	10.9	0.2	2.7	3.7	13.4
Saskatchewan-Southeastern Parklds.	33.7	2.2	1.3	0.7	0.8	3.8	0.6	14.5	0.1	1.3	1.0	7.4
Central Saskatchewan Parklands	53.8	4.1	2.4	1.3	1.4	6.8	1.3	20.3	0.5	1.8	2.0	11.9
Northern Saskatchewan	4.3	0.3	0.3	0.1	—	0.6	0.1	0.3	1.4	0.1	0.3	0.8

OCCUPATION OF THE HEAD OF THE HOUSEHOLD, 1964 ESTIMATES (continued)

Economic regions	Total households (000)	White collar				Blue collar		Other occupations				Hsld. head not in labor force (000)
		Mana-gerial (000)	Profes-sional (000)	Cleri-cal (000)	Sales (000)	Crafts-men, etc. (000)	Labor-ers (000)	Primary		Trans-port (000)	Serv-ices (000)	
								Farm-ers (000)	Others (000)			
Alberta	*377.0*	*38.7*	*29.1*	*22.5*	*18.6*	*68.4*	*10.9*	*59.2*	*6.0*	*21.0*	*28.8*	*73.8*
Medicine Hat-Palliser	11.3	1.0	0.7	0.5	0.4	2.3	0.3	1.8	—	0.7	0.5	3.1
Lethbridge Prairie	29.0	3.0	1.8	1.1	1.4	5.1	0.9	7.7	0.2	1.5	1.3	5.0
Alberta Rocky Mountains-Foothills	5.7	0.6	0.4	0.3	0.1	1.4	0.4	0.2	0.7	0.5	0.8	0.3
Calgary-South Central Alberta	115.4	13.2	10.4	9.7	7.4	21.1	3.1	10.3	0.9	6.3	9.5	23.5
Red Deer Environs	20.4	1.8	1.1	0.6	0.7	3.1	0.5	5.1	0.4	0.9	1.6	4.6
East-Central Alberta Prairie	28.6	2.3	1.3	0.6	0.7	3.5	0.5	11.8	0.2	1.1	1.1	5.5
Edmonton-Parklands	131.9	14.1	11.9	8.9	7.0	26.8	4.1	12.1	1.5	8.4	11.2	25.9
Northeastern Alberta	10.6	0.7	0.5	0.2	0.2	1.2	0.3	3.6	0.3	0.4	1.9	1.3
Northwestern Alberta-Peace River	24.1	2.0	1.0	0.6	0.7	3.9	0.8	6.6	1.8	1.2	0.9	4.6
British Columbia	*489.0*	*50.7*	*37.7*	*25.7*	*23.0*	*115.6*	*17.1*	*14.5*	*15.9*	*29.3*	*40.1*	*119.4*
East Kootenay	9.8	1.0	0.6	0.4	0.3	2.9	0.6	0.3	1.1	0.7	0.5	1.4
West Kootenay	20.0	1.8	1.7	0.8	0.5	6.0	1.1	0.4	1.1	1.4	1.0	4.2
Okanagan Valley	27.9	3.1	1.6	1.0	1.2	5.5	0.9	2.9	0.8	1.4	1.2	8.3
South-Central British Columbia	18.6	2.0	1.0	0.6	0.6	4.7	1.0	1.3	1.0	1.4	1.0	4.0
Vancouver-Lower Fraser	279.2	30.5	23.6	17.5	15.9	62.7	8.1	6.0	4.7	16.5	21.4	72.3
Victoria-Vancouver Island	89.5	7.5	6.4	3.7	3.3	19.2	2.8	1.6	3.8	4.8	12.5	23.9
Northwestern British Columbia	14.2	1.4	1.2	0.7	0.3	4.1	0.8	0.1	2.0	1.0	1.1	1.5
North-Central British Columbia	20.0	2.3	1.0	0.7	0.6	6.3	1.5	0.9	1.2	1.4	0.9	3.2
Northeastern British Columbia	9.8	1.1	0.6	0.3	0.3	4.2	0.3	1.0	0.2	0.7	0.5	0.6
Yukon and Northwest Territories	*9.0*	*0.7*	*0.7*	*0.2*	*0.1*	*1.5*	*0.5*	—	*1.6*	*0.7*	*1.0*	*2.0*
Canada	*4,805.0*	*486.9*	*366.4*	*294.0*	*226.2*	*1,168.6*	*179.9*	*370.5*	*117.6*	*287.0*	*375.9*	*932.0*

OCCUPATION OF THE HEAD OF THE HOUSEHOLD, 1964 ESTIMATES (continued)

Metropolitan centers	Total households	White collar				Blue collar		Other occupations			Hsld. head not in labor force
		Managerial	Professional	Clerical	Sales	Craftsmen etc.	Laborers	Primary occupations	Transport	Services	
Calgary	91,200	12,000	10,200	8,300	6,400	19,000	2,700	1,000	5,700	9,000	16,900
Edmonton	100,500	12,200	10,600	8,400	6,600	22,800	3,500	1,500	7,200	10,000	17,700
Halifax	46,000	5,200	4,400	3,900	2,100	9,400	1,300	300	2,700	11,400	5,300
Hamilton	113,000	11,200	9,600	7,700	6,100	40,200	4,500	2,600	6,200	7,400	17,500
Kitchener	45,300	5,200	3,400	3,300	2,800	17,300	1,300	900	2,100	2,700	6,300
London	56,500	6,400	5,600	4,800	4,200	13,700	1,700	1,000	3,400	6,500	9,200
Montréal	610,800	70,500	61,300	54,500	38,500	167,800	22,200	3,300	42,800	50,800	99,100
Ottawa	120,000	15,200	16,300	14,900	5,800	21,500	3,700	1,100	6,300	18,200	17,000
Québec	91,400	9,800	9,000	8,500	6,400	22,200	3,200	900	6,700	9,000	15,700
Regina	33,900	4,400	3,600	3,600	2,600	7,100	900	500	2,200	3,300	5,700
Saint John	26,300	2,900	1,900	2,100	1,400	7,000	1,000	300	2,000	2,100	5,600
St. John's	19,200	1,500	1,500	1,800	1,100	4,600	700	300	1,600	1,900	4,200
Saskatoon	29,100	3,300	3,200	2,300	2,100	5,600	900	500	2,100	2,800	6,300
Sudbury	26,800	2,100	1,800	1,100	1,100	7,400	1,400	6,000	1,400	1,600	2,900
Toronto	537,600	76,400	62,100	52,200	37,200	139,200	15,100	4,600	29,600	40,400	80,800
Vancouver	250,900	28,800	22,500	17,200	15,500	58,100	7,300	5,900	15,100	20,500	60,000
Victoria	53,200	4,400	4,500	3,100	2,300	9,300	1,400	1,200	2,500	8,200	16,300
Windsor	55,600	5,500	4,300	4,400	2,500	17,700	1,800	600	3,300	4,300	11,200
Winnipeg	135,300	15,800	11,900	13,100	8,600	32,400	5,300	1,300	9,500	14,300	23,100
Total metropolitan cities	2,442,600	292,800	247,700	215,200	153,300	622,300	79,900	33,800	152,400	224,400	420,800
Canada	4,805,000	486,900	366,400	294,000	226,200	1,168,600	179,900	488,100	287,000	375,900	932,000
Metropolitan cities' share of Canada (%)	50.8	60.1	67.6	73.2	67.8	53.3	44.4	6.9	53.1	59.7	45.2

EDUCATIONAL ATTAINMENT OF THE HEAD OF THE HOUSEHOLD, 1964 ESTIMATES

Economic regions	Total no. of households	No schooling	Elementary 1-4 years	Over 4 years	Secondary	Some university	University degree	Average schooling No. of years	Index Canada =100
Newfoundland	94,000	6,300	21,900	30,000	32,000	2,300	1,500	6.7	79
St. John's-Southeastern Nfld.	58,500	3,500	12,700	18,600	21,200	1,500	1,000	6.9	81
Central Nfld.	16,400	1,100	4,500	5,300	4,900	400	200	6.3	74
Western Nfld.	16,500	1,400	4,100	5,300	5,200	300	200	6.3	74
Labrador	2,600	300	600	800	700	100	100	6.5	76
Prince Edward Island	24,000	200	1,800	11,300	9,400	700	600	8.0	94
Nova Scotia	178,000	2,400	14,700	65,100	83,500	5,800	6,500	8.4	99
Sydney-Cape Breton	36,800	600	4,100	16,100	14,200	900	900	7.8	92
Northern Nova Scotia	34,500	400	2,900	13,500	15,700	900	1,100	8.2	96
Halifax-South Shore	83,700	1,100	6,200	27,800	41,600	3,300	3,700	8.7	102
Annapolis Valley	23,000	300	1,500	7,700	12,000	700	800	8.6	101
New Brunswick	137,000	4,200	17,200	60,300	46,700	4,300	4,300	7.6	89
Moncton-Southeastern N.B.	30,400	800	3,600	13,900	9,900	1,100	1,100	7.7	91
Saint John-Southern N.B.	39,300	700	2,500	16,200	17,500	1,200	1,200	8.3	98
Upper Saint John Valley	37,800	1,100	4,200	15,800	14,200	1,200	1,300	7.8	92
Northeastern N.B.	29,500	1,600	6,900	14,400	5,100	800	700	6.3	74
Québec	1,262,000	10,700	167,900	489,000	485,600	45,200	63,600	8.1	95
North Shore-New Québec	17,700	200	3,700	7,300	5,100	700	700	7.4	87
Gaspé Peninsula-South Shore	68,200	1,500	23,500	30,300	11,400	700	800	5.8	68
Saguenay Valley-Lake St. John	46,700	400	6,400	25,000	11,800	1,300	1,800	7.4	87
Metro Québec-Eastern Laurentides	138,800	1,500	22,700	61,100	41,300	4,800	7,400	7.7	91
Trois Rivières-St. Maurice Valley	65,600	600	9,200	29,800	22,300	1,500	2,200	7.6	89
Sherbrooke-Eastern Townships	102,200	1,100	17,600	45,500	32,500	2,500	3,000	7.4	87
Metro Montréal and its Environs	749,600	4,400	69,200	256,800	342,400	31,600	45,200	8.7	102
Western Québec	32,800	500	7,900	16,600	6,200	700	900	6.6	78
Hull-Western Laurentides	40,400	500	7,700	16,600	12,600	1,400	1,600	7.5	88

Ontario	*1,737,000*	*15,600*	*82,200*	*660,100*	*816,600*	*61,700*	*100,800*	*8.8*	*104*
Ottawa-Ottawa Valley	144,200	1,400	7,200	44,900	69,400	6,900	14,400	9.4	111
Kingston-Upper St. Lawrence	66,000	700	4,000	27,700	28,300	1,900	3,400	8.5	100
Peterborough-Central Lake Ontario	93,800	900	4,100	39,600	43,800	2,100	3,300	8.5	100
Metro Toronto and its Environs	604,500	3,700	24,100	198,000	305,000	27,600	46,100	9.3	109
Hamilton/St. Catharines-Niagara	211,900	1,700	8,500	82,500	103,300	6,500	9,400	8.7	102
London-Lake Erie	118,100	900	3,800	45,600	59,200	3,200	5,400	8.8	104
Windsor/Sarnia-Lake St. Clair	125,100	1,200	5,500	48,900	59,800	4,000	5,700	8.7	102
Kitchener-Midlands	105,900	800	3,100	48,200	46,800	2,700	4,300	8.5	100
Lake Huron-Georgian Bay	85,100	1,100	5,300	42,200	32,300	1,700	2,500	8.0	94
Northeastern Ontario: Clay Belt	52,100	900	5,800	25,100	17,100	1,400	1,800	7.7	91
Northeastern Ontario: Nickel Range	43,400	700	3,700	20,500	15,600	1,300	1,600	8.0	94
Northeastern Ontario: Sault	31,300	400	2,000	12,500	14,500	800	1,100	8.4	99
Lakehead-Northwestern Ontario	55,600	1,200	5,100	24,400	21,500	1,600	1,800	7.9	93
Manitoba	*248,000*	*7,400*	*22,100*	*82,000*	*115,800*	*10,500*	*10,200*	*8.4*	*99*
Metro Winnipeg and its Environs	182,500	4,600	14,200	53,000	93,300	8,700	8,700	8.7	102
Southwestern Manitoba Prairie	40,400	1,200	3,500	17,900	15,900	1,000	900	7.8	92
West-Central Manitoba Parklands	14,700	700	2,700	7,300	3,600	200	200	6.6	78
Northern Manitoba	10,400	900	1,700	3,800	3,000	600	400	7.2	85
Saskatchewan	*250,000*	*7,900*	*22,900*	*105,200*	*97,900*	*8,100*	*8,000*	*7.9*	*93*
Regina-Southeastern Plains	63,000	1,500	4,000	23,100	29,000	2,400	3,000	8.5	100
Saskatchewan Palliser	41,200	1,100	2,800	16,600	18,700	1,100	900	8.1	95
Saskatoon-Central Plains	54,000	1,200	3,100	18,400	26,800	2,100	2,400	8.7	102
Saskatchewan-Southeastern Parklds	33,700	1,400	5,100	17,600	8,200	900	500	6.9	81
Central Saskatchewan Parklands	53,800	2,100	6,900	27,800	14,400	1,500	1,100	7.1	84
Northern Saskatchewan	4,300	600	1,000	1,700	800	100	100	5.8	68

EDUCATIONAL ATTAINMENT OF THE HEAD OF THE HOUSEHOLD, 1964 ESTIMATES (continued)

Economic regions	Total no. of households	Schooling of the head of household						Average schooling	
		No schooling	Elementary 1–4 years	Elementary Over 4 years	Secondary	Some university	University degree	No. of years	Index Canada =100
Alberta	377,000	6,800	21,700	122,200	191,500	15,600	19,200	8.8	104
Medicine Hat-Palliser	11,300	200	800	3,800	5,800	400	300	8.5	100
Lethbridge Prairie	29,000	600	1,800	10,900	13,300	1,300	1,100	8.5	100
Alberta Rocky Mountains-Foothills	5,700	100	500	2,200	2,400	300	200	8.3	98
Calgary-South Central Alberta	115,400	1,300	3,400	29,100	68,500	5,300	7,800	9.5	112
Red Deer Environs	20,400	500	1,200	7,700	9,700	700	600	8.4	99
East-Central Alberta Prairie	28,600	600	2,400	13,500	10,700	800	600	7.8	92
Edmonton-Parklands	131,900	2,200	7,100	39,200	69,700	5,800	7,900	9.0	106
Northeastern Alberta	10,600	500	1,800	4,800	3,000	300	200	6.9	81
Northwestern Alberta-Peace River	24,100	800	2,700	11,000	8,400	700	500	7.5	88
British Columbia	489,000	6,100	19,300	140,200	270,100	28,100	25,200	9.2	108
East Kootenay	9,800	100	600	3,800	4,600	400	300	8.5	100
West Kootenay	20,000	400	1,100	6,500	10,200	900	900	8.8	104
Okanagan Valley	27,900	400	1,500	8,700	14,900	1,300	1,100	8.9	105
South-Central British Columbia	18,600	400	1,000	6,700	9,000	900	600	8.6	101
Vancouver-Lower Fraser	279,200	2,900	9,700	73,600	159,500	17,100	16,400	9.4	111
Victoria-Vancouver Island	89,500	900	2,500	24,000	52,200	5,300	4,600	9.4	111
Northwestern British Columbia	14,200	300	1,100	6,000	5,300	900	600	8.3	98
North-Central British Columbia	20,000	500	1,500	8,000	8,600	900	500	8.2	96
Northeastern British Columbia	9,800	200	300	2,900	5,800	400	200	8.9	105
Yukon and Northwest Territories	9,000	2,100	600	1,600	3,900	400	400	7.1	84
Canada	4,805,000	69,700	392,300	1,767,000	2,153,000	182,700	240,300	8.5	100

EDUCATIONAL ATTAINMENT OF THE HEAD OF THE HOUSEHOLD, 1964 ESTIMATES (continued)

Metropolitan centers	Total no. of households	Schooling of the head of household						Average schooling	
		No schooling	Elementary 1-4 years	Elementary Over 4 years	Secondary	Some university	University degree	No. of years	Index Canada =100
Calgary	91,200	400	1,900	20,500	55,900	4,800	7,700	9.9	116
Edmonton	100,500	1,000	3,900	25,100	57,300	5,400	7,800	9.5	112
Halifax	46,000	200	1,400	11,500	26,700	2,800	3,400	9.7	114
Hamilton	113,000	800	4,000	40,800	57,600	3,900	5,900	8.9	105
Kitchener	45,300	100	1,300	19,100	21,200	1,400	2,200	8.8	104
London	56,500	100	1,100	16,500	32,400	2,200	4,200	9.5	112
Montréal	610,800	3,700	46,000	192,500	293,100	31,300	44,200	9.0	106
Ottawa	120,000	700	5,100	30,400	62,400	7,200	14,200	9.9	116
Québec	91,400	100	6,700	37,500	36,300	4,100	6,700	8.7	102
Regina	33,900	400	1,500	9,400	18,200	1,700	2,700	9.4	111
Saint John	26,300	200	1,200	9,600	13,200	1,000	1,100	8.8	104
St. John's	19,200	400	1,500	5,500	10,200	900	700	8.7	102
Saskatoon	29,100	400	1,200	8,300	15,200	1,700	2,300	9.4	111
Sudbury	26,800	400	2,200	11,800	10,500	800	1,100	8.1	95
Toronto	537,600	3,600	18,500	157,400	286,500	26,500	45,100	9.5	112
Vancouver	250,900	1,600	7,400	62,800	146,500	16,500	16,100	9.6	113
Victoria	53,200	300	1,000	12,300	32,500	3,800	3,300	9.8	115
Windsor	55,600	600	3,000	20,300	26,900	2,200	2,600	8.7	102
Winnipeg	135,300	2,100	7,200	33,200	76,600	8,000	8,200	9.3	109
Total metropolitan cities	2,442,600	17,100	116,100	724,500	1,279,200	126,200	179,500	9.3	109
Canada	4,805,000	69,700	392,300	1,767,000	2,153,000	182,700	240,300	8.5	100
Metropolitan cities' share of Canada (%)	50.8	24.7	29.6	41.0	59.4	69.1	74.7	—	—

EDUCATION / 713

(*Text continued from page 701*)

fits accrue — better health standards, improved housing, more creative recreational patterns, and a keener desire for the finer things of life. In this respect, statistics on schooling may be used as a convenient yardstick for measuring the "quality" of the population in a particular region.

As a rule, people with more formal education stand apart from those with lower education — they live differently, think differently, buy differently. In a better-educated locality, the pressure is stronger on the manufacturers for superior quality and good taste in design. The market tends to become heterogeneous as buyers become more discriminating and ask for wider choices so as not to ape the Joneses. The demand is greater for the type of goods and services associated with the "eggheads" — well-written books and magazines, paintings, stereo-sets, tape-recorders, photographic equipment, gourmet foods, imported wines and liqueurs, etc. Savings in the form of insurance and investments also appear to rank high in the value scale of the educated consumer.

Conversely, in a region of low educational attainment the demand is brisk for lurid and sensational publications, honky-tonk amusements, mass-produced items, and sometimes even for sucker products ranging from false cures for ailments to astrological guides to behavior. The consumers are apt to be emotional, their decisions less sound, and their selectivity of merchandise not so exacting. They tend to stick to the nationally advertised products of well-known manufacturers and avoid the private brands of the retailers. The latter are generally purchased by better-educated persons who have a keener sense of judgment and know how to get maximum benefit from their shopping dollar.

Another significant factor about education is its close correlation to "leadership" status. Persons with more education are pace-setters rather than the followers in the acceptance of new products, new services, new ideas, new habits, new status symbols. Among the less educated, there are very few experimenters and innovators.

Education has some effect, too, on the character of local politics and the types of political campaigns waged. The kinds of appeals the candidates can make to an electorate are undoubtedly of a different order when the average voter has not progressed beyond elementary school than when he has at least a high school diploma.

The manner of communicating and the channels of communication also change with academic attainment. U.S. experience shows that the penetration of text as opposed to picture magazines is three or four times greater in households where the head holds a university degree. Similarly, with network television, general drama and travelogues are favored more strongly among the higher educated, while situation comedies and Westerns fare better among the masses.

Chapter 23

REGIONAL DATA BY RETAIL TRADE, MANUFACTURING AND AGRICULTURE

The ensuing tables provide regional statistics for three major categories of industries: retail trade, manufacturing, and agriculture. Such data can be useful, among other things, for determining the territorial potential of the product and for allocating the sales efforts by regions on a scientific basis.

Manufacturing

The statistics on manufacturing include: number of establishments, total employees, salaries and wages, and value of factory shipments. The figures are only for economic regions. They were not available for metropolitan centers at the time of publication.

Agriculture

The tables on agriculture cover the distribution of farm income. These statistics, compiled from the 1961 census reports, give a bird's-eye view of the main features of the farm market.

Retail trade

The data reflect the amount of buying power in an area and the conversion of that power into actual purchases. In addition to total retail sales, estimates are also published for sales in six major types of stores: grocery and combination; drug; clothing; hardware; furniture, appliance and radio; and motor vehicle. The figures have been obtained from the Financial Post's *Survey of 1965/66 Markets and Business Year Book*. The subsequent table gives the number of retail outlets by selected categories. The information is based on the actual count taken at the time of the 1961 census.

PRINCIPAL STATISTICS OF THE MANUFACTURING INDUSTRIES, 1962

Economic regions	Establishments (no.)	Total employees (no.)	Salaries and wages ($000)	Value of factory shipments ($000)	% of Canada
Newfoundland	*331*	*9,826*	*36,882*	*143,925*	*0.54*
St. John's-Southeastern Nfld.	197	5,743	14,895	64,267	0.24
Central Nfld.	67	1,732	9,979	29,081	0.11
Western Nfld.	67	2,351	12,008	50,577	0.19
Labrador.					
Prince Edward Island	*157*	*1,834*	*4,849*	*35,130*	*0.13*
Nova Scotia	*1,030*	*28,984*	*100,670*	*426,677*	*1.60*
Sydney-Cape Breton	134	6,024	26,390	88,693	0.33
Northern Nova Scotia	264	6,315	19,357	74,773	0.28
Halifax-South Shore	502	13,683	47,355	222,805	0.84
Annapolis Valley	130	2,962	7,568	40,406	0.15
New Brunswick	*722*	*22,555*	*78,558*	*401,142*	*1.50*
Moncton-Southeastern N.B.	165	3,817	12,043	54,521	0.20
Saint John-Southern N.B.	210	9,569	33,572	200,704	0.75
Upper Saint John Valley	347	9,169	32,943	145,917	0.55
Northeastern N.B.					
Québec	*11,104*	*436,991*	*1,741,492*	*7,936,347*	*29.71*
North Shore-New Québec	64	2,404	14,223	81,727	0.31
Gaspé Peninsula-South Shore	732	8,997	26,471	145,581	0.54
Saguenay Valley-Lake St. John	328	13,584	70,830	350,519	1.31
Metro Québec-Eastern Laurentides	1,245	33,878	123,031	511,968	1.92
Trois Rivières-St. Maurice Valley	626	25,289	102,083	485,867	1.82
Sherbrooke-Eastern Townships	1,033	42,871	145,061	675,506	2.53
Metro Montréal and its Environs	6,672	298,085	1,208,905	5,338,576	19.98
Western Québec	208	3,761	14,674	173,774	0.65
Hull-Western Laurentides	196	8,122	36,214	172,829	0.65

Ontario	12,586	637,912	2,914,851	13,342,555	49.95
Ottawa-Ottawa Valley	609	20,593	83,882	307,935	1.15
Kingston-Upper St. Lawrence	375	19,409	86,130	433,539	1.62
Peterborough-Central Lake Ontario	663	26,357	112,873	497,736	1.86
Metro Toronto and its Environs	5,570	275,602	1,262,098	5,609,834	21.00
Hamilton/St. Catharines-Niagara	1,418	107,977	534,502	2,333,317	8.74
London-Lake Erie	754	35,418	145,690	713,071	2.67
Windsor/Sarnia-Lake St. Clair	799	43,251	220,655	1,258,706	4.71
Kitchener-Midlands	1,037	51,922	205,549	869,619	3.26
Lake Huron-Georgian Bay	688	17,524	61,152	248,949	0.93
Northeastern Ontario: Clay Belt	227	7,671	35,311	155,672	0.58
Northeastern Ontario: Nickel Range	139	10,813	53,908	405,386	1.52
Northeastern Ontario: Sault	81	10,394	58,636	232,080	0.87
Lakehead-Northwestern Ontario	226	10,981	54,465	276,711	1.04
Manitoba	1,461	40,561	159,698	836,572	3.13
Metro Winnipeg and its Environs*	1,158	36,564	142,297	687,851	2.58
Southwestern Manitoba Prairie	153	1,594	5,381	25,423	0.09
West-Central Manitoba Parklands	89	250	691	5,088	0.02
Northern Manitoba*	61	2,153	11,329	118,210	0.44
Saskatchewan	720	12,963	53,529	375,223	1.40
Regina-Southeastern Plains	176	4,605	20,473	129,057	0.48
Saskatchewan Palliser	96	1,521	6,229	55,635	0.21
Saskatoon-Central Plains	169	3,751	15,518	104,264	0.39
Saskatchewan-Southeastern Parklands	92	840	2,693	19,448	0.07
Central Saskatchewan Parklands	} 187	2,246	8,616	66,819	0.25
Northern Saskatchewan					

* DBS has combined census division 16 of Northern Manitoba with 19 of Metro Winnipeg and its Environs.

PRINCIPAL STATISTICS OF THE MANUFACTURING INDUSTRIES, 1962 (continued)

Economic regions	Estab-lishments (no.)	Total employees (no.)	Salaries and wages ($000)	Value of factory shipments ($000)	% of Canada
Alberta	*1,681*	*40,064*	*171,099*	*1,017,237*	*3.81*
Medicine Hat-Palliser	47	2,081	8,364	49,049	0.18
Lethbridge Prairie	135	2,799	10,035	67,183	0.25
Alberta Rocky Mountains-Foothills	25	473	1,870	7,470	0.03
Calgary-South Central Alberta	488	11,700	52,170	303,282	1.14
Red Deer Environs	105	1,020	3,562	30,250	0.11
East-Central Alberta Prairie	96	746	2,960	20,981	0.08
Edmonton-Parklands	620	18,727	82,551	495,354	1.85
Northeastern Alberta	23	87	239	2,199	0.01
Northwestern Alberta-Peace River	142	2,431	9,348	41,469	0.16
British Columbia	*3,622*	*101,780*	*478,906*	*2,194,598*	*8.22*
East Kootenay	83	1,847	7,727	30,553	0.11
West Kootenay	134	6,487	32,226	149,721	0.56
Okanagan Valley	240	3,930	15,129	57,898	0.22
South Central British Columbia	209	3,120	13,114	61,426	0.23
Vancouver-Lower Fraser	1,998	56,843	264,921	1,197,992	4.49
Victoria-Vancouver Island	388	15,061	75,571	346,920	1.30
Northwestern British Columbia	76	7,946	43,611	232,512	0.87
North-Central British Columbia	429	5,887	23,911	101,732	0.38
Northeastern British Columbia	65	659	2,696	15,844	0.06
Yukon and Northwest Territories	*16*	*153*	*725*	*3,589*	*0.01*
Canada	*33,430*	*1,333,623*	*5,741,259*	*26,712,995*	*100.00*

Note: Some personnel engaged in non-manufacturing activities at head offices and sales offices could not be distributed by regions and are not, therefore, included. The actual total for the number of employees in Canada was 1,391,426 and total wages and salaries amounted to $6,102,995,000.

(Source: DBS, *Daily Bulletin Supplement* —5, August 26, 1965.)

DISTRIBUTION OF FARM INCOME, 1961

Economic regions	Number of farms	Total	Distribution of farms in each region by the value of the product sold (%)							
			$25,000 and over	$15,000 to 24,999	$10,000 to 14,999	$5,000 to 9,999	$3,750 to 4,999	$2,500 to 3,749	$1,200 to 2,499	Non-commercial
Newfoundland	*1,752*	*100.0*	*2.1*	*1.5*	*1.7*	*4.3*	*1.8*	*4.6*	*10.0*	*74.0*
St. John's-Southeastern Nfld.	1,218	100.0	2.5	1.9	2.2	4.4	1.7	3.5	8.3	75.5
Central Nfld.	113	100.0	2.6	3.5	—	11.5	1.8	6.2	19.5	54.9
Western Nfld.	421	100.0	0.7	—	0.5	2.4	1.9	7.4	12.3	74.8
Labrador	—									
Prince Edward Island	*7,335*	*100.0*	*0.7*	*1.1*	*2.5*	*12.2*	*9.6*	*13.3*	*22.4*	*38.2*
Nova Scotia	*12,518*	*100.0*	*1.3*	*1.5*	*2.2*	*7.5*	*4.2*	*7.4*	*15.4*	*60.5*
Sydney-Cape Breton	1,975	100.0	0.6	0.7	1.3	4.9	3.1	6.4	12.3	70.7
Northern Nova Scotia	4,600	100.0	0.5	0.9	2.0	6.8	4.4	8.0	16.8	60.6
Halifax-South Shore	2,846	100.0	1.0	1.0	1.4	5.3	3.3	6.1	14.9	67.0
Annapolis Valley	3,097	100.0	3.2	3.5	3.9	12.2	5.4	8.2	15.6	48.0
New Brunswick	*11,786*	*100.0*	*1.1*	*1.6*	*2.3*	*8.4*	*4.6*	*8.1*	*17.3*	*56.6*
Moncton-Southeastern N.B.	2,789	100.0	0.6	1.1	1.1	6.0	3.0	6.8	19.3	62.1
Saint John-Southern N.B.	2,212	100.0	0.8	1.4	2.9	10.6	5.9	8.8	20.2	49.4
Upper Saint John Valley	4,301	100.0	2.1	2.7	4.0	11.9	6.4	11.1	17.1	44.7
Northeastern N.B.	2,484	100.0	0.3	0.4	0.4	2.8	2.2	3.5	13.0	77.4
Québec	*95,777*	*100.0*	*0.6*	*1.0*	*2.5*	*12.4*	*9.0*	*15.2*	*24.6*	*34.7*
North Shore-New Québec	219	100.0	0.5	—	0.5	3.6	4.6	8.2	24.2	58.4
Gaspé Peninsula-South Shore	15,903	100.0	—	0.2	0.5	4.7	5.6	12.6	25.7	50.7
Saguenay Valley-Lake St. John	4,349	100.0	0.2	0.5	1.9	11.9	9.7	15.7	24.3	35.8
Metro Québec-Eastern Laurentides	16,236	100.0	0.4	0.7	1.6	11.4	8.9	15.6	27.3	34.1
Trois Rivières-St. Maurice Valley	8,197	100.0	1.0	1.0	2.1	11.7	10.2	17.9	28.9	27.2
Sherbrooke-Eastern Townships	16,568	100.0	0.7	1.4	2.9	15.0	10.8	17.8	24.5	26.9
Metro Montréal and its Environs	24,946	100.0	1.1	1.8	5.0	19.3	10.9	15.2	20.6	26.1
Western Québec	5,229	100.0	—	—	0.1	3.5	4.7	10.3	23.0	58.4
Hull-Western Laurentides	4,130	100.0	0.2	0.6	1.1	7.4	7.1	14.0	27.6	42.0

Economic regions	Number of farms	Total	Distribution of farms in each region by the value of the product sold (%)							
			$25,000 and over	$15,000 to 24,999	$10,000 to 14,999	$5,000 to 9,999	$3,750 to 4,999	$2,500 to 3,749	$1,200 to 2,499	Non-commercial
Ontario	121,333	100.0	4.0	4.8	7.1	19.7	9.4	12.5	17.0	25.5
Ottawa-Ottawa Valley	10,059	100.0	1.0	1.9	4.5	15.0	10.5	15.5	22.0	29.6
Kingston-Upper St. Lawrence	9,235	100.0	0.7	1.5	3.3	16.5	10.6	15.9	22.6	28.9
Peterborough-Central Lake Ontario	13,659	100.0	1.7	2.1	4.1	16.3	9.2	13.8	20.8	32.0
Metro Toronto and its Environs	8,409	100.0	4.4	6.3	9.5	19.6	7.7	9.6	15.3	27.6
Hamilton/St. Catharines-Niagara	10,940	100.0	4.9	5.2	8.1	17.1	6.7	9.8	15.7	32.5
London-Lake Erie	15,102	100.0	13.9	10.6	9.5	20.3	8.3	8.8	10.9	17.7
Windsor/Sarnia-Lake St. Clair	13,825	100.0	3.3	5.7	9.0	23.5	10.1	12.9	15.3	20.2
Kitchener-Midlands	15,614	100.0	3.8	7.2	11.4	28.8	10.8	11.6	12.1	14.3
Lake Huron-Georgian Bay	17,563	100.0	1.9	2.8	5.4	20.2	11.3	15.2	19.5	23.7
Northeastern Ontario: Clay Belt	2,781	100.0	0.2	0.9	2.3	10.5	5.9	9.3	21.1	49.8
Northeastern Ontario: Nickel Range	1,569	100.0	0.7	0.4	1.7	9.3	7.4	14.0	20.4	46.1
Northeastern Ontario: Sault	708	100.0	—	1.3	4.2	12.2	6.1	9.3	24.0	42.9
Lakehead-Northwestern Ontario	1,869	100.0	0.4	0.8	3.6	13.4	6.8	10.3	20.2	44.5
Manitoba	43,306	100.0	0.9	2.0	4.6	20.7	12.2	15.7	21.3	22.6
Metro Winnipeg and its Environs	19,601	100.0	1.3	2.5	4.7	17.1	9.4	13.2	21.4	30.4
Southwestern Manitoba Prairie	16,103	100.0	0.7	2.1	5.7	29.2	16.7	17.3	17.5	10.8
West-Central Manitoba Parklands	7,482	100.0	0.1	0.6	1.6	12.0	10.2	19.0	29.3	27.2
Northern Manitoba	120	100.0	0.8	2.5	4.2	8.3	5.0	13.3	21.7	44.2
Saskatchewan	93,924	100.0	0.7	2.4	6.4	25.9	14.1	18.2	19.9	12.4
Regina-Southeastern Plains	15,936	100.0	0.7	2.3	6.5	30.3	15.6	19.4	17.3	7.9
Saskatchewan Palliser	18,443	100.0	1.5	4.9	11.6	35.0	13.3	14.7	12.7	6.3
Saskatoon-Central Plains	14,041	100.0	0.9	3.7	9.3	32.7	15.1	15.8	14.7	7.8
Saskatchewan-Southeastern Parklds	18,896	100.0	0.3	0.8	2.4	17.5	15.1	21.9	26.6	15.4
Central Saskatchewan Parklands	26,268	100.0	0.5	1.3	4.0	19.3	12.5	18.5	24.6	19.3
Northern Saskatchewan	340	100.0	—	0.3	0.9	12.1	7.3	15.6	24.4	39.4

Alberta	73,212	*100.0*	2.7	*4.3*	7.0	21.8	11.2	14.8	18.4	19.8
Medicine Hat-Palliser	2,165	100.0	6.2	10.0	14.7	34.3	10.8	9.5	8.4	6.1
Lethbridge Prairie	7,381	100.0	8.4	10.3	13.3	28.8	9.4	9.7	9.8	10.3
Alberta Rocky Mountains/Foothills	175	100.0	5.2	4.0	6.3	9.7	7.4	9.7	22.3	35.4
Calgary-South Central Alberta	11,297	100.0	6.3	10.4	13.7	29.6	9.6	10.0	10.2	10.2
Red Deer Environs	6,551	100.0	2.2	3.7	6.6	22.4	12.0	15.2	17.5	20.4
East-Central Alberta Prairie	15,387	100.0	1.2	2.5	5.9	24.5	14.3	18.2	20.5	12.9
Edmonton-Parklands	15,834	100.0	0.9	1.8	3.7	16.4	10.7	16.6	22.3	27.6
Northeastern Alberta	4,494	100.0	0.1	0.4	1.7	11.4	11.1	17.7	25.1	32.5
Northwestern Alberta/Peace River	9,928	100.0	0.2	0.7	2.1	14.0	10.1	15.4	24.6	32.9
British Columbia	*19,934*	*100.0*	*3.6*	*4.4*	*5.8*	*12.7*	*5.7*	*8.7*	*13.8*	*45.3*
East Kootenay	397	100.0	1.5	1.5	2.3	6.8	9.1	9.8	20.9	48.1
West Kootenay	1,012	100.0	1.1	2.2	3.3	7.8	3.3	8.5	13.3	60.5
Okanagan Valley	4,460	100.0	2.0	2.2	5.2	13.5	7.3	11.6	16.6	41.6
South Central British Columbia	1,732	100.0	3.8	2.2	3.0	8.8	5.0	9.3	16.5	51.4
Vancouver-Lower Fraser	7,369	100.0	5.9	7.6	8.6	15.4	5.1	6.6	10.3	40.5
Victoria-Vancouver Island	2,059	100.0	4.4	5.4	5.2	11.0	3.6	5.5	9.2	55.7
Northwestern British Columbia	136	100.0	2.9	2.9	5.9	8.1	5.9	3.7	14.7	55.9
North-Central British Columbia	1,362	100.0	1.0	1.0	1.9	8.5	5.1	9.4	19.4	53.7
Northeastern British Columbia	1,407	100.0	0.7	0.9	3.7	13.7	8.8	13.9	19.8	38.5
Yukon and Northwest Territories	*26*	*100.0*	—	—	—	—	*3.8*	*3.8*	*3.8*	*88.6*
Canada	480,903	*100.0*	2.0	3.0	5.4	18.8	10.3	14.4	19.6	26.5

(Source: DBS, *Census of Canada, 1961.* Bulletin 96-522.)

RETAIL SALES BY SELECTED OUTLETS, 1964 ESTIMATES

Economic regions	Total retail sales		Grocery and combination		Drug	
	Amount ($000)	% of Canada	Amount ($000)	% of Canada	Amount ($000)	% of Canada
Newfoundland	*331,800*	*1.65*	*63,900*	*1.54*	*5,900*	*1.23*
St. John's-Southeastern Nfld.	203,800	1.01	42,800	1.03	3,900	0.81
Central Nfld.	59,400	0.30	8,800	0.21	900	0.19
Western Nfld.	61,000	0.30	12,200	0.30	1,100	0.23
Labrador	7,600	0.04	100	—	—	—
Prince Edward Island	*96,800*	*0.48*	*17,000*	*0.41*	*1,500*	*0.31*
Nova Scotia	*700,500*	*3.49*	*168,900*	*4.08*	*17,200*	*3.58*
Sydney-Cape Breton	163,500	0.81	43,200	1.04	2,700	0.56
Northern Nova Scotia	114,700	0.57	30,400	0.74	2,700	0.56
Halifax-South Shore	344,600	1.72	78,700	1.90	9,500	1.98
Annapolis Valley	77,700	0.39	16,600	0.40	2,300	0.48
New Brunswick	*572,000*	*2.85*	*137,900*	*3.33*	*16,200*	*3.37*
Moncton-Southeastern N.B.	134,500	0.67	31,400	0.76	4,000	0.83
Saint John-Southern N.B.	173,400	0.87	44,000	1.06	5,300	1.10
Upper Saint John Valley	157,000	0.78	33,800	0.82	4,200	0.88
Northeastern N.B.	107,100	0.53	28,700	0.69	2,700	0.56
Québec	*5,076,300*	*25.30*	*1,209,600*	*29.21*	*116,500*	*24.24*
North Shore-New Québec	87,300	0.44	12,000	0.29	1,200	0.25
Gaspé Peninsula-South Shore	226,800	1.13	42,200	1.02	3,200	0.66
Saguenay Valley-Lake St. John	212,800	1.06	54,400	1.31	3,500	0.73
Metro Québec-Eastern Laurentides	577,200	2.88	125,100	3.02	13,200	2.75
Trois Rivières-St. Maurice Valley	232,600	1.16	57,800	1.40	4,800	1.00
Sherbrooke-Eastern Townships	386,600	1.93	88,300	2.13	6,100	1.27
Metro Montréal and its Environs	3,096,500	15.43	760,000	18.35	80,900	16.83
Western Québec	127,300	0.63	32,600	0.79	1,600	0.33
Hull-Western Laurentides	129,200	0.64	37,200	0.90	2,000	0.42

RETAIL SALES BY SELECTED OUTLETS, 1964 ESTIMATES (continued)

Economic regions	Clothing Amount ($000)	Clothing % of Canada	Hardware Amount ($000)	Hardware % of Canada	Furniture, appliance and radio Amount ($000)	Furniture, appliance and radio % of Canada	Motor vehicle Amount ($000)	Motor vehicle % of Canada
Newfoundland	*8,900*	*0.97*	*3,200*	*0.88*	*6,000*	*0.96*	*51,800*	*1.58*
St. John's-Southeastern Nfld.	5,800	0.63	2,000	0.55	3,900	0.63	34,000	1.04
Central Nfld.	2,000	0.22	1,000	0.27	900	0.14	8,200	0.25
Western Nfld.	1,000	0.11	200	0.06	1,200	0.19	8,500	0.26
Labrador	100	0.01	—	—	—	—	1,100	0.03
Prince Edward Island	*4,000*	*0.44*	*200*	*0.05*	*1,700*	*0.27*	*10,800*	*0.33*
Nova Scotia	*29,900*	*32.6*	*8,700*	*2.38*	*15,100*	*2.43*	*127,700*	*3.90*
Sydney-Cape Breton	7,600	0.83	2,500	0.68	3,300	0.53	29,100	0.89
Northern Nova Scotia	4,800	0.52	1,400	0.38	1,800	0.29	22,300	0.68
Halifax-South Shore	15,100	1.65	3,100	0.85	7,900	1.27	60,100	1.83
Annapolis Valley	2,400	0.26	1,700	0.47	2,100	0.34	16,200	0.50
New Brunswick	*22,600*	*2.46*	*9,000*	*2.46*	*23,700*	*3.81*	*110,300*	*3.36*
Moncton-Southeastern N.B.	6,000	0.65	1,000	0.27	6,600	1.06	22,600	0.69
Saint John-Southern N.B.	5,300	0.58	1,900	0.52	6,300	1.01	35,000	1.07
Upper Saint John Valley	7,100	0.77	4,900	1.34	5,200	0.84	35,800	1.09
Northeastern N.B.	4,200	0.46	1,200	0.33	5,600	0.90	16,900	0.51
Québec	*299,500*	*32.63*	*98,700*	*27.02*	*205,300*	*33.00*	*743,100*	*22.68*
North Shore-New Québec	4,400	0.48	1,100	0.30	2,900	0.47	13,700	0.42
Gaspé Peninsula-South Shore	15,100	1.64	4,500	1.23	11,100	1.78	43,000	1.31
Saguenay Valley-Lake St. John	22,000	2.40	3,200	0.88	12,100	1.94	35,800	1.09
Metro Québec-Eastern Laurentides	36,200	3.94	9,100	2.49	21,500	3.46	82,800	2.53
Trois Rivières-St. Maurice Valley	15,200	1.66	5,400	1.48	6,700	1.08	34,000	1.04
Sherbrooke-Eastern Townships	24,300	2.65	7,300	2.00	17,800	2.86	69,100	2.11
Metro Montréal and its Environs	169,500	18.47	64,300	17.60	122,500	19.69	423,700	12.93
Western Québec	9,300	1.01	2,100	0.57	5,400	0.87	20,000	0.61
Hull-Western Laurentides	3,500	0.38	1,700	0.47	5,300	0.85	21,000	0.64

RETAIL SALES BY SELECTED OUTLETS, 1964 ESTIMATES (continued)

Economic regions	Total retail sales		Grocery and combination		Drug	
	Amount ($000)	% of Canada	Amount ($000)	% of Canada	Amount ($000)	% of Canada
Ontario	*7,406,800*	*36.91*	*1,562,500*	*37.73*	*189,700*	*39.47*
Ottawa-Ottawa Valley	630,300	3.14	128,200	3.10	14,200	2.96
Kingston-Upper St. Lawrence	259,400	1.29	60,800	1.47	6,200	1.29
Peterborough-Central Lake Ontario	340,100	1.70	73,700	1.78	7,900	1.64
Metro Toronto and its Environs	2,894,800	14.43	580,400	14.01	83,900	17.46
Hamilton/St. Catharines-Niagara	843,500	4.20	195,400	4.72	23,700	4.93
London-Lake Erie	499,600	2.49	87,600	2.11	10,500	2.19
Windsor/Sarnia-Lake St. Clair	458,300	2.28	103,400	2.50	12,400	2.58
Kitchener-Midlands	401,000	2.00	85,600	2.07	8,400	1.75
Lake Huron-Georgian Bay	321,200	1.60	70,300	1.70	7,500	1.56
Northeastern Ontario: Clay Belt	217,300	1.08	52,300	1.26	4,200	0.87
Northeastern Ontario: Nickel Range	179,800	0.90	42,800	1.03	2,900	0.60
Northeastern Ontario: Sault	126,500	0.63	28,900	0.70	3,000	0.62
Lakehead-Northwestern Ontario	235,000	1.17	53,100	1.28	4,900	1.02
Manitoba	*970,700*	*4.84*	*165,300*	*3.99*	*24,500*	*5.10*
Metro Winnipeg and its Environs	743,900	3.71	135,300	3.27	19,300	4.02
Southwestern Manitoba Prairie	141,500	0.71	19,300	0.47	3,400	0.71
West-Central Manitoba Parklands	44,300	0.22	5,600	0.13	1,100	0.23
Northern Manitoba	41,000	0.20	5,100	0.12	700	0.14
Saskatchewan	*1,153,500*	*5.75*	*145,000*	*3.50*	*20,800*	*4.33*
Regina-Southeastern Plains	336,200	1.68	43,600	1.05	6,600	1.37
Saskatchewan Palliser	196,400	0.98	23,300	0.56	3,300	0.69
Saskatoon-Central Plains	274,900	1.37	36,900	0.89	5,500	1.14
Saskatchewan-Southeastern Parklds.	111,600	0.56	13,400	0.33	2,000	0.42
Central Saskatchewan Parklands	221,300	1.10	26,600	0.64	3,200	0.67
Northern Saskatchewan	13,100	0.06	1,200	0.03	200	0.04

RETAIL SALES BY SELECTED OUTLETS, 1964 ESTIMATES (continued)

Economic regions	Clothing		Hardware		Furniture, appliance and radio		Motor vehicle	
	Amount ($000)	% of Canada	Amount ($000)	% of Canada	Amount ($000)	% of Canada	Amount ($000)	% of Canada
Ontario	*328,700*	*35.82*	*108,700*	*29.76*	*228,600*	*36.75*	*1,150,900*	*35.12*
Ottawa-Ottawa Valley	29,400	3.20	7,300	2.00	19,400	3.12	83,600	2.55
Kingston-Upper St. Lawrence	10,400	1.13	4,600	1.26	7,000	1.12	37,500	1.14
Peterborough-Central Lake Ontario	12,700	1.38	6,300	1.72	10,200	1.64	52,100	1.59
Metro Toronto and its Environs	130,400	14.21	33,100	9.06	84,100	13.52	457,200	13.95
Hamilton/St. Catharines-Niagara	35,800	3.90	10,000	2.74	27,600	4.44	113,600	3.47
London-Lake Erie	20,700	2.26	8,300	2.27	16,300	2.62	114,200	3.48
Windsor/Sarnia-Lake St. Clair	22,300	2.43	7,600	2.08	21,200	3.41	65,400	2.00
Kitchener-Midlands	19,900	2.17	7,000	1.92	13,000	2.09	66,400	2.03
Lake Huron-Georgian Bay	11,800	1.29	9,200	2.52	9,700	1.56	52,800	1.61
Northeastern Ontario: Clay Belt	12,300	1.34	4,800	1.31	6,200	1.00	33,400	1.02
Northeastern Ontario: Nickel Range	7,800	0.85	2,800	0.77	5,600	0.90	23,900	0.73
Northeastern Ontario: Sault	6,500	0.71	3,700	1.01	3,100	0.50	16,800	0.51
Lakehead-Northwestern Ontario	8,700	0.95	4,000	1.10	5,200	0.83	34,000	1.04
Manitoba	*29,200*	*3.18*	*19,500*	*5.34*	*24,800*	*3.99*	*130,700*	*3.99*
Metro Winnipeg and its Environs	20,400	2.22	11,300	3.10	19,400	3.12	92,400	2.82
Southwestern Manitoba Prairie	4,900	0.53	6,000	1.64	3,700	0.60	27,900	0.85
West-Central Manitoba Parklands	2,000	0.22	1,200	0.33	1,000	0.16	6,400	0.20
Northern Manitoba	1,900	0.21	1,000	0.27	700	0.11	4,000	0.12
Saskatchewan	*33,500*	*3.65*	*42,700*	*11.69*	*22,100*	*3.55*	*258,900*	*7.90*
Regina-Southeastern Plains	9,600	1.05	9,700	2.65	7,100	1.14	72,100	2.20
Saskatchewan Palliser	6,100	0.66	7,000	1.92	3,600	0.58	46,600	1.42
Saskatoon-Central Plains	9,500	1.03	9,500	2.60	5,900	0.95	57,400	1.75
Saskatchewan-Southeastern Parklds	2,900	0.32	7,300	2.00	1,900	0.30	24,500	0.75
Central Saskatchewan Parklands	5,300	0.58	8,900	2.44	3,600	0.58	56,700	1.73
Northern Saskatchewan	100	0.01	300	0.08	—	—	1,600	0.05

RETAIL SALES BY SELECTED OUTLETS, 1964 ESTIMATES (continued)

Economic regions	Total retail sales		Grocery and combination		Drug	
	Amount ($000)	% of Canada	Amount ($000)	% of Canada	Amount ($000)	% of Canada
Alberta..........	1,663,600	8.29	300,100	7.25	35,100	7.30
Medicine Hat-Palliser.....	48,200	0.24	8,700	0.21	900	0.19
Lethbridge Prairie........	128,400	0.64	24,000	0.58	2,900	0.60
Alberta Rocky Mountains-Foothills...	25,400	0.13	4,800	0.12	1,000	0.21
Calgary-South Central Alberta........	540,900	2.70	107,200	2.59	10,400	2.16
Red Deer Environs.........	91,200	0.45	13,700	0.33	2,400	0.50
East-Central Alberta Prairie........	96,500	0.48	15,900	0.38	2,100	0.44
Edmonton-Parklands.........	612,300	3.05	108,600	2.62	13,300	2.77
Northeastern Alberta........	32,300	0.16	3,700	0.09	500	0.10
Northwestern Alberta-Peace River.....	88,400	0.44	13,500	0.33	1,600	0.33
British Columbia........	2,095,600	10.44	371,300	8.96	53,200	11.07
East Kootenay........	39,900	0.20	6,400	0.15	800	0.17
West Kootenay........	79,600	0.40	16,800	0.41	1,700	0.35
Okanagan Valley....	117,200	0.58	23,000	0.55	3,200	0.67
South Central British Columbia.	82,100	0.41	15,800	0.38	1,500	0.31
Vancouver-Lower Fraser.....	1,206,400	6.01	207,400	5.01	33,600	6.99
Victoria-Vancouver Island.....	363,600	1.81	68,300	1.65	8,500	1.77
Northwestern British Columbia....	60,800	0.30	11,300	0.27	1,400	0.29
North-Central British Columbia....	95,000	0.47	16,600	0.40	1,700	0.35
Northeastern British Columbia....	51,000	0.26	5,700	0.14	800	0.17
Yukon and Northwest Territories...........	—		—		—	
Canada*.................	20,067,600	100.00	4,141,500	100.00	480,600	100.00

* The Yukon and the Northwest Territories' figures are not available and hence not included in the totals for Canada.

(Source: *Financial Post*, "1965/66 Survey of Markets and Business Year Book.")

RETAIL SALES BY SELECTED OUTLETS, 1964 ESTIMATES (continued)

Economic regions	Clothing		Hardware		Furniture, appliance and radio		Motor vehicle	
	Amount ($000)	% of Canada	Amount ($000)	% of Canada	Amount ($000)	% of Canada	Amount ($000)	% of Canada
Alberta	69,500	7.57	46,600	12.76	42,700	6.86	296,100	9.04
Medicine Hat-Palliser	2,400	0.26	600	0.16	2,000	0.32	9,200	0.28
Lethbridge Prairie	6,700	0.73	4,500	1.23	3,600	0.58	26,200	0.80
Alberta Rocky Mountains-Foothills	1,300	0.14	900	0.25	300	0.05	5,000	0.15
Calgary-South Central Alberta	20,500	2.23	11,200	3.07	14,900	2.39	90,600	2.77
Red Deer Environs	4,400	0.48	4,100	1.12	2,200	0.35	19,100	0.58
East-Central Alberta Prairie	3,600	0.39	7,300	2.00	2,000	0.32	16,800	0.51
Edmonton-Parklands	27,300	2.98	13,600	3.72	15,900	2.56	107,400	3.28
Northeastern Alberta	800	0.09	900	0.25	600	0.10	6,600	0.20
Northwestern Alberta-Peace River	2,500	0.27	3,500	0.96	1,200	0.19	15,200	0.47
British Columbia	92,000	10.02	28,000	7.66	52,100	8.38	396,400	12.10
East Kootenay	1,500	0.16	1,200	0.33	800	0.13	7,800	0.24
West Kootenay	2,900	0.32	1,400	0.38	2,000	0.32	16,000	0.49
Okanagan Valley	5,300	0.58	3,100	0.85	4,100	0.66	24,300	0.74
South Central British Columbia	3,600	0.39	1,700	0.46	1,600	0.26	14,500	0.44
Vancouver-Lower Fraser	55,800	6.08	10,600	2.90	29,400	4.73	231,300	7.06
Victoria-Vancouver Island	14,500	1.58	5,300	1.45	10,100	1.62	58,500	1.79
Northwestern British Columbia	3,000	0.33	1,200	0.33	800	0.13	10,200	0.31
North-Central British Columbia	4,000	0.43	3,100	0.85	1,700	0.27	21,400	0.65
Northeastern British Columbia	1,400	0.15	400	0.11	1,600	0.26	12,400	0.38
Yukon and Northwest Territories	—		—		—		—	
Canada*	917,800	100.00	365,300	100.00	622,100	100.00	3,276,700	100.00

* The Yukon and the Northwest Territories' figures are not available and hence not included in the totals for Canada.

(Source: *Financial Post:* "1965/66 Survey of Markets and Business Year Book.")

RETAIL SALES BY SELECTED OUTLETS, 1964 ESTIMATES (continued)

Metropolitan centers	Total retail sales		Grocery and combination		Drug	
	Amount ($000)	% of Canada	Amount ($000)	% of Canada	Amount ($000)	% of Canada
Calgary	460,400	2.30	94,300	2.28	8,600	1.79
Edmonton	517,500	2.58	95,100	2.30	11,400	2.37
Halifax	241,100	1.20	56,400	1.36	7,000	1.46
Hamilton	468,200	2.33	103,100	2.49	13,200	2.75
Kitchener	195,200	0.97	45,200	1.09	3,700	0.77
London	289,800	1.44	45,700	1.10	6,500	1.35
Montréal	2,526,800	12.59	626,100	15.12	70,500	14.67
Ottawa	539,500	2.69	118,900	2.87	12,200	2.54
Québec	432,300	2.16	96,800	2.34	11,600	2.41
Regina	220,000	1.10	27,600	0.67	5,000	1.04
Saint John	129,900	0.65	33,400	0.81	3,900	0.81
St. John's	122,500	0.61	21,700	0.52	2,900	0.60
Saskatoon	181,600	0.91	25,900	0.63	4,000	0.83
Sudbury	138,300	0.69	33,600	0.81	2,000	0.42
Toronto	2,597,200	12.94	510,000	12.31	76,100	15.83
Vancouver	1,091,100	5.44	181,800	4.39	30,200	6.28
Victoria	208,900	1.04	36,300	0.88	5,200	1.08
Windsor	204,400	1.02	47,600	1.15	5,800	1.21
Winnipeg	615,900	3.07	113,500	2.74	16,400	3.41

Metropolitan centers	Clothing		Hardware		Furniture, appliance and radio		Motor vehicle	
	Amount ($000)	% of Canada	Amount ($000)	% of Canada	Amount ($000)	% of Canada	Amount ($000)	% of Canada
Calgary	16,600	1.81	6,600	1.81	13,700	2.20	73,800	2.25
Edmonton	24,600	2.68	8,300	2.27	14,900	2.39	86,000	2.62
Halifax	11,500	1.25	1,300	0.36	5,100	0.82	40,700	1.24
Hamilton	18,000	1.96	4,400	1.20	13,300	2.14	60,400	1.84
Kitchener	10,300	1.12	2,000	0.55	7,500	1.21	29,100	0.89
London	9,500	1.07	2,700	0.74	8,300	1.33	76,000	2.32
Montréal	142,200	15.49	51,000	13.96	99,800	16.04	320,400	9.78
Ottawa	24,300	2.65	4,600	1.26	18,400	2.96	70,600	2.15
Québec	29,400	3.20	7,300	2.00	15,800	2.54	60,700	1.85
Regina	7,900	0.86	2,800	0.77	6,200	1.00	43,000	1.31
Saint John	4,800	0.52	900	0.25	4,900	0.79	28,100	0.86
St. John's	4,700	0.51	1,000	0.27	3,200	0.51	29,800	0.91
Saskatoon	7,500	0.82	2,800	0.77	4,900	0.79	33,500	1.02
Sudbury	6,900	0.73	2,000	0.55	4,700	0.76	21,000	0.64
Toronto	119,100	12.98	28,100	7.69	77,500	12.46	396,500	12.10
Vancouver	50,900	5.55	7,900	2.16	26,200	4.21	205,300	6.26
Victoria	8,000	0.87	2,500	0.68	5,800	0.93	36,200	1.10
Windsor	11,800	1.29	2,400	0.66	10,700	1.72	25,800	0.79
Winnipeg	16,900	1.84	7,300	2.00	16,100	2.59	71,400	2.18

RETAIL SALES BY SELECTED OUTLETS, 1964 ESTIMATES (continued)

Major urban areas	Total retail sales		Grocery and combination		Drug	
	Amount ($000)	% of Canada	Amount ($000)	% of Canada	Amount ($000)	% of Canada
Brantford	73,000	0.36	17,000	0.41	1,600	0.33
Chicoutimi-Jonquière	115,100	0.57	30,000	0.72	2,100	0.44
Drummondville	42,400	0.21	8,600	0.21	800	0.17
Fort William-Port Arthur	123,200	0.61	28,700	0.69	2,600	0.54
Guelph	57,000	0.28	12,200	0.30	1,600	0.33
Kingston	91,100	0.45	22,100	0.53	2,300	0.48
Moncton	98,200	0.49	20,800	0.50	2,900	0.60
Niagara Falls	63,000	0.31	17,500	0.42	2,500	0.52
Oshawa	115,800	0.58	26,900	0.65	2,800	0.58
Peterborough	81,600	0.41	16,200	0.39	2,100	0.44
St. Catharines	115,900	0.58	28,100	0.68	3,100	0.64
St. Jean	41,500	0.21	10,400	0.25	1,200	0.25
Sarnia	73,100	0.36	16,700	0.40	1,900	0.40
Sault Ste. Marie*	99,400	0.50	24,500	0.59	2,000	0.42
Shawinigan	50,800	0.25	14,300	0.35	1,100	0.23
Sherbrooke	100,900	0.50	20,500	0.50	2,000	0.42
Sydney-Glace Bay	112,200	0.56	31,600	0.76	2,200	0.46
Timmins	41,100	0.21	13,400	0.32	800	0.17
Trois Rivières	96,700	0.48	23,400	0.57	2,400	0.50
Valleyfield	33,900	0.17	9,200	0.22	700	0.15
Total of metropolitan centers and major urban areas	12,806,500	63.82	2,705,100	65.32	334,900	69.69
Canada	20,067,600	100.00	4,141,500	100.00	480,600	100.00

* Figures for the municipal area of the city before the amalgamation.

(Source: *Financial Post*, "1965/66 Survey of Markets and Business Year Book.")

Major urban areas	Clothing		Hardware		Furniture, appliance and radio		Motor vehicle	
	Amount ($000)	% of Canada	Amount ($000)	% of Canada	Amount ($000)	% of Canada	Amount ($000)	% of Canada
Brantford	4,800	0.52	700	0.19	2,700	0.43	9,700	0.30
Chicoutimi-Jonquière	12,000	1.31	1,000	0.27	7,100	1.14	22,500	0.69
Drummondville	2,600	0.28	800	0.22	2,200	0.35	8,800	0.27
Fort William-Port Arthur	4,600	0.49	1,200	0.33	2,600	0.42	20,200	0.62
Guelph	3,400	0.37	500	0.14	1,800	0.29	9,000	0.27
Kingston	3,800	0.41	1,600	0.44	2,500	0.40	11,100	0.34
Moncton	4,900	0.53	300	0.08	4,600	0.74	19,900	0.61
Niagara Falls	3,100	0.34	500	0.14	2,200	0.35	8,700	0.27
Oshawa	5,400	0.59	1,200	0.33	2,900	0.47	21,100	0.64
Peterborough	3,800	0.40	400	0.11	2,500	0.40	10,200	0.31
St. Catharines	6,100	0.65	1,900	0.52	4,200	0.67	16,500	0.50
St. Jean	3,100	0.34	1,000	0.27	1,700	0.27	5,900	0.18
Sarnia	3,500	0.38	700	0.19	3,600	0.58	9,900	0.30
Sault Ste. Marie*	5,800	0.63	3,500	0.96	2,800	0.45	13,300	0.41
Shawinigan	4,400	0.48	1,000	0.27	2,300	0.37	6,800	0.21
Sherbrooke	7,900	0.86	600	0.16	4,500	0.72	17,300	0.53
Sydney-Glace Bay	5,700	0.62	2,000	0.55	3,000	0.48	20,800	0.63
Timmins	2,900	0.32	700	0.19	1,300	0.21	5,600	0.17
Trois Rivières	7,400	0.81	1,300	0.36	3,400	0.55	18,300	0.56
Valleyfield	1,800	0.20	1,900	0.52	2,000	0.32	4,000	0.12
Total of metropolitan centers and major urban areas	621,700	67.73	168,700	46.19	416,900	67.00	1,967,900	60.04
Canada	917,800	100.00	365,300	100.00	622,100	100.00	3,276,700	100.00

*Figures for the municipal area of the city before the amalgamation.

(Source: *Financial Post*, "1965/66 Survey of Markets and Business Year Book.")

NUMBER OF RETAIL STORES IN SELECTED CATEGORIES, 1961 CENSUS

Economic regions	Food group				General merchandise group			Automotive group				
	Bakery products stores	Confectionery stores	Grocery and combination stores	Meat markets	Department and mail order stores	General stores	Variety stores	Automobile dealers	Used car dealers	Accessories, tire & battery shops	Service stations	Garages
Newfoundland	*13*	*456*	*2,208*	*47*	*79*	*977*	*18*	*37*	*3*	*6*	*228*	*96*
St. John's-Southeastern Nfld.	8	303	1,543	45	44	515	6	18	3	3	145	56
Central Nfld.	3	50	356	—	13	215	3	8	—	1	34	17
Western Nfld.	2	102	296	2	15	213	8	8	—	2	49	21
Labrador	—	1	13	—	7	34	1	3	—	—	—	2
Prince Edward Island	*6*	*15*	*269*	*16*	*15*	*110*	*5*	*22*	*2*	*13*	*120*	*54*
Nova Scotia	86	350	2,120	65	117	458	82	172	19	60	858	212
Sydney-Cape Breton	20	162	496	5	24	98	14	32	3	14	164	32
Northern Nova Scotia	24	65	481	23	35	117	18	46	5	13	222	50
Halifax-South Shore	33	94	910	30	35	166	36	65	6	24	343	88
Annapolis Valley	9	29	233	7	23	77	14	29	5	9	129	42
New Brunswick	*63*	*189*	*1,921*	*33*	*76*	*371*	*60*	*127*	*23*	*46*	*681*	*221*
Moncton-Southeastern N.B.	15	44	355	5	9	71	17	18	8	7	168	46
Saint John-Southern N.B.	29	24	479	11	20	68	14	36	10	13	153	43
Upper Saint John Valley	10	37	420	13	24	112	13	43	3	18	192	81
Northeastern N.B.	9	84	667	4	23	120	16	30	2	8	168	51
Québec	*1,012*	*2,271*	*11,176*	*1,133*	*356*	*1,758*	*477*	*786*	*157*	*379*	*4,197*	*2,420*
North Shore-New Québec	6	24	146	9	34	72	4	14	—	7	48	40
Gaspé Peninsula-South Shore	76	145	1,572	93	31	400	39	80	6	25	394	211
Saguenay Valley-Lake St. John	36	121	562	31	22	105	25	42	3	18	259	110
Metro Québec-Eastern Laurentides	128	177	1,601	186	35	301	47	81	16	35	572	374
Trois Rivières-St. Maurice Valley	90	179	764	112	30	100	33	46	14	33	249	199
Sherbrooke-Eastern Townships	95	190	1,066	104	33	180	53	105	30	50	461	344
Metro Montréal and its Environs	543	1,293	4,684	561	128	380	244	337	84	183	1,869	976
Western Québec	17	49	345	4	35	107	15	46	2	15	152	78
Hull-Western Laurentides	21	93	436	33	8	113	17	35	2	13	193	88

Ontario	*1,167*	*1,667*	*7,675*	*1,147*	*713*	*1,528*	*837*	*1,356*	*497*	*639*	*7,250*	*2,081*
Ottawa-Ottawa Valley	58	164	667	61	55	144	61	98	52	39	505	191
Kingston-Upper St. Lawrence	24	60	456	24	30	148	35	69	27	31	341	114
Peterborough-Central Lake Ontario	58	73	521	41	58	200	59	122	33	44	602	147
Metro Toronto and its Environs	488	336	2,002	466	94	106	246	273	125	148	1,756	452
Hamilton/St. Catharines-Niagara	151	290	911	153	65	72	72	153	80	79	940	279
London-Lake Erie	80	61	444	88	53	134	83	111	38	50	532	206
Windsor/Sarnia-Lake St. Clair	83	155	553	105	54	86	78	108	59	67	590	174
Kitchener-Midlands	69	85	444	106	64	123	57	122	37	62	489	166
Lake Huron-Georgian Bay	71	45	598	59	74	228	72	135	16	54	643	172
Northeastern Ontario: Clay Belt	26	113	366	11	50	99	26	60	4	23	274	60
Northeastern Ontario: Nickel Range	17	116	199	16	21	57	17	27	16	11	221	44
Northeastern Ontario: Sault	11	62	150	5	17	25	8	29	5	6	123	29
Lakehead-Northwestern Ontario	31	107	364	12	78	106	23	49	5	25	234	47
Manitoba	*176*	*132*	*1,541*	*104*	*116*	*559*	*34*	*239*	*42*	*44*	*768*	*376*
Metro Winnipeg and its Environs	121	74	1,130	63	46	274	21	112	35	30	537	203
Southwestern Manitoba Prairie	37	29	260	32	23	161	7	83	7	6	158	136
West-Central Manitoba Parklands	12	12	108	6	15	96	2	32	—	8	59	36
Northern Manitoba	6	17	43	3	32	28	4	12	—	—	14	1
Saskatchewan	*96*	*181*	*1,478*	*157*	*138*	*869*	*58*	*364*	*30*	*88*	*1,068*	*572*
Regina-Southeastern Plains	21	40	315	35	18	131	11	62	10	16	256	114
Saskatchewan Palliser	15	33	255	26	19	131	10	78	4	18	183	110
Saskatoon-Central Plains	23	44	254	30	16	119	15	69	10	16	193	98
Saskatchewan-Southeastern Parklds.	17	23	235	30	27	177	6	65	2	11	160	113
Central Saskatchewan Parklands	19	39	399	34	35	282	16	87	4	27	261	135
Northern Saskatchewan	1	2	20	2	23	29	—	3	—	—	15	2

NUMBER OF RETAIL STORES IN SELECTED CATEGORIES, 1961 CENSUS (continued)

Economic regions	Food group				General merchandise group			Automotive group				
	Bakery products stores	Confectionery stores	Grocery and combination stores	Meat markets	Department and mail order stores	General stores	Variety stores	Automobile dealers	Used car dealers	Accessories, tire & battery shops	Service stations	Garages
Alberta	225	194	1,630	215	183	707	114	390	80	125	1,533	527
Medicine Hat-Palliser	7	15	55	1	7	15	2	12	3	2	61	22
Lethbridge Prairie	15	30	129	22	22	52	5	48	5	15	137	46
Alberta Rocky Mountains-Foothills	3	6	28	3	5	8	1	9	—	—	35	3
Calgary-South Central Alberta	75	45	437	56	31	105	27	87	24	33	413	103
Red Deer Environs	16	14	74	19	14	42	13	36	8	11	98	35
East-Central Alberta Prairie	15	20	187	30	30	107	18	64	2	11	170	93
Edmonton-Parklands	83	45	504	59	28	177	36	80	34	40	450	149
Northeastern Alberta	3	9	75	4	9	71	3	17	2	6	37	25
Northwestern Alberta-Peace River	8	10	141	21	37	130	9	37	2	7	132	51
British Columbia	400	179	2,491	376	188	423	182	311	79	117	1,905	408
East Kootenay	6	4	51	11	8	24	4	18	2	4	66	13
West Kootenay	18	17	133	17	19	39	8	23	3	7	103	18
Okanagan Valley	24	15	166	24	22	27	22	36	5	3	164	40
South Central British Columbia	10	10	108	11	13	59	6	17	3	7	114	24
Vancouver-Lower Fraser	241	80	1,291	216	51	64	103	120	53	50	929	202
Victoria-Vancouver Island	82	37	511	74	31	87	20	41	13	25	313	58
Northwestern British Columbia	6	10	72	7	12	43	7	17	—	3	41	11
North-Central British Columbia	10	5	113	10	19	59	9	26	—	12	113	27
Northeastern British Columbia	3	1	46	6	13	21	3	13	—	6	62	15
Yukon and Northwest Territories	3	1	16	2	49	29	—	9	—	1	15	9
Canada	3,247	5,635	32,525	3,295	2,030	7,789	1,867	3,813	932	1,518	18,623	6,976

NUMBER OF RETAIL STORES IN SELECTED CATEGORIES, 1961 CENSUS

Metropolitan centers	Food				General merchandise			Automobile				
	Bakery products stores	Confectionery stores	Grocery & combination stores	Meat markets	Department and mail order stores	General stores	Variety stores	Automobile dealers	Used car dealers	Accessories, tires & battery shops	Service stations	Garages
Calgary	62	29	303	24	17	9	21	31	21	24	275	39
Edmonton	63	24	337	31	17	9	26	38	32	33	305	72
Halifax	22	29	328	9	11	4	23	28	4	14	124	37
Hamilton	82	113	389	86	17	23	24	51	38	25	416	124
Kitchener	19	36	148	33	17	8	15	30	20	17	183	51
London	37	29	140	30	10	9	46	26	17	19	211	53
Montréal	344	906	3,153	339	71	57	181	180	62	128	1,144	441
Ottawa	41	160	481	49	23	15	38	46	37	27	324	97
Québec	44	63	835	79	12	17	33	37	10	22	254	142
Regina	12	17	117	14	7	3	6	16	7	9	78	17
Saint John	21	16	263	9	9	6	5	16	5	6	75	16
St. John's	5	152	235	21	14	6	3	11	—	3	45	25
Saskatoon	14	17	91	9	6	6	7	15	9	9	68	14
Sudbury	13	82	110	14	8	5	8	17	16	6	112	26
Toronto	450	291	1,734	423	66	43	206	196	117	118	1,386	365
Vancouver	219	71	1,118	193	32	22	84	86	46	39	739	166
Victoria	50	23	259	41	8	9	10	13	10	10	150	23
Windsor	39	108	211	48	9	4	18	17	32	21	216	53
Winnipeg	94	47	763	42	21	11	18	46	29	25	340	64

NUMBER OF RETAIL STORES IN SELECTED CATEGORIES, 1961 CENSUS (continued)

Major urban areas	Food				General merchandise			Automotive				
	Bakery products stores	Confectionery stores	Grocery & combination stores	Meat markets	Department and mail order stores	General stores	Variety stores	Automobile dealers	Used car dealers	Accessories, tires and battery shops	Service stations	Garages
Brantford	9	43	49	9	7	1	5	9	9	7	69	19
Chicoutimi-Jonquière	6	36	189	7	7	8	11	17	—	6	77	27
Drummondville	12	36	78	5	5	3	8	11	11	8	30	23
Fort William-Port Arthur	12	67	158	7	10	3	14	13	3	17	87	14
Guelph	10	26	39	10	8	—	5	12	5	8	42	8
Kingston	8	7	76	4	10	4	7	15	15	7	57	18
Moncton	9	27	98	1	5	—	8	10	6	5	65	14
Niagara Falls	11	11	67	4	7	2	8	11	4	9	55	21
Oshawa	10	20	82	6	7	—	13	18	6	11	82	17
Peterborough	8	10	31	6	7	2	9	14	9	6	62	15
St. Catharines	19	50	121	15	9	2	10	26	15	14	124	20
St. Jean	5	20	78	4	4	2	4	10	—	8	25	7
Sarnia	10	15	51	6	7	1	20	12	12	8	64	12
Sault Ste. Marie	6	36	75	4	6	1	5	15	5	4	52	13
Shawinigan	6	29	135	3	3	1	12	10	1	9	26	16
Sherbrooke	5	27	129	10	4	—	7	20	3	11	69	40
Sydney-Glace Bay	16	122	281	1	15	20	12	19	2	11	70	14
Timmins	4	21	96	4	7	2	5	10	1	3	35	5
Trois Rivières	11	63	172	7	9	3	10	14	8	10	56	25
Valleyfield	5	24	49	3	3	1	5	9	1	4	20	15
Total of metropolitan centers and major urban areas	1,813	2,903	13,069	1,610	515	320	950	1,175	628	721	7,612	2,168

Economic regions	Apparel and accessories group				Hardware and some furnishings group				Other retail stores group					
	Men's and boys' clothing stores	Women's ready-to-wear stores	Family clothing and furnishing stores	Shoe stores	Hardware stores	Furniture stores	Household appliance stores	Furniture, radio, television and appliance stores	Drug stores	Fuel dealers	Book and stationery stores	Cameras, and photographic equipment stores	Jewelry stores	Sporting goods stores
Newfoundland	*10*	*16*	*82*	*19*	*30*	*13*	*16*	*27*	*58*	*23*	*4*	*3*	*24*	*4*
St. John's-Southeastern Nfld.	8	10	44	13	21	9	15	8	41	17	3	3	14	3
Central Nfld.	—	—	19	2	4	2	—	10	8	1	—	—	5	—
Western Nfld.	2	6	18	4	5	2	1	9	9	2	1	—	5	1
Labrador	—	—	1	—	—	—	—	—	—	3	1	—	—	1
Prince Edward Island	*9*	*15*	*8*	*8*	*3*	*7*	*5*	*3*	*27*	*13*	*3*	*10*	*13*	*1*
Nova Scotia	*103*	*108*	*132*	*92*	*110*	*53*	*66*	*58*	*179*	*55*	*36*	—	*84*	*20*
Sydney-Cape Breton	23	19	36	18	18	11	14	13	29	6	4	—	18	5
Northern Nova Scotia	22	22	20	20	23	13	12	11	34	14	9	6	21	1
Halifax-South Shore	47	47	57	40	43	21	27	26	91	24	18	4	31	10
Annapolis Valley	11	20	19	14	26	8	13	8	25	11	5	3	14	4
New Brunswick	*67*	*88*	*98*	*52*	*75*	*53*	*41*	*26*	*115*	*64*	*14*	—	*71*	*8*
Moncton-Southeastern N.B.	17	15	18	11	17	12	7	3	26	15	3	2	13	2
Saint John-Southern N.B.	24	15	21	13	27	14	12	9	39	23	5	—	18	3
Upper Saint John Valley	15	33	27	15	19	12	12	10	29	16	2	1	25	2
Northeastern N.B.	11	25	32	13	12	15	10	4	21	10	4	1	15	1
Québec	*867*	*1,156*	*1,116*	*1,021*	*1,007*	*671*	*303*	*370*	*1,199*	*596*	*264*	*65*	*911*	*189*
North Shore-New Québec	15	12	23	3	7	8	2	4	9	4	1	2	8	—
Gaspé Peninsula-South Shore	56	76	138	44	45	55	27	38	48	10	9	2	66	7
Saguenay Valley-Lake St. John	33	28	88	30	26	41	9	25	45	10	5	2	41	6
Metro Québec-Eastern Laurentides	94	123	135	111	126	79	45	50	145	59	21	4	119	19
Trois Rivières-St. Maurice Valley	51	65	79	49	54	38	20	27	65	39	8	4	72	11

NUMBER OF RETAIL STORES IN SELECTED CATEGORIES, 1961 CENSUS (continued)

Economic regions	Apparel and accessories group				Hardware and some furnishings group					Other retail stores group				
	Men's and boys' clothing stores	Women's ready-to-wear stores	Family clothing and furnishing stores	Shoe stores	Hardware stores	Furniture stores	Household appliance stores	Furniture, radio, television and appliance stores	Drug stores	Fuel dealers	Book and stationery stores	Cameras and photographic equipment stores	Jewelry stores	Sporting goods stores
Sherbrooke-Eastern Townships...	75	96	112	94	95	102	47	35	79	53	18	2	99	20
Metro Montréal and its Environs.	500	705	459	659	601	312	141	158	762	391	191	48	447	119
Western Québec..................	28	36	53	16	25	18	5	21	22	13	4	1	33	4
Hull-Western Laurentides.......	15	15	29	15	28	18	7	12	24	17	7	—	26	3
Ontario..........................	*1,404*	*1,694*	*830*	*1,278*	*1,640*	*866*	*736*	*367*	*1,944*	*715*	*336*	*199*	*1,074*	*377*
Ottawa-Ottawa Valley...........	95	106	51	103	80	64	51	31	127	57	29	14	69	24
Kingston-Upper St. Lawrence...	53	57	31	47	60	47	26	9	59	41	11	6	38	14
Peterborough-Central Lake Ontario.	60	75	47	63	96	45	51	17	88	66	13	8	58	27
Metro Toronto and its Environs..	517	744	272	483	555	290	190	86	772	160	129	89	338	140
Hamilton/St. Catharines-Niagara..	197	192	76	163	173	92	107	50	258	85	42	24	141	48
London-Lake Erie................	79	87	54	78	137	66	73	37	122	52	25	13	85	23
Windsor/Sarnia-Lake St. Clair..	99	109	70	84	147	78	79	32	143	33	16	14	86	28
Kitchener-Midlands.............	84	91	54	94	115	73	61	17	112	78	31	8	83	19
Lake Huron-Georgian Bay.......	73	88	70	75	128	59	44	26	108	58	14	12	63	20
Northeastern Ontario: Clay Belt.	53	52	41	28	56	26	30	21	52	27	5	5	38	6
Northeastern Ontario: Nickel Range.	30	26	17	15	33	13	8	13	29	20	5	1	17	4
Northeastern Ontario: Sault.....	20	37	18	22	19	5	5	13	26	19	3	4	20	10
Lakehead-Northwestern Ontario.....	44	30	29	23	41	8	11	15	48	19	13	4	38	14
Manitoba........................	*87*	*150*	*131*	*81*	*243*	*62*	*52*	*41*	*305*	*58*	*32*	*11*	*111*	*20*
Metro Winnipeg and its Environs....	55	107	85	64	123	44	36	29	227	36	29	8	67	13
Southwestern Manitoba Prairie....	18	29	28	12	95	10	11	9	57	17	2	—	31	3
West-Central Manitoba Parklands..	7	10	9	2	17	5	4	1	14	3	—	1	8	2
Northern Manitoba..............	7	4	9	3	8	3	1	2	7	2	1	2	5	2

Saskatchewan	*97*	*161*	*128*	*71*	*372*	*54*	*61*	*34*	*307*	*58*	*31*	*15*	*135*	*29*
Regina-Southeastern Plains	25	42	17	16	83	7	17	7	76	20	6	5	30	8
Saskatchewan Palliser	16	26	27	13	62	12	10	4	51	16	4	4	21	7
Saskatoon-Central Plains	30	46	25	20	69	15	18	9	75	7	11	4	37	5
Saskatchewan-Southeastern Parklds.	6	22	26	7	71	5	5	5	43	5	2	1	16	2
Central Saskatchewan Parklands	20	25	31	15	84	15	11	9	60	10	8	1	29	7
Northern Saskatchewan	—	—	2	—	3	—	—	—	2	—	—	—	2	—
Alberta	*201*	*255*	*184*	*142*	*419*	*107*	*125*	*57*	*443*	*54*	*46*	*39*	*208*	*81*
Medicine Hat-Palliser	8	12	8	6	9	5	11	2	13	2	1	2	9	3
Lethbridge Prairie	22	31	19	17	40	16	11	6	41	7	—	—	26	4
Alberta Rocky Mountains-Foothills	2	10	12	3	6	—	2	—	13	1	—	4	4	7
Calgary-South Central Alberta	67	82	47	47	110	39	25	20	118	13	14	16	58	31
Red Deer Environs	16	16	11	7	27	7	9	4	21	4	2	5	18	4
East-Central Alberta Prairie	14	21	26	12	82	10	11	3	39	12	4	1	16	5
Edmonton-Parklands	54	60	41	41	103	25	43	17	162	8	21	9	57	21
Northeastern Alberta	5	5	5	4	10	1	5	4	10	2	1	1	5	—
Northwestern Alberta-Peace River	13	18	15	5	32	4	8	1	26	5	3	1	15	6
British Columbia	*292*	*471*	*176*	*272*	*367*	*146*	*134*	*113*	*484*	*149*	*119*	*64*	*314*	*154*
East Kootenay	8	6	10	6	17	2	5	3	9	2	3	1	10	4
West Kootenay	16	19	12	9	20	5	7	4	19	11	3	5	19	10
Okanagan Valley	21	34	10	20	27	9	12	14	25	5	4	8	21	11
South-Central British Columbia	13	15	8	9	15	7	3	5	15	9	2	1	17	7
Vancouver-Lower Fraser	161	277	88	158	186	95	70	55	303	73	85	31	169	73
Victoria-Vancouver Island	41	79	24	47	67	20	25	21	82	33	18	9	50	37
Northwestern British Columbia	10	18	9	11	13	3	5	2	13	7	1	4	10	5
North-Central British Columbia	16	16	11	7	20	3	3	5	12	7	3	2	13	3
Northeastern British Columbia	6	7	4	5	2	2	4	4	6	2	—	3	5	4
Yukon and Northwest Territories	*4*	*5*	*3*	*2*	*7*	*1*	*—*	*1*	*5*	*6*	*1*	*—*	*6*	*—*
Canada	*3,141*	*4,119*	*2,888*	*3,038*	*4,273*	*2,033*	*1,539*	*1,097*	*5,066*	*1,791*	*886*	*409*	*2,951*	*883*

NUMBER OF RETAIL STORES IN SELECTED CATEGORIES, 1961 CENSUS (continued)

Metropolitan centers	Apparel and accessories				Hardware and home furnishings				Other retail					
	Men's & boys' clothing stores	Women's ready-to-wear stores	Family clothing & furnishing stores	Shoe stores	Hardware stores	Furniture stores	Household appliance stores	Furniture, radio, television, and appliance stores	Drug stores	Fuel dealers	Book and stationery stores	Cameras and photo supplies stores	Jewelry stores	Sporting goods stores
Calgary	47	64	26	41	57	30	18	16	90	5	13	15	41	28
Edmonton	43	48	24	36	57	23	36	12	132	5	20	9	46	19
Halifax	28	26	21	23	23	11	13	13	63	13	13	5	19	8
Hamilton	102	85	24	71	87	42	44	18	134	47	25	12	57	27
Kitchener	40	45	14	38	24	24	24	8	40	22	13	6	34	11
London	30	38	16	31	47	25	28	14	62	13	10	9	33	13
Montréal	393	564	277	526	452	205	87	97	633	244	168	44	330	85
Ottawa	67	67	35	74	58	37	28	26	99	38	29	14	54	21
Québec	63	80	54	86	82	31	33	21	112	44	19	3	75	16
Regina	18	28	3	12	17	6	14	5	43	7	5	4	19	5
Saint John	15	8	8	11	13	7	8	5	25	9	4	2	12	1
St. John's	7	7	17	5	12	4	4	4	28	12	2	3	10	2
Saskatoon	18	32	9	15	17	13	14	4	40	3	8	4	23	5
Sudbury	24	20	9	13	20	10	6	10	20	12	5	1	13	2
Toronto	469	681	237	441	477	254	158	74	702	124	116	82	298	126
Vancouver	142	248	69	134	151	85	62	43	271	55	77	29	139	61
Victoria	16	36	8	28	32	12	18	6	49	19	14	5	21	22
Windsor	39	42	30	33	61	28	29	12	68	13	7	8	31	14
Winnipeg	44	91	62	50	80	34	20	21	188	21	27	7	49	11

NUMBER OF RETAIL STORES IN SELECTED CATEGORIES, 1961 CENSUS (continued)

Major urban areas	Apparel and accessories				Hardware and home furnishings				Drug stores	Fuel dealers	Other retail		Jewelry stores	Sporting goods stores
	Men's and boys' clothing stores	Women's ready-to-wear stores	Family clothing and furnishing stores	Shoe stores	Hardware stores	Furniture stores	Household appliance stores	Furniture, radio, television and appliance stores			Book and stationery stores	Cameras and photo supplies stores		
Brantford	16	21	8	13	11	8	11	1	16	6	3	2	17	4
Chicoutimi-Jonquière	16	12	27	21	13	18	6	11	23	4	2	1	20	5
Drummondville	8	12	15	15	11	11	7	2	13	2	2	1	12	3
Fort William-Port Arthur	26	18	4	15	13	4	6	8	23	13	7	4	18	7
Guelph	14	11	3	10	9	9	5	2	17	13	4	—	9	2
Kingston	14	20	2	17	10	11	10	1	24	10	2	3	9	4
Moncton	9	10	6	7	5	3	7	1	17	12	3	—	6	2
Niagara Falls	21	25	4	14	10	9	7	3	26	3	7	1	11	7
Oshawa	23	23	10	17	19	14	10	5	19	4	6	1	14	7
Peterborough	12	17	3	12	7	6	5	2	19	9	3	3	12	1
St. Catharines	32	30	11	23	19	9	14	11	30	13	6	6	21	6
St. Jean	8	12	14	12	7	9	5	4	13	11	3	—	9	2
Sarnia	13	20	9	13	11	9	14	4	22	2	3	2	11	4
Sault Ste. Marie	13	22	9	18	10	4	2	9	15	13	3	1	12	6
Shawinigan	18	15	18	12	12	10	5	8	13	12	2	1	20	3
Sherbrooke	14	22	14	19	13	15	8	6	21	14	7	—	20	5
Sydney-Glace Bay	23	18	23	17	14	10	14	12	24	4	4	—	16	5
Timmins	11	11	7	6	8	2	5	6	11	2	—	2	8	2
Trois Rivières	16	25	19	17	15	8	7	6	31	11	2	2	24	4
Valleyfield	8	14	2	9	9	7	5	3	8	7	3	2	4	1
Total of metropolitan centers and major urban areas	1,920	2,568	1,151	1,955	1,993	1,057	797	514	3,184	871	647	294	1,577	557

(Source: DBS, *Census of Canada, 1961*, Bulletin 97-501.)

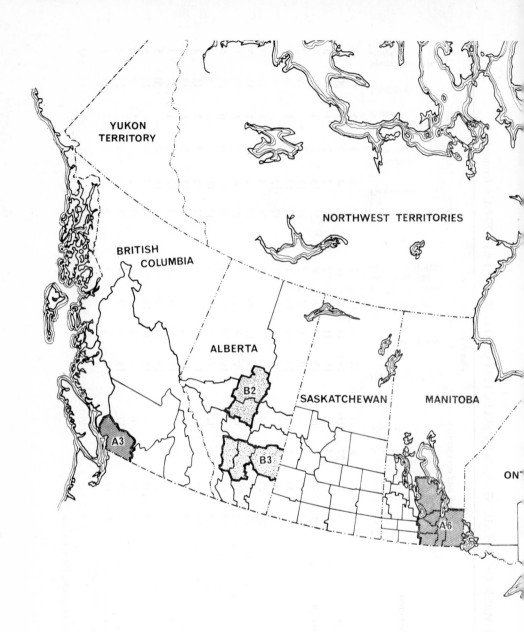

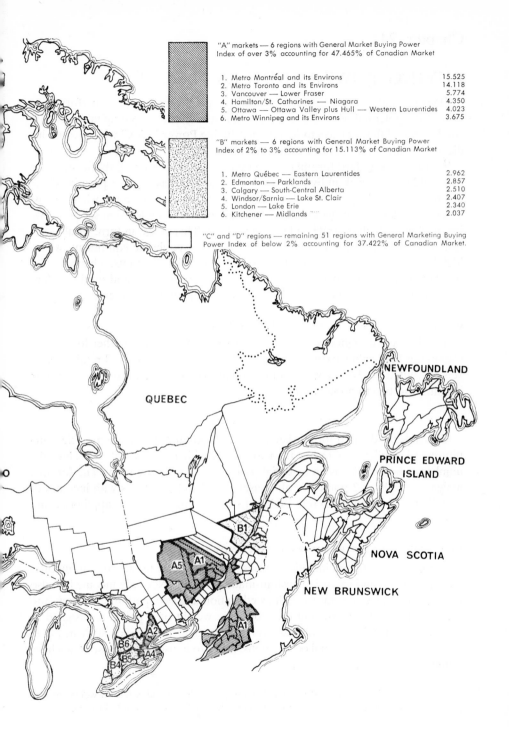

"A" markets — 6 regions with General Market Buying Power Index of over 3% accounting for 47.465% of Canadian Market

1.	Metro Montréal and its Environs	15.525
2.	Metro Toronto and its Environs	14.118
3.	Vancouver — Lower Fraser	5.774
4.	Hamilton/St. Catharines — Niagara	4.350
5.	Ottawa — Ottawa Valley plus Hull — Western Laurentides	4.023
6.	Metro Winnipeg and its Environs	3.675

"B" markets — 6 regions with General Market Buying Power Index of 2% to 3% accounting for 15.113% of Canadian Market

1.	Metro Québec — Eastern Laurentides	2.962
2.	Edmonton — Parklands	2.857
3.	Calgary — South-Central Alberta	2.510
4.	Windsor/Sarnia — Lake St. Clair	2.407
5.	London — Lake Erie	2.340
6.	Kitchener — Midlands	2.037

"C" and "D" regions — remaining 51 regions with General Marketing Buying Power Index of below 2% accounting for 37.422% of Canadian Market.

NEWFOUNDLAND

QUEBEC

PRINCE EDWARD ISLAND

B1

NOVA SCOTIA

A5 A1

NEW BRUNSWICK

A1

A2

B6
B5 A4
B4 B5

Chapter 24

BUYING POWER INDICES

One essential feature of successful marketing is the measuring of performance against the potential of each region. The statistics in the preceding tables can be combined in different ways to prepare a "Buying Power Index" which would indicate the sales potential of a region.

There is no standard formula for computing such an index. Experience is the only guide, since each individual product or service has its own peculiar characteristic. For example, the index for table salt or a loaf of bread, where population is the key factor, would differ from an index for a television set or a sewing machine, which is largely a family purchase. This index, in turn, would vary from one for overseas travel and custom-made stereophonic equipment, where high levels of income and education are the major determinants. Theoretically, one can prepare as many buying indices as there are products and services. Here are examples of three indices intended to cover the majority of cases.

GENERAL MARKET BUYING POWER INDEX

This index is designed for many consumer goods that are neither low-priced staples nor high value luxury goods and are sold through standard retail outlets. It is computed by giving a weight of five points to retail sales, three to disposable income, and two to population.*

HOME MARKET BUYING POWER INDEX

This index is devised for marketers who sell products for the home (e.g., furniture and appliances) rather than for an individual's personal use. Here the number of households is an essential part of the composite index. The formula assigns a weight of 2 points for all households, 4 to households with incomes of $5,000 and over, and 4 to retail sales of stores selling furniture, appliances and radios.

QUALITY MARKET BUYING POWER INDEX

Items in this category include luxuries, top-of-the-line models of automobiles and appliances, and exclusive custom-made products. Not only income but also other factors affecting status, such as education and occupation, are taken into consideration. In constructing the index, the weight of 3 points is assigned to households earning $10,000 and over a year, 3 to households with heads in managerial and professional occupations, and 4 to households whose heads have a university degree.

---

* For a low-priced food product, one can compile a similar index with a weight of 4 to population, 4 to grocery and combination store sales, and 2 to disposable income.

The Buying Power Index gives the "par" figure for each region or market on a percentage basis. In other words, it indicates what share of the Canadian market a region provides for a particular product or service based on its established potential. Comparison of "par" figures with current sales on a percentage basis will permit the segregation of territories which are getting their fair portion of the business from those above "average" in their performance and those not producing the sales they are capable of.

It must be always remembered that the index is intended only as an advisory guide. On occasions, when setting the quota for the region, the "par" figure may have to be slightly modified to take into account certain special factors. At times it may prove desirable to set a quota above the par to serve as a spur to particularly good salesmen. In other cases, it may be psychologically prudent to fix the quota below the level of potential: a competitor may be solidly entrenched, the product may not be available in enough retail stores, the dealers or distributors may be too lethargic to adopt aggressive merchandising methods. Judgment must also play an important part.

To establish sales control for a product with national distribution and national sales effort, the following procedure is recommended:

• Set up the sales territories in such a way that their boundaries coincide with the economic region or a group of economic regions.

• Calculate the percentage of the company's total sales made in each area.

• Enter the Buying Power Index for each territory. This is done by adding together the BPI's for the economic regions comprising that territory. For example, suppose the whole of Nova Scotia is considered as one market; then the Quality Buying Power Index would be 2.574.

• Compute the Index of Performance for each territory by dividing the percentage of the company's total sales by the respective Buying Power Index of that region. The resulting figures will show the relation between the company's sales and "par" for the area.

Territory or region	Sales in dollars	% of Canada	Quantity market BPI	Index of performance
1. East and West Kootenay	2,708	0.498	0.494	101
2. Okanagan Valley	2,491	0.458	0.462	99
3. South-Central B.C.	2,012	0.370	0.287	129
4. Vancouver-Lower Fraser	17,871	3.286	6.707	49
5. Victoria-Vancouver Island	4,862	0.894	1.753	51
6. Northern B.C.	5,428	0.998	0.762	131
. .	.	.	.	.
. .	.	.	.	.
. .	.	.	.	.
Canada	543,860	100.000	100.000	100

In the example above, territories 1 and 2 are performing as they should, 3 and 6 are doing extraordinarily well, while 4 and 5 are well below par.

The type of action taken on the basis of this information will depend upon the marketing managers. Some like to follow the line of least resistance. They feel it is hopeless to buck the tide, and prefer to back the winner by concentrating their efforts in an area where they are already in a strong competitive position and ahead of the par. Others follow the policy of obtaining a maximum volume of sales, and they realize that their best chances of success are normally in territories as yet not exploited to the full potential. When the latter course is adopted, it may be worthwhile to pick out all below-par territories and analyze the socio-economic characteristics of their population with the help of the statistics provided for each region in Part III A. Perhaps some unusual demographic feature, rather than a lack of sales effort, may be having an adverse effect on the demand for the product.

When the sales are confined to a province, the index of performance can still be computed simply by adjusting the base of the Buying Power Index. Suppose a manufacturer sells his product only in British Columbia. Then that province's Quality Market Buying Power Index of 10.465% would become 100%, and the regional figures would be converted as follows:

Territory or region	Quality market BPI	Province at 100%
East and West Kootenay	0.494	4.721
Okanagan Valley	0.462	4.415
South-Central B.C.	0.287	2.742
Vancouver-Lower Fraser	6.707	64.090
Victoria-Vancouver Island	1.753	16.751
Northern B.C.	0.762	7.281
Total	10.465	100.000

Similarly, if the distribution is confined only to the 19 metropolitan centers, then the total BPI of these centers, 69.847, would be converted into 100. In fact, with slight modifications, one can apply these indices for all types of marketing analyses.

BUYING POWER INDICES, 1964

Economic regions	General market buying power index		Home market buying power index		Quality market buying power index	
	% of Canada	Rank	% of Canada	Rank	% of Canada	Rank
Newfoundland	*1.803*	—	*1.189*	—	*0.911*	—
St. John's-Southeastern Nfld.	1.078	26	0.739	28	0.566	30
Central Nfld.	0.329	53	0.197	55	0.134	57
Western Nfld.	0.336	51	0.221	53	0.175	53
Labrador	0.060	63	0.032	63	0.036	63
Prince Edward Island	*0.472*	*44*	*0.290*	*51*	*0.251*	*51*
Nova Scotia	*3.453*	—	*2.743*	—	*2.574*	—
Sydney-Cape Breton	0.807	30	0.626	35	0.387	39
Northern Nova Scotia	0.566	39	0.391	42	0.421	37
Halifax-South Shore	1.688	16	1.399	17	1.473	14
Annapolis Valley	0.392	50	0.327	48	0.293	46
New Brunswick	*2.751*	—	*2.814*	—	*1.823*	—
Moncton-Southeastern N.B.	0.639	36	0.735	29	0.446	35
Saint John-Southern N.B.	0.779	31	0.789	27	0.569	29
Upper Saint John Valley	0.752	32	0.698	31	0.514	32
Northeastern N.B.	0.581	38	0.592	36	0.294	45
Québec	*26.162*	—	*28.448*	—	*26.731*	—
North Shore-New Québec	0.498	42	0.464	40	0.347	41
Gaspé Peninsula-South Shore	1.296	20	1.239	19	0.598	26
Saguenay Valley-Lake St. John	1.183	24	1.368	18	0.807	23
Metro Québec-Eastern Laurentides	2.962	7	3.025	8	3.024	8
Trois Rivières-St. Maurice Valley	1.282	21	1.136	22	0.986	20
Sherbrooke-Eastern Townships	1.964	13	2.150	13	1.346	16
Metro Montréal and its Environs	15.525	1	17.586	1	18.534	2
Western Québec	0.690	35	0.680	32	0.428	36
Hull-Western Laurentides	0.762	*	0.800	*	0.661	*
Ontario	*37.120*	—	*38.757*	—	*41.311*	—
Ottawa-Ottawa Valley	3.261	5	3.313	5	4.988	4
Kingston-Upper St. Lawrence	1.300	19	1.192	21	1.193	18
Peterborough-Central Lake Ontario	1.734	15	1.725	15	1.388	15
Metro Toronto and its Environs	14.118	2	14.856	2	19.016	1
Hamilton/St. Catharines-Niagara	4.350	4	4.775	4	4.121	5
London-Lake Erie	2.340	11	2.516	10	2.306	11
Windsor/Sarnia-Lake St. Clair	2.407	10	3.077	7	2.356	10
Kitchener-Midlands	2.037	12	2.166	12	1.889	12
Lake Huron-Georgian Bay	1.551	17	1.414	16	1.082	19
Northeastern Ontario: Clay Belt	1.132	25	1.009	24	0.796	24
Northeastern Ontario: Nickel Range	0.993	28	0.965	26	0.707	25
Northeastern Ontario: Sault	0.690	34	0.699	30	0.587	27
Lakehead-Northwestern Ontario	1.207	23	1.050	23	0.882	22

* Included with Ottawa-Ottawa Valley.

BUYING POWER INDICES (continued)

Economic regions	General market buying power index % of Canada	Rank	Home market buying power index % of Canada	Rank	Quality market buying power index % of Canada	Rank
Manitoba	*4.904*	—	*4.437*	—	*4.268*	—
Metro Winnipeg and its Environs	3.675	6	3.497	6	3.609	6
Southwestern Manitoba Prairie	0.739	33	0.576	38	0.397	38
West-Central Manitoba Parklands	0.234	56	0.171	58	0.117	59
Northern Manitoba	0.256	54	0.193	56	0.145	55
Saskatchewan	*5.241*	—	*3.986*	—	*3.610*	—
Regina-Southeastern Plains	1.472	18	1.204	20	1.287	17
Saskatchewan Palliser	0.890	29	0.656	34	0.473	33
Saskatoon-Central Plains	1.211	22	1.000	25	0.949	21
Saskatchewan-Southeastern Parklands.	0.563	40	0.408	41	0.271	49
Central Saskatchewan Parklands	1.014	27	0.679	33	0.576	28
Northern Saskatchewan	0.091	61	0.039	62	0.054	62
Alberta	*7.874*	—	*7.288*	—	*7.868*	—
Medicine Hat-Palliser	0.230	57	0.238	52	0.159	54
Lethbridge Prairie	0.608	37	0.584	37	0.540	31
Alberta Rocky Mountains-Foothills	0.117	60	0.091	61	0.093	60
Calgary-South Central Alberta	2.510	9	2.502	11	2.979	9
Red Deer Environs	0.423	47	0.332	47	0.300	43
East-Central Alberta Prairie	0.497	43	0.371	44	0.292	47
Edmonton-Parklands	2.857	8	2.762	9	3.152	7
Northeastern Alberta	0.184	59	0.114	60	0.091	61
Northwestern Alberta-Peace River	0.448	45	0.294	50	0.262	50
British Columbia	*10.133*	—	*9.894*	—	*10.465*	—
East Kootenay	0.198	58	0.172	57	0.131	58
West Kootenay	0.406	48	0.390	43	0.363	40
Okanagan Valley	0.542	41	0.558	39	0.462	34
South Central British Columbia	0.398	49	0.337	46	0.287	48
Vancouver-Lower Fraser	5.774	3	5.729	3	6.707	3
Victoria-Vancouver Island	1.797	14	1.852	14	1.753	13
Northwestern British Columbia	0.335	52	0.294	49	0.323	42
North-Central British Columbia	0.439	46	0.351	45	0.297	44
Northeastern British Columbia	0.244	55	0.211	54	0.142	56
Yukon and Northwest Territories	*0.087*	*62*	*0.154*	*59*	*0.188*	*52*
Canada	*100.000*	—	*100.000*	—	*100.000*	—

BUYING POWER INDICES, 1964

Metropolitan centers	General market buying power index		Home market buying power index		Quality market buying power index	
	% of Canada	Rank	% of Canada	Rank	% of Canada	Rank
Calgary	2.048	9	2.190	9	2.797	7
Edmonton	2.333	7	2.429	7	2.933	6
Halifax	1.107	11	0.954	14	1.214	11
Hamilton	2.421	6	2.592	6	2.530	9
Kitchener	0.955	14	1.136	12	0.954	15
London	1.274	10	1.327	11	1.497	10
Montréal	12.500	1	14.788	1	17.392	2
Ottawa	2.818	5	2.999	4	4.672	4
Québec	2.062	8	2.251	8	2.569	8
Regina	0.895	15	0.905	15	1.033	14
Saint John	0.570	18	0.617	18	0.483	18
St. John's	0.518	19	0.426	19	0.345	19
Saskatoon	0.738	16	0.718	17	0.800	16
Sudbury	0.690	17	0.721	16	0.508	17
Toronto	12.444	2	13.516	2	18.136	1
Vancouver	5.157	3	5.244	3	6.461	3
Victoria	0.983	13	1.093	13	1.181	12
Windsor	1.090	12	1.496	10	1.088	13
Winnipeg	2.899	4	2.893	5	3.254	5
Total of metropolitan cities	53.502	—	58.295	—	69.847	—
Canada	100.000	—	100.000	—	100.000	—

INDEX